Options, Futures, and Other Derivatives

THIRD EDITION

JOHN C. HULL
University of Toronto

PRENTICE HALL International, Inc.

Acquisitions Editor: Paul Donnelly
Associate Editor: Teresa Cohan
Editorial Assistant: MaryBeth Sanok
Editor-in-Chief: James Boyd
Marketing Manager: Susan McLaughlin
Production Editor: David Salierno
Production Coordinator: David Cotugno
Managing Editor: Carol Burgett
Manufacturing Buyer: Ken Clinton
Cover Design: Bruce Kenselaar
Composition: Publication Services
Cover Art/Photo: Ed Pritchard/Tony Stone Images

ISBN 0-13-264367-7

Prentice-Hall International (UK) Limited, *London*
Prentice-Hall of Australia Pty. Limited, *Sydney*
Prentice-Hall Canada, Inc., *Toronto*
Prentice-Hall Hispanoamericana, S.A., *Mexico*
Prentice-Hall of India Private Limited, *New Delhi*
Prentice-Hall of Japan, Inc., *Tokyo*
Simon & Schuster Asia Pte. Ltd., *Singapore*
Editora Prentice-Hall do Brasil, Ltda., *Rio de Janeiro*
Prentice-Hall, Inc., Upper Saddle River, New Jersey

Printed in the United States of America

10 9 8 7 6 5 4 3 2

To My Family

Brief Contents

1 INTRODUCTION 1

2 FUTURES MARKETS AND THE USE OF FUTURES
FOR HEDGING 16

3 FORWARD AND FUTURES PRICES 45

4 INTEREST RATE FUTURES 78

5 SWAPS 111

6 OPTIONS MARKETS 138

7 PROPERTIES OF STOCK OPTION PRICES 156

8 TRADING STRATEGIES INVOLVING OPTIONS 177

9 INTRODUCTION TO BINOMIAL TREES 194

10 MODEL OF THE BEHAVIOR OF STOCK PRICES 209

11 THE BLACK–SCHOLES ANALYSIS 228

12 OPTIONS ON STOCK INDICES, CURRENCIES,
AND FUTURES CONTRACTS 261

13 GENERAL APPROACH TO PRICING DERIVATIVES 288

14 THE MANAGEMENT OF MARKET RISK 308

15 NUMERICAL PROCEDURES 343

16 INTEREST RATE DERIVATIVES AND THE USE
OF BLACK'S MODEL 387

17 INTEREST RATE DERIVATIVES AND MODELS
OF THE YIELD CURVE 416

18 EXOTIC OPTIONS 457

19 ALTERNATIVES TO BLACK–SCHOLES
FOR OPTION PRICING 490

20 CREDIT RISK AND REGULATORY CAPITAL 517

21 REVIEW OF KEY CONCEPTS 539

Contents

PREFACE   xvii

1 INTRODUCTION   1

    1.1   Forward Contracts   1
    1.2   Futures Contracts   3
    1.3   Options   4
    1.4   Other Derivatives   9
    1.5   Types of Traders   10
    1.6   Summary   13
           Questions and Problems   13

**2 FUTURES MARKETS AND THE USE OF FUTURES
FOR HEDGING**   16

    2.1   Trading Futures Contracts   16
    2.2   Specification of the Futures Contract   17
    2.3   Operation of Margins   20
    2.4   Newspaper Quotes   24
    2.5   Convergence of Futures Price to Spot Price   28
    2.6   Settlement   29
    2.7   Regulation   30
    2.8   Hedging Using Futures   31
    2.9   Optimal Hedge Ratio   35
    2.10   Rolling the Hedge Forward   37

2.11   Accounting and Tax   38

2.12   Summary   40

Suggestions for Further Reading   41

Questions and Problems   42

3   FORWARD AND FUTURES PRICES   45

3.1   Some Preliminaries   45

3.2   Forward Contracts on a Security That Provides
No Income   51

3.3   Forward Contracts on a Security That Provides
a Known Cash Income   52

3.4   Forward Contracts on a Security That Provides
a Known Dividend Yield   54

3.5   General Result   55

3.6   Forward Prices versus Futures Prices   55

3.7   Stock Index Futures   57

3.8   Forward and Futures Contracts on Currencies   63

3.9   Futures on Commodities   65

3.10   The Cost of Carry   67

3.11   Delivery Choices   68

3.12   Futures Prices and the Expected Future Spot Price   68

3.13   Summary   71

Suggestions for Further Reading   72

Questions and Problems   73

Appendix 3A   Proof That Forward and Futures Prices Are
Equal When Interest Rates Are Constant   76

4   INTEREST RATE FUTURES   78

4.1   Some Preliminaries   78

4.2   Forward Rate Agreements   87

4.3   Treasury Bond and Treasury Note Futures   88

4.4   Treasury Bill Futures   95

4.5   Eurodollar Futures   99

4.6   Duration   100

4.7   Duration-Based Hedging Strategies   102

4.8   Limitations of Duration   104

4.9   Summary   106
        Suggestions for Further Reading   107
        Questions and Problems   107

5   **SWAPS**   111

5.1   Mechanics of Interest Rate Swaps   111
5.2   The Comparative Advantage Argument   118
5.3   Valuation of Interest Rate Swaps   121
5.4   Currency Swaps   125
5.5   Valuation of Currency Swaps   128
5.6   Other Swaps   130
5.7   Credit Risk   132
5.8   Summary   133
        Suggestions for Further Reading   134
        Questions and Problems   134

6   **OPTIONS MARKETS**   138

6.1   Exchange-Traded Options   138
6.2   Over-the-Counter Options   139
6.3   Specification of Stock Options   140
6.4   Newspaper Quotes   145
6.5   Trading   146
6.6   Commissions   147
6.7   Margins   148
6.8   The Options Clearing Corporation   150
6.9   Regulation   151
6.10   Taxation   151
6.11   Warrants and Convertibles   153
6.12   Summary   154
        Suggestions for Further Reading   154
        Questions and Problems   154

7   **PROPERTIES OF STOCK OPTION PRICES**   156

7.1   Factors Affecting Option Prices   156
7.2   Assumptions and Notation   158

7.3   Upper and Lower Bounds for Option Prices   159
7.4   Early Exercise: Calls on a Non-Dividend-Paying Stock   162
7.5   Early Exercise: Puts on a Non-Dividend-Paying Stock   165
7.6   Put–Call Parity   167
7.7   Effect of Dividends   170
7.8   Empirical Research   172
7.9   Summary   173
         Suggestions for Further Reading   174
         Questions and Problems   174

8   TRADING STRATEGIES INVOLVING OPTIONS   177

8.1   Strategies Involving a Single Option and a Stock   177
8.2   Spreads   179
8.3   Combinations   187
8.4   Other Payoffs   190
8.5   Summary   190
         Suggestions for Further Reading   191
         Questions and Problems   192

9   INTRODUCTION TO BINOMIAL TREES   194

9.1   One-Step Binomial Model   194
9.2   Risk-Neutral Valuation   198
9.3   Two-Step Binomial Trees   199
9.4   Put Example   202
9.5   American Options   203
9.6   Delta   204
9.7   Using Binomial Trees in Practice   205
9.8   Summary   206
         Suggestions for Further Reading   207
         Questions and Problems   207

10   MODEL OF THE BEHAVIOR OF STOCK PRICES   209

10.1   The Markov Property   209
10.2   Wiener Processes   210
10.3   The Process for Stock Prices   215

10.4 Review of the Model 217

10.5 The Parameters 219

10.6 Ito's Lemma 220

10.7 Summary 222

Suggestions for Further Reading 223

Questions and Problems 223

Appendix 10A Derivation of Ito's Lemma 225

11 THE BLACK–SCHOLES ANALYSIS 228

11.1 Lognormal Property of Stock Prices 228

11.2 The Distribution of the Rate of Return 230

11.3 Estimating Volatility from Historical Data 232

11.4 Concepts Underlying the Black–Scholes Differential Equation 235

11.5 Derivation of the Black–Scholes Differential Equation 237

11.6 Risk–Neutral Valuation 239

11.7 Black–Scholes Pricing Formulas 240

11.8 Cumulative Normal Distribution Function 243

11.9 Warrants Issued by a Company on Its Own Stock 244

11.10 Implied Volatilities 246

11.11 The Causes of Volatility 247

11.12 Dividends 249

11.13 Summary 253

Suggestions for Further Reading 255

Questions and Problems 256

Appendix 11A Exact Procedure for Calculating Values of American Calls on Dividend-Paying Stocks 259

Appendix 11B Calculation of Cumulative Probability in Bivariate Normal Distribution 260

12 OPTIONS ON STOCK INDICES, CURRENCIES, AND FUTURES CONTRACTS 261

12.1 Extending Black–Scholes 261

12.2 Pricing Formulas 263

12.3 Options on Stock Indices 264

12.4   Currency Options   269

12.5   Futures Options   273

12.6   Summary   280

Suggestions for Further Reading   281

Questions and Problems   282

Appendix 12A   Derivation of Differential Equation Satisfied by a Derivative Dependent on a Stock Paying a Continuous Dividend Yield   284

Appendix 12B   Derivation of Differential Equation Satisfied by a Derivative Dependent on a Futures Price   286

13   GENERAL APPROACH TO PRICING DERIVATIVES   288

13.1   Single Underlying Variable   288

13.2   Interest Rate Risk   292

13.3   Securities Dependent on Several State Variables   293

13.4   Is It Necessary to Estimate the Market Price of Risk?   296

13.5   Derivatives Dependent on Commodity Prices   297

13.6   Quantos   298

13.7   Summary   302

Suggestions for Further Reading   302

Questions and Problems   303

Appendix 13A   Generalization of Ito's Lemma   304

Appendix 13B   Derivation of the General Differential Equation Satisfied by Derivatives   305

14   THE MANAGEMENT OF MARKET RISK   308

14.1   Example   308

14.2   Naked and Covered Positions   309

14.3   A Stop-Loss Strategy   310

14.4   More Sophisticated Hedging Schemes   312

14.5   Delta Hedging   312

14.6   Theta   321

14.7   Gamma   323

14.8   Relationship among Delta, Theta, and Gamma   327

14.9   Vega   328

14.10   Rho   330

14.11   Scenario Analysis   331

14.12   Portfolio Insurance   333

14.13   Summary   337

Suggestions for Further Reading   338

Questions and Problems   339

Appendix 14A   Taylor Series Expansions
and Hedge Parameters   342

15   NUMERICAL PROCEDURES   343

15.1   Binomial Trees   343

15.2   Using the Binomial Tree for Options on Indices,
Currencies, and Futures Contracts   350

15.3   Binomial Model for a Dividend-Paying Stock   352

15.4   Extensions of the Basic Tree Approach   356

15.5   Alternative Procedures for Constructing Trees   358

15.6   Monte Carlo Simulation   361

15.7   Variance Reduction Procedures   365

15.8   Finite Difference Methods   368

15.9   Analytic Approximations in Option Pricing   379

15.10   Summary   380

Suggestions for Further Reading   381

Questions and Problems   382

Appendix 15A   Analytic Approximation to American Option
Prices of Macmillan, and Barone-Adesi
and Whaley   384

**16   INTEREST RATE DERIVATIVES AND THE USE
OF BLACK'S MODEL**   387

16.1   Exchange-Traded Interest Rate Options   387

16.2   Embedded Bond Options   389

16.3   Mortgage-Backed Securities   389

16.4   Option-Adjusted Spread   391

16.5   Black's Model   392

16.6   European Bond Options   395

16.7   Interest Rate Caps   397

16.8   European Swap Options   401

16.9   Accrual Swaps   404

16.10   Spread Options   405

16.11   Convexity Adjustments   406

16.12   Summary   411

Suggestions for Further Reading   412

Questions and Problems   412

Appendix 16A   Proof of the Convexity Adjustment Formula   414

17   INTEREST RATE DERIVATIVES AND MODELS
OF THE YIELD CURVE   416

17.1   Introduction to Equilibrium Models   416

17.2   One-Factor Models   417

17.3   The Rendleman and Bartter Model   418

17.4   The Vasicek Model   419

17.5   The Cox, Ingersoll, and Ross Model   422

17.6   Two-Factor Models   423

17.7   Introduction to No-Arbitrage Models   424

17.8   Modeling Forward Rates   428

17.9   Developing Markov Models   431

17.10   Ho and Lee Model   431

17.11   Hull and White Model   433

17.12   Interest Rate Trees   436

17.13   A General Tree-Building Procedure   438

17.14   Nonstationary Models   449

17.15   Forward Rates and Futures Rates   450

17.16   Summary   452

Suggestions for Further Reading   453

Questions and Problems   454

18   EXOTIC OPTIONS   457

18.1   Types of Exotic Options   457

18.2   Basic Numerical Procedures   469

18.3   Path-Dependent Derivatives   469

18.4   Lookback Options   474

18.5   Barrier Options   476

18.6   Options on Two Correlated Assets   480

18.7   Hedging Issues   482

18.8   Static Options Replication   483

18.9   Summary   485

Suggestions for Further Reading   486

Questions and Problems   487

**19   ALTERNATIVES TO BLACK–SCHOLES
FOR OPTION PRICING**   490

19.1   Known Changes in the Interest Rate
and Volatility   490

19.2   Merton's Stochastic Interest Rate Model   491

19.3   Pricing Biases   492

19.4   Alternative Models   494

19.5   Overview of Pricing Biases   499

19.6   Stochastic Volatility   499

19.7   How Black–Scholes Is Used in Practice   502

19.8   Implied Trees   505

19.9   Empirical Research   507

19.10   Summary   510

Suggestions for Further Reading   511

Questions and Problems   512

Appendix 19A   Pricing Formulas for Alternative Models   514

20   CREDIT RISK AND REGULATORY CAPITAL   517

20.1   Background   518

20.2   Adjusting the Prices of Options for Credit Risk   521

20.3   Contracts That Can Be Assets or Liabilities   523

20.4   Historical Default Experience   527

20.5   Valuation of Convertible Bonds   528

20.6   The BIS Capital Requirements   531

20.7   Reducing Exposure to Credit Risk   534

20.8   Summary   535

Suggestions for Further Reading   536

Questions and Problems   536

21   REVIEW OF KEY CONCEPTS   539

21.1   Riskless Hedges   539
21.2   Traded Securities versus Other Underlying Variables   540
21.3   Risk-Neutral Valuation   540
21.4   Those Big Losses   541
21.5   A Final Word   541

MAJOR EXCHANGES   543

GLOSSARY OF NOTATION   545

TABLE FOR $N(x)$ WHEN $x \leq 0$ 548

TABLE FOR $N(x)$ WHEN $x \geq 0$ 549

AUTHOR INDEX   551

SUBJECT INDEX   555

Preface

This book is appropriate for graduate and advanced undergraduate elective courses in business, economics, and financial engineering. It is also suitable for practitioners who want to acquire a working knowledge of how derivatives can be analyzed.

One of the key decisions that must be made by an author who is writing in the area of derivatives concerns the use of mathematics. If the level of mathematical sophistication is too high, the material is likely to be inaccessible to many students and practitioners. If it is too low, some important issues will inevitably be treated in a rather superficial way. In this book, great care has been taken in the use of mathematics. Nonessential mathematical material has been either eliminated or included in end-of-chapter appendices. Concepts that are likely to be new to many readers have been explained carefully, and many numerical examples have been included.

The feature of this book that distinguishes it from others in the same area is that it provides a unifying approach to the valuation of all derivatives—not just futures and options. This book assumes that the reader has taken an introductory course in finance and an introductory course in probability and statistics. No prior knowledge of options, futures contracts, swaps, and so on is assumed. It is not therefore necessary for students to take an elective course in investments prior to taking a course based on this book.

CHANGES IN THIS EDITION

This edition contains more material than the second edition. Also, the material in the second edition has been updated, and the organization of the material has been improved in a number of places. The changes include:

1. There are now three chapters on interest rate derivatives (Chapters 4, 16 and 17). Most of Chapters 16 and 17 is new. Chapter 16 includes material on mortgage-backed securities; the way in which Black's model is used by market participants to value a range of different interest rate derivatives; and the convexity adjustments necessary when Black's model is used. Chapter 17 includes material on both equilibrium and no-arbitrage models of the

term structure. It provides an updated and detailed description of procedures for constructing interest rate trees. It also deals with the convexity adjustments necessary when Eurodollar futures are used to construct the zero curve.

2. A new chapter, Chapter 10, introduces one- and two-step binomial trees and shows how they can be analyzed using either no-arbitrage or risk-neutral valuation arguments.

3. Major changes have been made to the chapter on exotic options (Chapter 18). There is much more material on how to value barrier options, path-dependent options, lookback options, and options on two correlated assets. Static options replication is also covered.

4. Major changes have been made to the chapter on credit risk (Chapter 20). This now has more emphasis on discrete models and covers the valuation of convertible bonds.

5. New topics and new material have been introduced in many other places. For example, accounting and tax are covered in Chapters 2 and 6; day count conventions are discussed in Chapter 4; the material on swaps in Chapter 5 has been revised; there is more material on quantos in Chapter 13; the scenario analysis approach to risk management is discussed in Chapter 14; the material on Monte Carlo variance reduction procedures and finite difference methods in Chapter 15 has been increased; GARCH and the implied tree technique are discussed in Chapter 19.

6. New questions and problems have been added. As in the previous edition, those that are more difficult than average have been asterisked.

Readers of the first and second editions might have noticed that I have made a small change in the book's title. *Options, Futures, and Other Derivative Securities* has now become *Options, Futures, and Other Derivatives*.

ACKNOWLEDGMENTS

Many people have played a part in the production of this book. The academics and practitioners who have made excellent and useful suggestions include Emilio Barone, Giovanni Barone-Adesi, Alex Bergier, George Blazenko, Laurence Booth, Phelim Boyle, Peter Carr, Don Chance, J.-P. Chateau, Ren-Raw Chen, Michel Crouhy, Emanuel Derman, Dieter Dorp, Scott Drabin, Jerome Duncan, Steinar Ekern, David Fowler, Dajiang Gao, Jörgen Hallbeck, Ian Hawkins, Michael Hemler, Steve Heston, Kiyoshi Kato, Kevin Kneafsy, Bill Margrabe, Izzy Nelkin, Paul Potvin, Eric Reiner, Gordon Roberts, Chris Robinson, Cheryl Rosen, John Rumsey, Klaus Schurger, Michael Selby, Piet Sercu, Duane Stock, Edward Thorpe, Yisong Tian, P.V. Viswanath, Ton Vorst, George Wang, Jason Wei, Bob Whaley, and Alan White. I am particularly grateful to Eduardo

Schwartz, who read the original manuscript for the first edition and made many comments that led to significant improvements.

The first two editions of this book were very popular with practitioners, and much of the material in the book has been greatly influenced by the informal contacts I have had with practitioners. The students in my elective courses on derivatives at the University of Toronto have also influenced the evolution of the book.

Alan White, a colleague at the University of Toronto (formerly a colleague at York University), deserves a special acknowledgment. Alan and I have been carrying out joint research in the area of derivatives for many years. During that time we have spent countless hours discussing different issues concerning derivatives. Many of the new ideas in this book, and many of the new ways used to explain old ideas, are as much Alan's as mine. Alan read the original version of this book very carefully and made many excellent suggestions for improvement.

I would like to thank Michelle Wang and Bernie Hildebrandt for excellent research assistance. The staff at Prentice Hall have been a continual source of encouragement to me as this project has progressed. I would particularly like to thank Scott Barr (my original editor), Leah Jewell (editor of the second edition), Paul Donnelly (my current editor), and David Salierno (production editor).

John C. Hull

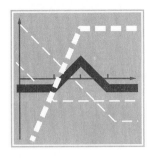

Chapter 1

Introduction

A *derivative* (or *derivative security*) is a financial instrument whose value depends on the values of other, more basic underlying variables. In recent years, derivatives have become increasingly important in the field of finance. Futures and options are now traded actively on many exchanges. Forward contracts, swaps, and many different types of options are regularly traded outside exchanges by financial institutions and their corporate clients in what are termed the *over-the-counter* markets. Other, more specialized derivatives often form part of a bond or stock issue.

Derivatives are also known as *contingent claims,* and these two terms are used interchangeably throughout the book. Very often the variables underlying derivatives are the prices of traded securities. A stock option, for example, is a derivative whose value is contingent on the price of a stock. However, as we shall see, derivatives can be contingent on almost any variable, from the price of hogs to the amount of snow falling at a certain ski resort.

This book has two objectives. The first is to explore the properties of those derivatives that are commonly encountered in practice; the second is to provide a theoretical framework within which all derivatives can be valued and hedged. In this opening chapter, we take a first look at forward contracts, futures contracts, and options. In later chapters, these instruments and the way they are traded are discussed in more detail.

1.1 FORWARD CONTRACTS

A *forward contract* is a particularly simple derivative. It is an agreement to buy or sell an asset at a certain future time for a certain price. The contract is usually between two financial institutions or between a financial institution and one of its corporate clients. It is not normally traded on an exchange.

One of the parties to a forward contract assumes a *long position* and agrees to buy the underlying asset on a certain specified future date for a certain specified price. The other party assumes a *short position* and agrees to sell the asset on the same date for the same price. The specified price in a forward contract will be referred to as the *delivery price.* At the time the contract is entered into, the delivery

1

price is chosen so that the value of the forward contract to both parties is zero.[1] This means that it costs nothing to take either a long or a short position.

A forward contract is settled at maturity. The holder of the short position delivers the asset to the holder of the long position in return for a cash amount equal to the delivery price. A key variable determining the value of a forward contract at any given time is the market price of the asset. As already mentioned, a forward contract is worth zero when it is first entered into. Later it can have a positive or a negative value, depending on movements in the price of the asset. For example, if the price of the asset rises sharply soon after the initiation of contract, the value of a long position in the forward contract becomes positive and the value of a short position in the forward contract becomes negative.

Forward Price

The *forward price* for a certain contract is defined as the delivery price which would make that contract have zero value. It follows that the forward price and the delivery price are equal at the time the contract is entered into. As time passes, the forward price is liable to change, whereas the delivery price, of course, remains the same. The two are not therefore equal, except by chance, at any time after the start of the contract. Generally, the forward price at any given time varies with the maturity of the contract being considered. For example, the forward price for a contract to buy or sell in three months is typically different from that for a contract to buy or sell in six months.

Corporations frequently enter into forward contracts on foreign exchange. Table 1.1 provides quotes for the pound sterling–U.S. dollar exchange rate on May 8, 1995. The first quote indicates that, ignoring commissions and other transactions costs, sterling can be bought or sold in the spot market (i.e., for virtually immediate delivery) at the rate of $1.6080 per pound; the second quote indicates that the forward price (or forward exchange rate) for a contract to buy or sell sterling in 30 days is $1.6076 per pound; the third quote indicates that the forward price for a contract to buy or sell sterling in 90 days is $1.6056 per pound; and so on.

Payoffs from Forward Contracts

Suppose that an investor entered into a long forward contract on May 8, 1995 to buy 1 million pounds sterling in 90 days at an exchange rate of 1.6056. This

TABLE 1.1 Spot and Forward Foreign Exchange Quotes on Sterling, May 8, 1995

Spot	1.6080
30-day forward	1.6076
90-day forward	1.6056
180-day forward	1.6018

[1]In Chapter 3 we explain the way in which this delivery price can be calculated.

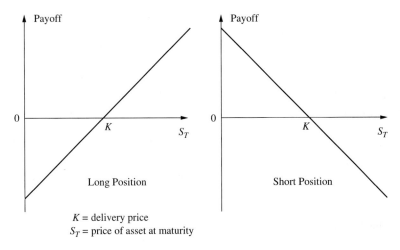

K = delivery price
S_T = price of asset at maturity

Figure 1.1   Payoffs from forward contracts.

contract would obligate the investor to buy 1 million pounds for U.S. $1,605,600. If the spot exchange rate rose to, say, 1.6500, at the end of the 90 days the investor would gain U.S. $44,400 ($= 1,650,000 - 1,605,600$) since the pounds, as soon as they have been purchased, can be sold for U.S. $1,650,000. Similarly, if the spot exchange rate fell to 1.5500 at the end of the 90 days, the investor would lose U.S. $55,600 since the forward contract would lead to the investor paying U.S. $55,600 more than the market price for the sterling.

In general, the payoff from a long position in a forward contract on one unit of an asset is

$$S_T - K$$

where K is the delivery price and S_T is the spot price of the asset at maturity of the contract. This is because the holder of the contract is obligated to buy an asset worth S_T for K. Similarly, the payoff from a short position in a forward contract on one unit of an asset is

$$K - S_T$$

These payoffs can be positive or negative. They are illustrated in Figure 1.1. Since it costs nothing to enter into a forward contract, the payoff from the contract is also the investor's total gain or loss from the contract.

1.2 FUTURES CONTRACTS

Like a forward contract, a *futures contract* is an agreement between two parties to buy or sell an asset at a certain time in the future for a certain price. Unlike forward contracts, futures contracts are normally traded on an exchange. To make trading possible, the exchange specifies certain standardized features of the contract. As the two parties to the contract do not necessarily know each other, the

exchange also provides a mechanism which gives the two parties a guarantee that the contract will be honored.

The largest exchanges on which futures contracts are traded are the Chicago Board of Trade (CBOT) and the Chicago Mercantile Exchange (CME). On these and other exchanges, a very wide range of commodities and financial assets form the underlying assets in the various contracts. The commodities include pork bellies, live cattle, sugar, wool, lumber, copper, aluminum, gold, and tin. The financial assets include stock indices, currencies, Treasury bills, and Treasury bonds.

One way in which a futures contract is different from a forward contract is that an exact delivery date is usually not specified. The contract is referred to by its delivery month, and the exchange specifies the period during the month when delivery must be made. For commodities, the delivery period is often the entire month. The holder of the short position has the right to choose the time during the delivery period when he or she will make delivery. Usually, contracts with several different delivery months are traded at any one time. The exchange specifies the amount of the asset to be delivered for one contract; how the futures price is to be quoted; and possibly, limits on the amount by which the futures price can move in any one day. In the case of a commodity, the exchange also specifies the product quality and the delivery location. Consider, for example, the wheat futures contract currently traded on the Chicago Board of Trade. The size of the contract is 5,000 bushels. Contracts for five delivery months (March, May, July, September, and December) are available for up to 18 months into the future. The exchange specifies the grades of wheat that can be delivered and the places where delivery can be made.

Futures prices are regularly reported in the financial press. Suppose that on September 1, the December futures price of gold is quoted at $500. This is the price, exclusive of commissions, at which investors can agree to buy or sell gold for December delivery. It is determined on the floor of the exchange in the same way as other prices (i.e., by the laws of supply and demand). If more investors want to go long than to go short, the price goes up; if the reverse is true, the price goes down.[2]

Further details on issues such as margin requirements, daily settlement procedures, delivery procedures, bid–ask spreads, and the role of the exchange clearinghouse are given in Chapter 2.

1.3 OPTIONS

Options on stocks were first traded on an organized exchange in 1973. Since then there has been a dramatic growth in options markets. Options are now traded on many exchanges throughout the world. Huge volumes of options are also traded

---

[2]In Chapter 3 we discuss the relationship between a futures price and the spot price of the underlying asset (gold, in this case).

over the counter by banks and other financial institutions. The underlying assets include stocks, stock indices, foreign currencies, debt instruments, commodities, and futures contracts.

There are two basic types of options. A *call option* gives the holder the right to buy the underlying asset by a certain date for a certain price. A *put option* gives the holder the right to sell the underlying asset by a certain date for a certain price. The price in the contract is known as the *exercise price* or *strike price;* the date in the contract is known as the *expiration date, exercise date,* or *maturity.* Amer-*ican options* can be exercised at any time up to the expiration date. *European options* can be exercised only on the expiration date itself.[3] Most of the options that are traded on exchanges are American. However, European options are gen-erally easier to analyze than American options, and some of the properties of an American option are frequently deduced from those of its European counterpart.

It should be emphasized that an option gives the holder the right to do some-thing. The holder does not have to exercise this right. This fact distinguishes options from forwards and futures, where the holder is obligated to buy or sell the underlying asset. Note that whereas it costs nothing to enter into a forward or futures contract, there is a cost to entering into an option contract.

Examples

Consider the situation of an investor who buys 100 European call options on IBM stock with a strike price of $100. Suppose that the current stock price is $98, the expiration date of the option is in two months, and the option price is $5. Since the options are European, the investor can exercise only on the expiration date. If the stock price on this date is less than $100, he or she will clearly choose not to exercise. (There is no point in buying for $100 a stock that has a market value of less than $100.) In these circumstances the investor loses the entire initial investment of $500. If the stock price is above $100 on the expiration date, the options will be exercised. Suppose, for example, that the stock price is $115. By exercising the options, the investor is able to buy 100 shares for $100 per share. If the shares are sold immediately, the investor makes a gain of $15 per share, or $1,500, ignoring transactions costs. When the initial cost of the options is taken into account, the net profit to the investor is $10 per option, or $1,000. (This calculation ignores the time value of money.) Figure 1.2 shows the way in which the investor's net profit or loss per option varies with the terminal stock price. Note that in some cases the investor exercises the options but takes a loss overall. Consider the situation when the stock price is $103 on the expiration date. The investor exercises the options but takes a loss of $200 overall. This is better than the loss of $500 that would be incurred if the options were not exercised.

Whereas the purchaser of a call option is hoping that the stock price will increase, the purchaser of a put option is hoping that it will decrease. Consider an

---

[3]Note that the terms *American* and *European* do not refer to the location of the option or the exchange. Some options trading on North American exchanges are European.

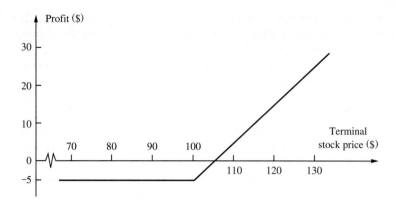

Figure 1.2   Profit from buying an IBM European call option: option price = $5, strike price = $100.

investor who buys 100 European put options on Exxon with a strike price of $70. Suppose that the current stock price is $66, the expiration date of the option is in three months, and the option price is $7. Since the options are European, they will be exercised only if the stock price is below $70 at the expiration date. Suppose that the stock price is $50 on this date. The investor can buy 100 shares for $50 per share and, under the terms of the put option, sell the same shares for $70, to realize a gain of $20 per share, or $2,000. (Again, transactions costs are ignored.) When the initial cost of the option is taken into account, the investor's net profit is $13 per option, or $1,300. Of course, if the final stock price is above $70, the put option expires worthless and the investor loses $7 per option, or $700. Figure 1.3 shows the way in which the investor's profit or loss per option varies with the terminal stock price.

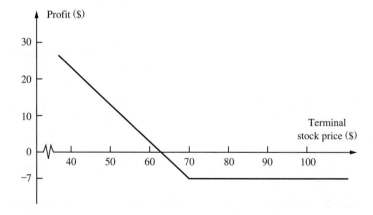

Figure 1.3   Profit from buying an Exxon European put option: option price = $7, strike price = $70.

As already mentioned, stock options are generally American rather than European. This means that the investors in the examples just given do not have to wait until the expiration date before exercising the options. We will see in later chapters that there are some circumstances under which it is optimal to exercise American options prior to maturity.

Option Positions

There are two sides to every option contract. On one side is the investor who has taken the long position (i.e., has bought the option). On the other side is the investor who has taken a short position (i.e., has sold or *written* the option). The writer of an option receives cash up front but has potential liabilities later. His or her profit or loss is the reverse of that for the purchaser of the option. Figures 1.4 and 1.5 show the variation of the profit and loss with the final stock price for writers of the options considered in Figures 1.2 and 1.3.

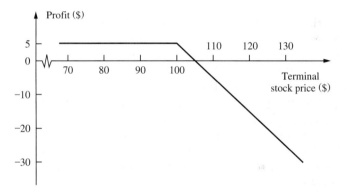

Figure 1.4   Profit from writing an IBM European call option: option price = $5, strike price = $100.

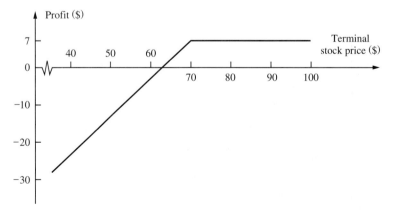

Figure 1.5   Profit from writing an Exxon European put option: option price = $7, strike price = $70.

Payoffs

Four basic option positions are possible:

1. A long position in a call option.
2. A long position in a put option.
3. A short position in a call option.
4. A short position in a put option.

It is often useful to characterize European option positions in terms of the payoff to the investor at maturity. The initial cost of the option is then not included in the calculation. If X is the strike price and S_T is the final price of the underlying asset, the payoff from a long position in a European call option is

$$\max(S_T - X, 0)$$

This reflects the fact that the option will be exercised if $S_T > X$ and will not be exercised if $S_T \leq X$. The payoff to the holder of a short position in the European call option is

$$- \max(S_T - X, 0)$$

or

$$\min(X - S_T, 0)$$

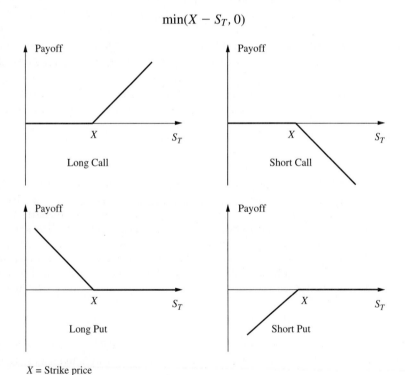

$X =$ Strike price
$S_T =$ Price of asset at maturity

Figure 1.6   Payoffs from positions in European options.

The payoff to the holder of a long position in a European put option is

$$\max(X - S_T, 0)$$

and the payoff from a short position in a European put option is

$$-\max(X - S_T, 0)$$

or

$$\min(S_T - X, 0)$$

Figure 1.6 illustrates these payoffs graphically.

1.4 OTHER DERIVATIVES

The call and put options described in Section 1.3 are sometimes termed "plain vanilla" or "standard" derivatives. In recent years, banks and other financial institutions have been very imaginative in designing nonstandard derivatives to meet the needs of clients. Sometimes these are sold by financial institutions directly to their corporate clients. On other occasions, they are added to bond or stock issues to make these issues more attractive to investors. Some nonstandard derivatives are simply portfolios of two or more "plain vanilla" call and put options. Others are far more complex. The possibilities for designing new interesting nonstandard derivatives seems to be virtually limitless. Nonstandard derivatives are sometimes termed *exotic options* or just *exotics*. In Chapter 18 we discuss a large number of different types of exotics and consider how they can be valued.

We now give examples of three derivatives which, although they appear to be complex, can be decomposed into portfolios of plain vanilla call and put options.[4]

Example 1.1: Standard Oil's Bond Issue

In 1986 Standard Oil issued some bonds where the holder received no interest. At the bond's maturity the company promised to pay $1,000 plus an additional amount based on the price of oil at that time. The additional amount was equal to the product of 170 and the excess (if any) of the price of a barrel of oil at maturity over $25. However, the maximum additional amount paid was restricted to $2,550 (which corresponds to a price of $40 per barrel). These bonds provided holders with a stake in a commodity that was critically important to the fortunes of the company. If the price of the commodity went up, the company was in a good position to provide the bondholder with the additional payment.

Example 1.2: ICON

In 1985, Bankers Trust developed *index currency option notes* (ICONs). These are bonds in which the amount received by the holder at maturity varies with a foreign exchange

---

[4]See Problems 1.14, 1.21, and 1.22 at the end of the chapter for an indication as to how the decomposition can be accomplished.

rate. Two exchange rates, X_1 and X_2, are specified with $X_1 > X_2$. If the exchange rate at the bond's maturity is above X_1, the bondholder receives the full face value. If it is less than X_2, the bondholder receives nothing. Between X_2 and X_1, a portion of the full face value is received. Bankers Trust's first issue of an ICON was for the Long Term Credit Bank of Japan. The ICON specified that if the yen–U.S. dollar exchange rate, S, is greater than 169 yen per dollar at maturity (in 1995), the holder of the bond receives \$1,000. If it is less than 169 yen per dollar, the amount received by holder of the bond is

$$1,000 - \max\left[0, 1,000\left(\frac{169}{S} - 1\right)\right]$$

When the exchange rate is below 84.5, nothing is received by the holder at maturity.

Example 1.3: Range Forward Contract

Range forward contracts or *flexible forwards* are popular in foreign exchange markets. Suppose that on May 8, 1995, a U.S. company finds that it will require sterling in 90 days' time and faces the exchange rates shown in Table 1.1. It could enter into a 90-day forward contract to buy at 1.6056. A range forward contract is an alternative. Under this contract an exchange band straddling 1.6056 is set. Suppose that the chosen band runs from 1.5700 to 1.6400. The range forward contract is then designed to ensure that if the spot rate in 90 days is less than 1.5700, the company pays 1.5700; if it is between 1.5700 and 1.6400, the company pays the spot rate; if it is greater than 1.6400, the company pays 1.6400.

Other More Complex Examples

As mentioned earlier, there is virtually no limit to the innovations that are possible in the derivatives area. Some of the options traded over the counter have payoffs dependent on maximum value attained by a variable during a period of time; some have payoffs dependent on the average value of a variable during a period of time; some have exercise prices that are functions of time; some have features where exercising one option automatically gives the holder another option; some have payoffs dependent on the square of some future interest rate; and so on.

Up to now, the variables underlying options and other derivatives have usually been stock prices, stock indices, interest rates, exchange rates, and commodity prices. However, other variables can be, and on occasion have been, used. For example, ski slope operators have been known to issue bonds where the payoff depends on the total snow falling at a certain resort, and banks have been known to create deposit instruments where the interest paid depends on the performance of the local football team.

1.5 TYPES OF TRADERS

Traders of derivatives can be categorized as hedgers, speculators, or arbitrageurs. We now take a first look at each of these.

Hedgers

Hedgers are interested in reducing a risk that they already face. Suppose that a U.S. company knows that it is due to pay £1,000,000 to one of its British suppliers in 90 days. It is faced with a significant foreign exchange risk. The cost, in U.S. dollars, of making the payment depends on the sterling exchange rate in 90 days. Using the rates quoted in Table 1.1, the company can choose to hedge by entering into a long forward contract to buy £1,000,000 in 90 days for $1,605,600. The effect is to lock in the exchange rate that will apply to the sterling it requires.

This hedge using forward exchange rates requires no initial payment. In some circumstances it saves the company a significant amount of money. For example, if the exchange rate rises to 1.7000, the company ends up $94,400 better off if it hedges. In other circumstances, the company may wish that it had not hedged. For example, if the exchange rate falls to 1.5000, hedging leads to an outcome that is $105,600 worse than no hedging. This example emphasizes that the purpose of hedging is to make the outcome more certain. It does not necessarily improve the outcome.

As an alternative to a forward contract, the company could buy a call option to acquire £1,000,000 at a certain exchange rate, say 1.6000, in 90 days. If the actual exchange rate in 90 days proves to be above 1.6000, the company exercises the option and buys the sterling it requires for $1,600,000. If the actual exchange rate proves to be below 1.6000, the company buys the sterling in the market in the usual way (and throws the options away since they are worthless). This option strategy enables the company to insure itself against adverse exchange rate movements while benefiting from favorable movements. Of course, this insurance is achieved at a cost. Whereas forward contracts require no initial payment, option contracts can be quite expensive.

Speculators

Whereas hedgers want to eliminate an exposure to movements in the price of an asset, speculators wish to take a position in the market. Either they are betting that a price will go up or they are betting that it will go down.

Forward contracts can be used for speculation. An investor who thinks that sterling will increase in value relative to the U.S. dollar can speculate by taking a long position in a 90-day forward contract on sterling. Suppose that in the situation depicted in Table 1.1, the actual spot sterling exchange rate in 90 days proves to be 1.7000. An investor who enters into a long position in a 90-day forward contract will be able to purchase pounds for $1.6056 when they are worth $1.7000. He or she will realize a gain of $0.0944 per pound.

There is an important difference between speculating using forward markets and speculating by buying the underlying asset (in this case, a currency) in the spot market. Buying a certain amount of the underlying asset in the spot market requires an initial cash payment equal to the total value of what is bought.

Entering into a forward contract on the same amount of the asset requires no initial cash payment.[5] Speculating using forward markets therefore provides an investor with a much higher level of leverage than speculating using spot markets.

Options when used for speculation also give extra leverage. To illustrate this point, suppose that a stock price is $32 and an investor who feels that it will rise buys call options with a strike price of $35 for $0.50 per option. If the price does not go above $35 during the life of the option, the investor will lose $0.50 per option (or 100% of the investment). However, if the price rises to $40, the investor will realize a profit of $4.50 per option (or 900% of the original investment).

Arbitrageurs

Arbitrageurs are a third important group of participants in derivatives markets. Arbitrage involves locking in a riskless profit by entering simultaneously into transactions in two or more markets. In later chapters we show how arbitrage is sometimes possible when the futures price of an asset gets out of line with its cash price. We also discuss how arbitrage arguments can be used in option pricing. In this section we illustrate the concept of arbitrage with a very simple example.

Consider a stock that is traded on stock exchanges in both New York and London. Suppose that the stock price is $172 in New York and £100 in London at a time when the exchange rate is $1.7500 per pound. An arbitrageur could simultaneously buy 100 shares of the stock in New York and sell them in London to obtain risk-free profit of

$$100 \times (\$1.75 \times 100 - \$172)$$

or $300 in the absence of transactions costs. Transactions costs would probably eliminate the profit for a small investor. However, large investment houses face very low transactions costs in both the stock market and the foreign exchange market. They would find the arbitrage opportunity very attractive and would try to take as much advantage of it as possible.

Arbitrage opportunities such as the one that has just been described cannot last for long. As arbitrageurs buy the stock in New York, the forces of supply and demand will cause the dollar price to rise. Similarly, as they sell the stock in London, the sterling price will be driven down. Very quickly, the two prices will become equivalent at the current exchange rate. Indeed, the existence of profit-hungry arbitrageurs makes it unlikely that a major disparity between the sterling price and the dollar price could ever exist in the first place.

Generalizing from this example, we can say that the very existence of arbitrageurs means that, in practice, only very small arbitrage opportunities are observed in the prices that are quoted in most financial markets. In this book, most

---

[5]In practice, when entering into a forward contract with a speculator, a financial institution may require the speculator to deposit some funds up front. These funds, which usually earn interest, are generally a relatively small proportion of the value of the assets underlying the contract. They serve as a guarantee that the contract will be honored by the speculator.

of our arguments concerning futures prices and the values of option contracts are based on the assumption that there are no arbitrage opportunities.

1.6 SUMMARY

One of the interesting developments in financial markets over the last 15 to 20 years has been the growing popularity of derivatives or contingent claims. In many situations, both hedgers and speculators find it more attractive to trade a derivative on an asset than to trade the asset itself. Some derivatives are traded on exchanges. Others are made available to corporate clients by financial institutions or added to new issues of securities by underwriters. There seems to be no shortage of new ideas in this area. Much of this book is concerned with the valuation of derivatives. The aim is to present a unifying framework within which all derivatives—not just options or futures—can be valued.

In this chapter we have taken a first look at forward, futures, and options contracts. A forward or futures contract involves an obligation to buy or sell an asset at a certain time in the future for a certain price. There are two types of options: calls and puts. A call option gives the holder the right to buy an asset by a certain date for a certain price. A put option gives the holder the right to sell an asset by a certain date for a certain price. Forwards, futures, and options are now traded on a wide range of different assets.

Derivatives have been very successful innovations in capital markets. Three main types of traders can be identified: hedgers, speculators, and arbitrageurs. Hedgers are in the position where they face risk associated with the price of an asset. They use derivatives to reduce or eliminate this risk. Speculators wish to bet on future movements in the price of an asset. They use derivatives to get extra leverage. Arbitrageurs are in business to take advantage of a discrepancy between prices in two different markets. If, for example, they see the futures price of an asset getting out of line with the cash price, they will take offsetting positions in the two markets to lock in a profit.

QUESTIONS AND PROBLEMS

1.1. What is the difference between a long forward position and a short forward position?

1.2. Explain carefully the difference between hedging, speculation, and arbitrage.

1.3. What is the difference between entering into a long forward contract when the forward price is $50 and taking a long position in a call option with a strike price of $50?

1.4. An investor enters into a short cotton futures contract when the futures price is 50 cents per pound. The contract is for the delivery of 50,000 pounds. How much does the investor gain or lose if the cotton price at the end of the contract is (a) 48.20 cents per pound; (b) 51.30 cents per pound?

1.5. Suppose that you write a put option contract on 100 IBM shares with a strike price of $120 and an expiration date in three months. The current price of IBM stock is $121. What have you committed yourself to? How much could you gain or lose?

1.6. You would like to speculate on a rise in the price of a certain stock. The current stock price is $29 and a three-month call with a strike of $30 costs $2.90. You have $5,800 to invest. Identify two alternative strategies, one involving an investment in the stock and the other involving investment in the option. What are the potential gains and losses from each?

1.7. Suppose that you own 5,000 shares worth $25 each. How can put options be used to provide you with insurance against a decline in the value of your holding over the next four months?

1.8. When first issued, a stock provides funds for a company. Is the same true of a CBOE stock option? Discuss.

1.9. Explain why a forward contract can be used for either speculation or hedging.

1.10. Suppose that a European call option to buy a share for $50 costs $2.50 and is held until maturity. Under what circumstances will the holder of the option make a profit? Under what circumstances will the option be exercised? Draw a diagram illustrating how the profit from a long position in the option depends on the stock price at maturity of the option.

1.11. Suppose that a European put option to sell a share for $60 costs $4.00 and is held until maturity. Under what circumstances will the seller of the option (i.e., the party with the short position) make a profit? Under what circumstances will the option be exercised? Draw a diagram illustrating how the profit from a short position in the option depends on the stock price at maturity of the option.

1.12. An investor writes a European-style September call option with a strike price of $20. It is now May, the stock price is $18, and the option price is $2. Describe the investor's cash flows if the option is held until September and the stock price is $25 at this time.

1.13. An investor writes a European-style December put option with a strike price of $30. The price of the option is $4. Under what circumstances does the investor make a gain?

1.14. Show that the Standard Oil bond described in Section 1.4 is a combination of a regular bond, a long position in call options on oil with a strike price of $25, and a short position in call options on oil with a strike price of $40.

1.15. A company knows that it is due to receive a certain amount of a foreign currency in four months. What type of option contract is appropriate for hedging?

1.16. The price of gold is currently $500 per ounce. The forward price for delivery in one year is $700. An arbitrageur can borrow money at 10% per annum. What should the arbitrageur do? Assume that the cost of storing gold is zero.

1.17. The Chicago Board of Trade offers a futures contract on long-term Treasury bonds. Characterize the investors likely to use this contract.

1.18. The current price of a stock is $94 and three-month call options with a strike price of $95 currently sell for $4.70. An investor who feels that the price of the stock will increase is trying to decide between buying 100 shares and buying 2,000 call options ($=$ 20 contracts). Both strategies involve an investment of $9,400. What

advice would you give? How high does the stock price have to rise for the option strategy to be more profitable?

1.19. "Options and futures are zero-sum games." What do you think is meant by this statement?

1.20. Describe the payoff from the following portfolio: a long forward contract on an asset and a long European put option on the asset with the same maturity as the forward contract and a strike price that is equal to the forward price of the asset at the time the portfolio is set up.

1.21. Show that an ICON such as the one described in Section 1.4 is a combination of a regular bond and two options.

1.22. Show that a range forward contract such as the one described in Section 1.4 is a combination of two options. How can a range forward contract be constructed so that it has zero value?

1.23. On July 1, 1996, a company enters into a forward contract to buy 10 million Japanese yen on January 1, 1997. On September 1, 1996, it enters into a forward contract to sell 10 million Japanese yen on January 1, 1997. Describe the payoff from this strategy.

1.24. Suppose that sterling–U.S. dollar spot and forward exchange rates are as given in Table 1.1. What opportunities are open to an investor in the following situations?
  (a) A 180-day European call option to buy £1 for $1.5700 costs 2 cents.
  (b) A 90-day European put option to sell £1 for $1.6400 costs 2 cents.

1.25. "A long forward contract is equivalent to a long position in a European call option and a short position in a European put option." Explain this statement.

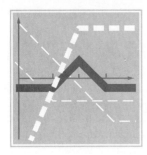

Chapter 2

Futures Markets and the Use of Futures for Hedging

Futures contracts were introduced in Chapter 1. They are agreements to buy or sell an asset in the future for a certain price. Unlike forward contracts, they are usually traded on an exchange. In this chapter we explain the way in which exchanges organize the trading of futures contracts. We discuss issues such as the specification of contracts, the operation of margin accounts, and the way in which quotes are made. We also discuss how futures contracts are used for hedging purposes.

2.1 TRADING FUTURES CONTRACTS

Suppose that it is March and you call your broker with instructions to buy one July corn futures contract (5,000 bushels) on the Chicago Board of Trade (CBOT) at the current market price. What happens? As a first step in the process, the broker passes your instructions on to a representative at the CBOT. From there, the instructions are sent by messenger to a trader on the floor of the exchange. This trader assesses the best price currently available and uses hand signals to indicate to other traders that he or she is willing to buy one contract at that price. If another trader indicates a willingness to take the other side of the position (i.e., short one July contract), the deal will be done. If not, the trader representing you will have to signal a willingness to trade at a higher price. Eventually, someone will be found to take the other side of the transaction. Confirmation that your instructions have been carried out and a notification of the price obtained are sent back to you through your broker.

There are two types of traders in the trading pits on the floor of an exchange. These are *commission brokers,* who execute trades for other people and earn commissions; and *locals,* who trade for their own account. There are many different types of orders that can be passed on to a commission broker. In the example just given, the instructions were to take a long position in one July corn contract at the current market price. This is a *market order.* Another popular type of order is a *limit order.* This specifies a certain price and requests that the transaction be executed only if that price or a better one is obtained.

Closing Out Positions

Closing out a position involves entering into a trade opposite to the original one. For example, if an investor goes long one July corn futures contract on March 6, he or she can close out the position on April 20 by shorting one July corn futures contract. If an investor shorts one July contract on March 6, he or she can close out the position on April 20 by going long one July contract. In each case, the investor's total gain or loss reflects the change in the futures price between March 6 and April 20.

The vast majority of the futures contracts that are initiated are closed out in this way. The delivery of the underlying asset is relatively rare. Despite this, it is important to understand the delivery arrangements. This is because it is the possibility of final delivery that ties the futures price to the cash price.

2.2 SPECIFICATION OF THE FUTURES CONTRACT

When developing a new contract, an exchange must specify in some detail the exact nature of the agreement between the two parties. In particular, it must specify the asset, the contract size (i.e., exactly how much of the asset will be delivered under one contract), how prices will be quoted, where delivery will be made, when delivery will be made, and how the price paid will be determined. Sometimes alternatives are specified for the asset that will be delivered and for the delivery arrangements. It is the party with the short position (the party that has agreed to sell) that chooses between these alternatives.

The Asset

When the asset is a commodity, there may be quite a variation in the quality of what is available in the marketplace. When specifying the asset, it is therefore important that the exchange stipulate the grade or grades of the commodity that are acceptable. The New York Cotton Exchange has specified the asset in its orange juice futures contract as

> US Grade A, with Brix value of not less than 57 degrees, having a Brix value to acid ratio of not less than 13 to 1 nor more than 19 to 1, with factors of color and flavor each scoring 37 points or higher and 19 for defects, with a minimum score of 94.

The Chicago Mercantile Exchange in its random-length lumber futures contract has specified that

> Each delivery unit shall consist of nominal 2 × 4s of random lengths from 8 feet to 20 feet, grade-stamped Construction and Standard, Standard and better, or #1 and #2; however, in no case may the quantity of Standard grade or #2 exceed 50 percent. Each delivery unit shall be manufactured in California, Idaho,

Montana, Nevada, Oregon, Washington, Wyoming, or Alberta or British Columbia, Canada, and contain lumber produced from and grade-stamped Alpine fir, Englemann spruce, hem-fir, lodgepole pine and/or spruce pine fir.

In the case of some commodities, a range of grades can be delivered, but the price received is adjusted depending on the grade chosen. For example, in the Chicago Board of Trade corn futures contract, the standard grade is "No. 2 Yellow," but substitutions are allowed at differentials established by the exchange.

The financial assets in futures contracts are generally well defined and unambiguous. For example, there is no need to specify the grade of a Japanese yen. However, there are some interesting features of the Treasury bond and Treasury note futures contracts traded on the Chicago Board of Trade. The underlying asset in the Treasury bond contract is any long-term U.S. Treasury bond that has a maturity of greater than 15 years and is not callable within 15 years. In the Treasury note futures contract, the underlying asset is any long-term Treasury note with a maturity no less than 6.5 years and not greater than 10 years. In both of these cases, the exchange has a formula for adjusting the price received according to the coupon and maturity date of the bond delivered. This is discussed in Chapter 4.

Contract Size

The contract size specifies the amount of the asset that has to be delivered under one contract. This is an important decision for the exchange. If the contract size is too large, many investors who wish to hedge relatively small exposures or who wish to take relatively small speculative positions will be unable to use the exchange. On the other hand, if the contract size is too small, trading may be expensive since there is a cost associated with each contract traded.

The correct size for a contract clearly depends on the likely user. Whereas the value of what is delivered under a futures contract on an agricultural product might be $10,000 to $20,000, it is much higher for some financial futures. For example, under the Treasury bond futures contract traded on the Chicago Board of Trade, instruments with a face value of $100,000 are delivered.

Delivery Arrangements

As already mentioned, the vast majority of the futures contracts that are initiated do not lead to delivery of the underlying asset. They are closed out prior to maturity. The delivery arrangements are nevertheless important in understanding the relationship between the futures price and the spot price of the asset.

The place where delivery will be made must be specified by the exchange. This is particularly important for commodities where there may be significant transportation costs. In the case of the Chicago Mercantile Exchange random-length lumber contract, the delivery location is specified as

On track and shall either be unitized in double-door boxcars or, at no additional cost to the buyer, each unit shall be individually paper-wrapped and loaded on flat-

cars. Par delivery of hem-fir in California, Idaho, Montana, Nevada, Oregon, and Washington, and in the province of British Columbia.

When alternative delivery locations are specified, the price received by the party with the short position is sometimes adjusted according to the location chosen by that party. For example, in the case of the corn futures contract traded by the Chicago Board of Trade, delivery can be made at Chicago, Burns Harbor, Toledo, or St. Louis. Deliveries at Toledo and St. Louis are made at a discount of 4 cents per bushel from the Chicago contract price.

A futures contract is referred to by its delivery month. The exchange must specify the precise period during the month when delivery can be made. For many futures contracts, the delivery period is the entire month.

The delivery months vary from contract to contract and are chosen by the exchange to meet the needs of market participants. For example, currency futures on the Chicago Mercantile Exchange have delivery months of March, June, September, and December; corn futures traded on the Chicago Board of Trade have delivery months of March, May, July, September, and December. At any given time, contracts trade for the closest delivery month and a number of subsequent delivery months. The exchange specifies when trading in a particular month's contract will begin. The exchange also specifies the last day on which trading can take place for a given contract. This is generally a few days before the last day on which delivery can be made.

Price Quotes

The futures price is quoted in a way that is convenient and easy to understand. For example, crude oil futures prices on the New York Mercantile Exchange (NYMEX) are quoted in dollars per barrel to two decimal places (i.e., to the nearest cent). Treasury bond and Treasury note futures prices on the Chicago Board of Trade are quoted in dollars and 32nds of a dollar. The minimum price movement that can occur in trading is consistent with the way in which the price is quoted. Thus it is $0.01 (or 1 cent per barrel) for the oil futures and one-32nd of a dollar for the Treasury bond and Treasury note futures.

Daily Price Movement Limits

For most contracts, daily price movement limits are specified by the exchange. For example, at the time of writing, the daily price movement limit for oil futures is $1. If the price moves down by an amount equal to the daily price limit, the contract is said to be *limit down*. If it moves up by the limit, it is said to be *limit up*. A *limit move* is a move in either direction equal to the daily price limit. Normally, trading on a contract ceases for the day once the contract is limit up or limit down, but in some instances, the exchange has the authority to step in and change the limits.

The purpose of daily price limits is to prevent large price movements occurring because of speculative excesses. However, these limits can become an

artificial barrier to trading when the price of the underlying commodity is advancing or declining rapidly. Whether price limits are, on balance, good for futures markets is controversial.

Position Limits

Position limits are the maximum number of contracts that a speculator may hold. In the Chicago Mercantile Exchange random-length lumber contract, for example, the position limit at the time of writing is 1,000 contracts, with no more than 300 in any one delivery month. Bona fide hedgers are not affected by position limits. The purpose of the limits is to prevent speculators from exercising undue influence on the market.

2.3 OPERATION OF MARGINS

If two investors get in touch with each other directly and agree to trade an asset in the future for a certain price, there are obvious risks. One of the investors may regret the deal and try to back out. Alternatively, the investor simply may not have the financial resources to honor the agreement. One of the key roles of the exchange is to organize trading so that contract defaults are minimized. This is where margins come in.

Marking to Market

To illustrate how margins work, consider an investor who contacts his or her broker on Monday, June 3, 1996, to buy two December 1996 gold futures contracts on the New York Commodity Exchange (COMEX). We suppose that the current futures price is $400 per ounce. Since the contract size is 100 ounces, the investor has contracted to buy a total of 200 ounces at this price. The broker will require the investor to deposit funds in what is termed a *margin account.* The amount that must be deposited at the time the contract is first entered into is known as the *initial margin.* This is determined by the broker. We will suppose this is $2,000 per contract, or $4,000 in total. At the end of each trading day, the margin account is adjusted to reflect the investor's gain or loss. This is known as *marking to market* the account.

Suppose, for example, that by the end of trading June 3, the futures price has dropped from $400 to $397. The investor has a loss of 200 × $3, or $600. This is because the 200 ounces of December gold, which he or she contracted to buy at $400, can now be sold for only $397. The balance in the margin account would therefore be reduced by $600 to $3,400. Similarly, if the price of December gold rose to $403 by the end of the first day, the balance in the margin account would be increased by $600 to $4,600. A trade is first marked to market at the close of the day on which it takes place. It is then marked to market at the close of trading on each subsequent day. If the delivery period is reached and delivery is made by

the party with the short position, the price received is generally the futures price at the time the contract was last marked to market.[1]

Note that marking to market is not merely an arrangement between broker and client. When there is a $600 decrease in the futures price so that the margin account of an investor with a long position is reduced by $600, the investor's broker has to pay the exchange $600 and the exchange passes the money on to the broker of an investor with a short position. Similarly, when there is an increase in the futures price, brokers for parties with short positions pay money to the exchange, and brokers for parties with long positions receive money from the exchange. We give more details of the mechanism by which this happens later in this section.

Maintenance Margin

The investor is entitled to withdraw any balance in the margin account in excess of the initial margin. To ensure that the balance in the margin account never becomes negative, a *maintenance margin,* which is somewhat lower than the initial margin, is set. If the balance in the margin account falls below the maintenance margin, the investor receives a *margin call* and is requested to top up the margin account to the initial margin level within a very short period of time. The extra funds deposited are known as a *variation margin.* If the investor does not provide the variation margin, the broker closes out the position by selling the contract. In the case of the investor in the preceding example, the broker would close out the position by selling on behalf of the investor 200 ounces of gold for delivery in December.

Table 2.1 illustrates the operation of the margin account for one possible sequence of futures prices in the case of the investor considered here. The maintenance margin is assumed for the purpose of the illustration to be $1,500 per contract, or $3,000 total. On June 11 the balance in the margin account falls $340 below the maintenance margin level. This triggers a margin call from the broker for additional margin of $1,340. The table assumes that the investor does in fact provide this margin by close of trading on June 12. On June 17, the balance in the margin account again falls below the maintenance margin level and a margin call for $1,260 is sent out. The investor provides this margin by close of trading on the next business day, June 18. On June 24, the investor decides to close out the position by shorting the two contracts. The futures price on that day is 392.30 and the investor has taken a cumulative loss of $1,540. Note that the investor has excess margin on June 12, 19, 20, and 21. The table assumes that this is not withdrawn.

Further Details

Some brokers allow an investor to earn interest on the balance in his or her margin account. The balance in the account does not therefore represent a true

---

[1]This may be adjusted for the quality of the asset delivered and the delivery location as described earlier.

TABLE 2.1   Operation of Margins for a Long Position in Two Gold Futures Contracts

The initial margin is $2,000 per contract, or $4,000 total; the maintenance margin is $1,500 per contract, or $3,000 total. The contract is entered into on Monday, June 3 at $400 and closed out on June 24 at $392.30. The numbers in the second column, except for the first and last numbers, are the futures price at the close of trading.

Day	Futures Price (dollars)	Daily Gain (Loss) (dollars)	Cumulative Gain (Loss) (dollars)	Margin Account Balance (dollars)	Margin Call (dollars)
	400.00			4,000	
June 3	397.00	(600)	(600)	3,400	
June 4	396.10	(180)	(780)	3,220	
June 5	398.20	420	(360)	3,640	
June 6	397.10	(220)	(580)	3,420	
June 7	396.70	(80)	(660)	3,340	
June 10	395.40	(260)	(920)	3,080	
June 11	393.30	(420)	(1,340)	2,660	1,340
June 12	393.60	60	(1,280)	4,060	
June 13	391.80	(360)	(1,640)	3,700	
June 14	392.70	180	(1,460)	3,880	
June 17	387.00	(1,140)	(2,600)	2,740	1,260
June 18	387.00	0	(2,600)	4,000	
June 19	388.10	220	(2,380)	4,220	
June 20	388.70	120	(2,260)	4,340	
June 21	391.00	460	(1,800)	4,800	
June 24	392.30	260	(1,540)	5,060	

cost, provided that the interest rate is competitive with that which could be earned elsewhere. To satisfy the initial margin requirements (but not subsequent margin calls), an investor can sometimes deposit securities with the broker. Treasury bills are usually accepted in lieu of cash, at about 90% of their face value. Shares are also sometimes accepted in lieu of cash—but at about 50% of their face value.

The effect of the marking to market is that a futures contract is settled daily rather than all at the end of its life. At the end of each day, the investor's gain (loss) is added to (subtracted from) the margin account. This brings the value of the contract back to zero. A futures contract is, in effect, closed out and rewritten at a new price each day.

Minimum levels for initial and maintenance margins are set by the exchange. Individual brokers may require greater margins from their clients than those specified by the exchange. However, brokers cannot require lower margins than those specified by the exchange. Margin levels are determined by the variability of the price of the underlying asset. The higher this variability, the higher the margin levels. A maintenance margin is usually about 75% of the initial margin.

Margin requirements may depend on the objectives of the trader. A bona fide hedger, such as a company that produces the commodity on which the futures contract is written, is often subject to lower margin requirements than a speculator. This is because there is deemed to be less risk of default. What are known as day trades and spread transactions often give rise to lower margin requirements than hedge transactions. A *day trade* is a trade where the trader announces to the broker that he or she plans to close out the position in the same day. Thus if the trader has taken a long position, the plan is to take an offsetting short position later in the day; if the trader has taken a short position, the plan is to take an offsetting long position later in the day. A *spread transaction* is one where the trader simultaneously takes a long position in a contract with one delivery month and a short position in a contract on the same underlying asset with another delivery month.

Note that margin requirements are the same on short futures positions as they are on long futures positions. It is just as easy to take a short futures position as it is to take a long futures position. The cash market does not have this symmetry. Taking a long position in the cash market involves buying the asset and presents no problems. Taking a short position involves selling an asset that you do not own. This is a more complex transaction that may or may not be possible in a particular market. It is discussed further in Chapter 3.

Clearinghouse and Clearing Margins

The *exchange clearinghouse* is an adjunct of the exchange and acts as an intermediary or middleman in futures transactions. It guarantees the performance of the parties to each transaction. The clearinghouse has a number of members, all with offices close to the clearinghouse. Brokers who are not clearinghouse members themselves must channel their business through a member. The main task of the clearinghouse is to keep track of all the transactions that take place during a day so that it can calculate the net position of each of its members.

Just as an investor is required to maintain a margin account with his or her broker, a clearinghouse member is required to maintain a margin account with the clearinghouse. This is known as a *clearing margin*. The margin accounts for clearinghouse members are adjusted for gains and losses at the end of each trading day in the same way as the margin accounts of investors. However, in the case of the clearinghouse member, there is an original margin but no maintenance margin. Every day, the account balance for each contract must be maintained at an amount equal to the original margin times the number of contracts outstanding. Thus, depending on transactions during the day and price movements, the clearinghouse member may have to add funds to its margin account at the end of the day. Alternatively, it may find that it can remove funds from the account at this time. Brokers who are not clearinghouse members must maintain a margin account with a clearinghouse member.

In the calculation of clearing margins, the exchange clearinghouse calculates the number of contracts outstanding on either a gross or a net basis. The

gross basis adds the total of all long positions entered into by clients to the total of all the short positions entered into by clients. The *net basis* allows these to be offset against each other. Suppose that a clearinghouse member has two clients, one with a long position in 20 contracts, the other with a short position in 15 contracts. Gross margining would calculate the clearing margin on the basis of 35 contracts; net margining would calculate the clearing margin on the basis of 5 contracts. Most exchanges currently use net margining.

It should be stressed that the purpose of the margining system is to reduce the possibility of market participants sustaining losses because of defaults. Overall, the system has been very successful. Losses arising from defaults on major exchanges have been virtually nonexistent.

2.4 NEWSPAPER QUOTES

Many newspapers carry futures quotations. In the *Wall Street Journal,* futures quotations can currently be found in the Money and Investing section. Table 2.2 shows the quotations for commodities as they appeared in the *Wall Street Journal* on Friday, May 12, 1995. These refer to the trading that took place on the preceding day (Thursday, May 11, 1995). The quotations for index futures and currency futures are given in Chapter 3. The quotations for interest rate futures are given in Chapter 4.

The asset underlying the futures contract, the exchange it is traded on, the contract size, and how the price is quoted are all shown at the top of each section. The first asset in Table 2.2 is corn, traded on the Chicago Board of Trade. The contract size is 5,000 bushels and the price is quoted in cents per bushel. The months in which particular contracts are traded are shown in the first column. Corn contracts with maturities in May 1995, July 1995, September 1995, December 1995, March 1996, May 1996, July 1996, and December 1996 were traded on May 11, 1995.

Prices

The first three numbers in each row show the opening price, the highest price achieved in trading during the day, and the lowest price achieved in trading during the day. The opening price is representative of the prices at which contracts were trading immediately after the opening bell. For July corn on May 11, 1995, the opening price was 258 cents per bushel; during the day, the price traded between $256\frac{1}{2}$ cents and $258\frac{3}{4}$ cents.

Settlement Price

The fourth number in the row is the *settlement price.* This is the average of the prices at which the contract traded immediately before the bell signaling the end of trading for the day. The fifth number is the change in the settlement price

TABLE 2.2 Commodity Futures Quotes from the *Wall Street Journal,* May 12, 1995

FUTURES PRICES

Thursday, May 11, 1995.

Open Interest Reflects Previous Trading Day.

GRAINS AND OILSEEDS

CORN (CBT) 5,000 bu.; cents per bu.

	Open	High	Low	Settle	Change	Lifetime High	Lifetime Low	Open Interest
May	252	252¾	250¾	252¼	....	285	228	4,233
July	258	258¾	256½	258	- ¼	285½	232½	141,648
Sept	262¾	263½	261½	262¾	....	270½	238	33,922
Dec	266¼	267½	264¾	266¾	....	268	235½	141,307
Mr96	272½	273½	271	272¾	....	274	249½	14,723
May	276¼	277	275	276¾	....	277¾	259½	1,352
July	278¼	279¼	277¼	278¾	....	280	254	7,351
Dec	253¾	253¾	252¾	253½	+ ¼	258½	239	4,373

Est vol 38,000; vol Wed 38,592; open Int 348,967, +987.

OATS (CBT) 5,000 bu.; cents per bu.

	Open	High	Low	Settle	Change	Lifetime High	Lifetime Low	Open Interest
May	143	143	143	143	....	151	122¼	420
July	148½	149¼	147¾	148½	- ¼	149¼	127½	11,368
Sept	151½	151¾	150¾	151¼	....	151¾	132	1,547
Dec	154¼	155	154	154¼	+ ¼	155	136	2,391
Mr96	156½	157½	156½	157½	+ ¼	157½	142	394

Est vol 3,000; vol Wed 3,286; open Int 16,126, +570.

SOYBEANS (CBT) 5,000 bu.; cents per bu.

	Open	High	Low	Settle	Change	Lifetime High	Lifetime Low	Open Interest
May	564½	564½	558	559¼	- 4¼	705½	553¼	2,544
July	574¼	574¼	568	569½	- 4¼	706½	559¼	62,841
Aug	579	579½	573	574¼	- 4¼	612	562½	11,408
Sept	583	583	578	578¾	- 4¼	615	564¾	5,980
Nov	592	592	585½	587¼	- 4	645	573¼	37,479
Ja96	600	600	595	595½	- 4½	626½	582½	3,266
Mar	606½	606½	603	603¾	- 3¾	632½	590½	943
May	613	613	613	609¾	- 4¼	637	602	285
July	616½	616½	614	613¼	- 4¼	641½	599½	1,760
Nov	597½	597½	594½	596¼	- ¼	615½	585	2,190

Est vol 33,000; vol Wed 23,141; open Int 128,699, -932.

SOYBEAN MEAL (CBT) 100 tons; $ per ton.

	Open	High	Low	Settle	Change	Lifetime High	Lifetime Low	Open Interest
May	164.00	164.30	162.80	163.90	- .40	207.00	155.30	2,345
July	168.40	168.70	166.80	167.80	- .50	206.00	159.80	40,783
Aug	170.40	170.40	168.80	169.50	- .60	182.60	162.10	10,183
Sept	172.20	172.30	170.50	171.40	- .30	182.70	164.00	8,523
Oct	173.50	173.70	172.10	172.90	- .20	183.20	166.00	9,989
Dec	176.80	176.80	175.10	176.30	....	186.40	169.30	13,880
Ja96	178.30	178.30	176.20	176.60	- .40	187.30	171.00	1,364

Est vol 15,000; vol Wed 14,229; open Int 87,135, -1,791.

SOYBEAN OIL (CBT) 60,000 lbs.; cents per lb.

	Open	High	Low	Settle	Change	Lifetime High	Lifetime Low	Open Interest
May	25.29	25.30	24.77	24.83	- .43	28.05	22.85	1,616
July	25.06	25.06	24.66	24.76	- .26	27.85	22.76	33,679
Aug	25.05	25.05	24.70	24.83	- .18	27.20	22.73	9,219
Sept	25.04	25.04	24.72	24.87	- .15	26.80	22.75	8,618
Oct	24.98	24.98	24.64	24.81	- .17	26.60	22.75	6,603
Dec	24.90	24.95	24.58	24.74	- .15	26.30	22.80	15,108
Ja96	24.91	24.91	24.65	24.75	- .16	26.10	23.25	931
Mar	24.85	24.85	24.73	24.85	- .10	25.87	23.85	1,110

Est vol 19,500; vol Wed 11,918; open int 76,925, -1,190.

WHEAT (CBT) 5,000 bu.; cents per bu.

	Open	High	Low	Settle	Change	Lifetime High	Lifetime Low	Open Interest
May	367½	369	366½	366¾	+ 2¼	398½	325	966
July	367½	370	367¼	368	+ 3½	370	316½	15,021
Sept	369	371¼	368¾	369½	+ 3½	377	329	5,245
Dec	377½	380	377½	378¾	+ 3¼	381	336½	3,176
Mr96	380½	381½	380	380½	+ 3	382	344½	592

Est vol 3,620; vol Wed 3,305; open int 24,141, +174.

WHEAT (MPLS) 5,000 bu.; cents per bu.

	Open	High	Low	Settle	Change	Lifetime High	Lifetime Low	Open Interest
May	408	409	400	403	- 3½	419¼	332½	226
July	389	389	385½	387½	+ 2½	395	324½	8,950
Sept	380	380	377¼	379¼	+ 2½	381	336¾	4,466
Dec	382	383½	381	382¼	+ 2¾	386	345	1,559

Est vol 4,738; vol Wed 4,794; open Int 15,227, +750.

CANOLA (WPG) 20 metric tons; Can. $ per ton

	Open	High	Low	Settle	Change	Lifetime High	Lifetime Low	Open Interest
June	395.00	395.50	385.20	387.50	- 7.70	483.00	346.50	7,846
Aug	405.50	405.50	395.50	398.80	- 6.30	459.50	362.00	7,232
Sept	386.00	386.00	378.50	383.00	- 2.80	426.90	350.00	3,809
Nov	383.50	384.10	375.50	378.70	- 5.20	425.50	331.00	14,872
Ja96	392.00	392.00	383.00	386.30	- 5.40	430.20	383.00	3,933
Mar	393.00	393.60	390.00	392.00	- 6.00	419.20	390.00	172

Est vol 3,650; vol Wed 4,186; open int 37,864, +254.

WHEAT (WPG) 20 metric tons; Can. $ per ton

	Open	High	Low	Settle	Change	Lifetime High	Lifetime Low	Open Interest
May	153.50	153.50	153.50	153.50	- .10	157.80	100.30	364
July	153.20	153.40	153.00	153.40	+ .20	156.00	101.00	3,911
Oct	143.10	143.20	143.00	143.20	+ .10	146.50	105.00	2,325
Dec		....	....	142.00	....	145.40	130.40	2,801
Mr96	143.00	143.20	143.00	143.20	+ .20	146.50	137.50	654

Est vol 782; vol Wed 291; open int 10,055, +80.

LIVESTOCK AND MEAT

CATTLE–FEEDER (CME) 50,000 lbs.; cents per lb.

	Open	High	Low	Settle	Change	Lifetime High	Lifetime Low	Open Interest
May	63.10	63.60	63.05	63.40	+ .22	76.45	62.25	2,658
Aug	64.60	65.15	64.40	64.67	+ .07	73.10	63.55	5,516
Sept	64.60	64.90	64.30	64.60	....	72.15	63.60	1,035
Oct	64.55	64.95	64.35	64.65	+ .10	71.95	63.85	2,058
Nov	65.40	65.75	65.25	65.45	+ .05	72.15	64.90	473
Ja96	65.30	65.60	65.15	65.40	+ .02	71.52	64.85	151

Est vol 1,780; vol Wed 3,440; open Int 11,960, +19.

CATTLE–LIVE (CME) 40,000 lbs.; cents per lb.

	Open	High	Low	Settle	Change	Lifetime High	Lifetime Low	Open Interest
June	59.50	59.87	59.00	59.27	+ .17	72.50	58.65	28,336
Aug	58.95	59.37	58.75	59.07	+ .27	68.10	57.75	15,508
Oct	61.10	61.50	60.85	61.20	+ .30	67.55	60.25	9,917
Dec	62.75	62.87	62.45	62.75	+ .22	67.25	61.75	3,709
Fb96	63.75	63.75	63.40	63.67	+ .20	68.20	62.80	3,275
Apr	64.50	64.65	64.37	64.62	+ .20	68.32	63.90	1,428

Est vol 12,921; vol Wed 25,557; open int 62,217, +268.

HOGS (CME) 40,000 lbs.; cents per lb.

	Open	High	Low	Settle	Change	Lifetime High	Lifetime Low	Open Interest
June	41.50	41.80	40.95	41.50	+ .10	51.55	39.95	12,295
July	42.05	42.35	41.75	42.22	+ .07	49.00	40.65	6,442
Aug	42.00	42.20	41.72	42.15	+ .07	47.00	40.60	4,892
Oct	40.10	40.42	40.10	40.10	- .05	43.15	38.30	4,375
Dec	41.25	41.40	41.12	41.15	+ .05	44.22	39.00	1,491
Fb96	42.07	42.25	42.07	42.17	+ .10	45.20	41.00	526
Apr	41.55	41.65	41.47	41.60	+ .10	44.02	40.55	214
June	45.65	45.75	45.60	45.75	+ .12	47.12	45.20	131

Est vol 5,778; vol Wed 6,545; open int 30,382, -193.

FOOD AND FIBER

COCOA (CSCE)–10 metric tons; $ per ton.

	Open	High	Low	Settle	Change	Lifetime High	Lifetime Low	Open Interest
May	1,295	1,287	1,262	1,271	- 24	1,612	1,111	114
July	1,299	1,302	1,265	1,276	- 24	1,600	1,225	28,850
Sept	1,320	1,322	1,295	1,302	- 23	1,611	1,263	19,470
Dec	1,357	1,358	1,332	1,337	- 23	1,633	1,290	11,929
Mr96	1,396	1,395	1,371	1,375	- 23	1,676	1,350	5,636
May	1,415	1,403	1,401	1,396	- 23	1,642	1,390	4,514
July	1,430	1,405	1,405	1,409	- 23	1,595	1,405	2,900
Sept		....	....	1,428	- 23	1,557	1,445	2,735
Dec	1,465	1,460	1,460	1,451	- 23	1,578	1,460	1,552

Est vol 12,368; vol Wed 3,485; open int 77,700, -259.

from the preceding day. In the case of the July 1995 corn futures contract, the settlement price was 258 cents on May 11, 1995, down 0.25 cent from May 10, 1995.

TABLE 2.2   Commodity Futures Quotes from the *Wall Street Journal*, May 12, 1995 *(Continued)*

FUTURES PRICES

COFFEE (CSCE) – 37,500 lbs.; cents per lb.

	Open	High	Low	Settle	Change	Lifetime High	Lifetime Low	Open Interest
May	171.25	172.00	166.00	166.65	– 4.60	244.40	82.50	66
July	174.00	179.80	168.50	169.90	– 4.90	245.10	85.00	18,639
Sept	176.50	178.05	170.50	172.45	– 4.65	238.00	89.00	8,490
Dec	178.50	179.90	174.00	174.20	– 4.30	242.00	151.00	5,588
Mr96	180.50	180.75	176.75	177.20	– 3.95	203.50	151.35	1,852

Est vol 9,549; vol Wed 4,995; open int 34,759, +153.

SUGAR – WORLD (CSCE) – 112,000 lbs.; cents per lb.

	Open	High	Low	Settle	Change	Lifetime High	Lifetime Low	Open Interest
July	11.57	11.58	11.12	11.18	– .38	15.21	10.57	61,827
Oct	10.74	10.75	10.38	10.42	– .32	14.25	10.38	33,042
Mr96	10.54	10.55	10.25	10.28	– .30	13.39	10.25	20,781
May	10.48	10.50	10.20	10.20	– .30	13.25	10.20	6,106
July	10.32	10.17	10.15	10.05	– .30	12.91	10.15	7,749
Oct	10.11	10.11	9.87	9.88	– .27	12.50	9.87	1,410

Est vol 20,874; vol Wed 8,140; open int 130,959, +319.

SUGAR – DOMESTIC (CSCE) – 112,000 lbs.; cents per lb.

	Open	High	Low	Settle	Change	Lifetime High	Lifetime Low	Open Interest
July	22.88	22.92	22.88	22.92	+ .05	22.97	22.00	3,189
Sept	22.71	22.76	22.71	22.76	+ .03	22.86	21.95	2,438
Nov	....	....		22.16	....	22.27	21.80	1,943
Ja96	21.86	21.87	21.86	21.86	– .01	22.03	21.75	783
Mar	21.85	21.85	21.85	21.87	– .01	21.98	21.78	1,071
May	....	....		21.95	....	21.96	21.80	305
July	....	....		21.95	....	21.95	21.88	666

Est vol 1,759; vol Wed 560; open int 10,407, +39.

COTTON (CTN) – 50,000 lbs.; cents per lb.

	Open	High	Low	Settle	Change	Lifetime High	Lifetime Low	Open Interest
July	102.29	102.29	102.29+	2.00	....	108.20	69.30	18,803
Oct	87.78	87.78	87.10	87.66 +	1.88	87.78	66.80	8,533
Dec	81.90	82.60	81.78	81.83 +	1.03	82.60	66.25	29,970
Mr96	83.15	83.60	82.80	82.80 +	.91	83.60	68.00	8,245
May	83.82	84.20	83.40	83.40 +	.60	84.20	72.70	2,974
Jly	na	84.70	83.95	83.95 +	1.05	84.70	76.00	1,249
Oct	na	79.75	78.80	78.83 –	.07	79.75	77.00	370

Est vol 12,000; vol Wed 9,680; open int 70,385, –61.

ORANGE JUICE (CTN) – 15,000 lbs.; cents per lb.

	Open	High	Low	Settle	Change	Lifetime High	Lifetime Low	Open Interest
May	na	103.50	103.30	103.50 +	.95	126.50	96.65	25
July	105.90	107.65	105.75	107.15 +	.85	129.00	100.50	13,831
Sept	110.00	111.55	109.70	111.00 +	.90	132.00	102.50	6,749
Nov	na	109.00	108.25	108.50 +	.45	129.00	105.00	2,159
Ja96	na	110.50	109.25	110.50 +	.55	129.20	105.50	2,608
Mar	....	....		112.50 +	.55	130.20	109.00	804
May	....	....		114.00 +	.55	126.00	113.50	402

Est vol 1,500; vol Wed 628; open int 26,378, +4.

					Lifetime	Open
Open	High	Low	Settle	Change	High Low	Interest

METALS AND PETROLEUM

COPPER-HIGH (Cmx.Div.NYM) – 25,000 lbs.; cents per lb.

	Open	High	Low	Settle	Change	Lifetime High	Lifetime Low	Open Interest
May	125.80	126.35	124.60	126.15 +	.65	139.40	76.85	3,462
June	124.70	125.25	124.70	126.00 +	.95	136.20	106.30	1,454
July	124.25	125.75	123.60	125.40 +	1.15	134.50	78.00	32,390
Aug	123.30	123.30	123.30	124.70 +	1.00	131.70	111.40	634
Sept	122.90	124.00	122.10	123.80 +	.90	130.50	79.10	5,959
Oct	....	....		123.10 +	.70	127.50	113.00	433
Nov	121.70	121.70	121.70	122.30 +	.50	126.30	113.95	371
Dec	121.00	122.00	120.50	121.60 +	.30	127.00	88.00	4,043
Ja95	....	....		120.70 +	.10	125.10	88.50	266
Mar	118.60	118.60	118.60	118.90 –	.30	123.70	99.20	1,559
May	116.50	116.50	116.50	116.80 –	.50	121.00	107.00	336
July	....	....		114.80 –	1.05	119.00	105.50	291
Sept	....	....		113.40 –	1.20	117.00	105.25	195
Dec	114.35	114.35	114.00	113.40 –	1.20	116.80	112.00	149

Est vol 9,000; vol Wed 5,376; open int 51,548, –63.

GOLD (Cmx.Div.NYM) – 100 troy oz.; $ per troy oz.

	Open	High	Low	Settle	Change	Lifetime High	Lifetime Low	Open Interest
May	....	....		383.50 –	.10	398.20	397.00	0
June	385.00	385.70	383.60	384.40 –	.10	430.00	351.00	62,584
Aug	387.00	388.90	386.60	387.60 –	.10	414.50	380.50	30,564
Oct	391.60	391.60	390.80	390.90	....	419.20	387.20	7,057
Dec	393.00	395.00	393.00	394.20 +	.10	439.50	358.00	17,373
Fb96	....	....		397.40 +	.20	424.50	393.60	11,078
Apr	....	....		400.80 +	.30	430.20	398.70	6,968
June	405.00	405.00	405.00	404.30 +	.40	447.00	370.90	6,831
Aug	....	....		407.60 +	.50	423.00	423.00	629
Oct	....	....		411.10 +	.70	432.20	418.00	114
Dec	413.50	413.50	413.50	414.70 +	.90	447.50	379.60	4,546
Fb97	....	....		418.30 +	1.00	....	....	110
June	....	....		425.40 +	1.10	456.00	429.20	3,359
Dec	....	....		435.90 +	1.10	477.00	402.00	3,752
Ju98	....	....		446.70 +	1.10	489.50	454.70	3,032
Dec	....	....		457.50 +	1.10	505.00	456.50	3,514
Ju99	....	....		468.60 +	1.10	520.00	485.30	3,950
Dec	....	....		479.80 +	1.10	506.00	490.00	1,932

Est vol 22,000; vol Wed 41,522; open int 167,393, –2,813.

PLATINUM (NYM) – 50 troy oz.; $ per troy oz.

	Open	High	Low	Settle	Change	Lifetime High	Lifetime Low	Open Interest
July	432.00	435.00	430.00	430.10 –	1.80	478.50	403.50	14,616
Oct	434.00	437.00	433.00	432.10 –	1.80	469.00	407.00	4,472
Ja96	437.00	439.00	436.00	434.00 –	1.80	463.50	409.10	1,516
Apr	440.00	440.00	440.00	437.00 –	1.80	467.50	429.50	698

Est vol 2,620; vol Wed 5,826; open int 21,350, –1,334.

SILVER (Cmx.Div.NYM) – 5,000 troy oz.; ¢ per troy oz.

	Open	High	Low	Settle	Change	Lifetime High	Lifetime Low	Open Interest
May	538.0	546.0	532.0	532.4 –	7.3	616.0	418.0	552
July	546.5	551.0	535.0	537.2 –	7.3	621.0	403.0	57,951
Sept	552.0	556.5	542.0	542.9 –	7.3	625.5	446.0	12,328
Dec	558.5	564.5	548.5	550.9 –	7.3	682.0	434.0	15,579
Mr96	566.0	573.0	566.0	559.2 –	7.3	638.0	466.5	10,174
May	....	....		564.9 –	7.3	646.0	475.0	5,633
July	....	....		570.7 –	7.3	642.0	480.0	4,426
Sept	579.0	579.0	579.0	576.8 –	7.3	579.0	488.0	3,183
Dec	594.0	599.0	592.0	586.1 –	7.3	670.0	454.0	2,110
Jl97	....	....		609.7 –	7.3	655.0	550.0	537
Dec	....	....		627.6 –	7.3	695.0	502.0	567
Dc98	....	....		673.7 –	7.3	734.0	586.0	157
Jl99	....	....		701.1 –	7.3	....	....	101

Est vol 22,000; vol Wed 42,339; open int 113,371, –4,458.

CRUDE OIL, Light Sweet (NYM) 1,000 bbls.; $ per bbl.

	Open	High	Low	Settle	Change	Lifetime High	Lifetime Low	Open Interest
June	19.78	19.88	19.25	19.41 –	.34	21.21	15.73	77,655
July	19.56	19.68	19.12	19.24 –	.30	20.42	16.05	63,503
Aug	19.39	19.40	18.90	19.03 –	.26	20.00	16.16	36,860
Sept	19.12	19.15	18.75	18.82 –	.22	19.84	16.28	26,169
Oct	18.92	18.94	18.58	18.66 –	.20	19 34	16.42	16,329
Nov	18.75	18.80	18.50	18.52 –	.19	19.15	17.15	16,199
Dec	18.60	18.65	18.36	18.40 –	.17	20.80	16.50	17,996
Ja96	18.34	18.34	18.34	18.30 –	.15	19.08	17.30	15,231
Feb	....	....		18.23 –	.14	18.84	17.38	9,842
Mar	18.24	18.24	18.08	18.16 –	.13	18.80	17.15	8,199
Apr	....	....		18.09 –	.12	18.46	17.53	5,355
May	....	....		18.05 –	.12	18.50	17.64	4,565
June	18.18	18.23	17.97	18.05 –	.11	20.40	17.22	15,557
July	....	....		18.04 –	.11	18.75	17.63	3,643
Aug	....	....		18.04 –	.11	19.36	17.59	1,774
Sept	....	....		18.04 –	.11	18.47	17.80	3,943
Oct	18.18	18.18	18.14	18.03 –	.11	18.35	17.97	1,555
Nov	....	....		18.02 –	.11	18.25	18.15	1,016
Dec	18.19	18.19	17.95	18.02 –	.11	20.40	17.65	14,510
Mr97	18.23	18.23	18.23	18.07 –	.10	18.38	18.03	509
June	....	....		18.12 –	.10	19.60	17.85	8,044
Dec	18.30	18.30	18.25	18.29 –	.07	19.20	18.05	10,303
Dc98	18.80	18.80	18.80	18.68 –	.03	18.80	18.80	419
Dc99	....	....		19.17	....	....	....	260

Est vol 147,281; vol Wed 125,214; open int 359,436, –9,927.

The settlement price is important because it is used for calculating daily gains and losses and margin requirements. In the case of the July 1995 corn futures contract, an investor with a long position in one contract would find that his or her margin account balance decreased by $12.50 (= $5,000 \times 0.25$ cent)

TABLE 2.2   Commodity Futures Quotes from the *Wall Street Journal*, May 12, 1995 *(Continued)*

FUTURES PRICES

HEATING OIL NO. 2 (NYM) 42,000 gal.; $ per gal.

	Open	High	Low	Settle	Change	Lifetime High	Lifetime Low	Open Int
June	.5000	.5045	.4875	.4909	− .0086	.5350	.4550	33,147
July	.5010	.5055	.4900	.4928	− .0081	.5430	.4640	21,514
Aug	.5060	.5070	.4945	.4963	− .0076	.5400	.4725	11,378
Sept	.5125	.5125	.5025	.5033	− .0071	.5310	.4815	6,373
Oct	.5200	.5200	.5110	.5123	− .0066	.5395	.4915	5,009
Nov	.5280	.5285	.5200	.5213	− .0061	.5440	.5000	4,544
Dec	.5365	.5380	.5270	.5298	− .0061	.5760	.5085	11,290
Ja96	.5405	.5405	.5310	.5338	− .0056	.5525	.5135	8,261
Feb	.5325	.5325	.5270	.5293	− .0051	.5930	.5150	6,254
Mar	.5190	.5190	.5170	.5188	− .0046	.5490	.5100	2,054
Apr	.5115	.5120	.5075	.5098	− .0041	.5450	.5050	837
May	....	....		.5023	− .0036	.5175	.5005	642
June	....	....		.4993	− .0036	.5100	.5000	2,064
July	....	....		.5018	− .0036	.5050	.5010	1,155
Aug	....	....		.5063	− .0036	....	....	347
Sept	....	....		.5148	− .0036	.5250	.5130	152

Est vol 30,232; vol Wed 30,232; open int 115,021, −1,424.

GASOLINE-NY Unleaded (NYM) 42,000 gal.; $ per gal.

	Open	High	Low	Settle	Change	Lifetime High	Lifetime Low	Open Int
June	.6330	.6416	.6250	.6328	− .0001	.6505	.5240	36,605
July	.6150	.6210	.6030	.6105	− .0035	.6285	.5160	19,999
Aug	.5990	.6015	.5875	.5925	− .0040	.6100	.5300	7,895
Sept	.5836	.5850	.5720	.5765	− .0050	.5945	.5220	3,685
Oct	.5634	.5635	.5555	.5580	− .0045	.5715	.5150	2,754
Nov	.5480	.5480	.5495	.5495	− .0040	.5640	.5085	1,747
Dec	.5440	.5450	.5400	.5420	− .0035	.5580	.5050	2,050

Est vol 33,353; vol Wed 29,400; open int 74,735, +1,811.

NATURAL GAS, (NYM) 10,000 MMBtu.; $ per MMBtu's

	Open	High	Low	Settle	Change	Lifetime High	Lifetime Low	Open Int
June	1.676	1.680	1.645	1.651	− .027	2.245	1.475	23,698
July	1.732	1.740	1.710	1.720	− .020	2.214	1.520	22,475
Aug	1.765	1.770	1.745	1.751	− .015	2.234	1.545	14,215
Sept	1.770	1.780	1.755	1.763	− .013	2.267	1.560	15,570
Oct	1.810	1.813	1.800	1.803	− .010	2.280	1.625	11,332
Nov	1.890	1.895	1.885	1.886	− .010	2.360	1.720	7,695
Dec	1.975	1.975	1.960	1.964	− .010	2.444	1.797	11,908
Ja96	1.990	1.990	1.976	1.979	− .010	2.416	1.817	11,780
Feb	1.920	1.925	1.920	1.914	− .010	2.295	1.760	4,918
Mar	....	....		1.864	− .010	2.220	1.710	4,580
Apr	1.824	1.824	1.820	1.814	− .010	2.105	1.650	3,124
May	1.826	1.826	1.820	1.816	− .010	2.055	1.650	2,933
June	1.825	1.825	1.825	1.822	− .009	1.910	1.660	2,482
July	....	....		1.827	− .009	1.890	1.675	2,745
Aug	1.840	1.840	1.840	1.832	− .009	1.905	1.695	1,249
Sept	1.840	1.840	1.840	1.837	− .009	1.920	1.755	1,654
Oct	1.870	1.870	1.870	1.859	− .009	1.930	1.852	1,277
Nov	1.945	1.945	1.934	1.927	− .009	1.945	1.910	1,140

Est vol 20,708; vol Wed 18,711; open int 144,775, −1,092.

BRENT CRUDE (IPE) 1,000 net bbls.; $ per bbl.

	Open	High	Low	Settle	Change	Lifetime High	Lifetime Low	Open Int
June	18.50	18.64	18.22	18.31	− .13	19.38	15.70	43,218
July	18.05	18.17	17.73	17.78	− .23	18.82	15.71	48,638
Aug	17.71	17.82	17.45	17.48	− .20	18.42	15.83	19,386
Sept	17.52	17.57	17.26	17.27	− .21	18.10	15.89	13,118
Oct	17.39	17.44	17.15	17.15	− .20	17.93	16.10	11,804
Nov	17.22	17.34	17.17	17.05	− .16	17.80	16.13	4,112
Dec	17.11	17.22	16.96	16.96	− .14	17.60	15.95	13,808
Ja96	....	....		16.88	− .12	17.40	16.24	2,883
Feb	16.99	16.99	16.97	16.80	− .11	17.43	16.18	3,349
Mar	....	....		16.72	− .12	17.09	16.37	1,092
Apr	16.73	16.83	16.69	16.69	− .09	17.30	16.45	1,926
May	16.80	16.80	16.67	16.67	− .09	17.16	16.80	555

Est vol 59,319; vol Wed 44,576; open int 163,889, +869.

GAS OIL (IPE) 100 metric tons; $ per ton

	Open	High	Low	Settle	Change	Lifetime High	Lifetime Low	Open Int
May	155.25	156.75	154.00	154.25	....	167.00	143.25	9,782
June	154.00	155.00	153.00	153.25	....	168.75	143.75	30,020
July	154.00	154.75	153.75	153.75	+ .25	163.00	145.50	18,515
Aug	155.75	155.75	154.75	....	....	162.00	147.75	6,691

Est vol 59,319; vol Wed 44,576; open int 163,889, +869.

> **EXCHANGE ABBREVIATIONS**
> (for commodity futures and futures options)
>
> CBT-Chicago Board of Trade; CME-Chicago Mercantile Exchange; CMX-COMEX (Div. of New York Mercantile Exchange); CTN-New York Cotton Exchange; FINEX-Financial Exchange (Div. of New York Cotton Exchange; IPE-International Petroleum Exchange; KC-Kansas City Board of Trade; LIFFE-London International Financial Futures Exchange; MATIF-Marche a Terme International de France; ME-Montreal Exchange; MCE-MidAmerica Commodity Exchange; MPLS-Minneapolis Grain Exchange; NYFE-New York Futures Exchange (Sub. of New York Cotton Exchange); NYM-New York Mercantile Exchange; SFE-Sydney Futures Exchange; TFE-Toronto Futures Exchange; WPG-Winnipeg Commodity Exchange.

between May 10 and May 11, 1995. Similarly, an investor with a short position in one contract would find that the margin balance increased by $12.50 between May 10, 1995 and May 11, 1995.

Lifetime Highs and Lows

The sixth and seventh numbers show the highest futures price and the lowest futures price achieved in the trading of the particular contract. The highest and lowest prices for the July 1995 corn futures contract were 285.50 cents and 232.50 cents. (The contract had traded for over a year on May 11, 1995.)

Open Interest and Volume of Trading

The final column in Table 2.2 shows the *open interest* for each contract. This is the total number of the contracts outstanding. It is the sum of all the long positions, or equivalently, it is the sum of all the short positions. Because

of problems in compiling the data, the open interest information is one trading day older than the price information. Thus, in the *Wall Street Journal* of May 12, 1995, the open interest is for the close of trading on May 10, 1995. In the case of the July 1995 corn futures contract, the open interest was 141,648 contracts.

At the end of each commodity's section, Table 2.2 shows the estimated volume of trading in contracts of all maturities on May 11, 1995 and the actual volume of trading in these contracts on May 10, 1995. It also shows the total open interest for all contracts on May 10, 1995 and the change in this open interest from May 9, 1995. For all corn futures contracts, the estimated trading volume was 38,000 contracts on May 11, 1995 and the actual trading volume was 38,592 contracts on May 10, 1995. The open interest for all contracts was 348,967 on May 10, 1995—up 987 from the preceding day.

It sometimes happens that the volume of trading in a day is greater than the open interest at the end of the day. This is indicative of a large number of day trades.

Patterns of Futures Prices

A number of different patterns of futures prices can be picked out from Table 2.2. The futures price of platinum on the New York Mercantile Exchange increases as the time to maturity increases. This is known as a *normal market.* By contrast, the futures price of copper on the New York Commodity Exchange is a decreasing function of the time to maturity. This is known as an *inverted market.* For hogs, the pattern is mixed. The futures price is sometimes an increasing and sometimes a decreasing function of maturity. The factors determining the pattern observed for a commodity are discussed in Chapter 3.

2.5 CONVERGENCE OF FUTURES PRICE TO SPOT PRICE

As the delivery month of a futures contract is approached, the futures price converges to the spot price of the underlying asset. When the delivery period is reached, the futures price equals—or is very close to—the spot price.

To show why this is so, suppose first that the futures price is above the spot price during the delivery period. This gives rise to a clear arbitrage opportunity for traders:

1. Short a futures contract.
2. Buy the asset.
3. Make delivery.

This is certain to lead to a profit equal to the amount by which the futures price exceeds the spot price. As traders exploit this arbitrage opportunity, the futures price will fall. Suppose next that the futures price is below the spot price during the delivery period. Companies interested in acquiring the asset will find

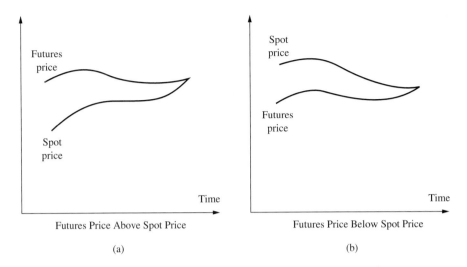

Figure 2.1   Relationship between futures price and spot price as the delivery month is approached.

it attractive to enter into a long futures contract and then wait for delivery to be made. As they do this, the futures price will tend to rise.

Figure 2.1 illustrates the convergence of the futures price to the spot price. In Figure 2.1a the futures price is above the spot price prior to the delivery month. (This corresponds to platinum in Table 2.2.) In Figure 2.1b the futures price is below the spot price prior to the delivery month. (This corresponds to copper in Table 2.2.)

2.6 SETTLEMENT

When the exchange has provided alternatives as to when, where, and what will be delivered, it is the party with the short position that makes the choice. When it is ready to deliver, the party with the short position sends a *notice of intention to deliver* to the exchange. The price paid is normally the most recent settlement price (with a possible adjustment for the quality of asset that is chosen and the delivery location). The exchange then selects a party with an outstanding long position to accept delivery.

Cash Settlement

Some financial futures, such as those on stock indices, are settled in cash. This is because it is inconvenient or impossible to deliver the underlying asset. In the case of the futures contract on the S&P 500, for example, delivering the underlying asset would involve delivering a portfolio of 500 stocks. When a contract is settled in cash, it is marked to market at the end of the last trading day and all

positions are declared closed. The settlement price on the last trading day is set equal to the closing spot price of the underlying asset. This ensures that the futures price converges to the spot price.

One exception to the rule that the settlement price on the last trading day equals the closing spot price is the S&P 500 futures contract. This bases the final settlement price on the opening price of the index the morning after the last trading day. This procedure is designed to avoid some of the problems connected with the fact that stock index futures, stock index options, and options on stock index futures all expire on the same day. Arbitrageurs often take large offsetting positions in these three contracts and there may be chaotic trading and significant price movements toward the end of an expiration day as they attempt to close out their positions. The media have coined the term *triple witching hour* to describe trading during the last hour of an expiration day.

2.7 REGULATION

Futures markets in the United States are currently regulated federally by the Commodity Futures Trading Commission (CFTC), which was established in 1974. This body is responsible for licensing futures exchanges and approving contracts. All new contracts and changes to existing contracts must be approved by the CFTC. To be approved, the contract must have some useful economic purpose. Usually, this means that it must serve the needs of hedgers as well as speculators.

The CFTC looks after the public interest. It is responsible for ensuring that prices are communicated to the public and that futures traders report their outstanding positions if they are above certain levels. The CFTC also licenses all individuals who offer their services to the public in the futures area. The backgrounds of these people are investigated and there are minimum capital requirements. The CFTC deals with complaints brought by the public and ensures that disciplinary action is taken against individuals when this is appropriate. It has the authority to force exchanges to take disciplinary action against members who are in violation of exchange rules.

In 1982, the National Futures Association (NFA) was formed. This led to some of the responsibilities of the CFTC being shifted to the futures industry itself. The NFA is an organization of people who participate in the futures industry. Its objective is to prevent fraud and ensure that the market operates in the best interests of the general public. The NFA requires its members to pass an exam. It is authorized to monitor trading and take disciplinary action where appropriate. It has set up an efficient system for arbitrating disputes between individuals and its members.

From time to time, other bodies, such as the Securities and Exchange Commission (SEC), the Federal Reserve Board, and the U.S. Treasury Department, have claimed jurisdictional rights over some aspects of futures trading. These bodies are concerned about the effects of futures trading on the spot markets

for securities such as stocks, Treasury bills, and Treasury bonds. The SEC currently has an effective veto over the approval of new stock or bond index futures contracts. However, the basic responsibility for all futures and options on futures rests with the CFTC.

Trading Irregularities

Most of the time, futures markets operate efficiently and in the public interest. However, from time to time, trading irregularities do come to light. One type of trading irregularity occurs when an investor group tries to "corner the market."[2] The investor group takes a huge long futures position and tries to exercise some control over the supply of the underlying commodity. As the maturity of the futures contracts is approached, the investor group does not close out its position, and the number of outstanding futures contracts may exceed the amount of the commodity available for delivery. The holders of short positions realize that they will find it difficult to deliver and become desperate to close out their positions. The result is a large rise in both futures and spot prices. Regulators usually deal with this type of abuse of the market by increasing margin requirements, imposing stricter position limits, prohibiting trades that increase a speculator's open position, and forcing market participants to close out their positions.

Other types of trading irregularities can involve the traders on the floor of the exchange. These received some publicity early in 1989 when it was announced that the FBI had carried out a two-year investigation, using undercover agents, of trading on the Chicago Board of Trade and the Chicago Mercantile Exchange. The investigation was initiated because complaints were filed by a large agricultural concern. The alleged offenses included overcharging customers, not paying customers the full proceeds of sales, and traders using their knowledge of customer orders to trade first for themselves.

2.8 HEDGING USING FUTURES

A company that knows that it is due to sell an asset at a particular time in the future can hedge by taking a short futures position. This is known as a *short hedge*. If the price of the asset goes down, the company does not fare well on the sale of the asset but makes a gain on the short futures position. If the price of the asset goes up, the company gains from the sale of the asset but takes a loss on the futures position. Similarly, a company that knows that it is due to buy an asset in the future can hedge by taking a long futures position. This is known as a *long hedge*. It is important to recognize that futures hedging does not necessarily improve the overall financial outcome. In fact, we can expect a futures hedge to

---

[2]Possibly the best known example of this is the activities of the Hunt brothers in the silver market in 1979–1980. Between the middle of 1979 and the beginning of 1980, their activities led to a price rise from $9 per ounce to $50 per ounce.

make the outcome worse roughly 50% of the time. What the futures hedge does do is reduce risk by making the outcome more certain.

There are a number of reasons why hedging using futures contracts works less than perfectly in practice.

1. The asset whose price is to be hedged may not be exactly the same as the asset underlying the futures contract.
2. The hedger may be uncertain as to the exact date when the asset will be bought or sold.
3. The hedge may require the futures contract to be closed out well before its expiration date.

These problems give rise to what is termed *basis risk.*

Basis Risk

The *basis* in a hedging situation is defined as follows:[3]

$$\text{basis} = \text{spot price of asset to be hedged} - \text{futures price of contract used}$$

If the asset to be hedged and the asset underlying the futures contract are the same, the basis should be zero at the expiration of the futures contract. Prior to expiration, as shown in Table 2.2 and illustrated in Figure 2.1, the basis may be positive or negative.

When the spot price increases by more than the futures price, the basis increases. This is referred to as a *strengthening of the basis.* When the futures price increases by more than the spot price, the basis declines. This is referred to as a *weakening of the basis.*

To examine the nature of basis risk we use the following notation:

S_1: spot price at time t_1
S_2: spot price at time t_2
F_1: futures price at time t_1
F_2: futures price at time t_2
b_1: basis at time t_1
b_2: basis at time t_2

We will assume that a hedge is put in place at time t_1 and closed out at time t_2. As an example we consider the case where the spot and futures price at the time the hedge is initiated are $2.50 and $2.20, respectively, and that at the time the hedge

---

[3]This is the usual definition. However, the alternative definition,

$$\text{basis} = \text{futures price} - \text{spot price}$$

is sometimes used, particularly when the futures contract is on a financial asset.

is closed out they are \$2.00 and \$1.90, respectively. This means that $S_1 = 2.50$, $F_1 = 2.20$, $S_2 = 2.00$, and $F_2 = 1.90$.

From the definition of the basis,

$$b_1 = S_1 - F_1$$

$$b_2 = S_2 - F_2$$

In our example, $b_1 = 0.30$ and $b_2 = 0.10$.

Consider first the situation of a hedger who knows that the asset will be sold at time t_2 and takes a short futures position at time t_1. The price realized for the asset is S_2 and the profit on the futures position is $F_1 - F_2$. The effective price that is obtained for the asset with hedging is therefore

$$S_2 + F_1 - F_2 = F_1 + b_2$$

In our example, this is \$2.30. The value of F_1 is known at time t_1. If b_2 were also known at this time, a perfect hedge (i.e., a hedge eliminating all uncertainty about the price obtained) would result. The hedging risk is the uncertainty associated with b_2. This is known as *basis risk*. Consider next a situation where a company knows that it will buy the asset at time t_2 and initiates a long hedge at time t_1. The price paid for the asset is S_2 and the loss on the futures position is $F_1 - F_2$. The effective price that is paid with hedging is therefore

$$S_2 + F_1 - F_2 = F_1 + b_2$$

This is the same expression as before; it is \$2.30 in the example. The value of F_1 is known at time t_1 and the term b_2 represents basis risk.

For investment assets such as currencies, stock indices, gold, and silver, the basis risk tends to be fairly small. This is because, as we will see in Chapter 3, arbitrage arguments lead to a well-defined relationship between the futures price and the spot price of an investment asset. The basis risk for an investment asset arises mainly from uncertainty as to the level of the risk-free interest rate and the asset's yield in the future. In the case of a commodity such as oil, corn, or copper, imbalances between supply and demand and the difficulties sometimes associated with storing the commodity can lead to large variations in the basis and therefore a much higher basis risk.

The asset that gives rise to the hedger's exposure is sometimes different from the asset underlying the hedge.[4] The basis risk is then usually greater. Define S_2^* as the price of the asset underlying the futures contract at time t_2. As before, S_2 is the price of the asset being hedged at time t_2. By hedging, a company ensures that the price that will be paid (or received) for the asset is

$$S_2 + F_1 - F_2$$

---

[4]For example, airlines sometimes use the NYMEX heating oil futures contract to hedge their exposure to the price of jet fuel. See the article by Nikkhah referenced at the end of this chapter for a description of this.

This can be written

$$F_1 + (S_2^* - F_2) + (S_2 - S_2^*)$$

The terms $S_2^* - F_2$ and $S_2 - S_2^*$ represent the two components of the basis. The $S_2^* - F_2$ term is the basis that would exist if the asset being hedged were the same as the asset underlying the futures contract. The $S_2 - S_2^*$ term is the basis arising from the difference between the two assets.

Note that basis risk can lead to an improvement or a worsening of a hedger's position. Consider a short hedge. If the basis strengthens unexpectedly, the hedger's position improves, whereas if the basis weakens unexpectedly, the hedger's position worsens. For a long hedge, the reverse holds.

Choice of Contract

One key factor affecting basis risk is the choice of the futures contract to be used for hedging. This choice has two components:

1. The choice of the asset underlying the futures contract.
2. The choice of the delivery month.

If the asset being hedged exactly matches an asset underlying a futures contract, the first choice is generally fairly easy. In other circumstances, it is necessary to carry out a careful analysis to determine which of the available futures contracts has futures prices that are most closely correlated with the price of the asset being hedged.

The choice of the delivery month is likely to be influenced by several factors. It might be assumed that when the expiration of the hedge corresponds to a delivery month, the contract with that delivery month is chosen. In fact, a contract with a later delivery month is usually chosen in these circumstances. This is because futures prices are in some instances quite erratic during the delivery month. Also, a long hedger runs the risk of having to take delivery of the physical asset if he or she holds the contract during the delivery month. This can be expensive and inconvenient.

In general, basis risk increases as the time difference between the hedge expiration and the delivery month increases. A good rule of thumb is therefore to choose a delivery month that is as close as possible to, but later than, the expiration of the hedge. Suppose that the delivery months are March, June, September, and December for a particular contract. For hedge expirations in December, January, and February, the March contract will be chosen; for hedge expirations in March, April, and May, the June contract will be chosen; and so on. This rule of thumb assumes that there is sufficient liquidity in all contracts to meet the hedger's requirements. In practice, liquidity tends to be greatest in short-maturity futures contracts. Therefore, in some situations the hedger may be inclined to use short-maturity contracts and roll them forward. This strategy is explained at the end of this chapter.

Example 2.1

It is March 1. A U.S. company expects to receive 50 million Japanese yen at the end of July. Yen futures contracts on the Chicago Mercantile Exchange have delivery months of March, June, September, and December. One contract is for the delivery of 12.5 million yen. The company therefore shorts four September yen futures contracts on March 1. When the yen are received at the end of July, the company closes out its position. We suppose that the futures price on March 1 in cents per yen is 0.7800 and that the spot and futures prices when the contract is closed out are 0.7200 and 0.7250, respectively. This means that the basis is –0.0050 when the contract is closed out. The effective price obtained in cents per yen is the final spot price plus the gain on the futures:

$$0.7200 + 0.0550 = 0.7750$$

This can also be written as the initial futures price plus the final basis:

$$0.7800 - 0.0050 = 0.7750$$

The company receives a total of 50×0.00775 million dollars, or \$387,500.

Example 2.2

It is June 8 and a company knows that it will need to purchase 20,000 barrels of crude oil at some time in October or November. Oil futures contracts are currently traded for delivery every month on NYMEX and the contract size is 1,000 barrels. The company therefore decides to use the December contract for hedging and takes a long position in 20 December contracts. The futures price on June 8 is \$18.00 per barrel. The company finds that it is ready to purchase the crude oil on November 10. It therefore closes out its futures contract on that date. The spot price and futures price on November 10 are \$20.00 per barrel and \$19.10 per barrel, respectively, so that the basis is \$0.90. The effective price paid is \$18.90 per barrel, or \$378,000 in total. This can be calculated as the final spot price of \$20.00 less the gain on the futures of \$1.10; or as the initial futures price, \$18.00, plus the final basis, \$0.90.

2.9 OPTIMAL HEDGE RATIO

The hedge ratio is the ratio of the size of the position taken in futures contracts to the size of the exposure. Up to now we have always assumed a hedge ratio of 1.0. We now show that if the objective of the hedger is to minimize risk, a hedge ratio of 1.0 is not necessarily optimal.

Define:

ΔS: change in spot price, S, during a period of time equal to the life of the hedge

ΔF: change in futures price, F, during a period of time equal to the life of the hedge

σ_S: standard deviation of ΔS

σ_F: standard deviation of ΔF

ρ: coefficient of correlation between ΔS and ΔF

h: hedge ratio

When the hedger is long the asset and short futures, the change in the value of the hedger's position during the life of the hedge is

$$\Delta S - h \, \Delta F$$

For a long hedge it is

$$h \, \Delta F - \Delta S$$

In either case the variance, v, of the change in value of the hedged position is given by

$$v = \sigma_S^2 + h^2 \sigma_F^2 - 2h\rho\sigma_S\sigma_F$$

so that

$$\frac{\partial v}{\partial h} = 2h\sigma_F^2 - 2\rho\sigma_S\sigma_F$$

Setting this equal to zero, and noting that $\partial^2 v / \partial h^2$ is positive, we see that the value of h that minimizes the variance is

$$h = \rho \frac{\sigma_S}{\sigma_F} \tag{2.1}$$

The optimal hedge ratio is therefore the product of the coefficient of correlation between ΔS and ΔF and the ratio of the standard deviation of ΔS to the standard deviation of ΔF. Figure 2.2 shows how the variance of the value of the hedger's position depends on the hedge ratio chosen.

If $\rho = 1$ and $\sigma_F = \sigma_S$, the optimal hedge ratio, h, is 1.0. This is to be expected since in this case the futures price mirrors the spot price perfectly. If $\rho = 1$ and $\sigma_F = 2\sigma_S$, the optimal hedge ratio h is 0.5. This result is also as expected since in this case the futures price always changes by twice as much as the spot price.

Example 2.3

A company knows that it will buy 1 million gallons of jet fuel in three months. The standard deviation of the change in the price per gallon of jet fuel over a three-month

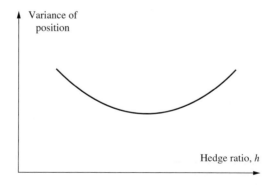

Figure 2.2   Dependence of variance of hedger's position on hedge ratio.

period is calculated as 0.032. The company chooses to hedge by buying futures contracts on heating oil. The standard deviation of the change in the futures price over a three-month period is 0.040 and the coefficient of correlation between the three-month change in the price of jet fuel and the three-month change in the futures price is 0.8. The optimal hedge ratio is therefore

$$0.8 \times \frac{0.032}{0.040} = 0.64$$

One heating oil futures contract is on 42,000 gallons. The company should therefore buy

$$0.64 \times \frac{1,000,000}{42,000} = 15.2$$

contracts. Rounding to the nearest whole number 15 contracts are required.

2.10 ROLLING THE HEDGE FORWARD

Sometimes, the expiration date of the hedge is later than the delivery dates of all the futures contracts that can be used. The hedger must then roll the hedge forward. This involves closing out one futures contract and taking the same position in a futures contract with a later delivery date. Hedges can be rolled forward many times. Consider a company that wishes to use a short hedge to reduce the risk associated with the price to be received for an asset at time T. If there are futures contracts 1, 2, 3, ..., n (not all necessarily in existence at the present time) with progressively later delivery dates, the company can use the following strategy:

Time t_1: short futures contract 1

Time t_2: close out futures contract 1
            short futures contract 2

Time t_3: close out futures contract 2
            short futures contract 3

$$\vdots$$

Time t_n: close out futures contract $n - 1$
            short futures contract n

Time T: close out futures contract n

In this strategy there are n basis risks or sources of uncertainty. At time T there is uncertainty about the difference between the futures price for contract n and the spot price of the asset being hedged. In addition, on each of the $n - 1$ occasions when the hedge is rolled forward, there is uncertainty about the difference between the futures price for the contract being closed out and the futures price for the new contract being entered into. (We will refer to the latter as the *rollover basis*.) In many situations the hedger has some flexibility on the exact time when a switch is made from one contract to the next. This can be used to reduce the rollover basis risk. For example, if the rollover basis is unattractive at

the beginning of the period during which the rollover must be made, the hedger can delay the rollover in the hope that the rollover basis will improve.

Example 2.4

In April 1996, a company realizes that it will have 100,000 barrels of oil to sell in June 1997 and decides to hedge its risk with a hedge ratio of 1.0. The current spot price is $19. Although futures contracts are traded for every month of the year up to 18 months in the future (see Table 2.2), we suppose that only the first six delivery months have sufficient liquidity to meet the company's needs. The company therefore shorts 100 October 1996 contracts. In September 1996 it rolls the hedge forward into the March 1997 contract. In February 1997 it rolls the hedge forward again into the July 1997 contract.

One possible outcome is that the price of oil drops from $19 to $16 per barrel between April 1996 and June 1997. Suppose that the October 1996 futures contract is shorted at $18.20 per barrel and closed out at $17.40 per barrel for a profit of $0.80 per barrel; the March 1997 contract is shorted at $17.00 per barrel and closed out at $16.50 per barrel for a profit of $0.50 per barrel; the July 1997 contract is shorted at $16.30 per barrel and closed out at $15.90 per barrel for a profit of $0.40 per barrel. In this case the futures contracts provide a total of $1.70 per barrel compensation for the $3 per barrel oil price decline.

Metallgesellschaft

Sometimes rolling the hedge forward can lead to cash flow problems. This was illustrated dramatically by the activities of a German company, Metallgesellschaft (MG), in the early 1990s.

MG sold a huge volume of 5- to 10-year heating oil and gasoline fixed-price supply contracts to its customers at 6 to 8 cents above market prices. It hedged its exposure with long positions in short futures contracts that were rolled over. As it turned out, the price of oil fell and there were margin calls on the futures position. This put considerable short-term cash flow pressures on MG. The members of MG who instigated the hedging strategy argued that these short-term cash outflows were offset by positive cash flows that would ultimately be realized on the long-term fixed-price contracts. However, the company's senior management and their bankers became concerned about the huge cash drain. As a result, the company closed out all the hedge positions and agreed with their customers that the fixed-price contracts would be abandoned. The result was a loss to MG of $1.33 billion.[5]

2.11 ACCOUNTING AND TAX

The full details of the accounting and tax treatment of futures contracts are beyond the scope of this book. An investor who wants detailed information on this should consult experts. In this section we provide some general background information.

[5]For a discussion of MG, see "MG's Trial by Essay," *RISK,* October 1994, pp. 228–34, and M. Miller and C. Culp, "Risk Management Lessons from Metallgesellschaft," *Journal of Applied Corporate Finance,* Fall 1994.

Accounting

FASB Statement No. 52, Foreign Currency Translation, established accounting standards in the United States for foreign currency futures. FASB Statement No. 80, Accounting for Futures Contracts, established accounting standards in the United States for all other contracts. The two statements require changes in market value to be recognized when they occur unless the contract qualifies as a hedge. If the contract does qualify as a hedge, gains or losses are generally recognized for accounting purposes in the same period in which the gains or losses from the item being hedged are recognized.

Consider an investor who in September 1996 takes a long position in a March 1997 corn futures contract and closes out the position at the end of February 1997. Suppose that the futures prices are 150 cents per bushel when the contract is entered into, 170 cents per bushel at the end of 1996, and 180 cents per bushel when the contract is closed out. One contract is for the delivery of 5,000 bushels. If the investor is a speculator, the gains for accounting purposes are

$$5,000 \times \$0.20 = \$1,000$$

in 1996 and

$$5,000 \times \$0.10 = \$500$$

in 1997. If the investor is hedging the purchase of 5,000 bushels of corn in 1997, the entire gain of $1,500 is realized in 1997 for accounting purposes.

The treatment of hedging gains and losses is sensible. If the investor in our example is a company that is hedging the purchase of 5,000 bushels of corn at the end of February 1997, the effect of the futures contract is to ensure that the price paid is close to 150 cents per bushel. The accounting treatment reflects that this price is paid in 1997. The 1996 accounting calculations are unaffected by the futures transaction.

Tax

Under the U.S. tax rules, two key issues are the nature of a taxable gain or loss and the timing of the recognition of the gain or loss. Gains or losses are either classified as capital gains/losses or as part of ordinary income. At the time of writing, capital gains are taxed at the same rate as ordinary income while the ability to deduct capital losses is restricted. For a noncorporate taxpayer, capital losses are deductible only to the extent of capital gains plus ordinary income up to $3,000. A noncorporate taxpayer can carry forward a net capital loss for an unlimited period of time. For a corporate taxpayer, capital losses are deductible only to the extent of capital gains. A corporation may carry back a capital loss three years. Any excess can be carried forward for five years.

Generally, positions in futures contracts and foreign currency contracts are treated as if they are sold on the last day of the tax year. Any gains or losses on contracts other than foreign currency contracts are treated as capital

gains/losses. Gains or losses on foreign currency contracts are treated as ordinary income/losses.

Hedging transactions are exempt from the foregoing rule. A hedging transaction is defined under the tax regulations as a transaction entered into in the normal course of business primarily for one of the following reasons:

1. To reduce the risk of price changes or currency fluctuations with respect to property that is held or to be held by the taxpayer for the purposes of producing ordinary income.
2. To reduce the risk of price or interest rate changes or currency fluctuations with respect to borrowings made by the taxpayer.

Gains or losses from hedging transactions are treated as ordinary income. The timing of the recognition of gains or losses from hedging transactions generally matches the timing of the recognition of income or deduction from the hedged items.

2.12 SUMMARY

In this chapter we have looked at how futures markets operate. In futures markets, contracts are traded on an exchange, and it is necessary for the exchange to define carefully the precise nature of what it is that is traded, the procedures that will be followed, and the regulations that will govern the market. By contrast, forward contracts are negotiated directly over the telephone by two relatively sophisticated individuals. As a result, there is no need to standardize the product, and an extensive set of rules and procedures is not required. The main differences between futures and forward contracts are summarized in Table 2.3.

A very high proportion of futures contracts that are initiated do not lead to the delivery of the underlying asset. They are closed out prior to the delivery period being reached. But it is the possibility of final delivery that drives the determination of the futures price. For each futures contract, there is a range of days during which delivery can be made and a well-defined delivery procedure.

TABLE 2.3 Comparison of Forward and Futures Contracts

Forwards	Futures
Private contract between two parties	Traded on an exchange
Not standardized	Standardized contract
Usually one specified delivery date	Range of delivery dates
Settled at end of contract	Settled daily
Delivery or final cash settlement usually takes place	Contract usually closed out prior to maturity

Some contracts, such as those on stock indices, are settled in cash rather than by delivery of the underlying asset.

The specification of contracts is an important activity for a futures exchange. The two sides to any contract must know what can be delivered, where delivery can take place, and when delivery can take place. They also need to know such details as the trading hours, how prices will be quoted, maximum price movements, and so on.

Margins are an important aspect of futures markets. An investor keeps a margin account with his or her broker. This is adjusted daily to reflect gains or losses, and the broker may require the account to be topped up from time to time if adverse price movements have taken place. The broker must either be a clearinghouse member or must maintain a margin account with a clearinghouse member. Each clearinghouse member maintains a margin account with the exchange clearinghouse. The balance in the account is adjusted daily to reflect gains and losses on the business for which the clearinghouse member is responsible. The exchange ensures that information on prices is collected in a systematic way and relayed within a matter of seconds to investors throughout the world. Many newspapers, such as the *Wall Street Journal,* carry each day a summary of the preceding day's trading.

Futures contracts can be used to hedge a company's exposure to a price of a commodity. A position in the futures markets is taken to offset the effect of the price of the commodity on the rest of the company's business. An important concept in futures hedging is basis. This is the difference between the spot price of an asset and its futures price. The risk in a hedge is the uncertainty about the value of the basis at the maturity of the hedge. This is known as basis risk.

The hedge ratio is the ratio of the size of the position taken in futures contracts to the size of the exposure. If a hedger wishes to minimize the variance of his or her total position, it may be optimal to use a hedge ratio different from 1.0. When there is no liquid futures contract that matures later than the expiration of the hedge, a strategy known as rolling the hedge forward is sometimes used. This involves entering into a sequence of futures contracts. When the first futures contract is near expiration, it is closed out and the hedger enters into a second contract with a later delivery month. When the second contract is close to expiration, it is closed out and the hedger enters into a third contract with a later delivery month; and so on. Rolling the hedge works well if there is a close correlation between changes in the futures prices and changes in the spot prices.

SUGGESTIONS FOR FURTHER READING

On Futures Markets

Chance, D., *An Introduction to Options and Futures.* Orlando, Fla.: Dryden Press, 1989.
Chicago Board of Trade, *Commodity Trading Manual.* Chicago: 1989.

Duffie, D., *Futures Markets.* Englewood Cliffs, N.J.: Prentice Hall, 1989.

Horn, F. F., *Trading in Commodity Futures.* New York: New York Institute of Finance, 1984.

Kolb, R., *Understanding Futures Markets.* Glenview, Ill.: Scott, Foresman, 1985.

Schwarz, E. W., J. M. Hill, and T. Schneeweis, *Financial Futures.* Homewood, Ill.: Richard D. Irwin, 1986.

Teweles, R. J., and F. J. Jones, *The Futures Game.* New York: McGraw-Hill, 1987.

On Hedging

Chicago Board of Trade, *Introduction to Hedging.* Chicago: 1984.

Ederington, L. H., "The Hedging Performance of the New Futures Market," *Journal of Finance,* 34 (March 1979), 157–70.

Frankcle, C. T., "The Hedging Performance of the New Futures Market: Comment," *Journal of Finance,* 35 (December 1980), 1273–79.

Johnson, L. L., "The Theory of Hedging and Speculation in Commodity Futures Markets." *Review of Economics Studies,* 27 (October 1960), 139–51.

Miller, M., and C. Culp, "Risk Management Lessons from Metallgesellschaft," *Journal of Applied Corporate Finance,* Fall 1994.

Nikkhah, S., "How End Users Can Hedge Fuel Costs in Energy Markets," *Futures* (October 1987), 66–67.

Stulz, R. M., "Optimal Hedging Policies," *Journal of Financial and Quantitative Analysis,* 19 (June 1984), 127–40.

QUESTIONS AND PROBLEMS

2.1. Distinguish between the terms *open interest* and *trading volume.*

2.2. What is the difference between a local and a commission broker?

2.3. What is the difference between the operation of the margin accounts administered by the clearinghouse and those administered by a broker?

2.4. What are the most important aspects of the design of a new futures contract?

2.5. Explain how margins protect investors against the possibility of default.

2.6. Under what circumstances are (a) a short hedge and (b) a long hedge appropriate?

2.7. Explain what is meant by basis risk when futures contracts are used for hedging.

2.8. Does a perfect hedge always lead to a better outcome than an imperfect hedge? Explain your answer.

2.9. Under what circumstances does a minimum variance hedge portfolio lead to no hedging at all?

2.10. Suppose that you enter into a short futures contract to sell July silver for $5.20 per ounce on the New York Commodity Exchange. The size of the contract is 5,000 ounces. The initial margin is $4,000 and the maintenance margin is $3,000. What change in the futures price will lead to a margin call? What happens if you do not meet the margin call?

2.11. The party with a short position in a futures contract sometimes has options as to the precise asset that will be delivered, where delivery will take place, when delivery will take place, and so on. Do these options increase or decrease the futures price? Explain your reasoning.

2.12. A company enters into a short futures contract to sell 5,000 bushels of wheat for 250 cents per bushel. The initial margin is $3,000 and the maintenance margin is $2,000. What price change would lead to a margin call? Under what circumstances could $1,500 be withdrawn from the margin account?

2.13. An investor enters into two long futures contracts on frozen orange juice. Each contract is for the delivery of 15,000 pounds. The current futures price is 160 cents per pound; the initial margin is $6,000 per contract; and the maintenance margin is $4,500 per contract. What price change would lead to a margin call? Under what circumstances could $2,000 be withdrawn from the margin account?

2.14. At the end of one day, a clearinghouse member is long 100 contracts and the settlement price is $50,000 per contract. The original margin is $2,000 per contract. On the following day, the member becomes responsible for clearing an additional 20 long contracts. These were entered into at a price of $51,000 per contract. The settlement price at the end of this day is $50,200. How much does the member have to add to its margin account with the exchange clearinghouse?

2.15. Suppose that the standard deviation of quarterly changes in the price of a commodity is $0.65, the standard deviation of quarterly changes in a futures price on the commodity is $0.81, and the coefficient of correlation between the two changes is 0.8. What is the optimal hedge ratio for a three-month contract? What does it mean?

2.16. "Speculation in futures markets is pure gambling. It is not in the public interest to allow speculators to buy seats on a futures exchange." Discuss this viewpoint.

2.17. Identify the most actively traded contracts in Table 2.2. Consider each of the following sections separately: grains and oilseeds, livestock and meat, food and fiber, and metals and petroleum.

2.18. What do you think would happen if an exchange started trading a contract where the quality of the underlying asset was incompletely specified?

2.19. "When a futures contract is traded on the floor of the exchange, it may be the case that the open interest increases by one, stays the same, or decreases by one." Explain this statement.

2.20. In the Chicago Board of Trade's corn futures contract, the following delivery months are available: March, May, July, September, and December. Which contract should be used for hedging when the expiration of the hedge is in:
   (a) June?
   (b) July?
   (c) January?

2.21. Does a perfect hedge always succeed in locking in the current spot price of an asset for a future transaction? Explain your answer.

2.22. Explain why a short hedger's position improves when the basis strengthens unexpectedly and worsens when the basis weakens unexpectedly.

2.23. Imagine that you are the treasurer of a Japanese company exporting electronic equipment to the United States. Discuss how you would design a foreign exchange

hedging strategy and the arguments you would use to sell the strategy to your fellow executives.

2.24. "If the minimum variance hedge ratio is calculated as 1.0, the hedge must be perfect." Is this statement true? Explain your answer.

2.25. "If there is no basis risk, the optimal hedge ratio is always 1.0." Is this statement true? Explain your answer.

2.26. The standard deviation of monthly changes in the spot price of live cattle is (in cents per pound) 1.2. The standard deviation of monthly changes in the futures price of live cattle for the closest contract is 1.4. The correlation between the futures price changes and the spot price changes is 0.7. It is now October 15. A beef producer is committed to purchasing 200,000 pounds of live cattle on November 15. The producer wants to use the December live cattle futures contracts to hedge its risk. Each contract is for the delivery of 40,000 pounds of cattle. What strategy should the beef producer follow?

2.27. A pig farmer expects to have 90,000 pounds of live hogs to sell in three months. The live hogs futures contract on the Chicago Mercantile Exchange is for the delivery of 30,000 pounds of hogs. How can the farmer use this for hedging? From the farmer's viewpoint, what are the pros and cons of hedging?

2.28. It is now July 1996. A mining company has just discovered a small deposit of gold. It will take six months to construct the mine. The gold will then be extracted on a more or less continuous basis for one year. Futures contracts on gold are available on the New York Commodity Exchange. The delivery months range from August 1996 to April 1998 and are at two-month intervals. Each contract is for the delivery of 100 ounces. Discuss how the mining company might use futures markets for hedging.

2.29. An airline executive has argued: "There is no point in our using oil futures. There is just as much chance that the price of oil in the future will be less than the futures price as that it will be greater than this price." Discuss this viewpoint.

2.30. What is the effect of using a hedge ratio of 1.5 instead of 1.0 in Example 2.4 of Section 2.10?

2.31. "Shareholders can hedge the risks faced by a company. There is no need for the company itself to hedge." Discuss this viewpoint.

2.32. "A company that uses a certain commodity in its manufacturing operations should pass price changes on to its customers. Hedging is then unnecessary." Discuss this viewpoint.

2.33. "Company treasurers should not hedge. They will be blamed when a loss is experienced on the position taken in the hedging instrument." Discuss this viewpoint.

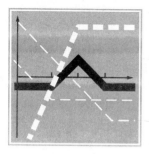

Chapter 3

Forward and Futures Prices

In this chapter we discuss how forward prices and futures prices are related to the price of the underlying asset. Forward contracts are generally easier to analyze than futures contracts because there is no daily settlement. Consequently, most of the analysis in the first part of the chapter is directed toward determining forward prices rather than futures prices. Luckily, for many of the contracts that are traded, it can be argued that the forward price and futures price of an asset are very close to each other when the maturities of the two contracts are the same. This means that results obtained for forward prices can be assumed to be true for futures prices as well.

In the first part of the chapter, key results are provided for forward contracts on:

1. Securities providing no income.
2. Securities providing a known cash income.
3. Securities providing a known dividend yield.

In the second part of the chapter we use these results to calculate futures prices for contracts on stock indices, foreign exchange, gold, and silver.

In this chapter we draw an important distinction between assets that are held solely for investment by a significant number of investors and those that are held almost exclusively for consumption. Futures and forward prices on the former can be determined in a relatively straightforward way, whereas those on the latter cannot. Later in the book we will find it necessary to make the same distinction when valuing options and other more complicated derivatives.

3.1 SOME PRELIMINARIES

Before we get into the calculation of forward prices, it is useful to present some preliminary material.

Continuous Compounding

In this book the interest rates used will be compounded continuously except where stated otherwise. Readers used to working with interest rates that are compounded annually, semiannually, or in some other way may find this frustrating. However, continuously compounded interest rates are used to such a great extent when options and other complex derivatives are being priced that it makes sense to get used to working with them now.

Consider an amount A invested for n years at an interest rate of R per annum. If the rate is compounded once per annum, the terminal value of the investment is

$$A(1 + R)^n$$

If it is compounded m times per annum, the terminal value of the investment is

$$A\left(1 + \frac{R}{m}\right)^{mn} \tag{3.1}$$

Suppose that $A = \$100$, $R = 10\%$ per annum, and $n = 1$, so that we are considering one year. When we compound once per annum ($m = 1$), this formula shows that the $\$100$ grows to

$$\$100 \times 1.1 = \$110$$

When we compound twice a year ($m = 2$), the formula shows that the $\$100$ grows to

$$\$100 \times 1.05 \times 1.05 = \$110.25$$

When we compound four times a year ($m = 4$), the formula shows that the $\$100$ grows to

$$\$100 \times 1.025^4 = \$110.38$$

Table 3.1 shows the effect of increasing the compounding frequency further (i.e., of increasing m). The limit as m tends to infinity is known as *continuous compounding*. With continuous compounding, it can be shown that an amount A invested for n years at rate R grows to

$$Ae^{Rn} \tag{3.2}$$

where e is the mathematical constant, 2.71828. In the example in Table 3.1, $A = 100$, $n = 1$, and $R = 0.1$, so that the value to which A grows with continuous compounding is

$$100e^{0.1} = 110.52$$

This is (to two decimal places) the same as the value using daily compounding. For most practical purposes, continuous compounding can be thought of as being equivalent to daily compounding. Compounding a sum of money at a

TABLE 3.1   Compounding Frequency

The effect of increasing the compounding frequency on the value of $100 at the end of one year when the interest rate is 10% per annum

Compounding Frequency	Value of $100 at End of One Year (dollars)
Annually ($m = 1$)	110.00
Semiannually ($m = 2$)	110.25
Quarterly ($m = 4$)	110.38
Monthly ($m = 12$)	110.47
Weekly ($m = 52$)	110.51
Daily ($m = 365$)	110.52

continuously compounded rate R for n years involves multiplying it by e^{Rn}. Discounting it at a continuously compounded rate R for n years involves multiplying by e^{-Rn}.

Suppose that R_c is a rate of interest with continuous compounding and R_m is the equivalent rate with compounding m times per annum. From the results in (3.1) and (3.2), we must have

$$Ae^{R_c n} = A\left(1 + \frac{R_m}{m}\right)^{mn}$$

or

$$e^{R_c} = \left(1 + \frac{R_m}{m}\right)^{m}$$

This means that

$$R_c = m \ln\left(1 + \frac{R_m}{m}\right) \qquad (3.3)$$

and

$$R_m = m(e^{R_c/m} - 1) \qquad (3.4)$$

These equations can be used to convert a rate where the compounding frequency is m times per annum to a continuously compounded rate, and vice versa. The function ln is the natural logarithm function. It is defined so that if $y = \ln x$, then $x = e^{y}$.

Example 3.1

Consider an interest rate that is quoted as 10% per annum with semiannual compounding. From using equation (3.3) with $m = 2$ and $R_m = 0.1$, the equivalent rate with continuous

compounding is

$$2 \ln (1 + 0.05) = 0.09758$$

or 9.758% per annum.

Example 3.2

Suppose that a lender quotes the interest rate on loans as 8% per annum with continuous compounding and that interest is actually paid quarterly. From using equation (3.4) with $m = 4$ and $R_c = 0.08$, the equivalent rate with quarterly compounding is

$$4(e^{0.02} - 1) = 0.0808$$

or 8.08% per annum. This means that on a $10,000 loan, interest payments of $202 would be required each quarter.

Finally, we note that a rate expressed with a compounding frequency of m_1 can be converted to a rate with a compounding frequency of m_2. From equation (3.1)

$$A\left(1 + \frac{R_{m_1}}{m_1}\right)^{m_1 n} = A\left(1 + \frac{R_{m_2}}{m_2}\right)^{m_2 n}$$

so that

$$R_{m_2} = \left[\left(1 + \frac{R_{m_1}}{m_1}\right)^{m_1/m_2} - 1\right] m_2$$

Short Selling

Some of the arbitrage strategies presented in this chapter involve short selling. This is a trading strategy that yields a profit when the price of a security goes down and a loss when it goes up. It involves selling securities that are not owned and buying them back later.

To explain the mechanics of short selling, we suppose that an investor contacts a broker to short 500 IBM shares. The broker immediately borrows 500 IBM shares from another client and sells them in the open market in the usual way, depositing the sale proceeds to the investor's account. Providing there are shares that can be borrowed, the investor can continue to maintain the short position for as long as desired. At some stage, however, the investor will choose to instruct the broker to close out the position. The broker then uses funds in the investor's account to purchase 500 IBM shares and replaces them in the account of the client from which the shares were borrowed. The investor makes a profit if the stock price has declined and a loss if it has risen. If at any time while the contract is open, the broker runs out of shares to borrow, the investor is what is known as *short-squeezed* and must close out the position immediately even though he or she may not be ready to do so.

Regulators currently only allow shares to be sold short on an *uptick,* that is, when the most recent movement in the price of the security was an increase. A broker requires significant initial margins from clients with short positions, and as with futures contracts, if there are adverse movements (i.e., increases) in the price of the security, additional margin may be required. The proceeds of the initial sales of the security normally form part of the initial margin requirement. Some brokers pay interest on margin accounts, and marketable securities such as Treasury bills can be deposited with a broker to meet initial margin requirements. As in the case of futures contracts, the margin does not therefore represent a real cost.

An investor with a short position must pay to his or her broker any income, such as dividends or interest, that would normally be received on the securities that have been shorted. The broker will transfer this to the account of the client from whom the securities have been borrowed. Consider the position of an investor who shorts 500 IBM shares in April when the price per share is $120 and closes out his or her position by buying them back in July when the price per share is $100. Suppose that a dividend of $4 per share is paid in May. The investor receives $500 \times \$120 = \$60,000$ in April when the short position is initiated. The dividend leads to a payment by the investor of $500 \times \$4 = \$2,000$ in May. The investor also pays $500 \times \$100 = \$50,000$ when the position is closed out in July. The net gain is, therefore,

$$\$60,000 - \$2,000 - \$50,000 = \$8,000$$

Assumptions

In this chapter we assume that there are some market participants for which the following are true:

1. There are no transactions costs.
2. All trading profits (net of trading losses) are subject to the same tax rate.
3. The market participants can borrow money at the same risk-free rate of interest as they can lend money.
4. The market participants take advantage of arbitrage opportunities as they occur.

Note that we do not require these assumptions to be true for all market participants. All that we require is that they be true for a subset of all market participants, for example, large investment houses. This is not unreasonable. As discussed in Chapter 1, the fact that these market participants are prepared to take advantage of arbitrage opportunities as they occur means that in practice arbitrage opportunities disappear almost as soon as they arise. An implication of the assumptions is therefore that market prices are such that there are no arbitrage opportunities.

Repo Rate

The relevant risk-free rate of interest for many arbitrageurs operating in the futures market is what is known as the *repo rate*. A *repo* or *repurchase agreement* is an agreement where the owner of securities agrees to sell them to a counterparty and buy them back at a slightly higher price later. The counterparty is providing a loan. The difference between the price at which the securities are sold and the price at which they are repurchased is the interest earned by the counterparty. If structured carefully a repo involves very little risk to either side. For example, if the borrowing company does not keep to its side of the agreement, the lender is able to keep the borrower's securities. The repo rate is only slightly higher than the Treasury bill rate. The most common type of repo is an *overnight repo* where the agreement is renegotiated each day. However, longer-term arrangements, known as *term repos,* are sometimes used.

Notation

Some of the notation that will be used in this chapter is as follows:

T: time when the forward contract matures (years)

t: current time (years)

S: price of asset underlying the forward contract at time t

S_T: price of asset underlying the forward contract at time T (unknown at the current time, t)

K: delivery price in the forward contract

f: value of a long forward contract at time t

F: forward price at time t

r: risk-free rate of interest per annum at time t, with continuous compounding, for an investment maturing at time T

The variables T and t are measured in years from some date (it does not matter when) prior to the start of the contract. The variable of interest for the purposes of our current analysis is of course $T - t$, which is the time remaining, measured in years, in the forward contract. There is a reason for defining two separate variables, t and T. This will become apparent in later chapters when we consider the effect on the price of a derivative of time passing. At this stage, the reader can conveniently think in terms of $T - t$ as a single variable.

It is important to realize that the forward price, F, is quite different from the value of the forward contract, f. As explained in Chapter 1, the forward price at any given time is the delivery price that would make the contract have a zero value. When a contract is initiated, the delivery price is normally set equal to the forward price so that $F = K$ and $f = 0$. As time passes, both f and F change. The analysis and the examples in the next few sections should make clear the distinction between the two variables.

3.2 FORWARD CONTRACTS ON A SECURITY THAT PROVIDES NO INCOME

The easiest forward contract to value is one written on a security that provides the holder with no income. Non-dividend-paying stocks and discount bonds are examples of such securities.[1]

For there to be no arbitrage opportunities, the relationship between the forward price, F, and the spot price, S, for a no-income security must be

$$F = Se^{r(T-t)} \tag{3.5}$$

To show this, suppose first that $F > Se^{r(T-t)}$. An investor can borrow S dollars for a period of time $T - t$ at the risk-free interest rate of r, buy the asset, and take a short position in the forward contract. At time T, the asset is sold under the terms of the forward contract for F, and $Se^{r(T-t)}$ is used to repay the loan. A profit of $F - Se^{r(T-t)}$ is therefore realized at time T.

Suppose next that $F < Se^{r(T-t)}$. An investor can take a long position in the forward contract and short the asset. The short position leads to a cash inflow of S that can be invested at rate r for a period of time $T - t$. At time T, the asset is purchased under the terms of the forward contract for F, the short position is closed out, and a profit of $Se^{r(T-t)} - F$ is realized.

Example 3.3

Consider a forward contract on a non-dividend-paying stock that matures in three months. Suppose that the stock price is $40, and the three-month risk-free rate of interest is 5% per annum. In this case $T - t = 0.25$, $r = 0.05$, and $S = 40$, so that

$$F = 40e^{0.05 \times 0.25} = 40.50$$

This would be the delivery price in a forward contract negotiated today. If the actual forward price in the market is greater than $40.50, an arbitrageur can borrow money, buy the stock, and short the forward contract for a net profit. If the forward price is less than $40.50, an arbitrageur can short the stock, invest the proceeds, and take a long forward position. Again a net profit is realized.

We now use rather more formal arguments to provide a relationship between the value of a long forward contract, f, and its delivery price, K. Consider the following two portfolios:

Portfolio A: one long forward contract on the security plus an amount of cash equal to $Ke^{-r(T-t)}$
Portfolio B: one unit of the security

In portfolio A, the cash, assuming that it is invested at the risk-free rate, will grow to an amount K at time T. It can then be used to pay for the security at the maturity

---

[1] Some of the contracts that are used as examples in the first half of this chapter (e.g., forward contracts on non-dividend-paying stocks) do not normally arise in practice. But they do form useful examples for developing our ideas.

of the forward contract. Both portfolios will therefore consist of one unit of the security at time T. It follows that they must be equally valuable at the earlier time, t. If this were not true, an investor could make a riskless profit by buying the less expensive portfolio and shorting the more expensive one.

It follows that

$$f + Ke^{-r(T-t)} = S$$

or

$$f = S - Ke^{-r(T-t)} \tag{3.6}$$

When a forward contract is initiated, the forward price equals the delivery price specified in the contract and is chosen so that the value of the contract is zero. The forward price, F, is therefore that value of K which makes $f = 0$ in equation (3.6), that is,

$$F = Se^{r(T-t)}$$

This is in agreement with equation (3.5).

Example 3.4

Consider a long six-month forward contract on a one-year discount bond when the delivery price is $950. We assume that the six-month risk-free rate of interest (continuously compounded) is 6% per annum and that the current bond price is $930. In this case $T - t = 0.50$, $r = 0.06$, $K = 950$, $S = 930$, and equation (3.6) shows that the value, f, of the long forward contract is given by

$$f = 930 - 950e^{-0.5 \times 0.06} = 8.08$$

Similarly, the value of a short forward is -8.08.

3.3 FORWARD CONTRACTS ON A SECURITY THAT PROVIDES A KNOWN CASH INCOME

In this section we consider a forward contract on a security that will provide a perfectly predictable cash income to the holder. Examples are stocks paying known dividends and coupon-bearing bonds. Define I as the present value, using the risk-free discount rate, of income to be received during the life of the forward contract.

For there to be no arbitrage, the relationship between F and S must be

$$F = (S - I)e^{r(T-t)} \tag{3.7}$$

To show this, suppose first that $F > (S - I)e^{r(T-t)}$. An arbitrageur can borrow S dollars to buy the asset, and short a forward contract. The asset is sold for F at time T under the terms of the forward contract. Assuming that the income received is used to pay off part of the loan, an amount $(S - I)e^{r(T-t)}$ of the loan

remains to be repaid at time T. A profit of $F - (S - I)e^{r(T-t)}$ is therefore realized at time T.

Suppose next that $F < (S - I)e^{r(T-t)}$. An arbitrageur can short the asset, invest the proceeds, and take a long position in the forward contract. In this case, a profit of $(S - I)e^{r(T-t)} - F$ is realized at time T.

Example 3.5

Consider a 10-month forward contract on a stock with a price of $50. We assume that the risk-free rate of interest (continuously compounded) for all maturities is 8% per annum. We also assume that dividends of $0.75 per share are expected after three months, six months, and nine months. The present value of the dividends, I, is given by

$$I = 0.75e^{-0.08 \times 3/12} + 0.75e^{-0.08 \times 6/12} + 0.75e^{-0.08 \times 9/12} = 2.162$$

The variable $T - t$ is 0.8333 year so that the forward price, F, is given by

$$F = (50 - 2.162)e^{0.08 \times 0.8333} = 51.14$$

If the forward price were less than this, an arbitrageur would short the stock and buy forward contracts. If the forward price were greater than this, an arbitrageur would short forward contracts and buy the stock.

Again we can use rather more formal arguments to relate the value of a long forward contract, f, to its delivery price, K. We change portfolio B in the preceding section to:

Portfolio B: one unit of the security plus borrowings of amount I at the risk-free rate

The income from the security can be used to repay the borrowings so that this portfolio has the same value as one unit of the security at time T. Portfolio A also has this value at time T. The two portfolios must therefore have the same value at time t, that is,

$$f + Ke^{-r(T-t)} = S - I$$

or

$$f = S - I - Ke^{-r(T-t)} \tag{3.8}$$

The forward price, F, is, as before, the value of K that makes f zero. Using equation (3.8), we obtain

$$F = (S - I)e^{r(T-t)}$$

which is in agreement with equation (3.7).

Example 3.6

Consider a five-year bond with a price of $900. Suppose that a forward contract on the bond with a delivery price of $910 has a maturity of one year. Coupon payments of $60 are expected after six months and after twelve months. The second coupon payment is immediately prior to the delivery date in the forward contract. The continuously compounded

risk-free rates of interest for six months and one year are 9% per annum and 10% per annum. In this case $S = 900$, $K = 910$, $r = 0.10$, $T - t = 1$, and

$$I = 60e^{-0.09 \times 0.5} + 60e^{-0.10 \times 1.0} = 111.65$$

and the value, f, of a long position in the forward contract using equation (3.8) is given by

$$f = 900 - 111.65 - 910e^{-0.10 \times 1.0} = -35.05$$

The value of a short position is $+35.05$. Note that there is no accrued interest at the beginning and end of the contract in this example. Complications arising from accrued interest are discussed in Chapter 4.

3.4 FORWARD CONTRACTS ON A SECURITY THAT PROVIDES A KNOWN DIVIDEND YIELD

As explained in later sections, both currencies and stock indices can be regarded as securities that provide known dividend yields. In this section we provide a general analysis of forward contracts on such securities.

A known dividend yield means that the income when expressed as a percentage of the security price is known. We assume that the dividend is paid continuously at an annual rate q. To illustrate what this means, suppose that $q = 0.05$, so that the dividend yield is 5% per annum. When the security price is $10, dividends in the next small interval of time are paid at the rate of 50 cents per annum; when the security price is $100, dividends in the next small interval of time are paid at the rate of $5 per annum; and so on.

To value the forward contract, portfolio B in Section 3.2 can be replaced by:

Portfolio B: $e^{-q(T-t)}$ of the security with all income being reinvested in the security

The security holding in portfolio B grows as a result of the dividends that are paid, so that at time T exactly one unit of the security is held. Portfolios A and B are therefore worth the same at time T. From equating their values at time t, we obtain

$$f + Ke^{-r(T-t)} = Se^{-q(T-t)}$$

or

$$f = Se^{-q(T-t)} - Ke^{-r(T-t)} \tag{3.9}$$

and the forward price, F, is given by the value of K that makes f zero:

$$F = Se^{(r-q)(T-t)} \tag{3.10}$$

Note that if the dividend yield rate varies during the life of the forward contract, equation (3.10) is still correct with q equal to the average dividend yield rate.

Example 3.7

Consider a six-month forward contract on a security that is expected to provide a continuous dividend yield of 4% per annum. The risk-free rate of interest (with continuous compounding) is 10% per annum. The stock price is $25 and the delivery price is $27. In this case $S = 25$, $K = 27$, $r = 0.10$, $q = 0.04$, and $T - t = 0.5$. From equation (3.9) the value of a long position, f, is given by

$$f = 25e^{-0.04 \times 0.5} - 27e^{-0.1 \times 0.5} = -1.18$$

From equation (3.10) the forward price, F, is given by

$$F = 25e^{0.06 \times 0.5} = 25.76$$

3.5 GENERAL RESULT

The value of a forward contract at the time it is first entered into is zero. At a later stage it may prove to have a positive or a negative value. There is a general result, applicable to all forward contracts, that gives the value of a long forward contract, f, in terms of the originally negotiated delivery price, K, and the current forward price, F. This is

$$f = (F - K)e^{-r(T-t)} \tag{3.11}$$

To see why equation (3.11) is correct, we compare a long forward contract with delivery price F with an otherwise identical long forward contract that has a delivery price of K. The difference between the two is only in the amount that will be paid for the underlying asset at time T. Under the first contract this amount is F; under the second contract it is K. A cash outflow difference of $F - K$ at time T translates to a difference of $(F - K)e^{-r(T-t)}$ at time t. The contract with a delivery price F is, therefore, less valuable than the contract with delivery price K by an amount $(F - K)e^{-r(T-t)}$. The value of the contract that has a delivery price of F is by definition zero. It follows that the value of the contract with a delivery price of K is $(F - K)e^{-r(T-t)}$. This proves equation (3.11).

It is easy to verify that the relationship in equation (3.11) is consistent with the formulas derived for F and f in each of Sections 3.2, 3.3, and 3.4.

3.6 FORWARD PRICES VERSUS FUTURES PRICES

Appendix 3A provides an arbitrage argument to show that when the risk-free interest rate is constant and the same for all maturities, the forward price for a contract with a certain delivery date is the same as the futures price for a contract with the same delivery date. The argument in Appendix 3A can be extended to cover situations where the interest rate is a known function of time.

When interest rates vary unpredictably (as they do in the real world), forward and futures prices are in theory no longer the same. We can get a sense of

the nature of the relationship by considering the situation where the price of the underlying asset, S, is strongly positively correlated with interest rates. When S increases, an investor who holds a long futures position makes an immediate gain because of the daily settlement procedure. Since increases in S tend to occur at the same time as increases in interest rates, this gain will tend to be invested at a higher-than-average rate of interest. Similarly, when S decreases, the investor will make an immediate loss. This loss will tend to be financed at a lower-than-average rate of interest. An investor holding a forward contract rather than a futures contract is not affected in this way by interest rate movements. It follows that, *ceteris paribus,* a long futures contract will be more attractive than a long forward contract. Hence, when S is strongly positively correlated with interest rates, futures prices will tend to be higher than forward prices. When S is strongly negatively correlated with interest rates, a similar argument shows that forward prices will tend to be higher than futures prices.

The theoretical differences between forward and futures prices for contracts that last only a few months are in most circumstances sufficiently small to be ignored.[2] In most of this book we therefore assume that forward and futures contracts are the same. The symbol F will be used to represent both the futures price and the forward price of an asset.

As the life of a futures contract increases, the differences between forward and futures contracts are liable to become significant and it is then dangerous to assume that forward and futures prices are perfect substitutes for each other. This point is discussed further in connection with Eurodollar futures in Chapters 4 and 17.

Empirical Research

Some empirical research that has been carried out comparing forward and futures contracts is listed at the end of the chapter. Cornell and Reinganum studied forward and futures prices on the British pound, Canadian dollar, German mark, Japanese yen, and Swiss franc between 1974 and 1979. They found very few statistically significant differences between the two prices. Their results were confirmed by Park and Chen, who as part of their study looked at the British pound, deutschemark, Japanese yen, and Swiss franc between 1977 and 1981.

French studied copper and silver during the period 1968–1980. The results for silver show that the futures price and the forward price are significantly different (at the 5% confidence level) with the futures price generally above the forward price. The results for copper are less clear cut. Park and Chen looked at gold, silver, silver coin, platinum, copper, and plywood between 1977 and 1981. Their

---

[2]In practice, there are a number of factors, not reflected in theoretical models, that may cause forward and futures prices to be different. These factors include taxes, transactions costs, and the treatment of margins. Also, in some instances, futures contracts are more liquid and easier to trade than are forward contracts.

results are similar to those of French for silver. The forward and futures prices are significantly different, with the futures price above the forward price. Rendleman and Carabini studied the Treasury bill market between 1976 and 1978. They also found statistically significant differences between futures and forward prices.

3.7 STOCK INDEX FUTURES

A *stock index* tracks the changes in the value of a hypothetical portfolio of stocks. The weight of a stock in the portfolio equals the proportion of the portfolio invested in the stock. The percentage increase in the value of a stock index over a small interval of time is usually defined so that it is equal to the percentage increase in the total value of the stocks comprising the portfolio at that time. A stock index is not usually adjusted for cash dividends. In other words, any cash dividends received on the portfolio are ignored when percentage changes in most indices are being calculated.

It is worth noting that if the hypothetical portfolio of stocks remains fixed, the weights assigned to individual stocks in the portfolio do not remain fixed. If the price of one particular stock in the portfolio rises more sharply than others, more weight is given to that stock automatically. A corollary to this is that if the weights of the stocks in the portfolio are specified as constant over time, the hypothetical portfolio will change each day. If the price of one particular stock in the portfolio rises more sharply than others, the holding of the stock must be reduced to maintain the weighting.

Stock Indices

Table 3.2 shows futures prices for contracts on a number of different stock indices as they were reported in the *Wall Street Journal* of May 12, 1995. The prices refer to the close of trading on May 11, 1995. The *Standard & Poor's 500 (S&P 500) Index* is based on a portfolio of 500 different stocks: 400 industrials, 40 utilities, 20 transportation companies, and 40 financial institutions. The weights of the stocks in the portfolio at any given time reflect the stock's total market capitalization (= stock price × number of shares outstanding). This index accounts for 80% of the market capitalization of all the stocks listed on the New York Stock Exchange. One futures contract, traded on the Chicago Mercantile Exchange, is on 500 times the index. The *Standard & Poor's MidCap 400 Index* is similar to the S&P 500, but based on a portfolio of 400 stocks that have somewhat lower market capitalizations.

The *Nikkei 225 Stock Average* is based on a portfolio of 225 of the largest stocks trading on the Tokyo Stock Exchange. Stocks are weighted according to their prices. One futures contract (traded on the Chicago Mercantile Exchange) is on five times the index. The *CAC-40 Index* is based on 40 large stocks trading in France. The *FT-SE 100 Index* is based on a portfolio of 100 major U.K. shares

TABLE 3.2   Stock Index Futures Quotes from the *Wall Street Journal,*
May 12, 1995

```
S&P 500 INDEX (CME) $500 times index
                                       Open
     Open High  Low  Settle Chg  High  Low  Interest
June 525.30 526.80 523.45 526.65 + 1.25 527.90 449.50 195,648
Sept 529.45 530.90 527.85 530.90 + 1.30 532.10 456.30 20,709
Dec  533.00 534.00 533.00 535.00 + 1.40 536.20 474.45  4,671
Mr96 537.60 537.60 537.60 539.30 + 1.40 540.80 511.00  1,445
  Est vol 83,492; vol Wed 75,739; open int 222,419, -226.
  Indx prelim High 524.89; Low 522.70; Close 524.37 +.01
S&P MIDCAP 400 (CME) $500 times index
June 187.40 188.80 187.05 188.65 + .95 188.80 165.50  9,168
  Est vol 428; vol Wed 355; open int 9,214, +2.
  The index: High 187.91; Low 186.74; Close 187.89 +.87
NIKKEI 225 STOCK AVERAGE (CME) - $5 times index
June 16660. 16830. 16660. 16820. - 750 22050. 15510. 32,668
Sept  ....   ....  16905. - 750 20625. 15700.   208
  Est vol 1,563; vol Wed 1,274; open int 32,932, +293.
  The index: High 16872.87; Low 16461.73;Close16461.73
  -364.76
GSCI (CME) - $250 times nearby index
June 180.80 181.00 178.90 179.40 - .90 184.50 172.00 12,904
Aug   ....   ....  177.30 - .90 180.50 172.30   124
```

```
  Est vol 564; vol Wed 445; open int 13,032, +53.
  The index: High 181.14; Low 178.69; Close 179.31 -1.25
CAC-40 STOCK INDEX (MATIF) - FFr 200 per index pt.
May  1992. 2017. 1988.  2008. + 11. 2017. 1729. 39,542
June 1972. 1999. 1971.5 1991. + 13. 2042. 1711. 31,923
July 1974. 1991.5 1974. 1992. + 12. 1991.5 1039.5  384
Sept 2010. 2010. 2010.  2011.5 + 11. 2017. 1736. 11,348
Dec   ....  ....        2041.5 + 11. 2038.5 1913.  2,445
Mr96  ....  ....        2073.5 + 11. 2010.5 1946.5  762
  Est vol 43,489; vol.Wed 31,632; open int 86,404, +1,544.
FT-SE 100 INDEX (LIFFE) - £25 per index point
June 3300.0 3342.0 3296.0 3324.0 + 160.0 3342.0 2960.0 71,229
Sept  ....   ....   ....  3347.0 + 160.0 3294.0 3000.5  2,147
Dec   ....   ....   ....  3376.0 + 160.0 3241.0 3200.0   180
  Est vol 21,850; vol Wed 13,309; open int 73,556, +844.
ALL ORDINARIES SHARE PRICE INDEX (SFE)
  A$25 times index
June 2093. 2101. 2049. 2055. - 28.0 2200. 1861. 91,293
Sept  ....  ....  2081. - 28.0 2114. 1882.  6,701
Dec   ....  ....  2097. - 28.0 2128. 1913.  1,902
Mr96  ....  ....  2123. - 28.0 2150. 1950.   914
  Est vol 9,370; vol Wed 10,350; open int 100,810, +3,133.
  The index: High 2071.3; Low 2034.5; Close 2036.4 -20.5
```

listed on the London Stock Exchange. The *All Ordinaries Share Price Index* is a broadly based index reflecting the value of a portfolio of Australian stocks.

Other stock indices that sometimes underlie derivatives in the United States are the *New York Stock Exchange (NYSE) Composite Index* and the *Major Market Index (MMI).* The NYSE Composite Index is based on a portfolio of all the stocks listed on the New York Stock Exchange with weights reflecting market capitalizations. The MMI is based on a portfolio of 20 blue-chip stocks listed on the New York Stock Exchange with weights reflecting prices. The latter is very closely correlated to the widely quoted *Dow Jones Industrial Average,* which is also based on relatively few stocks.

In the GSCI index futures contract shown in Table 3.2, the underlying asset is the *Goldman Sachs Commodity Index.* This is not a stock index. It is a broadly based index of commodity prices. All the major commodity groups, such as energy, livestock, grains and oilseeds, food and fiber, and metals, are represented in the GSCI. Studies by Goldman Sachs have shown that the GSCI is negatively related to the S&P 500 index, with the correlation being in the range −0.30 to −0.40.

As mentioned in Section 2.6, futures contracts on stock indices are settled in cash, not by delivery of the underlying asset. All contracts are marked to market on the last trading day and the positions are deemed to be closed. For most contracts, the settlement price on the last trading day is set at the closing value of the index on that day. But as discussed in Section 2.6, for the S&P 500 it is set as the value of the index calculated from opening prices the next day. For the futures on the S&P 500, the last trading day is the Thursday before the third Friday of the delivery month.

Futures Prices of Stock Indices

Most indices can be thought of as securities that pay dividends. The security is the portfolio of stocks underlying the index, and the dividends paid by the security are the dividends that would be received by the holder of this portfolio. To a reasonable approximation, the dividends can be assumed to be paid continuously. If q is the dividend yield rate, equation (3.10) gives the futures price, F, as

$$F = Se^{(r-q)(T-t)} \tag{3.12}$$

Example 3.8

Consider a three-month futures contract on the S&P 500. Suppose that the stocks underlying the index provide a dividend yield of 3% per annum, that the current value of the index is 400, and that the continuously compounded risk-free interest rate is 8% per annum. In this case, $r = 0.08$, $S = 400$, $T - t = 0.25$, and $q = 0.03$, and the futures price, F, is given by

$$F = 400e^{0.05 \times 0.25} = 405.03$$

In practice, the dividend yield on the portfolio underlying an index varies week by week throughout the year. For example, a large proportion of the dividends on NYSE stocks are paid in the first week of February, May, August, and November of each year. The value of q that is used should represent the average annualized dividend yield during the life of the contract. The dividends used for estimating q should be those for which the ex-dividend date is during the life of the futures contract. Looking at Table 3.2, we see that the futures prices for the S&P 500 appear to be increasing with maturity at about 3.2% per annum. This corresponds to the situation where the risk-free interest rate exceeds the dividend yield by about 3.2% per annum.

If an analyst is unhappy working in terms of dividend yields, he or she can estimate the dollar amount of dividends that will be paid by the portfolio underlying the index and the timing of those dividends. The index can then be considered to be a security providing known income, and the result in equation (3.7) can be used to calculate the futures price. This approach is useful for indices in countries such as Japan, France, and Germany, where all stocks tend to pay dividends on the same dates.

Index Arbitrage

If $F > Se^{(r-q)(T-t)}$, profits can be made by buying the stocks underlying the index and shorting futures contracts. If $F < Se^{(r-q)(T-t)}$, profits can be made by doing the reverse, that is, shorting or selling the stocks underlying the index and taking a long position in futures contracts. These strategies are known as *index arbitrage*. When $F < Se^{(r-q)(T-t)}$, index arbitrage is often done by a pension fund that owns an indexed portfolio of stocks. When $F > Se^{(r-q)(T-t)}$, it is often done by a corporation holding short-term money market investments. For indices

involving many stocks, index arbitrage is sometimes accomplished by trading a relatively small representative sample of stocks whose movements closely mirror those of the index. Often, index arbitrage is implemented using *program trading.* This means that a computer system is used to generate the trades.

October 19, 1987

In normal market conditions, F is very close to $Se^{(r-q)(T-t)}$. However, it is interesting to note what happened on October 19, 1987, when the market fell by over 20% and the volume of shares traded on the New York Stock Exchange (604 million) easily exceeded all previous records. For most of the day, futures prices were at a significant discount to the underlying index. For example, at the close of trading, the S&P 500 index was at 225.06 (down 57.88 on the day) while the futures price for December delivery on the S&P 500 was 201.50 (down 80.75 on the day). This was largely because the delays in processing orders to sell equity made index arbitrage too risky. On the next day, October 20, 1987, the New York Stock Exchange placed temporary restrictions on the way in which program trading could be done. The result was that the breakdown of the traditional linkage between stock indices and stock index futures continued. At one point, the futures price for the December contract was 18% less than the S&P 500 index.

The Growth Rate of Index Futures Prices

In this section we show that the growth rate of an index futures price equals the excess return of the underlying index over the risk-free rate. As usual we define S, F, q, and T as the current index price, the current futures price, the dividend yield on the index, and the maturity date of the futures contract. We consider the futures price at some earlier time τ. Define:

F_τ: index futures price at time τ

S_τ: spot price of index at time τ

If the portfolio underlying the index provides an excess return over the risk-free rate of x, the total return is $x + r$. Of this, q is realized in the form of dividends and $x + r - q$ is realized in the form of capital gains. Hence

$$S_\tau = Se^{(x+r-q)(\tau-t)}$$

From equation (3.10),

$$F = Se^{(r-q)(T-t)}$$

and

$$F_\tau = S_\tau e^{(r-q)(T-\tau)}$$

It follows from these three equations that

$$F_\tau = Fe^{x(\tau-t)}$$

showing that the growth rate of the futures price equals the excess return on the index.

Hedging Using Index Futures

Stock index futures can be used to hedge the risk in a well-diversified port-folio of stocks. Readers familiar with the capital asset pricing model will know that the relationship between the return on a portfolio of stocks and the return on the market (i.e., the stock market as a whole) is described by a parameter β ($=$ beta). This is the slope of the best-fit line obtained when the excess return on the portfolio over the risk-free rate is regressed against the excess return on the market over the risk-free rate. When $\beta = 1.0$, the return on the portfolio tends to mirror the return on the market; when $\beta = 2.0$, the excess return on the portfolio tends to be twice as great as the excess return on the market; when $\beta = 0.5$, it tends to be half as great; and so on.

The analysis in the preceding section shows that the excess return on the index over the risk-free rate equals the growth rate of the futures price. The return on the index is a reasonable proxy for the return on the market. The growth rate of an index futures price can therefore be considered to be equal to the excess return of the market over the risk-free rate. It follows from the capital asset pricing model that the expected excess return on a portfolio is its β times the proportional change in an index futures price. To hedge a portfolio we therefore need to use index futures contracts with a total underlying asset value equal to the portfolio's beta times the value of the portfolio. Define:

Π: value of the portfolio

$\mathcal{F}$: underlying asset value of one futures contract (if one futures contract is on m times the index, $\mathcal{F} = mF$)

It follows that the optimal number of contracts to short when hedging is

$$\beta \frac{\Pi}{\mathcal{F}}$$

Example 3.9

A company wishes to hedge a portfolio worth \$2,100,000 using an S&P 500 index futures contract with four months to maturity. The current futures price is 300 and the β of the portfolio is 1.5. The value of one futures contract is $300 \times 500 = \$150,000$. The correct number of futures contracts to short, therefore, is

$$1.5 \times \frac{2,100,000}{150,000} = 21$$

A stock index hedge, if effective, should result in the value of the hedged po-sition growing at close to the risk-free interest rate. The excess return on the port-folio (whether positive or negative) is offset by the gain or loss on the futures. It is natural to ask why the hedger should go to the trouble of using futures contracts. If the hedger's objective is to earn the risk-free interest rate, he or she can simply sell the portfolio and invest the proceeds in Treasury bills.

One possibility is that the hedger feels that the stocks in the portfolio have been chosen well. He or she might be very uncertain about the performance of the market as a whole but confident that the stocks in the portfolio will outperform the market (after appropriate adjustments have been made for the β of the portfolio). A hedge using index futures removes the risk arising from market moves and leaves the hedger exposed only to the performance of the portfolio relative to the market. Another possibility is that the hedger is planning to hold a portfolio for a long period of time and requires short-term protection in an uncertain market situation. The alternative strategy of selling the portfolio and buying it back later might involve unacceptably high transactions costs.

Changing Beta

Stock index futures can be used to change the beta of a portfolio. Consider the situation in Example 3.9. To reduce the beta of the portfolio from 1.5 to 0, 21 contracts are required. To reduce beta to 1.0, it is necessary to short only one-third of 21 or 7 contracts; to increase the beta from 1.5 to 3.0, a long position in 21 contracts is required; and so on. In general, to change the beta of the portfolio from β to β^* where $\beta > \beta^*$, a short position in

$$(\beta - \beta^*)\frac{\Pi}{\mathcal{F}}$$

contracts is required. When $\beta < \beta^*$, a long position in

$$(\beta^* - \beta)\frac{\Pi}{\mathcal{F}}$$

contracts is required.

The Nikkei Index

Equation (3.12) does not apply to the futures contract on the Nikkei 225. The reason for this is quite subtle. Define S_F as the value of the Nikkei 225 index. This is the value of a portfolio measured in yen. The variable underlying the CME futures contract on the Nikkei 225 is a variable with a *dollar value* of $5S_F$. In other words, the futures contract takes a variable that is measured in yen and treats it as though it were dollars. We cannot invest in a portfolio whose value will always be $5S_F$ dollars. The best we can do is to invest in one that is always worth $5S_F$ yen or in one that is always worth $5QS_F$ dollars, where Q is the dollar value of 1 yen. The variable underlying the Nikkei 225 is therefore a dollar amount that does not equal the price of a traded security. Consequently, we cannot derive a theoretical futures price using arbitrage arguments. In Chapter 13 we show how other arguments can be used to produce a formula for the CME Nikkei 225 futures price.

3.8 FORWARD AND FUTURES CONTRACTS ON CURRENCIES

We now move on to consider forward and futures contracts on foreign currencies. The variable, S, is the current price in dollars of one unit of the foreign currency; K is the delivery price agreed to in the forward contract. A foreign currency has the property that the holder of the currency can earn interest at the risk-free interest rate prevailing in the foreign country. (For example, the holder can invest the currency in a foreign-denominated bond.) We define r_f as the value of this foreign risk-free interest rate with continuous compounding.

The two portfolios that enable us to price a forward contract on a foreign currency are

Portfolio A: one long forward contract plus an amount of cash equal to $Ke^{-r(T-t)}$

Portfolio B: an amount $e^{-r_f(T-t)}$ of the foreign currency

Both portfolios will become worth the same as one unit of the foreign currency at time T. They must therefore be equally valuable at time t. Hence

$$f + Ke^{-r(T-t)} = Se^{-r_f(T-t)}$$

or

$$f = Se^{-r_f(T-t)} - Ke^{-r(T-t)} \tag{3.13}$$

The forward price (or forward exchange rate), F, is the value of K that makes $f = 0$ in equation (3.13). Hence

$$F = Se^{(r-r_f)(T-t)} \tag{3.14}$$

This is the well-known interest rate parity relationship from the field of international finance. From the discussion earlier in this chapter, F is, to a reasonable approximation, also the futures price.

Note that equations (3.13) and (3.14) are identical to equations (3.9) and (3.10), respectively, with q replaced by r_f. This is because a foreign currency is analogous to a security paying a known dividend yield. The "dividend yield" is the risk-free rate of interest in the foreign currency. To see why this is so, note that interest earned on a foreign currency holding is denominated in the foreign currency. Its value when measured in the domestic currency is therefore proportional to the value of the foreign currency.

Table 3.3 shows futures prices on May 12, 1995 for contracts trading on the Japanese yen, deutschemark, Canadian dollar, British pound, Swiss franc, and Australian dollar in the International Monetary Market of the Chicago Mercantile Exchange. The futures exchange rate is quoted as the value of the foreign currency in U.S. dollars (or, in the case of the yen, the value of the foreign currency in U.S. cents). This can be confusing because spot and forward rates on most currencies are quoted the other way around, that is, as the number of units

TABLE 3.3   Foreign Exchange Futures
Quotes from the *Wall Street Journal*, May
12, 1995

CURRENCY

	Open	High	Low	Settle	Change	Lifetime High	Lifetime Low	Open Interest
JAPAN YEN (CME) – 12.5 million yen; $ per yen (.00)								
June	1.1971	1.2014	1.1660	1.1729	– .0255	1.2625	.9915	64,735
Sept	1.2070	1.2070	1.1801	1.1869	– .0256	1.2670	1.0175	4,517
Dec	1.2115	1.2115	1.1943	1.2007	– .0256	1.2813	1.0300	834
Mr96	1.2120	1.2130	1.2112	1.2147	– .0254	1.2990	1.0465	427
June	1.2330	1.2330	1.2260	1.2285	– .0254	1.3130	1.0780	142
Est vol 32,263; vol Wed 20,935; open int 70,655, +491.								
DEUTSCHEMARK (CME) – 125,000 marks; $ per mark								
June	.7217	.7225	.6957	.6988	– .0229	.7448	.5980	66,024
Sept	.7210	.7210	.6988	.7014	– .0230	.7450	.6290	3,720
Dec	.7132	.7155	.7028	.7037	– .0232	.7480	.6580	832
Mr96	....	....	....	.7058	– .0233	.7505	.6525	98
Est vol 48.871; vol Wed 37,660; open int 70,647, –251.								
CANADIAN DOLLAR (CME) – 100,000 dlrs.; $ per Can $								
June	.7370	.7400	.7361	.7393	+ .0023	.7600	.6948	45,125
Sept	.7363	.7385	.7360	.7376	+ .0023	.7438	.6920	3,692
Dec	.7350	.7365	.7350	.7363	+ .0023	.7400	.6895	2,234
Mr96	.7350	.7355	.7350	.7350	+ .0023	.7355	.6900	657
June	.7335	.7340	.7335	.7337	+ .0023	.7340	.6905	252
Est vol 5,220; vol Wed 4,715; open int 51,960, +992.								
BRITISH POUND (CME) – 62,500 pds.; $ per pound								
June	1.5860	1.5860	1.5524	1.5594	– .0236	1.6530	1.5330	24,420
Sept	1.5700	1.5700	1.5490	1.5562	– .0234	1.6480	1.5410	322
Est vol 20,299; vol Wed 9,262; open int 24,829, +239.								
SWISS FRANC (CME) – 125,000 francs; $ per franc								
June	.8734	.8734	.8356	.8381	– .0341	.9038	.7193	26,604
Sept	.8710	.8710	.8415	.8436	– .0344	.9085	.7605	2,625
Dec	.8650	.8650	.8485	.8489	– .0347	.9138	.7834	641
Est vol 29,515; vol Wed 20,915; open int 29,913, –382.								
AUSTRALIAN DOLLAR (CME) – 100,000 dlrs.; $ per A.$								
June	.7275	.7353	.7275	.7317	+ .0054	.7762	.7187	8,556
Est vol 650; vol Wed 1,008; open int 8,633, +242.								

of the foreign currency per U.S. dollar. A forward quote on the Canadian dollar
of 1.4000 would become a futures quote of 0.7143.

When the foreign interest rate is greater than the domestic interest rate
$(r_f > r)$, equation (3.14) shows that F is always less than S and that F decreases
as the maturity of the contract, T, increases. Similarly, when the domestic interest
rate is greater than the foreign interest rate $(r > r_f)$, equation (3.14) shows that F
is always greater than S and that F increases as T increases. On May 12, 1995, interest rates in Japan, Germany, and Switzerland were all lower than in the United
States. This corresponds to the $r_f < r$ situation and explains why futures prices
for these currencies increase with maturity. Interest rates in Canada and Britain
were higher than in the United States. This corresponds to the $r_f > r$ situation
and explains why futures prices for these currencies decrease with maturity.

Example 3.10

The futures price of the Japanese yen in Table 3.3 appears to be increasing at a rate of
about 4.7% per annum with the maturity. For example, the June 1996 settlement price
is about 4.7% higher than the June 1995 settlement price. This suggests that the short-
term risk-free interest rate was about 4.7% per annum higher in the United States than in
Japan.

3.9 FUTURES ON COMMODITIES

We now move on to consider commodity futures contracts. Here it will prove to be important to distinguish between commodities that are held by a significant number of investors solely for investment (e.g., gold and silver) and those that are held primarily for consumption. Arbitrage arguments can be used to obtain exact futures prices in the case of investment commodities. However, it turns out that they can only be used to give an upper bound to the futures price in the case of consumption commodities.

Gold and Silver

Although they have some commercial uses, gold and silver are held by a significant number of investors solely for investment. If storage costs are zero, they can be considered as being analogous to securities paying no income. Using the notation introduced earlier, S is the current spot price of gold. As shown by equation (3.5), the futures price, F, should be given by

$$F = Se^{r(T-t)} \tag{3.15}$$

Storage costs can be regarded as negative income. If U is the present value of all the storage costs that will be incurred during the life of a futures contract, it follows from equation (3.7) that

$$F = (S + U)e^{r(T-t)} \tag{3.16}$$

If the storage costs incurred at any time are proportional to the price of the commodity, they can be regarded as providing a negative dividend yield. In this case, from equation (3.10),

$$F = Se^{(r+u)(T-t)} \tag{3.17}$$

where u is the storage costs per annum as a proportion of the spot price.

Example 3.11

Consider a one-year futures contract on gold. Suppose that it costs $2 per ounce per year to store gold, with the payment being made at the end of the year. Assume that the spot price is $450 and the risk-free rate is 7% per annum for all maturities. This corresponds to $r = 0.07$, $S = 450$, $T - t = 1$, and

$$U = 2e^{-0.07} = 1.865$$

The futures price, F, is given by

$$F = (450 + 1.865)e^{0.07} = 484.63$$

Other Commodities

For commodities that are not held primarily for investment purposes, the arbitrage arguments leading to equations (3.15), (3.16), and (3.17) need to be reviewed carefully. Suppose that instead of equation (3.16), we have

$$F > (S + U)e^{r(T-t)} \tag{3.18}$$

To take advantage of this, an arbitrageur should implement the following strategy:

1. Borrow an amount $S + U$ at the risk-free rate and use it to purchase one unit of the commodity and to pay storage costs.
2. Short a futures contract on one unit of the commodity.

If we regard the futures contract as a forward contract, this is certain to lead to a profit of $F - (S + U)e^{r(T-t)}$ at time T. There is no problem with implementing the strategy for any commodity. However, as arbitrageurs do so, there will be a tendency for S to increase and F to decrease until equation (3.18) is no longer true. We conclude that equation (3.18) cannot hold for any significant length of time.

Suppose next that

$$F < (S + U)e^{r(T-t)} \tag{3.19}$$

We might try to take advantage of this using a strategy analogous to that for a forward contract on a non-dividend-paying stock when the forward price is too low. However, this would involve shorting the commodity in such a way that the storage costs are paid to the person with the short position. This is not usually possible.

For gold and silver, we can argue that there are many investors who hold the commodity solely for investment. When they observe the inequality in equation (3.19), they will find it profitable to:

1. Sell the commodity, save the storage costs, and invest the proceeds at the risk-free interest rate.
2. Buy the futures contract.

The result is a riskless profit at maturity of $(S + U)e^{r(T-t)} - F$ relative to the position the investors would have been in if they had held the gold or silver. It follows that equation (3.19) cannot hold for long. Since neither equation (3.18) nor equation (3.19) can hold for long, we must have $F = (S + U)e^{r(T-t)}$.

For commodities that are not, to any significant extent, held for investment, this argument cannot be used. Individuals and companies who keep the commodity in inventory do so because of its consumption value—not because of its value as an investment. They are reluctant to sell the commodity and buy futures contracts since futures contracts cannot be consumed. There is therefore nothing to stop equation (3.19) from holding. Since equation (3.18) cannot hold, all we can assert for a consumption commodity is

$$F \leq (S + U)e^{r(T-t)} \tag{3.20}$$

If storage costs are expressed as a proportion, u, of the spot price, the equivalent result is

$$F \leq Se^{(r+u)(T-t)} \tag{3.21}$$

Convenience Yields

When $F < Se^{(r+u)(T-t)}$, users of the commodity must feel that there are benefits from ownership of the physical commodity that are not obtained by the holder of a futures contract. These benefits may include the ability to profit from temporary local shortages or the ability to keep a production process running. The benefits are sometimes referred to as the *convenience yield* provided by the product. If the dollar amount of storage costs is known and has a present value, U, the convenience yield, y, is defined so that

$$Fe^{y(T-t)} = (S + U)e^{r(T-t)}$$

If the storage costs per unit are a constant proportion, u, of the spot price, y is defined so that

$$Fe^{y(T-t)} = Se^{(r+u)(T-t)}$$

or

$$F = Se^{(r+u-y)(T-t)} \tag{3.22}$$

The convenience yield simply measures the extent to which the left-hand side is less than the right-hand side in equation (3.20) or in equation (3.21). Consider, for example, copper in Table 2.2. The futures price of copper decreases as the maturity of the contract increases. This indicates that the convenience yield, y, is greater than $r + u$. For investment assets such as gold, the convenience yield must be zero; otherwise, there are arbitrage opportunities.

The convenience yield reflects the market's expectations concerning the future availability of the commodity. The greater the possibility that shortages will occur during the life of the futures contract, the higher the convenience yield. If users of the commodity have high inventories, there is very little chance of shortages in the near future and the convenience yield tends to be low. On the other hand, low inventories tend to lead to high convenience yields.

3.10 THE COST OF CARRY

The relationship between futures prices and spot prices can be summarized in terms of what is known as the *cost of carry*. This measures the storage cost plus the interest that is paid to finance the asset less the income earned on the asset. For a non-dividend-paying stock, the cost of carry is r since there are no storage costs and no income is earned; for a stock index, it is $r - q$ since income is earned at rate q on the asset; for a currency, it is $r - r_f$; for a commodity with storage costs that are a proportion u of the price, it is $r + u$; and so on.

Define the cost of carry as c. For an investment asset, the futures price is

$$F = Se^{c(T-t)} \tag{3.23}$$

For a consumption asset, it is

$$F = Se^{(c-y)(T-t)} \qquad (3.24)$$

where y is the convenience yield.

3.11 DELIVERY CHOICES

Whereas a forward contract normally specifies that delivery is to take place on a particular day, a futures contract often allows the party with the short position to choose to deliver at any time during a certain period. (Typically, the party has to give a few days notice of its intention to deliver.) This introduces a complication into the determination of futures prices. Should the maturity of the futures contract be assumed to be the beginning, middle, or end of the delivery period? Even though most futures contracts are closed out prior to maturity, it is important to know when delivery would have taken place, in order to calculate the theoretical futures price.

If the futures price is an increasing function of the time to maturity, it can be seen from equation (3.24) that the benefits from holding the asset (including convenience yield and net of storage costs) are less than the risk-free rate. It is then usually optimal for the party with the short position to deliver as early as possible. This is because the interest earned on the cash received outweighs the benefits of holding the asset. As a general rule, futures prices in these circumstances should therefore be calculated on the basis that delivery will take place at the beginning of the delivery period. If futures prices are decreasing as maturity increases, the reverse is true: It is usually optimal for the party with the short position to deliver as late as possible and futures prices should, as a general rule, be calculated on the assumption that this will happen.

3.12 FUTURES PRICES AND THE EXPECTED FUTURE SPOT PRICE

One question that is often raised is whether the futures price of an asset is equal to its expected future spot price. If you had to guess what the price of an asset will be in 3 months, is the futures price an unbiased estimate? John Maynard Keynes and John Hicks in the 1930s argued that if hedgers tend to hold short positions and speculators tend to hold long positions, the futures price will be below the expected future spot price. This is because speculators require compensation for the risks they are bearing. They will trade only if there is an expectation that the futures price will rise over time. Hedgers, on the other hand, because they are reducing their risks, are prepared to enter into contracts where the expected payoff is slightly negative. If hedgers tend to hold long positions while speculators hold short positions, Keynes and Hicks argue that the futures price must be above the

expected future spot price. The reason is similar. To compensate speculators for the risks they are bearing, there must be an expectation that the futures prices will decline over time.

The situation where the futures price is below the expected future spot price is known as *normal backwardation;* the situation where the futures price is above the expected future spot price is known as *contango.* We now consider the factors determining normal backwardation and contango from the point of view of the trade-offs that have to be made between risk and return in capital markets.

Risk and Return

In general, the higher the risk of an investment, the higher the expected return demanded by an investor. The capital asset pricing model, which was out-lined in Section 3.7, leads to the conclusion that there are two types of risk in the economy: systematic and nonsystematic. Nonsystematic risk should not be important to an investor. This is because it can be almost completely eliminated by holding a well-diversified portfolio. An investor should not therefore require a higher expected return for bearing nonsystematic risk. Systematic risk, by con-trast, cannot be diversified away. It arises from a correlation between returns from the investment and returns from the stock market as a whole. An investor in general requires a higher expected return than the risk-free interest rate for bear-ing positive amounts of systematic risk. Also, an investor is prepared to accept a lower expected return than the risk-free interest rate when the systematic risk in an investment is negative.

The Risk in a Futures Position

Consider a speculator who takes a long futures position in the hope that the price of the asset will be above the futures price at maturity. We suppose that the speculator puts the present value of the futures price into a risk-free investment at time t while simultaneously taking a long futures position. We assume that the futures contract can be treated as a forward contract and that the delivery date is T. The proceeds of the risk-free investment are used to buy the asset on the delivery date. The asset is then immediately sold for its market price. This means that the cash flows to the speculator are

Time t: $-Fe^{-r(T-t)}$
Time T: $+S_T$

where S_T is the price of the asset at time T.

The present value of this investment is

$$-Fe^{-r(T-t)} + E(S_T)e^{-k(T-t)}$$

where k is the discount rate appropriate for the investment (i.e., the expected return required by investors on the investment) and E denotes expected value. Assuming that all investment opportunities in securities markets have zero net

present value,

$$-Fe^{-r(T-t)} + E(S_T)e^{-k(T-t)} = 0$$

or

$$F = E(S_T)e^{(r-k)(T-t)} \tag{3.25}$$

The value of k depends on the systematic risk of the investment. If S_T is un-correlated with the level of the stock market, the investment has zero systematic risk. In this case, $k = r$ and equation (3.25) shows that $F = E(S_T)$. If S_T is pos-itively correlated with the level of the stock market, the investment has positive systematic risk. In this case, $k > r$ and equation (3.25) shows that $F < E(S_T)$. Finally, if S_T is negatively correlated with the stock market, the investment has negative systematic risk. This means that $k < r$ and equation (3.25) shows that $F > E(S_T)$.

Empirical Evidence

If $F = E(S_T)$, the futures price will drift up or down only if the market changes its views about the expected future spot price. Over a long period of time, we can reasonably assume that the market revises its expectations about future spot prices upward as often as it does so downward. It follows that when $F = E(S_T)$, the average profit from holding futures contracts over a long period of time should be zero. The $F < E(S_T)$ situation corresponds to the positive sys-tematic risk situation. Since the futures price and the spot price must be equal at maturity of the futures contract, it implies that a futures price should, on average, drift up and a trader should over a long period of time make positive profits from consistently holding long futures positions. Similarly, the $F > E(S_T)$ situation implies that a trader should over a long period of time make positive profits from consistently holding short futures positions.

How do futures prices behave in practice? Some of the empirical work that has been carried out is listed at the end of this chapter. The results are mixed. Houthakker's study looked at futures prices for wheat, cotton, and corn during the period 1937–1957. It showed that it was possible to earn significant profits from taking long futures positions. This suggests that an investment in corn has positive systematic risk and $F < E(S_T)$. Telser's study contradicted the findings of Houthakker. His data covered the period 1926–1950 for cotton and 1927–1954 for wheat and gave rise to no significant profits for traders taking either long or short positions. To quote from Telser, "The futures data offer no evidence to contradict the simple . . . hypothesis that the futures price is an unbiased estimate of the expected future spot price." Gray's study looked at corn futures prices during the 1921–1959 period and resulted in similar findings to those of Telser. Dusak's study used data on corn, wheat, and soybeans during 1952–1967 and took a different approach. It attempted to estimate the systematic risk of an in-vestment in these commodities by calculating the correlation of movements in the

commodity prices with movements in the S&P 500. The results suggest that there is no systematic risk and lend support to the $F = E(S_T)$ hypothesis. However, other work by Chang using the same commodities and more advanced statistical techniques supports the $F < E(S_T)$ hypothesis.

3.13 SUMMARY

In many situations the futures price of a contract with a certain delivery date can be considered to be the same as the forward price for a contract with the same delivery date. It can be shown that, in theory, the two should be exactly the same when interest rates are perfectly predictable and should be close to each other for short-life contracts when interest rates vary unpredictably.

For the purposes of understanding futures (or forward) prices, it is convenient to divide futures contracts into two categories: those where the underlying asset is held for investment by a significant number of investors and those where the underlying asset is held primarily for consumption purposes. In the case of investment assets, we have considered three different situations:

1. The asset provides no income.
2. The asset provides a known dollar income.
3. The asset provides a known dividend yield.

The results are summarized in Table 3.4. They enable futures prices to be obtained for contracts on stock indices, currencies, gold, and silver.

In the case of consumption assets, it is not possible to obtain the futures price as a function of the spot price and other observable variables. A parameter known as the asset's convenience yield becomes important. This measures the extent to

TABLE 3.4   Forward/Futures Contracts on Investment Assets

Summary of results for a contract with maturity T on an asset with price S when the risk-free interest rate for a T-year period is r

Asset	Value of Long Forward Contract with Delivery Price K	Forward/Futures Price
Provides no income	$S - Ke^{-r(T-t)}$	$Se^{r(T-t)}$
Provides known income with present value, I	$S - I - Ke^{-r(T-t)}$	$(S - I)e^{r(T-t)}$
Provides known dividend yield, q	$Se^{-q(T-t)} - Ke^{-r(T-t)}$	$Se^{(r-q)(T-t)}$

which users of the commodity feel that there are benefits from ownership of the physical asset that are not obtained by the holders of the futures contract. These benefits may include the ability to profit from temporary local shortages or the ability to keep a production process running. It is possible to obtain only an upper bound for the futures price of consumption assets using arbitrage arguments.

The concept of a cost of carry is sometimes useful. The cost of carry is the storage cost of the underlying asset plus the cost of financing it minus the income received from it. In the case of investment assets, the futures price is greater than the spot price by an amount reflecting the cost of carry. In the case of consumption assets, the futures price is greater than the spot price by an amount reflecting the cost of carry net of the convenience yield.

If we assume that the capital asset pricing model is true, the relationship between the futures price and the expected future spot price depends on whether the spot price is positively or negatively correlated with the level of the stock market. Positive correlation will tend to lead to a futures price lower than the expected future spot price. Negative correlation will tend to lead to a futures price higher than the expected future spot price. Only when the correlation is zero will the theoretical futures price be equal to the expected future spot price.

SUGGESTIONS FOR FURTHER READING

On Empirical Research Concerning Forward and Futures Prices

Cornell, B., and M. Reinganum, "Forward and Futures Prices: Evidence from Foreign Exchange Markets," *Journal of Finance,* 36 (December 1981), 1035–45.

French, K., "A Comparison of Futures and Forward Prices," *Journal of Financial Economics,* 12 (November 1983), 311–42.

Park, H. Y., and A. H. Chen, "Differences between Futures and Forward Prices: A Further Investigation of Marking to Market Effects," *Journal of Futures Markets,* 5 (February 1985), 77–88.

Rendleman, R., and C. Carabini, "The Efficiency of the Treasury Bill Futures Markets," *Journal of Finance,* 34 (September 1979), 895–914.

Viswanath, P. V., "Taxes and the Futures-Forward Price Difference in the 91-day T-Bill Market," *Journal of Money Credit and Banking,* 21, 2 (May 1989), 190–205.

On Empirical Research Concerning the Relationship between Futures Prices and Expected Future Spot Prices

Chang, E. C., "Returns to Speculators and the Theory of Normal Backwardation," *Journal of Finance,* 40 (March 1985), 193–208.

Dusak, K., "Futures Trading and Investor Returns: An Investigation of Commodity Risk Premiums," *Journal of Political Economy,* 81 (December 1973), 1387–1406.

Gray, R. W., "The Search for a Risk Premium," *Journal of Political Economy,* 69 (June 1961), 250–60.

Houthakker, H. S., "Can Speculators Forecast Prices?" *Review of Economics and Statistics,* 39 (1957), 143–51.

Telser, L. G., "Futures Trading and the Storage of Cotton and Wheat," *Journal of Political Economy,* 66 (June 1958), 233–55.

On the Theoretical Relationship between Forward and Futures Prices

Cox, J. C., J. E. Ingersoll, and S. A. Ross, "The Relation between Forward Prices and Futures Prices," *Journal of Financial Economics*, 9 (December 1981), 321–46.

Jarrow, R. A., and G. S. Oldfield, "Forward Contracts and Futures Contracts," *Journal of Financial Economics,* 9 (December 1981), 373–82.

Kane, E. J., "Market Incompleteness and Divergences between Forward and Futures Interest Rates," *Journal of Finance,* 35 (May 1980), 221–34.

Margrabe, W., "A Theory of Forward and Futures Prices," Working Paper, Wharton School, University of Pennsylvania, 1976.

Richard, S., and M. Sundaresan, "A Continuous Time Model of Forward and Futures Prices in a Multigood Economy," *Journal of Financial Economics,* 9 (December 1981), 347–72.

Other

Hicks, J. R., *Value and Capital.* Oxford: Oxford University Press, 1939.

Keynes, J. M., *A Treatise on Money.* London: Macmillan, 1930.

QUESTIONS AND PROBLEMS

3.1. A bank quotes you a rate of interest of 14% per annum with quarterly compounding. What is the equivalent rate with (a) continuous compounding, and (b) annual compounding?

3.2. Explain what happens when an investor shorts a certain share.

3.3. Suppose that you enter into a six-month forward contract on a non-dividend-paying stock when the stock price is $30 and the risk-free interest rate (with continuous compounding) is 12% per annum. What is the forward price?

3.4. A stock index currently stands at 350. The risk-free interest rate is 8% per annum (with continuous compounding) and the dividend yield on the index is 4% per annum. What should the futures price for a four-month contract be?

3.5. Explain carefully why the futures price of gold can be calculated from its spot price and other observable variables, whereas the futures price of copper cannot.

3.6. Explain carefully the meaning of the terms *convenience yield* and *cost of carry.* What is the relationship between the futures price, the spot price, the convenience yield, and the cost of carry?

3.7. Is the futures price of a stock index greater than or less than the expected future value of the index? Explain your answer.

3.8. A person receives $1,100 in one year in return for an investment of $1,000 now. What is the percentage return per annum with:
   (a) Annual compounding?
   (b) Semiannual compounding?
   (c) Monthly compounding?
   (d) Continuous compounding?

3.9. What rate of interest with continuous compounding is equivalent to 15% per annum with monthly compounding?

3.10. A deposit account pays 12% per annum with continuous compounding, but interest is actually paid quarterly. How much interest will be paid each quarter on a $10,000 deposit?

3.11. A one-year-long forward contract on a non-dividend-paying stock is entered into when the stock price is $40 and the risk-free rate of interest is 10% per annum with continuous compounding.
   (a) What are the forward price and the initial value of the forward contract?
   (b) Six months later, the price of the stock is $45 and the risk-free interest rate is still 10%. What are the forward price and the value of the forward contract?

3.12. A stock is expected to pay a dividend of $1 per share in two months and again in five months. The stock price is $50 and the risk-free rate of interest is 8% per annum with continuous compounding for all maturities. An investor has just taken a short position in a six-month forward contract on the stock.
   (a) What are the forward price and the initial value of the forward contract?
   (b) Three months later, the price of the stock is $48 and the risk-free rate of interest is still 8% per annum. What are the forward price and the value of the short position in the forward contract?

3.13. The risk-free rate of interest is 7% per annum with continuous compounding and the dividend yield on a stock index is 3.2% per annum. The current value of an index is 150. What is the six-month futures price?

3.14. Assume that the risk-free interest rate is 9% per annum with continuous compounding and that the dividend yield on a stock index varies throughout the year. In February, May, August, and November, the dividend yield is 5% per annum. In other months it is 2% per annum. Suppose that the value of the index on July 31, 1996 is 300. What is the futures price for a contract deliverable on December 31, 1996?

3.15. Suppose that the risk-free interest rate is 10% per annum with continuous compounding and the dividend yield on a stock index is 4% per annum. The index is standing at 400 and the futures price for a contract deliverable in four months is 405. What arbitrage opportunities does this create?

3.16. Estimate the difference between risk-free rates of interest in Germany and the United States from the information in Table 3.3.

3.17. The two-month interest rates in Switzerland and the United States with continuous compounding are 3% and 8% per annum, respectively. The spot price of the Swiss franc is $0.6500. The futures price for a contract deliverable in two months is $0.6600. What arbitrage opportunities does this create?

3.18. The current price of silver is $9 per ounce. The storage costs are $0.24 per ounce per year payable quarterly in advance. Assuming that interest rates of all maturities equal 10% per annum with continuous compounding, calculate the futures price of silver for delivery in nine months.

3.19. A bank offers a corporate client a choice between borrowing cash at 11% per annum and borrowing gold at 2% per annum. (If gold is borrowed, interest and principal must be repaid in gold. Thus 100 ounces borrowed today would require 102 ounces to be repaid in one year.) The risk-free interest rate is 9.25% per annum and storage costs are 0.5% per annum. Discuss whether the rate of interest on the gold loan is too high or too low in relation to the rate of interest on the cash loan. The interest rates on the two loans are expressed with annual compounding. The risk-free interest rate and storage cost are expressed with continuous compounding.

3.20. Suppose that F_1 and F_2 are two futures contracts on the same commodity with maturity dates of t_1 and t_2 and $t_2 > t_1$. Prove that

$$F_2 \le (F_1 + U)e^{r(t_2 - t_1)}$$

where r is the risk-free interest rate (assumed to be constant) and U is the cost of storing the commodity between times t_1 and t_2 discounted to time t_1 at the risk-free rate. For the purposes of this problem, assume that a futures contract is the same as a forward contract.

3.21. When a known cash outflow in a foreign currency is hedged by a company using a forward contract, there is no foreign exchange risk. When it is hedged using futures contracts, the marking to market process does leave the company exposed to some risk. Explain the nature of this risk. In particular, consider whether the company is better off using a futures contract or a forward contract when:
(a) The value of the foreign currency falls rapidly during the life of the contract.
(b) The value of the foreign currency rises rapidly during the life of the contract.
(c) The value of the foreign currency first rises and then falls back to its initial level.
(d) The value of the foreign currency first falls and then rises back to its initial level.

Assume that the forward price equals the futures price.

3.22. It is sometimes argued that a forward exchange rate is an unbiased predictor of future exchange rates. Under what circumstances is this so?

3.23. A company that is uncertain about the exact date when it will pay a foreign currency sometimes wishes to negotiate with its bank a forward contract where there is a period during which delivery can be made. The company wants to reserve the right to choose the exact delivery date to fit in with its own cash flows. Put yourself in the position of the bank. How would you price the product that the client wants?

3.24. What is the difference between the way in which prices are quoted in the foreign exchange futures market, the foreign exchange spot market, and the foreign exchange forward market?

3.25. The forward price on the German mark for delivery in 45 days is quoted as 1.8204. The futures price for a contract that will be delivered in 45 days is 0.5479. Explain these two quotes. Which is more favorable for an investor wanting to sell marks?

3.26. The Value Line Index is designed to reflect changes in the value of a portfolio of over 1,600 equally weighted stocks. Prior to March 9, 1988, the change in the index from one day to the next was calculated as the *geometric* average of the changes in the prices of the stocks underlying the index. In these circumstances, does equation (3.12) correctly relate the futures price of the index to its cash price? If not, does the equation overstate or understate the futures price?

3.27. A company has a $10 million portfolio with a beta of 1.2. How can it use futures contracts on the S&P 500 to hedge its risk? The index is currently standing at 270.

3.28. "When the convenience yield is high, long hedges are likely to be particularly attractive to a company that knows it will require a certain quantity of a commodity on a certain future date." Discuss.

3.29. A U.S. company is interested in using the futures contracts traded on the CME to hedge its German mark exposure. Define r as the interest rate (all maturities) on the U.S. dollar and r_f as the interest rate (all maturities) on the mark. Assume that r and r_f are constant and suppose that the company uses a contract expiring at time T to hedge an exposure at time τ $(T > \tau)$. Show that the optimal hedge ratio is

$$e^{(r_f - r)(T - \tau)}$$

APPENDIX 3A: PROOF THAT FORWARD AND FUTURES PRICES ARE EQUAL WHEN INTEREST RATES ARE CONSTANT

In this appendix we show that forward and futures prices are equal when interest rates are constant. Suppose that a futures contract lasts for n days and that F_i is the futures price at the end of day i $(0 < i < n)$. Define δ as the risk-free rate per day (assumed constant). Consider the following strategy:[3]

1. Take a long futures position of e^{δ} at the end of day 0 (i.e., at the beginning of the contract).
2. Increase the long position to $e^{2\delta}$ at the end of day 1.
3. Increase the long position to $e^{3\delta}$ at the end of day 2.

And so on.

     This strategy is summarized in Table 3.5. By the beginning of day i, the investor has a long position of $e^{\delta i}$. The profit (possibly negative) from the position on day i is

$$(F_i - F_{i-1})e^{\delta i}$$

---

[3]This strategy was proposed by J. C. Cox, J. E. Ingersoll, and S. A. Ross, "The Relationship between Forward Prices and Futures Prices," *Journal of Financial Economics,* 9 (December 1981), 321–46.

TABLE 3.5   Investment Strategy to Show That Futures and Forward Prices Are Equal

Day	0	1	2	$\cdots$	$n-1$	n
Futures price	F_0	F_1	F_2	$\cdots$	F_{n-1}	F_n
Futures position	e^{δ}	$e^{2\delta}$	$e^{3\delta}$	$\cdots$	$e^{n\delta}$	0
Gain/loss	0	$(F_1 - F_0)e^{\delta}$	$(F_2 - F_1)e^{2\delta}$	$\cdots$	$\cdots$	$(F_n - F_{n-1})e^{n\delta}$
Gain/loss compounded to day n	0	$(F_1 - F_0)e^{n\delta}$	$(F_2 - F_1)e^{n\delta}$	$\cdots$	$\cdots$	$(F_n - F_{n-1})e^{n\delta}$

Assume that this is compounded at the risk-free rate until the end of day n. Its value at the end of day n is

$$(F_i - F_{i-1})e^{\delta i}e^{(n-i)\delta} = (F_i - F_{i-1})e^{n\delta}$$

The value at the end of day n of the entire investment strategy is therefore

$$\sum_{i=1}^{n}(F_i - F_{i-1})e^{n\delta}$$

This is

$$[(F_n - F_{n-1}) + (F_{n-1} - F_{n-2}) + \cdots + (F_1 - F_0)]e^{n\delta} = (F_n - F_0)e^{n\delta}$$

Since F_n is the same as the terminal asset price, S_T, the terminal value of the investment strategy can be written

$$(S_T - F_0)e^{n\delta}$$

An investment of F_0 in a risk-free bond combined with the strategy just given yields

$$F_0 e^{n\delta} + (S_T - F_0)e^{n\delta} = S_T e^{n\delta}$$

at time T. No investment is required for all the long futures positions described. It follows that an amount F_0 can be invested to give an amount $S_T e^{n\delta}$ at time T.

Suppose next that the forward price at the end of day 0 is G_0. By investing G_0 in a riskless bond and taking a long forward position of $e^{n\delta}$ forward contracts, an amount $S_T e^{n\delta}$ is also guaranteed at time T. Thus, there are two investment strategies, one requiring an initial outlay of F_0, the other requiring an initial outlay of G_0, both of which yield $S_T e^{n\delta}$ at time T. It follows that in the absence of arbitrage opportunities

$$F_0 = G_0$$

In other words, the futures price and the forward price are identical. Note that in this proof there is nothing special about the time period of one day. The futures price based on a contract with weekly settlements is also the same as the forward price when corresponding assumptions are made.

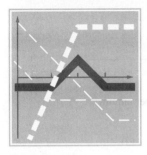

Chapter 4
Interest Rate Futures

An interest rate futures contract is a futures contract on an asset whose price is dependent on the level of interest rates. In this chapter we describe the mechanics of how interest rate futures contracts work and how prices are quoted. We also explain the way in which futures prices can be related to spot prices, discuss the concept of duration, and consider hedging strategies involving interest rate futures.

Hedging a company's exposure to interest rates is more complicated than hedging its exposure to, say, the price of copper. This is because an entire term structure is necessary to provide a full description of the level of interest rates, whereas the price of copper can be described by a single number. When wishing to hedge its interest rate exposure, a company must decide not only the maturity of the hedge it requires but also the maturity of the interest rate to which it is exposed. It must then find a way of using available interest rate futures contracts so that an appropriate hedge is obtained.

4.1 SOME PRELIMINARIES

Before we describe the nature of interest rate futures contracts, it is appropriate to review a few topics concerned with the term structure of interest rates.

Spot and Forward Interest Rates

The n-year spot interest rate is the interest rate on an investment that is made for a period of time starting today and lasting for n years. Thus the three-year spot rate is the rate of interest on an investment lasting three years, the five-year spot rate is the rate of interest on an investment lasting five years, and so on. The investment considered should be a "pure" n-year investment with no intermediate payments. This means that all the interest and the principal is repaid to the investor at the end of year n. The n-year spot rate is also referred to as the *n-year zero-coupon yield*. This is because it is, by definition, the yield on a bond that pays no coupons.

TABLE 4.1   Calculation of Forward Rates

Year (n)	Spot Rate for an n-year Investment (% per annum)	Forward Rate for nth Year (% per annum)
1	10.0	
2	10.5	11.0
3	10.8	11.4
4	11.0	11.6
5	11.1	11.5

Forward interest rates are the rates of interest implied by current spot rates for periods of time in the future. To illustrate how they are calculated, we suppose that the spot rates are as shown in the second column of Table 4.1. The rates are assumed to be continuously compounded. Thus the 10% per annum rate for one year means that in return for an investment of $100 today, the investor receives $100e^{0.1} = \$110.52$ in one year; the 10.5% per annum rate for two years means that in return for an investment of $100 today, the investor receives $100e^{0.105 \times 2} = \$123.37$ in two years; and so on.

The forward interest rate in Table 4.1 for year 2 is 11% per annum. This is the rate of interest that is implied by the spot rates for the period of time between the end of the first year and the end of the second year. It can be calculated from the one-year spot interest rate of 10% per annum and the two-year spot interest rate of 10.5% per annum. It is the rate of interest for year 2 that when combined with 10% per annum for year 1, gives 10.5% per annum overall for the two years. To show that the correct answer is 11% per annum, suppose that $100 is invested. A rate of 10% for the first year and 11% for the second year yields

$$100e^{0.1}e^{0.11} = \$123.37$$

at the end of the second year. A rate of 10.5% per annum for 2 years yields

$$100e^{0.105 \times 2}$$

which is also $123.37. This example illustrates the general result that when interest rates are continuously compounded and rates in successive time periods are combined, the overall equivalent rate is simply the arithmetic average of the rates (10.5% is the average of 10% and 11%). The result is only approximately true when the rates are not continuously compounded.

The forward rate for the third year is the rate of interest that is implied by a 10.5% per annum two-year spot rate and a 10.8% per annum three-year spot rate. It is 11.4% per annum. This is because an investment for two years at 10.5% per annum averaged with an investment for one year at 11.4% per annum gives an overall return for the three years of 10.8% per annum. The other forward rates can be calculated similarly and are shown in the third column of the table. In general, if r is the spot rate of interest applying for T years and r^* is the spot rate

of interest applying for T^* years where $T^* > T$, the forward interest rate for the period of time between T and T^*, $\hat{r}$, is given by

$$\hat{r} = \frac{r^*T^* - rT}{T^* - T} \tag{4.1}$$

To illustrate the use of this formula, consider the calculation of the year 4 forward rate from the data in Table 4.1: $T = 3$, $T^* = 4$, $r = 0.108$, and $r^* = 0.11$, and the formula gives $\hat{r} = 0.116$.

Zero-Coupon Yield Curve

The *zero-coupon yield curve* is a curve showing the relationship between spot rates (i.e., zero-coupon yields) and maturity. Figure 4.1 shows the zero-coupon yield curve for the data in Table 4.1. It is important to distinguish between the zero-coupon yield curve and a yield curve for coupon-bearing bonds. In a situation such as that shown in Figure 4.1, where the yield curve is upward sloping, the zero-coupon yield curve will always be above the yield curve for coupon-bearing bonds. This is because the yield on a coupon-bearing bond is affected by the fact that the investor gets some payments before the maturity of the bond and the required rates of return corresponding to these payment dates are lower than those corresponding to the final payment date.

Analysts sometimes also look at the curve relating forward rates to the maturity of the forward contract. The forward rates can be defined so that they correspond to three months or six months or any other convenient time period. Equation (4.1) can be rewritten

$$\hat{r} = r^* + (r^* - r)\frac{T}{T^* - T}$$

This shows that if the yield curve is upward sloping with $r^* > r$, then $\hat{r} > r^* > r$, so that forward rates are higher than zero-coupon yields. Taking limits as T^*

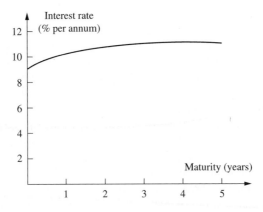

Figure 4.1   Zero-coupon yield curve for the data in Table 4.1.

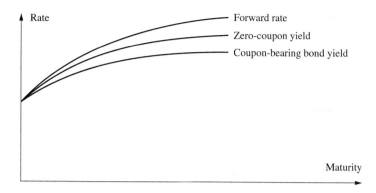

Figure 4.2   Situation when yield curve is upward sloping.

approaches T (so that r^* approaches r) we see that the forward rate for a very short period of time beginning at time T is

$$r + T\frac{\partial r}{\partial T}$$

This is known as the *instantaneous forward rate* for a maturity T.

   Figure 4.2 shows the zero-coupon yield curve, coupon-bearing-bond yield curve, and forward rate curve when the yield curve is upward sloping. For the reasons just given, the forward rate curve is above the zero-coupon yield curve, which is in turn above the coupon-bearing bond yield curve. Figure 4.3 shows the situation when the yield curve is downward sloping. Arguments similar to those for the upward-sloping yield curve show that in this situation the coupon-bearing bond yield curve is above the zero-coupon yield curve, which is in turn above the forward rate curve.

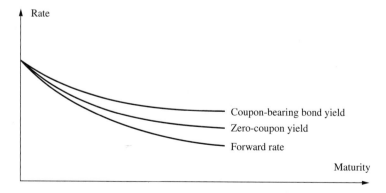

Figure 4.3   Situation when yield curve is downward sloping.

Determination of Zero-Coupon Yield Curve

In practice, spot rates (or zero-coupon yields) cannot always be observed directly. What can be observed are the prices of coupon-bearing bonds. An important issue therefore is how the zero-coupon yield curve can be extracted from the prices of coupon-bearing bonds.

One commonly used approach is known as the *bootstrap method.* To illustrate it, consider the data in Table 4.2 on the prices of six bonds. Since the first three bonds pay no coupons, the continuously compounded spot rates corresponding to the maturities of these bonds can easily be calculated. The first bond provides a return of 2.5 on an investment of 97.5 over three months. Using equation (3.3), the three-month rate with continuous compounding is

$$4 \ln \left(1 + \frac{2.5}{97.5}\right) = 0.1013$$

or 10.13% per annum. Similarly, the six-month rate is

$$2 \ln \left(1 + \frac{5.1}{94.9}\right) = 0.1047$$

or 10.47% per annum. The one-year rate is

$$\ln \left(1 + \frac{10}{90.0}\right) = 0.1054$$

or 10.54% per annum.

The fourth bond lasts 1.5 years. The payments are as follows:

6 months: $ 4
1 year: 4
1.5 years: 104

TABLE 4.2   Data for Bootstrap Method

Bond Principal (dollars)	Time to Maturity (years)	Annual Coupon[a] (dollars)	Bond Price (dollars)
100	0.25	0	97.5
100	0.50	0	94.9
100	1.00	0	90.0
100	1.50	8	96.0
100	2.00	12	101.6
100	2.75	10	99.8

[a]Half of the stated coupon is assumed to be paid every six months.

From our earlier calculations, we know that the discount rate for the payment at the end of six months is 10.47% and the discount rate for the payment at the end of one year is 10.54%. We also know that the bond's price, $96, must equal the present value of all the payments received by the bondholder. Suppose that the 1.5-year spot rate is denoted by R. It follows that

$$4e^{-0.1047 \times 0.5} + 4e^{-0.1054 \times 1.0} + 104e^{-R \times 1.5} = 96$$

This reduces to

$$e^{-1.5R} = 0.85196$$

or

$$R = -\frac{\ln(0.85196)}{1.5} = 0.1068$$

The 1.5-year spot rate is therefore 10.68%. This is the only spot rate that is consistent with the six-month and one-year spot rate and consistent with the data in Table 4.2.

The two-year spot rate can be calculated similarly from the six-month, one-year, and 1.5-year spot rates and the information on the fifth bond in Table 4.2. If R is the two-year spot rate,

$$6e^{-0.1047 \times 0.5} + 6e^{-0.1054 \times 1.0} + 6e^{-0.1068 \times 1.5} + 106e^{-R \times 2.0} = 101.6$$

This gives $R = 0.1081$, or 10.81%.

So far we have points on the zero-coupon curve corresponding to five different maturities. Points corresponding to other intermediate maturities are obtained by linear interpolation. The sixth bond provides cash flows as follows:

3 months:	$	5
9 months:		5
1.25 years:		5
1.75 years:		5
2.25 years:		5
2.75 years:		105

The discount rate corresponding to the first cash flow has already been determined as 10.13%. Using linear interpolation, the discount rates for the next three cash flows are 10.505, 10.61, and 10.745%. The present value of the first four cash flows is therefore

$$5e^{-0.1013 \times 0.25} + 5e^{-0.10505 \times 0.75} + 5e^{-0.1061 \times 1.25} + 5e^{-0.10745 \times 1.75} = 18.018$$

The present value of the last two cash flows is therefore

$$99.8 - 18.018 = 81.782$$

Suppose that the 2.75-year spot rate is R. Using linear interpolation, the 2.25-year spot rate is

$$0.1081 \times \frac{2}{3} + \frac{R}{3}$$

or $0.0721 + R/3$. An equation for R is, therefore,

$$5e^{-2.25\times(0.0721+R/3)} + 105e^{-2.75\times R} = 81.782$$

This can be solved by trial and error or by using a numerical procedure such as Newton–Raphson to give $R = 0.1087$.[1] The 2.75-year interest rate is 10.87%.

Figure 4.4 plots the zero-coupon yield curve that is constructed from the prices of the six bonds in Table 4.2. If other longer maturity bonds were available, a complete term structure could be obtained.

Variations on the methodology described here are sometimes used in practice. For example, one can interpolate between the yields on the 2.75-year bond and the 2.0-year bond in Table 4.2 to calculate the notional yield on a 2.5-year bond. The zero-coupon yield curve can then be constructed in the way that has been described using the notional 2.5-year bond instead of the 2.75-year bond.[2]

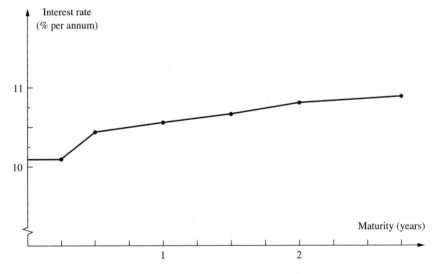

Figure 4.4   Zero-coupon yield curve for data in Table 4.2.

[1]The Newton–Raphson procedure is designed to solve an equation of the form $f(x) = 0$. It starts with a guess of the solution: $x = x_0$. It then produces successively better estimates of the solution: $x = x_1$, $x = x_2$, $x = x_3$, ... using the formula $x_{i+1} = x_i - f(x_i)/f'(x_i)$. Usually, x_2 is extremely close to the true solution.

[2]The coupon on the 2.5-year bond can be chosen by interpolating between the coupons on the 2.0- and 2.75-year coupon bond. Alternatively, it can be assumed equal to the bond's yield.

Day Count Conventions

In Section 3.1 we discussed the interpretation of the compounding frequency that is used when an interest rate is quoted. We now discuss the day count convention. This is a quite separate issue from compounding frequency. The day count defines the way in which interest accrues over time. Generally, we know the interest earned over some reference period (e.g., the time between coupon payments) and we are interested in calculating the interest earned over some other period.

The day count convention is usually expressed as X/Y. When we are calculating the interest earned between two dates, X defines the way in which the number of days between the two dates is calculated and Y defines the way in which the total number of days in the reference period is measured. The interest earned between the two dates is

$$\frac{\text{number of days between dates}}{\text{number of days in reference period}} \times \text{interest earned in reference period}$$

Three day count conventions that are commonly used in practice are:

1. Actual/actual (in period)
2. 30/360
3. Actual/360

In the United States actual/actual (in period) is used for Treasury bonds; 30/360 is used for corporate and municipal bonds; and actual/360 is used for Treasury bills and other money market instruments.

The use of actual/actual (in period) for Treasury bonds indicates that accrued interest is based on the ratio of the actual days elapsed to the actual number of days in the period between coupon payments. Suppose that the bond principal is $100, coupon payment dates are March 1 and September 1, the coupon rate is 8%, and we wish to calculate the interest earned between March 1 and July 3. The reference period is from March 1 to September 1. There are 184 (actual) days in this period and interest of $4 is earned during the period. There are 124 (actual) days between March 1 and July 3. The interest earned between March 1 and July 3 is therefore

$$\frac{124}{184} \times 4 = \$2.6957$$

The use of 30/360 for corporate and municipal bonds indicates that we assume 30 days per month and 360 days per year when carrying out calculations. Using 30/360, the total number of days between March 1 and September 1 is 180. The total number of days between March 1 and July 3 is $4 \times 30 + 2 = 122$. In

a corporate bond with the same terms as the Treasury bond just considered, the interest earned between March 1 and July 3 would therefore be

$$\frac{122}{180} \times 4 = \$2.7111$$

The use of actual/360 for a money market instrument indicates that the reference period is 360 days. The interest earned during part of a year is calculated by dividing the actual number of elapsed days by 360 and multiplying by the rate. The interest earned in 90 days is therefore exactly one-fourth of the quoted rate. Note that the interest earned in a whole year of 365 days is 365/360 times the quoted rate.

Theories of the Term Structure

A number of different theories of the term structure have been proposed. The simplest is the *expectations theory*. This conjectures that long-term interest rates should reflect expected future short-term interest rates. More precisely, it argues that a forward interest rate corresponding to a certain period is equal to the expected future spot interest rate for that period. Another theory is known as the *market segmentation theory*. This conjectures that there need be no relationship between short-, medium-, and long-term interest rates. Under the theory, different institutions invest in bonds of different maturity and do not switch maturities. The short-term interest rate is determined by supply and demand in the short-term bond market, the medium-term interest rate is determined by supply and demand in the medium-term bond market, and so on.

The theory that is in some ways most appealing is known as *liquidity preference theory*. This argues that forward rates should always be higher than expected future spot interest rates. The basic assumption underlying the theory is that investors prefer to preserve their liquidity and invest funds for short periods of time. Borrowers, on the other hand, usually prefer to borrow at fixed rates for long periods of time. If the interest rates offered by banks and other financial intermediaries were such that the forward rate equaled the expected future spot rate, long-term interest rates would equal the average of expected future short-term interest rates. In the absence of any incentive to do otherwise, investors would tend to deposit their funds for short time periods and borrowers would tend to choose to borrow for long time periods. Financial intermediaries would then find themselves financing substantial amounts of long-term fixed-rate loans with short-term deposits. This would involve excessive interest rate risk. In practice, to match depositors with borrowers and avoid interest rate risk, financial intermediaries raise long-term interest rates relative to expected future short-term interest rates. This reduces the demand for long-term fixed-rate borrowing and encourages investors to deposit their funds for long terms.

Liquidity preference theory leads to a situation in which long rates are greater than the average of expected future short rates. It is also consistent with

the empirical result that yield curves tend to be upward sloping more often than they are downward sloping.

4.2 FORWARD RATE AGREEMENTS

A *forward rate agreement* (FRA) is a forward contract where the parties agree that a certain interest rate will apply to a certain principal during a specified future period of time. An FRA is generally settled in cash at the beginning of the specified period of time. In this section we explain how forward rate agreements can be valued in terms of forward rates.

Consider a forward rate agreement where it is agreed at time zero that an interest rate of R_K will be earned for the period of time between T and T^* on a principal of 100. Suppose further that r is the spot interest rate for maturity T and r^* is the spot interest rate for maturity T^*. The forward rate agreement is an agreement to the following cash flows:

Time T : -100
Time T^*: $+100e^{R_K(T^*-T)}$

The value of the agreement at time zero, $V(0)$, can be found by taking the present value of these cash flows:

$$V(0) = 100e^{R_K(T^*-T)}e^{-r^*T^*} - 100e^{-rT} \tag{4.2}$$

The variable, $V(0)$, is zero when

$$R_K(T^* - T) - r^*T^* = -rT$$

or

$$R_K = \frac{r^*T^* - rT}{T^* - T}$$

Comparing this with equation (4.1), we see that the value of a forward rate agreement is zero when the agreed rate, R_K, equals the forward interest rate, $\hat{r}$. The agreed rate in an FRA should therefore always equal the forward rate at the time the contract is initiated.

If R is the interest rate at time T for the period between T and T^*, the cash settlement received at time T can be calculated from the cash flows given above as

$$-100 + 100e^{R_K(T^*-T)}e^{-R(T^*-T)} \tag{4.3}$$

Consider now the value of the FRA at time t ($0 \le t \le T$). Define r, r^*, and $\hat{r}$ as spot and forward rates with the same maturities as before but observed at time t rather than time zero. Similar to equation (4.2), the value of the FRA at time t is

$$V(t) = 100e^{R_K(T^*-T)}e^{-r^*(T^*-t)} - 100e^{-r(T-t)}$$

From equation (4.1), $\hat{r}(T^* - T) + r(T - t) = r^*(T^* - t)$, so this can be written

$$V(t) = [-100 + 100e^{R_K(T^*-T)}e^{-\hat{r}(T^*-T)}]e^{-r(T-t)}$$

This is the present value of the expression in equation (4.3) when $R = \hat{r}$.

This shows that we can always value FRAs by calculating the present value of cash flows on the assumption that the current forward rates are realized. This will prove to be a useful result in the valuation of swaps in Chapter 5.

4.3 TREASURY BOND AND TREASURY NOTE FUTURES

Table 4.3 shows interest rate futures quotes as they appeared in the *Wall Street Journal* on May 12, 1995. The most popular long-term interest rate futures con-

TABLE 4.3   Interest Rate Futures Quotes from the *Wall Street Journal,* May 12, 1995

INTEREST RATE

TREASURY BONDS (CBT)-$100,000; pts. 32nds of 100%

	Open	High	Low	Settle	Change	Lifetime High	Low	Open Interest
June	109-12	109-31	108-24	109-10	− 21	113-15	94-27	387,665
Sept	108-30	109-17	108-10	108-28	− 21	112-15	94-10	32,343
Dec	108-16	109-01	107-29	108-14	− 11	111-23	93-27	4,541
Mr96	108-08	108-17	107-17	108-00	− 11	110-14	93-13	851
June	....	....	....	107-16	....	107-18	93-06	57

Est vol 600,000; vol Wed 639,722; op int 425,523, +8,324.

TREASURY BONDS (MCE)-$50,000; pts. 32nds of 100%

	Open	High	Low	Settle	Change	Lifetime High	Low	Open Interest
June	109-16	110-00	108-24	109-14	+ 7	110-29	95-20	15,496
Sept	109-01	109-11	108-11	109-00	+ 7	110-14	98-19	554

Est vol 7,500; vol Wed 9,799; open int 16,124, −1,774.

TREASURY NOTES (CBT)-$100,000; pts. 32nds of 100%

	Open	High	Low	Settle	Change	Lifetime High	Low	Open Interest
June	108-03	108-12	107-15	107-29	− 7	109-09	97-27	253,213
Sept	107-16	107-27	107-01	107-13	− 7	108-25	97-11	30,087
Dec	106-31	107-04	106-22	106-30	− 6	108-06	96-30	1,141
Mr96	....	....	....	106-15	− 6	107-12	98-20	148

Est vol 125,000; vol Wed 151,331; open int 284,591, −6,293.

5 YR TREAS NOTES (CBT)-$100,000; pts. 32nds of 100%

	Open	High	Low	Settle	Change	Lifetime High	Low	Open Interest
June	106-02	106-08	105-18	05-275	− 7.0	106-28	99-06	197,014
Sept	105-27	05-295	105-10	05-185	− 7.5	06-185	99-07	20,694

Est vol 75,700; vol Wed 79,504; open int 217,709, +1,783.

2 YR TREAS NOTES (CBT)-$200,000; pts. 32nds of 100%

	Open	High	Low	Settle	Change	Lifetime High	Low	Open Interest
June	03-055	03-065	02-285	03-005	− 4	103-16	99-24	27,414
Sept	102-28	102-28	02-255	02-275	− 4	03-075	101-20	154

Est vol 4,200; vol Wed 3,485; open int 27,568, −613.

30-DAY FEDERAL FUNDS (CBT)-$5 million; pts. of 100%

	Open	High	Low	Settle	Change	Lifetime High	Low	Open Interest
May	93.99	93.99	93.98	93.99	....	94.00	92.60	3,890
June	94.00	94.00	93.99	94.00	....	94.03	92.82	3,811
July	94.05	94.05	94.01	94.02	− .03	94.10	92.65	2,167
Aug	94.05	94.05	94.02	94.04	− .03	94.14	93.10	846
Sept	94.09	94.09	94.03	94.06	− .04	94.18	93.40	1,050
Oct	94.06	94.07	94.05	94.07	− .05	94.21	93.75	186

Est vol 2,000; vol Wed 3,052; open int 12,045, +910.

TREASURY BILLS (CME) - $1 mil.; pts. of 100%

	Open	High	Low	Settle	Chg	Discount Settle	Chg	Open Interest
June	94.38	94.39	94.32	94.34	− .05	5.66	+ .05	11,538
Sept	94.44	94.45	94.33	94.37	− .07	5.63	+ .07	11,569
Dec	94.29	94.33	94.26	94.34	− .06	5.66	+ .06	11,513
Mr96	....	....	....	94.33	− .12	5.67	+ .12	239

Est vol 3,291; vol Wed 6,454; open int 34,859, −493.

LIBOR-1 MO. (CME) - $3,000,000; points of 100%

	Open	High	Low	Settle	Chg	Yield Settle	Chg	Open Interest
May	93.94	93.94	93.92	93.93	− .01	6.07	+ .01	19,979
June	93.95	93.97	93.93	93.95	− .01	6.05	+ .01	12,938
July	94.01	94.01	93.94	93.96	− .05	6.06	+ .05	4,490
Aug	94.00	94.00	93.94	93.94	− .06	6.06	+ .06	2,515
Sept	94.07	94.07	93.98	94.01	− .09	5.99	+ .09	364
Oct	94.10	94.10	94.00	94.02	-- .10	5.98	+ .10	426
Nov	94.00	94.00	94.00	93.99	− .10	6.01	+ .10	275
Dec	93.97	93.98	93.82	93.89	− .08	6.11	+ .08	336

Est vol 7,694; vol Wed 7,531; open int 41,352, +517.

MUNI BOND INDEX (CBT)-$1,000; times Bond Buyer MBI

	Open	High	Low	Settle	Chg	High	Low	Open Interest
June	92-10	92-27	91-30	92-14	+ 7	93-05	83-25	19,935
Sept	113-00	113-17	112-28	113-11	+ 13	113-22	108-29	144

Est vol 7,500; vol Wed 9,510; open int 20,080, +550.
The index: Close 92-30; Yield 6.19.

EURODOLLAR (CME) - $1 million; pts of 100%

	Open	High	Low	Settle	Chg	Yield Settle	Chg	Open Interest
June	93.94	93.94	93.88	93.90	− .04	6.10	+ .04	421,604
Sept	94.04	94.06	93.91	93.96	− .09	6.04	+ .09	367,596
Dec	93.96	94.00	93.79	93.89	− .08	6.11	+ .08	312,919
Mr96	93.95	94.02	93.81	93.90	− .08	6.10	+ .08	262,262
June	93.86	93.89	93.68	93.76	− .09	6.32	+ .09	187,946
Sept	93.77	93.77	93.55	93.65	− .09	6.35	+ .09	163,410
Dec	93.59	93.60	93.36	93.47	− .10	6.53	+ .10	128,944
Mr97	93.55	93.55	93.33	93.43	− .10	6.57	+ .10	99,564
June	93.50	93.50	93.28	93.37	− .09	6.63	+ .09	88,041
Sept	93.43	93.43	93.26	93.32	− .08	6.68	+ .08	70,281
Dec	93.33	93.34	93.18	93.24	− .07	6.76	+ .07	60,990
Mr98	93.30	93.31	93.18	93.23	− .05	6.77	+ .05	57,289
June	93.23	93.24	93.14	93.17	− .04	6.83	+ .04	53,448
Sept	93.17	93.19	93.09	93.13	− .02	6.87	+ .02	42,103
Dec	93.08	93.10	93.01	93.05	− .01	6.95	+ .01	35,220
Mr99	93.07	93.08	93.00	93.04	− .01	6.96	+ .01	29,660
June	93.00	93.02	92.93	92.98	....	7.02	....	23,301
Sept	92.94	92.96	92.87	92.92	....	7.08	....	15,421
Dec	92.85	92.87	92.78	92.83	....	7.17	....	12,559
Mr00	92.85	92.87	92.78	92.83	....	7.17	....	10,254
June	92.75	92.77	92.73	92.76	+ .01	7.24	− .01	7,355
Sept	92.69	92.71	92.67	92.70	+ .01	7.30	− .01	7,855
Dec	92.58	92.62	92.58	92.61	+ .01	7.39	− .01	7,018
Mr01	92.57	92.61	92.57	92.60	+ .01	7.40	− .01	5,746
June	92.51	92.54	92.49	92.52	+ .01	7.48	− .01	6,497
Sept	92.41	92.46	92.41	92.44	+ .01	7.56	− .01	8,154

tracts is the Treasury bond futures contract traded on the Chicago Board of Trade. In this contract, any government bond with more than 15 years to maturity on the first day of the delivery month and not callable within 15 years from that day can be delivered. As will be explained later, the exchange has developed a procedure for adjusting the price received by the party with the short position according to the particular bond delivered.

The Treasury note and five-year Treasury note futures contract are also actively traded. In the Treasury note futures contract, any government bond (or note) with a maturity between $6\frac{1}{2}$ and 10 years can be delivered. As in the case of the Treasury bond futures contract, there is a way of adjusting the price received by the party with the short position according to the particular note delivered. In the five-year Treasury note futures contract, any of the four most recently auctioned Treasury notes can be delivered.

The rest of our discussion in this section focuses on Treasury bond futures. However, many of the points made are applicable to the other contracts on bonds.

TABLE 4.3   Interest Rate Futures Quotes from the *Wall Street Journal,* May 12, 1995 (*Continued*)

```
Dec    92.34 92.36 92.32 92.35 + .01  7.65 -  .01   7,772
Mr02   92.31 92.35 92.31 92.34 + .01  7.66 -  .01   4,497
June   92.24 92.31 92.24 92.27 + .01  7.73 -  .01   3,524
Sept   92.17 92.24 92.17 92.20 + .01  7.80 -  .01   2,628
Dec    92.08 92.13 92.08 92.11 + .01  7.89 -  .01   1,924
Mr03   92.08 92.13 92.08 92.11 + .01  7.89 -  .01   2,043
June   92.04 92.11 92.04 92.01 + .01  7.99 -  .01   5,057
Sept   92.00 92.04 91.99 92.00 + .01  8.00 -  .01   3,175
Dec    91.91 91.94 91.90 91.91 + .01  8.09 -  .01   3,841
Mr04   91.90 91.93 91.89 91.90 + .01  8.10 -  .01   4,052
June   91.85 91.88 91.82 91.84 + .01  8.16 -  .01   3,287
Sept   ....  ....  ....  91.78 + .01  8.22 -  .01   3,358
Dec    ....  ....  ....  91.68 + .01  8.32 -  .01   2,475
Mr05   91.67 91.73 91.67 91.69 + .01  8.31 -  .01   2,845
   Est vol 966,942; vol Wed 859,945; open int 2,535,955, -6,318.
STERLING (LIFFE) - £500,000; pts of 100%
                                      Lifetime       Open
     Open  High  Low  Settle Change High  Low  Interest
June  93.03 93.08 92.88 92.91 - .17 94.92 91.42  79,070
Sept  92.62 92.67 92.44 92.47 - .19 94.72 91.01  84,088
Dec   92.31 92.36 92.13 92.17 - .17 94.53 90.71  63,050
Mr96  92.10 92.14 91.92 91.98 - .15 94.35 90.50  38,879
June  91.91 91.96 91.75 91.82 - .13 94.14 90.38  38,228
Sept  91.72 91.79 91.60 91.66 - .12 92.55 90.30  26,712
Dec   91.56 91.65 91.49 91.52 - .13 92.25 90.20  23,557
Mr97  91.49 91.55 91.39 91.43 - .12 92.05 90.05  19,218
June  91.42 91.44 91.33 91.37 - .13 91.50 89.92  13,866
Sept  91.41 91.41 91.30 91.34 - .12 91.45 90.10  10,061
Dec   91.40 91.40 91.34 91.34 - .13 91.41 90.58   6,535
Mr98  91.36 91.36 91.35 91.34 - .13 91.45 90.89   2,213
   Est vol 130,447; vol Wed 110,287; open int 405,477, -3,826.
LONG GILT (LIFFE) - £50,000; 32nds of 100%
June  105-21 106-03 104-29 105-04 - 0-25 106-12 100-01 99,263
Sept  105-05 105-12 104-24 104-24 - 0-25 105-30 101-11  1,468
   Est vol 103,805; vol Wed 107,697; open int 100,731, +11,178.
EUROMARK (LIFFE) - DM 1,000,000; pts of 100%
June  95.46 95.48 95.38 95.40 - .08 95.91 93.15125,760
Sept  95.37 95.42 95.25 35.25 - .17 95.87 93.35136,245
Dec   95.27 95.29 95.03 95.06 - .25 95.77 93.04129,026
Mr96  95.13 95.15 94.88 94.90 - .27 95.86 92.84 82,809
June  94.88 94.89 94.66 94.66 - .25 95.50 92.63 50,285
Sept  94.52 94.54 94.40 94.35 - .22 94.62 92.42 45,590
Dec   94.18 94.20 94.06 94.02 - .20 94.26 92.26 39,055
Mr97  93.87 93.90 93.78 93.74 - .17 93.99 92.20 26,094
June  93.62 93.64 93.54 93.50 - .16 93.70 92.06 18,322
Sept  93.43 93.47 93.37 93.31 - .16 93.51 91.94 12,007
Dec   93.30 93.30 93.25 93.16 - .16 93.35 92.00  8,055

Mr98  93.18 93.20 93.15 93.09 - .13 93.24 92.59  2,104
   Est vol 198,694; vol Wed 204,783; open int 675,352, +1,787.
EUROSWISS (LIFFE) - SFr 1,000,000; pts of 100%
June  96.61 96.64 96.47 96.48 - .17 96.72 94.42 25,108
Sept  96.56 96.56 96.41 96.40 - .19 96.66 94.38 10,319
Dec   96.40 96.41 96.26 96.26 - .18 96.47 94.70  6,554
Mr96  96.21 96.22 96.07 96.07 - .18 96.33 95.32  1,982
   Est vol 17,227; vol Wed 6,336; open int 43,963, +152.
3-MONTH EURO LIRA (LIFFE) - Itl 1,000,000; pts of 100%
June  89.95 90.08 89.81 89.95 - -.07 92.37 87.25 37,259
Sept  89.83 89.87 89.66 89.76 - .07 92.18 87.75 28,653
Dec   89.70 89.80 89.67 89.64 - .10 90.22 87.59 13,699
Mr96  89.59 89.67 89.55 89.56 - .07 89.67 87.90  7,389
June  89.52 89.52 89.46 89.46 - .07 89.60 87.97  4,011
Sept  89.50 89.50 89.47 89.44 - .05 89.50 87.84  2,080
   Est vol 13,707; vol Wed 24,263; open int 93,091, +6,160.
GERMAN GOVT. BOND (LIFFE)
250,000 marks; pts of 100%
June  93.96 94.27 93.75 93.79 - .41 94.48 87.60 191,262
Sept  93.43 93.66 93.21 93.22 - .41 93.87 89.35  8,556
   Est vol 173,552; vol Wed 181,370; open int 199,818, +6,046.
ITALIAN GOVT. BOND (LIFFE)
ITL 200,000,000; pts of 100%
June  100.62 101.55 100.40 100.67 - .43 101.70 91.44 44,874
Sept  100.95 100.25 100.05 100.04 - .53 101.10 91.12  2,389
   Est vol 55,544; vol Wed 70,993; open int 47,263, +676.
CANADIAN BANKERS ACCEPTANCE (ME) - C$1,000,000
June  92.88 92.89 92.80 92.84 - .03 95.33 90.47 26,701
Sept  93.19 na    na    na    -  na  95.11 90.42  na
Dec   93.16 93.16 93.04 93.06 - .13 94.79 90.15 13,660
Mr96  93.14 93.14 93.03 93.03 - .17 93.28 89.95 14,529
June  93.05 93.05 92.80 92.98 - .17 93.25 89.92  9,258
Sept  93.00 93.00 92.92 92.93 - .16 93.21 90.17  5,732
Dec   92.96 92.96 92.90 92.88 - .18 93.15 90.20  1,640
Mr97  92.93 92.93 92.80 92.80 - .18 92.92 92.08   281
   Est vol 9,699; vol Wed 8,532; open int 95,655, +2,223.
10 YR. CANADIAN GOVT. BONDS (ME) - C$100,000
June  106.29 106.30 105.65 105.92 - .45 107.52 99.70 22,449
Sept  ....   ....   ....   105.52 - .45 103.40 102.46   628
   Est vol na; vol Wed 4,135; open int 23,077, +1,574.
10 YR. FRENCH GOVT. BONDS (MATIF)
FFr 500,000; 100ths of 100%
June  115.32 115.78 115.18 115.44 - .04 115.92 107.66136,255
Sept  114.74 115.16 114.64 114.88 - .02 115.00 107.70 12,251
Dec   114.46 114.84 114.42 114.60 - .02 114.84 108.47  1,694
   Est vol 184,903; vol Wed 212,521; open int 150,200, +11,343.
```

Quotes for Treasury Bonds

Treasury bond prices are quoted in dollars and 32nds of a dollar. The quoted price is for a bond with a face value of $100. Thus a quote of 90-05 means that the indicated price for a bond with a face value of $100,000 is $90,156.25.

The quoted price is not the same as the cash price that is paid by the purchaser. The quoted price is sometimes referred to as the *clean price* and the cash price as the *dirty price*. The relationship between the cash price and the quoted price is

cash price $=$ quoted price $+$ accrued interest since last coupon date

To illustrate this formula, suppose that it is March 5, 1997 and the bond under consideration is an 11% coupon bond maturing on July 10, 2010 with a quoted price of 95-16 (or $95.50). As mentioned in Section 4.1, government bonds accrue interest on an actual/actual (in period) basis and interest is paid semiannually. The most recent coupon date in this case is January 10, 1997 and the next coupon date is July 10, 1997. The number of days between January 10, 1997 and March 5, 1997 is 54, while the number of days between January 10, 1997 and July 10, 1997 is 181. On $100 face value of bonds, the coupon payment is $5.50 on January 10 and July 10. The accrued interest on March 5, 1997 is the share of the July 10 coupon accruing to the bondholder and is calculated as

$$\frac{54}{181} \times \$5.5 = \$1.64$$

The cash price per $100 face value for the July 10, 2010 bond is therefore

$$\$95.50 + \$1.64 = \$97.14$$

The cash price of a $100,000 bond is $97,140.

Treasury bond futures prices are quoted in the same way as the Treasury bond prices themselves. Table 4.3 shows that the settlement price for the September contract on May 11, 1995 was 108-28 or $108\frac{28}{32}$. One contract involves the delivery of $100,000 of face value of bond. Thus a $1 change in the quoted futures price would lead to a $1,000 change in the value of the futures contract. Delivery can take place at any time during the delivery month.

Conversion Factors

As mentioned, there is a provision in the Treasury bond futures contract for the party with the short position to choose to deliver any bond with a maturity over 15 years and not callable within 15 years. When a particular bond is delivered, a parameter known as its *conversion factor* defines the price received by the party with the short position. The quoted price applicable to the delivery is the product of the conversion factor and the quoted futures price. Taking accrued interest into

account, we have the following relationship for each $100 face value of the bond delivered:

$$\begin{array}{c} \text{cash received by party} \\ \text{with short position} \end{array} = \begin{array}{c} \text{quoted futures} \\ \text{price} \end{array} \times \begin{array}{c} \text{conversion factor} \\ \text{for bond delivered} \end{array}$$

$$+ \begin{array}{c} \text{accrued interest since last} \\ \text{coupon date on bond delivered} \end{array}$$

Each contract is for the delivery of $100,000 face value of bonds. Suppose that the quoted futures price is 90-00, the conversion factor for the bond delivered is 1.3800, and the accrued interest on this bond at the time of delivery is $3.00 per $100 face value. The cash received by the party with the short position when it delivers the bond (and the cash paid by the party with the long position when it takes delivery) is

$$(1.3800 \times 90.00) + 3.00 = \$127.20$$

per $100 face value. A party with the short position in one contract would therefore deliver bonds with face value of $100,000 and receive $127,200.

The conversion factor for a bond is equal to the value of the bond on the first day of the delivery month on the assumption that the interest rate for all maturities equals 8% per annum (with semiannual compounding). The bond maturity and the times to the coupon payment dates are rounded down to the nearest three months for the purposes of the calculation. This enables the CBOT to produce comprehensive tables. If, after the rounding, the bond lasts for an exact number of half years, the first coupon is assumed to be paid in six months. If after rounding the bond does not last for an exact number of six months (i.e., there is an extra three months), the first coupon is assumed to be paid after three months and accrued interest is subtracted.

Example 4.1

Consider a 14% coupon bond with 20 years and two months to maturity. For the purposes of calculating the conversion factor, the bond is assumed to have exactly 20 years to maturity. The first coupon payment is assumed to be made after six months. Coupon payments are then assumed to be made at six-month intervals until the end of the 20 years when the principal payment is made. We will work in terms of a $100 face value bond. On the assumption that the discount rate is 8% per annum with semiannual compounding (or 4% per six months), the value of the bond is

$$\sum_{i=1}^{40} \frac{7}{1.04^i} + \frac{100}{1.04^{40}} = 159.38$$

Dividing by the face value, the credit conversion factor is 1.5938.

Example 4.2

Consider a 14% coupon bond with 18 years and four months to maturity. For the purposes of calculating the conversion factor, the bond is assumed to have exactly 18 years and three

months to maturity. Discounting all the payments back to a point in time three months from today gives a value of

$$7 + \sum_{i=1}^{36} \frac{7}{1.04^i} + \frac{100}{1.04^{36}} = 163.72$$

The interest rate for a three-month period is $\sqrt{1.04} - 1$ or 1.9804%. Hence discounting back to the present gives the bond's value as $163.72/1.019804 = 160.55$. Subtracting the accrued interest of 3.5, this becomes 157.05. The conversion factor is therefore 1.5705.

Cheapest-to-Deliver Bond

At any given time, there are many bonds that can be delivered in the CBOT Treasury bond futures contract. These vary widely as far as coupon and maturity is concerned. The party with the short position can choose which of the available bonds is "cheapest" to deliver. Since the party with the short position receives

(quoted futures price × conversion factor) + accrued interest

and the cost of purchasing a bond is

quoted price + accrued interest

the cheapest-to-deliver bond is the one for which

quoted price − (quoted futures price × conversion factor)

is least. This can be found by examining each of the bonds in turn.

Example 4.3

The party with the short position has decided to deliver and is trying to choose between the three bonds in Table 4.4. Assume that the current quoted futures price is 93-08 or 93.25. The cost of delivering each of the bonds is as follows:

Bond 1: $99.50 − (93.25 × 1.0382) = 2.69$
Bond 2: $143.50 − (93.25 × 1.5188) = 1.87$
Bond 3: $119.75 − (93.25 × 1.2615) = 2.12$

The cheapest-to-deliver bond is bond 2.

TABLE 4.4 Deliverable Bonds in Example 4.3

Bond	Quoted Price	Conversion Factor
1	99.50	1.0382
2	143.50	1.5188
3	119.75	1.2615

A number of factors determine the cheapest-to-deliver bond. When yields are in excess of 8%, there is a tendency for the conversion factor system to favor the delivery of low-coupon long-maturity bonds. When yields are less than 8%, there is a tendency for it to favor the delivery of high-coupon, short-maturity bonds. Also, when the yield curve is upward sloping, there is a tendency for bonds with a long time to maturity to be favored; whereas when it is downward sloping, there is a tendency for bonds with a short time to maturity to be delivered. Finally, some bonds tend to sell for more than their theoretical value. Examples are low-coupon bonds and bonds where the coupons can be stripped from the bond. These bonds are unlikely to prove to be cheapest to deliver in any circumstances.

The Wild Card Play

Trading in the CBOT Treasury bond futures contracts ceases at 2 p.m. (Chicago time). However, Treasury bonds themselves continue trading until 4 p.m. Furthermore, the party with the short position has until 8 p.m. to issue to the clearinghouse a notice of intention to deliver. If the notice is issued, the invoice price is calculated on the basis of the settlement price that day. This is the price at which trading was being done just before the bell at 2 p.m.

This gives the party with the short position an option known as the *wild card play*. If bond prices decline after 2 p.m., he or she can issue a notice of intention to deliver and proceed to buy cheapest-to-deliver bonds in preparation for delivery. If the bond price does not decline, the party with the short position keeps the position open and waits until the next day when the same strategy can be used.

Like the other options open to the party with the short position, the wild card option is not free. Its value is reflected in the futures price, which is lower than it would be without the option.

Determining the Quoted Futures Price

An exact theoretical futures price for the Treasury bond contract is difficult to determine because the short party's options concerned with the timing of delivery and choice of the bond that is delivered cannot easily be valued. However, if we assume that both the cheapest-to-deliver bond and the delivery date are known, the Treasury bond futures contract is a futures contract on a security providing the holder with known income. Equation (3.7) then shows that futures price, F, is related to the spot price, S, by

$$F = (S - I)e^{r(T-t)} \qquad (4.4)$$

where I is the present value of the coupons during the life of the futures contract, T is the time when the futures contract matures, t is the current time, and r is the risk-free interest rate applicable to the period between times t and T.

In equation (4.4), F is the cash futures price and S is the cash bond price. The correct procedure to determine the quoted futures price is therefore as follows:

1. Calculate the cash price of the cheapest-to-deliver bond from the quoted price.
2. Calculate the cash futures price from the cash bond price using equation (4.4).
3. Calculate the quoted futures price from the cash futures price.
4. Divide the quoted futures price by the conversion factor to allow for the difference between the cheapest-to-deliver bond and the standard 15-year 8% bond.

The procedure is best illustrated with an example.

Example 4.4

Suppose that in a T-bond futures contract, it is known that the cheapest-to-deliver bond will be a 12% coupon bond with a conversion factor of 1.4000. Suppose also that it is known that delivery will take place in 270 days' time. Coupons are payable semiannually on the bond. As illustrated in Figure 4.5, the last coupon date was 60 days ago, the next coupon date is in 122 days' time, and the next-but-one coupon date is in 305 days' time. The term structure is flat and the rate of interest (with continuous compounding) is 10% per annum. We assume that the current quoted bond price is $120. The cash price of the bond is obtained by adding to this quoted price the proportion of the next coupon payment that accrues to the holder. The cash price is therefore

$$120 + \frac{60}{60 + 122} \times 6 = 121.978$$

A coupon payment of $6 will be received after 122 days ($= 0.3342$ year). The present value of this is

$$6e^{-0.3342 \times 0.1} = 5.803$$

The futures contract lasts for 270 days ($= 0.7397$ year). The cash futures price if the contract were written on the 12% bond would therefore be

$$(121.978 - 5.803)e^{0.7397 \times 0.1} = 125.094$$

Figure 4.5   Time chart for Example 4.4.

At delivery, there are 148 days of accrued interest. The quoted futures price if the contract were written on the 12% bond would therefore be

$$125.094 - 6 \times \frac{148}{148 + 35} = 120.242$$

The contract is in fact written on a standard 8% bond, and 1.4000 standard bonds are considered equivalent to each 12% bond. The quoted futures price should therefore be

$$\frac{120.242}{1.4000} = 85.887$$

4.4 TREASURY BILL FUTURES

We now move on to consider futures contracts dependent on the short rate. In the Treasury bill futures contract, the underlying asset is a 90-day Treasury bill. Under the terms of the contract, the party with the short position must deliver $1 million of Treasury bills on one of three successive business days. The first delivery day is the first day of the delivery month on which a 13-week Treasury bill is issued and a one-year Treasury bill has 13 weeks remaining to maturity. In practice, this means that the Treasury bill may have 89 or 90 or 91 days to expiration when it is delivered.

A Treasury bill is what is known as a *discount instrument*. It pays no coupons, and the investor receives the face value at maturity. Prior to maturity of the futures contract, the underlying asset can be viewed as a Treasury bill with a maturity longer than 90 days. For example, if the futures contract matures in 160 days, the underlying asset is a 250-day Treasury bill.

Suppose that we are at time 0, the futures contract matures in T years, and the Treasury bill underlying the futures contract matures in T^* years. (The difference between T^* and T is 90 days.) We suppose further that r and r^* are the continuously compounded interest rates for risk-free investments maturing at times T and T^*, respectively. Assuming that the Treasury bill underlying the futures contract has a face value of $100, its current value, V^*, is given by

$$V^* = 100e^{-r^*T^*}$$

Since no income is paid on the instrument, we know from equation (3.5) that the futures price, F, is e^{rT} times this; that is,

$$F = 100e^{-r^*T^*} e^{rT} = 100e^{rT - r^*T^*}$$

From equation (4.1) this reduces to

$$F = 100e^{-\hat{r}(T^* - T)}$$

where $\hat{r}$ is the forward rate for the time period between T and T^*. This expression shows that the futures price of a Treasury bill is the price it will have if the 90-day

interest rate on the delivery date proves to be equal to the current forward rate. This is analogous to the result in Section 4.2 for FRAs.

Arbitrage Opportunities

If the forward interest rate implied by the Treasury bill futures price is different from that implied by the rates on Treasury bills themselves, there is a potential arbitrage opportunity. Suppose that the 45-day Treasury bill rate is 10%, the 135-day Treasury bill rate is 10.5%, and the rate corresponding to the Treasury bill futures prices for a contract maturing in 45 days is 10.6% (with all rates being continuously compounded on an actual/actual basis). The forward rate for the period between 45 and 135 days implied by the Treasury bill rates is, from equation (4.1),

$$\frac{135 \times 10.5 - 45 \times 10}{90} = 10.75\%$$

This is greater than the 10.6% forward rate implied by the futures price. An arbitrageur should attempt to borrow for the period of time between 45 and 135 days at 10.6% and invest at 10.75%. This is achieved by the following strategy:

1. Short the futures contract.
2. Borrow 45-day money at 10% per annum.
3. Invest the borrowed money for 135 days at 10.5% per annum.

We will refer to this as a *Type 1 arbitrage*. The first trade ensures that a Treasury bill yielding 10.6% can be sold after 45 days have elapsed. It in effect locks in a rate of interest of 10.6% on borrowed funds for this time period. The second and third trades ensure that a rate of interest of 10.75% is earned during the time period.

If, instead, the rate of interest corresponding to the Treasury bill futures were greater than 10.75%, the opposite strategy would be appropriate:

1. Take a long position in the futures contract.
2. Borrow 135-day money at 10.5% per annum.
3. Invest the borrowed money for 45 days at 10.0% per annum.

We will refer to this as a *Type 2 arbitrage*.

Both of these arbitrage possibilities involve borrowing at, or close to, the Treasury bill rate. As discussed in Chapter 3, repos provide a way in which companies that own portfolios of marketable securities can do this for short periods of time. In testing for arbitrage opportunities in the Treasury bill market, traders frequently calculate what is known as the *implied repo rate*. This is the rate of interest on a short-term Treasury bill implied by the futures price for a contract maturing at the same time as the short-term Treasury bill and the price of a Treasury

bill maturing 90 days later than the short-term Treasury bill. If the implied repo rate is greater than the actual short-term Treasury bill rate, a Type 1 arbitrage is in principle possible. If the implied repo rate is less than the short-term Treasury bill rate, a Type 2 arbitrage is in principle possible.

Example 4.5

The cash price (per $100 face value) of a Treasury bill maturing in 146 days is $95.21 and the cash futures price for a 90-day Treasury bill futures contract maturing in 56 days is $96.95. Since 90 days is 0.2466 year and 146 days is 0.4000 year, the continuously compounded 146-day rate, r^*, is

$$-\frac{1}{0.4000} \ln 0.9521 = 0.1227$$

or 12.27%, and the continuously compounded forward rate, $\hat{r}$, implied by the futures price, is

$$-\frac{1}{0.2466} \ln 0.9695 = 0.1256$$

or 12.56%. Rearranging equation (4.1), we see that the continuously compounded 56-day rate, r, implied by r^* and $\hat{r}$, is

$$r = \frac{r^* T^* - \hat{r}(T^* - T)}{T}$$

This is the implied repo rate. In this case it is

$$\frac{12.27 \times 146 - 12.56 \times 90}{56} = 11.80\%$$

If the 56-day rate is less than 11.80% per annum, a Type 1 arbitrage is indicated. If it is greater than 11.80%, a Type 2 arbitrage is indicated.

Quotes for Treasury Bills

As mentioned in Section 4.1, the actual/360 day count convention is used for Treasury bills in the United States. Treasury bill price quotes are for a Treasury bill with a face value of $100. Suppose that Y is the cash price of a Treasury bill that has a face value of $100 and n days to maturity. The price is quoted as

$$\frac{360}{n}(100 - Y)$$

This is referred to as the *discount rate*. It is the annualized dollar return provided by the Treasury bill in 360 days expressed as a percentage of the face value. If for a 90-day Treasury bill, the cash price, Y, were 98, the quoted price would be 8.00.

The discount rate is not the same as the rate of return earned on the Treasury bill. The latter is calculated as the dollar return divided by the cost. In the preceding example, where the quoted price is 8.00, the rate of return would be

2/98, or 2.04%, per 90 days. This amounts to

$$\frac{2}{98} \times \frac{360}{90} = 0.0816$$

or 8.16% per annum on an actual/360 basis. Alternatively, it is

$$\frac{2}{98} \times \frac{365}{90} = 0.0828$$

or 8.28% per annum on an actual/365 basis. Both of these rates are expressed with a compounding period of 90 days.[3] When converted to semiannual compounding, the second rate is sometimes referred to as the *bond equivalent yield* because it is directly comparable with the yields quoted on government bonds.

A 90-day Treasury bill futures contract is for delivery of $1 million of Treasury bills. Treasury bill futures prices are not quoted in the same way as the prices of Treasury bills themselves. The following relationship is used:[4]

$$\begin{array}{c} \text{Treasury bill futures} \\ \text{price quote} \end{array} = 100 - \begin{array}{c} \text{corresponding Treasury bill} \\ \text{price quote} \end{array}$$

If Z is the quoted futures price and Y is the cash futures price, this means that

$$Z = 100 - 4(100 - Y)$$

or, equivalently,

$$Y = 100 - 0.25(100 - Z)$$

Since there are 1 million dollars face value of Treasury bills underlying one Treasury bill futures contract, the contract price is

$$10,000[100 - 0.25(100 - Z)] \tag{4.5}$$

Thus the futures quote of 94.44 for September 1995 Treasury bills in Table 4.3 corresponds to a price of $100 - 0.25(100 - 94.44) = \$98.61$ per $100 of 90-day Treasury bills or a contract price of $986,100.

The amount that is paid or received by each side in the marking to market process equals the change in the contract price. For example, when the futures price changes by one basis point (i.e., by 0.01), the amount paid by one side and received by the other side on one contract is $10,000 \times 0.25 \times 0.01$ or $25. If 90-day Treasury bills are delivered by the party with the short position, the price received is the contract price in equation (4.5). If the Treasury bills that are delivered have 89 days to maturity, the price received is calculated by replacing the 0.25 in the

---

[3]It is interesting to note in passing that the compounding frequency convention for a money market instrument such as a Treasury bill is generally to set the compounding period equal to the life of the instrument. This means that the yields on money market instruments of different maturities are not directly comparable.

[4]The reason for quoting Treasury bill futures prices in this way is to ensure that the bid quote is below the ask quote.

preceding formula by 89/360, or 0.2472. If they have 91 days to maturity, the 0.25 in the formula becomes 91/360, or 0.2528.

Example 4.6

Suppose that the 140-day interest rate is 8% per annum and the 230-day rate is 8.25% per annum (with continuous compounding and actual/actual being used for both rates). The forward rate for the time period between day 140 and day 230 is

$$\frac{0.0825 \times 230 - 0.08 \times 140}{90} = 0.0864$$

or 8.64%. Since 90 days $= 0.2466$ year, the futures price for $100 of 90-day Treasury bills deliverable in 140 days is

$$100e^{-0.0864 \times 0.2466} = 97.89$$

This would be quoted as $100 - 4(100 - 97.89) = 91.56$. (This calculation ignores the difference between futures and forward contracts.)

4.5 EURODOLLAR FUTURES

As shown in Table 4.3, the Eurodollar futures contract traded on the Chicago Mercantile Exchange (CME) is a very popular contract. The total open interest exceeded 2.5 million contracts on May 11, 1995. A Eurodollar is a dollar deposited in a U.S. or foreign bank outside the United States. The Eurodollar interest rate is the rate of interest earned on Eurodollars deposited by one bank with another bank. It is also known as the London Interbank Offer Rate (LIBOR). Eurodollar interest rates are generally higher than the corresponding Treasury bill interest rates because a bank has to pay a higher rate of interest than the Federal government on borrowed funds. The interest rate underlying the Eurodollar futures contract is a 90-day rate.

On the surface, a Eurodollar futures contract appears to be structurally the same as the Treasury bill futures contract. Suppose the quoted futures price is Z. The formula for calculating the value of one contract from the quoted futures price is equation (4.5), the same as that used for Treasury bill futures. The quote of 93.96 for the September 1995 contract in Table 4.3 corresponds to a Eurodollar interest rate quote of 6.04 and a contract price of

$$10,000[100 - 0.25(100 - 93.96)] = \$984,900$$

However, there are some important differences between the Treasury bill and Eurodollar futures contracts. For a Treasury bill, the contract price converges at maturity to the price of a 90-day $1 million face value Treasury bill, and if a contract is held until maturity, this is the instrument delivered. A Eurodollar futures contract is settled in cash on the second London business day before the third Wednesday of the month. The final marking to market sets the contract price

equal to

$$10,000(100 - 0.25R)$$

where R is the quoted Eurodollar rate at that time. This quoted Eurodollar rate is the actual 90-day rate on Eurodollar deposits with quarterly compounding. It is not a discount rate. The Eurodollar futures contract is therefore a futures contract on an interest rate, whereas the Treasury bill futures contract is a futures contract on the price of a Treasury bill or a discount rate.

We made the point in Section 3.6 that futures prices and forward prices may not be the same for long-dated contracts. This point is particularly relevant to Eurodollar futures contracts since they have maturities up to 10 years. Eurodollar futures are regularly used to calculate zero-coupon LIBOR rates. For contracts lasting only a year or two it is reasonable to assume that the futures price is the forward price, or equivalently, that the rate calculated from the futures price is a forward interest rate. For longer-dated contracts this is far less reasonable. The adjustments that are necessary to convert a futures rate to a forward rate are discussed in Section 17.15.

4.6 DURATION

Duration is an important concept in the use of interest rate futures for hedging. The duration of a bond is a measure of how long, on average, the holder of the bond has to wait before receiving cash payments. A zero-coupon bond that matures in n years has a duration of n years. However, a coupon-bearing bond maturing in n years has a duration of less than n years. This is because some of the cash payments are received by the holder prior to year n.

Suppose that the current time is 0 and a bond provides the holder with payments c_i at time t_i ($1 \le i \le n$). The price, B, and continuously compounded yield, y, are related by

$$B = \sum_{i=1}^{n} c_i e^{-yt_i} \qquad (4.6)$$

The duration, D, of the bond is defined as

$$D = \frac{\sum_{i=1}^{n} t_i c_i e^{-yt_i}}{B} \qquad (4.7)$$

This can be written

$$D = \sum_{i=1}^{n} t_i \left[\frac{c_i e^{-yt_i}}{B} \right]$$

The term in square brackets is the ratio of the present value of the payment at time t_i to the bond price. The bond price is the present value of all payments. The

duration is therefore a weighted average of the times when payments are made with the weight applied to time t_i being equal to the proportion of the bond's total present value provided by the payment at time t_i. The sum of the weights is 1.0. We now show why duration is an important concept in hedging.

From equation (4.6),

$$\frac{\partial B}{\partial y} = -\sum_{i=1}^{n} c_i t_i e^{-yt_i} \tag{4.8}$$

and from equation (4.7) this can be written

$$\frac{\partial B}{\partial y} = -BD \tag{4.9}$$

If we make a small parallel shift to the yield curve increasing all interest rates by a small amount Δy, the yields on all bonds also increase by Δy. Equation (4.9) shows that the bond's price increases by ΔB, where

$$\frac{\Delta B}{\Delta y} = -BD \tag{4.10}$$

or

$$\frac{\Delta B}{B} = -D \Delta y$$

This shows that the percentage change in a bond price is equal to its duration multiplied by the size of the parallel shift in the yield curve.

Example 4.7

Consider a three-year 10% coupon bond with a face value of $100. Suppose that the yield on the bond is 12% per annum with continuous compounding. This means that $y = 0.12$. Coupon payments of $5 are made every six months. Table 4.5 shows the calculations necessary to determine the bond's duration. The present values of the payments using the yield as the discount rate are shown in column 3. (For example, the present value of the first payment is $5e^{-0.12 \times 0.5} = 4.709$.) The sum of the numbers in column 3 give the bond's price as $94.213. The weights are calculated by dividing the numbers in column

TABLE 4.5   Calculation of Duration

Time (yrs)	Payment ($)	Present Value	Weight	Time × Weight
0.5	5	4.709	0.050	0.025
1.0	5	4.435	0.047	0.047
1.5	5	4.176	0.044	0.066
2.0	5	3.933	0.042	0.084
2.5	5	3.704	0.039	0.098
3.0	105	73.256	0.778	2.334
	130	94.213	1.000	2.654

3 by 94.213. The sum of the numbers in column 5 gives the duration as 2.654 years. From equation (4.10),

$$\Delta B = -94.213 \times 2.654 \, \Delta y$$

that is,

$$\Delta B = -250.04 \, \Delta y$$

If $\Delta y = +0.001$ so that y increases to 0.121, this formula indicates that we expect ΔB to be -0.25. In other words, we expect the bond price to go down to $94.213 - 0.250 = 93.963$. By recomputing the bond price for a yield of 12.1%, the reader can verify that this is indeed what happens.

The duration of a bond portfolio can be defined as a weighted average of the durations of the individual bonds in the portfolio with the weights being proportional to the bond prices. Equation (4.10) then shows that the proportional effect of a parallel shift of Δy in the yield curve is the duration of the portfolio multiplied by the Δy.

This analysis is based on the assumption that y is expressed with continuous compounding. If y is expressed with annual compounding, a similar analysis to that just given shows that equation (4.10) becomes

$$\Delta B = -\frac{BD \, \Delta y}{1 + y}$$

More generally, if y is expressed with a compounding frequency of m times per year,

$$\Delta B = -\frac{BD \, \Delta y}{1 + y/m}$$

The expression

$$\frac{D}{1 + y/m}$$

is sometimes referred to as *modified duration*.

4.7 DURATION-BASED HEDGING STRATEGIES

Consider the situation where a position in an interest-rate-dependent asset such as a bond portfolio or a money market security is being hedged using an interest rate futures contract. Define

F: contract price for the interest rate futures contract

D_F: duration of asset underlying futures contract

S: value of asset being hedged

D_S: duration of asset being hedged

We assume that the change in the yield, Δy, is the same for all maturities, which means that only parallel shifts in the yield curve can occur. From equation (4.10) it is approximately true that

$$\Delta S = -SD_S\,\Delta y \tag{4.11}$$

To a reasonable approximation, it is also true that

$$\Delta F = -FD_F\,\Delta y \tag{4.12}$$

The number of contracts required to hedge against an uncertain Δy is therefore

$$N^* = \frac{SD_S}{FD_F} \tag{4.13}$$

This is the *duration-based hedge ratio*.[5] It is sometimes also called the *price sensitivity hedge ratio*. Using it has the effect of making the duration of the entire position zero.

When the hedging instrument is a Treasury bond futures contract, the hedger must base D_F on an assumption that one particular bond will be delivered. This means that the hedger must estimate which of the available bonds is likely to be cheapest to deliver at the time the hedge is put in place. If, subsequently, the interest rate environment changes so that it looks as though a different bond will be cheapest to deliver, the performance of the hedge may be worse than expected.

Example 4.8

On May 20, a corporate treasurer learns that $3.3 million will be received on August 5. The funds will be needed for a major capital investment the following February. The treasurer therefore plans to invest the funds in six-month Treasury bills as soon as they are received. The current yield on six-month Treasury bills, expressed with semiannual compounding, is 11.20%. The treasurer is concerned that this may decline between May 20 and August 5 and decides to hedge using Treasury bill futures. The quoted price for the September T-bill futures contract is 89.44. In this case the company will lose money if interest rates go down. The hedge must therefore provide a positive profit when rates go down or, equivalently, when Treasury bill prices go up. This means that a long hedge is required.

To calculate the number of T-bill futures contracts that should be purchased, we note that the asset underlying the futures contract lasts for three months. Since it is a discount instrument, its duration is also three months, or 0.25 year. Similarly, the six-month Treasury bill investment planned by the treasurer has a duration of six months, or

---

[5]If yields are defined with a compounding frequency of m, equation (4.13) becomes

$$N^* = \frac{SD_S(1 + y_F/m)}{FD_F(1 + y_S/m)}$$

where y_S and y_F are the yields on S and F. This is not the same as equation (4.13) except when $y_S = y_F$. The reason for the difference is that the assumption that $\Delta y_S = \Delta y_F$ when yields are continuously compounded is not quite the same assumption as $\Delta y_S = \Delta y_F$ when yields are compounded once a year.

0.50 year. Each T-bill futures contract is for the delivery of $1 million of T-bills. The contract price is

$$10,000[100 - 0.25(100 - 89.44)] = \$973,600$$

The number of contracts that should be purchased is, using equation (4.13),

$$\frac{3,300,000}{973,600} \times \frac{0.5}{0.25} = 6.78$$

Rounding to the nearest whole number, the treasurer should purchase seven contracts.

Example 4.9

It is August 2 and a fund manager with $10 million invested in government bonds is concerned that interest rates are expected to be highly volatile over the next 3 months. The fund manager decides to use the December T-bond futures contract to hedge the value of the portfolio. The current futures price is 93-02, or 93.0625. Since each contract is for the delivery of $100,000 face value of bonds, the futures contract price is $93,062.50.

The average duration of the bond portfolio over the next three months will be 6.80 years. The cheapest-to-deliver bond in the T-bond contract is expected to be a 20-year 12% per annum coupon bond. The yield on this bond is currently 8.80% per annum, and the duration will be 9.20 years at maturity of the futures contract.

The fund manager requires a short position in T-bond futures to hedge the bond portfolio. If interest rates go up, a gain will be made on the short futures position and a loss will be made on the bond portfolio. If interest rates decrease, a loss will be made on the short position, but there will be a gain on the bond portfolio. The number of bond futures contracts that should be shorted can be calculated from equation (4.13) as

$$\frac{10,000,000}{93,062.50} \times \frac{6.80}{9.20} = 79.42$$

Rounding to the nearest whole number, the portfolio manager should short 79 contracts.

4.8 LIMITATIONS OF DURATION

The duration concept provides a simple approach to interest rate risk management. However, the hedge to which it gives rise is far from perfect. There are two main reasons for this. The first concerns a concept known as *convexity*. The second concerns the underlying assumption of parallel shifts in the yield curve.

Convexity

For very small parallel shifts in the yield curve, the change in value of a portfolio depends solely on its duration. When moderate or large changes in interest rates are considered, a factor known as *convexity* is sometimes important. Figure 4.6 shows the relationship between the percentage change in value and change

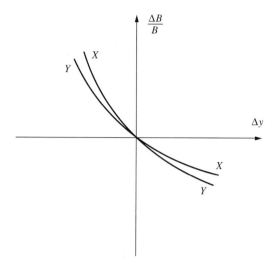

Figure 4.6   Bond portfolios with different convexities.

in yield for two portfolios having the same duration. The figure shows that both portfolios change in value by the same percentage for small yield changes and is consistent with equation (4.10). For large interest rate changes, the portfolios behave differently. Portfolio X has more convexity or curvature than portfolio Y. Its value increases by a greater percentage amount than that of portfolio Y when yields decline, and its value decreases by less than that of portfolio Y when yields increase. The convexity of a bond portfolio tends to be greatest when the portfolio provides payments evenly over a long period of time. It is least when the payments are concentrated around one particular point in time.

A measure of convexity is

$$\frac{\partial^2 B}{\partial y^2} = \sum_{i=1}^{n} c_i t_i^2 e^{-y t_i}$$

This is a measure of the curvature of the relationship between ΔB and Δy in Figure 4.6. When managing portfolios of assets and liabilities some financial institutions try to match both duration and this convexity measure of the assets with those of the liabilities.

Nonparallel Shifts

One serious problem with the duration concept is that it assumes all interest rates change by the same amount. In practice, short-term rates are usually more volatile than, and are not closely correlated with, long-term rates. Sometimes it even happens that short- and long-term rates move in opposite directions to each other. For this reason, financial institutions often hedge their interest rate exposure by dividing the zero-coupon yield curve up into segments and ensuring that they

are hedged against a movement in each segment. Suppose that the ith segment is the part of the zero-coupon yield curve between time t_i and t_{i+1}. A financial institution would examine the effect of a small increase Δy in all the zero-coupon yields for maturities between t_i and t_{i+1} while keeping the rest of the zero-coupon yield curve unchanged. If the exposure were unacceptable, further trades would be undertaken in carefully selected instruments to reduce it. In the context of a bank managing a portfolio of assets and liabilities, this approach is sometimes referred to as *GAP management.*

4.9 SUMMARY

In this chapter we have discussed three of the most popular interest rate futures contracts: the Treasury bond, Treasury bill, and Eurodollar contracts. We have also considered different ways in which these contracts can be used for hedging. Since bond prices are inversely related to interest rates, a short hedge provides protection against an increase in interest rates; a long hedge provides protection against a decrease in interest rates.

In the Treasury bond futures contract, the party with the short position has a number of interesting delivery options:

1. Delivery can be made on any day during the delivery month.
2. There are a number of alternative bonds that can be delivered.
3. On any day during the delivery month, the notice of intention to deliver at the 2 p.m. settlement price can be made any time up to 8 p.m.

These options all tend to reduce the futures price.

The concept of duration is important in hedging interest rate risk. Duration measures how long, on average, an investor has to wait before receiving payments. It is a weighted average of the times until payments are received, with the weight for a particular payment time being proportional to the present value of the payment.

A key result underlying the duration-based hedging scheme described in this chapter is

$$\Delta B = -BD\,\Delta y$$

where B is a bond price, D is its duration, Δy is a small change in its yield (continuously compounded), and ΔB is the resultant small change in B. The equation enables a hedger to assess the sensitivity of a bond to small changes in its yield. It also enables the hedger to assess the sensitivity of an interest rate futures price to small changes in the yield of the underlying bond. If the hedger is prepared to assume that Δy is the same for all bonds, the result enables the hedger to calculate the number of futures contracts necessary to protect a bond or bond portfolio against small changes in interest rates.

The key assumption underlying the duration-based hedging scheme is that all interest rates change by the same amount. This means that only parallel shifts

in the term structure are allowed for. In practice, short-term interest rates are generally more volatile than long-term interest rates, and hedge performance is liable to be poor if the duration of the bond underlying the futures contract and the duration of the asset being hedged are markedly different.

SUGGESTIONS FOR FURTHER READING

Allen, S. L., and A. D. Kleinstein, *Valuing Fixed Income Investments and Derivative Securities.* New York: New York Institute of Finance, 1991.

Chicago Board of Trade, *Interest Rate Futures for Institutional Investors.* Chicago: 1987.

Fabozzi, F. J., *Fixed Income Mathematics: Analytical and Statistical Techniques.* Chicago: Probus, 1993.

Figlewski, S., *Hedging with Financial Futures for Institutional Investors.* Cambridge, Mass.: Ballinger, 1986.

Gay, G. D., R. W. Kolb, and R. Chiang, "Interest Rate Hedging: An Empirical Test of Alternative Strategies," *Journal of Financial Research,* 6 (Fall 1983), 187–97.

Klemkosky, R. C., and D. J. Lasser, "An Efficiency Analysis of the T-Bond Futures Market," *Journal of Futures Markets,* 5 (1985), 607–20.

Kolb, R. W., *Interest Rate Futures: A Comprehensive Introduction.* Richmond, Va.: R. F. Dame, 1982.

Kolb, R. W., and R. Chiang, "Improving Hedging Performance Using Interest Rate Futures," *Financial Management,* 10 (Autumn 1981), 72–79.

Resnick, B. G., "The Relationship between Futures Prices for U.S. Treasury Bonds," *Review of Research in Futures Markets,* 3 (1984), 88–104.

Resnick, B. G., and E. Hennigar, "The Relationship between Futures and Cash Prices for U.S. Treasury Bonds," *Review of Research in Futures Markets,* 2 (1983), 282–99.

Senchak, A. J., and J. C. Easterwood, "Cross Hedging CDs with Treasury Bill Futures," *Journal of Futures Markets,* 3 (1983), 429–38.

Veit, W. T., and W. W. Reiff, "Commercial Banks and Interest Rate Futures: A Hedging Survey," *Journal of Futures Markets,* 3 (1983), 283–93.

QUESTIONS AND PROBLEMS

4.1. Suppose that spot interest rates with continuous compounding are as follows:

Maturity (years)	Rate (% per annum)
1	8.0
2	7.5
3	7.2
4	7.0
5	6.9

Calculate forward interest rates for the second, third, fourth, and fifth years.

4.2. The term structure is upward sloping. Put the following in order of magnitude:
   (a) The five-year spot rate.
   (b) The yield on a five-year coupon-bearing bond.
   (c) The forward rate corresponding to the period between 5 and $5\frac{1}{4}$ years in the future.

   What is the answer to this question when the term structure is downward sloping?

4.3. The six-month and the one-year spot rates are both 10% per annum. For a bond that lasts 18 months and pays a coupon of 8% per annum (with a coupon payment having just been made), the yield is 10.4% per annum. What is the bond's price? What is the 18-month spot rate? All rates are quoted with semiannual compounding.

4.4. It is January 9, 1997. The price of a Treasury bond with a 12% coupon that matures on October 12, 2005 is quoted as 102-07. What is the cash price?

4.5. The price of a 90-day Treasury bill is quoted as 10.00. What continuously compounded return does an investor earn on the Treasury bill for the 90-day period?

4.6. What assumptions does a duration-based hedging scheme make about the way in which the term structure moves?

4.7. It is January 30. You are managing a bond portfolio worth $6 million. The average duration of the portfolio is 8.2 years. The September Treasury bond futures price is currently 108-15 and the cheapest-to-deliver bond has a duration of 7.6 years. How should you hedge against changes in interest rates over the next seven months?

4.8. Suppose that spot interest rates with continuous compounding are as follows:

Maturity (years)	Rate (% per annum)
1	12.0
2	13.0
3	13.7
4	14.2
5	14.5

   Calculate forward interest rates for the second, third, fourth, and fifth years.

4.9. Suppose that spot interest rates with continuous compounding are as follows:

Maturity (months)	Rate (% per annum)
3	8.0
6	8.2
9	8.4
12	8.5
15	8.6
18	8.7

   Calculate forward interest rates for the second, third, fourth, fifth, and sixth quarters.

4.10. The cash prices of six-month and one-year Treasury bills are 94.0 and 89.0. A $1\frac{1}{2}$-year bond that will pay coupons of $4 every six months currently sells for $94.84. A two-year bond that will pay coupons of $5 every six months currently sells for $97.12. Calculate the six-month, one-year, $1\frac{1}{2}$-year, and two-year spot rates.

4.11. A 10-year 8% coupon bond currently sells for $90. A 10-year 4% coupon bond currently sells for $80. What is the 10-year spot rate? (*Hint:* Consider taking a long position in two of the 4% coupon bonds and a short position in one of the 8% coupon bonds.)

4.12. Explain carefully why liquidity preference theory is consistent with the observation that the term structure tends to be upward sloping more often than it is downward sloping.

4.13. It is May 5, 1998. The quoted price of a government bond with a 12% coupon that matures on July 27, 2001 is 110-17. What is the cash price?

4.14. Suppose that the T-bond futures price is 101-12. Which of the following four bonds is cheapest to deliver?

Bond	Price	Conversion Factor
1	125-05	1.2131
2	142-15	1.3792
3	115-31	1.1149
4	144-02	1.4026

4.15. It is July 30, 1996. The cheapest-to-deliver bond in a September 1996 Treasury bond futures contract is a 13% coupon bond, and delivery is expected to be made on September 30, 1996. Coupon payments on the bond are made on February 4 and August 4 each year. The term structure is flat and the rate of interest with semiannual compounding is 12% per annum. The conversion factor for the bond is 1.5. The current quoted bond price is $110. Calculate the quoted futures price for the contract.

4.16. An investor is looking for arbitrage opportunities in the Treasury bond futures market. What complications are created by the fact that the party with a short position can choose to deliver any bond with a maturity of over 15 years?

4.17. Suppose that the Treasury bill futures price for a contract maturing in 33 days is quoted as 90.04 and the discount rate for a 123-day Treasury bill is 10.03. What is the implied repo rate? How can it be used?

4.18. Suppose that the nine-month interest rate is 8% per annum and the six-month interest rate is 7.5% per annum (both with continuous compounding). Estimate the futures price of 90-day Treasury bills with a face value of $1 million for delivery in six months. How would the price be quoted?

4.19. Assume that a bank can borrow or lend money at the same interest rate in Eurodollar markets. The 90-day rate is 10% per annum and the 180-day rate is 10.2% per annum both expressed with continuous compounding. The Eurodollar futures price for a contract maturing in 90 days is quoted as 89.5. What arbitrage opportunities are open to the bank?

4.20. A Canadian company wishes to create a Canadian T-bill futures contract from a U.S. Treasury bill futures contract and forward contracts on foreign exchange. Using an example, explain how this can be done. For the purposes of this problem, assume that a futures contract is the same as a forward contract.

4.21. A five-year bond with a yield of 11% (continuously compounded) pays an 8% coupon at the end of each year.
    (a) What is the bond's price?
    (b) What is the bond's duration?
    (c) Use the duration to calculate the effect on the bond's price of a 0.2% decrease in its yield.
    (d) Recalculate the bond's price on the basis of a 10.8% per annum yield and verify that the result is in agreement with your answer to (c).

4.22. Portfolio A consists of a one-year discount bond with a face value of $2,000 and a 10-year discount bond with a face value of $6,000. Portfolio B consists of a 5.95 year discount bond with a face value of $5,000. The current yield on all bonds is 10% per annum.
    (a) Show that both portfolios have the same duration.
    (b) Show that the percentage changes in the values of the two portfolios for a 10-basis-point increase in yields is the same.
    (c) What are the percentage changes in the values of the two portfolios for a 5% per annum increase in yields?
    (d) Which portfolio has the higher convexity?

4.23. Suppose that a bond portfolio with a duration of 12 years is hedged using a futures contract where the underlying asset has a duration of four years. What is likely to be the impact on the hedge of the fact that the 12-year rate is less volatile than the four-year rate?

4.24. Suppose that it is February 20 and a treasurer realizes that on July 17, the company will have to issue $5 million of commercial paper with a maturity of 180 days. If the paper were issued today, it would realize $4,820,000. (In other words, the company would receive $4,820,000 for its paper and have to redeem it at $5,000,000 in 180 days' time.) The September Eurodollar futures price is quoted as 92.00. How should the treasurer hedge the company's exposure?

4.25. On August 1, a portfolio manager has a bond portfolio worth $10 million. The duration of the portfolio is 7.1 years. The December Treasury bond futures price is currently 91-12, and the cheapest-to-deliver bond has a duration of 8.8 years. How should the portfolio manager immunize the portfolio against changes in interest rates over the next two months?

4.26. How can the portfolio manager change the duration of the portfolio to 3.0 years in Problem 4.25?

4.27. Between February 28, 1997 and March 1, 1997 you have a choice between owning a government bond paying a 10% coupon and a corporate bond paying a 10% coupon. Consider carefully the day count conventions discussed in Section 4.1 and decide which of the two bonds you would prefer to own. Ignore the risk of default.

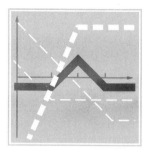

Chapter 5
Swaps

Swaps are private agreements between two companies to exchange cash flows in the future according to a prearranged formula. They can be regarded as portfolios of forward contracts. The study of swaps is therefore a natural extension of the study of forward and futures contracts.

The first swap contracts were negotiated in 1981. Since then, the market has grown very rapidly. Hundreds of billions of dollars of contracts are currently negotiated each year. In this chapter we discuss how swaps are designed, how they are used, and how they can be valued. We also consider briefly the nature of the credit risk facing financial institutions when they trade swaps and other similar financial contracts. This last topic is covered in more detail in Chapter 20.

5.1 MECHANICS OF INTEREST RATE SWAPS

The most common type of swap is a "plain vanilla" interest rate swap. In this, one party, B, agrees to pay to the other party, A, cash flows equal to interest at a predetermined fixed rate on a notional principal for a number of years. At the same time, party A agrees to pay party B cash flows equal to interest at a floating rate on the same notional principal for the same period of time. The currencies of the two sets of interest cash flows are the same. The life of the swap can range from two years to over 15 years.

London Interbank Offer Rate

The floating rate in many interest rate swap agreements is the London Interbank Offer Rate (LIBOR). LIBOR is the rate of interest offered by banks on deposits from other banks in Eurocurrency markets. One-month LIBOR is the rate offered on one-month deposits, three-month LIBOR is the rate offered on three-month deposits, and so on. LIBOR rates are determined by trading between banks and change continuously as economic conditions change. Just as prime is often the reference rate of interest for floating-rate loans in the domestic financial market, LIBOR is frequently a reference rate of interest for loans in

international financial markets. To understand how it is used, consider a loan where the rate of interest is specified as six-month LIBOR plus 0.5% per annum. The life of the loan is divided into six-month periods. For each period, the rate of interest is set 0.5% per annum above the six-month LIBOR rate at the beginning of the period. Interest is paid at the end of the period. As mentioned in Section 4.5, three-month LIBOR is the rate of interest underlying the very popular Eurodollar futures contract that trades on the Chicago Mercantile Exchange.

Example

Consider a three-year swap initiated on March 1, 1996, where company B agrees to pay to company A a rate of 5% per annum on a notional principal of $100 million and in return company A agrees to pay to company B the six-month LIBOR rate on the same notional principal. We assume the agreement specifies that payments are to be exchanged every six months and the 5% interest rate is quoted with semiannual compounding. This swap can be represented diagrammatically as shown in Figure 5.1.

The first exchange of payments would take place on September 1, 1996, six months after the initiation of the agreement. Company B would pay to company A $2.5 million. This is the interest on the $100 million principal for six months at 5%. Company A would pay to company B interest on the $100 million principal at the six-month LIBOR rate prevailing six months prior to September 1, 1996; that is, on March 1, 1996. Suppose that the six-month LIBOR rate on March 1, 1996 is 4.2%. Company A pays to company B $0.5 \times 0.042 \times \$100$ or $2.1 million. Note that there is no uncertainty about this first exchange of payments since it is determined by the LIBOR rate at the time the contract is entered into.

The second exchange of payments would take place on March 1, 1997, one year after initiation of the agreement. Company B would pay $2.5 million to company A. Company A would pay interest on the $100 million principal to company B at the six-month LIBOR rate prevailing six months prior to March 1, 1997; that is, on September 1, 1996. Suppose that the six-month LIBOR rate on September 1, 1996 is 4.8%. Company A pays $0.5 \times 0.048 \times \$100$, or $2.4 million to company B.

In total there are six exchanges of payment on the swap. The fixed payments are always $2.5 million. The floating-rate payments on a payment date are calculated using the six-month LIBOR rate prevailing six months before the payment date. An interest rate swap is generally structured so that one side remits the difference between the two payments to the other side. In the example given, company B would pay company A $0.4 million ($= 2.5$ million $- 2.1$ million) on September 1, 1996 and $0.1 million ($= 2.5$ million $- 2.4$ million) on March 1, 1997.

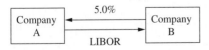

Figure 5.1   Interest rate swap between companies A and B.

TABLE 5.1   Cash Flows (Millions of Dollars) to Company B in a $100 Million Three-Year Interest Rate Swap When a Fixed Rate of 5% Is Paid and LIBOR Is Received

Date	LIBOR Rate (%)	Floating Cash Flow	Fixed Cash Flow	Net Cash Flow
Mar. 1, 1996	4.20			
Sept. 1, 1996	4.80	+2.10	−2.50	−0.40
Mar. 1, 1997	5.30	+2.40	−2.50	−0.10
Sept. 1, 1997	5.50	+2.65	−2.50	+0.15
Mar. 1, 1998	5.60	+2.75	−2.50	+0.25
Sept. 1, 1998	5.90	+2.80	−2.50	+0.30
Mar. 1, 1999	6.40	+2.95	−2.50	+0.45

Table 5.1 provides a complete example of the payments that would be made under the swap for one particular set of six-month LIBOR rates. The table shows the swap cash flows from the perspective of company B. Note that the $100 million principal is used only for the calculation of interest payments. The principal itself is not exchanged. This is why it is termed the *notional principal.*

If the principal were exchanged at the end of the life of the swap, the nature of the deal would not be changed in any way. This is because the principal is the same for both the fixed and floating payments. Exchanging $100 million for $100 million at the end of the life of the swap is a transaction that would have no financial value to either party. Table 5.2 shows the cash flows in Table 5.1 with a final exchange of principal added in. The cash flows in the third column of this table are the cash flows from a long position in a floating-rate bond. The cash flows in the fourth column of the table are the cash flows from a short position in a fixed-rate bond. The table shows that the swap can be regarded as the exchange of a fixed-rate bond for a floating-rate bond. Company B, whose position is described by Table 5.2, is long a floating-rate bond and short a fixed-rate bond. Company A is long a fixed-rate bond and short a floating-rate bond.

TABLE 5.2   Cash Flows (Millions of Dollars) from Table 5.1 When There Is a Final Exchange of Principal

Date	LIBOR Rate (%)	Floating Cash Flow	Fixed Cash Flow	Net Cash Flow
Mar. 1, 1996	4.20			
Sept. 1, 1996	4.80	+2.10	−2.50	−0.40
Mar. 1, 1997	5.30	+2.40	−2.50	−0.10
Sept. 1, 1997	5.50	+2.65	−2.50	+0.15
Mar. 1, 1998	5.60	+2.75	−2.50	+0.25
Sept. 1, 1998	5.90	+2.80	−2.50	+0.30
Mar. 1, 1999	6.40	+102.95	−102.50	+0.45

This characterization of the cash flows in the swap helps to explain why the floating rate in the swap is set six months before it is paid. On a floating-rate instrument interest is generally set at the beginning of the period over which it will apply and is paid at the end of the period. A "plain vanilla" interest-rate swap such as the one in Table 5.2 is designed so that the payments on the floating side correspond to the interest paid on a floating-rate loan.

Using the Swap to Transform a Liability

For company B the swap could be used to transform a floating-rate loan into a fixed-rate loan. Suppose that company B has arranged to borrow $100 million at LIBOR plus 80 basis points. (One basis point is one hundredth of 1%, so the rate is LIBOR plus 0.8%.) After company B has entered into the swap it has three sets of cash flows:

1. It pays LIBOR plus 0.8% to its outside lenders.
2. It receives LIBOR under the terms of the swap.
3. It pays 5% under the terms of the swap.

These three sets of cash flows net out to an interest rate payment of 5.8%. Thus for company B the swap could have the effect of transforming borrowings at a floating rate of LIBOR plus 80 basis points into borrowings at a fixed rate of 5.8%.

For company A the swap could have the effect of transforming a fixed-rate loan into a floating-rate loan. Suppose that company A has a three-year $100 million loan outstanding on which it pays 5.2%. After it has entered into the swap it has three sets of cash flows:

1. It pays 5.2% to its outside lenders.
2. It pays LIBOR under the terms of the swap.
3. It receives 5% under the terms of the swap.

These three sets of cash flows net out to an interest rate payment of LIBOR plus 0.2% (or LIBOR plus 20 basis points). Thus for company A the swap could have the effect of transforming borrowings at a fixed rate of 5.2% into borrowings at a floating rate of LIBOR plus 20 basis points. These potential uses of the swap by companies A and B are illustrated in Figure 5.2.

Using the Swap to Transform an Asset

Swaps can also be used to transform the nature of an asset. Consider company B in our example. The swap could have the effect of transforming an asset earning a fixed rate of interest into an asset earning a floating rate of interest. Suppose that company B owns $100 million in bonds that will return 4.7% over the

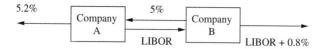

Figure 5.2   Companies A and B each use the swap to transform a liability.

next three years. After company B has entered into the swap it has three sets of
cash flows:

1. It receives 4.7% on the bonds.
2. It receives LIBOR under the terms of the swap.
3. It pays 5% under the terms of the swap.

These three sets of cash flows net out to an interest rate inflow of LIBOR minus
30 basis points. Thus one possible use of the swap for company B is to transform
an asset earning 4.7% into an asset earning LIBOR minus 30 basis points.

Consider next company A. The swap could have the effect of transforming
an asset earning a floating rate of interest into an asset earning a fixed rate of
interest. Suppose that company A has an investment of $100 million that yields
LIBOR minus 25 basis points. After it has entered into the swap it has three sets
of cash flows:

1. It receives LIBOR minus 25 basis points on its investment.
2. It pays LIBOR under the terms of the swap.
3. It receives 5% under the terms of the swap.

These three sets of cash flows net out to an interest rate inflow of 4.75%. Thus one
possible use of the swap for company A is to transform an asset earning LIBOR
minus 25 basis points into an asset earning 4.75%. These potential uses of the
swap by companies A and B are illustrated in Figure 5.3.

Role of Financial Intermediary

Usually, two nonfinancial companies do not get in touch with each other
directly to arrange a swap in the way indicated in Figures 5.2 and 5.3. They each
deal with a financial intermediary such as a bank or other financial institution.
"Plain vanilla" fixed-for-floating swaps on U.S. interest rates are usually structured so that the financial institution earns about 3 basis points (= 0.03%) on a
pair of offsetting transactions.

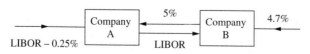

Figure 5.3   Companies A and B each use the swap to transform an asset.

Figure 5.4   Interest rate swap from Figure 5.2 when financial intermediary is used.

Figure 5.4 shows what the role of the financial institution might be in the situation in Figure 5.2. The financial institution enters into two offsetting swap transactions with companies A and B. Assuming that neither A nor B defaults, the financial institution is certain to make a profit of 0.03% (3 basis points) per year on the principal of $100 million. (This amounts to $30,000 per year for the three-year period.) Company B ends up borrowing at 5.815% (instead of 5.8% as in Figure 5.2). Company A ends up borrowing at LIBOR plus 21.5 basis points (instead of at LIBOR plus 20 basis points as in Figure 5.2).

Figure 5.5 illustrates the role of the financial institution in the situation in Figure 5.3. Again the financial institution is certain to make a profit of 3 basis points if neither company defaults on the swap. Company B ends up earning LIBOR minus 31.5 basis points (instead of LIBOR minus 30 basis points as in Figure 5.3). Company A ends up earning 4.735% (instead of 4.75% as in Figure 5.5).

Note that in each case the financial institution has two separate contracts, one with company A and the other with company B. In most instances, company A will not even know that the financial institution has entered into an offsetting swap with company B, and vice versa. If one of the companies defaults, the financial institution still has to honor its agreement with the other company. The 3-basis-point spread earned by the financial institution is partly to compensate it for the default risk it is bearing.

Pricing Schedules

The fixed rate in the "plain vanilla" swap we have been considering is normally quoted as a certain number of basis points above the Treasury note (TN) yield. Table 5.3 shows an *indication pricing schedule* that was used by swap traders working for financial institutions at 1:30 p.m. New York time on May 11, 1995. It indicates the prices quoted to prospective counterparties. For example, it indicates that for a five-year swap where the financial institution will pay fixed and receive six-month LIBOR, the fixed rate should be set 23 basis points above the current five-year Treasury note rate of 6.49%. In other words, the financial institution should set the fixed rate at 6.72%. When it is negotiating

Figure 5.5   Interest rate swap from Figure 5.3 when financial institution is used.

TABLE 5.3   Indication Pricing for Interest Rate Swaps at 1:30 p.m. New York Time on May 11, 1995 (TN = Treasury note; bps = basis points)

Maturity (years)	Bank Pays Fixed Rate	Bank Receives Fixed Rate	Current TN Rate (%)
2	2-yr TN + 17 bps	2-yr TN + 20 bps	6.23
3	3-yr TN + 19 bps	3-yr TN + 22 bps	6.35
4	4-yr TN + 21 bps	4-yr TN + 24 bps	6.42
5	5-yr TN + 23 bps	5-yr TN + 26 bps	6.49
7	7-yr TN + 27 bps	7-yr TN + 30 bps	6.58
10	10-yr TN + 31 bps	10-yr TN + 34 bps	6.72

a five-year swap where it will receive fixed and pay six-month LIBOR for five years, the schedule indicates that it should set the fixed rate at 26 basis points above the current five-year Treasury note rate, or at 6.75%. The bank's profit or its bid–asked spread from negotiating two offsetting five-year swaps would be 3 basis points (= 0.03%) per annum.[1]

At any given time, swap spreads are determined by supply and demand. If more market participants want to receive fixed than receive floating, swap spreads tend to fall. If the reverse is true, swap spreads tend to rise. Table 5.3 would be updated regularly as market conditions changed.

The day count conventions discussed in Section 4.1 affect payments on a swap. Since it is a money market rate, six-month LIBOR is quoted on an actual/360 basis with semiannual compounding. The Treasury note rate is quoted on an actual/actual (in period) basis with semiannual compounding. This can be confusing. To make a six-month LIBOR rate comparable with a Treasury note rate in a 365-day year, either the six-month LIBOR rate must be multiplied by 365/360 or the Treasury note rate must be multiplied by 360/365. A LIBOR-based floating-rate cash flow on a swap payment date is calculated as $QRn/360$ where Q is the principal, R is the relevant LIBOR rate, and n is the number of days since the last payment date.[2]

Warehousing

In practice, it is unlikely that two companies will contact a financial institution at exactly the same time and want to take opposite positions in exactly

---

[1] In the early days of swaps, bid–asked spreads as high as 100 basis points were possible. As Table 5.3 indicates, the market is now much more competitive.

[2] Some of the numbers calculated earlier in this chapter are not perfectly accurate. For example, in Table 5.1 the first floating-rate cash flow in millions of dollars would be

$$100 \times 0.042 \times \frac{184}{360} = 2.1467$$

the same swap. For this reason, most large financial institutions are prepared to warehouse interest rate swaps. This involves entering into a swap with one counterparty, then hedging the interest rate risk until a counterparty wanting to take an opposite position is found. The interest rate futures contracts discussed in Chapter 4 are one way of carrying out the hedging.

5.2 THE COMPARATIVE ADVANTAGE ARGUMENT

An explanation commonly put forward to explain the popularity of swaps concerns comparative advantages. Consider the use of an interest rate swap to transform a liability. Some companies, it is argued, have a comparative advantage when borrowing in fixed-rate markets, while other companies have a comparative advantage in floating-rate markets. When obtaining a new loan, it makes sense for a company to go to the market where it has a comparative advantage. This may lead to a company borrowing fixed when it wants floating, or borrowing floating when it wants fixed. The swap is used to transform the fixed-rate loan into a floating-rate loan, or vice versa.

Example

Suppose that two companies, A and B, both wish to borrow $10 million for five years and have been offered the rates shown in Table 5.4. We assume that company B wants to borrow at a fixed rate of interest, while company A wants to borrow floating funds at a rate linked to six-month LIBOR. Company B clearly has a lower credit rating than company A since it pays a higher rate of interest than company A in both fixed and floating markets.

A key feature of the rates offered to companies A and B is that the difference between the two fixed rates is greater than the difference between the two floating rates. Company B pays 1.20% more than company A in fixed-rate markets and only 0.70% more than company A in floating-rate markets. Company B appears to have a comparative advantage in floating-rate markets, while company A appears to have a comparative advantage in fixed-rate markets.[3] It is this apparent

TABLE 5.4   Borrowing Rates That Provide a Basis for the Comparative Advantage Argument

	Fixed	Floating
Company A	10.00%	6-month LIBOR + 0.30%
Company B	11.20%	6-month LIBOR + 1.00%

[3]Note that B's comparative advantage in floating-rate markets does not imply that B pays less than A in this market. It means that the extra amount that B pays over the amount paid by A is less in this market. One of my students summarized the situation as follows: "A pays more less in fixed-rate markets; B pays less more in floating-rate markets."

Figure 5.6   Swap agreement between A and B when rates in Table 5.4 apply.

anomaly that can lead to the swap being negotiated. Company A borrows fixed-rate funds at 10% per annum. Company B borrows floating-rate funds at LIBOR plus 1.00% per annum. They then enter into a swap agreement to ensure that A ends up with floating-rate funds and B ends up with fixed-rate funds.

To understand how the swap might work, we assume that A and B get in touch with each other directly. The sort of swap they might negotiate is shown in Figure 5.6. Company A agrees to pay company B interest at six-month LIBOR on $10 million. In return, company B agrees to pay company A interest at a fixed rate of 9.95% per annum on $10 million.

Company A has three sets of interest rate cash flows:

1. It pays 10.00% per annum to outside lenders.
2. It receives 9.95% per annum from B.
3. It pays LIBOR to B.

The net effect of the three cash flows is that A pays LIBOR plus 0.05% per annum. This is 0.25% per annum less than it would pay if it went directly to floating-rate markets. Company B also has three sets of interest rate cash flows:

1. It pays LIBOR + 1.00% per annum to outside lenders.
2. It receives LIBOR from A.
3. It pays 9.95% per annum to A.

The net effect of the three cash flows is that B pays 10.95% per annum. This is 0.25% per annum less than it would pay if it went directly to fixed-rate markets.

The swap arrangement appears to improve the position of both A and B by 0.25% per annum. The total gain is therefore 0.50% per annum. This could have been calculated in advance. The total apparent gain from an interest rate swap agreement is always $|a - b|$, where a is the difference between the interest rates facing the two companies in fixed-rate markets, and b is the difference between the interest rates facing the two companies in floating-rate markets. In this case, $a = 1.20\%$ and $b = 0.70\%$.

If A and B did not deal directly with each other and used a financial institution as in Figures 5.4 and 5.5, the financial institution would probably earn a spread of about 3 basis points. This means that the total apparent gain to A and B would be only 47 basis points.

Criticism of the Comparative Advantage Argument

The comparative advantage argument for explaining the attractiveness of interest rate swaps is open to question. Why in Table 5.4 should the spreads between the rates offered to A and B be different in fixed and floating markets? Now that the swap market has been in existence for some time, we might reasonably expect these types of differences to have been arbitraged away.

The reason why spread differentials appear to continue to exist may be due in part to the nature of the contracts available to companies in fixed and floating markets. The 10.0 and 11.2% rates available to A and B in fixed-rate markets are likely to be the rates at which the companies can issue five-year fixed-rate bonds. The LIBOR + 0.3% and LIBOR + 1.0% rates available to A and B in floating-rate markets are six-month rates. In the floating-rate market, the lender usually has the opportunity to review the floating rates every six months. If the creditworthiness of A or B has declined, the lender has the option of increasing the spread over LIBOR that is charged. In extreme circumstances the lender can refuse to roll over the loan at all. The providers of fixed-rate finance do not have the option to change the terms of the loan in this way.[4]

The spreads between the rates offered to A and B are a reflection of the extent to which B is more likely to default than A. During the next six months there is very little chance that either A or B will default. As we look further ahead, default statistics show that the probability of a default by a company with a low credit rating (such as B) increases faster than the probability of a default by a company with a high credit rating (such as A). This is why the spread between the five-year rates is greater than the spread between the six-month rates.

After negotiating a floating-rate loan at LIBOR + 1.0% and entering into the swap shown in Figure 5.6, we argued that B obtained a fixed-rate loan at 10.95%. The arguments we are now presenting show that this is not really the case. In practice, the rate paid is 10.95% only if B can continue to borrow floating-rate funds at a spread of 1.0% over LIBOR. For example, if the credit rating of B declines so that the floating-rate loan is rolled over at LIBOR + 2.0%, the rate paid by B increases to 11.95%. The relatively high five-year borrowing rate offered to B in Table 5.4 suggests that the market considers that B's spread over six-month LIBOR for borrowed funds is expected to rise. Assuming that this is so, B's expected average borrowing rate if it enters into the swap is greater than 10.95%.

The swap in Figure 5.6 locks in LIBOR + 0.1% for company A for the whole of the next five years, not just for the next six months. Unless there is a strong reason for supposing that company A's credit rating will improve, it appears to be a good deal for company A. The downside of the arrangement to company A is the possibility of a default by the counterparty. Figure 5.6 shows the counterparty

---

[4]If two companies negotiate floating-rate loans where the spread over LIBOR is guaranteed in advance regardless of changes in their credit rating, the difference between the rates they pay does in practice equal the difference between the rates they face in fixed-rate markets.

to be company B, but, as explained earlier, a financial institution is likely to act as intermediary as in Figure 5.4. Company A then has to take the creditworthiness of the financial institution into account when making its decision.

5.3 VALUATION OF INTEREST RATE SWAPS

If we assume no possibility of default, an interest rate swap can be valued either as a long position in one bond combined with a short position in another bond, or as a portfolio of forward rate agreements.

Relationship of Swap Value to Bond Prices

As illustrated in Table 5.2, a swap can be characterized as the difference between two bonds. Consider the swap between the financial institution and company B in Figure 5.4. Although the principal is not exchanged, we can assume without changing the value of the swap that at the end of its life, A pays B the notional principal of $100 million and B pays A the same notional principal. The swap is then the same as an arrangement in which:

1. Company B has lent the financial institution $100 million at the six-month LIBOR rate.
2. The financial institution has lent company B $100 million at a fixed rate of 5.015% per annum.

To put this another way, the financial institution has sold a $100 million floating-rate (LIBOR) bond to company B and has purchased a $100 million fixed -rate (5.015% per annum) bond from company B. The value of the swap to the financial institution is therefore the difference between the values of two bonds.

Suppose that it is now time zero and that under the terms of a swap, a financial institution receives fixed payments of k dollars at times t_i ($1 \leq i \leq n$) and makes floating payments at the same times. Define:

> V: value of swap to financial institution
> B_{fix}: value of fixed-rate bond underlying the swap
> B_{fl}: value of floating-rate bond underlying the swap
> Q: notional principal in swap agreement

It follows that:

$$V = B_{\text{fix}} - B_{\text{fl}} \tag{5.1}$$

It is customary to discount the cash flows in a swap at LIBOR rates. The implicit assumption is that the risk associated with swap cash flows is the same as the

risk associated with the cash flows on a loan in the interbank market.[5] A LIBOR zero-coupon yield curve is usually calculated from Eurodollar futures quotes and swap quotes such as those on Table 5.3. For this purpose it is assumed that a swap entered into at the average of the bid and offer quote has a value of zero. (For, example, in Table 5.3 this means that a five-year swap where 6.735% is exchanged for 6-month LIBOR is worth zero.) The floating-rate bond underlying such a swap is worth par. It follows that the fixed-rate bond is also worth par. An indication schedule such as Table 5.3 therefore defines a number of fixed-rate bonds that are worth par. These are known as *par yield bonds*. The bootstrap procedure described in Section 4.1 is used to determine the zero-coupon yield curve from Eurodollar futures quotes and these par yield bonds. This zero-coupon yield curve defines the appropriate discount rates to use in evaluating equation (5.1) for an existing swap.

To see how Equation (5.1) is used, define r_i as the discount rate corresponding to maturity t_i. Since B_{fix} is the value of a bond that pays k at time $t_i (1 \le i \le n)$ and the principal amount of Q at time t_n,

$$B_{\text{fix}} = \sum_{i=1}^{n} ke^{-r_i t_i} + Qe^{-r_n t_n}$$

Consider next the floating-rate bond, B_{fl}. Immediately after a payment date, B_{fl}, is always equal to notional principal, Q. Between payment dates, we can use the fact that B_{fl} will equal Q immediately after the next payment date. In our notation, the time until the next payment date is t_1 so that

$$B_{\text{fl}} = Qe^{-r_1 t_1} + k^* e^{-r_1 t_1}$$

where k^* is the floating-rate payment (already known) that will be made at time t_1.

In the situation where the financial institution is paying fixed and receiving floating, B_{fix} and B_{fl} are calculated in the same way and

$$V = B_{\text{fl}} - B_{\text{fix}}$$

The value of the swap is zero when it is first negotiated. During its life it may have a positive or negative value.

Example 5.1

Suppose that under the terms of a swap, a financial institution has agreed to pay six-month LIBOR and receive 8% per annum (with semiannual compounding) on a notional principal of $100 million. The swap has a remaining life of 1.25 years. The relevant discount rates with continuous compounding for three-month, nine-month, and 15-month maturities are 10.0%, 10.5%, and 11.0%, respectively. The six-month LIBOR rate at the last payment date was 10.2% (with semiannual compounding). In this case, $k = \$4$

---

[5]This is an approximation. For example, the cash flows on a swap with the Federal government should clearly be discounted at a lower rate than the cash flows on the same swap with a BBB-rated counterparty.

million and $k^* = \$5.1$ million, so that

$$B_{\text{fix}} = 4e^{-0.25 \times 0.1} + 4e^{-0.75 \times 0.105} + 104e^{-1.25 \times 0.11}$$

$$= \$98.24 \text{ million}$$

$$B_{\text{fl}} = 5.1e^{-0.25 \times 0.1} + 100e^{-0.25 \times 0.1}$$

$$= \$102.51 \text{ million}$$

Hence the value of the swap is $98.24 - 102.51 = -\$4.27$ million. If the bank has been in the opposite position of paying fixed and receiving floating, the value of the swap would be $+\$4.27$ million. Note that a more precise calculation would take account of the actual/360 day count convention for LIBOR in calculating k^* (see footnote 2). It would also take account of the precise timing of the fixed rate payments.

Relationship of Swap Value to Forward Rate Agreements

Forward rate agreements were introduced in Section 4.2. They are agreements that a certain interest rate will apply for a certain period of time in the future. An interest rate swap can be decomposed into a series of forward rate agreements. This is best illustrated by returning to the swap agreement between the financial institution and company B in Figure 5.4. In this agreement the financial institution has agreed that a rate of 5.015% per annum will apply for periods in the future regardless of prevailing market rates. The agreement for each period is a forward rate agreement (FRA). The entire swap is a portfolio of FRAs.

As shown in Section 4.2, an FRA can be valued by calculating the present value of the difference between the interest that will be paid under the FRA and the interest that would be paid if the forward interest rate applied. This means that FRAs can be valued on the basis that forward interest rates are realized. Since a swap is a portfolio of forward interest rate agreements, a swap also can be valued by making the assumption that forward interest rates are realized. The procedure is:[6]

1. Calculate forward rates for each of the LIBOR rates that will determine swap cash flows.
2. Calculate swap cash flows on the assumption that the LIBOR rates will equal the forward rates.
3. Set the swap value equal to the present value of these cash flows.

Example 5.2

Consider again the situation in Example 5.1. The cash flows that will be exchanged in three months have already been determined. A rate of 8% will be exchanged for 10.2%. The value of the exchange to the financial institution is

$$0.5 \times 100 \times (0.08 - 0.102)e^{-0.1 \times 0.25} = -1.07$$

---

[6]Note that this procedure does not always work for nonstandard swaps. This point will be discussed in later chapters.

To calculate the value of the exchange in nine months, we must first calculate the forward rate corresponding to the period between three and nine months. Using equation (4.1), this is

$$\frac{0.75 \times 0.105 - 0.25 \times 0.10}{0.5} = 0.1075$$

or 10.75% with continuous compounding. Using equation (3.4), this becomes 11.044% with semiannual compounding. The value of the FRA corresponding to the exchange in nine months is therefore

$$0.5 \times 100 \times (0.08 - 0.11044)e^{-0.75 \times 0.105} = -1.41$$

To calculate the value of the exchange in 15 months, we must first calculate the forward rate corresponding to the period between nine and 15 months. Using equation (4.1), this is

$$\frac{1.25 \times 0.11 - 0.75 \times 0.105}{0.5} = 0.1175$$

or 11.75% with continuous compounding. Using equation (3.4), this becomes 12.102% with semiannual compounding. The value of the FRA corresponding to the exchange in 15 months is therefore

$$0.5 \times 100 \times (0.08 - 0.12102)e^{-1.25 \times 0.11} = -1.79$$

The total value of the swap is

$$-1.07 - 1.41 - 1.79 = -4.27$$

or −$4.27 million. This is in agreement with the calculation based on bond prices in Example 5.1.

At the time the swap is entered into, it is worth approximately zero. This means that the sum of the value of the FRAs underlying the swap is zero at this time. It does not mean that the value of each individual FRA is zero. In general, some will have positive values while others have negative values.

Consider again the forward contracts underlying the swap between the financial institution and company B in Figure 5.4. For the financial institution,

value of FRA < 0 when forward interest rate > 5.015%

value of forward contract = 0 when forward interest rate = 5.015%

value of forward contract > 0 when forward interest rate < 5.015%

Suppose that the term structure is upward sloping at the time the swap is negotiated. This means that the forward interest rates increase as the maturity of the FRA increases. Since the sum of the values of the FRAs is zero, this must mean that the forward interest rate is greater than 5.015% for the early payment dates

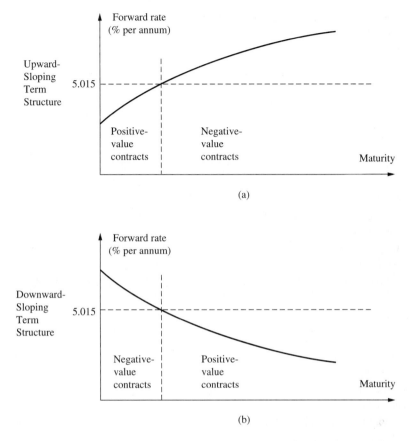

Figure 5.7   Value of forward contracts underlying financial institution's swap with Company B in Figure 5.4 when term structure is upward sloping and downward sloping.

and less than 5.015% for the later payment dates. The value to the financial institution of the FRAs corresponding to early payment dates are therefore positive, while those corresponding to later payment dates are negative. If the term structure is downward sloping at the time the swap is negotiated, the reverse is true. This situation is illustrated in Figure 5.7.

5.4 CURRENCY SWAPS

Another popular type of swap is known as a *currency swap.* In its simplest form, this involves exchanging principal and fixed-rate interest payments on a loan in one currency for principal and fixed-rate interest payments on an approximately equivalent loan in another currency.

Reasons for Currency Swaps

A currency swap can be used to transform a loan in one currency into a loan in another currency. To illustrate how a currency swap works, we suppose that company A and company B are offered the fixed five-year rates of interest in U.S. dollars and sterling shown in Table 5.5. This table shows that sterling interest rates are generally higher than U.S. interest rates. Also, company A is more creditworthy than company B since it is offered a more favorable rate of interest in both currencies. From the point of a swap trader the interesting aspect of Table 5.5 is that the differences between the rates offered to A and B in the two markets are not the same. Company B pays 2.0% more than company A in the U.S. dollar market and only 0.4% more than company A in the sterling market.

This situation is analogous to that in Table 5.4. Company A has a comparative advantage in the U.S. dollar market, while company B has a comparative advantage in the sterling market. In Section 5.2 we argued that comparative advantages are largely illusory when fixed and floating rates are compared. Here we are comparing the rates offered in two different currencies and it is more likely that the comparative advantages are genuine. The comparative advantage shown in Table 5.5 might arise from the situation where company A is an American company that is better known to U.S. investors and company B is a U.K. company that is better known to British investors. More likely, it arises from the tax environments in which A and B operate. (We suppose that the rates in Table 5.5 have been adjusted to reflect the differential impact of taxes.) We suppose that A wants to borrow sterling while B wants to borrow dollars. This creates a perfect situation for a currency swap. Company A and company B each borrow in the market where they have a comparative advantage; that is, company A borrows dollars while company B borrows sterling. They then use a currency swap to transform A's loan into a sterling loan and B's loan into a dollar loan.

As already mentioned, the difference between the dollar interest rates is 2.0% while the difference between the sterling interest rates is 0.4%. By analogy with the interest rate swap case, we expect the total gain to all parties to be 2.0% − 0.4% = 1.6% per annum.

There are many ways in which the swap can be organized. Figure 5.8 shows one possible arrangement. Company A borrows dollars while company B borrows

TABLE 5.5   Borrowing Rates
Motivating Currency Swap

Quoted rates have been adjusted to reflect tax advantages/disadvantages.

	Dollars	Sterling
Company A	8.00%	11.6%
Company B	10.00%	12.0%

Figure 5.8   Currency swap.

sterling. The effect of the swap is to transform the U.S. dollar interest rate of 8.0% per annum to a sterling interest rate of 11.0% per annum for company A. This makes company A 0.6% per annum better off than it would be if it went directly to sterling markets. Similarly, company B exchanges a sterling loan at 12% for a dollar loan at 9.4% and ends up 0.6% better off than it would be if it went directly to dollar markets. The financial intermediary gains 1.4% per annum on its dollar cash flows and loses 1.0% per annum on its sterling cash flows. Ignoring the difference between the two currencies it makes a net gain of 0.4% per annum. As predicted, the total gain to all parties is 1.6% per annum.

A currency swap agreement requires the principal to be specified in each of the two currencies. The principal amounts are usually exchanged at the beginning and at the end of the life of the swap. They are chosen so that they are approximately equal at the exchange rate at the beginning of the swap's life. In the example in Figure 5.8, the principal amounts might be $15 million and £10 million. Initially, the principal amounts flow in the opposite direction to the arrows in Figure 5.8. The interest payments during the life of the swap and the final principal payment flow in the same direction as the arrows. Thus, at the outset of the swap, company A pays $15 million and receives £10 million. Each year during the life of the swap contract, company A receives $1.20 million (= 8% of $15 million) and pays £1.10 million (= 11% of £10 million). At the end of the life of the swap, it pays a principal of £10 million and receives a principal of $15 million.

The reader may feel that the swap in Figure 5.8 is unsatisfactory because the financial institution is exposed to foreign exchange risk. Each year, it makes a gain of $210,000 (= 1.4% of $15 million) and a loss of £100,000 (= 1% of £10 million). However, the financial institution can avoid this risk by buying £100,000 per annum in the forward market for each year of the life of the swap. This will lock in a net gain in U.S. dollars. If we tried to redesign the swap so that the financial institution makes a 0.4% spread in dollars and a zero spread in sterling, we might come up with the arrangement in Figure 5.9 or Figure 5.10. In Figure 5.9, company B bears some foreign exchange risk because it pays 1.0%

Figure 5.9   Alternative arrangement for currency swap; company B bears some foreign exchange risk.

Figure 5.10   Alternative arrangement for currency swap; company A bears some foreign exchange risk.

per annum in sterling and 8.4% in dollars. In Figure 5.10, company A bears some foreign exchange risk because it receives 1.0% per annum in dollars and pays 12.0% in sterling. In general, it makes sense for the financial institution to bear the foreign exchange risk because it is in the best position to hedge it.

Like interest rate swaps, currency swaps are frequently warehoused by financial institutions. The financial institution then carefully monitors its exposures to various currencies so that it can hedge its risk.

5.5 VALUATION OF CURRENCY SWAPS

In the absence of default risk, a currency swap can be decomposed into a position in two bonds in a similar way to an interest rate swap. Consider the position of company B in Figure 5.8. It is long a sterling bond that pays interest at 12.0% per annum and short a dollar bond that pays interest at 9.4% per annum. In general, if V is the value of a swap such as the one in Figure 5.8 to the party paying U.S. dollar interest rates,

$$V = SB_F - B_D$$

where B_F is the value, measured in the foreign currency, of the foreign-denominated bond underlying the swap, B_D is the value of the U.S. dollar bond underlying the swap, and S is the spot exchange rate (expressed as number of units of domestic currency per unit of foreign currency). The value of a swap can therefore be determined from the term structure of interest rates in the domestic currency, the term structure of interest rates in the foreign currency, and the spot exchange rate.

Example 5.3

Suppose that the term structure of interest rates is flat in both Japan and the United States. The Japanese rate is 4% per annum and the U.S. rate is 9% per annum (both with continuous compounding). A financial institution has entered into a currency swap where it receives 5% per annum in yen and pays 8% per annum in dollars once a year. The principals in the two currencies are $10 million and 1,200 million yen. The swap will last for another three years and the current exchange rate is 110 yen = $1. In this case

$$B_D = 0.8e^{-0.09 \times 1} + 0.8e^{-0.09 \times 2} + 10.8e^{-0.09 \times 3}$$
$$= \$9.64 \text{ million}$$

$$B_F = 60e^{-0.04 \times 1} + 60e^{-0.04 \times 2} + 1,260e^{-0.04 \times 3}$$
$$= 1,230.55 \text{ million yen}$$

The value of the swap is

$$\frac{1,230.55}{110} - 9.64 = \$1.55 \text{ million}$$

If the financial institution had been paying yen and receiving dollars, the value of the swap would have been −$1.55 million.

Decomposition into Forward Contracts

An alternative decomposition of the currency swap is into a series of forward contracts. Suppose that in Figure 5.8 there is one payment date per year. On each payment date company B has agreed to exchange an inflow of £1.2 million (= 12% of £10 million) for an outflow of $1.41 million (= 9.4% of $15 million). In addition, at the final payment date, it has agreed to exchange a £10 million inflow for a $15 million outflow. Each of these exchanges represents a forward contract. Suppose that t_i $(1 \leq i \leq n)$ is the time of the ith settlement date, r_i $(1 \leq i \leq n)$ is the continuously compounded U.S. dollar interest rate applicable to a time period of length t_i, and F_i $(1 \leq i \leq n)$ is the forward exchange rate applicable to time t_i. In Chapter 3 we showed that the value of a long forward contract is in all circumstances the present value of the amount by which the forward price exceeds the delivery price. The value to company B of the forward contract corresponding to the exchange of interest payments at time t_i is, therefore,

$$(1.2F_i - 1.41)e^{-r_i t_i}$$

for $1 \leq i \leq n$. The value to company B of the forward contract corresponding to the exchange of principal payments at time t_n is

$$(10F_n - 15)e^{-r_n t_n}$$

This shows that the value of a currency swap can always be calculated from forward exchange rates and the term structure of domestic interest rates.

Example 5.4

Consider again the situation in Example 5.3. The current spot rate is 110 yen per dollar, or 0.009091 dollar per yen. Since the difference between the dollar and yen interest rates is 5% per annum, equation (3.14) can be used to give the one-year, two-year, and three-year forward exchange rates as

$$0.009091e^{0.05 \times 1} = 0.0096$$
$$0.009091e^{0.05 \times 2} = 0.0100$$
$$0.009091e^{0.05 \times 3} = 0.0106$$

respectively. The exchange of interest involves receiving 60 million yen and paying $0.8 million. The risk-free interest rate in dollars is 9% per annum. From equation (3.11) the

values of the forward contracts corresponding to the exchange of interest are therefore (in millions of dollars)

$$(60 \times 0.0096 - 0.8)e^{-0.09 \times 1} = -0.21$$

$$(60 \times 0.0101 - 0.8)e^{-0.09 \times 2} = -0.16$$

$$(60 \times 0.0106 - 0.8)e^{-0.09 \times 3} = -0.13$$

The final exchange of principal involves receiving 1,200 million yen and paying $10 million. From equation (3.11), the value of the forward contract corresponding to this is (in millions of dollars)

$$(1,200 \times 0.0106 - 10)e^{-0.09 \times 3} = 2.04$$

The total value of the swap is $2.04 - 0.13 - 0.16 - 0.21 = \$1.54$ million, which (allowing for rounding errors) is in agreement with the result of the calculations in Example 5.3.

Assume that the principal amounts in the two currencies are exactly equivalent at the start of a currency swap. At this time, the total value of the swap is zero. However, as in the case of interest rate swaps, this does not mean that each of the individual forward contracts underlying the swap has zero value. It can be shown that when interest rates in two currencies are different, the payer of the low-interest-rate currency is in the position where the forward contracts corresponding to the early exchanges of cash flows have positive values and the forward contract corresponding to final exchange of principals has a negative expected value. The payer of the high-interest-rate currency is likely to be in the opposite position; that is, the early exchanges of cash flows have negative values and the final exchange has a positive expected value.

For the payer of the low-interest-rate currency, there will be a tendency for the swap to have a negative value during most of its life. This is because the forward contracts corresponding to the early exchanges of payments have positive values, and once these exchanges have taken place, there is a tendency for the remaining forward contracts to have, in total, a negative value. For the payer of the high-interest-rate currency, the reverse is true. There is a tendency for the value of the swap to be positive during most of its life. These results are important when the credit risk in the swap is being evaluated.

5.6 OTHER SWAPS

A swap in its most general form is a contract that involves the exchange of cash flows according to a formula that depends on the value of one or more underlying variables. There is, therefore, no limit to the number of different types of swaps that can be invented.

In an interest-rate swap, a number of different floating reference rates can be used. Six-month LIBOR is the most common. Among the others used are: the three-month LIBOR, the one-month commercial paper rate, the Treasury bill rate,

and the municipal bond tax-exempt rate. Swaps can be constructed to swap one floating rate (say, LIBOR) for another floating rate (say, prime). This allows a financial institution to hedge an exposure arising from assets subject to one floating rate being financed by liabilities that are subject to a different floating rate.

The principal in a swap agreement can be varied throughout the term of the swap to meet the needs of a counterparty. In an *amortizing swap,* the principal reduces in a predetermined way. This might be designed to correspond to the amortization schedule on a loan. In a *step-up swap,* the principal increases in a predetermined way. This might be designed to correspond to the drawdowns on a loan agreement. *Deferred swaps* or *forward swaps* in which parties do not begin to exchange interest payments until some future date can also be arranged.

One popular swap is an agreement to exchange a fixed interest rate in one currency for a floating interest rate in another currency. As such, it is a combination of the "plain vanilla" interest rate swap and currency swap discussed in this chapter.

Swaps can be extendable or puttable. In an *extendable swap,* one party has the option to extend the life of the swap beyond the specified period. In a *puttable swap,* one party has the option to terminate the swap early. Options on swaps or *swaptions* are also available. An option on an interest-rate swap is in essence an option to exchange a fixed-rate bond for a floating-rate bond. Since the floating-rate bond is worth its face value at the start of a swap, swaptions can be considered as options on the value of the fixed-rate bond with a strike price equal to the face value. Swaptions are discussed further in Chapter 16.

A *constant maturity swap* (CMS swap) is an agreement to exchange a LIBOR rate for a swap rate. (An example is an agreement to exchange 6-month LIBOR for the 10-year swap rate every six months for the next five years.) A *constant maturity Treasury swap* (CMT swap) is a similar agreement to exchange a LIBOR rate for a particular Treasury rate (e.g., the 10-year Treasury rate.) An index amortizing rate swap (sometimes also called an *indexed principal swap*) is a swap where the principal reduces in a way dependent on the level of interest rates. (The lower the interest rate, the greater the reduction in the principal.) A *differential swap* or *diff swap* is a swap where a floating interest rate in the domestic currency is exchanged for a floating interest rate in a foreign currency, with both interest rates being applied to the same domestic principal.

An *equity swap* is an agreement to exchange the dividends and capital gains realized on an equity index for either a fixed or a floating rate of interest. Equity swaps can be used by portfolio managers to switch from an investment in bonds to an investment in equity, or vice versa. *Commodity swaps* are now becoming increasingly popular. A company that consumes 100,000 barrels of oil per year could agree to pay \$2 million each year for the next 10 years and to receive in return $100,000S$, where S is the current market price of oil per barrel. This would in effect lock in its oil cost at \$20 per barrel. Similarly, an oil producer might agree to the opposite exchange. This would have the effect of locking in the price it realized for its oil at \$20 per barrel.

5.7 CREDIT RISK

Contracts such as swaps that are private arrangements between two companies entail credit risks. Consider a financial institution that has entered into offsetting contracts with two companies, A and B (see Figure 5.4 or Figure 5.8). If neither party defaults, the financial institution remains fully hedged. A decline in the value of one contract will always be offset by an increase in the value of the other contract. However, there is a chance that one party will get into financial difficulties and default. The financial institution then still has to honor the contract it has with the other party.

Suppose that some time after the initiation of the contracts in Figure 5.4, the contract with company B has a positive value to the financial institution while the contract with company A has a negative value. If company B defaults, the financial institution is liable to lose the whole of the positive value it has in this contract. To maintain a hedged position, it would have to find a third party willing to take company B's position. To induce the third party to take the position, it would have to pay the third party an amount roughly equal to the value of its contract with B prior to the default.

A financial institution has credit risk exposure from a swap only when the value of the swap to the financial institution is positive. What happens when this value is negative and the counterparty gets into financial difficulties? In theory, the financial institution could realize a windfall gain since a default would lead to it getting rid of a liability. In practice, it is likely that the counterparty would choose to sell the contract to a third party or rearrange its affairs in some way so that its positive value in the contract is not lost. The most realistic assumption for the financial institution is therefore as follows. If the counterparty goes bankrupt, there will be a loss if the value of the swap to the financial institution is positive, and there will be no effect on the financial institution's position if the value of the swap to the financial institution is negative. This situation is summarized in Figure 5.11.

Sometimes a financial institution can predict in advance which of two offsetting contracts is likely to have a positive value. Consider the currency swap in Figure 5.8. Sterling interest rates are higher than U.S. interest rates. This means that as time passes the financial institution is likely to find that its swap with A has a negative value while its swap with B has a positive value. The creditworthiness of B is therefore far more important than the creditworthiness of A.

In general, the expected loss from a default on a currency swap is greater than the expected loss from a default on an interest rate swap. This is because, in the case of a currency swap, principal amounts in different currencies are exchanged. In the case of both types of swaps, the expected loss from a default is much greater than the expected loss from a default on a regular loan with approximately the same principal as the swap.

It is important to distinguish between the credit risk and market risk to a financial institution in any contract. As discussed earlier, the credit risk arises

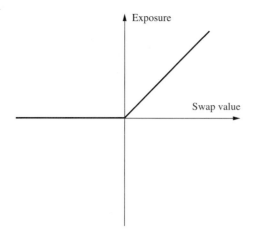

Figure 5.11   Credit exposure in a swap.

from the possibility of a default by the counterparty when the value of the contract to the financial institution is positive. The market risk arises from the possibility that market variables such as interest rates and exchange rates will move in such a way that the value of a contract to the financial institution becomes negative. Market risks can be hedged by entering into offsetting contracts; credit risks cannot be hedged. Credit risk issues are discussed further in Chapter 20. Market risk is discussed further in Chapter 14.

5.8 SUMMARY

The two most common types of swaps are interest rate swaps and currency swaps. In an interest rate swap, one party agrees to pay the other party interest at a fixed rate on a notional principal for a number of years. In return, it receives interest at a floating rate on the same notional principal for the same period of time. In a currency swap, one party agrees to pay interest on a principal amount in one currency. In return, it receives interest on a principal amount in another currency.

Principal amounts are not usually exchanged in an interest rate swap. In a currency swap, principal amounts are usually exchanged at both the beginning and the end of the life of the swap. For a party paying interest in the foreign currency, the foreign principal is received and the domestic principal is paid at the beginning of the life of the swap. At the end of the life of the swap, the foreign principal is paid and the domestic principal is received.

An interest rate swap can be used to transform a floating-rate loan into a fixed-rate loan, or vice versa. A currency swap can be used to transform a loan in one currency into a loan in another currency. In essence, a swap is a long position in one bond combined with a short position in another bond. Alternatively, it can be considered as a portfolio of forward contracts.

Swaps are usually arranged by financial institutions. Ideally, to eliminate interest rate or exchange rate risk, a financial institution would like to enter into offsetting swap agreements with two parties at the same time. In practice, financial institutions frequently warehouse swaps. This means that they enter into a swap agreement with one party and then hedge their risk on a day-to-day basis while they attempt to find a party wanting to take the opposite position.

When a financial institution enters into a pair of offsetting swaps with different counterparties, it is exposed to credit risk. If one of the counterparties defaults when the financial institution has positive value in its swap with that counterparty, the financial institution loses money since it still has to honor its swap agreement with the other counterparty.

SUGGESTIONS FOR FURTHER READING

Bicksler, J., and A. H. Chen, "An Economic Analysis of Interest Rate Swaps," *Journal of Finance,* 41, 3 (1986), 645–55.

Hull, J., "Assessing Credit Risk in a Financial Institution's Off-Balance Sheet Commitments," *Journal of Financial and Quantitative Analysis,* 24 (December 1989), 489–502.

Hull J., and A. White, "The Impact of Default Risk on the Prices of Options and Other Derivative Securities," *Journal of Banking and Finance,* 19 (1995), 299–322.

International Swaps and Derivatives Association, "Code of Standard Working, Assumptions and Provisions for Swaps." New York.

Layard-Liesching, R., "Swap Fever," *Euromoney,* Supplement (January 1986), 108–13.

Marshall, J. F., and K. R. Kapner, *Understanding Swap Finance.* Cincinnati, Ohio: South-Western, 1990.

Smith, C. W., C. W. Smithson, and L. M. Wakeman, "The Evolving Market for Swaps," *Midland Corporate Finance Journal,* 3 (Winter 1986), 20–32.

Turnbull, S. M., "Swaps: A Zero Sum Game," *Financial Management,* 16 (Spring 1987), 15–21.

Wall, L. D., and J. J. Pringle, "Alternative Explanations of Interest Rate Swaps: A Theoretical and Empirical Analysis," *Financial Management,* 18, 2 (Summer 1989), 59–73.

QUESTIONS AND PROBLEMS

5.1. Companies A and B have been offered the following rates per annum on a $20 million five-year loan:

	Fixed Rate	Floating Rate
Company A	12.0%	LIBOR + 0.1%
Company B	13.4%	LIBOR + 0.6%

Company A requires a floating-rate loan; company B requires a fixed-rate loan. Design a swap that will net a bank, acting as intermediary, 0.1% per annum and appear to be equally attractive to both companies.

5.2. Company X wishes to borrow U.S. dollars at a fixed rate of interest. Company Y wishes to borrow Japanese yen at a fixed rate of interest. The amounts required by the two companies are roughly the same at the current exchange rate. The companies have been quoted the following interest rates, which have been adjusted to reflect the tax situations of the two companies:

	Yen	Dollars
Company X	5.0%	9.6%
Company Y	6.5%	10.0%

Design a swap that will net a bank, acting as intermediary, 50 basis points per annum. Make the swap equally attractive to the two companies and ensure that all foreign exchange risk is assumed by the bank.

5.3. A $100 million interest rate swap has a remaining life of 10 months. Under the terms of the swap, six-month LIBOR is exchanged for 12% per annum (compounded semi-annually). The average of the bid and ask rate being exchanged for six-month LIBOR in swaps of all maturities is currently 10% per annum with continuous compounding. The six-month LIBOR rate was 9.6% per annum two months ago. What is the current value of the swap to the party paying floating? What is its value to the party paying fixed?

5.4. What is meant by *warehousing swaps?*

5.5. A currency swap has a remaining life of 15 months. It involves exchanging interest at 14% on £20 million for interest at 10% on $30 million once a year. The term structure of interest rates in both the United Kingdom and the United States is currently flat and if the swap were negotiated today, the interest rates exchanged would be 8% in dollars and 11% in sterling. All interest rates are quoted with annual compounding. The current exchange rate is 1.6500. What is the value of the swap to the party paying sterling? What is the value of the swap to the party paying dollars?

5.6. Explain the difference between the credit risk and the market risk in a financial contract. Which of the risks can be hedged?

5.7. Explain why a bank is subject to credit risk when it enters into two offsetting swap contracts.

5.8. Companies X and Y have been offered the following rates per annum on a $5 million investments

	Fixed Rate	Floating Rate
Company X	8.0%	LIBOR
Company Y	8.8%	LIBOR

Company X requires a fixed-rate investment; company Y requires a floating-rate investment. Design a swap that will net a bank, acting as intermediary, 0.2% per annum and which will appear to be equally attractive to X and Y.

5.9. Company A, a British manufacturer, wishes to borrow U.S. dollars at a fixed rate of interest. Company B, a U.S. multinational, wishes to borrow sterling at a fixed rate of interest. They have been quoted the following rates per annum (adjusted for tax effects):

	Sterling	Dollars
Company A	11.0%	7.0%
Company B	10.6%	6.2%

Design a swap that will net a bank, acting as intermediary, 10 basis points per annum and which will produce a gain of 15 basis points per annum for each of the two companies.

5.10. Under the terms of an interest rate swap, a financial institution has agreed to pay 10% per annum and to receive three-month LIBOR in return on a notional principal of $100 million with payments being exchanged every three months. The swap has a remaining life of 14 months. The average of the bid and ask fixed rate currently being swapped for three-month LIBOR is 12% per annum for all maturities. The three-month LIBOR rate one month ago was 11.8% per annum. All rates are compounded quarterly. What is the value of the swap?

5.11. Suppose that the term structure of interest rates is flat in the United States and Germany. The dollar interest rate is 11% per annum, while the mark interest rate is 8% per annum. The current exchange rate is 2.1 marks = $1. Under the terms of a swap agreement, a financial institution pays 5% per annum in marks and receives 10% per annum in dollars. The principals in the two currencies are $10 million and 20 million marks. Payments are exchanged every year with one exchange having just taken place. The swap will last two more years. What is the value of the swap to the financial institution? Assume that all interest rates are continuously compounded.

5.12. A financial institution has entered into an interest rate swap with company X. Under the terms of the swap, it receives 10% per annum and pays six-month LIBOR on a principal of $10 million for five years. Payments are made every six months. Suppose that company X defaults on the sixth payment date (end of year 3) when the interest rate (with semiannual compounding) is 8% per annum for all maturities. What is the loss to the financial institution? Assume that six-month LIBOR was 9% per annum halfway through year 3.

5.13. A financial institution has entered into a 10-year currency swap with company Y. Under the terms of the swap, it receives interest at 3% per annum in Swiss francs and pays interest at 8% per annum in U.S. dollars. Interest payments are exchanged once a year. The principal amounts are $7 million and 10 million francs. Suppose that company Y defaults at the end of year 6 when the exchange rate is $0.80 per

franc. What is the cost to the financial institution? Assume that at the end of year 6, the interest rate is 3% per annum in Swiss francs and 8% per annum in U.S. dollars for all maturities. All interest rates are quoted with annual compounding.

5.14. Companies A and B face the following interest rates:

	A	B
U.S. dollars (floating rate)	LIBOR + 0.5%	LIBOR + 1.0%
German marks (fixed rate)	5.0%	6.5%

Assume that A wants to borrow dollars at a floating rate of interest and B wants to borrow marks at a fixed rate of interest. A financial institution is planning to arrange a swap and requires a 50-basis-point spread. If the swap is to appear to be equally attractive to A and B, what rates of interest will A and B end up paying?

5.15. Company X is based in the United Kingdom and would like to borrow U.S. $50 million at a fixed rate of interest for five years in U.S. funds. As the company is not well known in the United States, this has proved to be impossible. However, the company has been quoted 12% per annum on fixed-rate five-year sterling funds. Company Y is based in the United States and would like to borrow the equivalent of U.S. $50 million in sterling funds for five years at a fixed rate of interest. It has been unable to get a quote, but has been offered U.S.$ funds at 10.5% per annum. Five-year government bonds currently yield 9.5% per annum in the United States and 10.5% in the United Kingdom. Suggest an appropriate currency swap that will net the financial intermediary 0.5% per annum.

5.16. After it hedges its foreign exchange risk using forward contracts, is the financial institution's average spread in Figure 5.8 likely to be greater than or less than 40 basis points? Explain your answer.

5.17. How can a deferred swap be created from two other swaps?

5.18. "Companies with high credit risks are the ones that cannot access fixed-rate markets directly. They are the companies that are most likely to be paying fixed and receiving floating in an interest rate swap." Assume that this is true. Do you think it increases or decreases the risk of a financial institution's swap portfolio? Assume that companies are most likely to default when interest rates are high.

5.19. How can a financial institution that warehouses interest rate swaps monitor its exposure to interest rate changes?

5.20. Why is the expected loss from a default on a swap less than the expected loss from the default on a loan with the same principal?

5.21. A bank finds that its assets are not matched with its liabilities. It is taking floating-rate deposits and making fixed-rate loans. How can swaps be used to offset the risk?

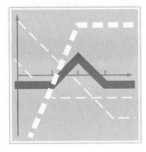

Chapter 6
Options Markets

Options were introduced in Chapter 1. It will be recalled that a call option is the right to buy an asset for a certain price; a put option is the right to sell an asset for a certain price. A European option can be exercised only at the end of its life; an American option can be exercised at any time during its life. In this chapter we explain the way in which options markets are organized, the terminology used, how the contracts are traded, how margin requirements are set, and so on. Options are fundamentally different from the forward, futures, and swap contracts discussed in the last few chapters. An option gives the holder of the option the right to do something. The holder does not have to exercise this right. By contrast, in a forward, futures, or swap contract, the two parties have entered into a binding commitment.

6.1 EXCHANGE-TRADED OPTIONS

Options trade on many different exchanges throughout the world. The underlying assets include stocks, foreign currencies, stock indices, and many different futures contracts.

Stock Options

The exchanges trading stock options in the United States are the Chicago Board Options Exchange (CBOE), the Philadelphia Exchange (PHLX), the American Stock Exchange (AMEX), the Pacific Stock Exchange (PSE), and the New York Stock Exchange (NYSE). Options trade on over 500 different stocks. Among the most actively traded options contracts are those on IBM, Kodak, and General Motors. One contract gives the holder the right to buy or sell 100 shares at the specified strike price. This is convenient since the shares themselves are normally traded in lots of 100.

Foreign Currency Options

The major exchange for trading foreign currency options is the Philadelphia Exchange. It offers both European and American contracts on the Australian

dollar, British pound, Canadian dollar, deutschemark, French franc, Japanese yen, and Swiss franc. The size of one contract depends on the currency. For example, in the case of the British pound, one contract gives the holder the right to buy or sell £31,250; in the case of the Japanese yen, one contract gives the holder the right to buy or sell 6.25 million yen.

Index Options

Many different index options trade in the United States. The two most popular are those on the S&P 100 and S&P 500 traded on the CBOE. The S&P 500 option is European, whereas the S&P 100 option is American. One contract is to buy or sell 100 times the index at the specified strike price. Settlement is in cash rather than by delivering the portfolio underlying the index. Consider, for example, one call contract on the S&P 100 with a strike price of 280. If it is exercised when the value of the index is 292, the writer of the contract pays the holder $(292 - 280) \times 100 = \$1,200$. This cash payment is based on the index value at the end of the day on which exercise instructions are issued. Not surprisingly, investors usually wait until the end of a day before issuing these instructions.

Futures Options

In a futures option (or option on futures), the underlying asset is a futures contract. The futures contract normally matures shortly after the expiration of the option. Futures options are now available for most of the assets on which futures contracts are traded. When the holder of a call option exercises, he or she acquires from the writer a long position in the underlying futures contract plus a cash amount equal to the excess of the futures price over the strike price. When the holder of a put option exercises, he or she acquires a short position in the underlying futures contract plus a cash amount equal to the excess of the strike price over the futures price. In both cases, the futures contracts have zero value and can be closed out immediately. The payoff from a futures option is therefore the same as the payoff from a stock option with the stock price replaced by the futures price. The most actively traded futures option is the Treasury bond futures option traded on the Chicago Board of Trade. The contracts on corn, soybeans, crude oil, live cattle, gold, Eurodollars, and some currencies are also popular.

6.2 OVER-THE-COUNTER OPTIONS

Not all options are traded on exchanges. Over-the-counter options markets, where financial institutions and corporations trade directly with each other, are very popular. Trading is particularly active in over-the-counter options on foreign exchange and interest rates.

The main advantage of an over-the-counter option is that it can be tailored by a financial institution to meet the needs of a corporate client. The strike price

and maturity do not have to correspond to those of exchange-traded options. Also, nonstandard features can be incorporated into the design of the option. Two examples of options involving nonstandard features are Bermudan and Asian options. A *Bermudan option* is exercisable only on certain specified days during its life. In an *Asian* option, the payoff is defined in terms of the average value of the underlying asset during a certain time period rather than in terms of its final value. In Chapter 18 we give many other examples of nonstandard over-the-counter options.

6.3 SPECIFICATION OF STOCK OPTIONS

In the rest of this chapter we focus on exchange-traded stock options. The contract specifications and trading of index options, currency options, and futures options are discussed further in Chapter 12.

A stock option contract is an American-style option contract to buy or sell 100 shares of the stock. Details of the contract, such as the expiration date, the strike price, what happens when dividends are declared, how large a position investors can hold, and so on, are specified by the exchange.

Expiration Dates

One of the items used to describe a stock option is the month in which the expiration date occurs. Thus, a January call on IBM is a call option on IBM with an expiration date in January. The precise expiration date is 10:59 p.m. Central Time on the Saturday immediately following the third Friday of the expiration month. The last day on which options trade is the third Friday of the expiration month. An investor with a long position in an option normally has until 4:30 p.m. Central Time on that Friday to instruct his or her broker to exercise the option. The broker then has until 10:59 p.m. the next day to complete the paperwork notifying the exchange that the exercise is to take place.

Stock options are on a January, February, or March cycle. The January cycle consists of the months of January, April, July, and October. The February cycle consists of the months of February, May, August, and November. The March cycle consists of the months of March, June, September, and December. If the expiration date for the current month has not yet been reached, options trade with expiration dates in the current month, the following month, and the next two months in its cycle. If the expiration date of the current month has passed, options trade with expiration dates in the next month, the next-but-one month, and the next two months of the expiration cycle. For example, IBM is on a January cycle. At the beginning of January, options are traded with expiration dates in January, February, April, and July; at the end of January, they are traded with expiration dates in February, March, April, and July; at the beginning of May, they are traded with expiration dates in May, June, July, and October; and so on. When one option reaches expiration, trading in another is started.

Longer-dated stock options known as *long-term equity anticipation securities* or LEAPS also trade on exchanges. These have January expiration dates up to two years into the future. In May 1995, options on a range of stocks traded with expiration dates of January 1996 and January 1997.

Strike Prices

The exchange chooses the strike prices at which options can be written. For stock options, strike prices are normally spaced $2\frac{1}{2}$, \$5, or \$10 apart. (An exception occurs when there has been a stock split or a stock dividend, as will be described shortly.) The usual rule followed by exchanges is to use a $2\frac{1}{2}$ spacing for strike prices when the stock price is less than \$25, a \$5 spacing when it is between \$25 and \$200, and a \$10 spacing when it is greater than \$200. For example, when the price of a stock is 12, we might expect to see options trading with strike prices of 10, $12\frac{1}{2}$, and 15; when it is 100, we might expect to see strike prices of 90, 95, 100, 105, and 110.

When a new expiration date is introduced, the two strike prices closest to the current stock price are usually selected by the exchange. If one of these is very close to the existing stock price, the third strike price closest to the current stock price may also be selected. If the stock price moves outside the range defined by the highest and lowest strike price, trading is usually introduced in an option with a new strike price. To illustrate these rules, suppose that the stock price is \$53 when trading in the October options starts. Call and put options would first be offered with strike prices of 50 and 55. If the stock price rose above \$55, a strike price of 60 would be offered; if it fell below \$50, a strike price of 45 would be offered; and so on.

Terminology

For any given asset at any given time, there may be many different option contracts trading. Consider a stock where there are four expiration dates and five strike prices. If call and put options trade with every expiration date and every strike price, there are a total of 40 different contracts. All options of the same type (calls or puts) are referred to as an *option class*. For example, IBM calls are one class while IBM puts are another class. An *option series* consists of all the options of a given class with the same expiration date and strike price. In other words, an option series refers to a particular contract that is traded. The IBM 110 January calls are an option series.

Options are referred to as *in the money, at the money,* or *out of the money.* An in-the-money option is one that would lead to a positive cash flow to the holder if it were exercised immediately. Similarly, an at-the-money option would lead to zero cash flow if it were exercised immediately, and an out-of-the-money option would lead to a negative cash flow if it were exercised immediately. If S is the stock price and X is the strike price, a call option is in the money when $S > X$, at the money when $S = X$, and out of the money when $S < X$. A put option is in

the money when $S < X$, at the money when $S = X$, and out of the money when $S > X$. Clearly, an option will be exercised only if it is in the money. In the absence of transactions costs, an in-the-money option will always be exercised on the expiration date if it has not been exercised previously.

The *intrinsic value* of an option is defined as the maximum of zero and the value it would have if it were exercised immediately. For a call option, the intrinsic value is therefore max $(S-X, 0)$. For a put option, it is max $(X-S, 0)$. An in-the-money American option must be worth at least as much as its intrinsic value since the holder can realize a positive intrinsic value by exercising immediately. Often it is optimal for the holder of an in-the-money American option to wait rather than exercise immediately. The option is then said to have *time value*. The total value of an option can be thought of as the sum of its intrinsic value and its time value.

Flex Options

Some exchanges now offer *flex options*. These are options where the traders on the floor of the exchange agree to nonstandard terms. These nonstandard terms might involve a strike price or an expiration date that is different from those usually offered by the exchange. Flex options are an attempt by the exchanges to regain business from the over-the-counter markets.

Dividends and Stock Splits

The early over-the-counter options were dividend protected. If a company declared a cash dividend, the strike price for options on the company's stock was reduced on the ex-dividend day by the amount of the dividend. Now, both exchange-traded and over-the-counter options are not generally adjusted for cash dividends. As we will see in Chapter 11, this has significant implications for the way in which options are valued.

Exchange-traded options are adjusted for stock splits. A stock split occurs when the existing shares are "split" into more shares. For example, in a 3-for-1 stock split, three new shares are issued to replace each existing share. Since a stock split does not change the assets or the earning ability of a company, we should not expect it to have any effect on the wealth of the company's shareholders. All else being equal, the 3-for-1 stock split just referred to should cause the stock price to go down to one-third of its previous value. In general, an n-for-m stock split should cause the stock price to go down to m/n of its previous value. The terms of option contracts are adjusted to reflect expected changes in a stock price arising from a stock split. After an n-for-m stock split, the exercise price is reduced to m/n of its previous value and the number of shares covered by one contract is increased to n/m of its previous value. If the stock price reduces in the way expected, the positions of both the writer and the purchaser of a contract remain unchanged.

Example 6.1

Consider a call option to buy 100 shares of a company for $30 per share. Suppose that the company makes a 2-for-1 stock split. The terms of the option contract are then changed so that it gives the holder the right to purchase 200 shares for $15 per share.

Stock options are adjusted for stock dividends. A stock dividend involves a company issuing more shares to its existing shareholders. For example, a 20% stock dividend means that investors receive one new share for each five already owned. Like a stock split, a stock dividend has no effect on either the assets or the earning power of a company. The stock price can be expected to go down as a result of a stock dividend. The 20% stock dividend referred to is essentially the same as a 6-for-5 stock split. All else being equal, it should cause the stock price to decline to five-sixths of its previous value. The terms of an option are adjusted to reflect the expected price decline arising from a stock dividend in the same way as they are for that arising from a stock split.

Example 6.2

Consider a put option to sell 100 shares of a company for $15 per share. Suppose that the company declares a 25% stock dividend. This is equivalent to a 5-for-4 stock split. The terms of the option contract are changed so that it gives the holder the right to sell 125 shares for $12.

Adjustments are also made for rights issues. A rights issue gives existing shareholders the right to buy more shares at a specified price. The basic procedure is to calculate the theoretical price of the rights and then to reduce the strike price by this amount. As pointed out by Brown, this procedure leaves the option holder slightly worse off than he or she was before the issue.[1]

Position Limits and Exercise Limits

The exchange specifies a *position limit* for each stock upon which options are traded. This defines the maximum number of option contracts that an investor can hold on one side of the market. For this purpose, long calls and short puts are considered to be on the same side of the market. Also, short calls and long puts are considered to be on the same side of the market. The *exercise limit* equals the position limit. It defines the maximum number of contracts that can be exercised by any individual (or group of individuals acting together) in any period of five consecutive business days. For Digital Equipment, the position limit/exercise limit is at the time of writing 8,000 contracts.

Position limits and exercise limits are designed to prevent the market from being unduly influenced by the activities of an individual investor or group of investors. However, whether they are really necessary is a controversial issue.

---

[1] See R. L. Brown, "Adjusting Option Contracts to Reflect Capitalization Changes," *Journal of Business Finance and Accounting,* 16 (1989), 247–54.

TABLE 6.1 Stock Option Quotations from the *Wall Street Journal* on May 12, 1995

Option/Strike		Exp.	–Call– Vol.	–Call– Last	–Put– Vol.	–Put– Last
ADC Tel	30	Aug	40	3 1/4	...	...
ADT	10	Jun	75	1 11/16	...	...
AGCO	30	May	93	6	...	...
36 3/8	35	May	35	1 3/16	...	...
AL Phr	17 1/2	Dec	...	...	35	1 11/16
...	17 1/2	Dec	...	...	35	1 11/16
A M R	65	May	220	3 1/4	90	1/4
68 1/4	65	Jun	...	...	234	1 1/8
68 1/4	70	May	147	1/2	30	2 5/16
68 1/4	70	Jun	172	1 1/2	...	...
A S A	40	Jun	10	3 3/8	168	5/16
42 7/8	45	May	180	1/16	484	2 5/8
42 7/8	45	Jun	551	7/16	65	2 15/16
42 7/8	45	Aug	33	1 5/16	15	3 1/4
42 7/8	45	Nov	2	2 1/8	40	3 5/8
42 7/8	55	Aug	32	1/8	...	...
AST Rs	17 1/2	May	110	1/4	100	3/8
17 1/4	17 1/2	Jun	...	...	100	1 1/8
AT&T	50	May	38	1 3/8	3	1/8
51 1/2	50	Jul	15	2 1/4	104	5/8
51 1/2	50	Oct	10	3 3/8	62	1 1/4
51 1/2	55	Jul	225	3/8	5	3 3/4
51 1/2	55	Oct	189	1	...	...
AbbeyH	35	May	50	15/16	...	...
35 1/4	35	Aug	100	3 1/8	...	...
Abbt L	35	May	52	5 1/2	...	...
40 1/2	35	Aug	32	6	...	...
40 1/2	40	May	199	15/16	...	...
40 1/2	40	Jun	80	1 1/2	25	1
40 1/2	40	Aug	119	2	31	1 3/16
Aclaim	12 1/2	Jun	50	3 7/8	...	...
16 1/4	12 1/2	Jul	100	4 1/4	...	...
16 1/4	15	May	511	1 1/2	5	3/16
16 1/4	15	Jun	20	1 15/16	50	5/8
16 1/4	17 1/2	Jun	285	5/8	...	...
16 1/4	17 1/2	Jul	241	7/8	510	2 5/8
Actava	7 1/2	Jun	100	1 9/16	...	...
Actel	12 1/2	May	150	3/16	...	...
Adaptc	25	Jul	10	6 1/4	1000	15/16
30 5/8	30	May	162	1 3/16	10	7/8
30 5/8	30	Jun	5	2 3/16	330	1 3/4
30 5/8	30	Jul	...	...	345	2 5/8
30 5/8	35	Jul	101	1 1/16	...	...
AdobeS	50	Jun	225	6	...	...
55 1/2	55	May	303	1 5/8	...	...
A M D	25	Oct	...	...	258	3/8
37 1/8	30	Jul	64	7 3/4	55	5/16
37 1/8	35	May	564	2 5/8	732	3/16
37 1/8	35	Jun	322	3 3/8	52	15/16
37 1/8	35	Jul	415	4	429	1 3/8
37 1/8	35	Oct	72	5 1/4	20	2 3/8
37 1/8	40	May	249	1/4	435	3 1/4
37 1/8	40	Jun	292	7/8	21	3 1/8
37 1/8	40	Jul	691	1 3/4	...	...
37 1/8	40	Oct	86	2 3/4	...	...
AdvTis	7 1/2	Sep	...	...	120	1 11/16
Aetna	60	May	45	3/4	...	...
59 3/4	60	Jul	50	2 1/4	...	...
Agnico	12 1/2	Nov	...	...	76	1 3/4
AirPd	45	Jun	35	8	...	...
Airgas	22 1/2	Jul	160	2 13/16	...	...
24 1/2	25	May	43	3/16	...	...
Airtch	22 1/2	Jul	60	4	...	...
AlaskA	15	May	1500	1 3/8	...	...
16 1/2	15	Jun	1500	1 3/4	...	...
Alcan	30	Sep	82	1 1/4	...	...
Alcatl	20	Dec	50	5/8	...	...
Aldila	7 1/2	Jun	80	1/8	...	...
AlnSem	40	May	38	2 1/4	...	...
AldSgnl	40	Jun	125	1 3/4	...	...
40 3/4	45	Dec	105	1 3/16	50	4 1/2
Alltel	22 1/2	Oct	...	...	35	3/4
Altera	80	May	94	5 1/2	...	...
85 1/4	80	Jun	210	8 1/2	65	3
85 1/4	85	May	84	2 5/16	30	2 1/4
85 1/4	85	Jun	105	5 1/4	1	4 3/4
85 1/4	90	Jun	108	3 1/4	...	...
Alcoa	40	May	36	4 5/8	...	...
44 1/2	40	Jun	60	5 1/8	...	...
44 1/2	40	Jul	2	5 1/4	50	1/2
44 1/2	45	May	205	7/16	...	...
44 1/2	45	Jun	130	1 1/4	...	...

Option/Strike		Exp.	–Call– Vol.	–Call– Last	–Put– Vol.	–Put– Last
22 7/8	22 1/2	Oct	272	2 1/2	27	1 3/8
22 7/8	25	May	149	1/16	26	2
22 7/8	25	Jun	580	1/4	3	2
22 7/8	25	Jul	579	5/8	20	2 1/2
22 7/8	25	Oct	39	1 5/16	22	2 3/4
22 7/8	30	Oct	49	3/8	27	7 1/8
BattlM	10	May	35	3/16	...	...
9 5/8	10	Jun	307	1/2	...	...
9 5/8	10	Jul	117	5/8	94	3/4
9 5/8	10	Oct	200	1 1/8	31	1
9 5/8	12 1/2	Jun	100	1/16	...	...
BausLm	40	May	145	3/8	...	...
39 3/4	40	Jun	...	...	50	1 9/16
Baxter	30	Aug	100	5 1/8	...	...
35 1/8	30	Nov	100	5 3/8	...	...
BayNtw	35	May	67	1 5/8	115	7/8
35 1/4	35	Jun	274	2 1/2	33	1 3/4
35 1/4	40	Jun	51	13/16	...	...
BearSt o	21 3/8	Oct	100	1 1/4	...	...
BedBth	22 1/2	Jun	35	1 3/8	...	...
BellAtl	55	May	269	1 3/8	...	...
BellSo	65	Oct	42	1 11/16	...	...
Benfcl	45	Jun	298	1 1/4	...	...
BergBr	25	May	184	7/16	...	...
23 5/8	30	May	50	1/16	...	...
23 5/8	30	Jun	53	1/4	...	...
BestBuy	25	May	89	3/4	107	1/2
25 1/4	25	Jun	146	1 9/16	21	1 7/16
25 1/4	30	Jun	53	3/16	61	5 1/4
25 1/4	30	Sep	140	1 3/16	4	6
Beth S	15	May	88	3/8	8	3/8
14 7/8	15	Jun	40	3/4	...	...
14 7/8	15	Jul	88	1 1/4	...	...
14 7/8	17 1/2	Jul	45	5/16	3	2 13/16
BetzLb	45	Jul	200	1/2	...	...
Bevrly	12 1/2	Jun	...	...	43	5/16
Biogen	40	May	200	7/8	25	1 3/8
39 1/4	40	Jun	66	1 3/4	40	2 3/8
39 1/4	45	Jul	42	1 1/4	5	6 1/2
Biomet	17 1/2	Jul	70	7/16	...	...
Blk Dk	30	Jun	...	...	183	1 1/4
Block	45	Jun	65	1/2	...	...
40 3/4	45	Jul	33	1 1/4	13	4
40 3/4	45	Oct	34	1 9/16	...	...
BoatBn	35	Oct	35	13/16	...	...
Boeing	50	May	108	4 1/2	19	1/16
54 3/8	55	Aug	1233	2 1/2	33	2 1/4
54 3/8	60	Jun	60	1/4	...	...
54 3/8	60	Nov	33	1 5/16	...	...
Bois C	40	Aug	155	5/16	...	...
Bombay	5	Sep	...	...	35	1/8
BordCh	12 1/2	Aug	300	3 5/8	...	...
16 1/4	15 3/4	Nov	112	1 5/8	...	...
Borlnd	10	Jul	40	5/8	...	...
BostCh	17 1/2	May	71	4 1/8	15	1/16
22 3/4	17 1/2	Jun	257	4	40	1/4
22 3/4	20	May	538	2 5/8	10	1/16
22 3/4	20	Jun	51	2 5/8	37	9/16
22 3/4	20	Jul	92	2 13/16	1570	1 1/4
22 3/4	20	Oct	25	3 5/8	37	2 1/16
22 3/4	22 1/2	May	237	5/8	20	15/16
22 3/4	22 1/2	Jun	161	1	10	1 7/8
22 3/4	22 1/2	Jul	69	1 1/2	1500	2 1/2
22 3/4	22 1/2	Oct	60	2 3/16	120	3 1/2
BostSc	22 1/2	Nov	190	7 1/4	...	...
28	25	Jun	40	3 1/2	...	...
Bowatr	30	Jun	40	8 5/8	...	...
38 5/8	40	Dec	40	3	...	...
Bradles	7 1/2	Nov	...	...	50	7/16
BredTc	20	Jun	50	1 3/8	...	...
20	20	Jul	28	1 1/2	40	1 3/8
Brnker	17 1/2	Jul	60	7/8	3	1 3/16
BrMSq	60	Sep	45	6 3/4	5	1/2
65 3/4	60	Dec	...	...	45	5/8
65 3/4	70	Sep	82	5/8	...	...
65 3/4	70	Dec	41	1 1/4	1	4 1/2
BrtPet	80	Jul	42	8	...	...
BrdbdT	20	Nov	35	5 5/8	...	...
BrodSf	45	Jun	10	5 3/8	143	2
47 7/8	50	May	45	3/4	127	3
47 7/8	50	Jun	16	2 11/16	113	4 1/2
Brktre	15	Jun	72	3	...	...

Option/Strike		Exp.	–Call– Vol.	–Call– Last	–Put– Vol.	–Put– Last
60 7/8	60	Aug	245	3 1/4	89	1 1/2
60 7/8	60	Nov	62	4 1/4	1	2 3/8
60 7/8	65	Aug	93	3/4	...	...
60 7/8	65	Nov	127	1 3/4	...	...
CCFems	20	Jun	281	3/4	...	...
CoeurM	17 1/2	May	50	2	10	1/16
19 1/4	20	May	70	3/16	15	3/4
19 1/4	20	Aug	35	1 5/8	...	...
ColgPl	70	Jun	...	...	130	5/8
ColDta	15	Jun	101	4 1/4	...	...
18 7/8	20	May	38	3/8	93	1 3/16
18 7/8	20	Jun	54	1 1/16	25	2 7/16
ColuGs	30	Jun	50	5/8	...	...
ColHsp	40	May	96	1 1/2	25	1/8
41 3/8	40	Jun	60	2 3/4	...	...
41 3/8	40	Aug	351	3 1/4	110	1 3/8
41 3/8	45	May	...	...	50	3 3/4
Comcst	15	Oct	51	2	...	...
Cmc sp	15	Oct	26	2 1/16	59	1 1/8
16 1/2	17 1/2	Jul	160	3/4	...	...
16 1/2	20	Jul	150	3/16	...	...
Comeric	25	May	40	4 1/8	...	...
CmpUSA	20	May	238	5 5/8	...	...
25 1/2	22 1/2	May	102	2 5/8	6	1/16
25 1/2	22 1/2	Aug	50	4 1/4	205	1 1/8
25 1/2	25	May	135	11/16	16	3/8
25 1/2	25	Jun	51	1 9/16	15	1 3/16
25 1/2	30	Nov	43	1 11/16	...	...
ChileT	70	May	...	...	60	1/8
77 5/8	75	May	50	3	31	9/16
77 5/8	75	Jun	138	5 7/8	238	2
77 5/8	80	May	32	1 3/16	10	3 3/8
77 5/8	80	Jun	305	3 1/8	...	...
Compaq	30	May	4073	8 1/4	...	...
38	30	Jul	3980	8 3/4	76	1/4
38	35	May	236	3 1/4	179	1/8
38	35	Jun	66	3 7/8	32	5/8
38	35	Jul	223	4 1/2	167	1 1/16
38	35	Oct	257	6	166	2
38	40	May	654	1/4	200	2 1/4
38	40	Jun	540	15/16	19	2 3/4
38	40	Jul	170	1 13/16	70	3 3/8
38	40	Oct	60	3 1/4	6	4 1/8
38	45	Jul	412	1/2	...	...
CmprsL	10	Jul	100	3/4	...	...
CmpAsc	65	May	112	4 5/8	...	...
69 1/2	70	May	563	1 1/16	36	1 3/4
69 1/2	70	Jul	50	3 7/8	...	...
69 1/2	75	Jul	463	1 7/8	...	...
CompSc	50	May	110	1/4	20	2 5/8
Comvrs	12 1/2	Oct	60	3 1/8	...	...
ConAgr	30	Jun	96	3 1/8	...	...
Conrail	50	May	50	3 7/8	...	...
53	50	Jun	100	4 3/8	...	...
53	50	Oct	53	5 5/8	...	...
53	60	Jul	111	5/8	...	...
ConPap	45	May	80	8	...	...
CnStor	20	Oct	36	7/8	...	...
CtAirB	15	May	80	1 15/16	...	...
16 7/8	15	Jun	119	2 1/2	...	...
16 7/8	17 1/2	Dec	...	...	42	3 1/8
CtlMed	10	Jun	50	1/2	...	...
CtrlDt	10	Jun	...	...	40	5/8
CoopTr	25	May	150	1/4	...	...
CorTher	12 1/2	May	...	...	315	3/8
16 1/4	15	May	85	1 3/4	175	5/8
16 1/4	15	Jun	50	3	40	1 3/4
16 1/4	17 1/2	May	136	5/8	...	...
CoramH	12 1/2	May	2195	6 3/8	...	...
17 7/8	15	Aug	420	4 3/8	...	...
17 7/8	17 1/2	May	326	1 3/8	35	1/2
17 7/8	17 1/2	Jun	187	1 7/8	...	...
17 7/8	20	May	257	1/8	108	1 1/4
17 7/8	20	Jun	142	1/2	30	1 11/16
17 7/8	20	Aug	53	1	50	1 5/16
17 7/8	22 1/2	Jun	...	...	40	3 1/4
Cordis	75	May	50	5/16	...	...
Corng	35	May	50	1/4	15	1 1/8
33 5/8	35	Aug	100	1 1/2	...	...
33 5/8	35	Nov	100	2 1/4	...	...
Cvntry	17 1/2	Jun	40	5	...	...
22 1/4	25	May	90	1/8	...	...

6.4 NEWSPAPER QUOTES

Many newspapers carry option quotations. In the *Wall Street Journal,* stock option quotations can currently be found under the heading "Listed Options" in the Money and Investing section. Table 6.1 shows the quotations as they appeared in the *Wall Street Journal* of Friday May 12, 1995. These refer to trading that took place on the previous day (i.e., Thursday, May 11, 1995).

The company on whose stock the option is written, together with the closing stock price, are listed in the first column. The strike price and maturity month appear in the second and third columns. If the specified call option with the specified strike price and the specified maturity month traded during the previous day, the next two columns show the volume of trading and price at last trade for the call option. The final two columns show the same for a put option.

The quoted price is the price of an option to buy or sell one share. As mentioned earlier, one contract is for the purchase or sale of 100 shares. A contract, therefore, costs 100 times the price shown. Since most options are priced at less than $10 and some are priced at less than $1, investors do not have to be extremely wealthy to trade options.

The *Wall Street Journal* also shows the total call volume, put volume, call open interest, and put open interest for each exchange. The numbers for Thursday, May 11, 1995 are shown in Table 6.2. The volume is the total number of contracts traded on the day. The open interest is the number of contracts outstanding.

From Table 6.1 it appears that there were arbitrage opportunities on May 11, 1995. For example, a May call on AT&T with a strike price of 50 is quoted as $1\frac{3}{8}$. Since the stock price is $51\frac{1}{2}$, it appears that this call could be purchased and then exercised immediately for a profit of $\frac{1}{8}$. In fact, arbitrage opportunities such as this almost certainly did not exist. For both options and stocks, Table 6.1 gives the prices at which the last trade took place on May 11, 1995. The last trade for the May AT&T call with a strike price of 50 probably occurred much earlier in the day than the last trade on the stock. If an option trade had been attempted at the time of the last trade on the stock, the call price would have been higher than $1\frac{3}{8}$.

TABLE 6.2   Volume and Open Interest, May 11, 1995

Exchange	Call Volume	Call Open Interest	Put Volume	Put Open Interest
Chicago Board	336,569	6,342,979	272,657	5,012,108
American	134,336	3,631,612	53,997	1,982,079
Philadelphia	48,952	1,728,799	20,758	1,005,127
Pacific	71,697	1,502,984	25,723	856,178
New York	7,657	886,403	1,347	453,058
Total	599,211	14,092,777	374,482	9,308,550

6.5 TRADING

Options trading is in many respects similar to futures trading (see Chapter 2). An exchange has a number of members (individuals and firms) who are referred to as having seats on the exchange. Membership in an exchange entitles one to go on the floor of the exchange and trade with other members.

Market Makers

Most options exchanges (including the CBOE) use a market maker system to facilitate trading. A *market maker* for a certain option is a person who will quote both a bid and an ask price on the option whenever he or she is asked to do so. The bid is the price at which the market maker is prepared to buy and the ask is the price at which the market maker is prepared to sell. At the time the bid and the ask are quoted, the market maker does not know whether the trader who asked for the quotes wants to buy or sell the option. The ask is, of course, higher than the bid, and the amount by which the ask exceeds the bid is referred to as the *bid–ask spread.* The exchange sets upper limits for the bid–ask spread. Typically, it must be no more than $0.25 for options priced at less than $0.50, $0.50 for options priced between $0.50 and $10, $0.75 for options priced between $10 and $20, and $1 for options priced over $20.

The existence of the market maker ensures that buy and sell orders can always be executed at some price without delays. Market makers therefore add liquidity to the market. The market makers themselves make their profits from the bid–ask spread. To hedge their risks, they use some of the schemes discussed in Chapter 14.

Floor Broker

Floor brokers execute trades for the general public. When an investor contacts his or her broker to buy or sell an option, the broker relays the order to the firm's floor broker in the exchange on which the option trades. If the brokerage house does not have its own floor broker, it generally has an arrangement whereby it uses either an independent floor broker or the floor broker of another firm.

The floor broker trades either with another floor broker or with the market maker. A floor broker may be on commission or may be paid a salary by the brokerage house for which he or she executes trades.

Order Book Official

Many orders that are relayed to floor brokers are limit orders. This means that they can be executed only at the specified price or a more favorable price. Often, when a limit order reaches a floor broker, it cannot be executed immediately. (For example, a limit order to buy a call at $5 cannot be executed immediately when the market maker is quoting a bid of 4\frac{3}{4}$ and an ask of 5\frac{1}{4}$.) In most

exchanges, the floor broker will then pass the order to a person known as an *order book official* (or board broker). This person enters the order into a computer along with other public limit orders. This ensures that as soon as the limit price is reached, the order is executed. The information on all outstanding limit orders is available to all traders.

The market maker/order book official system can be contrasted with the *specialist system* which is used in a few options exchanges (e.g., AMEX and PHLX) and is the most common system for trading stocks. Under the specialist system, a person known as a specialist is responsible for being a market maker and keeping a record of limit orders. Unlike an order book official, a specialist does not make information on limit orders available to other traders.

Offsetting Orders

An investor who has purchased an option can close out his or her position by issuing an offsetting order to sell the same option. Similarly, an investor who has written an option can close out his or her position by issuing an offsetting order to buy the same option. If, when an option contract is traded, neither investor is offsetting an existing position, the open interest increases by one contract. If one investor is offsetting an existing position and the other is not, the open interest stays the same. If both investors are offsetting existing positions, the open interest goes down by one contract.

6.6 COMMISSIONS

For the retail investor, commissions vary significantly from broker to broker. Discount brokers generally charge lower commissions than those charged by full-service brokers. The actual amount charged is usually calculated as a fixed cost plus a proportion of the dollar amount of the trade. Table 6.3 shows the sort of

TABLE 6.3   Typical Commission Schedule for a Discount Broker

Dollar Amount of Trade	Commission[a]
< $2,500	$20 + 0.02 of the dollar amount
$2,500 to $10,000	$45 + 0.01 of the dollar amount
> $10,000	$120 + 0.0025 of the dollar amount

[a]Maximum commission is $30 per contract for the first five contracts plus $20 per contract for each additional contract. Minimum commission is $30 per contract for the first contract plus $2 per contract for each additional contract.

schedule that might be offered by a discount broker. Under this schedule, the purchase or sale of one contract always costs $30 (since both the maximum and minimum commission is $30 for the first contract). The purchase of eight contracts when the option price is $3 would cost $20 + (0.02 × 2,400) = $68 in commissions.

If an option position is closed out by entering into an offsetting trade, the commission must be paid again. If the option is exercised, an investor pays the same commission as he or she would when placing an order to buy or sell the underlying stock. Typically, this is 1 to 2% of the stock's value.

Consider an investor who buys one call contract with a strike price of $50 when the stock price is $49. We suppose the option price is $4.50, so the cost of the contract is $450. Using the schedule in Table 6.3, the commission paid when the option is bought is $30. Suppose that the stock price rises and the option is exercised when it reaches $60. Assuming that the investor pays a 1.5% commission on stock trades, the commission payable when the option is exercised is

$$0.015 \times \$60 \times 100 = \$90$$

The total commission paid is, therefore, $120 and the net profit to the investor is

$$\$1,000 - \$450 - \$120 = \$430$$

Note that if the investor could sell the option for $10 instead of exercising it, he or she would save $60 in commissions. (This is because the commission payable when an option is sold is only $30 in our example.) In general, the commission system tends to push investors in the direction of selling options rather than exercising them.

A hidden cost in option trading (and in stock trading) is the market maker's bid–ask spread. Suppose that in the example just considered, the bid price was $4.00 and the ask price was $4.50 at the time the option was purchased. We can reasonably assume that a "fair" price for the option is halfway between the bid and the ask price, or $4.25. The cost to the buyer and to the seller of the market maker system is the difference between the fair price and the price paid. This is $0.25 per option, or $25 per contract.

6.7 MARGINS

When shares are purchased, an investor can either pay cash or use a margin account. The initial margin required is usually 50% of the value of the shares, and the maintenance margin is usually 25% of the value of the shares. The margin account operates in the same way as it does for an investor entering into a futures contract (see Chapter 2).

When call and put options are purchased, the option price must be paid in full. Investors are not allowed to buy options on margin. This is because options

already contain substantial leverage. Buying on margin would raise this leverage to an unacceptable level. When an investor writes options, he or she is required to maintain funds in a margin account. This is because the investor's broker and the exchange want to be satisfied that the investor will not default if the option is exercised. The size of the margin required depends on the circumstances.

Writing Naked Options

Consider first the situation where a stock option is naked. This means that the option position is not combined with an offsetting position in the underlying stock. The initial margin is the greater of the results of the following two calculations:

1. A total of 100% of the proceeds of the sale plus 20% of the underlying share price less the amount if any by which the option is out of the money.
2. A total of 100% of the proceeds of the sale plus 10% of the underlying share price.

For options on a broadly based index, the 20% in the preceding calculations is replaced by 15%. This is because an index is usually less volatile than the price of an individual stock.

Example 6.3

An investor writes four naked call option contracts on a stock. The option price is $5, the strike price is $40, and the stock price is $38. Since the option is $2 out of the money, the first calculation gives

$$400(5 + 0.2 \times 38 - 2) = 4{,}240$$

The second calculation gives

$$400(5 + 0.1 \times 38) = 3{,}520$$

The initial margin requirement is therefore $4,240. Note that if the option had been a put, it would be $2 in the money and the margin requirement would be

$$400(5 + 0.2 \times 38) = \$5{,}040$$

In both cases the proceeds of the sale, $2,000, can be used to form part of the margin account.

A calculation similar to the initial margin calculation (but with the current market price replacing the proceeds of sale) is repeated every day. Funds can be withdrawn from the margin account when the calculation indicates that the margin required is less than the current balance in the margin account. When the calculation indicates that a significantly greater margin is required, a margin call will be made.

Writing Covered Calls

Writing covered calls involves writing call options when the shares that might have to be delivered are already owned. Covered calls are far less risky than naked calls since the worst that can happen is that the investor is required to sell shares already owned at below their market value. If covered call options are out of the money, no margin is required. The shares owned can be purchased using a margin account as described previously, and the price received for the option can be used to partially fulfill this margin requirement. If the options are in the money, no margin is required for the options. However, for the purposes of calculating the investor's equity position, the share price is reduced by the extent (if any) to which the option is in the money. This may limit the amount that the investor can withdraw from the margin account if the share price increases.

Example 6.4

An investor decides to buy 200 shares of a certain stock on margin and to write two call option contracts on the stock. The stock price is $63, the strike price is $65, and the price of the option is $7. Since the options are out of the money, the margin account allows the investor to borrow 50% of the price of the stock, or $6,300. The investor is also able to use the price received for the option, $7 × 200 or $1,400, to finance the purchase of the shares. The shares cost $63 × 200 = $12,600. The minimum cash initially required from the investor for his or her trades is, therefore,

$$\$12,600 - \$6,300 - \$1,400 = \$4,900$$

In Chapter 8 we discuss more complicated option trading strategies, such as spreads, combinations, straddles, strangles, and so on. There are special rules for determining the margin requirements when these trading strategies are used.

6.8 THE OPTIONS CLEARING CORPORATION

The Options Clearing Corporation (OCC) performs much the same sort of function for options markets as the clearinghouse does for futures markets (see Chapter 2). It guarantees that the option writer will fulfill his or her obligations under the terms of the option contract and keeps a record of all long and short positions. The OCC has a number of members, and all option trades must be cleared through a member. If a brokerage house is not itself a member of an exchange's OCC, it must arrange to clear its trades with a member. Members are required to have a certain minimum amount of capital and to contribute to a special fund that can be used if any member defaults on an option obligation.

When purchasing an option, the buyer must pay for it in full by the morning of the next business day. These funds are deposited with the OCC. The writer of the option maintains a margin account with his or her broker, as described earlier. The broker maintains a margin account with the OCC member that clears its trades. The OCC member, in turn, maintains a margin account with the OCC. The

margin requirements described in the preceding section are the margin requirements imposed by the OCC on its members. A brokerage house may require higher margins from its clients. However, it cannot require lower margins.

Exercising an Option

When an investor wishes to exercise an option, the investor notifies his or her broker. The broker in turn notifies the OCC member that clears its trades. This member then places an exercise order with the OCC. The OCC randomly selects a member with an outstanding short position in the same option. The member, using a procedure established in advance, selects a particular investor who has written the option. If the option is a call, this investor is required to sell stock at the strike price. If it is a put, the investor is required to buy stock at the strike price. The investor is said to be *assigned.* When an option is exercised, the open interest goes down by one.

At the expiration of the option, all in-the-money options should be exercised unless the transactions costs are so high as to wipe out the payoff from the option. Some brokerage firms will automatically exercise options for their clients at expiration when it is in their clients' interest to do so. Many exchanges also have rules for exercising stock options that are in the money at expiration.

6.9 REGULATION

Options markets are regulated in a number of ways. Both the exchanges and the Options Clearing Corporations have rules governing the behavior of traders. In addition, there are both federal and state regulatory authorities. In general, options markets have demonstrated a willingness to regulate themselves. There have been no major scandals or defaults by OCC members. Investors can have a high level of confidence in the way the market is run.

The Securities and Exchange Commission is responsible for regulating options markets in stocks, stock indices, currencies, and bonds at the federal level. The Commodity Futures Trading Commission is responsible for regulating markets for options on futures. The major options markets are in the states of Illinois and New York. These states actively enforce their own laws on unacceptable trading practices.

6.10 TAXATION

Determining the tax implications of options strategies can be tricky and an investor who is in doubt about his or her position should consult a tax specialist. The general rule for all investors is that gains and losses from the trading of stock options are taxed as capital gains or losses. The way in which capital gains and losses are taxed in the United States was discussed in Section 2.11. The holder

of an option recognizes a gain or loss when (a) the option is allowed to expire unexercised or (b) the option is sold or (c) the option is exercised. If a call option is exercised, the writer is deemed to have sold stock at the strike price plus the original call price. The party with a long position is deemed to have purchased the stock at the strike price plus the call price. (This is then used as a basis for calculating this party's gain or loss when the stock is eventually sold.) If a put option is exercised, the party with a long position is deemed to have sold stock for the strike price less the original put price. The writer is deemed to have bought stock for the strike price less the original put price. (This is used as a basis for calculating the writer's gain or loss when the stock is eventually sold.) In all cases, brokerage commissions are deductible.

Wash Sale Rule

One tax consideration in option trading in the United States is the wash sale rule. To understand this rule, imagine an investor who buys a stock when the price is $60 and plans to keep it for the long term. If the stock price drops to $40, the investor might be tempted to sell the stock and then immediately repurchase it so that the $20 loss is realized for tax purposes. To prevent this sort of thing, the tax authorities have ruled that when the repurchase is within 30 days of the sale (i.e., between 30 days before the sale and 30 days after the sale) any loss on the sale is not deductible. This rule is relevant to options traders because for the purposes of the wash sale rule, a call option on a stock is regarded as the same security as the stock itself. Thus, selling a stock at a loss and buying a call option within a 30-day period will lead to the loss being disallowed.

Tax Planning Using Options

Tax practitioners sometimes use options and other derivatives to minimize tax costs or maximize tax benefits. One simple transaction is a cross-border arbitrage. A company buys an option in one tax jurisdiction where the cost of the option can be offset against tax immediately while selling an identical option in another jurisdiction where the income arising from the option sale is taxed only when the option is exercised or expires. Other transactions are more complex. For example, it is sometimes advantageous for a United States corporation to sell an in-the-money option on one of its assets to a related entity in a foreign jurisdiction. The U.S. corporation is not taxed on the income until the option is exercised. The result is that the corporation has obtained a loan from the foreign entity without withholding tax being charged on the interest. If carefully structured, options can also be used to create a hybrid instrument that is treated as equity for rating or financial reporting purposes and as debt for tax purposes. As a debt instrument, the corporation obtains the tax benefit on the interest/dividend it pays. This can significantly reduce its cost of capital.

Tax authorities in many jurisdictions have proposed legislation designed to combat the use of derivatives for tax purposes. Before entering into any tax-

motivated transaction a treasurer should explore in detail how the structure could be unwound in the event of legislative change and how costly this process could be.

6.11 WARRANTS AND CONVERTIBLES

For the exchange-traded options that have been described so far, the writers and purchasers meet on the floor of the exchange and, as trading takes place, the number of contracts outstanding fluctuates. A warrant is an option that arises in a quite different way. *Warrants* are issued (i.e., written) by a company or a financial institution. In some cases they are subsequently traded on an exchange. The number of contracts outstanding is determined by the size of the original issue and changes only when options are exercised or expire. Warrants are bought and sold in much the same way as stocks and there is no need for an Options Clearing Corporation to become involved. When a warrant is exercised, the original issuer settles up with the current holder of the warrant.

Call warrants are frequently issued by companies on their own stock. For example, in a debt issue a company might offer investors a package consisting of bonds plus call warrants on its stock. If the warrants are exercised, the company issues new treasury stock to the warrant holders in return for the strike price specified in the contract. The strike price and exercise date of the warrants do not have to correspond to those of the regular exchange-traded call options. Typically, warrants have longer maturities than regular exchange-traded call options.

Put and call warrants are also sometimes issued by a financial institution to satisfy a demand in the market. The underlying asset is typically an index, a currency, or a commodity. For example, at the end of the 1980s there was a great deal of interest in put warrants on the Japanese Nikkei 225 index. Once a warrant like this has been issued, it is often traded on an exchange. The financial institution typically settles in cash when the warrant is exercised. The financial institution is paid for the warrant up front but must hedge its risk. The techniques for doing this are described in Chapter 14.

Convertible bonds are debt instruments with embedded options issued by corporations. The holder has the right to exchange a convertible bond for equity in the issuing company at certain times in the future according to a certain exchange ratio. Very often, the convertible is *callable*. This means that it can be repurchased by the issuer at a certain price at certain times in the future. Once the bonds have been called, the holder can always choose to convert prior to repurchase. Thus the effect of a call provision is often to give the issuer the right to force conversion of the bonds into equity at an earlier time than the holders would otherwise choose. The company provides the holder with new treasury stock in exchange for the bonds when the convertible is converted. If, as a rough approximation, interest rates are assumed constant and call provisions are ignored, a convertible can be regarded as a regular debt instrument plus call warrants.

6.12 SUMMARY

Options trade on a wide range of different assets on exchanges and in the over-the-counter market. An exchange must specify the terms of the option contracts it trades. In particular, it must specify the size of the contract, the precise expiration time, and the strike price. Over-the-counter options can be tailored to the particular needs of corporations and do not have to correspond to those traded on exchanges.

The terms of a stock option are not adjusted for cash dividends. However, they are adjusted for stock dividends and stock splits. The aim of the adjustment is to keep the positions of both the writer and the buyer of a contract unchanged.

Most options exchanges use a market-maker system. A market maker is a person who is prepared to quote both a bid (price at which he or she is prepared to buy) and an ask (price at which he or she is prepared to sell). Market makers improve the liquidity of the market and ensure that there is never any delay in executing market orders. They themselves make a profit from the difference between their bid and ask prices (known as their bid–ask spread). The exchange has rules specifying upper limits for the bid–ask spread.

Writers of options have potential liabilities and are required to maintain margins with their brokers. The broker, if not a member of the Options Clearing Corporation, will maintain a margin account with a firm that is a member. This firm will in turn maintain a margin account with the Options Clearing Corporation. The Options Clearing Corporation is responsible for keeping a record of all outstanding contracts, handling exercise orders, and so on.

SUGGESTIONS FOR FURTHER READING

Chance, D. M., *An Introduction to Options and Futures Markets.* Orlando, Fla.: Dryden Press, 1989.

Chicago Board Options Exchange, *Reference Manual.* Chicago: 1982.

Chicago Board Options Exchange, *Understanding Options.* Chicago: 1985.

Clasing, H. K., *The Dow Jones–Irwin Guide to Put and Call Trading.* Homewood, Ill.: Dow Jones–Irwin, 1978.

Cox, J. C., and M. Rubinstein, *Options Markets.* Englewood Cliffs, N.J.: Prentice Hall, 1985.

Gastineau, G., *The Stock Options Manual.* New York: McGraw-Hill, 1979.

McMillan, L. G., *Options as a Strategic Investment.* New York: New York Institute of Finance, 1986.

QUESTIONS AND PROBLEMS

6.1. Explain why brokers require margins from clients when they write options but not when they buy options.

6.2. A stock option is on a February–May–August–November cycle. What options trade on (a) April 1 and (b) May 30?

6.3. A company declares a 3-for-1 stock split. Explain how the terms of a call option with a strike price of $60 change.

6.4. Explain the difference between the specialist system and the market maker/order book official system for the organization of trading at an exchange.

6.5. Explain carefully the difference between writing a call option and buying a put option.

6.6. The treasurer of a corporation is trying to choose between the use of options and forward contracts to hedge the corporation's foreign exchange risk. Discuss the advantages and disadvantages of each.

6.7. Consider an exchange-traded call option contract to buy 500 shares with exercise price $40 and maturity in four months. Explain how the terms of the option contract change when there is
(a) A 10% stock dividend.
(b) A 10% cash dividend.
(c) A 4-for-1 stock split.

6.8. "If most of the call options on a stock are in the money, it is likely that the stock price has risen rapidly in the last few months." Discuss this statement.

6.9. What is the effect of an unexpected cash dividend on (a) a call option price and (b) a put option price?

6.10. Options on General Motors' stock are on a March–June–September–December cycle. What options trade on (a) March 1; (b) June 30; and (c) August 5?

6.11. Explain why the market maker's bid–ask spread represents a real cost to options investors.

6.12. An investor writes five naked call option contracts. The option price is $3.50, the strike price is $60.00, and the stock price is $57.00. What is the initial margin requirement?

6.13. An investor buys 500 shares of a stock and sells five call option contracts on the stock. The strike price is $30. The price of the option is $3. What is the investor's minimum cash investment (a) if the stock price is $28 and (b) if the stock price is $32?

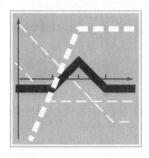

Chapter 7

Properties of Stock Option Prices

In this chapter we discuss the factors affecting stock option prices. We use a number of different arbitrage arguments to explore the relationships between European option prices, American option prices, and the underlying asset price. We show that it is never optimal to exercise an American call option on a non-dividend-paying stock prior to expiration, but that there are some circumstances under which the early exercise of an American put option on such a stock is optimal.

7.1 FACTORS AFFECTING OPTION PRICES

There are six factors affecting the price of a stock option:

1. The current stock price
2. The strike price
3. The time to expiration
4. The volatility of the stock price
5. The risk-free interest rate
6. The dividends expected during the life of the option

In this section we consider what happens to option prices when one of these factors changes with all the others remaining fixed. The results are summarized in Table 7.1.

Stock Price and Strike Price

If it is exercised at some time in the future, the payoff from a call option will be the amount by which the stock price exceeds the strike price. Call options therefore become more valuable as the stock price increases and less valuable as the strike price increases. For a put option, the payoff on exercise is the amount by which the strike price exceeds the stock price. Put options therefore behave in the opposite way to call options. They become less valuable as the stock price increases and more valuable as the strike price increases.

TABLE 7.1 Summary of the Effect on the Price of a Stock Option of Increasing One Variable While Keeping All Others Fixed

Variable	European Call	European Put	American Call	American Put
Stock price	+	−	+	−
Strike price	−	+	−	+
Time to expiration	?	?	+	+
Volatility	+	+	+	+
Risk-free rate	+	−	+	−
Dividends	−	+	−	+

Time to Expiration

Consider next the effect of the expiration date. Both put and call American options become more valuable as the time to expiration increases. To see this, consider two options that differ only as far as the expiration date is concerned. The owner of the long-life option has all the exercise opportunities open to the owner of the short-life option—and more. The long-life option must therefore always be worth at least as much as the short-life option.

European put and call options do not necessarily become more valuable as the time to expiration increases. This is because it is not true that the owner of a long-life European option has all the exercise opportunities open to the owner of a short-life European option. The owner of the long-life European option can exercise only at the maturity of that option. Consider two European call options on a stock, one with an expiration date in one month, the other with an expiration date in two months. Suppose that a very large dividend is expected in six weeks. The dividend will cause the stock price to decline. It is possible that this will lead to the short-life option being worth more than the long-life option.

Volatility

The precise way in which the volatility is defined is discussed in Chapter 11. Roughly speaking, the volatility of a stock price is a measure of how uncertain we are about future stock price movements. As volatility increases, the chance that the stock will do very well or very poorly increases. For the owner of a stock, these two outcomes tend to offset each other. However, this is not so for the owner of a call or put. The owner of a call benefits from price increases but has limited downside risk in the event of price decreases since the most that he or she can lose is the price of the option. Similarly, the owner of a put benefits from price decreases but has limited downside risk in the event of price increases. The values of both calls and puts therefore increase as volatility increases.

Risk-Free Interest Rate

The risk-free interest rate affects the price of an option in a less clear-cut way. As interest rates in the economy increase, the expected growth rate of the stock price tends to increase. However, the present value of any future cash flows received by the holder of the option decreases. These two effects both tend to decrease the value of a put option. Hence, put option prices decline as the risk-free interest rate increases. In the case of calls, the first effect tends to increase the price while the second effect tends to decrease it. It can be shown that the first effect always dominates the second effect; that is, the prices of calls always increase as the risk-free interest rate increases.

It should be emphasized that these results assume that all other variables remain fixed. In practice when interest rates rise (fall), stock prices tend to fall (rise). The net effect of an interest rate change and the accompanying stock price change may be different from that just given.

Dividends

Dividends have the effect of reducing the stock price on the ex-dividend date. This is bad news for the value of call options and good news for the value of put options. The values of call options are therefore negatively related to the sizes of any anticipated dividends, and the values of put options are positively related to the sizes of any anticipated dividends.

7.2 ASSUMPTIONS AND NOTATION

We now move on to derive some relationships between option prices that do not require any assumptions about volatility and the probabilistic behavior of stock prices. The assumptions we do make are similar to those we made when deriving forward and futures prices in Chapter 3. We assume that there are some market participants, such as large investment banks, for which

1. There are no transactions costs.
2. All trading profits (net of trading losses) are subject to the same tax rate.
3. Borrowing and lending at the risk-free interest rate is possible.

We assume that these market participants are prepared to take advantage of arbitrage opportunities as they arise. As discussed in Chapters 1 and 3, this means that any available arbitrage opportunities disappear very quickly. For the purposes of our analyses, it is therefore reasonable to assume that there are no arbitrage opportunities.

We will use the following notation:

S: current stock price
X: strike price of option
T: time of expiration of option
t: current time
S_T: stock price at time T
r: risk-free rate of interest for maturity T (continuously compounded)
C: value of American call option to buy one share
P: value of American put option to sell one share
c: value of European call option to buy one share
p: value of European put option to sell one share
σ: volatility of stock price

It should be noted that r is the nominal rate of interest, not the real rate of interest. We can assume that $r > 0$. Otherwise, a risk-free investment would provide no advantages over cash. (Indeed, if $r < 0$, cash would be preferable to a risk-free investment.)

7.3 UPPER AND LOWER BOUNDS FOR OPTION PRICES

In this section we derive upper and lower bounds for option prices. These do not depend on any particular assumptions about the factors mentioned in Section 7.2 (except $r > 0$). If the option price is above the upper bound or below the lower bound, there are profitable opportunities for arbitrageurs.

Upper Bounds

An American or European call option gives the holder the right to buy one share of a stock for a certain price. No matter what happens, the option can never be worth more than the stock. Hence, the stock price is an upper bound to the option price:

$$c \leq S \quad \text{and} \quad C \leq S$$

If these relationships are not true, an arbitrageur can easily make a riskless profit by buying the stock and selling the call option.

An American or European put option gives the holder the right to sell one share of a stock for X. No matter how low the stock price becomes, the option can never be worth more than X. Hence

$$p \leq X \quad \text{and} \quad P \leq X$$

For European options, we know that at time T, the option will not be worth more than X. It follows that it must now not be worth more than the present value of X:

$$p \le Xe^{-r(T-t)}$$

If this were not true, an arbitrageur could make a riskless profit by writing the option and investing the proceeds of the sale at the risk-free interest rate.

Lower Bound for Calls on Non-Dividend-Paying Stocks

A lower bound for the price of a European call option on a non-dividend-paying stock is

$$S - Xe^{-r(T-t)}$$

We first illustrate this with a numerical example and then present a more formal argument.

Suppose that $S = \$20$, $X = \$18$, $r = 10\%$ per annum, and $T - t = 1$ year. In this case,

$$S - Xe^{-r(T-t)} = 20 - 18e^{-0.1} = 3.71$$

or $3.71. Consider the situation where the European call price is $3.00, which is less than the theoretical minimum of $3.71. An arbitrageur can buy the call and short the stock. This provides a cash inflow of $20.00 − $3.00 = $17.00. If invested for one year at 10% per annum, the $17.00 grows to $17e^{0.1} = \$18.79$. At the end of the year, the option expires. If the stock price is greater than $18, the arbitrageur exercises the option, closes out the short position, and makes a profit of

$$\$18.79 - \$18.00 = \$0.79$$

If the stock price is less than $18, the stock is bought in the market and the short position is closed out. The arbitrageur then makes an even greater profit. For example, if the stock price is $17, the arbitrageur's profit is

$$\$18.79 - \$17.00 = \$1.79$$

For a more formal argument, we consider the following two portfolios:

Portfolio A: one European call option plus an amount of cash equal to $Xe^{-r(T-t)}$

Portfolio B: one share

In portfolio A, if the cash is invested at the risk-free interest rate, it will grow to X at time T. If $S_T > X$, the call option is exercised at time T and portfolio A is worth S_T. If $S_T < X$, the call option expires worthless and the portfolio is worth X. Hence, at time T, portfolio A is worth

$$\max(S_T, X)$$

Portfolio B is worth S_T at time T. Hence, portfolio A is always worth as much as, and is sometimes worth more than, portfolio B at time T. It follows that it must be worth more than portfolio B today. Hence

$$c + Xe^{-r(T-t)} > S$$

or

$$c > S - Xe^{-r(T-t)}$$

Since the worst that can happen to a call option is that it expires worthless, its value must be positive. This means that $c > 0$ and therefore

$$c > \max(S - Xe^{-r(T-t)}, 0) \tag{7.1}$$

Example 7.1

Consider a European call option on a non-dividend-paying stock when the stock price is $51, the exercise price is $50, the time to maturity is six months, and the risk-free rate of interest is 12% per annum. In this case, $S = 51$, $X = 50$, $T - t = 0.5$, and $r = 0.12$. From equation (7.1), a lower bound for the option price is $S - Xe^{-r(T-t)}$, or

$$51 - 50e^{-0.12 \times 0.5} = \$3.91$$

Lower Bound for European Puts on Non-Dividend-Paying Stocks

For a European put option on a non-dividend-paying stock, a lower bound for the price is

$$Xe^{-r(T-t)} - S$$

Again, we first illustrate this with a numerical example and then present a more formal argument.

Suppose that $S = \$37$, $X = \$40$, $r = 5\%$ per annum, and $T - t = 0.5$ year. In this case,

$$Xe^{-r(T-t)} - S = 40e^{-0.05 \times 0.5} - 37 = 2.01$$

or $2.01. Consider the situation where the European put price is $1.00, which is less than the theoretical minimum of $2.01. An arbitrageur can borrow $38.00 for six months to buy both the put and the stock. At the end of the six months, the arbitrageur will be required to repay $38e^{0.05 \times 0.5} = \$38.96$. If the stock price is below $40.00, the arbitrageur exercises the option to sell the stock for $40.00, repays the loan, and makes a profit of

$$\$40.00 - \$38.96 = \$1.04$$

If the stock price is greater than $40.00, the arbitrageur discards the option, sells the stock, and repays the loan for an even greater profit. For example, if the stock price is $42.00, the arbitrageur's profit is

$$\$42.00 - \$38.96 = \$3.04$$

For a more formal argument, we consider the following two portfolios:

Portfolio C: one European put option plus one share
Portfolio D: an amount of cash equal to $Xe^{-r(T-t)}$

If $S_T < X$, the option in portfolio C is exercised at time T and the portfolio becomes worth X. If $S_T > X$, the put option expires worthless and the portfolio is worth S_T at time T. Hence portfolio C is worth

$$\max{(S_T,\ X)}$$

at time T. Assuming that the cash is invested at the risk-free interest rate, portfolio D is worth X at time T. Hence, portfolio C is always worth as much as, and is sometimes worth more than, portfolio D at time T. It follows that in the absence of arbitrage opportunities, portfolio C must be worth more than portfolio D today. Hence

$$p + S > Xe^{-r(T-t)}$$

or

$$p > Xe^{-r(T-t)} - S$$

Since the worst that can happen to a put option is that it expires worthless, its value must be positive. This means that

$$p > \max{[Xe^{-r(T-t)} - S,\ 0]} \tag{7.2}$$

Example 7.2

Consider a European put option on a non-dividend-paying stock when the stock price is $38, the exercise price is $40, the time to maturity is three months, and the risk-free rate of interest is 10% per annum. In this case, $S = 38$, $X = 40$, $T - t = 0.25$, and $r = 0.10$. From equation (7.2), a lower bound for the option price is $Xe^{-r(T-t)} - S$, or

$$40e^{-0.1 \times 0.25} - 38 = \$1.01$$

7.4 *EARLY EXERCISE: CALLS ON A NON-DIVIDEND-PAYING STOCK*

In this section we show that it is never optimal to exercise an American call option on a non-dividend-paying stock early. To illustrate the general nature of the argument, consider an American call option on a non-dividend-paying stock with one month to expiration when the stock price is $50 and the strike price is $40. The option is deep in the money and the investor who owns the option might well be tempted to exercise it immediately. However, if the investor plans to hold the stock for more than one month, this is not the best strategy. A better course of action is to keep the option and exercise it at the end of the month. The $40 strike

price is then paid out one month later than it would be if the option were exercised immediately. This means that interest is earned on the $40 for one month. Since the stock pays no dividend, no income from the stock is sacrificed. A further advantage of waiting rather than exercising immediately is that there is some chance (however remote) that the stock price will be below $40 in one month. In this case, the option expires worthless and the investor is glad that the decision to exercise early was not taken!

This argument shows that there are no advantages to exercising early if the investor plans to keep the stock for the rest of the life of the option (one month, in this case). What if the investor thinks the stock is currently overpriced and is wondering whether to exercise the option and sell the stock? In this case, the investor is better off selling the option than exercising it.[1] The option will be bought by another investor who does want to hold the stock. Such investors must exist. Otherwise the current stock price would not be $50. The price obtained for the option will be greater than its intrinsic value of $10 for the reasons just mentioned. In fact, equation (7.1) shows that the market price of the option must always be greater than

$$50 - 40e^{-0.1 \times 0.08333} = \$10.33$$

Otherwise, there are arbitrage opportunities.

To present a more formal argument, consider again the following two portfolios:

Portfolio E: one American call option plus an amount of cash equal to $Xe^{-r(T-t)}$

Portfolio F: one share

The value of the cash in portfolio E at expiration of the option is X. At some earlier time τ, it is $Xe^{-r(T-\tau)}$. If the call option is exercised at time τ, the value of portfolio E is

$$S - X + Xe^{-r(T-\tau)}$$

This is always less than S when $\tau < T$ since $r > 0$. Portfolio E is therefore always worth less than portfolio F if the call option is exercised prior to maturity. If the call option is held to expiration, the value of portfolio E at time T is

$$\max(S_T, X)$$

The value of portfolio F is S_T. There is always some chance that $S_T < X$. This means that portfolio E is always worth as much as, and is sometimes worth more than, portfolio F.

---

[1] As an alternative strategy, the investor can keep the option and short the stock. This locks in a better profit than $10.

We have shown that portfolio E is worth less than portfolio F if the option is exercised immediately, but is worth at least as much as portfolio F if the holder of the option delays exercise until the expiration date. It follows that a call option on a non-dividend-paying stock should never be exercised prior to the expiration date. An American call option on a non-dividend-paying stock is therefore worth the same as the corresponding European call option on the same stock:

$$C = c$$

For a quicker proof, we can use equation (7.1):

$$c > S - Xe^{-r(T-t)}$$

Since the owner of an American call has all the exercise opportunities open to the owner of the corresponding European call, we must have

$$C \geq c$$

Hence

$$C > S - Xe^{-r(T-t)}$$

Since $r > 0$, it follows from this that $C > S - X$. If it were optimal to exercise early, C would equal $S - X$. We deduce that it can never be optimal to exercise early.

Figure 7.1 shows the general way in which the call price varies with S. It indicates that the call price is always above its intrinsic value of $\max(S - X, 0)$. As r, σ, or $T - t$ increase, the call price moves in the direction indicated by the arrows (i.e., farther away from the intrinsic value).

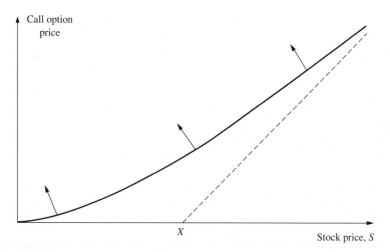

Figure 7.1   Variation of price of an American or European call option on a non-dividend-paying stock with the price, S.

To summarize, one reason why a call option should not be exercised early can be considered as being due to the insurance that it provides. When held instead of the stock itself, a call option in effect insures the holder against the stock price falling below the exercise price. Once the option has been exercised and the exercise price has been exchanged for the stock price, this insurance vanishes. Another reason is concerned with the time value of money. The later the strike price is paid out the better.

7.5 EARLY EXERCISE: PUTS ON A NON-DIVIDEND-PAYING STOCK

It can be optimal to exercise an American put option on a non-dividend-paying stock early. Indeed, at any given time during its life, a put option should always be exercised early if it is sufficiently deeply in the money. To illustrate this, consider an extreme situation. Suppose that the strike price is $10 and the stock price is virtually zero. By exercising immediately, an investor makes an immediate gain of $10. If the investor waits, the gain from exercising might be less than $10 but it cannot be more than $10 since negative stock prices are impossible. Furthermore, receiving $10 now is preferable to receiving $10 in the future. It follows that the option should be exercised immediately.

It is instructive to consider the following two portfolios:

Portfolio G: one American put option plus one share
Portfolio H: an amount of cash equal to $Xe^{-r(T-t)}$

If the option is exercised at time $\tau < T$, portfolio G becomes worth X while portfolio H is worth $Xe^{-r(T-\tau)}$. Portfolio G is therefore worth more than portfolio H. If the option is held to expiration, portfolio G becomes worth

$$\max(X, S_T)$$

while portfolio H is worth X. Portfolio G is therefore worth at least as much as, and possibly more than, portfolio H. Note the difference between this situation and the one in the preceding section. Here we cannot argue that early exercise is undesirable since portfolio G looks more attractive than portfolio H regardless of the decision on early exercise.

Like a call option, a put option can be viewed as providing insurance. A put option, when held in conjunction with the stock, insures the holder against the stock price falling below a certain level. However, a put option is different from a call option in that it may be optimal for an investor to forgo this insurance and exercise early in order to realize the strike price immediately. In general, the early exercise of a put option becomes more attractive as S decreases, as r increases, and as σ decreases.

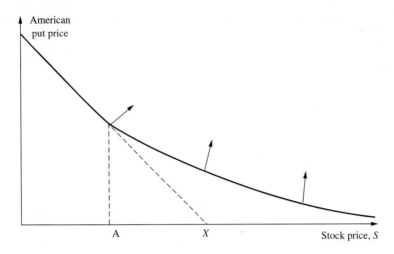

Figure 7.2   Variation of price of an American put option with the stock price, S.

It will be recalled from equation (7.2) that

$$p > Xe^{-r(T-t)} - S$$

For an American put with price P, the stronger condition

$$P \geq X - S$$

must always hold since immediate exercise is always possible.

Figure 7.2 shows the general way in which the price of an American put varies with S. Provided that $r > 0$, it is always optimal to exercise an American put immediately when the stock price is sufficiently low. When early exercise is optimal, the value of the option is $X - S$. The curve representing the value of the put therefore merges into the put's intrinsic value, $X - S$, for a sufficiently small value of S. In Figure 7.2, this value of S is shown as point A. The value of the put moves in the direction indicated by the arrows when r decreases, when σ increases, and when T increases.

Since there are some circumstances when it is desirable to exercise an American put option early, it follows that an American put option is always worth more than the corresponding European put option. Since an American put is sometimes worth its intrinsic value (see Figure 7.2), it follows that a European put option must sometimes be worth less than its intrinsic value. Figure 7.3 shows the variation of the European put price with the stock price. Note that point B in Figure 7.3, at which the price of the option is equal to its intrinsic value, must represent a higher value of the stock price than point A in Figure 7.2. Point E in Figure 7.3 is where $S = 0$ and the European put price is $Xe^{-r(T-t)}$.

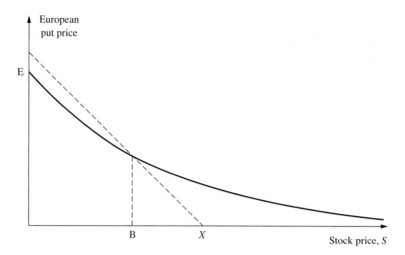

Figure 7.3   Variation of price of a European put option with the stock price, S.

7.6 PUT–CALL PARITY

It will be recalled that P and C are the prices of American put and call options, while p and c are the prices of European put and call options. The variables, P, p, C, and c are all functions of S, X, r, $T - t$, and σ. We have shown that for a non-dividend-paying stock,

$$C = c$$

$$P > p \quad \text{when} \quad r > 0$$

We now derive an important relationship between p and c for a non-dividend-paying stock. Consider the following two portfolios:

> *Portfolio A:* one European call option plus an amount of cash equal to $Xe^{-r(T-t)}$

> *Portfolio C:* one European put option plus one share

Both are worth

$$\max(S_T, X)$$

at expiration of the options. Since the options are European, they cannot be exercised prior to the expiration date. The portfolios must therefore have identical values today. This means that

$$c + Xe^{-r(T-t)} = p + S \tag{7.3}$$

This relationship is known as *put–call parity*. It shows that the value of a European call with a certain exercise price and exercise date can be deduced from the value of a European put with the same exercise price and date, and vice versa.

If equation (7.3) does not hold, there are arbitrage opportunities. Suppose that the stock price is $31, the exercise price is $30, the risk-free interest rate is 10% per annum, the price of a three-month European call option is $3, and the price of a three-month European put option is $2.25. In this case,

$$c + Xe^{-r(T-t)} = 3 + 30e^{-0.1 \times 0.25} = 32.26$$

$$p + S = 2.25 + 31 = 33.25$$

Portfolio C is overpriced relative to portfolio A. The correct arbitrage strategy is to buy the securities in portfolio A and short the securities in portfolio C. This involves buying the call and shorting both the put and the stock. The strategy generates a positive cash flow of

$$-3 + 2.25 + 31 = \$30.25$$

up front. When invested at the risk-free interest rate, this grows to $30.25e^{0.1 \times 0.25} = 31.02$ in three months. If the stock price at expiration of the option is greater than $30, the call will be exercised. If it is less than $30, the put will be exercised. In either case the investor ends up buying one share for $30. This share can be used to close out the short position. The net profit is therefore

$$\$31.02 - \$30.00 = \$1.02$$

For an alternative situation, suppose that the call price is $3 and the put price is $1. In this case

$$c + Xe^{-r(T-t)} = 3 + 30e^{-0.1 \times 0.25} = 32.26$$

$$p + S = 1 + 31 = 32.00$$

Portfolio A is overpriced relative to portfolio C. An arbitrageur can short the securities in portfolio A and buy the securities in portfolio C to lock in a profit. This involves shorting the call and buying both the put and the stock. The strategy involves an initial investment of

$$\$31 + \$1 - \$3 = \$29$$

at time zero. When financed at the risk-free interest rate, a repayment of $29e^{0.1 \times 0.25} = \$29.73$ is required at the end of the three months. As in the previous case, either the call or the put will be exercised. The short call and long put option position therefore leads to the stock being sold for $30.00. The net profit is therefore

$$\$30.00 - \$29.73 = \$0.27$$

Relationship between American Call and Put Prices

Put–call parity holds only for European options. However, it is possible to derive some relationships between American option prices for a non-dividend-paying stock. Since $P > p$, it follows from equation (7.3) that

$$P > c + Xe^{-r(T-t)} - S$$

and since $c = C$,

$$P > C + Xe^{-r(T-t)} - S$$

or

$$C - P < S - Xe^{-r(T-t)} \tag{7.4}$$

For a further relationship between C and P, consider

Portfolio I: one European call option plus an amount of cash equal to X
Portfolio J: one American put option plus one share

Both options have the same exercise price and expiration date. Assume that the cash in portfolio I is invested at the risk-free interest rate. If the put option is not exercised early portfolio J is worth

$$\max (S_T, \ X)$$

at time T. Portfolio I is worth

$$\max (S_T, \ X) + Xe^{r(T-t)} - X$$

at this time. Portfolio I is therefore worth more than portfolio J. Suppose next that the put option in portfolio J is exercised early, say, at time τ. This means that portfolio J is worth X at time τ. However, even if the call option were worthless, portfolio I would be worth $Xe^{r(\tau-t)}$ at time τ. It follows that portfolio I is worth more than portfolio J in all circumstances. Hence

$$c + X > P + S$$

Since $c = C$,

$$C + X > P + S$$

or

$$C - P > S - X$$

Combining this with equation (7.4), we obtain

$$S - X < C - P < S - Xe^{-r(T-t)} \tag{7.5}$$

Example 7.3

Consider the situation where an American call option on a non-dividend-paying stock with exercise price $20.00 and maturity in five months is worth $1.50. This must also be the value of a European call option on the same stock with the same exercise price and maturity. Suppose that the current stock price is $19.00 and the risk-free interest rate is 10% per annum. From a rearrangement of equation (7.3), the price of a European put with exercise price $20 and maturity in five months is

$$1.50 + 20e^{-0.1 \times 0.4167} - 19 = \$1.68$$

From equation (7.5),

$$19 - 20 < C - P < 19 - 20e^{-0.1 \times 0.4167}$$

or

$$1 > P - C > 0.18$$

showing that $P - C$ lies between $1.00 and $0.18. Since C is $1.50, P must lie between $1.68 and $2.50. In other words, upper and lower bounds for the price of an American put with the same strike price and expiration date as the American call are $2.50 and $1.68.

7.7 EFFECT OF DIVIDENDS

The results produced in Sections 7.3 to 7.6 have assumed that we are dealing with options on a non-dividend-paying stock. In this section we discuss the impact of dividends. In the United States, most exchange-traded stock options have less than eight months to maturity. The dividends payable during the life of the option can usually be predicted with reasonable accuracy. We will use D to denote the present value of the dividends during the life of the option. For this purpose a dividend is assumed to occur at the time of its ex-dividend date.

Lower Bound for Calls and Puts

We can redefine portfolios A and B as follows:

Portfolio A: one European call option plus an amount of cash equal to $D + Xe^{-r(T-t)}$

Portfolio B: one share

A similar argument to the one used to derive equation (7.1) shows that

$$c > S - D - Xe^{-r(T-t)} \tag{7.6}$$

We can also redefine portfolios C and D as follows:

Portfolio C: one European put option plus one share
Portfolio D: an amount of cash equal to $D + Xe^{-r(T-t)}$

A similar argument to the one used to derive equation (7.2) shows that

$$p > D + Xe^{-r(T-t)} - S \tag{7.7}$$

Early Exercise

When dividends are expected, we can no longer assert that an American call option will not be exercised early. Sometimes it is optimal to exercise an American call immediately prior to an ex-dividend date. This is because the dividend will cause the stock price to jump down, making the option less attractive. It is never optimal to exercise a call at other times. This point is discussed further in Chapter 11.

Put–Call Parity

Comparing the value at time T of the redefined portfolios A and C shows that when there are dividends, put–call parity [equation (7.3)] becomes

$$c + D + Xe^{-r(T-t)} = p + S \tag{7.8}$$

Dividends cause equation (7.5) to be modified to

$$S - D - X < C - P < S - Xe^{-r(T-t)} \tag{7.9}$$

To prove this inequality, consider

Portfolio I: one European call option plus an amount of cash equal to $D + X$
Portfolio J: one American put option plus a share

Regardless of what happens, it can be shown that portfolio I is worth more than portfolio J. Hence

$$P + S < c + D + X$$

Since a European call is never worth more than its American counterpart, or $c < C$, it follows that

$$P + S < C + D + X$$

or

$$S - D - X < C - P$$

This proves the first half of the inequality in equation (7.9). For a non-dividend-paying stock, we showed in equation (7.5) that

$$C - P < S - Xe^{-r(T-t)}$$

Since dividends decrease the value of a call and increase the value of a put, this inequality must also be true for options on a dividend-paying stock. This proves the second half of the inequality in equation (7.9).

7.8 EMPIRICAL RESEARCH

Empirical research to test the results in this chapter might seem to be relatively simple to carry out once the appropriate data have been assembled. In fact, there are a number of complications:

1. It is important to be sure that option prices and stock prices are being observed at exactly the same time. For example, testing for arbitrage opportunities by looking at the price at which the last trade is done each day is inappropriate. This point has already been made in connection with the numbers in Table 6.1.
2. It is important to consider carefully whether a trader could have taken advantage of any observed arbitrage opportunity. If the opportunity exists only momentarily, there might, in practice, be no way of exploiting it.
3. Transactions costs must be taken into account when determining whether arbitrage opportunities were possible.
4. Put–call parity holds only for European options. Exchange-traded stock options are American.
5. Dividends to be paid during the life of the option must be estimated.

Some of the empirical research that has been carried out is described in the papers by Bhattacharya, Galai, Gould and Galai, Klemkosky and Resnick, and Stoll that are referenced at the end of this chapter. Galai and Bhattacharya test whether option prices are ever less than their lower bounds; Stoll, Gould and Galai, and the two papers by Klemkosky and Resnick test whether put–call parity holds. We will consider the results of Bhattacharya and of Klemkosky and Resnick.

Bhattacharya's study examined whether the theoretical lower bounds for call options applied in practice. He used data consisting of the transaction prices for options on 58 stocks over a 196-day period between August 1976 and June 1977. The first test examined whether the options satisfied the condition that price be greater than intrinsic value, that is, whether $C > \max(S - X, 0)$. Over 86,000 option prices were examined and about 1.3% were found to violate this condition. In 29% of the cases, the violation disappeared by the next trade, indicating that in practice traders would not have been able to take advantage of it. When transactions costs were taken into account, the profitable opportunities created by the violation disappeared. Bhattacharya's second test examined whether options sold for less than the lower bound $S - D - Xe^{-r(T-t)}$ [see equation (7.6)]. He found that 7.6% of his observations did, in fact, sell for less than this lower bound. However, when transactions costs were taken into account, these did not give rise to profitable opportunities.

Klemkosky and Resnick's tests of put–call parity used data on option prices taken from trades between July 1977 and June 1978. They subjected their data

to several tests to determine the likelihood of options being exercised early and discarded data where early exercise was considered probable. By doing this they felt they were justified in treating American options as European. They identified 540 situations where the call price was too low relative to the put and 540 situations where the call price was too high relative to the put. After allowing for transactions costs, 38 of the first set of situations gave rise to profitable arbitrage opportunities and 147 of the second set of situations did so. The opportunities persisted when either a 5- or a 15-minute delay between the opportunity being noted and trades being executed was assumed. Klemkosky and Resnick's conclusion is that arbitrage opportunities were available to some traders, particularly market makers, during the period they studied.

7.9 SUMMARY

There are six factors affecting the value of a stock option: the current stock price, the strike price, the expiration date, the stock price volatility, the risk-free interest rate, and the dividends expected during the life of the option. The value of a call generally increases as the current stock price, the time to expiration, the volatility, and the risk-free interest rate increase. The value of a call decreases as the strike price and expected dividends increase. The value of a put generally increases as the strike price, the time to expiration, the volatility, and the expected dividends increase. The value of a put decreases as the current stock price and the risk-free interest rate increase.

It is possible to reach some conclusions about the values of stock options without making any assumptions about the probabilistic behavior of stock prices. For example, the price of a call option on a stock must always be worth less than the price of the stock itself. Similarly, the price of a put option on a stock must always be worth less than the option's strike price.

A call option on a non-dividend-paying stock must be worth more than

$$\max [S - Xe^{-r(T-t)}, 0]$$

where S is the stock price, X is the exercise price, r is the risk-free interest rate, and T is the time to expiration. A put option on a non-dividend-paying stock must be worth more than

$$\max [Xe^{-r(T-t)} - S, 0]$$

When dividends with present value D will be paid, the lower bound for a call option becomes

$$\max [S - D - Xe^{-r(T-t)}, 0]$$

and the lower bound for a put option becomes

$$\max [Xe^{-r(T-t)} + D - S, 0]$$

Put–call parity is a relationship between the price, c, of a European call option on a stock and the price, p, of a European put option on a stock. For a non-dividend-paying stock, it is

$$c + Xe^{-r(T-t)} = p + S$$

For a dividend-paying stock, the put–call parity relationship is

$$c + D + Xe^{-r(T-t)} = p + S$$

Put–call parity does not hold for American options. However, it is possible to use arbitrage arguments to obtain upper and lower bounds for the difference between the price of an American call and the price of an American put.

In future chapters we carry the analyses in this chapter further by making some specific assumptions about the probabilistic behavior of stock prices. This will enable us to derive exact pricing formulas for European stock options. It will also enable us to develop numerical procedures for pricing American options.

SUGGESTIONS FOR FURTHER READING

Bhattacharya, M., "Transaction Data Tests of Efficiency of the Chicago Board Options Exchange," *Journal of Financial Economics,* 12 (1983), 161–85.

Galai, D., "Empirical Tests of Boundary Conditions for CBOE Options," *Journal of Financial Economics,* 6 (1978), 187–211.

Gould, J. P., and D. Galai, "Transactions Costs and the Relationship Between Put and Call Prices," *Journal of Financial Economics,* 1 (1974), 105–29.

Klemkosky, R. C., and B. G. Resnick, "An Ex-ante Analysis of Put–Call Parity," *Journal of Financial Economics,* 8 (1980), 363–78.

Klemkosky, R. C., and B. G. Resnick, "Put–Call Parity and Market Efficiency," *Journal of Finance,* 34 (December 1979), 1141–55.

Merton, R. C., "The Relationship Between Put and Call Prices: Comment," *Journal of Finance,* 28 (March 1973), 183–84.

Merton, R. C., "Theory of Rational Option Pricing," *Bell Journal of Economics and Management Science,* 4 (Spring 1973), 141–83.

Stoll, H. R., "The Relationship Between Put and Call Option Prices," *Journal of Finance,* 24 (December 1969), 801–24.

QUESTIONS AND PROBLEMS

7.1. An investor buys a call with strike price X and writes a put with the same strike price. Describe the investor's position.

7.2. Explain why an American option is always worth at least as much as a European option on the same asset with the same strike price and exercise date.

7.3. Explain why an American option is always worth at least as much as its intrinsic value.

7.4. List the six factors affecting stock option prices.

7.5. What is a lower bound for the price of a four-month call option on a non-dividend-paying stock when the stock price is $28, the strike price is $25, and the risk-free interest rate is 8% per annum?

7.6. What is a lower bound for the price of a one-month European put option on a non-dividend-paying stock when the stock price is $12, the strike price is $15, and the risk-free interest rate is 6% per annum?

7.7. Give two reasons why the early exercise of an American call option on a non-dividend-paying stock is not optimal. The first reason should involve the time value of money. The second reason should apply even if interest rates are zero.

7.8. "The early exercise of an American put is a trade-off between the time value of money and the insurance value of a put." Explain this statement.

7.9. A European call and put option on a stock both have a strike price of $20 and an expiration date in three months. Both sell for $3. The risk-free interest rate is 10% per annum, the current stock price is $19, and a $1 dividend is expected in one month. Identify the arbitrage opportunity open to a trader.

7.10. Explain why the arguments leading to put–call parity for European options cannot be used to give a similar result for American options.

7.11. What is a lower bound for the price of a six-month call option on a non-dividend-paying stock when the stock price is $80, the strike price is $75, and the risk-free interest rate is 10% per annum?

7.12. What is a lower bound for the price of a two-month European put option on a non-dividend-paying stock when the stock price is $58, the strike price is $65, and the risk-free interest rate is 5% per annum?

7.13. A four-month European call option on a dividend-paying stock is currently selling for $5. The stock price is $64, the strike price is $60, and a dividend of $0.80 is expected in one month. The risk-free interest rate is 12% per annum for all maturities. What opportunities are there for an arbitrageur?

7.14. A one-month European put option on a non-dividend-paying stock is currently selling for 2\frac{1}{2}$. The stock price is $47, the strike price is $50, and the risk-free interest rate is 6% per annum. What opportunities are there for an arbitrageur?

7.15. Give an intuitive explanation of why the early exercise of an American put becomes more attractive as the risk-free rate increases and volatility decreases.

7.16. The price of a European call that expires in six months and has a strike price of $30 is $2. The underlying stock price is $29, and a dividend of $0.50 is expected in two months and in five months. The term structure is flat, with all risk-free interest rates being 10%. What is the price of a European put option that expires in six months and has a strike price of $30?

7.17. Explain carefully the arbitrage opportunities in Problem 7.16 if the European put price is $3.

7.18. The price of an American call on a non-dividend-paying stock is $4. The stock price is $31, the strike price is $30, and the expiration date is in three months. The risk-

free interest rate is 8%. Derive upper and lower bounds for the price of an American put on the same stock with the same strike price and expiration date.

7.19. Explain carefully the arbitrage opportunities in Problem 7.18 if the American put price is greater than the calculated upper bound.

7.20. Suppose that c_1, c_2, and c_3 are the prices of European call options with strike prices X_1, X_2, and X_3, respectively, where $X_3 > X_2 > X_1$ and $X_3 - X_2 = X_2 - X_1$. All options have the same maturity. Show that

$$c_2 \leq 0.5(c_1 + c_3)$$

(*Hint:* Consider a portfolio that is long one option with strike price X_1, long one option with strike price X_3, and short two options with strike price X_2.)

7.21. What is the result corresponding to that in Problem 7.20 for American put options?

7.22. Suppose that you are the manager and sole owner of a highly leveraged company. All the debt will mature in one year. If at that time the value of the company is greater than the face value of the debt, you will pay off the debt. If the value of the company is less than the face value of the debt, you will declare bankruptcy and the debtholders will own the company.

(a) Express your position as an option on the value of the company.

(b) Express the position of the debtholders in terms of options on the value of the company.

(c) What can you do to increase the value of your position?

7.23. Executive stock options are call options issued by a company to its executives. Usually, the strike price is close to the market price at the time the options are issued. If the options are exercised, the company issues new treasury stock. Executive stock options cannot usually be sold by the executive to another party and sometimes cease to exist if the executive leaves the company. Often, they last for as long as 10 years. They are frequently exercised well before the expiration date. Discuss the possible reasons why an executive might choose to exercise these options early.

C h a p t e r 8

Trading Strategies Involving Options

The profit pattern from an investment in a single stock option was discussed in Chapter 1. In this chapter we cover more fully the range of profit patterns obtainable using options. The profit patterns are explained on the assumption that the underlying asset is a stock. However, similar profit patterns can be obtained for other underlying assets.

In the first section we consider what happens when a position in a stock option is combined with a position in the stock itself. We then move on to discuss the profit patterns obtained when an investment is made in two or more different options on the same stock. One of the attractions of options is that they can be used to create a wide range of different payoff functions. Unless otherwise stated the options we consider are all European. Toward the end of this chapter, we will argue that if European options were available with every single possible strike price, any payoff function could in theory be created.

8.1 STRATEGIES INVOLVING A SINGLE OPTION AND A STOCK

There are a number of different trading strategies involving a single option on a stock and the stock itself. The profits from these are illustrated in Figure 8.1. In this figure, and in other figures throughout this chapter, the dashed line shows the relationship between profit and stock price for the individual securities comprising the portfolio, while the solid line shows the relationship between profit and stock price for the whole portfolio.

In Figure 8.1a the portfolio consists of a long position in a stock plus a short position in a call option. The investment strategy represented by this portfolio is known as *writing a covered call*. This is because the long stock position "covers" or protects the investor from the possibility of a sharp rise in the stock price. In Figure 8.1b a short position in a stock is combined with a long position in a call option. This is the reverse of writing a covered call. In Figure 8.1c the investment strategy involves buying a put option on a stock and the stock itself. This is sometimes referred to as a *protective put* strategy. In Figure 8.1d a short position in a put option is combined with a short position in the stock. This is the reverse of a protective put.

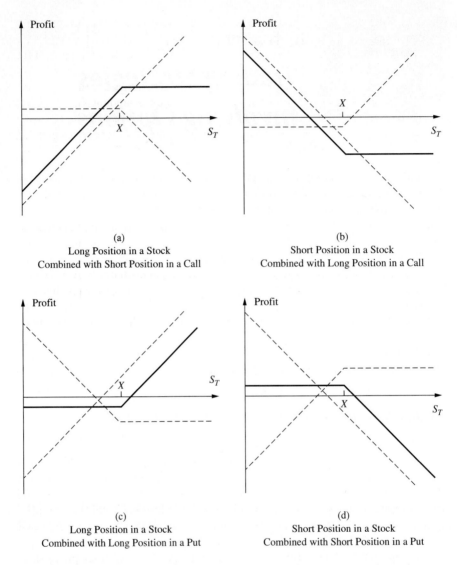

(a)
Long Position in a Stock
Combined with Short Position in a Call

(b)
Short Position in a Stock
Combined with Long Position in a Call

(c)
Long Position in a Stock
Combined with Long Position in a Put

(d)
Short Position in a Stock
Combined with Short Position in a Put

Figure 8.1 Profit from various trading strategies involving a single option and a stock.

The profit patterns in Figure 8.1(a–d) have the same general shape as the profit patterns discussed in Chapter 1 for short put, long put, long call, and short call, respectively. Put–call parity provides a way of understanding why this is so. It will be recalled from Chapter 7 that the put–call parity relationship is

$$p + S = c + Xe^{-r(T-t)} + D \qquad (8.1)$$

where p is the price of a European put, S is the stock price, c is the price of a European call, X is the strike price of both call and put, r is the risk-free interest rate, T is the maturity date of both call and put, and D is the present value of the dividends anticipated during the life of the option.

Equation (8.1) shows that a long position in a put combined with a long position in the stock is equivalent to a long call position plus an amount $Xe^{-r(T-t)} + D$ of cash. This explains why the profit pattern in Figure 8.1c is similar to the profit pattern from a long call position. The position in Figure 8.1d is the reverse of that in Figure 8.1c and therefore leads to a profit pattern similar to that from a short call position.

Equation (8.1) can be rearranged to become

$$S - c = Xe^{-r(T-t)} + D - p$$

This shows that a long position in a stock combined with a short position in a call is equivalent to a short put position plus an amount $= Xe^{-r(T-t)} + D$ of cash. This explains why the profit pattern in Figure 8.1a is similar to the profit pattern from a short put position. The position in Figure 8.1b is the reverse of that in Figure 8.1a and therefore leads to a profit pattern similar to that from a long put position.

8.2 SPREADS

A spread trading strategy involves taking a position in two or more options of the same type (i.e., two or more calls or two or more puts).

Bull Spreads

One of the most popular types of spreads is a *bull spread*. This can be created by buying a call option on a stock with a certain strike price and selling a call option on the same stock with a higher strike price. Both options have the same expiration date. The strategy is illustrated in Figure 8.2. The profits from the two option positions taken separately are shown by the dashed lines.

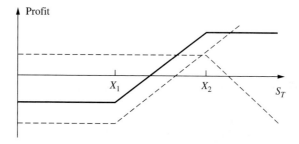

Figure 8.2   Bull spread created using call options.

TABLE 8.1   Payoff from a Bull Spread

Stock Price Range	Payoff from Long Call Option	Payoff from Short Call Option	Total Payoff
$S_T \geq X_2$	$S_T - X_1$	$X_2 - S_T$	$X_2 - X_1$
$X_1 < S_T < X_2$	$S_T - X_1$	0	$S_T - X_1$
$S_T \leq X_1$	0	0	0

The profit from the whole strategy is the sum of the profits given by the dashed lines and is indicated by the solid line. Since a call price always decreases as the strike price increases, the value of the option sold is always less than the value of the option bought. A bull spread, when created from calls, therefore requires an initial investment.

Suppose that X_1 is the strike price of the call option bought, X_2 is the strike price of the call option sold, and S_T is the stock price on the expiration date of the options. Table 8.1 shows the total payoff that will be realized from a bull spread in different circumstances. If the stock price does well and is greater than the higher strike price, the payoff is the difference between the two strike prices, $X_2 - X_1$. If the stock price on the expiration date lies between the two strike prices, the payoff is $S_T - X_1$. If the stock price on the expiration date is below the lower strike price, the payoff is zero. The profit in Figure 8.2 is calculated by subtracting the initial investment from the payoff.

A bull spread strategy limits both the investor's upside potential and his or her downside risk. We can describe the strategy by saying that the investor has a call option with a strike price equal to X_1 and has chosen to give up some upside potential by selling a call option with strike price X_2 ($X_2 > X_1$). In return for giving up the upside potential the investor reduces his or her initial outlay by the price of the option with strike price X_2. Three types of bull spreads can be distinguished:

1. Both calls initially out of the money.
2. One call initially in the money, the other call initially out of the money.
3. Both calls initially in the money.

The most aggressive bull spreads are those of type 1. They cost very little to set up and have a small probability of giving a relatively high payoff ($= X_2 - X_1$). As we move from type 1 to type 2 and from type 2 to type 3, the spreads become more conservative.

Example 8.1

An investor buys for $3 a call with a strike price of $30 and sells for $1 a call with a strike price of $35. The payoff from this bull spread strategy is $5 if the stock price is above $35

and zero when it is below \$30. If the stock price is between \$30 and \$35, the payoff is the amount by which the stock price exceeds \$30. The cost of the strategy is \$3 − \$1 = \$2. The profit is therefore as follows:

Stock Price Range	Profit
$S_T \leq 30$	−2
$30 < S_T < 35$	$S_T - 32$
$S_T \geq 35$	+3

Bull spreads can also be created by buying a put with a low strike price and selling a put with a high strike price. This is illustrated in Figure 8.3. Unlike the bull spread created using calls, bull spreads created from puts involve a positive cash flow to the investor up front. (This ignores margin requirements.) The final payoffs from bull spreads created using puts are lower than from those created using calls.

Bear Spreads

An investor entering into a bull spread is hoping that the stock price will increase. By contrast, an investor who enters into a *bear spread* is hoping that the stock price will decline. Like a bull spread, a bear spread can be created by buying a call with one strike price and selling a call with another strike price. However, in the case of a bear spread, the strike price of the option purchased is greater than the strike price of the option sold. This is illustrated in Figure 8.4, where the profit from the spread is shown by the solid line. A bear spread created from calls involves an initial cash inflow (when margin requirements are ignored) since the price of the call sold is greater than the price of the call purchased.

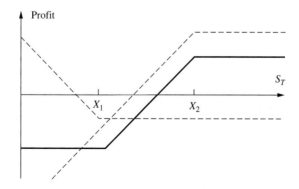

Figure 8.3   Bull spread created using put options.

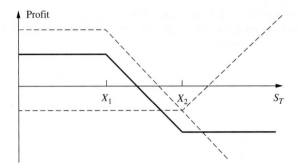

Figure 8.4   Bear spread created using call options.

TABLE 8.2   Payoff from a Bear Spread

Stock Price Range	Payoff from Long Call Option	Payoff from Short Call Option	Total Payoff
$S_T \geq X_2$	$S_T - X_2$	$X_1 - S_T$	$-(X_2 - X_1)$
$X_1 < S_T < X_2$	0	$X_1 - S_T$	$-(S_T - X_1)$
$S_T \leq X_1$	0	0	0

Assuming that the strike prices are X_1 and X_2 with $X_1 < X_2$, Table 8.2 shows the payoff that will be realized from a bear spread in different circumstances. If the stock price is greater than X_2, the payoff is negative at $-(X_2 - X_1)$. If the stock price is less than X_1, the payoff is zero. If the stock price is between X_1 and X_2, the payoff is $-(S_T - X_1)$. The profit is calculated by adding the initial cash inflow to the payoff.

Example 8.2

An investor buys for $1 a call with a strike price of $35 and sells for $3 a call with a strike price of $30. The payoff from this bear spread strategy is –$5 if the stock price is above $35 and zero if it is below $30. If the stock price is between $30 and $35, the payoff is $-(S_T - 30)$. The investment generates $3 - $1 = $2 up front. The profit is therefore as follows:

Stock Price Range	Profit
$S_T \leq 30$	+2
$30 < S_T < 35$	$32 - S_T$
$S_T \geq 35$	−3

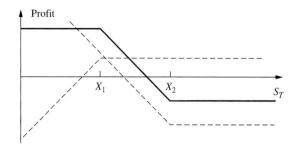

Figure 8.5   Bear spread created using put options.

Like bull spreads, bear spreads limit both the upside profit potential and the downside risk. Bear spreads can be created using puts instead of calls. The investor buys a put with a high strike price and sells a put with a low strike price. This is illustrated in Figure 8.5. Bear spreads created with puts require an initial investment. In essence, the investor has bought a put with a certain strike price and chosen to give up some of the profit potential by selling a put with a lower strike price. In return for the profit given up, the investor gets the price of the option sold.

Butterfly Spreads

A butterfly spread involves positions in options with three different strike prices. It can be created by buying a call option with a relatively low strike price, X_1; buying a call option with a relatively high strike price, X_3; and selling two call options with a strike price, X_2, halfway between X_1 and X_3. Generally, X_2 is close to the current stock price. The pattern of profits from the strategy is shown in Figure 8.6. A butterfly spread leads to a profit if the stock price stays close to X_2 but gives rise to a small loss if there is a significant stock price move in either

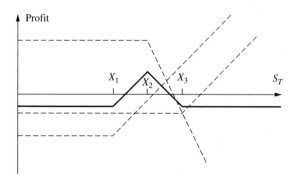

Figure 8.6   Butterfly spread using call options.

TABLE 8.3   Payoff from a Butterfly Spread

Stock Price Range	Payoff from First Long Call	Payoff from Second Long Call	Payoff from Short Calls	Total Payoff[a]
$S_T \leq X_1$	0	0	0	0
$X_1 < S_T \leq X_2$	$S_T - X_1$	0	0	$S_T - X_1$
$X_2 < S_T \leq X_3$	$S_T - X_1$	0	$-2(S_T - X_2)$	$X_3 - S_T$
$S_T > X_3$	$S_T - X_1$	$S_T - X_3$	$-2(S_T - X_2)$	0

[a]These payoffs are calculated using the relationship $X_2 = 0.5(X_1 + X_3)$.

direction. It is therefore an appropriate strategy for an investor who feels that large stock price moves are unlikely. The strategy requires a small investment initially. The payoff from a butterfly spread is shown in Table 8.3.

Suppose that a certain stock is currently worth $61. Consider an investor who feels that it is unlikely that there will be a significant price move in the next six months. Suppose that the market prices of six-month calls are as follows:

Strike Price (dollars)	Call Price (dollars)
55	10
60	7
65	5

The investor could create a butterfly spread by buying one call with a $55 strike price, buying one call with a $65 strike price, and selling two calls with a $60 strike price. It costs $10 + $5 − (2 × $7) = $1 to create the spread. If the stock price in six months is greater than $65 or less than $55, there is no payoff and the investor makes a net loss of $1. If the stock price is between $56 and $64, a profit is made. The maximum profit, $4, occurs when the stock price in six months is $60.

Butterfly spreads can be created using put options. The investor buys a put with a low strike price, buys a put with a high strike price, and sells two puts with an intermediate strike price. This is illustrated in Figure 8.7. The butterfly spread in the example just considered would be created by buying a put with a strike price of $55, buying a put with a strike price of $65, and selling two puts with a strike price of $60. If all options are European, the use of put options results in exactly the same spread as the use of call options. Put–call parity can be used to show that the initial investment is the same in both cases.

A butterfly spread can be sold or shorted by following the reverse strategy to that described earlier. Options are sold with strike prices of X_1 and X_3, and two options with the middle strike price X_2 are purchased. This strategy produces a modest profit if there is a significant movement in the stock price.

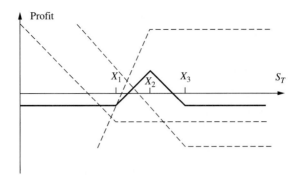

Figure 8.7   Butterfly spread using put options.

Calendar Spreads

Up to now we have assumed that the options used to create a spread all expire at the same time. We now move on to discuss calendar spreads where the options used have the same strike price and different expiration dates.

A calendar spread can be created by selling a call option with a certain strike price and buying a longer-maturity call option with the same strike price. The longer the maturity of an option, the more expensive it is. This calendar spread therefore requires an initial investment. Assuming that the long-maturity option is sold when the short-maturity option expires, the profit pattern given by a calendar spread is as shown in Figure 8.8. This is similar to the profit pattern from the butterfly spread in Figure 8.6. The investor makes a profit if the stock price at the expiration of the short-maturity option is close to the strike price of

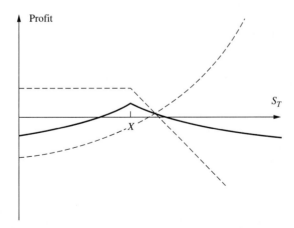

Figure 8.8   Calendar spread created using two calls.

the short-maturity option. However, a loss is incurred when the stock price is significantly above or significantly below this strike price.

To understand the profit pattern from a calendar spread, first consider what happens if the stock price is very low when the short-maturity option expires. The short-maturity option is worthless and the value of the long-maturity option is close to zero. The investor therefore incurs a loss that is only a little less than the cost of setting up the spread initially. Consider next what happens if the stock price, S_T, is very high when the short-maturity option expires. The short-maturity option costs the investor $S_T - X$ and the long-maturity option (assuming that early exercise is not optimal) is worth a little more than $S_T - X$, where X is the strike price of the options. Again the investor makes a net loss that is a little less than the cost of setting up the spread initially. If S_T is close to X, the short-maturity option costs the investor either a small amount or nothing at all. However, the long-maturity option is still quite valuable. In this case a significant net profit is made.

In a *neutral calendar spread*, a strike price close to the current stock price is chosen. A *bullish calendar spread* would involve a higher strike price, while a *bearish calendar spread* would involve a lower strike price.

Calendar spreads can be created with put options as well as call options. The investor buys a long-maturity put option and sells a short-maturity put option. As shown in Figure 8.9, the profit pattern is similar to that obtained from using calls.

A *reverse calendar spread* is the opposite to that shown in Figure 8.8 or 8.9. The investor buys a short-maturity option and sells a long-maturity option. This creates a small profit if the stock price at the expiration of the short-maturity option is well above or well below the strike price of the short-maturity option. However, it leads to a loss if it is close to the strike price.

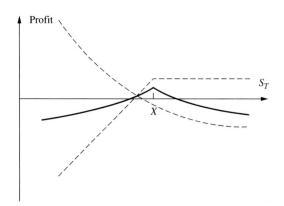

Figure 8.9   Calendar spread created using two puts.

Diagonal Spreads

Bull, bear, and calendar spreads can all be created from a long position in one call and a short position in another call. In the case of bull and bear spreads, the calls have different strike prices and the same expiration date. In the case of calendar spreads, the calls have the same strike price and different expiration dates. A *diagonal spread* is a spread which is such that both the expiration date and the strike price of the calls are different. There are several different types of diagonal spreads. Their profit patterns are generally variations on the profit patterns from the corresponding bull or bear spreads.

8.3 COMBINATIONS

A combination is an option trading strategy that involves taking a position in both calls and puts on the same stock. We consider what are known as *straddles*, *strips*, *straps*, and *strangles*.

Straddle

One popular combination is a *straddle*. This involves buying a call and put with the same strike price and expiration date. The profit pattern is shown in Figure 8.10. The strike price is denoted by X. If the stock price is close to this strike price at expiration of the options, the straddle leads to a loss. However, if there is a large move in either direction, a significant profit will result. The payoff from a straddle is calculated in Table 8.4.

A straddle is appropriate when an investor is expecting a large move in a stock price but does not know in which direction the move will be. Consider an investor who feels that the price of a certain stock, currently valued at $69 by the market, will move significantly in the next three months. The investor could create a straddle by buying both a put and a call with a strike price of $70 and an expiration date in three months. Suppose that the call costs $4 and the put

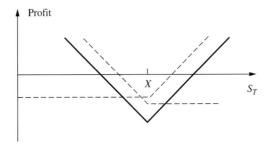

Figure 8.10   Straddle.

TABLE 8.4   Payoff from a Straddle

Range of Stock Price	Payoff from Call	Payoff from Put	Total Payoff
$S_T \leq X$	0	$X - S_T$	$X - S_T$
$S_T > X$	$S_T - X$	0	$S_T - X$

costs $3. If the stock price stays at $69, it is easy to see that the strategy costs the investor $6. (An up-front investment of $7 is required, the call expires worthless, and the put expires worth $1.) If the stock price moves to $70, a loss of $7 is experienced. (This is the worst that can happen.) However, if the stock price jumps up to $90, a profit of $13 is made; if the stock price moves down to $55, a profit of $8 is made; and so on.

A straddle would seem to be a natural strategy for the stock of a company that is subject to a takeover bid. If the bid is successful, the stock price can be expected to move up sharply. If it is unsuccessful, the stock price can be expected to move down sharply. In practice, it is not quite that easy to make money! Option prices for a stock whose price is expected to exhibit a large jump tend to be significantly higher than for a similar stock where no jump is expected.

The straddle in Figure 8.10 is sometimes referred to as a *bottom straddle* or *straddle purchase*. A *top straddle* or *straddle write* is the reverse position. It is created by selling a call and a put with the same exercise price and expiration date. It is a highly risky strategy. If the stock price on the expiration date is close to the strike price, it leads to a significant profit. However, the loss arising from a large move in either direction is unlimited.

Strips and Straps

A *strip* consists of a long position in one call and two puts with the same strike price and expiration date. A *strap* consists of a long position in two calls and one put with the same strike price and expiration date. The profit patterns from strips and straps are shown in Figure 8.11. In a strip, the investor is betting that there will be a big stock price move and considers a decrease in the stock price to be more likely than an increase. In a strap, the investor is also betting that there will be a big stock price move. However, in this case, an increase in the stock price is considered to be more likely than a decrease.

Strangles

In a *strangle*, sometimes called a *bottom vertical combination*, an investor buys a put and a call with the same expiration date and different strike prices. The profit pattern that is obtained is shown in Figure 8.12. The call strike price, X_2, is higher than the put strike price, X_1. The payoff function for a strangle is calculated in Table 8.5.

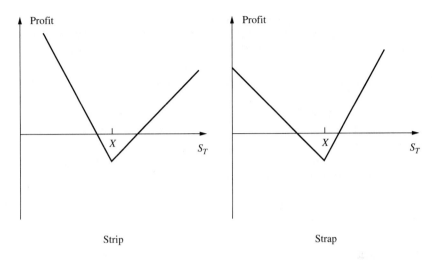

Figure 8.11   Profit patterns from strips and straps.

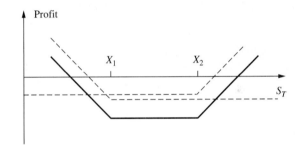

Figure 8.12   Strangle.

TABLE 8.5   Payoff from a Strangle

Range of Stock Price	Payoff from Call	Payoff from Put	Total Payoff
$S_T \leq X$	0	$X_1 - S_T$	$X_1 - S_T$
$X_1 < S_T < X_2$	0	0	0
$S_T \geq X_2$	$S_T - X_2$	0	$S_T - X_2$

A strangle is a similar strategy to a straddle. The investor is betting that there will be a large price move but is uncertain whether it will be an increase or a decrease. Comparing Figures 8.12 and 8.10, we see that the stock price has to move farther in a strangle than in a straddle for the investor to make a profit. However, the downside risk if the stock price ends up at a central value is less with a strangle.

The profit pattern obtained with a strangle depends on how close the strike prices are together. The farther they are apart, the less the downside risk and the farther the stock price has to move for a profit to be realized.

The sale of a strangle is sometimes referred to as a *top vertical combination*. It can be appropriate for an investor who feels that large stock price moves are unlikely. However, like the sale of a straddle, it is a risky strategy since the investor's potential loss is unlimited.

8.4 OTHER PAYOFFS

This chapter has demonstrated just a few of the ways in which options can be used to produce an interesting relationship between profit and stock price. If European options expiring at time T were available with every single possible strike price, any payoff function at time T could in theory be obtained. The easiest way to see this is in terms of butterfly spreads. It will be recalled that a butterfly spread is created by buying options with strike prices X_1 and X_3 and selling two options with strike price X_2, where $X_1 < X_2 < X_3$ and $X_3 - X_2 = X_2 - X_1$. Figure 8.13 shows the payoff from a butterfly spread. This could be described as a "spike." As X_1 and X_3 become closer together, the spike becomes smaller. By judiciously combining together a large number of very small spikes, any payoff function can be approximated.

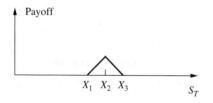

Figure 8.13   Payoff from a butterfly spread.

8.5 SUMMARY

A number of common trading strategies involve a single option and the underlying stock. For example, writing a covered call involves buying the stock and selling

a call option on the stock; a protective put involves buying a put option and buying the stock. The former is similar to selling a put option; the latter is similar to buying a call option.

Spreads involve either taking a position in two or more calls or taking a position in two or more puts. A bull spread can be created by buying a call (put) with a low strike price and selling a call (put) with a high strike price. A bear spread can be created by buying a call (put) with a high strike price and selling a call (put) with a low strike price. A butterfly spread involves buying calls (puts) with a low and high strike price and selling two calls (puts) with some intermediate strike price. A calendar spread involves selling a call (put) with a short time to expiration and buying a call (put) with a longer time to expiration. A diagonal spread involves a long position in one option and a short position in another option where both the strike price and expiration date are different.

Combinations involve taking a position in both calls and puts on the same stock. A straddle combination involves taking a long position in a call and a long position in a put with the same strike price and expiration date. A strip consists of a long position in one call and two puts with the same strike price and expiration date. A strap consists of a long position in two calls and one put with the same strike price and expiration date. A strangle consists of a long position in a call and a put with different strike prices and the same expiration date. There are many other ways in which options can be used to produce interesting payoffs. It is not surprising that option trading has steadily increased in popularity and continues to fascinate investors.

SUGGESTIONS FOR FURTHER READING

Bookstaber, R. M., *Option Pricing and Strategies in Investing*. Reading, Mass.: Addison-Wesley, 1981.

Chance, D. M., *An Introduction to Options and Futures*. Orlando, Fla.: Dryden Press, 1989.

Degler, W. H., and H. P. Becker, "Nineteen Option Strategies and When to Use Them," *Futures*, June 1984.

Gastineau, G., *The Stock Options Manual*, 2nd ed. New York: McGraw-Hill, 1979.

McMillan, L. G., *Options as a Strategic Investment*, 2nd ed. New York: New York Institute of Finance, 1986.

Slivka, R., "Call Option Spreading," *Journal of Portfolio Management*, 7 (Spring 1981), 71–76.

Welch, W. W., *Strategies for Put and Call Option Trading*. Cambridge, Mass.: Winthrop, 1982.

Yates, J. W., and R. W. Kopprasch, "Writing Covered Call Options: Profits and Risks," *Journal of Portfolio Management*, 6 (Fall 1980), 74–80.

QUESTIONS AND PROBLEMS

8.1. What is a protective put? What position in call options is equivalent to a protective put?

8.2. Explain two ways in which a bear spread can be created.

8.3. When is it appropriate for an investor to purchase a butterfly spread?

8.4. Call options on a stock are available with strike prices of $15, $17\frac{1}{2}$, and $20 and expiration dates in three months. Their prices are $4, $2, and $\frac{1}{2}$, respectively. Explain how the options can be used to create a butterfly spread. Construct a table showing how profit varies with stock price for the butterfly spread.

8.5. What trading strategy creates a reverse calendar spread?

8.6. What is the difference between a strangle and a straddle?

8.7. A call option with a strike price of $50 costs $2. A put option with a strike price of $45 costs $3. Explain how a strangle can be created from these two options. What is the pattern of profits from the strangle?

8.8. Analyze carefully the difference between a bull spread created from puts and a bull spread created from calls.

8.9. Explain how an aggressive bear spread can be created using put options.

8.10. Suppose that put options on a stock with strike price $30 and $35 cost $4 and $7, respectively. How can the options be used to create (a) a bull spread, and (b) a bear spread? Construct a table that shows the profit and payoff for both spreads.

8.11. Three put options on a stock have the same expiration date and strike prices of $55, $60, and $65. The market prices are $3, $5, and $8, respectively. Explain how a butterfly spread can be created. Construct a table showing the profit from the strategy. For what range of stock prices would the butterfly spread lead to a loss?

8.12. Use put–call parity to show that the cost of a butterfly spread created from European puts is identical to the cost of a butterfly spread created from European calls.

8.13. A diagonal spread is created by buying a call with strike price X_2 and exercise date T_2, and selling a call with strike price X_1 and exercise date T_1 ($T_2 > T_1$). Draw a diagram showing the profit when (a) $X_2 > X_1$ and (b) $X_2 < X_1$.

8.14. A call with a strike price of $60 costs $6. A put with the same strike price and expiration date costs $4. Construct a table that shows the profits from a straddle. For what range of stock prices would the straddle lead to a loss?

8.15. Construct a table showing the payoff from a bull spread when puts with strike prices X_1 and X_2 are used ($X_2 > X_1$).

8.16. An investor believes that there will be a big jump in a stock price but is uncertain as to the direction. Identify six different strategies the investor can follow and explain the differences between them.

8.17. How can a forward contract on a stock with a certain delivery price and delivery date be created from options?

8.18. A box spread is a combination of a bull call spread with strike prices X_1 and X_2 and a bear put spread with the same strike prices. The expiration dates of all options are the same. What are the characteristics of a box spread?

8.19. What is the result if the strike price of the put is higher than the strike price of the call in a strangle?

8.20. Draw a diagram showing the variation of an investor's profit and loss with the terminal stock price for a portfolio consisting of:

(a) One share and a short position in one call option.

(b) Two shares and a short position in one call option.

(c) One share and a short position in two call options.

(d) One share and a short position in four call options.

In each case, assume that the call option has an exercise price equal to the current stock price.

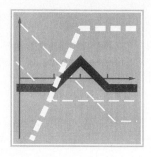

Chapter 9

Introduction to Binomial Trees

A useful and very popular technique for pricing an option or other derivative involves constructing what is known as a *binomial tree*. This is a tree that represents possible paths that might be followed by the underlying asset's price over the life of the derivative. In this chapter we take a first look at binomial trees and explain their relationship to an important principle known as *risk-neutral valuation*. The general approach we follow is similar to that in an important paper published by Cox, Ross, and Rubinstein in 1979.

The material in this chapter is intended to be introductory. More details on how numerical procedures involving binomial trees can be implemented in practice are provided in Chapter 15.

9.1 ONE-STEP BINOMIAL MODEL

We start by considering a very simple situation where a stock price is currently $20 and it is known that at the end of three months the stock price will be either $22 or $18. We suppose that the stock pays no dividends and that we are interested in valuing a European call option to buy the stock for $21 in three months. This option will have one of two values at the end of the three months. If the stock price turns out to be $22, the value of the option will be $1; if the stock price turns out to be $18, the value of the option will be zero. The situation is illustrated in Figure 9.1.

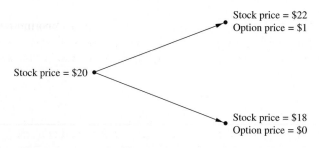

Figure 9.1   Stock price movements in numerical example.

It turns out that a relatively simple argument can be used to price the option in this example. The only assumption we need is that there are no arbitrage opportunities for an investor. We set up a portfolio of the stock and the option in such a way that there is no uncertainty about the value of the portfolio at the end of the three months. We then argue that since the portfolio has no risk, the return earned on it must equal the risk-free interest rate. This enables us to work out the cost of setting up the portfolio and therefore the option's price. Since there are two securities (the stock and the stock option) and only two possible outcomes, it is always possible to set up the riskless portfolio.

Consider a portfolio consisting of a long position in Δ shares of the stock and a short position in one call option. We will calculate the value of Δ that makes the portfolio riskless. If the stock price moves up from 20 to 22, the value of the shares is 22Δ and the value of the option is 1, so that the total value of the portfolio is $22\Delta - 1$. If the stock price moves down from 20 to 18, the value of the shares is 18Δ and the value of the option is zero, so that the total value of the portfolio is 18Δ. The portfolio is riskless if the value of Δ is chosen so that the final value of the portfolio is the same for both of the alternative stock prices. This means that

$$22\Delta - 1 = 18\Delta$$

or

$$\Delta = 0.25$$

A riskless portfolio is, therefore:

Long: 0.25 share
Short: 1 option

If the stock price moves up to 22, the value of the portfolio is

$$22 \times 0.25 - 1 = 4.5$$

If the stock price moves down to 18, the value of the portfolio is

$$18 \times 0.25 = 4.5$$

Regardless of whether the stock price moves up or down, the value of the portfolio is always 4.5 at the end of the life of the option.

Riskless portfolios must, in the absence of arbitrage opportunities, earn the risk-free rate of interest. Suppose that in this case the risk-free rate is 12% per annum. It follows that the value of the portfolio today must be the present value of 4.5, or

$$4.5e^{-0.12 \times 0.25} = 4.367$$

The value of the stock price today is known to be 20. Suppose that the option price is denoted by f. The value of the portfolio today is, therefore,

$$20 \times 0.25 - f = 5 - f$$

It follows that

$$5 - f = 4.367$$

or

$$f = 0.633$$

This shows that in the absence of arbitrage opportunities the current value of the option must be \$0.633. If the value of the option were more than 0.633, the portfolio would cost less than 4.367 to set up and would earn more than the risk-free rate. If the value of the option were less than 0.633, shorting the portfolio would provide a way of borrowing money at less than the risk-free rate.

Generalization

We can generalize the argument that has just been presented by considering a non-dividend-paying stock whose price is S and a derivative on the stock whose current price is f. The current time is time zero. We suppose that the derivative provides a payoff at time T and that during the life of the derivative the stock price can either move up from S to a new level Su or down from S to a new level Sd ($u > 1$; $d < 1$). The proportional increase in the stock price when there is an up movement is $u - 1$; the proportional decrease when there is a down movement is $1 - d$. If the stock price moves up to Su, we suppose that the payoff from the derivative is f_u; if the stock price moves down to Sd, we suppose the payoff from the derivative is f_d. The situation is illustrated in Figure 9.2.

As before, we imagine a portfolio consisting of a long position in Δ shares and a short position in one derivative. We calculate the value of Δ that makes the portfolio riskless. If there is an up movement in the stock price, the value of the portfolio at the end of the life of the derivative is

$$Su\Delta - f_u$$

If there is a down movement in the stock price, this becomes

$$Sd\Delta - f_d$$

The two are equal when

$$Su\Delta - f_u = Sd\Delta - f_d$$

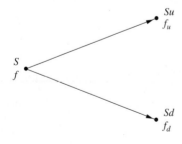

Figure 9.2   Stock and derivative prices in general one-step tree.

or

$$\Delta = \frac{f_u - f_d}{Su - Sd} \tag{9.1}$$

In this case the portfolio is riskless and must earn the risk-free interest rate. Equation (9.1) shows that Δ is the ratio of the change in the derivative price to the change in the stock price as we move between the nodes at time T.

Denoting the risk-free interest rate by r, the present value of the portfolio must be

$$(Su\Delta - f_u)e^{-rT}$$

The cost of setting up the portfolio is

$$S\Delta - f$$

It follows that

$$S\Delta - f = (Su\Delta - f_u)e^{-rT}$$

Substituting from equation (9.1) for Δ and simplifying, this equation reduces to

$$f = e^{-rT}[pf_u + (1 - p)f_d] \tag{9.2}$$

where

$$p = \frac{e^{rT} - d}{u - d} \tag{9.3}$$

Equations (9.2) and (9.3) enable a derivative to be priced using a one-step binomial model.

In the numerical example considered previously (see Figure 9.1), $u = 1.1$, $d = 0.9$, $r = 0.12$, $T = 0.25$, $f_u = 1$, and $f_d = 0$. From equation (9.3),

$$p = \frac{e^{0.03} - 0.9}{1.1 - 0.9} = 0.6523$$

and from equation (9.2),

$$f = e^{-0.03}(0.6523 \times 1 + 0.3477 \times 0) = 0.633$$

This agrees with the answer obtained earlier in this section.

Irrelevance of the Stock's Expected Return

The derivative pricing formula in equation (9.2) does not involve the probabilities of the stock price moving up or down. For example, we get the same price for a European option when the probability of an upward movement is 0.5 as we do when it is 0.9. This is surprising and seems counterintuitive. It is natural to assume that as the probability of an upward movement in the stock price increases, the value of a call option on the stock increases and the value of a put option on the stock decreases. This is not the case.

The key reason for this is that we are not valuing the option in absolute terms. We are calculating its value in terms of the price of the underlying stock. The probabilities of future up or down movements are already incorporated into the price of the stock. It turns out that we do not need to take them into account again when valuing the option in terms of the stock price.

9.2 RISK-NEUTRAL VALUATION

Although we do not need to make any assumptions about the probabilities of up and down movements to derive equation (9.2), it is natural to interpret the variable p in equation (9.2) as the probability of an up movement in the stock price. The variable $1 - p$ is then the probability of a down movement and the expression

$$p f_u + (1 - p) f_d$$

is the expected payoff from the derivative. With this interpretation of p, equation (9.2) then states that the value of the derivative today is its expected future value discounted at the risk-free rate.

We now investigate the expected return from the stock when the probability of an up movement is assumed to be p. The expected stock price at time T, $E(S_T)$, is given by

$$E(S_T) = pSu + (1 - p)Sd$$

or

$$E(S_T) = pS(u - d) + Sd$$

Substituting from equation (9.3) for p, this reduces to

$$E(S_T) = Se^{rT} \tag{9.4}$$

showing that the stock price grows on average at the risk-free rate. Setting the probability of the up movement equal to p is therefore equivalent to assuming that the return on the stock equals the risk-free rate.

We will refer to a world where everyone is risk neutral as a *risk-neutral world*. In such a world investors require no compensation for risk, and the expected return on all securities is the risk-free interest rate. Equation (9.4) shows that we are assuming a risk-neutral world when we set the probability of an up movement to p. Equation (9.2) shows that the value of the derivative is its expected payoff in a risk-neutral world discounted at the risk-free rate.

This result is an example of an important general principle in option pricing known as *risk-neutral valuation*. This states that we can with complete impunity assume that the world is risk neutral when pricing options and other derivatives. The prices we get are correct not just in a risk-neutral world but in other worlds as well.

One-Step Binomial Example Revisited

To illustrate the principle of risk-neutral valuation further, consider again the example in Figure 9.1. The stock price is currently $20 and will move either up to $22 or down to $18 at the end of three months. The derivative considered is a European call option with a strike price of $21 and an expiration date in three months. The risk-free interest rate is 12% per annum.

We denote the probability of an upward movement in the stock price in a risk-neutral world by p. In such a world the expected return on the stock must be the risk-free rate of 12%. This means that p must satisfy

$$22p + 18(1 - p) = 20e^{0.12 \times 0.25}$$

or

$$4p = 20e^{0.12 \times 0.25} - 18$$

That is, p must be 0.6523.

At the end of the three months the call option has a 0.6523 probability of being worth 1 and a 0.3477 probability of being worth zero. Its expected value is, therefore,

$$0.6523 \times 1 + 0.3477 \times 0 = \$0.6523$$

Discounting at the risk-free rate, the value of the option today is

$$0.6523e^{-0.12 \times 0.25}$$

or $0.633. This is the same as the value obtained earlier, demonstrating that no-arbitrage arguments and risk-neutral valuation give the same answer.

9.3 TWO-STEP BINOMIAL TREES

We can extend the analysis that has been given to a two-step binomial tree such as that shown in Figure 9.3. Here the stock price starts at $20 and in each of two time steps may go up by 10% or down by 10%. We suppose that each time step is three months in length and the risk-free interest rate is 12% per annum. As before, we consider an option with a strike price of $21.

The objective of our analysis is to calculate the option price at the initial node of the tree. This can be done by repeatedly applying the principles established earlier in this chapter. Figure 9.4 shows the same tree as Figure 9.3, but with both the stock price and the option price at each node. (The stock price is the upper number and the option price is the lower number.) The option prices at the final nodes of the tree are easily calculated. They are the payoffs from the option. At node D the stock price is 24.2 and the option's price is $24.2 - 21 = 3.2$; at nodes E and F the option is out of the money and its value is zero.

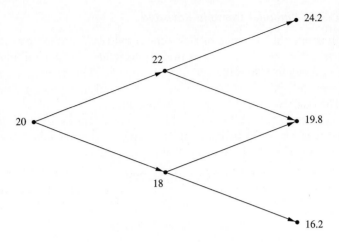

Figure 9.3   Stock prices in a two-step tree.

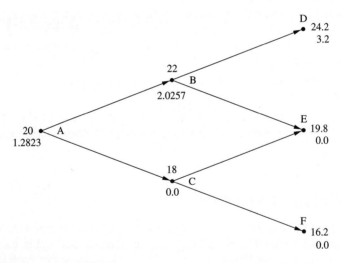

Figure 9.4   Stock and option prices in a two-step tree. The upper number at each node is the stock price; the lower number is the option price.

At node C the option price is zero, since node C leads to either node E or node F, and at both of these nodes the option price is zero. We calculate the option price at node B by focusing our attention on the part of the tree shown in Figure 9.5. Using the notation introduced earlier in the chapter, $u = 1.1$, $d = 0.9$, $r = 0.12$, $T = 0.25$, and $p = 0.6523$, and equation (9.2) gives the value of the option at node B as

$$e^{-0.12 \times 0.25}(0.6523 \times 3.2 + 0.3477 \times 0) = 2.0257$$

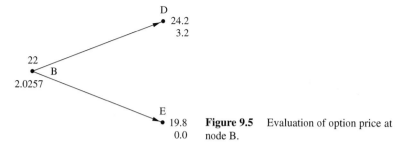

D
24.2
3.2

22
B
2.0257

E
19.8   **Figure 9.5**   Evaluation of option price at
0.0   node B.

It remains to calculate the option price at the initial node A. We do this by focusing on the first step of the tree. We know that the value of the option at node B is 2.0257 and that at node C it is zero. Equation (9.2) therefore gives the value at node A as

$$e^{-0.12 \times 0.25}(0.6523 \times 2.0257 + 0.3477 \times 0) = 1.2823$$

The price of the option is $1.2823.

Note that this example was constructed so that u and d (the proportional up and down movements) were the same at each node of the tree and so that the time steps were of the same length. This led to the risk-neutral probability, p, as calculated by equation (9.3), being the same at each node.

Generalization

We can generalize the case of two time steps by considering the situation shown in Figure 9.6. The stock price is initially S. During each time step, it

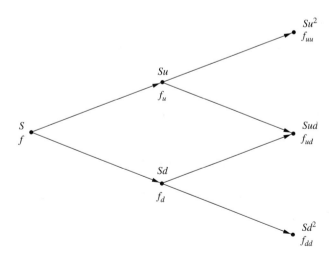

Figure 9.6   Stock and option prices in general two-step tree.

either moves up to u times its initial value or down to d times its initial value. The notation for the value of the derivative is shown on the tree. (For example, after two up movements the value of the derivative is f_{uu}.) We suppose that the risk-free interest rate is r and the length of the time step is Δt years.

Repeated application of equation (9.2) gives

$$f_u = e^{-r\Delta t}[pf_{uu} + (1-p)f_{ud}] \tag{9.5}$$

$$f_d = e^{-r\Delta t}[pf_{ud} + (1-p)f_{dd}] \tag{9.6}$$

$$f = e^{-r\Delta t}[pf_u + (1-p)f_d] \tag{9.7}$$

Substituting from equations (9.5) and (9.6) in (9.7), we get

$$f = e^{-2r\Delta t}[p^2 f_{uu} + 2p(1-p)f_{ud} + (1-p)^2 f_{dd}] \tag{9.8}$$

This is consistent with the principle of risk-neutral valuation mentioned earlier. The variables p^2, $2p(1-p)$, and $(1-p)^2$ are the probabilities of the upper, middle, and lower final nodes being reached. The derivative's price is equal to its expected payoff in a risk-neutral world discounted at the risk-free interest rate.

If we generalize the use of binomial trees still further by adding more steps to the tree, we find that the risk-neutral valuation principle continues to hold. The derivative's price is always equal to its expected payoff in a risk-neutral world, discounted at the risk-free interest rate.

9.4 PUT EXAMPLE

The procedures described in this chapter can be used to price any derivative dependent on a stock whose price changes are binomial. Consider, for example, a two-year European put with a strike price of 52 on a stock whose current price is 50. We suppose that there are two time steps of one year and in each time step the stock price either moves up by a proportional amount of 20% or down by a proportional amount of 20%. We also suppose that the risk-free interest rate is 5%.

The tree is shown in Figure 9.7. The value of the risk-neutral probability, p, is given by

$$p = \frac{e^{0.05 \times 1} - 0.8}{1.2 - 0.8} = 0.6282$$

The possible final stock prices are 72, 48, and 32. In this case $f_{uu} = 0$, $f_{ud} = 4$, $f_{dd} = 20$, and $\Delta t = 1$. Using equation (9.8), we have

$$f = e^{-2 \times 0.05 \times 1}(0.6282^2 \times 0 + 2 \times 0.6282 \times 0.3718 \times 4 + 0.3718^2 \times 20)$$

$$= 4.1923$$

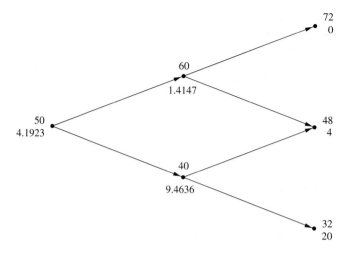

Figure 9.7 Use of two time-step tree to value European put option. At each node the upper number is the stock price; the lower number is the option price.

The value of the put is $4.1923. This result can also be obtained using equation (9.2) and working back through the tree one step at a time. Figure 9.7 shows the intermediate option prices that are calculated.

9.5 AMERICAN OPTIONS

Up to now the options we have considered have been European. We now move on to consider how American options can be valued using a binomial tree such as that shown in Figures 9.4 or 9.7. The procedure is to work back through the tree from the end to the beginning, testing at each node to see whether early exercise is optimal. The value of the option at the final nodes is the same as for the European option. At earlier nodes the value of the option is the greater of

1. The value given by equation (9.2).
2. The payoff from early exercise.

As an illustration, we consider how Figure 9.7 is affected if the option under consideration is American rather than European. The stock prices and their probabilities are of course unchanged. The values for the option at the final nodes are also unchanged. At node B, equation (9.2) gives the value of the option as 1.4147, while the payoff from early exercise is negative ($= -8$). Clearly, early exercise is not optimal at node B and the value of the option at this node is 1.4147. At node C, equation (9.2) gives the value of the option as 9.4636, while the payoff

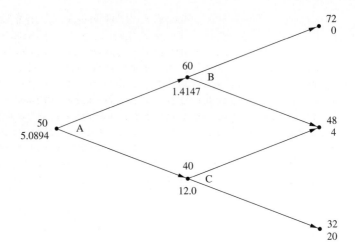

Figure 9.8   Use of two time-step tree to value American put option. At each node the upper number is the stock price; the lower number is the option price.

from early exercise is 12.0. In this case early exercise is optimal and the value of the option is 12.0. At the initial node A the value given by equation (9.2) is

$$e^{-0.05 \times 1}(0.6282 \times 1.4147 + 0.3718 \times 12.0) = 5.0894$$

while the payoff from early exercise is 2.0. In this case early exercise is not optimal. The value of the option is, therefore, $5.0894. Figure 9.8 shows the new tree values. More details on the use of binomial trees to value American options are provided in Chapter 15.

9.6 DELTA

At this stage it is appropriate to discuss *delta*, an important parameter in the pricing and hedging of options. The delta of a stock option is the ratio of the change in the price of a stock option to the change in the price of the underlying stock. It is the number of units of the stock we should hold for each option shorted to create a riskless hedge. It is the same as the Δ introduced earlier in this chapter. The construction of a riskless hedge is sometimes referred to as *delta hedging*. The delta of a call option is positive, whereas the delta of a put option is negative.

From Figure 9.1 we can calculate the value of the delta of the call option being considered as

$$\frac{1 - 0}{22 - 18} = 0.25$$

This is because when the stock price changes from 18 to 22, the option price changes from 0 to 1.

In Figure 9.4 the delta corresponding to stock price movements over the first time step is

$$\frac{2.0257 - 0}{22 - 18} = 0.5064$$

The delta for stock price movements over the second time step is

$$\frac{3.2 - 0}{24.2 - 19.8} = 0.7273$$

if there is an upward movement over the first time step and

$$\frac{0 - 0}{19.8 - 16} = 0$$

if there is a downward movement over the first time step.

In Figure 9.7, delta is

$$\frac{1.4147 - 9.4636}{60 - 40} = -0.4024$$

for the first time step and either

$$\frac{0 - 4}{72 - 48} = -0.1667$$

or

$$\frac{4 - 20}{48 - 32} = -1.0000$$

over the second time step.

The two-step examples show that delta changes over time. (In Figure 9.4 delta changes from 0.5064 to either 0.7273 or 0; in Figure 9.7 it changes from -0.4024 to either -0.1667 or -1.0000.)[1] This means that to maintain a riskless hedge using an option and the underlying stock, we need to adjust our holdings in the stock periodically. This is a feature of options that we return to in Chapters 11 and 14.

9.7 USING BINOMIAL TREES IN PRACTICE

The binomial models presented so far have been unrealistically simple. Clearly, an analyst can expect to obtain only a very rough approximation to an option price by assuming that stock price movements during the life of the option consist of one or two binomial steps.

---

[1]Note that the risk-neutral probability, p, does remain the same throughout the tree provided that the proportional up movement u, the proportional down movement d, and the time step Δt are kept constant.

When binomial trees are used in practice, the life of the option is typically divided into 30 or more time steps. In each time step there is a binomial stock price movement. With 30 time steps this means that 31 terminal stock prices and 2^{30}, or about 1 billion, possible stock price paths are considered.

The values of u and d are determined from the stock price volatility, σ. There are a number of different ways that this can be done. If we define Δt as the length of one time step, one possibility is to set

$$u = e^{\sigma \sqrt{\Delta t}}$$

and

$$d = \frac{1}{u}$$

The complete set of equations defining the tree is then

$$u = e^{\sigma \sqrt{\Delta t}} \qquad d = e^{-\sigma \sqrt{\Delta t}}$$

$$p = \frac{e^{r\Delta t} - d}{u - d}$$

Chapter 15 provides a further discussion of these formulas and practical issues involved in the construction and use of binomial trees.

9.8 SUMMARY

This chapter has provided a first look at the valuation of stock options and other derivatives. If stock price movements during the life of an option on the stock are governed by a one-step binomial tree, it is possible to set up a portfolio consisting of a stock option and the stock that is riskless. In a world where there are no arbitrage opportunities, riskless portfolios must earn the risk-free interest. This enables the stock option to be priced in terms of the underlying stock. It is interesting to note that no assumptions are required about the probabilities of up and down movements in the stock price at each node.

When stock price movements are governed by a multistep binomial tree, we can treat each binomial step separately and work back from the end of the life of the option to the beginning to obtain the current value of the option. Again only no-arbitrage arguments are used and no assumptions are required about the probabilities of up and down movements in the stock price at each node.

Another approach to valuing derivatives involves the use of what is known as risk-neutral valuation. This is a very important principle that states that it is permissible to assume that the world is risk neutral when valuing options and other derivatives in terms of the underlying asset. In this chapter we have shown using both numerical examples and algebra that no-arbitrage arguments and risk-neutral valuation lead to the same prices for a derivative.

The delta of an equity derivative, Δ, considers the effect of a small change in the underlying stock price on the derivative's price. It is the ratio of the change in the derivative's price to the change in the stock price. For a riskless position an investor should buy Δ shares for each option sold. An inspection of a typical binomial tree shows that delta is liable to change during the life of an option. This means that riskless positions do not automatically remain riskless. They must be adjusted periodically.

In Chapter 11 we discuss the Black–Scholes analytic approach to pricing stock options. In Chapters 12 and 13 we discuss other types of options. In Chapter 14 we move on to consider hedge statistics such as delta. In Chapter 15 we return to binomial trees and provide a more complete discussion of how they are used in practice.

SUGGESTIONS FOR FURTHER READING

Cox, J., S. Ross, and M. Rubinstein, "Option Pricing: A Simplified Approach," *Journal of Financial Economics,* 7 (October 1979), 229–64.

Rendleman, R. and B. Bartter, "Two State Option Pricing," *Journal of Finance,* 34 (1979), 1092–1110.

QUESTIONS AND PROBLEMS

9.1. A stock price is currently $40. It is known that at the end of one month it will be either $42 or $38. The risk-free interest rate is 8% per annum with continuous compounding. What is the value of a one-month European call option with a strike price of $39?

9.2. Explain the no-arbitrage and risk-neutral valuation approaches to valuing a European option using a one-step binomial tree.

9.3. What is the delta of a stock option?

9.4. A stock price is currently $50. It is known that at the end of six months it will be either $45 or $55. The risk-free interest rate is 10% per annum with continuous compounding. What is the the value of a six-month European put option with a strike price of $50?

9.5. A stock price is currently $100. Over each of the next two six-month periods it is expected to go up by 10% or down by 10%. The risk-free interest rate is 8% per annum with continuous compounding. What is the value of a one-year European call option with a strike price of $100?

9.6. For the situation considered in Problem 9.5, what is the value of a one-year European put option with a strike price of $100? Verify that the European call and European put prices satisfy put–call parity.

9.7. Consider the situation where stock price movements during the life of a European option are governed by a two-step binomial tree. Explain why it is not possible to

set up a position in the stock and the option that remains riskless for the whole of the life of the option.

9.8. A stock price is currently $50. It is known that at the end of two months it will be either $53 or $48. The risk-free interest rate is 10% per annum with continuous compounding. What is the value of a two-month European call option with a strike price of $49? Use no-arbitrage arguments.

9.9. A stock price is currently $80. It is known that at the end of four months it will be either $75 or $85. The risk-free interest rate is 5% per annum with continuous compounding. What is the value of a four-month European put option with a strike price of $80? Use no-arbitrage arguments.

9.10. A stock price is currently $50. It is known that at the end of six months it will be either $60 or $42. The risk-free rate of interest with continuous compounding is 12% per annum. Calculate the value of a six-month European call option on the stock with an exercise price of $48. Verify that no-arbitrage arguments and risk-neutral valuation arguments give the same answers.

9.11. A stock price is currently $40. It is known that at the end of three months it will be either $45 or $35. The risk-free rate of interest with quarterly compounding is 8% per annum. Calculate the value of a three-month European put option on the stock with an exercise price of $40. Verify that no-arbitrage arguments and risk-neutral valuation arguments give the same answers.

9.12. A stock price is currently $50. Over each of the next two three-month periods it is expected to go up by 6% or down by 5%. The risk-free interest rate is 5% per annum with continuous compounding. What is the value of a six-month European call option with a strike price of $51?

9.13. For the situation considered in Problem 9.12, what is the value of a six-month European put option with a strike price of $51? Verify that the European call and European put prices satisfy put–call parity. If the put option were American, would it ever be optimal to exercise it early at any of the nodes on the tree?

9.14. A stock price is currently $40. Over each of the next two three-month periods it is expected to go up by 10% or down by 10%. The risk-free interest rate is 12% per annum with continuous compounding.
(a) What is the value of a six-month European put option with a strike price of $42?
(b) What is the value of a six-month American put option with a strike price of $42?

9.15. Estimate using "trial and error" how high the strike price has to be in Problem 9.14 for it to be optimal to exercise the option immediately.

9.16. A stock price is currently $25. It is known that at the end of two months it will be either $23 or $27. The risk-free interest rate is 10% per annum with continuous compounding. Suppose that S_T is the stock price at the end of two months. What is the value of a derivative that pays off S_T^2 at this time?

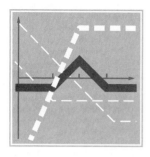

C h a p t e r 1 0

Model of the Behavior of Stock Prices

Any variable whose value changes over time in an uncertain way is said to follow a *stochastic process*. Stochastic processes can be classified as *discrete time* or *continuous time*. A discrete-time stochastic process is one where the value of the variable can change only at certain fixed points in time, whereas a continuous-time stochastic process is one where changes can take place at any time. Stochastic processes can also be classified as *continuous variable* or *discrete variable*. In a continuous-variable process, the underlying variable can take any value within a certain range, whereas in a discrete-variable process, only certain discrete values are possible.

In this chapter we derive a continuous-variable, continuous-time stochastic process for stock prices. An understanding of this process is the first step to understanding the pricing of options and other more complicated derivatives. It should be pointed out that in practice we do not observe stock prices following continuous-variable, continuous-time processes. Stock prices are restricted to discrete values (usually multiples of $\$\frac{1}{8}$) and changes can be observed only when the exchange is open. Nevertheless, the continuous-variable, continuous-time process proves to be a useful model for most purposes.

In this chapter we introduce what is known as *stochastic calculus*. This is an extension of regular calculus that deals with continuous-time stochastic processes. Many people feel that continuous-time stochastic processes are so complicated that they must be left entirely to "rocket scientists." This is not so. The biggest hurdle to understanding these processes is the notation. In this chapter we present a step-by-step approach aimed at getting the reader over this hurdle.

10.1 THE MARKOV PROPERTY

A *Markov process* is a particular type of stochastic process where only the present value of a variable is relevant for predicting the future. The past history of the variable and the way in which the present has emerged from the past are irrelevant.

Stock prices are usually assumed to follow a Markov process. Suppose that the price of IBM stock is $100 now. If the stock price follows a Markov process,

our predictions for the future should be unaffected by the price one week ago, one month ago, or one year ago. The only relevant piece of information is the fact that the price is now \$100.[1] Predictions for the future are uncertain and must be expressed in terms of probability distributions. The Markov property implies that the probability distribution of the price at any particular future time depends only on the current stock price of \$100.

The Markov property of stock prices is consistent with the weak form of market efficiency. This states that the present price of a stock impounds all the information contained in a record of past prices. If the weak form of market efficiency were not true, technical analysts could make above-average returns by interpreting charts of the past history of stock prices. There is very little evidence that they are in fact able to do this.

It is competition in the marketplace which tends to ensure that weak-form market efficiency holds. The very fact that there are many, many investors watching the stock market closely and trying to make a profit from it leads to a situation where a stock price at any given time impounds the information in past prices. Suppose that it is discovered that a particular pattern in past stock prices always gives a 65% chance of price rises in the near future. Investors would attempt to buy a stock as soon as the pattern was observed, and demand for the stock would immediately rise. This would lead to an immediate rise in its price and the observed effect would be eliminated, as would any profitable trading opportunities.

10.2 WIENER PROCESSES

Models of stock price behavior are usually expressed in terms of what are known as *Wiener processes.* A Wiener process is a particular type of Markov stochastic process. It has been used in physics to describe the motion of a particle that is subject to a large number of small molecular shocks and is sometimes referred to as *Brownian motion.*

The behavior of a variable, z, which follows a Wiener process, can be understood by considering the changes in its value in small intervals of time. Consider a small interval of time of length Δt and define Δz as the change in z during Δt. There are two basic properties Δz must have for z to be following a Wiener process:

Property 1. Δz is related to Δt by the equation

$$\Delta z = \epsilon \sqrt{\Delta t} \qquad (10.1)$$

where ϵ is a random drawing from a standardized normal distribution (i.e., a normal distribution with a mean of zero and a standard deviation of 1.0).

---

[1] Statistical properties of the stock price history of IBM may be useful in determining the characteristics of the stochastic process followed by the stock price (e.g., its volatility). The point being made here is that the particular path followed by the stock in the past is irrelevant.

Property 2. The values of Δz for any two different short intervals of time Δt are independent.

It follows from property 1 that Δz itself has a normal distribution with

$$\text{mean of } \Delta z = 0$$

$$\text{standard deviation of } \Delta z = \sqrt{\Delta t}$$

$$\text{variance of } \Delta z = \Delta t$$

Property 2 implies that z follows a Markov process.

Consider next the increase in the value of z during a relatively long period of time, T. This can be denoted by $z(T) - z(0)$. It can be regarded as the sum of the increases in z in N small time intervals of length Δt, where

$$N = \frac{T}{\Delta t}$$

Thus

$$z(T) - z(0) = \sum_{i=1}^{N} \epsilon_i \sqrt{\Delta t} \tag{10.2}$$

where the ϵ_i ($i = 1, 2, \ldots, N$) are random drawings from a standardized normal distribution. From property 2 the ϵ_i's are independent of each other. It follows from equation (10.2) that $z(T) - z(0)$ is normally distributed with[2]

$$\text{mean of } [z(T) - z(0)] = 0$$

$$\text{variance of } [z(T) - z(0)] = N\Delta t = T$$

$$\text{standard deviation of } [z(T) - z(0)] = \sqrt{T}$$

Thus in any time interval of length T, the increase in the value of a variable that follows a Wiener process is normally distributed with a mean of zero and a standard deviation of $\sqrt{T}$. It should now be clear why Δz is defined as the product of ϵ and $\sqrt{\Delta t}$ rather than as the product of ϵ and Δt. Variances are additive for independent normal distributions; standard deviations are not. It makes sense to define the stochastic process so that the variance rather than the standard deviation of changes is proportional to the length of the time interval considered.

Example 10.1

Suppose that the value, z, of a variable which follows a Wiener process is initially 25 and that time is measured in years. At the end of one year the value of the variable is normally

---

[2]This result is based on the following well-known property of normal distributions. If a variable Y is equal to the sum of N independent normally distributed variables X_i ($1 \leq i \leq N$), Y is itself normally distributed. The mean of Y is equal to the sum of the means of the X_i's. The variance of Y is equal to the sum of the variances of the X_i's.

distributed with a mean of 25 and a standard deviation of 1.0. At the end of two years it is normally distributed with a mean of 25 and a standard deviation of $\sqrt{2}$, or 1.414. Note that our uncertainty about the value of the variable at a certain time in the future, as measured by its standard deviation, increases as the square root of how far we are looking ahead.

In ordinary calculus it is usual to proceed from small changes to the limit as the small changes become closer to zero. Thus $\Delta y / \Delta x$ becomes dy/dx in the limit, and so on. We can proceed similarly when dealing with continuous-time stochastic processes. A Wiener process is the limit as $\Delta t \longrightarrow 0$ of the process described above for z. Figure 10.1 illustrates what happens to the path followed by z as the limit $\Delta t \longrightarrow 0$ is taken. Analogously to ordinary calculus, we write the limiting case of equation (10.1) as

$$dz = \epsilon \sqrt{dt}$$

Generalized Wiener Process

The basic Wiener process that has been developed so far has a drift rate of zero and a variance rate of 1.0. The drift rate of zero means that the expected value of z at any future time is equal to its current value. The variance rate of 1.0 means that the variance of the change in z in a time interval of length T equals T. A *generalized Wiener process* for a variable x can be defined in terms of dz as follows:

$$dx = a\,dt + b\,dz \qquad (10.3)$$

where a and b are constants.

To understand equation (10.3) it is useful to consider the two components on the right-hand side separately. The $a\,dt$ term implies that x has an expected drift rate of a per unit time. Without the $b\,dz$ term, the equation is

$$dx = a\,dt$$

which implies that

$$\frac{dx}{dt} = a$$

or

$$x = x_0 + at$$

where x_0 is the value of x at time zero. In a time interval of length T, x increases by an amount aT. The $b\,dz$ term on the right-hand side of equation (10.3) can be regarded as adding noise or variability to the path followed by x. The amount of this noise or variability is b times a Wiener process. In a small time interval Δt, the change in the value of x, Δx, is from equations (10.1) and (10.3) given by

$$\Delta x = a\,\Delta t + b\epsilon \sqrt{\Delta t}$$

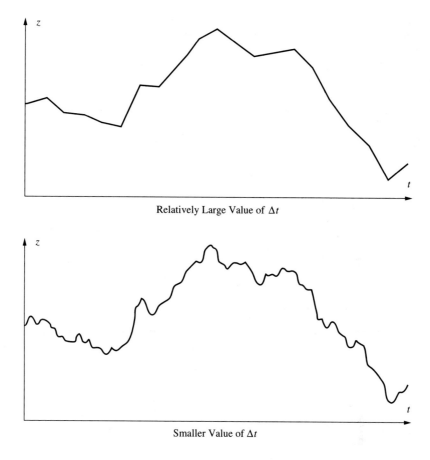

Relatively Large Value of Δt

Smaller Value of Δt

The True Process Obtained as $\Delta t \longrightarrow 0$

Figure 10.1   How a Wiener process is obtained when $\Delta t \longrightarrow 0$ in equation (10.1).

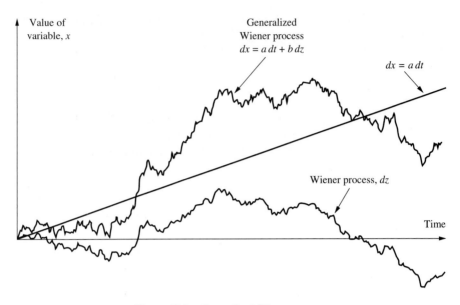

Figure 10.2   Generalized Wiener process.

where, as before, ϵ is a random drawing from a standardized normal distribution. Thus Δx has a normal distribution with

$$\text{mean of } \Delta x = a\Delta t$$

$$\text{standard deviation of } \Delta x = b\sqrt{\Delta t}$$

$$\text{variance of } \Delta x = b^2\Delta t$$

Similar arguments to those just given show that the change in the value of x in any time interval T is normally distributed with

$$\text{mean of change in } x = aT$$

$$\text{standard deviation of change in } x = b\sqrt{T}$$

$$\text{variance of change in } x = b^2T$$

Thus the generalized Wiener process given in equation (10.3) has an expected drift rate (i.e., average drift per unit time) of a and a variance rate (i.e., variance per unit of time) of b^2. It is illustrated in Figure 10.2.

Example 10.2

Consider the situation where the cash position of a company, measured in thousands of dollars, follows a generalized Wiener process with a drift of 20 per year and a variance rate of 900 per year. Initially, the cash position is 50. At the end of one year the cash position will have a normal distribution with a mean of 70 and a standard deviation of $\sqrt{900}$ or 30. At the end of six months it will have a normal distribution with a mean of 60 and a standard deviation of $30\sqrt{0.5} = 21.21$. Note that our uncertainty about the cash

position at some time in the future, as measured by its standard deviation, increases as the square root of how far ahead we are looking. Also, note that the cash position can become negative (which we can interpret as a situation where the company is borrowing funds).

Ito Process

A further type of stochastic process can be defined. This is known as an *Ito process.* It is a generalized Wiener process where the parameters a and b are functions of the value of the underlying variable, x, and time, t. Algebraically, an Ito process can be written

$$dx = a(x, t) dt + b(x, t) dz \qquad (10.4)$$

Both the expected drift rate and variance rate of an Ito process are liable to change over time.

10.3 THE PROCESS FOR STOCK PRICES

In this section we discuss the stochastic process followed by the price of a non-dividend-paying stock. The effects of dividends on the process are discussed in Chapter 11.

It is tempting to suggest that a stock price follows a generalized Wiener process; that is, that it has a constant expected drift rate and a constant variance rate. However, this model fails to capture a key aspect of stock prices. This is that the expected percentage return required by investors from a stock is independent of the stock's price. If investors require a 14% per annum expected return when the stock price is $10, then, *ceteris paribus,* they will also require a 14% per annum expected return when it is $50.

Clearly, the constant expected drift-rate assumption is inappropriate and needs to be replaced by the assumption that the expected drift, expressed as a proportion of the stock price, is constant. The latter implies that if S is the stock price, the expected drift rate in S is μS for some constant parameter, μ. Thus, in a short interval of time, Δt, the expected increase in S is $\mu S \Delta t$. The parameter, μ, is the expected rate of return on the stock, expressed in decimal form.

If the variance rate of the stock price is always zero, this model implies that

$$dS = \mu S \, dt$$

or

$$\frac{dS}{S} = \mu \, dt$$

so that

$$S = S_0 e^{\mu t} \qquad (10.5)$$

where S_0 is the stock price at time zero. Equation (10.5) shows that when the variance rate is zero, the stock price grows at a continuously compounded rate of μ per unit time.

In practice, of course, a stock price does exhibit volatility. A reasonable assumption is that the variance of the percentage return in a short period of time, Δt, is the same regardless of the stock price. In other words, an investor is just as uncertain as to his or her percentage return when the stock price is $50 as when it is $10. Define σ^2 as the variance rate of the proportional change in the stock price. This means that $\sigma^2 \Delta t$ is the variance of the proportional change in the stock price in time Δt and that $\sigma^2 S^2 \Delta t$ is the variance of the actual change in the stock price, S, during Δt. The instantaneous variance rate of S is therefore $\sigma^2 S^2$.

These arguments suggest that S can be represented by an Ito process which has instantaneous expected drift rate μS and instantaneous variance rate $\sigma^2 S^2$. This can be written as

$$dS = \mu S \, dt + \sigma S \, dz$$

or

$$\frac{dS}{S} = \mu \, dt + \sigma \, dz \qquad (10.6)$$

Equation (10.6) is the most widely used model of stock price behavior. The variable σ is usually referred to as the *stock price volatility*. The variable μ is its expected rate of return.

Example 10.3

Consider a stock that pays no dividends, has a volatility of 30% per annum, and provides an expected return of 15% per annum with continuous compounding. In this case $\mu = 0.15$ and $\sigma = 0.30$. The process for the stock price is

$$\frac{dS}{S} = 0.15 \, dt + 0.30 \, dz$$

If S is the stock price at a particular time and ΔS is the increase in the stock price in the next small interval of time,

$$\frac{\Delta S}{S} = 0.15 \Delta t + 0.30 \epsilon \sqrt{\Delta t}$$

where ϵ is a random drawing from a standardized normal distribution. Consider a time interval of one week or 0.0192 year and suppose that the initial stock price is $100. Then $\Delta t = 0.0192$, $S = 100$, and

$$\Delta S = 100(0.00288 + 0.0416 \epsilon)$$

or

$$\Delta S = 0.288 + 4.16 \epsilon$$

showing that the price increase is a random drawing from a normal distribution with mean $0.288 and standard deviation $4.16.

10.4 REVIEW OF THE MODEL

The model of stock price behavior that has been developed in this chapter [see equation (10.6)] is sometimes known as *geometric Brownian motion*. The discrete-time version of the model is

$$\frac{\Delta S}{S} = \mu \Delta t + \sigma \epsilon \sqrt{\Delta t} \tag{10.7}$$

The variable ΔS is the change in the stock price, S, in a small interval of time, Δt; and ϵ is a random drawing from a standardized normal distribution (i.e., a normal distribution with a mean of zero and standard deviation of 1.0). The parameter μ is the expected rate of return per unit time from the stock and the parameter σ is the volatility of the stock price. Both of these parameters are assumed constant.

The left-hand side of equation (10.7) is the proportional return provided by the stock in a short period of time Δt. The term $\mu \Delta t$ is the expected value of this return, while the term $\sigma \epsilon \sqrt{\Delta t}$ is the stochastic component of the return. The variance of the stochastic component (and therefore of the whole return) is $\sigma^2 \Delta t$.

Equation (10.7) shows that $\Delta S / S$ is normally distributed with mean $\mu \Delta t$ and standard deviation $\sigma \sqrt{\Delta t}$. In other words,

$$\frac{\Delta S}{S} \sim \phi(\mu \Delta t, \sigma \sqrt{\Delta t}) \tag{10.8}$$

where $\phi(m, s)$ denotes a normal distribution with mean m and standard deviation s.

Monte Carlo Simulation

Suppose that the expected return from the stock is 14% per annum and that the standard deviation of the return (i.e., the volatility) is 20% per annum. If time is measured in years, it follows that

$$\mu = 0.14$$

$$\sigma = 0.20$$

Suppose that $\Delta t = 0.01$ so that we are considering changes in the stock price in time intervals of length 0.01 year (or 3.65 days). It follows that $\Delta S / S$ is normal with mean 0.0014 ($= 0.14 \times 0.01$) and standard deviation 0.02 ($= 0.2 \times \sqrt{0.01}$), that is,

$$\frac{\Delta S}{S} \sim \phi(0.0014,\ 0.02) \tag{10.9}$$

A path for the stock price can be simulated by sampling repeatedly from $\phi(0.0014, 0.02)$. One procedure for doing this is to sample values, v_1, from a standardized normal distribution [i.e., $\phi(0, 1)$] and then convert these to samples, v_2, from $\phi(0.0014, 0.02)$ using

$$v_2 = 0.0014 + 0.02 v_1 \tag{10.10}$$

Table 10.1 shows one particular simulation of stock price movements. The initial stock price is assumed to be $20. For the first period the random number, v_1, sampled from $\phi(0, 1)$ is 0.52. Using equation (10.10), this gives a random sample of 0.0118 from $\phi(0.0014, 0.02)$. Using equation (10.9), $\Delta S = 20 \times 0.0118$, or 0.236. At the beginning of the next period the stock price is therefore $20.236, and so on. Note that the samples, v_2, must be independent of each other. Otherwise, the Markov property, discussed in Section 10.1, does not hold.

Table 10.1 assumes that stock prices are measured to the nearest 0.001, which of course is not the case. To get the stock price that would be quoted, the figures in the first column of the table should be rounded to the nearest $\$\frac{1}{8}$. It is important to realize that the table shows only one possible pattern of stock price movements. Different random samples would lead to different price movements. Any small time interval Δt can be used in the simulation. However, only in the limit as $\Delta t \longrightarrow 0$ is a true description of geometric Brownian motion obtained. The final stock price of 21.124 in Table 10.1 can be regarded as a random sample from the distribution of stock prices at the end of 10 time intervals or one-tenth of a year. By repeatedly simulating movements in the stock price, as in Table 10.1,

TABLE 10.1   Simulation of Stock Price When $\mu = 0.14$
and $\sigma = 0.20$ during Periods of Length 0.01 Year

Stock Price at Start of Period	Random Sample, v_1, from $\phi(0, 1)$	Corresponding Random Sample, v_2, from $\phi(0.0014, 0.02)$	Change in Stock Price during Period
20.000	0.52	0.0118	0.236
20.236	1.44	0.0302	0.611
20.847	−0.86	−0.0158	−0.329
20.518	1.46	0.0306	0.628
21.146	−0.69	−0.0124	−0.262
20.883	−0.74	−0.0134	−0.280
20.603	0.21	0.0056	0.115
20.719	−1.10	−0.0206	−0.427
20.292	0.73	0.0160	0.325
20.617	1.16	0.0246	0.507
21.124	2.56	0.0526	1.111

a complete probability distribution of the stock price at the end of one-tenth of a year is obtained.

10.5 THE PARAMETERS

The process for stock prices that has been developed in this chapter involves two parameters, μ and σ. The values of those parameters depend on the units in which time is measured. Here and elsewhere in this book, we assume that time is measured in years.

The parameter μ is the expected return earned by an investor in a short period of time. It is annualized and expressed as a proportion. Most investors require higher expected returns to induce them to take higher risks. It follows that the value of μ should depend on the risk of the return from the stock.[3] It should also depend on the level of interest rates in the economy. The higher the level of interest rates, the higher the expected return required on any given stock. On average, μ is about 8% greater than the return on a risk-free investment such as a Treasury bill.[4] Thus when the return on Treasury bills is 8% per annum, or 0.08, a typical value of μ is 0.16; that is, a typical expected return on a stock is 16% per annum.

Fortunately, we do not have to concern ourselves with the determinants of μ in any detail because the value of a derivative dependent on a stock is in general independent of μ. The parameter σ, the stock price volatility, is, by contrast, critically important to the determination of the value of most derivatives. Procedures for estimating σ empirically are discussed in Chapter 11. Typical values of σ for a stock are in the range 0.20 to 0.40 (i.e., 20 to 40%).

The standard deviation of the proportional change in the stock price in a small interval of time Δt is $\sigma \sqrt{\Delta t}$. As a rough approximation, the standard deviation of the proportional change in the stock price in a relatively long period of time, T, is $\sigma \sqrt{T}$. This means that as an approximation, volatility can be interpreted as the standard deviation of the change in the stock price in one year.

Note that the standard deviation of the proportional change in the stock price in a relatively long time interval, T, is not exactly $\sigma \sqrt{T}$. This is because proportional changes are not additive. (For example, a 10% increase in a stock price followed by a 20% increase leads to a total increase of 32%, not 30%.) In Section 10.6 the probability distribution of the change in the logarithm of the stock price over a relatively long period of time T will be shown to be normal. The volatility of a stock price is exactly equal to the standard deviation of the continuously compounded return provided by the stock in one year.

[3]More precisely, μ depends on that part of the risk which cannot be diversified away by the investor.

[4]See R. G. Ibbotson and R. A. Sinquefield, *Stocks, Bonds, Bills and Inflation: The Past and the Future* (Charlotteville, Va.: Financial Analyst Research Foundation, 1982), Exhibit 29, p. 71.

10.6 ITO'S LEMMA

The price of a stock option is a function of the underlying stock's price and time. More generally, we can say that the price of any derivative is a function of the stochastic variables underlying the derivative and time. A serious student of derivatives must therefore acquire some understanding of the behavior of functions of stochastic variables. An important result in this area was discovered by a mathematician, K. Ito, in 1951.[5] It is known as *Ito's lemma.*

Suppose that the value of a variable x follows an Ito process:

$$dx = a(x, t)\,dt + b(x, t)\,dz \tag{10.11}$$

where dz is a Wiener process and a and b are functions of x and t. The variable x has a drift rate of a and a variance rate of b^2. Ito's lemma shows that a function, G, of x and t follows the process

$$dG = \left(\frac{\partial G}{\partial x}a + \frac{\partial G}{\partial t} + \frac{1}{2}\frac{\partial^2 G}{\partial x^2}b^2\right)dt + \frac{\partial G}{\partial x}b\,dz \tag{10.12}$$

where the dz is the same Wiener process as in equation (10.11). Thus G also follows an Ito process. It has a drift rate of

$$\frac{\partial G}{\partial x}a + \frac{\partial G}{\partial t} + \frac{1}{2}\frac{\partial^2 G}{\partial x^2}b^2$$

and a variance rate of

$$\left(\frac{\partial G}{\partial x}\right)^2 b^2$$

A completely rigorous proof of Ito's lemma is beyond the scope of this book. In Appendix 10A we show that the lemma can be viewed as an extension of well-known results in differential calculus.

Earlier in this chapter we argued that

$$dS = \mu S\,dt + \sigma S\,dz \tag{10.13}$$

with μ and σ constant is a reasonable model of stock price movements. From Ito's lemma, it follows that the process followed by a function, G, of S and t is

$$dG = \left(\frac{\partial G}{\partial S}\mu S + \frac{\partial G}{\partial t} + \frac{1}{2}\frac{\partial^2 G}{\partial S^2}\sigma^2 S^2\right)dt + \frac{\partial G}{\partial S}\sigma S\,dz \tag{10.14}$$

Note that both S and G are affected by the same underlying source of uncertainty, dz. This proves to be very important in the derivation of the Black–Scholes results.

[5] See K. Ito, "On Stochastic Differential Equations," *Memoirs, American Mathematical Society*, 4 (1951), 1–51.

Application to Forward Contracts

To illustrate Ito's lemma, consider a forward contract on a non-dividend-paying stock. Assume that the risk-free rate of interest is constant and equal to r for all maturities. Define F as the forward price. From equation (3.5),

$$F = Se^{r(T-t)}$$

so that

$$\frac{\partial F}{\partial S} = e^{r(T-t)} \qquad \frac{\partial^2 F}{\partial S^2} = 0 \qquad \frac{\partial F}{\partial t} = -rSe^{r(T-t)}$$

Assume that S follows geometric Brownian motion with expected return μ and volatility σ. [This is the process in equation (10.13).] The process for F is, from equation (10.14), given by

$$dF = \left[e^{r(T-t)}\mu S - rSe^{r(T-t)} \right] dt + e^{r(T-t)}\sigma S \, dz$$

Substituting $F = Se^{r(T-t)}$, this becomes

$$dF = (\mu - r)F \, dt + \sigma F \, dz \qquad (10.15)$$

Like S, F follows geometric Brownian motion. It has an expected growth rate of $\mu - r$ rather than μ. This is analogous to a result we proved in Section 3.7 that the growth rate in a stock index futures price is the excess return of the index over the risk-free rate.

Application to the Logarithm of the Stock Price

We now use Ito's lemma to derive the process followed by $\ln S$. Define

$$G = \ln S$$

Since

$$\frac{\partial G}{\partial S} = \frac{1}{S} \qquad \frac{\partial^2 G}{\partial S^2} = -\frac{1}{S^2} \qquad \frac{\partial G}{\partial t} = 0$$

it follows from equation (10.14) that the process followed by G is

$$dG = \left(\mu - \frac{\sigma^2}{2} \right) dt + \sigma \, dz$$

Since μ and σ are constant, this equation indicates that G follows a generalized Wiener process. It has constant drift rate $\mu - \sigma^2/2$ and constant variance rate σ^2. From the results earlier in this chapter, this means that the change in G between the current time, t, and some future time, T, is normally distributed with

mean

$$\left(\mu - \frac{\sigma^2}{2}\right)(T - t)$$

and variance

$$\sigma^2(T - t)$$

The value of G at time t is $\ln S$. Its value at time T is $\ln S_T$, where S_T is the stock price at time T. Its change during the time interval $T - t$ is therefore

$$\ln S_T - \ln S$$

Hence

$$\ln S_T - \ln S \sim \phi\left[\left(\mu - \frac{\sigma^2}{2}\right)(T - t), \sigma\sqrt{T - t}\right]$$

10.7 SUMMARY

Stochastic processes describe the probabilistic evolution of the value of a variable through time. A Markov process is one where only the present value of the variable is relevant for predicting the future. The past history of the variable and the way in which the present has emerged from the past is irrelevant.

A Wiener process, dz, is a process describing the evolution of a normally distributed variable. The drift of the process is zero and the variance rate is 1 per unit time. This means that if the value of the variable is x at time zero, at time T it is normally distributed with mean x and standard deviation $\sqrt{T}$.

A generalized Wiener process describes the evolution of a normally distributed variable with a drift of a per unit time and a variance rate of b^2 per unit time, where a and b are constants. This means that if the value of the variable is x at time zero, at time T it is normally distributed with a mean of $x + aT$ and a standard deviation of $b\sqrt{T}$.

An Ito process is a process where the drift and variance rate of x can be a function of both x itself and time. The change in x in a very short period of time is normally distributed, but its change over longer periods of time is liable to be non-normal.

In this chapter we have developed a plausible Markov stochastic process for the behavior of a stock price over time. The process is widely used in the valuation of derivatives. It is known as geometric Brownian motion. Under this process, the proportional rate of return to the holder of the stock in any small interval of time is normally distributed and the returns in any two different small intervals of time are independent.

One way of gaining an intuitive understanding of a stochastic process for a variable is to simulate the behavior of the variable. This involves dividing a time interval into many small time steps and randomly sampling possible paths for the variable. The future probability distribution for the variable can then be calculated. Monte Carlo simulation is discussed further in Chapter 15.

Ito's lemma is a way of calculating the stochastic process followed by a function of a variable from the stochastic process followed by the variable itself. As we will see in Chapter 11, Ito's lemma is very important in the pricing of derivatives. A key point is that the Wiener process, dz, underlying the stochastic process for the variable is exactly the same as the Wiener process underlying the stochastic process for the function of the variable. Both are subject to the same underlying source of uncertainty.

SUGGESTIONS FOR FURTHER READING

On the Markov Property of Stock Prices

Brealey, R. A., *An Introduction to Risk and Return from Common Stock,* 2nd ed. Cambridge, Mass.: MIT Press, 1983.

Cootner, P. H. (ed.), *The Random Character of Stock Market Prices.* Cambridge, Mass.: MIT Press, 1964.

On Stochastic Processes

Cox, D. R., and H. D. Miller, *The Theory of Stochastic Processes.* London: Chapman & Hall, 1965.

Feller, W., *Probability Theory and Its Applications,* vols. 1 and 2. New York: John Wiley & Sons, 1950.

QUESTIONS AND PROBLEMS

10.1. What would it mean to assert that the temperature at a certain place follows a Markov process? Do you think that temperatures do, in fact, follow a Markov process?

10.2. Can a trading rule based on the past history of a stock's price ever produce returns that are consistently above average? Discuss.

*10.3. A company's cash position, measured in millions of dollars, follows a generalized Wiener process with a drift rate of 0.1 per month and a variance rate of 0.16 per month. The initial cash position is 2.0.

    (a) What are the probability distributions of the cash position after one month, six months, and one year?

    (b) What are the probabilities of a negative cash position at the end of six months and one year?

    (c) At what time in the future is the probability of a negative cash position greatest?

*10.4. A company's cash position, measured in millions of dollars, follows a generalized Wiener process with a drift rate of 1.5 per quarter and a variance rate of 4.0 per quarter. How high does the company's initial cash position have to be for the company to have a less than 5% chance of a negative cash position by the end of one year?

*10.5. Variables X_1 and X_2 follow generalized Wiener processes with drift rates μ_1 and μ_2 and variances σ_1^2 and σ_2^2. What process does $X_1 + X_2$ follow if:
(a) The changes in X_1 and X_2 in any short interval of time are uncorrelated?
(b) There is a correlation ρ between the changes in X_1 and X_2 in any short interval of time?

*10.6. Consider a variable, S, which follows the process

$$dS = \mu\, dt + \sigma\, dz$$

For the first three years, $\mu = 2$ and $\sigma = 3$; for the next three years, $\mu = 3$ and $\sigma = 4$. If the initial value of the variable is 5, what is the probability distribution of the value of the variable at the end of year 6?

10.7. Suppose that a stock price has an expected return of 16% per annum and a volatility of 30% per annum. When the stock price at the end of a certain day is $50, calculate the following:
(a) The expected stock price at the end of the next day.
(b) The standard deviation of the stock price at the end of the next day.
(c) The 95% confidence limits for the stock price at the end of the next day.

10.8. Stock A and stock B both follow geometric Brownian motion. Changes in any short interval of time are uncorrelated with each other. Does the value of a portfolio consisting of one of stock A and one of stock B follow geometric Brownian motion? Explain your answer.

10.9. Equation (10.7) can be written as

$$\Delta S = \mu S\Delta t + \sigma S\epsilon\sqrt{\Delta t}$$

where μ and σ are constant. Explain carefully the difference between this model and each of the following:

$$\Delta S = \mu\Delta t + \sigma\epsilon\sqrt{\Delta t}$$

$$\Delta S = \mu S\Delta t + \sigma\epsilon\sqrt{\Delta t}$$

$$\Delta S = \mu\Delta t + \sigma S\epsilon\sqrt{\Delta t}$$

Why is the model in equation (10.7) a more appropriate model of stock price behavior than any of these three alternatives?

10.10. It has been suggested that the short-term interest rate, r, follows the stochastic process

$$dr = (a - r)b\, dt + rc\, dz$$

where a, b, and c are positive constants and dz is a Wiener process. Describe the nature of this process.

10.11 Suppose that a stock price S follows geometric Brownian motion with expected return μ and volatility σ:

$$dS = \mu S\,dt + \sigma S\,dz$$

What is the process followed by the variable S^n? Show that S^n also follows geometric Brownian motion. The expected value of S_T, the stock price at time T, is $Se^{\mu(T-t)}$. What is the expected value of S_T^n?

*10.12. Suppose that x is the yield to maturity with continuous compounding on a discount bond that pays off \$1 at time T. Assume that x follows the process

$$dx = a(x_0 - x)\,dt + sx\,dz$$

where a, x_0, and s are positive constants and dz is a Wiener process. What is the process followed by the bond price?

*10.13. Suppose that x is the yield on a perpetual government bond that pays interest at the rate of \$1 per annum. Assume that x is expressed with continuous compounding, that interest is paid continuously on the bond, and that x follows the process

$$dx = a(x_0 - x)\,dt + sx\,dz$$

where a, x_0, and s are positive constants and dz is a Wiener process. What is the process followed by the bond price? What is the expected instantaneous return (including interest and capital gains) to the holder of the bond?

APPENDIX 10A: DERIVATION OF ITO'S LEMMA

In this appendix we show how Ito's lemma can be regarded as a natural extension of other, simpler results. Consider a continuous and differentiable function G of a variable x. If Δx is a small change in x and ΔG is the resulting small change in G, it is well known that

$$\Delta G \approx \frac{dG}{dx}\Delta x \qquad\qquad (10A.1)$$

In other words, ΔG is approximately equal to the rate of change of G with respect to x multiplied by Δx. The error involves terms of order Δx^2. If more precision is required, a Taylor series expansion of ΔG can be used:

$$\Delta G = \frac{dG}{dx}\Delta x + \frac{1}{2}\frac{d^2G}{dx^2}\Delta x^2 + \frac{1}{6}\frac{d^3G}{dx^3}\Delta x^3 + \cdots$$

For a continuous and differentiable function G of two variables, x and y, the result analogous to equation (10A.1) is

$$\Delta G \approx \frac{\partial G}{\partial x}\Delta x + \frac{\partial G}{\partial y}\Delta y \qquad\qquad (10A.2)$$

and the Taylor series expansion of ΔG is

$$\Delta G = \frac{\partial G}{\partial x}\Delta x + \frac{\partial G}{\partial y}\Delta y + \frac{1}{2}\frac{\partial^2 G}{\partial x^2}\Delta x^2 + \frac{\partial^2 G}{\partial x \partial y}\Delta x \, \Delta y + \frac{1}{2}\frac{\partial^2 G}{\partial y^2}\Delta y^2 + \cdots$$

(10A.3)

In the limit as Δx and Δy tend to zero, equation (10A.3) gives

$$dG = \frac{\partial G}{\partial x}dx + \frac{\partial G}{\partial y}dy$$

(10A.4)

A derivative is a function of a variable that follows a stochastic process. We now extend equation (10A.4) to cover such functions. Suppose that a variable x follows the general Ito process in equation (10.4):

$$dx = a(x, t)\, dt + b(x, t)\, dz$$

(10A.5)

and that G is some function of x and of time, t. By analogy with equation (10A.3), we can write

$$\Delta G = \frac{\partial G}{\partial x}\Delta x + \frac{\partial G}{\partial t}\Delta t + \frac{1}{2}\frac{\partial^2 G}{\partial x^2}\Delta x^2 + \frac{\partial^2 G}{\partial x \partial t}\Delta x \, \Delta t + \frac{1}{2}\frac{\partial^2 G}{\partial t^2}\Delta t^2 + \cdots$$

(10A.6)

Equation (10A.5) can be discretized to

$$\Delta x = a(x, t)\Delta t + b(x, t)\epsilon\sqrt{\Delta t}$$

or if arguments are dropped,

$$\Delta x = a\Delta t + b\epsilon\sqrt{\Delta t}$$

(10A.7)

This equation reveals an important difference between the situation in equation (10A.6) and the situation in equation (10A.3). When limiting arguments were used to move from equation (10A.3) to equation (10A.4), terms in Δx^2 were ignored because they were second-order terms. From equation (10A.7),

$$\Delta x^2 = b^2\epsilon^2\Delta t + \text{ terms of higher order in } \Delta t$$

(10A.8)

which shows that the term involving Δx^2 in equation (10A.6) has a component that is of order Δt and cannot be ignored.

The variance of a standardized normal distribution is 1.0. This means that

$$E(\epsilon^2) - [E(\epsilon)]^2 = 1$$

where E denotes expected value. Since $E(\epsilon) = 0$, it follows that $E(\epsilon^2) = 1$. The expected value of $\epsilon^2\Delta t$ is therefore Δt. It can be shown that the variance of $\epsilon^2\Delta t$ is of order Δt^2 and that as a result of this, $\epsilon^2\Delta t$ becomes nonstochastic and equal to its expected value of Δt as Δt tends to zero. It follows that the first term on the right-hand side of equation (10A.8) becomes nonstochastic and equal to $b^2\, dt$ as Δt tends to zero. Taking limits as Δx and Δt tend to zero in equation (10A.6), and

using this last result, we therefore obtain

$$dG = \frac{\partial G}{\partial x}dx + \frac{\partial G}{\partial t}dt + \frac{1}{2}\frac{\partial^2 G}{\partial x^2}b^2\,dt \qquad (10A.9)$$

This is Ito's lemma. Substituting for dx from equation (10A.5), equation (10A.9) becomes

$$dG = \left(\frac{\partial G}{\partial x}a + \frac{\partial G}{\partial t} + \frac{1}{2}\frac{\partial^2 G}{\partial x^2}b^2\right)dt + \frac{\partial G}{\partial x}b\,dz$$

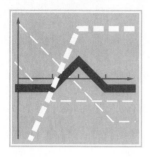

Chapter 11

The Black–Scholes Analysis

In the early 1970s, Fischer Black and Myron Scholes made a major breakthrough by deriving a differential equation that must be satisfied by the price of any derivative dependent on a non-dividend-paying stock.[1] They used the equation to obtain values for European call and put options on the stock. In this chapter we explain both the Black–Scholes analysis and the powerful technique known as risk-neutral valuation.

Before we start, it is appropriate to mention one point concerning the notation that will be used. When valuing forward contracts in Chapter 3, no assumptions were made about interest rates, and the variable r was used to denote the risk-free rate of interest for an investment maturing at time T. In this chapter and the next few chapters, we continue to denote the risk-free interest rate by r. However, except where otherwise stated, we assume that interest rates are constant and the same for all maturities. In Chapter 19 we discuss how this constant interest rate assumption can be relaxed in the Black–Scholes model.

11.1 LOGNORMAL PROPERTY OF STOCK PRICES

A variable has a lognormal distribution if the natural logarithm of the variable is normally distributed. In Section 10.6 we showed that if a stock price, S, follows geometric Brownian motion,

$$dS = \mu S \, dt + \sigma S \, dz$$

then

$$d \ln S = \left(\mu - \frac{\sigma^2}{2} \right) dt + \sigma \, dz$$

From this equation we see that the variable $\ln S$ follows a generalized Wiener process. The change in $\ln S$ between time t and T is normally distributed:

---

[1] See F. Black and M. Scholes, "The Pricing of Options and Corporate Liabilities," *Journal of Political Economy*, 81 (May–June 1973), 637–54.

$$\ln S_T - \ln S \sim \phi \left[\left(\mu - \frac{\sigma^2}{2} \right)(T - t), \sigma \sqrt{T - t} \right] \tag{11.1}$$

where S_T is the stock price at a future time T; S is the stock price at the current time, t; and $\phi(m, s)$ denotes a normal distribution with mean m and standard deviation s. From the properties of a normal distribution it follows from equation (11.1) that

$$\ln S_T \sim \phi \left[\ln S + \left(\mu - \frac{\sigma^2}{2} \right)(T - t), \sigma \sqrt{T - t} \right] \tag{11.2}$$

This shows that $\ln S_T$ is normally distributed so that S_T has a lognormal distribution. The standard deviation of $\ln S_T$ is proportional to $\sqrt{T - t}$. This means that our uncertainty about the logarithm of the stock price, as measured by its standard deviation, is proportional to the square root of how far ahead we are looking.

Example 11.1

Consider a stock with an initial price of $40, an expected return of 16% per annum, and a volatility of 20% per annum. From equation (11.2), the probability distribution of the stock price, S_T, in six months' time is given by

$$\ln S_T \sim \phi[\ln 40 + (0.16 - 0.04/2)0.5, 0.2 \sqrt{0.5}]$$

$$\ln S_T \sim \phi(3.759, 0.141)$$

There is a 95% probability that a normally distributed variable has a value within 1.96 standard deviations of its mean. Hence, with 95% confidence,

$$3.759 - 1.96 \times 0.141 < \ln S_T < 3.759 + 1.96 \times 0.141$$

This can be written

$$e^{3.759 - 1.96 \times 0.141} < S_T < e^{3.759 + 1.96 \times 0.141}$$

or

$$32.55 < S_T < 56.56$$

Thus there is a 95% probability that the stock price in six months will lie between 32.55 and 56.56.

A variable that has a lognormal distribution can take any value between zero and infinity. Figure 11.1 illustrates the shape of a lognormal distribution. Unlike the normal distribution, it is skewed so that the mean, median, and mode are all different. From equation (11.2) and the properties of the lognormal distribution, it can be shown that the expected value of S_T, $E(S_T)$, is given by[2]

$$E(S_T) = Se^{\mu(T-t)} \tag{11.3}$$

[2]For a discussion of the properties of the lognormal distribution, see J. Aitchison and J. A. C. Brown, *The Lognormal Distribution* (Cambridge: Cambridge University Press, 1966).

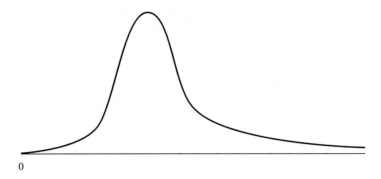

Figure 11.1   Lognormal distribution.

This fits in with the definition of μ as the expected rate of return. The variance of S_T, var(S_T), can be shown to be given by

$$\text{var}(S_T) = S^2 e^{2\mu(T-t)}[e^{\sigma^2(T-t)} - 1] \qquad (11.4)$$

Example 11.2

Consider a stock where the current price is $20, the expected return is 20% per annum, and the volatility is 40% per annum. The expected stock price in one year, $E(S_T)$, and the variance of the stock price in one year, var(S_T), are given by

$$E(S_T) = 20e^{0.2} = 24.43$$

$$\text{var}(S_T) = 400e^{0.4}(e^{0.16} - 1) = 103.54$$

The standard deviation of the stock price in one year is $\sqrt{103.54}$, or 11.18.

11.2 THE DISTRIBUTION OF THE RATE OF RETURN

The lognormal property of stock prices can be used to provide information on the probability distribution of the continuously compounded rate of return earned on a stock between times t and T. Define the continuously compounded rate of return per annum realized between t and T as η.[3] It follows that

$$S_T = Se^{\eta(T-t)}$$

and

$$\eta = \frac{1}{T-t} \ln \frac{S_T}{S} \qquad (11.5)$$

---

[3]It is important to distinguish between the continuously compounded rate of return, η, and the annualized return with no compounding (see Section 3.1). The latter is

$$\frac{1}{T-t} \left(\frac{S_T - S}{S} \right)$$

and is always greater than η.

Since

$$\ln S_T - \ln S = \ln \frac{S_T}{S}$$

Equation (11.1) implies that

$$\ln \frac{S_T}{S} \sim \phi \left[(\mu - \frac{\sigma^2}{2})(T - t), \sigma \sqrt{T - t} \right] \tag{11.6}$$

From the properties of normal distributions, it follows from equation (11.5) that

$$\eta \sim \phi \left(\mu - \frac{\sigma^2}{2}, \frac{\sigma}{\sqrt{T - t}} \right) \tag{11.7}$$

Thus the continuously compounded rate of return is normally distributed with mean $\mu - \sigma^2/2$ and standard deviation $\sigma/\sqrt{T - t}$.

Example 11.3

Consider a stock with an expected return of 17% per annum and a volatility of 20% per annum. The probability distribution for the actual rate of return (continuously compounded) realized over three years is normal with mean

$$0.17 - \frac{0.04}{2} = 0.15$$

or 15% per annum and standard deviation

$$\frac{0.2}{\sqrt{3}} = 0.1155$$

or 11.55% per annum. Since there is a 95% chance that a normally distributed variable will lie within 1.96 standard deviations of its mean, we can be 95% confident that the actual return realized over three years will be between -7.6% and $+37.6\%$ per annum.

What Is the Expected Rate of Return?

The result in equation (11.7) shows that the expected continuously compounded rate of return in time $T - t$ is $\mu - \sigma^2/2$. This may seem strange since in Chapter 10, μ was defined as the expected value of the rate of return in any short interval. How can this be different from the expected value of the continuously compounded rate of return in a longer time interval? To understand the difference between the two, we consider a numerical example. Suppose that the following is a sequence of the actual returns per annum realized on a stock in five consecutive years, measured using annual compounding:

$$15\%, \quad 20\%, \quad 30\%, \quad -20\%, \quad 25\%$$

The arithmetic mean of the returns is calculated by taking the sum of the returns and dividing by 5. It is 14%. However, an investor would earn less than 14% per

annum if he or she left money invested in the stock for the five years. The dollar value of $100 at the end of the five years would be

$$100 \times 1.15 \times 1.20 \times 1.30 \times 0.80 \times 1.25 = 179.40$$

By contrast a 14% return with annual compounding would give

$$100 \times 1.14^5 = 192.54$$

This example illustrates the general result that the mean of the returns earned in different years is not necessarily the same as the mean return per annum over several years with annual compounding. It can be shown that unless the returns happen to be the same in each year, the former is always greater than the latter.[4] The actual average return earned by the investor, with annual compounding, is

$$(1.7940)^{1/5} - 1 = 0.124$$

or 12.4% per annum.

There is, of course, nothing magical about the time period of one year in this example. Suppose that the time period over which returns are measured is made progressively shorter and the number of observations is increased. We can calculate the following two estimates:

1. The expected rate of return in a very short period of time. (This is obtained by calculating the arithmetic average of the returns realized in many very short periods of time.)
2. The expected continuously compounded rate of return over a five-year period. (This is obtained by calculating the average of the returns with continuous compounding realized over many five-year periods.)

The example just given indicates that we should expect estimate 1 to be greater than estimate 2. Our earlier results show that this is in fact the case. The expected rate of return in an infinitesimally short period of time is μ. The expected continuously compounded rate of return is $\mu - \sigma^2/2$.

These arguments show that the term *expected return* is ambiguous. It can refer either to μ or to $\mu - \sigma^2/2$. Unless otherwise stated, we will use it to refer to μ throughout this book.

11.3 ESTIMATING VOLATILITY FROM HISTORICAL DATA

To estimate the volatility of a stock price empirically, the stock price is usually observed at fixed intervals of time (e.g., every day, every week, or every month).

---

[4]Some readers may recognize this as equivalent to the statement that the arithmetic mean of a set of numbers is always greater than the geometric mean if the numbers are not all equal to each other.

Define:

$n+1$: number of observations
S_i : stock price at end of ith interval ($i = 0, 1, \ldots, n$)
τ : length of time interval in years

and let

$$u_i = \ln\left(\frac{S_i}{S_{i-1}}\right)$$

for $i = 1, 2, \ldots, n$.

Since $S_i = S_{i-1}e^{u_i}$, u_i is the continuously compounded return (not annualized) in the ith interval. The usual estimate, s, of the standard deviation of the u_i's is given by

$$s = \sqrt{\frac{1}{n-1}\sum_{i=1}^{n}(u_i - \bar{u})^2}$$

or

$$s = \sqrt{\frac{1}{n-1}\sum_{i=1}^{n}u_i^2 - \frac{1}{n(n-1)}\left(\sum_{i=1}^{n}u_i\right)^2}$$

where $\bar{u}$ is the mean of the u_i's.

From equation (11.1), the standard deviation of the u_i's is $\sigma\sqrt{\tau}$. The variable, s, is therefore an estimate of $\sigma\sqrt{\tau}$. It follows that σ itself can be estimated as s^*, where

$$s^* = \frac{s}{\sqrt{\tau}}$$

The standard error of this estimate can be shown to be approximately $s^*/\sqrt{2n}$.

Choosing an appropriate value for n is not easy. *Ceteris paribus,* more data generally lead to more accuracy. However, σ does change over time and data that are too old may not be relevant for predicting the future. A compromise that seems to work reasonably well is to use closing prices from daily data over the most recent 90 to 180 days. A rule of thumb that is often used is to set the time period over which the volatility is measured equal to the time period over which it is to be applied. Thus if the volatility is to be used to value a two-year option, two years of historical data are used.

There is an important issue concerned with whether time should be measured in calendar days or trading days when volatility parameters are being estimated and used. Later in this chapter we show that the empirical research carried out to date indicates that trading days should be used. In other words, days when the exchange is closed should be ignored for the purposes of the volatility calculation.

Example 11.4

Table 11.1 shows a possible sequence of stock prices over a 20-day period. Since

$$\sum u_i = 0.09531 \quad \text{and} \quad \sum u_i^2 = 0.00333$$

an estimate of the standard deviation of the daily return is

$$\sqrt{\frac{0.00333}{19} - \frac{0.09531^2}{380}} = 0.0123$$

Assuming that time is measured in trading days and that there are 252 trading days per year, $\tau = 1/252$ and the data give an estimate for the volatility per annum of $0.0123 \times \sqrt{252} = 0.195$. The estimated volatility is 19.5% per annum. The standard error of this estimate is

$$\frac{0.195}{\sqrt{2 \times 20}} = 0.031$$

or 3.1% per annum.

TABLE 11.1   Computation of Volatility

Day	Closing Stock Price (dollars)	Price Relative, S_i/S_{i-1}	Daily Return, $u_i = \ln(S_i/S_{i-1})$
0	20		
1	$20\frac{1}{8}$	1.00625	0.00623
2	$19\frac{7}{8}$	0.98758	−0.01250
3	20	1.00629	0.00627
4	$20\frac{1}{2}$	1.02500	0.02469
5	$20\frac{1}{4}$	0.98781	−0.01227
6	$20\frac{7}{8}$	1.03086	0.03040
7	$20\frac{7}{8}$	1.00000	0.00000
8	$20\frac{7}{8}$	1.00000	0.00000
9	$20\frac{3}{4}$	0.99401	−0.00601
10	$20\frac{3}{4}$	1.00000	0.00000
11	21	1.01205	0.01198
12	$21\frac{1}{8}$	1.00595	0.00593
13	$20\frac{7}{8}$	0.98817	−0.01190
14	$20\frac{7}{8}$	1.00000	0.00000
15	$21\frac{1}{4}$	1.01796	0.01780
16	$21\frac{3}{8}$	1.00588	0.00587
17	$21\frac{3}{8}$	1.00000	0.00000
18	$21\frac{1}{4}$	0.99415	−0.00587
19	$21\frac{3}{4}$	1.02353	0.02326
20	22	1.01149	0.01143

This analysis assumes that the stock pays no dividends, but it can be adapted to accommodate dividend-paying stocks. The return, u_i, during a time interval that includes an ex-dividend day is given by

$$u_i = \ln \frac{S_i + D}{S_{i-1}}$$

where D is the amount of the dividend. The return in other time intervals is still

$$u_i = \ln \frac{S_i}{S_{i-1}}$$

However, as tax factors play a part in determining returns around an ex-dividend date, it is probably best to discard altogether data for intervals that include an ex-dividend date.

11.4 CONCEPTS UNDERLYING THE BLACK–SCHOLES DIFFERENTIAL EQUATION

The Black–Scholes differential equation is an equation that must be satisfied by the price, f, of any derivative dependent on a non-dividend-paying stock. The equation is derived in the next section. Here we consider the nature of the arguments used.

The Black–Scholes analysis is analogous to the no-arbitrage analysis we used in Chapter 9 to value options when stock price changes are binomial. A riskless portfolio consisting of a position in the option and a position in the underlying stock is set up. In the absence of arbitrage opportunities, the return from the portfolio must be the risk-free interest rate, r.

The reason why a riskless portfolio can be set up is because the stock price and the option price are both affected by the same underlying source of uncertainty: stock price movements. In any short period of time, the price of a call option is perfectly positively correlated with the price of the underlying stock; the price of a put option is perfectly negatively correlated with the price of the underlying stock. In both cases, when an appropriate portfolio of the stock and the option is set up, the gain or loss from the stock position always offsets the gain or loss from the option position so that the overall value of the portfolio at the end of the short period of time is known with certainty.

Suppose, for example, that at a particular point in time the relationship between a small change in the stock price, ΔS, and the resultant small change in the price of a European call option, Δc, is given by

$$\Delta c = 0.4 \, \Delta S$$

This means that the slope of the line representing the relationship between c and S is 0.4, as indicated in Figure 11.2. The riskless portfolio would consist of

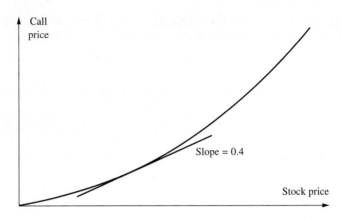

Figure 11.2   Relationship between c and S.

1. A long position in 0.4 share.
2. A short position in one call option.

There is one important difference between the Black–Scholes analysis and our analysis using a binomial model in Chapter 9. In Black–Scholes the position that is set up is riskless for only a very short period of time. (Theoretically, it remains riskless only for an instantaneously short period of time.) To remain riskless it must be adjusted or *rebalanced* frequently.[5] For example, the relationship between Δc and ΔS might change from $\Delta c = 0.4\,\Delta S$ today to $\Delta c = 0.5\,\Delta S$ in two weeks. This would mean that 0.5 rather than 0.4 shares must then be owned for each call option sold. It is nevertheless true that the return from the riskless portfolio in any very short period of time must be the risk-free interest rate. This is the key element in the Black–Scholes arguments and leads to their pricing formulas.

Assumptions

The assumptions we use to derive the Black–Scholes differential equation are as follows:

1. The stock price follows the process developed in Chapter 10 with μ and σ constant.
2. The short selling of securities with full use of proceeds is permitted.
3. There are no transactions costs or taxes. All securities are perfectly divisible.
4. There are no dividends during the life of the derivative.
5. There are no riskless arbitrage opportunities.
6. Security trading is continuous.
7. The risk-free rate of interest, r, is constant and the same for all maturities.

[5]We discuss the rebalancing of portfolios in more detail in Chapter 14.

As we discuss in Chapter 19, some of these assumptions can be relaxed. For example, μ, r, and σ can be known functions of t.

11.5 DERIVATION OF THE BLACK–SCHOLES DIFFERENTIAL EQUATION

We now derive the Black–Scholes differential equation. We assume that the stock price S follows the process discussed in Chapter 10:

$$dS = \mu S\,dt + \sigma S\,dz \tag{11.8}$$

Suppose that f is the price of a call option or other derivative contingent on S. The variable f must be some function of S and t. Hence from equation (10.14),

$$df = \left(\frac{\partial f}{\partial S}\mu S + \frac{\partial f}{\partial t} + \frac{1}{2}\frac{\partial^2 f}{\partial S^2}\sigma^2 S^2\right)dt + \frac{\partial f}{\partial S}\sigma S\,dz \tag{11.9}$$

The discrete versions of equations (11.8) and (11.9) are

$$\Delta S = \mu S \Delta t + \sigma S \Delta z \tag{11.10}$$

and

$$\Delta f = \left(\frac{\partial f}{\partial S}\mu S + \frac{\partial f}{\partial t} + \frac{1}{2}\frac{\partial^2 f}{\partial S^2}\sigma^2 S^2\right)\Delta t + \frac{\partial f}{\partial S}\sigma S \Delta z \tag{11.11}$$

where ΔS and Δf are the changes in f and S in a small time interval Δt. It will be recalled from the discussion of Ito's lemma in Section 10.6 that the Wiener processes underlying f and S are the same. In other words, the $\Delta z\,(= \epsilon \sqrt{\Delta t})$ in equations (11.10) and (11.11) are the same. It follows that by choosing a portfolio of the stock and the derivative, the Wiener process can be eliminated.

The appropriate portfolio is

$$-1: \quad \text{derivative}$$

$$+\frac{\partial f}{\partial S}: \quad \text{shares}$$

The holder of this portfolio is short one derivative and long an amount $\partial f/\partial S$ of shares. Define Π as the value of the portfolio. By definition

$$\Pi = -f + \frac{\partial f}{\partial S}S \tag{11.12}$$

The change $\Delta\Pi$ in the value of the portfolio in time Δt is given by

$$\Delta\Pi = -\Delta f + \frac{\partial f}{\partial S}\Delta S \tag{11.13}$$

Substituting equations (11.10) and (11.11) into equation (11.13) yields

$$\Delta\Pi = \left(-\frac{\partial f}{\partial t} - \frac{1}{2}\frac{\partial^2 f}{\partial S^2}\sigma^2 S^2\right)\Delta t \tag{11.14}$$

Since this equation does not involve Δz, the portfolio Π must be riskless during time Δt. The assumptions listed in the preceding section imply that the portfolio must instantaneously earn the same rate of return as other short-term risk-free securities. If it earned more than this return, arbitrageurs could make a riskless profit by shorting the risk-free securities and using the proceeds to buy the portfolio; if it earned less, they could make a riskless profit by shorting the portfolio and buying risk-free securities. It follows that

$$\Delta\Pi = r\Pi\,\Delta t$$

where r is the risk-free interest rate. Substituting from equations (11.12) and (11.14), this becomes

$$\left(\frac{\partial f}{\partial t} + \frac{1}{2}\frac{\partial^2 f}{\partial S^2}\sigma^2 S^2\right)\Delta t = r\left(f - \frac{\partial f}{\partial S}S\right)\Delta t$$

so that

$$\frac{\partial f}{\partial t} + rS\frac{\partial f}{\partial S} + \frac{1}{2}\sigma^2 S^2\frac{\partial^2 f}{\partial S^2} = rf \tag{11.15}$$

Equation (11.15) is the Black–Scholes differential equation. It has many solutions, corresponding to all the different derivatives that can be defined with S as the underlying variable. The particular derivative that is obtained when the equation is solved depends on the *boundary conditions* that are used. These specify the values of the derivative at the boundaries of possible values of S and t. In the case of a European call option, the key boundary condition is

$$f = \max(S - X, 0) \qquad \text{when } t = T$$

In the case of a European put option, it is

$$f = \max(X - S, 0) \qquad \text{when } t = T$$

One point that should be emphasized about the portfolio Π in the derivation of equation (11.15) is that it is not permanently riskless. It is riskless only for an infinitesimally short period of time. As S and t change, $\partial f/\partial S$ also changes. To keep the portfolio riskless, it is therefore necessary to change frequently the relative proportions of the derivative and the stock in the portfolio.

Example 11.5

A forward contract on a non-dividend-paying stock is a derivative dependent on the stock. As such, it should satisfy equation (11.15). From equation (3.6), the value of the forward contract, f, is given by

$$f = S - Ke^{-r(T-t)}$$

where K is the delivery price. This means that

$$\frac{\partial f}{\partial t} = -rKe^{-r(T-t)} \qquad \frac{\partial f}{\partial S} = 1 \qquad \frac{\partial^2 f}{\partial S^2} = 0$$

When these are substituted into the left-hand side of equation (11.15), we obtain

$$-rKe^{-r(T-t)} + rS$$

This equals rf, showing that equation (11.15) is indeed satisfied.

11.6 RISK–NEUTRAL VALUATION

Risk-neutral valuation was introduced in connection with the binomial model in Chapter 9. It is without doubt the single most important tool for the analysis of derivatives. It arises from one key property of the Black–Scholes differential equation (11.15). This property is that the equation does not involve any variables that are affected by the risk preferences of investors. The variables that do appear in the equation are the current stock price, time, stock price volatility, and the risk-free rate of interest. All are independent of risk preferences.

The Black–Scholes differential equation would not be independent of risk preferences if it involved the expected return on the stock, μ. This is because the value of μ does depend on risk preferences. The higher the level of risk aversion by investors, the higher μ will be for any given stock. It is fortunate that μ happens to drop out in the derivation of the equation.

The fact that the Black–Scholes differential equation is independent of risk preferences enables an ingenious argument to be used. If risk preferences do not enter the equation, they cannot affect its solution. Any set of risk preferences can therefore be used when evaluating f. In particular, the very simple assumption that all investors are risk neutral can be made.

In a world where investors are risk neutral, the expected return on all securities is the risk-free rate of interest, r. This is because risk-neutral investors do not require a premium to induce them to take risks. It is also true that the present value of any cash flow in a risk-neutral world can be obtained by discounting its expected value at the risk-free rate. The assumption that the world is risk neutral does therefore considerably simplify the analysis of derivatives. Consider a derivative such as a European option that pays off some function of the stock price at time T. First, the expected value of the derivative at time T is calculated on the assumption that the expected return from the stock is r rather than μ. This expected value is then discounted to the present time using a discount rate of r.

It is important to realize that the risk-neutrality assumption is merely an artificial device for obtaining solutions to the Black–Scholes differential equation. The solutions that are obtained are valid in all worlds, not just those where investors are risk neutral. When we move from a risk-neutral world to a risk-averse world, two things happen. The expected growth rate in the stock price

changes and the discount rate that must be used for any payoffs from the derivative changes. It happens that these two effects always offset each other exactly.

Application to Forward Contracts on a Stock

Forward contracts on a non-dividend-paying stock have already been valued in Section 3.2. They will be valued again in this section to provide a simple illustration of risk-neutral valuation. We make the assumption that interest rates are constant and equal to r. This is somewhat more restrictive than the assumption in Section 3.2. Consider a long forward contract that matures at time T with delivery price, K. As described in Chapter 1, the value of the contract at maturity is

$$S_T - K$$

where S_T is the stock price at time T. From the risk-neutral valuation argument, the value of the forward contract at time $t(< T)$ is its expected value at time T in a risk-neutral world, discounted to time t at the risk-free rate of interest. Denoting the value of the forward contract at time t by f, this means that

$$f = e^{-r(T-t)}\hat{E}(S_T - K) \tag{11.16}$$

where $\hat{E}$ denotes expected value in a risk-neutral world. Since K is a constant, equation (11.16) becomes

$$f = e^{-r(T-t)}\hat{E}(S_T) - Ke^{-r(T-t)} \tag{11.17}$$

The growth rate of the stock price, μ, becomes r in a risk-neutral world. Hence from equation (11.3),

$$\hat{E}(S_T) = Se^{r(T-t)} \tag{11.18}$$

Substituting equation (11.18) into equation (11.17) gives

$$f = S - Ke^{-r(T-t)} \tag{11.19}$$

This is in agreement with equation (3.6). Example 11.5 shows that this expression for f satisfies the Black–Scholes differential equation.

11.7 BLACK–SCHOLES PRICING FORMULAS

In their pathbreaking paper, Black and Scholes succeeded in solving their differential equation to obtain exact formulas for the prices of European call and put options. These formulas are presented in equations (11.22) and (11.23). In this section we indicate how a similar analysis to that just used for forward contracts can be used to derive the formulas.

The expected value of a European call option at maturity in a risk-neutral world is

$$\hat{E}[\max(S_T - X, 0)]$$

where, as before, $\hat{E}$ denotes expected value in a risk-neutral world. From the risk-neutral valuation argument the European call option price, c, is the value of this discounted at the risk-free rate of interest, that is,

$$c = e^{-r(T-t)}\hat{E}[\max(S_T - X, 0)] \tag{11.20}$$

In a risk-neutral world, $\ln S_T$ has the probability distribution in equation (11.2) with μ replaced by r; that is,

$$\ln S_T \sim \phi\left[\ln S + \left(r - \frac{\sigma^2}{2}\right)(T - t), \sigma\sqrt{T - t}\right] \tag{11.21}$$

Evaluating the right-hand side of equation (11.20) is an application of integral calculus.[6] The result is

$$c = SN(d_1) - Xe^{-r(T-t)}N(d_2) \tag{11.22}$$

where

$$d_1 = \frac{\ln(S/X) + (r + \sigma^2/2)(T - t)}{\sigma\sqrt{T - t}}$$

$$d_2 = \frac{\ln(S/X) + (r - \sigma^2/2)(T - t)}{\sigma\sqrt{T - t}} = d_1 - \sigma\sqrt{T - t}$$

and $N(x)$ is the cumulative probability distribution function for a variable that is normally distributed with a mean of zero and a standard deviation of 1 (i.e., it is the probability that such a variable will be less than x).

Equation (11.22) can be written

$$c = e^{-r(T-t)}[SN(d_1)e^{r(T-t)} - XN(d_2)]$$

The expression $N(d_2)$ is the probability that the option will be exercised in a risk-neutral world so that $XN(d_2)$ is the strike price times the probability that the strike price will be paid. The expression $SN(d_1)e^{r(T-t)}$ is the expected value of a variable that equals S_T if $S_T > X$ and zero otherwise in a risk-neutral world. This provides an interpretation of the terms in the Black–Scholes formula and shows that it is consistent with risk-neutral valuation.

Since $c = C$, equation (11.22) also gives the value of an American call option on a non-dividend-paying stock. The value of a European put can be

---

[6]If g is the probability density function of S_T in a risk-neutral world given by (11.21), equation (11.20) becomes

$$c = e^{-r(T-t)}\int_X^\infty (S_T - X)g(S_T)\,dS_T$$

Substituting $S_T = e^w$ converts this to an integral involving the normal rather than the lognormal distribution. The rest is tedious algebra!

calculated in a manner similar to a European call. Alternatively, put–call parity (see Chapter 7) can be used. The result is

$$p = Xe^{-r(T-t)}N(-d_2) - SN(-d_1) \qquad (11.23)$$

Unfortunately, no exact analytic formula for the value of an American put option on a non-dividend-paying stock has been produced. Numerical procedures and analytic approximations for calculating American put values are discussed in Chapter 15.

Note that to derive equations (11.22) and (11.23), it has been assumed that r is constant. In practice, when the equations are used, r is set equal to the risk-free rate of interest on an investment lasting for $T - t$, the life of the option.

Properties of the Black–Scholes Formulas

We now show that the Black–Scholes formulas have the right general properties by considering what happens when some of the parameters take extreme values.

When the stock price, S, becomes very large, a call option is almost certain to be exercised. It then becomes very similar to a forward contract with delivery price X. From equation (3.6), we therefore expect the call price to be

$$S - Xe^{-r(T-t)}$$

This is, in fact, the call price given by equation (11.22) since, when S becomes very large, both d_1 and d_2 become very large and $N(d_1)$ and $N(d_2)$ are both close to 1.0. When the stock price becomes very large, the price of a European put option, p, approaches zero. This is consistent with equation (11.23) since $N(-d_1)$ and $N(-d_2)$ are both close to zero.

Consider next what happens when the volatility σ approaches zero. Since the stock is virtually riskless, its price will grow at rate r to $Se^{r(T-t)}$ at time T and the payoff from a call option is

$$\max[Se^{r(T-t)} - X, 0]$$

Discounting at rate r, the value of the call today is

$$e^{-r(T-t)} \max[Se^{r(T-t)} - X, 0] = \max[S - Xe^{-r(T-t)}, 0]$$

To show that this is consistent with equation (11.22), consider first the case where $S > Xe^{-r(T-t)}$. This implies that $\ln(S/X) + r(T - t) > 0$. As σ tends to zero, d_1 and d_2 tend to $+\infty$ so that $N(d_1)$ and $N(d_2)$ tend to 1.0 and equation (11.22) becomes

$$c = S - Xe^{-r(T-t)}$$

When $S < Xe^{-r(T-t)}$, it follows that $\ln(S/X) + r(T - t) < 0$. As σ tends to zero, d_1 and d_2 tend to $-\infty$ so that $N(d_1)$ and $N(d_2)$ tend to zero and equation (11.22) gives a call price of zero. The call price is therefore always $\max[S - Xe^{-r(T-t)}, 0]$ as σ tends to zero. Similarly, it can be shown that the put price is always $\max[Xe^{-r(T-t)} - S, 0]$ as σ tends to zero.

11.8 CUMULATIVE NORMAL DISTRIBUTION FUNCTION

The only problem in applying equations (11.22) and (11.23) is in calculating the cumulative normal distribution function, N. Tables for $N(x)$ are provided at the end of this book. The function can also be evaluated directly using numerical procedures. Alternatively, a polynomial approximation can be used.[7] One such approximation that can easily be obtained using a hand calculator is

$$N(x) = \begin{cases} 1 - N'(x)(a_1 k + a_2 k^2 + a_3 k^3) & \text{when } x \geq 0 \\ 1 - N(-x) & \text{when } x < 0 \end{cases}$$

where

$$k = \frac{1}{1 + \gamma x}$$

$$\gamma = 0.33267$$

$$a_1 = 0.4361836$$

$$a_2 = -0.1201676$$

$$a_3 = 0.9372980$$

and

$$N'(x) = \frac{1}{\sqrt{2\pi}} e^{-x^2/2}$$

This provides values for $N(x)$ that are usually accurate to four decimal places and are always accurate to 0.0002.

For six-decimal-place accuracy, the following can be used:

$$N(x) = \begin{cases} 1 - N'(x)(a_1 k + a_2 k^2 + a_3 k^3 + a_4 k^4 + a_5 k^5) & \text{when } x \geq 0 \\ 1 - N(-x) & \text{when } x < 0 \end{cases}$$

where

$$k = \frac{1}{1 + \gamma x}$$

$$\gamma = 0.2316419$$

$$a_1 = 0.319381530$$

$$a_2 = -0.356563782$$

$$a_3 = 1.781477937$$

---

[7] See M. Abramowitz and I. Stegun, *Handbook of Mathematical Functions* (New York: Dover Publications, 1972).

$$a_4 = -1.821255978$$

$$a_5 = 1.330274429$$

and $N'(x)$ is defined as above.

Example 11.6

Consider the situation where the stock price six months from the expiration of an option is $42, the exercise price of the option is $40, the risk-free interest rate is 10% per annum, and the volatility is 20% per annum. This means that $S = 42, X = 40, r = 0.1, \sigma = 0.2, T - t = 0.5$,

$$d_1 = \frac{\ln 1.05 + 0.12 \times 0.5}{0.2\sqrt{0.5}} = 0.7693$$

$$d_2 = \frac{\ln 1.05 + 0.08 \times 0.5}{0.2\sqrt{0.5}} = 0.6278$$

and

$$Xe^{-r(T-t)} = 40e^{-0.05} = 38.049$$

Hence if the option is a European call, its value, c, is given by

$$c = 42N(0.7693) - 38.049N(0.6278)$$

If the option is a European put, its value, p, is given by

$$p = 38.049N(-0.6278) - 42N(-0.7693)$$

Using one of the polynomial approximations,

$$N(0.7693) = 0.7791 \qquad N(-0.7693) = 0.2209$$

$$N(0.6278) = 0.7349 \qquad N(-0.6278) = 0.2651$$

so that

$$c = 4.76 \qquad p = 0.81$$

The stock price has to rise by $2.76 for the purchaser of the call to break even. Similarly, the stock price has to fall by $2.81 for the purchaser of the put to break even.

11.9 WARRANTS ISSUED BY A COMPANY ON ITS OWN STOCK

The Black–Scholes formula, with some adjustments for the impact of dilution, can be used to value European warrants issued by a company on its own stock.[8]

---

[8] See F. Black and M. Scholes, "The Pricing of Options and Corporate Liabilities," *Journal of Political Economy,* 81 (May–June 1973), 637–59; D. Galai and M. Schneller, "Pricing Warrants and the Value of the Firm," *Journal of Finance,* 33 (1978), 1339–42; B. Lauterbach and P. Schultz, "Pricing Warrants: An Empirical Study of the Black–Scholes Model and Its Alternatives," *Journal of Finance,* 45 (1990), 1181–1209.

Consider a company with N outstanding shares and M outstanding European warrants. Suppose that each warrant entitles the holder to purchase γ shares from the company at time T at a price of X per share.

If V_T is the value of the company's equity (including the warrants) at time T and the warrant holders exercise, the company receives a cash inflow from the payment of the exercise price of $M\gamma X$ and the value of the company's equity increases to $V_T + M\gamma X$. This value is distributed among $N + M\gamma$ shares so that the share price immediately after exercise becomes

$$\frac{V_T + M\gamma X}{N + M\gamma}$$

The payoff to the warrant holder is therefore

$$\gamma\left(\frac{V_T + M\gamma X}{N + M\gamma} - X\right)$$

or

$$\frac{N\gamma}{N + M\gamma}\left(\frac{V_T}{N} - X\right)$$

The warrants should be exercised only if this payoff is positive. The payoff to the warrant holder is therefore

$$\frac{N\gamma}{N + M\gamma}\max\left(\frac{V_T}{N} - X, 0\right)$$

This shows that the value of the warrant is the value of

$$\frac{N\gamma}{N + M\gamma}$$

regular call options on V/N, where V is the value of the company's equity. The value of V is given by

$$V = NS + MW$$

where S is the stock price and W is the warrant price, so that

$$\frac{V}{N} = S + \frac{M}{N}W$$

The Black–Scholes formula in equation (11.22) therefore gives the warrant price W if:

1. The stock price S is replaced by $S + (M/N)W$.
2. The volatility σ is the volatility of the equity of the company (i.e., it is the volatility of the value of the shares plus the warrants, not just the shares).
3. The formula is multiplied by $(N\gamma)/(N + M\gamma)$.

When these adjustments are made we end up with a formula for W as a function of W. This can be solved numerically.

11.10 IMPLIED VOLATILITIES

The one parameter in the Black–Scholes pricing formulas that cannot be observed directly is the volatility of the stock price. In Section 11.3 we discussed how this can be estimated from a history of the stock price. At this stage it is appropriate to mention an alternative approach that uses what is termed an *implied volatility*. This is the volatility implied by an option price observed in the market.

To illustrate the basic idea, suppose that the value of a call on a non-dividend-paying stock is 1.875 when $S = 21$, $X = 20$, $r = 0.1$, and $T - t = 0.25$. The implied volatility is the value of σ, which when substituted into equation (11.22) gives $c = 1.875$. Unfortunately, it is not possible to invert equation (11.22) so that σ is expressed as a function of S, X, r, $T - t$, and c. However, an iterative search procedure can be used to find the implied σ. We could start by trying $\sigma = 0.20$. This gives a value of c equal to 1.76, which is too low. Since c is an increasing function of σ, a higher value of σ is required. We could next try a value of 0.30 for σ. This gives a value of c equal to 2.10, which is too high and means that σ must lie between 0.20 and 0.30. Next, a value of 0.25 can be tried for σ. This also proves to be too high, showing that σ lies between 0.20 and 0.25. Proceeding in this way the range for σ can be halved at each iteration and the correct value of σ can be calculated to any required accuracy.[9] In this example, the implied volatility is 0.235, or 23.5 percent per annum.

Implied volatilities can be used to monitor the market's opinion about the volatility of a particular stock. This does change over time. They can also be used to estimate the price of one option from the price of another option. Very often, several implied volatilities are obtained simultaneously from different options on the same stock and a composite implied volatility for the stock is then calculated by taking a suitable weighted average of the individual implied volatilities. The amount of weight given to each implied volatility in this calculation should reflect the sensitivity of the option price to the volatility. To illustrate this point, suppose that two implied volatility estimates are available. The first is 21% per annum and is based on an at-the-money option; the second is 26% per annum and is based on a deep-out-of-the-money option with the same maturity. The price of the at-the-money option is far more sensitive to volatility than the price of the deep-out-of-the-money option. It is therefore providing more information about the "true" implied volatility. We might therefore choose a weight of 0.9 for the at-the-money implied volatility and a weight of 0.1 for the deep-out-of-the-money

---

[9]This method is presented for illustration. Other more powerful methods, such as the Newton–Raphson method, are often used in practice. (See footnote 1 in Chapter 4 for further information on the Newton–Raphson method.)

option. The weighted-average implied volatility would then be

$$0.9 \times 0.21 + 0.1 \times 0.26 = 0.215$$

or 21.5% per annum. Different weighting schemes are discussed by Latane and Rendleman, by Chiras and Manaster, and by Whaley.[10] Beckers, after examining various weighting schemes, concluded that best results are obtained by using only the option whose price is most sensitive to σ.[11] Thus the Beckers approach would estimate 21 percent for the volatility in the example just mentioned.

11.11 THE CAUSES OF VOLATILITY

Some analysts have claimed that the volatility of a stock price is caused solely by the random arrival of new information about the future returns from the stock. Others have claimed that volatility is caused largely by trading. An interesting question, therefore, is whether the volatility of an exchange-traded instrument is the same when the exchange is open as when it is closed.

Fama and K. French have tested this question empirically.[12] They collected data on the stock price at the close of each trading day over a long period of time, and then calculated:

1. The variance of stock price returns between the close of trading on one day and the close of trading on the next trading day when there are no intervening nontrading days
2. The variance of the stock price returns between the close of trading on Fridays and the close of trading on Mondays

If trading and nontrading days are equivalent, the variance in situation 2 should be three times as great as the variance in situation 1. Fama found that it was only 22% higher. French's results were similar. He found that it was 19% higher.

These results suggest that volatility is far larger when the exchange is open than when it is closed. Proponents of the view that volatility is caused only by

[10]See H. Latane and R. J. Rendleman, "Standard Deviation of Stock Price Ratios Implied by Option Premia," *Journal of Finance,* 31 (May 1976), 369–82; D. P. Chiras and S. Manaster, "The Information Content of Option Prices and a Test of Market Efficiency," *Journal of Financial Economics,* 6 (1978), 213–34; R. E. Whaley, "Valuation of American Call Options on Dividend-Paying Stocks: Empirical Tests," *Journal of Financial Economics,* 10 (March 1982), 29–58.

[11]See S. Beckers, "Standard Deviations in Option Prices as Predictors of Future Stock Price Variability," *Journal of Banking and Finance,* 5 (September 1981), 363–82. The sensitivity of an option with respect to σ is measured by the partial derivative of its price with respect to σ. See Chapter 14 for how this can be calculated.

[12]See E. E. Fama, "The Behavior of Stock Market Prices," *Journal of Business,* 38 (January 1965), 34–105; K. R. French, "Stock Returns and the Weekend Effect," *Journal of Financial Economics,* 8 (March 1980), 55–69.

new information might be tempted to argue that most new information on stocks arrives during trading days.[13] However, studies of futures prices on agricultural commodities, which depend largely on the weather, have shown that they exhibit much the same behavior as stock prices; that is, they are much more volatile during trading hours. Presumably, news about the weather is equally likely to arise on any day. The only reasonable conclusion seems to be that volatility is to some extent caused by trading itself.[14]

What are the implications of all of this for the measurement of volatility and the Black–Scholes model? If daily data are used to measure volatility, the results suggest that days when the exchange is closed should be ignored. The volatility per annum can then be calculated from the volatility per trading day using the formula

$$\text{volatility per annum} = \frac{\text{volatility per}}{\text{trading day}} \times \sqrt{\frac{\text{number of trading}}{\text{days per annum}}}$$

This is the approach that was used in Section 11.3 and is the approach generally used by practitioners. The normal assumption in equity markets is that there are 252 trading days per year.

Although volatility appears to be a phenomenon that is related largely to trading days, interest is paid by the calendar day. This has led D. French[15] to suggest that when options are being valued, two time measures should be calculated:

$$\tau_1 : \frac{\text{trading days until maturity}}{\text{trading days per year}}$$

$$\tau_2 : \frac{\text{calendar days until maturity}}{\text{calendar days per year}}$$

and that the Black–Scholes formulas should be adjusted to

$$c = SN(d_1) - Xe^{-r\tau_2}N(d_2)$$

and

$$p = Xe^{-r\tau_2}N(-d_2) - SN(-d_1)$$

---

[13] In fact, this is questionable. Often important announcements (e.g., those concerned with sales and earnings) are made when exchanges are closed.

[14] For a discussion of this, see K. French and R. Roll, "Stock Return Variances: The Arrival of Information and the Reaction of Traders," *Journal of Financial Economics,* 17 (September 1986), 5–26. We consider one way in which trading can generate volatility when we discuss portfolio insurance schemes in Chapter 14.

[15] See D. W. French, "The Weekend Effect on the Distribution of Stock Prices: Implications for Option Pricing,"*Journal of Financial Economics,* 13 (September 1984), 547–59.

where

$$d_1 = \frac{\ln(S/X) + r\tau_2 + \sigma^2\tau_1/2}{\sigma\sqrt{\tau_1}}$$

$$d_2 = \frac{\ln(S/X) + r\tau_2 - \sigma^2\tau_1/2}{\sigma\sqrt{\tau_1}} = d_1 - \sigma\sqrt{\tau_1}$$

In practice, this adjustment makes little difference except for very short life options.

11.12 DIVIDENDS

Up to now we have assumed that the stock upon which the option is written pays no dividends. In practice, this is not usually true. In this section we modify the Black–Scholes model to take account of dividends. We assume that the amount and timing of the dividends during the life of an option can be predicted with certainty. As most traded stock options last for less than nine months, this is not an unreasonable assumption.

A dividend-paying stock can reasonably be expected to follow the stochastic process developed in Chapter 10 except when the stock goes ex-dividend. At this point the stock's price goes down by an amount reflecting the dividend paid per share. For tax reasons, the stock price may go down by somewhat less than the cash amount of the dividend. To take account of this, the word *dividend* in this section should be interpreted as the reduction in the stock price on the ex-dividend date caused by the dividend. Thus, if a dividend of $1 per share is anticipated and the share price normally goes down by 80% of the dividend on the ex-dividend date, the dividend should be assumed to be $0.80 for the purposes of the analysis.

European Options

European options can be analyzed by assuming that the stock price is the sum of two components: a riskless component that corresponds to the known dividends during the life of the option and a risky component. The riskless component at any given time is the present value of all the dividends during the life of the option discounted from the ex-dividend dates to the present at the risk-free rate. By the time the option matures, the dividends will have been paid and the riskless component will no longer exist. The Black–Scholes formula is therefore correct if S is put equal to the risky component of the stock price and σ is the volatility of the process followed by the risky component.[16] Operationally, this means that the Black–Scholes formula can be used provided that the stock price

---

[16]In theory this is not quite the same as the volatility of the stochastic process followed by the whole stock price. The volatility of the risky component is approximately equal to the volatility of the whole stock price multiplied by $S/(S - V)$, where V is the present value of the dividends. In practice, the two are often assumed to be the same.

is reduced by the present value of all the dividends during the life of the option, the discounting being done from the ex-dividend dates at the risk-free rate. A dividend is counted as being during the life of the option only if its ex-dividend date occurs during the life of the option.

Example 11.7

Consider a European call option on a stock when there are ex-dividend dates in two months and five months. The dividend on each ex-dividend date is expected to be $0.50. The current share price is $40, the exercise price is $40, the stock price volatility is 30% per annum, the risk-free rate of interest is 9% per annum, and the time to maturity is six months. The present value of the dividends is

$$0.5e^{-0.1667\times0.09} + 0.5e^{-0.4167\times0.09} = 0.9741$$

The option price can therefore be calculated from the Black–Scholes formula with $S = 39.0259$, $X = 40$, $r = 0.09$, $\sigma = 0.3$, and $T - t = 0.5$.

$$d_1 = \frac{\ln 0.9756 + 0.135 \times 0.5}{0.3\sqrt{0.5}} = 0.2017$$

$$d_2 = \frac{\ln 0.9756 + 0.045 \times 0.5}{0.3\sqrt{0.5}} = -0.0104$$

Using the polynomial approximation in Section 11.8 gives us

$$N(d_1) = 0.5800 \qquad N(d_2) = 0.4959$$

and from equation (11.22), the call price is

$$39.0259 \times 0.5800 - 40e^{-0.09\times0.5} \times 0.4959 = 3.67$$

or $3.67.

American Options

Consider next American call options. Earlier in this chapter we presented an argument to show that these should never be exercised early in the absence of dividends. An extension to the argument shows that when there are dividends, it is optimal to exercise only at a time immediately before the stock goes ex-dividend. We assume that n ex-dividend dates are anticipated and that $t_1, t_2, \ldots, t_n$ are moments in time immediately prior to the stock going ex-dividend with $t_1 < t_2 < t_3 < \cdots < t_n$. The dividends corresponding to these times will be denoted by $D_1, D_2, \ldots, D_n$, respectively.

We start by considering the possibility of early exercise just prior to the final ex-dividend date (i.e., at time t_n). If the option is exercised at time t_n, the investor receives

$$S(t_n) - X$$

If the option is not exercised, the stock price drops to $S(t_n) - D_n$. As shown by equation (7.1), the value of the option is then greater than

$$S(t_n) - D_n - Xe^{-r(T-t_n)}$$

It follows that if

$$S(t_n) - D_n - Xe^{-r(T-t_n)} \geq S(t_n) - X$$

that is,

$$D_n \leq X(1 - e^{-r(T-t_n)}) \tag{11.24}$$

it cannot be optimal to exercise at time t_n. On the other hand, if

$$D_n > X(1 - e^{-r(T-t_n)}) \tag{11.25}$$

for any reasonable assumption about the stochastic process followed by the stock price, it can be shown that it is always optimal to exercise at time t_n for a sufficiently high value of $S(t_n)$. The inequality in (11.25) will tend to be satisfied when the final ex-dividend date is fairly close to the maturity of the option (i.e., $T - t_n$ is small) and the dividend is large.

Consider next time t_{n-1}, the penultimate ex-dividend date. If the option is exercised at time t_{n-1}, the investor receives

$$S(t_{n-1}) - X$$

If the option is not exercised at time t_{n-1}, the stock price drops to $S(t_{n-1}) - D_{n-1}$ and the earliest subsequent time at which exercise could take place is t_n. Hence from equation (7.1) a lower bound to the option price if it is not exercised at time t_{n-1} is

$$S(t_{n-1}) - D_{n-1} - Xe^{-r(t_n-t_{n-1})}$$

It follows that if

$$S(t_{n-1}) - D_{n-1} - Xe^{-r(t_n-t_{n-1})} \geq S(t_{n-1}) - X$$

or

$$D_{n-1} \leq X(1 - e^{-r(t_n-t_{n-1})})$$

it is not optimal to exercise at time t_{n-1}. Similarly, for any $i < n$, if

$$D_i \leq X(1 - e^{-r(t_{i+1}-t_i)}) \tag{11.26}$$

it is not optimal to exercise at time t_i.

The inequality in (11.26) is approximately equivalent to

$$D_i \leq Xr(t_{i+1} - t_i)$$

Assuming that X is fairly close to the current stock price, the dividend yield on the stock would have to be either close to or above the risk-free rate of interest for this inequality not to be satisfied. This is not often the case.

We can conclude from this analysis that in most circumstances, the only time that needs to be considered for the early exercise of an American call is the final ex-dividend date, t_n. Furthermore, if inequality (11.26) holds for $i = 1, 2, \ldots, n - 1$ and inequality (11.24) holds, we can be certain that early exercise is never optimal.

Black's Approximation

Black suggests an approximate procedure for taking account of early exercise.[17] This involves calculating, as described earlier in this section, the prices of European options that mature at times T and t_n, and then setting the American price equal to the greater of the two. This approximation seems to work well in most cases. A more exact procedure suggested by Roll, Geske, and Whaley is given in Appendix 10A.[18]

Example 11.8

Consider the situation in Example 11.7, but suppose that the option is American rather than European. In this case $D_1 = D_2 = 0.5$, $S = 40$, $X = 40$, $r = 0.09$, t_1 occurs after two months, and t_2 occurs after five months.

$$X(1 - e^{-r(t_2 - t_1)}) = 40(1 - e^{-0.09 \times 0.25}) = 0.89$$

Since this is greater than 0.5, it follows [see inequality (11.26)] that the option should never be exercised on the first ex-dividend date.

$$X(1 - e^{-r(T - t_2)}) = 40(1 - e^{-0.09 \times 0.0833}) = 0.30$$

Since this is less than 0.5, it follows [see inequality (11.24)] that when it is sufficiently deeply in-the-money, the option should be exercised on its second ex-dividend date.

We now use Black's approximation to value the option. The present value of the first dividend is

$$0.5e^{-0.1667 \times 0.09} = 0.4926$$

so that the value of the option on the assumption that it expires just before the final ex-dividend date can be calculated using the Black–Scholes formula with $S = 39.5074$, $X = 40$, $r = 0.09$, $\sigma = 0.30$, and $T - t = 0.4167$. It is \$3.52. Black's approximation involves taking the greater of this and the value of the option when it can only be exercised at the end of six months. From Example 11.7 we know that the latter is \$3.67. Black's approximation therefore gives the value of the American call as \$3.67.

The value of the option given by the Roll, Geske, and Whaley (RGW) formula is \$3.72. There are two reasons for differences between RGW and Black's approximation (BA). The first concerns the timing of the early exercise decision and tends to make RGW greater than BA. In BA the assumption is that the holder has to decide today whether the option will be exercised after five months or after six months; RGW allows the decision on early exercise at the five-month point to depend on the stock price. The second concerns

[17] See F. Black, "Fact and Fantasy in the Use of Options," *Financial Analysts Journal,* 31 (July–August 1975), 36–41, 61–72.

[18] See R. Roll, "An Analytic Formula for Unprotected American Call Options on Stocks with Known Dividends," *Journal of Financial Economics,* 5 (1977), 251–58; R. Geske, "A Note on an Analytic Valuation Formula for Unprotected American Call Options on Stocks with Known Dividends," *Journal of Financial Economics,* 7 (1979), 375–80; R. Whaley, "On the Valuation of American Call Options on Stocks with Known Dividends," *Journal of Financial Economics,* 9 (June 1981), 207–11; R. Geske, "Comments on Whaley's Note," *Journal of Financial Economics,* 9 (June 1981), 213–15.

the way in which volatility is applied and tends to make BA greater than RGW. In BA when we assume exercise takes place after five months, the volatility is applied to the stock price less the present value of the first dividend; when we assume exercise takes place after six months, the volatility is applied to the stock price less the present value of both dividends. In RGW, it is always applied to the stock price less the present value of both dividends.

Whaley[19] has tested empirically three models for the pricing of American calls on dividend-paying stocks: (1) the formula in Appendix 10B, (2) Black's model, and (3) the European option pricing model described at the beginning of this section. He used 15,582 Chicago Board options. The models produced pricing errors with means of 1.08, 1.48, and 2.15%, respectively. The typical bid–ask spread on a call option is greater than 2.15% of the price. On average, therefore, all three models work well and within the tolerance imposed on the options market by trading imperfections.

Up to now, our discussion has centered around American call options. The results for American put options are less clear cut. Dividends make it less likely that an American put option will be exercised early. It can be shown that it is never worth exercising an American put for a period immediately prior to an ex-dividend date.[20] Indeed, if

$$D_i \geq X(1 - e^{-r(t_{i+1} - t_i)})$$

for all $i < n$ and

$$D_n \geq X(1 - e^{-r(T - t_n)})$$

an argument analogous to that just given shows that the put option should never be exercised early. In other cases, numerical procedures must be used to value a put.

11.13 SUMMARY

In this chapter we started by examining the properties of the process for stock prices introduced in Chapter 10. The process implies that the price of a stock at some future time, given its price today, is lognormal. It also implies that the continuously compounded return from the stock in a period of time is normally distributed. Our uncertainty about future stock prices increases as we look further ahead. The standard deviation of the logarithm of the stock price is proportional to the square root of how far ahead we are looking.

[19]See R. E. Whaley, "Valuation of American Call Options on Dividend Paying Stocks: Empirical Tests," *Journal of Financial Economics,* 10 (March 1982), 29–58.

[20]See H. E. Johnson, "Three Topics in Option Pricing," Ph.D. thesis, University of California, Los Angeles, 1981, p. 42.

To estimate the volatility, σ, of a stock price empirically, the stock price is observed at fixed intervals of time (e.g., every day, every week, or every month). For each time period, the natural logarithm of the ratio of the stock price at the end of the time period to the stock price at the beginning of the time period is calculated. The volatility is estimated as the standard deviation of these numbers divided by the square root of the length of the time period in years. Usually, days when the exchanges are closed are ignored in measuring time for the purposes of volatility calculations.

The differential equation for the price of any derivative dependent on a stock can be obtained by setting up a position in the option and the stock that is riskless. Since the derivative and the option price both depend on the same underlying source of uncertainty, this can always be done. The position that is set up remains riskless for only a very short period of time. However, the return on a riskless position must always be the risk-free interest rate if there are to be no arbitrage opportunities.

The expected return on the stock does not enter into the Black–Scholes differential equation. This leads to a useful result known as risk-neutral valuation. This result states that when valuing a derivative dependent on a stock price, we can assume that the world is risk neutral. This means that we can assume that the expected return from the stock is the risk-free interest rate and then discount expected payoffs at the risk-free interest rate. The Black–Scholes equations for European call and put options can be derived by either solving their differential equation or by using risk-neutral valuation.

An implied volatility is the volatility which, when used in conjunction with the Black–Scholes option pricing formula, gives the market price of the option. Traders monitor implied volatilities and sometimes use the implied volatility from one stock option price to calculate the price of another option on the same stock. Empirical results show that the volatility of a stock is much higher when the exchange is open than when it is closed. This suggests that to some extent trading itself causes stock price volatility.

The Black–Scholes results can easily be extended to cover European call and put options on dividend-paying stocks. The procedure is to use the Black–Scholes formula with the stock price reduced by the present value of the dividends anticipated during the life of the option, and the volatility equal to the volatility of the stock price net of the present value of these dividends.

In theory, American call options are liable to be exercised early immediately before any ex-dividend date. In practice, only the final ex-dividend date usually needs to be considered. Fischer Black has suggested an approximation. This involves setting the American call option price equal to the greater of two European call option prices. The first European call option expires at the same time as the American call option; the second expires immediately prior to the final ex-dividend date. A more exact approach involving bivariate normal distributions is explained in Appendix 10A.

SUGGESTIONS FOR FURTHER READING

On the Distribution of Stock Price Changes

Blattberg, R., and N. Gonedes, "A Comparison of the Stable and Student Distributions as Statistical Models for Stock Prices," *Journal of Business,* 47 (April 1974), 244–80.

Fama, E. F., "The Behavior of Stock Prices," *Journal of Business,* 38 (January 1965), 34–105.

Kon, S. J., "Models of Stock Returns—A Comparison," *Journal of Finance,* 39 (March 1984), 147–65.

Richardson, M., and T. Smith, "A Test for Multivariate Normality in Stock Returns," *Journal of Business,* 66 (1993), 295–321.

On the Black–Scholes Differential Equation

Black, F., and M. Scholes, "The Pricing of Options and Corporate Liabilities," *Journal of Political Economy,* 81 (May–June 1973), 637–59.

Merton, R. C., "Theory of Rational Option Pricing," *Bell Journal of Economics and Management Science,* 4 (Spring 1973), 141–83.

On Risk-Neutral Valuation

Cox, J. C., and S. A. Ross, "The Valuation of Options for Alternative Stochastic Processes," *Journal of Financial Economics,* 3 (1976), 145–66.

Smith, C. W., "Option Pricing: A Review," *Journal of Financial Economics,* 3 (1976), 3–54.

On the Black–Scholes Formula and Its Extensions

Black, F., "Fact and Fantasy in the Use of Options and Corporate Liabilities," *Financial Analysts Journal,* 31 (July–August 1975), 36–41, 61–72.

Black, F., and M. Scholes, "The Pricing of Options and Corporate Liabilities," *Journal of Political Economy,* 81 (May–June 1973), 637–59.

Merton, R. C., "Theory of Rational Option Pricing," *Bell Journal of Economics and Management Science,* 4 (Spring 1973), 141–83.

Smith, C. W., "Option Pricing: A Review," *Journal of Financial Economics,* 3 (March 1976), 3–51.

On Analytic Solutions to the Pricing of American Calls

Geske, R., "Comments on Whaley's Note," *Journal of Financial Economics,* 9 (June 1981), 213–15.

Geske, R., "A Note on an Analytic Valuation Formula for Unprotected American Call Options on Stocks with Known Dividends," *Journal of Financial Economics,* 7 (1979), 375–80.

Roll, R., "An Analytical Formula for Unprotected American Call Options on Stocks with Known Dividends," *Journal of Financial Economics,* 5 (1977), 251–58.

Whaley, R., "On the Valuation of American Call Options on Stocks with Known Dividends," *Journal of Financial Economics,* 9 (1981), 207–11.

QUESTIONS AND PROBLEMS

11.1. What does the Black–Scholes stock option pricing model assume about the probability distribution of the stock price in one year?

11.2. The volatility of a stock price is 30% per annum. What is the standard deviation of the proportional price change in one trading day?

11.3. Explain the principle of risk-neutral valuation.

11.4. Calculate the price of a three-month European put option on a non-dividend-paying stock with a strike price of $50 when the current stock price is $50, the risk-free interest rate is 10% per annum, and the volatility is 30% per annum.

11.5. What difference does it make to your calculations in Problem 11.4 if a dividend of $1.50 is expected in two months?

11.6. What is implied volatility? How can it be calculated?

11.7. A stock price is currently $50. Assume that the expected return from the stock is 18% and its volatility is 30%. What is the probability distribution for the stock price in two years? Calculate the mean and standard deviation of the distribution. Determine 95% confidence intervals.

11.8. A stock price is currently $40. Assume that the expected return from the stock is 15% and that its volatility is 25%. What is the probability distribution for the rate of return (with continuous compounding) earned over a two-year period?

11.9. A stock price follows geometric Brownian motion with an expected return of 16% and a volatility of 35%. The current price is $38.
    (a) What is the probability that a European call option on the stock with an exercise price of $40 and a maturity date in six months will be exercised?
    (b) What is the probability that a European put option on the stock with the same exercise price and maturity will be exercised?

11.10. Prove that with the notation in the chapter, a 95% confidence interval for S_T is between

$$Se^{(\mu-\sigma^2/2)(T-t)-1.96\sigma\sqrt{T-t}} \quad \text{and} \quad Se^{(\mu-\sigma^2/2)(T-t)+1.96\sigma\sqrt{T-t}}$$

11.11. A portfolio manager announces that the average of the returns realized in each year of the last 10 years is 20% per annum. In what respect is this statement misleading?

11.12. Suppose that observations on a stock price (in dollars) at the end of each of 15 consecutive weeks are as follows: $30\frac{1}{4}$, 32, $31\frac{1}{8}$, $30\frac{1}{8}$, $30\frac{1}{4}$, $30\frac{3}{8}$, $30\frac{5}{8}$, 33, $32\frac{7}{8}$, 33, $33\frac{1}{2}$, $33\frac{1}{2}$, $33\frac{3}{4}$, $33\frac{1}{2}$, $33\frac{1}{4}$. Estimate the stock price volatility. What is the standard error of your estimate?

*11.13. Assume that a non-dividend-paying stock has an expected return of μ and a volatility of σ. An innovative financial institution has just announced that it will trade a security which pays off a dollar amount equal to $\ln S_T$ at time T where S_T denotes the value of the stock price at time T.

   (a) Use risk-neutral valuation to calculate the price of the security at time t in terms of the stock price, S, at time t.

   (b) Confirm that your price satisfies the differential equation (11.15).

*11.14. If the security in Problem 11.13 is a success, the financial institution plans to offer another security which pays off a dollar amount equal to S_T^2 at time T.

   (a) Use risk-neutral valuation to calculate the price of the security at time t in terms of the stock price, S, at time t. (*Hint:* The expected value of S_T^2 can be calculated from the mean and variance of S_T given in Section 11.1.)

   (b) Confirm that your price satisfies the differential equation (11.15).

*11.15. Consider a derivative that pays off S_T^n at time T where S_T is the stock price at that time. When the stock price follows geometric Brownian motion, it can be shown that its price at time t ($t \le T$) has the form

$$h(t, T)S^n$$

where S is the stock price at time t and h is a function only of t and T.

   (a) By substituting into the Black–Scholes partial differential equation derive an ordinary differential equation satisfied by $h(t, T)$.

   (b) What is the boundary condition for the differential equation for $h(t, T)$?

   (c) Show that

$$h(t, T) = e^{[0.5\sigma^2 n(n-1)+r(n-1)](T-t)}$$

where r is the risk-free interest rate and σ is the stock price volatility.

11.16. What is the price of a European call option on a non-dividend-paying stock when the stock price is \$52, the strike price is \$50, the risk-free interest rate is 12% per annum, the volatility is 30% per annum, and the time to maturity is three months?

11.17. What is the price of a European put option on a non-dividend-paying stock when the stock price is \$69, the strike price is \$70, the risk-free interest rate is 5% per annum, the volatility is 35% per annum, and the time to maturity is six months?

11.18. Consider an option on a non-dividend-paying stock when the stock price is \$30, the exercise price is \$29, the risk-free interest rate is 5%, the volatility is 25% per annum, and the time to maturity is 4 months.

   (a) What is the price of the option if it is a European call?

   (b) What is the price of the option if it is an American call?

   (c) What is the price of the option if it is a European put?

   (d) Verify that put–call parity holds.

11.19. Assume that the stock in Problem 11.18 is due to go ex-dividend in $1\frac{1}{2}$ months. The expected dividend is 50 cents.

   (a) What is the price of the option if it is a European call?

    (b) What is the price of the option if it is a European put?

    (c) If the option is an American call, are there any circumstances under which it will be exercised early?

11.20. A call option on a non-dividend-paying stock has a market price of $2\frac{1}{2}$. The stock price is $15, the exercise price is $13, the time to maturity is 3 months, and the risk-free interest rate is 5% per annum. What is the implied volatility?

*11.21. With the notation used in this chapter:

    (a) What is $N'(x)$?

    (b) Show that $SN'(d_1) = Xe^{-r(T-t)}N'(d_2)$.

    (c) Calculate $\partial d_1/\partial S$ and $\partial d_2/\partial S$.

    (d) Show that

$$\frac{\partial c}{\partial t} = -rXe^{-r(T-t)}N(d_2) - SN'(d_1)\frac{\sigma}{2\sqrt{T-t}}$$

    where c is the price of a call option on a non-dividend-paying stock.

    (e) Show that $\partial c/\partial S = N(d_1)$.

    (f) Show that the Black–Scholes formula for the price of a call option on a non-dividend-paying stock does satisfy the Black–Scholes differential equation.

*11.22. Show that the Black–Scholes formula for a call option gives a price which tends to $\max(S - X, 0)$ as $t \longrightarrow T$.

11.23. Consider an American call option when the stock price is $18, the exercise price is $20, the time to maturity is six months, the volatility is 30% per annum, and the risk-free interest rate is 10% per annum. Two equal dividends are expected during the life of the option with ex-dividend dates at the end of two months and five months. How high can the dividends be without the American option being worth more than the corresponding European option?

11.24. Suppose that in Problem 11.23 each dividend is 40 cents per share. Use Black's approximation to value the option.

11.25. Explain carefully why Black's approach to evaluating an American call option on a dividend-paying stock may give an approximate answer even when only one dividend is anticipated. Does the answer given by Black's approach understate or overstate the true option value? Explain your answer.

11.26. Consider an American call option on a stock. The stock price is $70, the time to maturity is eight months, the risk-free rate of interest is 10% per annum, the exercise price is $65, and the volatility is 32%. Dividends of $1 are expected after three months and six months. Show that it can never be optimal to exercise the option on either of the two dividend dates. Calculate the price of the option.

11.27. Show that the probability that a European call option will be exercised in a risk-neutral world is, with the notation introduced in this chapter, $N(d_2)$. What is an expression for the value of a derivative that pays off $100 if the price of a stock at time T is greater than X?

APPENDIX 11A: EXACT PROCEDURE FOR CALCULATING VALUES OF AMERICAN CALLS ON DIVIDEND-PAYING STOCKS

The Roll, Geske, and Whaley formula for the value of an American call option on a stock paying a single dividend D_1 at time t_1 is

$$C = (S - D_1 e^{-r\tau_1})N(b_1) + (S - D_1 e^{-r\tau_1})M\left(a_1, -b_1; -\sqrt{\frac{\tau_1}{\tau}}\right)$$

$$- Xe^{-r\tau}M\left(a_2, -b_2; -\sqrt{\frac{\tau_1}{\tau}}\right) - (X - D_1)e^{-r\tau_1}N(b_2) \qquad (11A.1)$$

where

$$a_1 = \frac{\ln[(S - D_1 e^{-r\tau_1})/X] + (r + \sigma^2/2)\tau}{\sigma\sqrt{\tau}}$$

$$a_2 = a_1 - \sigma\sqrt{\tau}$$

$$b_1 = \frac{\ln[(S - D_1 e^{-r\tau_1})/\overline{S}] + (r + \sigma^2/2)\tau_1}{\sigma\sqrt{\tau_1}}$$

$$b_2 = b_1 - \sigma\sqrt{\tau_1}$$

$$\tau_1 = t_1 - t$$

$$\tau = T - t$$

The variable σ is the volatility of the stock price less the present value of the dividend. The function, $M(a, b; \rho)$, is the cumulative probability in a standardized bivariate normal distribution that the first variable is less than a and the second variable is less than b, when the coefficient of correlation between the variables is ρ. We give a procedure for calculating the M function in Appendix 11B. The variable $\overline{S}$ is the solution to

$$c(\overline{S}, t_1) = \overline{S} + D_1 - X$$

where $c(\overline{S}, t_1)$ denotes the Black–Scholes option price given by equation (11.22) when $S = \overline{S}$ and $t = t_1$. When early exercise is never optimal, $\overline{S} = \infty$. In this case $b_1 = b_2 = -\infty$ and equation (11A.1) reduces to the Black–Scholes equation with S replaced by $S - D_1 e^{-r\tau_1}$. In other situations $\overline{S} < \infty$ and the option should be exercised at time t_1 when $S(t_1) > \overline{S} + D_1$.

When several dividends are anticipated, early exercise is normally only ever optimal on the final ex-dividend date (see Section 11.12). It follows that the Roll, Geske, and Whaley formula can be used with S reduced by the present value of all dividends except the final one. The variable, D_1, should be set equal to the final dividend and t_1 should be set equal to the final ex-dividend date.

APPENDIX 11B: CALCULATION OF CUMULATIVE PROBABILITY IN BIVARIATE NORMAL DISTRIBUTION

As in Appendix 11A, we define $M(a, b; \rho)$ as the cumulative probability in a standardized bivariate normal distribution that the first variable is less than a and the second variable is less than b, when the coefficient of correlation between the variables is ρ. Drezner provides a way of calculating $M(a, b; \rho)$ to four-decimal-place accuracy.[21] If $a \leq 0$, $b \leq 0$, and $\rho \leq 0$,

$$M(a, b; \rho) = \frac{\sqrt{1 - \rho^2}}{\pi} \sum_{i, j = 1}^{4} A_i A_j f(B_i, B_j)$$

where

$$f(x, y) = \exp[a'(2x - a') + b'(2y - b') + 2\rho(x - a')(y - b')]$$

$$a' = \frac{a}{\sqrt{2(1 - \rho^2)}} \qquad b' = \frac{b}{\sqrt{2(1 - \rho^2)}}$$

$A_1 = 0.3253030 \qquad A_2 = 0.4211071 \qquad A_3 = 0.1334425 \qquad A_4 = 0.006374323$

$B_1 = 0.1337764 \qquad B_2 = 0.6243247 \qquad B_3 = 1.3425378 \qquad B_4 = 2.2626645$

In other circumstances where the product of a, b, and ρ is negative or zero, one of the following identities can be used:

$$M(a, b; \rho) = N(a) - M(a, -b; -\rho)$$

$$M(a, b; \rho) = N(b) - M(-a, b; -\rho)$$

$$M(a, b; \rho) = N(a) + N(b) - 1 + M(-a, -b; \rho)$$

In circumstances where the product of a, b, and ρ is positive, the identity

$$M(a, b; \rho) = M(a, 0; \rho_1) + M(b, 0; \rho_2) - \delta$$

can be used in conjunction with the previous results, where

$$\rho_1 = \frac{(\rho a - b)\, \text{sgn}(a)}{\sqrt{a^2 - 2\rho a b + b^2}} \qquad \rho_2 = \frac{(\rho b - a)\, \text{sgn}(b)}{\sqrt{a^2 - 2\rho a b + b^2}}$$

$$\delta = \frac{1 - \text{sgn}(a)\, \text{sgn}(b)}{4} \qquad \text{sgn}(x) = \begin{cases} +1 & \text{when } x \geq 0 \\ -1 & \text{when } x < 0 \end{cases}$$

[21]Z. Drezner, "Computation of the Bivariate Normal Integral," *Mathematics of Computation*, 32 (January 1978), 277–79. Note that the presentation here corrects a typo in Drezner's paper.

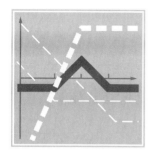

Chapter 12

Options on Stock Indices, Currencies, and Futures Contracts

In this chapter we tackle the problem of valuing options on stock indices, currencies, and futures contracts. As a first step, the analysis in Chapter 11 is extended to cover European options on a stock paying a continuous dividend. It is then argued that stock indices, currencies, and many futures prices are analogous to stocks paying continuous dividends. The basic results for options on a stock paying a continuous dividend can therefore be extended to value options on these other assets.

12.1 EXTENDING BLACK–SCHOLES

In this section we present a simple rule that enables results produced for European options on a non-dividend-paying stock to be extended so that they apply to European options on stocks paying a known continuous dividend. Consider the difference between a stock that provides a continuous dividend yield equal to q per annum and a similar stock that provides no dividends. As explained in Chapter 11, the payment of a dividend causes a stock price to drop by an amount equal to the dividend. The payment of a continuous dividend at rate q, therefore, causes the growth rate in the stock price to be less than it would otherwise be by an amount q. If, with a continuous dividend yield of q, the stock price grows from S at time t to S_T at time T, then in the absence of dividends, it would grow from S at time t to $S_T e^{q(T-t)}$ at time T. Alternatively, in the absence of dividends it would grow from $Se^{-q(T-t)}$ at time t to S_T at time T.

This argument shows that we get the same probability distribution for the stock price at time T in each of the following two cases:

1. The stock starts at price S and provides a continuous dividend yield equal to q.
2. The stock starts at price $Se^{-q(T-t)}$ and provides no dividend.

This leads to a simple rule: When valuing a European option lasting for time $T - t$ on a stock providing a known dividend yield equal to q, we reduce the current stock price from S to $Se^{-q(T-t)}$ and then value the option as though the stock pays no dividends.

Bounds for Option Prices

As a first application of this rule, consider the problem of determining bounds for the price of a European option on a stock providing a dividend yield equal to q. Substituting $Se^{-q(T-t)}$ for S into equation (7.1), we see that a lower bound for the European call option price, c, is given by

$$c > \max(Se^{-q(T-t)} - Xe^{-r(T-t)}, 0) \tag{12.1}$$

We can also prove this directly by considering the following two portfolios:

> *Portfolio A:* one European call option plus an amount of cash equal to $Xe^{-r(T-t)}$
>
> *Portfolio B:* $e^{-q(T-t)}$ shares with dividends being reinvested in additional shares

In portfolio A, the cash, if it is invested at the risk-free interest rate, will grow to X at time T. If $S_T > X$, the call option is exercised at time T and portfolio A is worth S_T. If $S_T < X$, the call option expires worthless and the portfolio is worth X. Hence, at time T, portfolio A is worth

$$\max(S_T, X)$$

Because of the reinvestment of dividends, portfolio B becomes one share at time T. It is, therefore, worth S_T at this time. It follows that portfolio A is always worth as much as, and is sometimes worth more than, portfolio B at time T. In the absence of arbitrage opportunities, this must also be true today. Hence

$$c + Xe^{-r(T-t)} > Se^{-q(T-t)}$$

or

$$c > Se^{-q(T-t)} - Xe^{-r(T-t)}$$

To obtain a lower bound for a European put option, we can similarly replace S by $Se^{-q(T-t)}$ in equation (7.2) to get

$$p > \max(Xe^{-r(T-t)} - Se^{-q(T-t)}, 0) \tag{12.2}$$

This result can also be proved directly by considering:

> *Portfolio C:* one European put option plus $e^{-q(T-t)}$ shares with dividends on the shares being reinvested in additional shares
>
> *Portfolio D:* an amount of cash equal to $Xe^{-r(T-t)}$

Put–Call Parity

Replacing S by $Se^{-q(T-t)}$ in equation (7.3), we obtain put–call parity for an option on a stock providing a continuous dividend yield equal to q:

$$c + Xe^{-r(T-t)} = p + Se^{-q(T-t)} \tag{12.3}$$

This result can also be proved directly by considering the following two portfolios:

Portfolio A: one European call option plus an amount of cash equal to $Xe^{-r(T-t)}$

Portfolio C: one European put option plus $e^{-q(T-t)}$ shares with dividends on the shares being reinvested in additional shares

Both portfolios are worth $\max(S_T, X)$ at time T. They must, therefore, be worth the same today and the put–call parity result in equation (12.3) follows.

12.2 PRICING FORMULAS

By replacing S by $Se^{-q(T-t)}$ in the Black–Scholes formulas, equations (11.22) and (11.23), we obtain the price, c, of a European call and the price, p, of a European put on a stock providing a continuous dividend yield at rate q as

$$c = Se^{-q(T-t)}N(d_1) - Xe^{-r(T-t)}N(d_2) \qquad (12.4)$$

$$p = Xe^{-r(T-t)}N(-d_2) - Se^{-q(T-t)}N(-d_1) \qquad (12.5)$$

Since

$$\ln\left(\frac{Se^{-q(T-t)}}{X}\right) = \ln\frac{S}{X} - q(T-t)$$

d_1 and d_2 are given by

$$d_1 = \frac{\ln(S/X) + (r - q + \sigma^2/2)(T - t)}{\sigma\sqrt{T-t}}$$

and

$$d_2 = \frac{\ln(S/X) + (r - q - \sigma^2/2)(T - t)}{\sigma\sqrt{T-t}} = d_1 - \sigma\sqrt{(T-t)}$$

These results were first derived by Merton.[1] As discussed in Section 11.12, the word *dividend* should, for the purposes of option valuation, be defined as the reduction in the price of the underlying asset on the ex-dividend date arising from the dividend. If the dividend yield is not constant during the life of the option, equations (12.4) and (12.5) are still true, with q equal to the average annualized dividend yield during the life of the option.

Risk-Neutral Valuation

Appendix 12A derives, in a similar way in Section 11.5, the differential equation that must be satisfied by any derivative whose price, f, depends on a

---

[1] See R. Merton, "Theory of Rational Option Pricing," *Bell Journal of Economics and Management Science*, 4 (Spring 1973), 141–83.

stock providing a continuous dividend. Like the basic differential equation, it does not involve any variable affected by risk preferences. The risk-neutral valuation procedure, described in Section 11.6, can therefore be used. In a risk-neutral world, the total return from the stock must be r. The dividends provide a return of q. The expected proportional growth rate in the stock price must therefore be $r - q$. To value a derivative dependent on a stock providing a continuous dividend yield equal to q, we therefore set the expected growth rate of the stock equal to $r - q$ and discount the expected payoff at rate r. This approach can be used to derive equations (12.4) and (12.5).

12.3 OPTIONS ON STOCK INDICES

Several exchanges trade options on stock indices. Some of the indices used track the movement of the U.S. stock market as a whole. Some are based on the

TABLE 12.1   Quotes for Stock Index Options from the *Wall Street Journal*, May 12, 1995

INDEX OPTIONS TRADING

S & P 100 INDEX(OEX)

Exp	Strike	Vol	Last	Chg	Open Int
May	385p	10	1/16	...	716
May	400p	20	1/16	...	4,299
May	405p	26	1/16	...	1,625
May	410p	25	1/16	...	3,515
May	415p	70	1/16	...	2,285
May	420p	10	1/16	...	11,477
Jun	420p	70	1/4	...	3,708
Jul	420p	79	7/16	− 1/16	1,139
May	425p	150	1/16	...	6,088
Jul	425p	5	9/16	− 1/8	116
May	430p	279	1/16	...	10,384
Jun	430p	10	1/4	− 1/16	3,402
Jul	430p	7	3/4	− 1/16	1,755
Aug	430p	5	1 3/8	...	86
May	435c	375	64 7/8	+ 4 3/8	1,434
May	435p	597	1/16	− 1/16	13,109
Jun	435p	100	5/16	...	2,692
May	440p	140	59 7/8	+ 1 7/8	3,847
May	440p	43	1/8	...	18,015
Jun	440p	169	3/8	− 1/16	9,042
Jul	440p	60	1	...	2,634
May	445c	92	55	+ 1	1,500
May	445c	408	1/16	+ 1/16	19,839
Jun	445c	4	54	− 1/2	208
Jun	445p	45	1/2	+ 1/16	7,212
Jul	445p	50	1 1/8	+ 1/8	91
May	450c	596	50	+ 1	5,564
May	450p	4,588	1/8	...	28,910
Jun	450c	89	50	...	3,085
Jun	450p	167	9/16	− 1/16	11,804
Jul	450p	13	1 1/4	− 1/16	4,110
May	455c	175	44	...	2,427
May	455p	1,266	1/8	− 1/16	28,115
Jun	455c	2	45 3/4	+ 1 3/4	901
Jun	455p	39	3/8	− 1/16	5,122
Jul	455c	30	47 1/2	...	118
Jul	455p	980	1 9/16	− 1/16	828
May	460c	704	40	+ 1/4	10,152
May	460p	2,303	3/16	...	32,272
Jun	460c	107	41 7/8	+ 2 3/4	4,531
Jun	460p	676	3/4	− 1/16	13,352
Jul	460c	2	44 1/8	+ 1 1/8	7,361
Jul	460p	114	1 3/4	− 1/8	18,055
Aug	460c	12	45 1/2	+ 1 3/4	149
Aug	460p	434	2 3/4	− 1/4	908
May	465c	862	34 3/4	− 1/8	9,409
May	465p	3,522	1/4	...	36,176
Jun	465c	105	35 3/8	+ 3/8	2,900
Jun	465p	552	15/16	− 1/8	14,602
Jul	465p	7	2 1/4	...	4,108
May	470c	1,479	30 1/4	+ 3/4	20,309
May	470p	5,087	1/4	− 1/8	55,905
Jun	470c	710	30 1/8	+ 1/8	9,330
Jun	470p	1,382	1 3/16	− 1/16	21,562
Jul	470c	5	34	...	9,462
Jul	470p	279	2 5/8	− 3/16	9,346
Aug	470c	2	36	+ 1 3/8	9,096
Aug	470p	101	3 5/8	− 3/8	8,585
May	475c	1,646	25	+ 1/2	22,141
May	475p	6,157	3/8	− 1/8	52,010
Jun	475c	110	26	− 1/8	9,523
Jun	475p	1,697	1 1/2	− 1/8	21,251
Jul	475c	746	30	+ 7/8	4,377
Jul	475p	680	3 1/4	− 1/8	4,535
May	480c	2,885	20 1/2	+ 7/8	26,182
May	480p	8,347	7/16	− 1/8	52,983
Jun	480c	2,030	22 1/8	+ 3/8	18,564
Jun	480p	5,824	1 7/8	− 1/4	29,555
Jul	480c	1,022	25 3/8	− 1/8	10,843
Jul	480p	1,085	3 3/4	− 1/8	6,156
Aug	480c	5	27 1/2	+ 1/4	2,591
Aug	480p	784	5 1/8	− 1/4	4,707
May	485c	2,341	15 3/8	+ 1/2	25,303
May	485p	12,700	11/16	− 3/16	49,528
Jun	485c	124	17 1/2	+ 1/4	11,834
Jun	485p	3,534	2 5/8	− 3/16	15,622
Jul	485c	500	22	+ 1 3/8	6,978
Jul	485p	680	4 1/2	− 3/8	4,035
May	490c	5,230	10 5/8	+ 1/2	23,853
May	490p	20,183	1	− 7/16	43,504
Jun	490c	1,144	13 1/2	− 1/8	15,503
Jun	490p	4,007	3 5/8	− 1/8	17,430
Jul	490c	154	16 3/4	...	11,209
Jul	490p	312	5 7/8	− 1/8	3,208
Aug	490c	460	19 3/4	+ 2	534
Aug	490p	483	7 1/4	− 1/4	1,928
May	495c	22,305	6 3/4	+ 5/8	33,516
May	495p	31,380	1 7/8	− 5/8	39,670
Jun	495c	4,529	10 1/8	+ 3/8	14,459
Jun	495p	6,483	4 7/8	− 1/2	13,994
Jul	495c	690	14	+ 3/4	7,155
Jul	495p	1,343	7 1/4	− 3/8	2,675
May	500c	31,500	3 1/4	+ 1/4	34,107
May	500p	19,586	3 1/2	− 7/8	16,187
Jun	500c	2,000	7	+ 1/4	14,864
Jun	500p	1,880	6 7/8	− 3/8	3,209
Jul	500c	5	10	...	3,873
Jul	500p	253	9	− 3/4	687
Aug	500c	19	12 1/4	+ 1/4	733
May	505c	13,351	13/16	...	20,538
May	505p	3,050	6 3/4	− 7/8	2,070
Jun	505c	2,256	4 5/8	+ 1/4	14,360
Jun	505p	31	10	− 1/4	223
Jul	505c	12	7 5/8	+ 3/8	4,556
Jul	505p	170	11	− 1 1/2	84
May	510c	3,561	7/16	...	11,122
Jun	510c	813	11 1/2	− 5 3/8	300
Jun	510c	3,582	2 3/4	+ 1/8	9,280
Jul	510c	1	14 1/4	...	5
Jul	510c	650	5 3/8	+ 1/4	9,380
Jul	510p	12	15 1/4	...	26
Aug	510c	21	7 1/2	+ 1/2	973
Aug	510p	2	16	− 1/2	294
May	515c	961	3/16	...	5,048
Jun	515c	938	1 11/16	+ 3/16	5,884
Jul	515c	364	3 3/4	+ 1/4	2,206
Jul	515p	1	17 7/8	...	2
May	520c	260	1/8	+ 1/16	930
May	520p	5	22 3/8	...	...
Jun	520c	1,102	15/16	+ 1/16	1,953
Jul	520c	35	2 1/4	...	2,581
Aug	520c	72	3 1/2	+ 1/8	1,147
Aug	520p	1	22 1/4	− 5 1/8	7
Jun	525c	1,401	9/16	+ 1/16	2,480
Jul	525c	215	1 7/16	+ 1/16	1,812

Call vol. 113,717   Open Int......502,398
Put vol. 155,302   Open Int........818,784

performance of a particular sector (e.g., mining, computer technology, and utilities). Some are designed to track the performance of a foreign stock market.

Quotes

Table 12.1 shows quotes on the three most popular index options as they appeared in the Money and Investing section of the *Wall Street Journal* of May 12, 1995. These quotes refer to the price at which the last trade was done on the preceding day.

The option on the S&P 500 Index is European, while those on the S&P 100 and Major Market Index are American. All are settled in cash rather than by delivering the securities underlying the index. This means that upon exercise of the option, the holder of a call option receives $S - X$ in cash and the writer of the option pays this amount in cash, where S is the value of the index and X is the strike price. Similarly, the holder of a put option receives $X - S$ in cash and the writer of the option pays this amount in cash. The cash payment is based on

TABLE 12.1 Quotes for Stock Index Options from the *Wall Street Journal,* May, 12, 1995 (*Continued*)

INDEX OPTIONS TRADING

MAJOR MARKET (XMI)					
Jun	395p	20	1/4	...	1,200
May	405p	80	1/16	– 1/16	826
May	410p	38	1/16	...	330
Jul	415p	52	1 1/16	– 1/16	1,450
Jul	420p	200	1 5/16	– 1/8	1,150
May	425c	1	40 5/8	+ 8 1/4	170
May	430c	3	34	+ 6 7/8	296
May	430p	228	3/16	...	1,520
Jun	430c	1	36 1/8	+ 3 1/2	131
May	435p	11	3/16	– 1/4	3,037
May	440p	103	3/8	– 3/16	1,995
Jun	440p	8	1 3/8	– 7/16	1,038
May	445c	60	20 3/4	+ 1 3/4	464
May	445p	36	3/8	– 1/4	1,336
Jun	445c	2	22 1/2	+ 5 3/8	268
Jun	445p	7	1 3/4	– 1/16	221
Jul	445p	148	3 1/2	– 7/8	750
May	450c	8	14 1/2	+ 1/4	550
May	450p	242	5/8	...	2,025
Jul	450p	2	4 1/8	– 1 3/4	116
May	455c	5	11 3/8	+ 2 1/4	329
May	455p	79	3/4	– 1/2	1,210
Jun	455c	51	14 1/4	+ 5 3/8	305
Jun	455p	8	3 1/4	– 1/2	135
May	460c	103	7 3/8	+ 1 3/8	325
May	460p	85	1 1/2	– 1/2	292
Jun	460p	43	4 1/2	– 1/2	106
May	465c	86	3 7/8	+ 1	297
May	465p	245	3 1/8	– 7/8	60
Jun	465c	10	7 1/4	+ 1 5/8	331
Jun	465p	75	5 5/8	– 1 1/4	156
Jul	465c	2	10	+ 1 3/4	202
Jul	465p	67	8 1/8	– 1 1/8	207
May	470c	79	1 5/16	+ 1/8	255
May	470p	83	5 1/4	– 4 7/8	42
Jun	470c	400	4 3/8	+ 7/8	90
Jun	470p	321	8 5/8	– 6 1/8	1
Jul	470c	100	8	+ 4 1/8	85
Jul	470p	3	10 5/8	– 3/4	7
May	475c	30	1/2	+ 1/8	255
Jun	480c	26	1 1/2	+ 1/4	38
Call vol.......... 955			Open Int..........8,637		
Put vol.........1,877			Open Int........52,718		
S & P 500 INDEX-AM (SPX)					
Jun	400p	180	1/16	– 1/16	18,195
Jun	410p	5	1/8	– 3/4	1,220
Jun	420p	5	1/8	...	4,570
May	440c	1,500	82 3/4	+ 16 1/4	5,635
Jun	450p	11	3/16	– 1/16	40,290
Jun	455p	15	1/4	– 1/8	7,623
Jun	460p	5	1/4	...	11,267
May	465c	5	60 1/4	+ 3/4	117
May	465p	100	1/16	– 1/16	3,497
Jun	465c	400	61	+ 11 1/8	7,116
Jun	465p	981	7/16	+ 1/16	13,876
Jun	470c	1,500	54	...	2,791
Jun	470p	100	7/16	– 1/16	17,837
May	475c	4	50 1/4	+ 2 3/4	1,496
May	475p	1,809	1/8	...	11,525
Jun	475p	380	9/16	...	28,407
May	480p	1,920	1/8	+ 1/16	15,162
Jun	480p	205	5/8	– 1/8	18,356
Jul	480p	110	1 5/8	– 1/8	2,542
May	485p	558	1/8	1/16	22,759
Jun	485c	4	41	1 1/2	9,700
Jun	485p	105	13/16	+ 1/16	26,292
May	490p	235	3/16	...	31,128
Jun	490p	22	1	– 1/4	16,895
Jul	490p	20	2 1/8	...	1,544
May	495c	325	29 3/4	+ 2	10,260
May	495p	606	3/16	– 1/16	15,195
Jun	495p	169	1 3/16	– 1/16	25,868
Jul	495p	15	2 5/8	– 1/8	8,362
May	500c	685	24 3/4	+ 2 1/8	23,477
May	500p	769	1/4	– 1/16	34,221
Jun	500c	3	25 3/4	+ 1/2	20,968
Jun	500p	128	1 7/16	+ 1/16	33,013
Jul	500p	26	3 3/8	...	2,425
May	505c	1,030	19 3/8	+ 3/8	32,854
May	505p	1,183	3/8	– 1/8	30,035
Jun	505p	640	1 7/8	– 1/4	37,557
Jul	505p	3	3 3/4	– 1/4	873
May	510c	66	16	+ 1 1/2	20,027
May	510p	894	7/16	– 5/16	25,956
Jun	510c	1,000	18 1/8	+ 7/8	31,403
Jun	510p	927	2 3/8	– 1/4	24,880
Jul	510p	131	4 7/8	+ 1/8	2,602
May	515c	544	10 1/4	+ 1/2	28,219
May	515p	2,862	3/4	– 3/8	21,337
Jun	515c	19	13 3/4	+ 1 3/8	29,940
Jun	515p	1,476	3 1/4	– 3/8	18,220
Jul	515p	24	5 3/4	– 1/4	3,061
May	520c	3,615	6 1/4	+ 1/8	26,760
May	520p	1,134	1 1/2	– 5/8	13,024
Jun	520c	210	10 5/8	+ 1 1/8	13,654
Jun	520p	1,677	4 3/8	– 5/8	17,202
Jul	520c	145	13 1/2	+ 1 3/4	1,408
Jul	520p	3,645	6 7/8	– 1/8	4,553
May	525c	2,376	3 1/4	+ 3/8	11,006
May	525p	1,054	3	– 7/8	3,527
Jun	525c	2,445	7 1/4	+ 1/4	35,972
Jun	525p	776	6 1/8	– 1 1/8	12,586
Jul	525c	436	10 3/4	+ 5/8	727
Jul	525p	166	9 1/8	– 1/4	390
May	530c	562	1 1/4	+ 1/8	7,740
May	530p	140	6 1/8	– 1 1/8	497
Jun	530c	1,452	4 7/8	+ 3/8	18,666
Jun	530p	53	9 1/2	+ 1/4	1,530
Jul	530p	25	11	– 1/8	3,124
May	535c	841	1/2	+ 1/16	4,195
May	535p	1	10 5/8	– 1 3/8	36
Jun	535c	313	2 11/16	– 1/8	10,578
Jun	535p	5	12	– 1 1/4	252
Jul	535c	530	5 1/2	– 1/2	6,880
Jul	535p	7	13 3/8	+ 5/8	507
May	540c	203	3/16	...	1,120
Jun	540c	310	1 11/16	+ 3/16	898
May	545c	100	1/16	...	...
May	550c	10	1/16	...	7,547
May	550p	100	25 1/4	– 4 1/4	1,201
Jun	550c	238	1/2	...	7,742
Jul	550c	150	1 3/4	– 1/8	6,070
Call vol...... 26,050			Open Int.......833,501		
Put vol....... 40,172			Open Int.... 1,243,562		

the index value at the end of the day on which the exercise instructions are issued. Each contract is for $100 times the value of the index.

Example 12.1

In Table 12.1, one August call option on the S&P 100 with strike price of 460 costs 45\frac{1}{2}$. One contract is on 100 times the index and costs $4,550. The value of the index at the close of trading on May 11, 1995 was 498.52, so that the option was in the money. If the option contract were exercised on May 11, 1995, the holder would receive $(498.52 - 460) \times 100 = \$3,852$ in cash.

In addition to relatively short-dated options, the exchanges trade longer-maturity contracts known as LEAPS. The acronym *LEAPS* stands for "long-term equity anticipation securities" and was originated by the CBOE. LEAPS last up to three years. The index is divided by 10 for the purposes of quoting the strike price and the option price. One contract is an option on 100 times one-tenth of the index (or 10 times the index). LEAPS on indices have expiration dates in December. Those on the S&P 100 and Major Market Index are American, while those on the S&P 500 are European. As mentioned in Chapter 6, the CBOE and several other exchanges also trade LEAPS on many individual stocks. These have expirations in January.

Another innovation of the CBOE is *CAPS*. These trade on the S&P 100 and S&P 500. These are options where the payout is capped so that it cannot exceed $30. The options are European except for the following: A call CAP is automatically exercised on a day when the index closes more than $30 above the strike price; a put CAP is automatically exercised on a day when the index closes more than $30 below the cap level.

As mentioned in Chapter 6, the CBOE also trades what are known as *flex options*. These are options where the traders can choose the expiration date, the strike price, whether the option is American or European, and the settlement basis.

Portfolio Insurance

Index options can be used by portfolio managers to limit their downside risk. Suppose that the value of an index is S. Consider a manager in charge of a well-diversified portfolio which has a β of 1.0 so that its value mirrors the value of the index. (See Section 3.7 for a discussion of β.) If for each $100S$ dollars in the portfolio, the manager buys one put option contract with exercise price X, the value of the portfolio is protected against the possibility of the index falling below X. For instance, suppose that the manager's portfolio is worth $500,000 and the value of the index is 250. The portfolio is worth 2,000 times the index. The manager can obtain insurance against the value of the portfolio dropping below $480,000 in the next three months by buying 20 put option contracts with a strike price of 240. To illustrate how this would work, consider the situation where the index drops to 225 in three months. The portfolio will be worth about

$450,000. However, the payoff from the options will be 20 × ($240 − $225) × 100 = $30,000, bringing the total value of the portfolio up to the insured value of $480,000.

When the Portfolio's Beta Is Not 1.0

Consider next a portfolio that has a β of 2.0 and is not therefore expected to mirror the index. Suppose that it currently has a value of $1 million. Suppose also that the current risk-free interest rate is 12% per annum, the dividend yield on both the portfolio and the index is expected to be 4% per annum, and the current value of the index is 250.

Table 12.2 shows the expected relationship between the level of the index and the value of the portfolio in three months. To illustrate the sequence of calculations necessary to derive the table, consider what happens when the value of the index in three months proves to be 260:

Value of index in three months	260
Return from change in index	10/250 or 4% per three months
Dividends from index	0.25 × 4 = 1% per three months
Total return from index	4 + 1 = 5% per three months
Risk-free interest rate	0.25 × 12 = 3% per three months
Excess return from index over risk-free interest rate	5 − 3 = 2% per three months
Excess return from portfolio over risk-free interest rate	2 × 2 = 4% per three months
Return from portfolio	3 + 4 = 7% per three months
Dividends from portfolio	0.25 × 4 = 1% per three months
Increase in value of portfolio	7 − 1 = 6% per three months
Value of portfolio	1 × 1.06 = $1.06 million

If S is the value of the index, β put contracts should be purchased for each $100S$ dollars in the portfolio. The strike price should be the value the index is

TABLE 12.2   Relation between Value of Index and Value of Portfolio for a Situation where $\beta = 2$

Value of Index in Three Months	Value of Portfolio in Three Months (millions of dollars)
270	1.14
260	1.06
250	0.98
240	0.90
230	0.82

expected to have when the value of the portfolio reaches the insured value. Suppose that the insured value is $0.90 million in our example. Table 12.2 shows that the appropriate strike price for the put options purchased is 240. In this case $100S = \$25,000$ and the value of the portfolio is $1 million. Since $1,000,000/25,000 = 40$ and $\beta = 2$, the correct strategy is to buy 80 put contracts with a strike price of 240.

To illustrate that this gives the required result, consider what happens if the value of the index falls to 230. As shown in Table 12.2, the value of the portfolio is $0.82 million. The put options pay off $(240 - 230) \times 80 \times 100 = \$80,000$ and this is exactly what is necessary to move the total value of the portfolio manager's position up from $0.82 million to the required level of $0.90 million.

Valuation

When options on stock indices are valued, it is usual to assume that the stock index follows geometric Brownian motion.[2] This means that equations (12.4) and (12.5) can be used to value European call and put options on an index with S equal to the value of the index, σ equal to the volatility of the index, and q equal to the dividend yield on the index.

Equations (12.4) and (12.5) were presented on the assumption that dividends are paid continuously and that the rate at which they are paid is constant. In fact, both of these assumptions can be relaxed. All that is required is that we be able to estimate the dividend yield in advance. The variable q should be set equal to the average dividend yield (continuously compounded and annualized) during the life of the option. For the purposes of calculating this average dividend yield, a dividend is counted as occurring during the life of the option if the ex-dividend date is during its life.

In the United States there is some seasonality in the way dividends are paid. For example, it is popular to pay dividends during the first week of February, May, August, and November. At any given time the correct value of q is therefore likely to depend on the life of the option. In some other countries the seasonality is even more pronounced. For example, in Japan all companies tend to have the same ex-dividend dates.

Example 12.2

Consider a European call option on the S&P 500 which is two months from maturity. The current value of the index is 310, the exercise price is 300, the risk-free interest rate is 8% per annum, and the volatility of the index is 20% per annum. Dividend yields of 0.2% and 0.3% are expected in the first month and the second month, respectively. In this case,

---

[2]This presents a theoretical problem since it is inconsistent to assume that both stock prices and a weighted average of stock prices follow geometric Brownian motion. For practical purposes, however, this inconsistency is not really important. Neither individual stocks nor stock indices follow geometric Brownian motion exactly, but for both it is a useful approximation.

$S = 310, X = 300, r = 0.08, \sigma = 0.2$, and $T - t = 0.1667$. The average dividend yield is 0.5% per two months or 3% per annum. Hence $q = 0.03$ and equation (12.4) gives

$$d_1 = \frac{\ln 1.03333 + 0.07 \times 0.1667}{0.2\sqrt{0.1667}} = 0.5444$$

$$d_2 = \frac{\ln 1.03333 + 0.03 \times 0.1667}{0.2\sqrt{0.1667}} = 0.4628$$

$$N(d_1) = 0.7069 \qquad N(d_2) = 0.6782$$

so that the call price, c, is given by

$$c = 310 \times 0.7069 e^{-0.03 \times 0.1667} - 300 \times 0.6782 e^{-0.08 \times 0.1667} = 17.28$$

One contract would cost $1,728.

As an alternative to estimating future dividend yields, we can attempt to predict the absolute amounts of the dividend that will be paid. The basic Black–Scholes formula can be used with S set equal to the initial value of the stock index less the present value of the dividends. This is the approach recommended in Section 11.12 for a stock paying known dividends. It is difficult to implement for a broadly based stock index since it requires a prediction of the dividends expected on every stock underlying the index.

In some circumstances it is optimal to exercise American put options on an index prior to the exercise date. To a lesser extent this is also true of American call options on an index. American stock index option prices are therefore always worth slightly more than the corresponding European stock index option prices. Numerical procedures and analytic approximations for valuing American index options are discussed in Chapter 15.

12.4 CURRENCY OPTIONS

The Philadelphia Exchange (PHLX) began trading in currency options in 1982. Since then the size of the market has grown very rapidly. The currencies currently traded include the Australian dollar, British pound, Canadian dollar, German mark, Japanese yen, French franc, Swiss franc, and European currency unit. For most of these currencies, the Philadelphia Exchange trades both European and American options. It also trades an option on the German mark–Japanese yen exchange rate. A significant amount of trading in foreign currency options is also done outside the organized exchanges. Many banks and other financial institutions are prepared to sell or buy foreign currency options that have exercise prices and exercise dates tailored to meet the needs of their corporate clients.

For a corporate client wishing to hedge a foreign exchange exposure, foreign currency options are an interesting alternative to forward contracts. A company

due to receive sterling at a known time in the future can hedge its risk by buying put options on sterling which mature at that time. This guarantees that the value of the sterling will not be less than the exercise price, while allowing the company to benefit from any favorable exchange rate movements. Similarly, a company due to pay sterling at a known time in the future can hedge by buying calls on sterling which mature at that time. This guarantees that the cost of the sterling will not be greater than a certain amount while allowing the company to benefit from favorable exchange rate movements. Whereas a forward contract locks in the exchange rate for a future transaction, an option provides a type of insurance. Of course, insurance is not free. It costs nothing to enter into a forward transaction, while options require that a premium be paid up front.

Quotes

Table 12.3 shows the closing prices of some of the currency options traded on the Philadelphia Exchange on May 11, 1995. Options are traded with maturity dates in March, June, September, and December for up to nine months into the future. They are also traded with maturity dates in each of the next two months. Options with expirations in June and December up to three years into the future also trade. The expiration date for regular PHLX currency options is the Friday before the third Wednesday of the expiration month. For the "EOM" options the expiration date is the last Friday of the month. Table 12.3 shows only the three contracts in each category with the shortest time to maturity.

The sizes of contracts are indicated at the beginning of each section in Table 12.3. The option prices are for the purchase or sale of one unit of a foreign currency with U.S. dollars. For the Japanese yen, the prices are in hundredths of a cent. For the other currencies they are in cents. Thus one call option contract on the British pound with strike price $162\frac{1}{2}$ cents and exercise month September would give the holder the right to purchase £31,250 for U.S. $50,781.25. The indicated price of the contract is $31,250 \times 1.86$ or $581.25. The spot exchange rate on sterling is shown as 156.25 cents per pound.

Valuation

To value currency options, we define S as the spot exchange rate, that is, the value of one unit of the foreign currency in U.S. dollars. We assume that exchange rates follow the same type of stochastic process as a stock: geometric Brownian motion. We define σ as the volatility of the exchange rate and r_f as the risk-free rate of interest in the foreign country.

As noted in Section 3.8, a foreign currency is analogous to a stock providing a known dividend yield. The owner of foreign currency receives a "dividend yield" equal to the risk-free interest rate, r_f, in the foreign currency. Since we are assuming the same stochastic process for stocks and foreign currencies, the formulas derived in Section 12.2 are correct with q replaced by r_f. The European

TABLE 12.3 Currency Option Prices on the Philadelphia Exchange, May 11, 1995

PHILADELPHIA OPTIONS

Thursday, May 11, 1995

		Calls Vol.	Calls Last	Puts Vol.	Puts Last
DMark					69.84
62,500 German Marks EOM-European style.					
74½	Jun	300	0.30	...	...
76½	Jun	300	0.11	...	0.01
Australian Dollar					73.29
50,000 Australian Dollars-cents per unit.					
72	Jun	...	...	30	0.50
74	May	100	0.12	...	...
British Pound					156.25
31,250 British Pound EOM-cents per unit.					
155	May	4	1.46	310	0.45
157½	May	255	0.80	550	1.20
160	May	5	0.25	...	...
31,250 British Pounds-European Style.					
150	Jun	12	6.80	6	0.36
150	Sep	...	...	62	1.75
155	Jun	1	2.60	1	1.40
157½	Jun	32	1.15	...	...
160	Jun	6	0.60	...	...
162½	Sep	500	1.86	...	...
31,250 British Pounds-European units.					
145	Sep	...	0.01	18	0.80
31,250 British Pounds-cents per unit.					
155	May	...	...	50	0.23
155	Jun	...	...	10	1.05
157½	May	35	0.35	1	0.63
157½	Jun	10	1.12	8	2.68
157½	Sep	9	3.60	...	...
162½	Jun	2	0.28	...	...
170	May	...	0.01	112	14.30
British Pound-GMark					223.75
31,250 British Pound-German Mark cross.					
216	Jun	...	...	323	1.50
224	Jun	320	1.80	...	...
31,250 British Pound-German mark EOM.					
224	May	4	1.04	...	...
Canadian Dollar					74.04
50,000 Canadian Dollars-cents per unit.					
72	Jun	5	2.01	...	...
72½	Jun	8	1.50	...	...
74	May	...	...	6	0.10
74	Sep	6	0.90	...	...
ECU					129.94
62,500 European Currency Units-cents per unit.					
132	May	6	0.11	...	...
French Franc					198.75
250,000 French Franc-European Style.					
17¼	Jun	4	28.60	...	0.01
250,000 French Francs-10ths of a cent per unit.					
19¾	May	...	...	42	0.44
20	Jun	...	...	40	3.40
250,000 French Francs-European Style.					
20¼	Jun	...	...	1	5.20
GMark-JYen					59.97
62,500 GMark-JYen cross EOM.					
59½	May	...	...	100	0.32
German Mark					69.84
62,500 German Mark-cents per unit.					
77	Sep	1	0.50	...	...
62,500 German Marks EOM-cents per unit.					
69½	Jun	...	...	3800	0.76
70	May	4	0.82	...	...
71½	May	2000	0.33	...	...
72	May	14	0.20	...	...
72	Jun	1000	0.94	...	...
72½	May	202	0.26	...	...
71	Jun	10	1.14	...	...
71	Sep	387	2.40	...	...
71½	May	15	0.09	15	0.43
72	Sep	2647	1.78	...	...
72½	May	...	...	10	1.49
72½	Jun	22	0.40	...	...
74	Sep	387	1.21	...	...
74½	Jun	22	0.15	...	...
75	Jun	200	0.19	...	0.01
75	Sep	2647	0.84	...	...
62,500 German Marks-cents per unit.					
64	Jun	...	...	10	0.01
64	Sep	...	...	10	0.23
65	Jun	...	...	17	0.06
65	Sep	...	...	3800	0.33
67	May	4	4.00	...	...
67	Jun	4	4.16	12	0.23
68	Jun	...	...	152	0.50
68	Sep	...	0.01	63	1.22
68½	May	...	...	20	0.05
69	May	...	...	1000	0.13
69	Jun	...	...	541	0.72
69	Sep	...	...	41	1.72
69½	May	525	0.50	1025	0.45
69½	Jun	...	...	301	0.95
70	May	...	...	1209	0.59
70	Jun	103	1.04	680	1.20
70	Sep	...	...	3860	1.90
70½	May	...	...	1023	0.80
70½	Jun	1	0.95	21	1.32
71	May	590	0.30	1347	1.30
71	Jun	10	0.66	15	1.92
71	Sep	...	...	12	2.06
71½	May	...	...	3273	0.80
71½	Jun	25	0.86	28	1.60
72	May	974	0.06	875	2.05
72	Jun	1125	0.52	33	2.68
72	Sep	3	1.40	6	3.08
72½	May	...	...	302	1.66
72½	Jun	80	0.58	73	2.14
73	May	...	...	9	3.20
73	Jun	221	0.28	14	2.90
73	Sep	...	...	12	3.95
73½	Jun	...	...	6	3.60
74	Jun	427	0.18	...	...
74	Sep	...	...	10	4.88
75½	Jun	7	0.13	...	...
76	Jun	5	0.10	...	...
Japanese Yen					116.47
6,250,000 Japanese Yen -100ths of a cent					
108	Jun	10	9.72	...	...
108	Sep	...	0.01	4	0.43
109	Jun	...	...	200	0.07
109	Sep	...	...	13	0.60
111	Jun	...	...	10	0.20
112	Sep	...	...	21	1.19
114	Jun	1000	4.00	30	0.70
115	May	364	1.42	3602	0.06
115	Jun	30	2.80	288	0.95
116	May	...	...	17	0.15
116	Jun	15	2.22	141	1.40
116	Sep	...	...	3	2.45
117	May	100	0.62	134	0.80
117	Jun	30	2.62	17	1.58
118	May	200	0.19	110	1.72
118	Jun	5	1.75	65	2.48
119	May	70	0.65	...	...
120	May	10	0.50	...	...
121	May	16	0.30	...	...
6,250,000 Japanese Yen-100ths of a cent pe					
130	Sep	13	0.65	...	0.01
6,250,000 Japanese Yen-100ths of a cent per unit.					
100	Sep	...	0.01	15	0.04
104	Sep	...	...	30	0.20
6,250,000 Japanese Yen-European Style					
117	May	...	...	50	0.15
117	Jun	...	...	150	1.85
121	May	47	0.03	...	...
Swiss Franc					83.65
62,500 Swiss Franc EOM-cents per unit.					
82	Jun	...	...	10	0.60
84	May	...	...	10	0.53
87	May	...	...	50	2.28
88	May	3	0.24	...	...
89	May	5	0.18	...	...
90	May	...	...	5	5.13
62,500 Swiss Francs EOM.					
84½	May	...	0.01	15	0.84
86½	May	10	0.95	...	...
62,500 Swiss Francs-European Style.					
78½	May	15	7.10	...	...
80	Jun	...	...	40	0.36
82½	Jun	...	...	63	0.64
85	Jun	...	...	5	1.44
86	May	...	...	10	1.90
88	May	...	...	5	1.18
89	May	...	...	5	2.40
89	Jun	5	0.40	...	...
94	Jun	267	0.04	...	...
95	Jun	63	0.04	...	0.01
96	Jun	257	0.02	...	0.01
62,500 Swiss Francs-cents per unit.					
78	Sep	5	7.92	25	0.72
80	Jun	...	...	12	0.17
80	Sep	5	6.32	8	0.95
81	Sep	20	4.96	7	1.45
81½	Jun	...	...	5	0.54
82	May	...	...	100	0.04
82	Jun	...	...	30	0.75
82	Sep	15	4.32	44	1.81
82½	Jun	...	...	100	0.69
83	May	...	...	145	0.20
83	Jun	...	...	108	0.98
83	Sep	5	3.60	32	1.84
83½	May	300	0.60	331	0.34
83½	Jun	5	2.02	...	...
84	May	...	...	97	0.59
84	Jun	300	1.51	417	1.81
84½	May	...	...	34	0.80
85	May	...	...	130	1.25
85	Jun	20	1.10	31	2.26
85	Sep	...	...	20	3.21
85½	May	...	...	10	1.55
85½	Jun	...	...	19	1.81
86	May	...	...	31	1.24
86	Jun	1	1.38	66	2.66
86	Sep	...	...	2	3.68
87	May	...	...	15	2.74
87	Jun	10	0.95	28	3.40
87	Sep	5	2.28	...	...
88	Jun	...	...	1	3.64
88	Sep	...	...	3	5.20

call price, c, and put price, p, are therefore given by

$$c = Se^{-r_f(T-t)}N(d_1) - Xe^{-r(T-t)}N(d_2) \tag{12.6}$$

$$p = Xe^{-r(T-t)}N(-d_2) - Se^{-r_f(T-t)}N(-d_1) \tag{12.7}$$

where

$$d_1 = \frac{\ln(S/X) + (r - r_f + \sigma^2/2)(T - t)}{\sigma\sqrt{T - t}}$$

and

$$d_2 = \frac{\ln(S/X) + (r - r_f - \sigma^2/2)(T - t)}{\sigma\sqrt{T - t}} = d_1 - \sigma\sqrt{T - t}$$

Both the domestic interest rate, r, and the foreign interest rate, r_f, are assumed to be constant and the same for all maturities. Put and call options on a currency are symmetrical in that a put option to sell X_A units of currency A for X_B units of currency B is the same as a call option to buy X_B units of currency B for X_A units of currency A.

From equation (3.14) the forward rate, F, for a maturity T is given by

$$F = Se^{(r-r_f)(T-t)}$$

This enables equations (12.6) and (12.7) to be simplified to

$$c = e^{-r(T-t)}[FN(d_1) - XN(d_2)] \tag{12.8}$$

$$p = e^{-r(T-t)}[XN(-d_2) - FN(-d_1)] \tag{12.9}$$

where

$$d_1 = \frac{\ln(F/X) + (\sigma^2/2)(T - t)}{\sigma\sqrt{T - t}}$$

$$d_2 = \frac{\ln(F/X) - (\sigma^2/2)(T - t)}{\sigma\sqrt{T - t}} = d_1 - \sigma\sqrt{T - t}$$

Note that the maturities of the forward contract and the option must be the same for equations (12.8) and (12.9) to apply.

Example 12.3

Consider a four-month European call option on the British pound. Suppose that the current exchange rate is 1.6000, the strike price is 1.6000, the risk-free interest rate in the United States is 8% per annum, the risk-free interest rate in Britain is 11% per annum, and the option price is 4.3 cents. In this case $S = 1.6$, $X = 1.6$, $r = 0.08$, $r_f = 0.11$, $T - t = 0.3333$, and $c = 0.043$. The implied volatility can be calculated by trial and error. A volatility of 20% gives an option price of 0.0639; a volatility of 10% gives an option price of 0.0285; and so on. The implied volatility is 14.1%.

In some circumstances it is optimal to exercise American currency options prior to maturity. Thus American currency options are worth more than their European counterparts. In general, call options on high-interest currencies and put options on low-interest currencies are the most likely to be exercised prior

to maturity. This is because a high-interest currency is expected to depreciate relative to the U.S. dollar and a low-interest currency is expected to appreciate relative to the U.S. dollar. Unfortunately, analytic formulas do not exist for the evaluation of American currency options. Numerical procedures and analytic approximations are discussed in Chapter 15.

12.5 FUTURES OPTIONS

Options on futures contracts or futures options are now traded on many different exchanges. They require the delivery of an underlying futures contract when exercised. If a call futures option is exercised, the holder acquires a long position in the underlying futures contract plus a cash amount equal to the current futures price minus the strike price. If a put futures option is exercised, the holder acquires a short position in the underlying futures contract plus a cash amount equal to the strike price minus the current futures price.

Example 12.4

Consider an investor who has a September futures call option on 25,000 pounds of copper with a strike price of 70 cents per pound. Suppose that the current futures price of copper for delivery in September is 80 cents. If the option is exercised, the investor receives $2,500(= 25,000 \times 10$ cents) plus a long position in a futures contract to buy 25,000 pounds of copper in September. If desired, the position in the futures contract can be closed out immediately at no cost. This would leave the investor with the $2,500 cash payoff.

Example 12.5

Consider an investor who has a December futures put option on 5,000 bushels of corn with a strike price of 200 cents per bushel. Suppose that the current futures price of corn for delivery in December is 180 cents. If the option is exercised, the investor receives $1,000(= 5,000 \times 20$ cents) plus a short position in a futures contract to sell 5,000 bushels of corn in December. If desired, the position in the futures contract can be closed out immediately at no cost. This would leave the investor with the $1,000 cash payoff.

Futures options are written on both financial futures and commodity futures. Table 12.4 shows the closing prices of a variety of futures options on May 11, 1995. The month shown is the expiration month of the underlying futures contract. The maturity date of the options contract is generally on, or a few days before, the earliest delivery date of the underlying futures contract. For example, the NYSE index futures option and the S&P index futures options both expire on the same day as the underlying futures contract while the IMM currency futures options expire two business days prior to the expiration of the futures contract. The quotes for the options on interest rate futures in Table 12.4 are discussed in Chapter 16.

TABLE 12.4 Closing Prices of Futures Options, May 11, 1995

FUTURES OPTIONS PRICES

Thursday, May 11, 1995.

AGRICULTURAL

CORN (CBT)
5,000 bu.; cents per bu.

Strike	Calls–Settle			Puts–Settle		
Price	Jly	Sep	Dec	Jly	Sep	Dec
240	18¼	25½	31¼	5	3⅛	5
250	11	19¾	24¾	3⅛	7¼	8½
260	6⅜	15⅝	20	8½	13	14
270	3¾	12⅝	16½	16	19½	19⅝
280	2¼	10¼	13⅜	....	....	26½
290	1⅜	8⅜	10¾	....	....	33⅝

Est vol 8,500 Wed 5,887 calls 3,275 puts
Op Int Wed 168,953 calls 88,785 puts

SOYBEANS (CBT)
5,000 bu.; cents per bu.

Strike	Calls–Settle			Puts–Settle		
Price	Jly	Aug	Sep	Jly	Aug	Sep
525	45	....	....	½	2¼	3
550	23¾	32½	39	4⅛	8¼	9¾
575	10⅝	21½	28	16½	21¾	23½
600	5⅝	14½	20¾	36	40	41
625	3⅜	10¾	16½	58½	60¾	....
650	2⅛	8¼	13¼	82¼	....	....

Est vol 6,000 Wed 3,569 calls 1,596 puts
Op Int Wed 112,753 calls 49,188 puts

SOYBEAN MEAL (CBT)
100 tons; $ per ton

Strike	Calls–Settle			Puts–Settle		
Price	Jly	Aug	Sep	Jly	Aug	Sep
160	8.40	10.85	....	.65	1.50	1.90
165	5.00	7.70	10.10	2.15	3.20	3.70
170	2.85	5.50	7.70	5.00	5.75	6.30
175	1.50	4.25	6.10	8.70	9.40	9.50
180	1.10	3.00	4.80	13.20	....	13.25
185	.90	2.50	3.90	....	....	17.25

Est vol 250 Wed 569 calls 157 puts
Op Int Wed 12,674 calls 11,268 puts

SOYBEAN OIL (CBT)
60,000 lbs.; cents per lb.

Strike	Calls–Settle			Puts–Settle		
Price	Jly	Aug	Sep	Jly	Aug	Sep
2400	1.010	....	....	.250	.450	.630
2450	....	....	....	.410	....	....
2500	.480	.800	.970	.740	.990	1.090
2600	.260	.560	.690	1.490	1.700	1.830
2700	.150	.390	.570	2.380	....	....
2800	.100	.300	....	3.330	....	....

Est vol 500 Wed 206 calls 521 puts
Op Int Wed 11,395 calls 8,305 puts

WHEAT (CBT)
5,000 bu.; cents per bu.

Strike	Calls–Settle			Puts–Settle		
Price	Jly	Sep	Dec	Jly	Sep	Dec
340	24¼	32¾	45	2⅝	5¾	6½
350	16¾	25½	37¾	5⅛	8¼	9¼
360	11½	19¾	31½	9½	12½	12¼
370	7½	15¼	25¾	15½	17½	16¼
380	4¾	12	21	22¾	....	21¼
390	3	9	17¼	31	....	....

Est vol 5,000 Wed 1,812 calls 1,085 puts
Op Int Wed 34,579 calls 24,866 puts

COTTON (CTN)
50,000 lbs.; cents per lb.

Strike	Calls–Settle			Puts–Settle		
Price	Jly	Oct	Dec	Jly	Oct	Dec
100	7.60	1.84	.84	2.74	....	18.45
101	6.97	....	....	3.11	....	....
102	6.39	....	....	3.52	....	....
103	5.84	....	....	3.96	....	....
104	5.32	....	....	4.44	....	....
105	1.20	....	....	4.95	....	....

Est vol 6,000 Wed 3,301 calls 4,077 puts
Op int Wed 80,149 calls 86,506 puts

ORANGE JUICE (CTN)
15,000 lbs.; cents per lb.

Strike	Calls–Settle			Puts–Settle		
Price	Jly	Aug	Sep	Jly	Aug	Sep
95	12.25	....	16.00	.35	....	.70
100	7.60	....	....	.65	....	1.10
105	3.70	7.75	....	1.25	....	2.20
110	1.45	4.50	....	4.00	....	3.80
115	.55	2.70	....	12.90	....	6.85
120	.15	1.45	....	....	....	10.50

Est vol 100 Wed 346 calls 264 puts
Op Int Wed 4,637 calls 4,943 puts

COFFEE (CSCE)
37,500 lbs.; cents per lb.

Strike	Calls–Settle			Puts–Settle		
Price	Jly	Aug	Sep	Jly	Aug	Sep
160	11.40	17.55	22.05	1.50	5.10	9.60
165	7.90	14.70	19.25	3.00	7.25	11.80
170	5.13	11.85	16.95	4.90	9.40	14.50
175	3.00	9.45	14.40	8.10	12.00	16.95
180	1.90	7.40	13.25	12.00	14.95	20.80
185	1.20	6.00	11.00	16.30	18.55	23.55

Est vol 2,345 Wed 1,642 calls 990 puts
Op Int Wed 28,841 calls 21,684 puts

SUGAR–WORLD (CSCE)
112,000 lbs.; cents per lb.

Strike	Calls–Settle			Puts–Settle		
Price	Jun	Jly	Aug	Jun	Jly	Aug
1000	1.19	1.27	0.70	0.01	0.09	0.28
1050	0.70	0.87	0.45	0.02	0.19	0.53
1100	0.26	0.54	0.35	0.08	0.36	0.90
1150	0.03	0.33	0.18	0.35	0.65	1.26
1200	0.01	0.20	0.12	0.83	1.02	1.70
1250	0.01	0.11	0.10	1.33	1.43	2.18

Est vol 3,697 Wed 1,696 calls 431 puts
Op int Wed 60,652 calls 45,329 puts

COCOA (CSCE)
10 metric tons; $ per ton

Strike	Calls–Settle			Puts–Settle		
Price	Jly	Aug	Sep	Jly	Aug	Sep
1200	83	121	137	7	19	35
1250	47	87	96	22	35	44
1300	27	59	69	49	57	67
1350	13	41	51	87	89	99
1400	6	27	35	130	125	133
1450	4	18	25	178	166	173

Est vol 1,255 Wed 394 calls 454 puts
Op Int Wed 27,326 calls 10,432 puts

OIL

CRUDE OIL (NYM)
1,000 bbls.; $ per bbl.

Strike	Calls–Settle			Puts–Settle		
Price	Jun	Jly	Aug	Jun	Jly	Aug
1850	.92	.97	....	.01	.23	.50
1900	.44	.65	.75	.03	.41	.72
1950	.10	.38	.53	.19	.63	1.00
2000	.02	.25	.35	.61	1.01	1.31
2050	.01	.14	.24	1.10	1.40	1.70
2100	.01	.09	.16	1.60	1.84	....

Est vol 29,150 Wed 14,408 calls 10,-877 puts
Op Int Wed 223,692 calls 133,069 puts

HEATING OIL No.2 (NYM)
42,000 gal.; $ per gal.

Strike	Calls–Settle			Puts–Settle		
Price	Jun	Jly	Aug	Jun	Jly	Aug
47	.0226	....	....	.0017	.0069	.0082

Strike	Calls–Settle			Puts–Settle		
Price	Jly	Aug	Sep	Jly	Aug	Sep
48	.0146	.0227	.0277	.0037	.0100	.0115
49	.0084	.0171	....	.0075	.0143	.0156
50	.0045	.0125	.0170	.0136	.0197	.0207
51	.0022	.0094	.0130	.0213	.0265	.0266
52	.0010	.0068	.0102	.0301	.0339	.0337

Est vol 2,562 Wed 1,123 calls 377 puts
Op Int Wed 25,268 calls 11,646 puts

GASOLINE–Unload (NYM)
42,000 gal.; $ per gal.

Strike	Calls–Settle			Puts–Settle		
Price	Jun	Jly	Aug	Jun	Jly	Aug
61	.0258	.0197	.0170	.0030	.0192	....
62	.0176	.0160	.0140	.0048	.0255	....
63	.0103	.0125	.0113	.0075	.0319	....
64	.0055	.0098	.0093	.0127	....	....
65	.0030	.0075	.0075	.0202	....	....
66	.0018	.0058	....	....	....	....

Est vol 4,182 Wed 2,671 calls 2,223 puts
Op Int Wed 42,020 calls 27,213 puts

NATURAL GAS (NYM)
10,000 MMBtu.; $ per MMBtu.

Strike	Calls–Settle			Puts–Settle		
Price	Jun	Jly	Aug	Jun	Jly	Aug
155	.107	.183	....	.006	.014	.018
160	.064	.145	.177	.013	.026	.027
165	.036	.109	.143	.035	.039	.043
170	.017	.079	.112	.066	.059	.061
175	.007	.050	.086	.106	.080	.085
180	.002	.033	.063	....	.113	.112

Est vol 3,746 Wed 568 calls 1,270 puts
Op Int Wed 24,998 calls 34,217 puts

BRENT CRUDE (IPE)
1,000 net bbls.; $ per bbl.

Strike	Calls–Settle			Puts–Settle		
Price	Jly	Aug	Sep	Jly	Aug	Sep
1700	0.97	0.91	0.86	na	0.43	0.59
1750	0.67	0.66	na	0.39	0.68	0.86
1800	0.43	0.45	0.44	0.65	0.97	1.17
1850	0.24	0.29	0.32	0.96	1.31	1.55
1900	0.13	0.18	0.21	1.35	1.70	1.94
1950	0.08	0.10	na	na	2.12	2.37

Est vol 5,703 Wed 225 calls 479 puts
Op Int Wed 33,278 calls 18,668 puts

GAS OIL (IPE)
100 metric tons; $ per ton

Strike	Calls–Settle			Puts–Settle		
Price	Jun	Jly	Aug	Jun	Jly	Aug
145	8.70	9.60	10.95	.45	.85	1.20
150	4.65	8.80	7.25	.40	2.05	2.50
155	1.90	3.30	6.30	3.65	4.55	4.55
160	.55	1.60	2.45	na	7.85	7.70
165	.15	.70	1.30	11.90	11.95	11.55
170	.05	.30	.65	18.80	16.55	15.90

Est vol 260 Wed 500 calls 190 puts
Op Int Wed 4,390 calls 1,979 puts

LIVESTOCK

CATTLE-FEEDER (CME)
50,000 lbs.; cents per lb.

Strike	Calls–Settle			Puts–Settle		
Price	May	Aug	Sep	May	Aug	Sep
61	....	....	....	0.15	....	....
62	1.67	4.12	....	0.27	1.45	1.75
63	0.95	....	....	0.55	....	....
64	0.40	2.82	3.15	1.00	2.20	2.55
65	0.15	....	....	1.75	....	....
66	0.05	1.87	2.15	2.65	3.20	3.55

Est vol 406 Wed 276 calls 379 puts
Op Int Wed 4,457 calls 5,744 puts

TABLE 12.4   Closing Prices of Futures Options, May 11, 1995
(*Continued*)

FUTURES OPTIONS PRICES

CATTLE-LIVE (CME)
40,000 lbs.; cents per lb.

Strike	Calls–Settle			Puts–Settle		
Price	Jun	Jly	Aug	Jun	Jly	Aug
57	...	...	...	0.50	...	1.30
58	2.10	...	2.67	0.82	...	1.65
59	1.50	...	2.20	1.22	...	2.12
60	1.02	...	1.72	1.75	...	2.65
61	0.67	...	1.35	2.40	...	3.20
62	0.42	...	1.02	3.15	...	3.90

Est vol 1,706   Wed 1,497 calls 1,282 puts
Op int Wed   22,901 calls 21,335 puts

HOGS–LIVE (CME)
40,000 lbs.; cents per lb.

Strike	Calls–Settle			Puts–Settle		
Price	Jun	Jly	Aug	Jun	Jly	Aug
40	1.90	2.87	3.05	0.40	0.67	0.92
41	1.25	2.22	...	0.75	1.00	...
42	0.75	1.65	1.85	1.25	1.42	1.70
43	0.45	1.20	...	1.95	1.97	...
44	0.22	0.80	1.07	2.72	2.55	2.90
45	0.12	0.60	...	3.60	...	...

Est vol 277   Wed 194 calls 143 puts
Op int Wed   6,938 calls 6,196 puts

METALS

COPPER (CMX)
25,000 lbs.; cents per lb.

Strike	Calls–Settle			Puts–Settle		
Price	Jly	Sep	Dec	Jly	Sep	Dec
118	8.65	8.65	8.40	1.25	2.90	4.90
120	7.00	7.30	7.20	1.60	3.50	5.70
125	3.65	4.70	5.05	3.25	5.90	8.35
130	1.55	2.85	3.90	6.15	8.95	12.05
135	0.75	1.65	3.00	10.35	12.55	16.10
140	0.30	0.90	2.10	14.90	18.80	20.15

Est vol 350   Wed 182 calls 239 puts
Op int Wed   5,187 calls 8,252 puts

GOLD (CMX)
100 troy ounces; $ per troy ounce

Strike	Calls–Settle			Puts–Settle		
Price	Jun	Jly	Aug	Jun	Jly	Aug
360	24.40	27.70	27.80	0.10	0.20	0.40
370	14.40	17.90	18.40	0.10	0.50	0.80
380	4.60	8.80	10.30	0.20	1.20	2.50
390	0.10	2.50	4.70	5.70	4.90	6.50
400	0.10	0.80	1.80	15.60	14.10	14.00
410	0.10	0.30	1.00	25.60	22.50	23.20

Est vol 28,000   Wed 11,951 calls 2,-616 puts
Op int Wed   183,448 calls 70,100 puts

SILVER (CMX)
5,000 troy ounces; cts per troy ounce

Strike	Calls–Settle			Puts–Settle		
Price	Jun	Jly	Sep	Jun	Jly	Sep
475	62.0	64.4	72.8	0.2	2.2	6.0
500	37.8	42.5	54.5	0.5	5.3	12.8
525	15.5	24.2	40.0	3.5	12.0	22.7
550	2.5	15.7	29.0	15.5	28.5	36.3
575	0.7	9.0	21.5	38.7	46.8	53.3
600	0.4	5.7	16.5	63.4	68.5	73.5

Est vol 8,000   Wed 8,659 calls 2,177 puts
Op int Wed   64,489 calls 31,905 puts

CURRENCY

JAPANESE YEN (CME)
12,500,000 yen; cents per 100 yen

Strike	Calls–Settle			Puts–Settle		
Price	Jun	July	Aug	Jun	July	Aug
11650	2.08	...	...	1.29	...	...
11700	1.81	...	...	1.52	1.61	...
11750	1.58	...	...	1.79	1.82	...
11800	1.37	...	...	2.08	2.05	...
11850	1.18	...	...	2.38	2.30	...
11900	1.03	...	...	2.73	2.57	...

Est vol 12,712   Wed 4,323 calls 3,999 puts
Op int Wed   48,148 calls 72,113 puts

DEUTSCHEMARK (CME)
125,000 marks; cents per mark

Strike	Calls–Settle			Puts–Settle		
Price	Jun	July	Aug	Jun	July	Aug
6900	1.57	...	...	0.69	0.95	...
6950	1.26	...	...	0.88	1.17	1.46
7000	1.00	1.53	...	1.12	1.39	1.69
7050	0.78	...	...	1.40	1.65	...
7100	0.62	1.09	1.40	1.73	1.94	2.25
7150	0.47	0.91	1.21	2.08	2.26	...

Est vol 24,736   Wed 5,114 calls 4,452 puts
Op int Wed   74,896 calls 77,322 puts

CANADIAN DOLLAR (CME)
100,000 Can.$, cents per Can.$

Strike	Calls–Settle			Puts–Settle		
Price	Jun	July	Aug	Jun	July	Aug
7300	1.06	...	...	0.13	...	...
7350	0.70	0.81	...	0.27	...	...
7400	0.44	0.65	...	0.51	...	...
7450	0.24	0.37	...	...	...	...
7500	0.12	...	...	1.18	...	...
7550	0.05	...	...	...	...	...

Est vol 1,330   Wed 403 calls 184 puts
Op int Wed   8,063 calls 6,079 puts

BRITISH POUND (CME)
62,500 pounds; cents per pound

Strike	Calls–Settle			Puts–Settle		
Price	Jun	July	Aug	Jun	July	Aug
1500	6.16	...	...	0.24	...	...
1525	4.02	...	...	0.60	...	...
1550	2.30	...	...	1.36	2.28	...
1575	1.16	...	...	2.72	...	...
1600	0.50	1.06	...	1.56	5.40	...
1625	0.24	...	...	6.78	...	...

Est vol 22,239   Wed 764 calls 681 puts
Op int Wed   23,226 calls 25,806 puts

SWISS FRANC (CME)
125,000 francs; cents per franc

Strike	Calls–Settle			Puts–Settle		
Price	Jun	July	Aug	Jun	July	Aug
8300	1.93	...	...	1.12	1.39	...
8350	...	...	...	1.34	...	...
8400	1.39	...	...	1.58	1.82	...
8450	...	...	...	1.86	...	...
8500	0.98	...	...	2.16	2.33	...
8550	0.81	...	...	2.49	...	...

Est vol 7,390   Wed 2,179 calls 2,093 puts
Op int Wed   15,437 calls 23,923 puts

INTEREST RATE

T-BONDS (CBT)
$100,000; points and 64ths of 100%

Strike	Calls–Settle			Puts–Settle		
Price	Jun	Sep	Dec	Jun	Sep	Dec
107	2-25	...	...	0-05	...	...
108	1-36	2-40	3-08	0-16	1-49	2-45
109	0-56	...	...	0-36	...	...
110	0-26	1-42	2-12	1-06	2-48	3-46
111	0-10	...	...	1-54	...	...
112	0-03	0-62	1-30	2-47	4-03	4-60

Est. vol. 195,000;
Wed vol. 116,329 calls; 101,408 puts
Op. int. Wed 383,068 calls; 529,761 puts

T-NOTES (CBT)
$100,000; points and 64ths of 100%

Strike	Calls–Settle			Puts–Settle		
Price	Jun	Sep	Dec	Jun	Sep	Dec
106	1-62	2-25	2-39	0-05	0-63	...
107	1-07	1-50	2-03	0-13	1-23	2-07
108	0-32	1-17	1-38	0-37	1-55	...
109	0-10	0-56	...	1-16	...	...
110	0-03	0-37	0-58	2-09	3-09	...
111	0-01	0-23	...	3-06	...	...

Est vol 50,000   Wed 21,647 calls 34,-449 puts
Op int Wed   174,458 calls 199,161 puts

5 YR TREAS NOTES (CBT)
$100,000; points and 64ths of 100%

Strike	Calls–Settle			Puts–Settle		
Price	Jun	Sep	Dec	Jun	Sep	Dec
10450	1-26	1-47	...	0-03	0-43	...
10500	0-62	1-26	...	0-06	0-54	...
10550	0-38	1-07	...	0-15	1-03	...
10600	0-20	0-57	...	0-29	1-19	...
10650	0-09	0-44	...	0-50	1-37	...
10700	0-04	0-34	...	...	...	...

Est vol 38,000   Wed 13,459 calls 24,-203 puts
Op int Wed   123,543 calls 195,916 puts

EURODOLLAR (CME)
$ million; pts. of 100%

Strike	Calls–Settle			Puts–Settle		
Price	May	Jun	Sep	May	Jun	Sep
9350	0.40	0.41	0.56	0.00	0.01	0.10
9375	0.15	0.18	0.38	0.00	0.03	0.17
9400	0.00	0.03	0.24	0.10	0.13	0.28
9425	0.00	0.01	0.14	...	0.36	0.43
9450	...	0.00	0.08	...	0.60	0.61
9475	...	0.00	0.04	...	0.85	0.82

Est. vol. 175,499;
Wed vol. 109,320 calls; 115,776 puts
Op. Int. Wed 973,212 calls; 1,336,946 puts

2 YR. MID-CURVE EURODOLLAR (CME)
$1,000,000 contract units; pts. of 100%

Strike	Calls–Settle			Puts–Settle		
Price	Jun	...	...	Jun	...	...
9300	0.45	...	...	0.08	...	...
9325	0.29	...	...	...	...	...
9350	0.15	...	...	...	...	...
9375	...	...	...	...	...	...
9400	...	...	...	...	...	...
9425	...	...	...	...	...	...

Est vol 150   Wed 00 calls 0 puts
Op int Wed   7,860 calls 6,835 puts

EUROMARK (LIFFE)
$1 million; pts. of 100%

Strike	Calls–Settle			Puts–Settle		
Price	May	Jun	Jly	May	Jun	Jly
9500	.44	.45	.40	...	.01	.06
9525	.20	.22	.21	.01	.03	.12
9550	.01	.06	.09	.07	.12	.25
9575	...	.02	.03	.31	.33	.44
9600	...	.01	.01	.56	.57	.67
9625	...	...	...	.81	.81	.91

Est vol   Thur 4,143 calls 8,824 puts
Op int Wed   174,070 calls 268,054 puts

LONG GILT (LIFFE)
£50,000; 64ths of 100%

Strike	Calls–Settle			Puts–Settle		
Price	Jun	Jly	Aug	Jun	Jly	Aug
103	2-35	2-33	2-48	0-05	0-27	0-42
104	1-42	1-48	2-03	0-12	0-42	0-61
105	0-59	1-10	1-30	0-29	1-04	1-24

TABLE 12.4 Closing Prices of Futures Options, May 11, 1995
(Continued)

FUTURES OPTIONS PRICES

Strike	Calls–Settle			Puts–Settle		
Price	Jun	Jly	Aug	Jun	Jly	Aug
106	0-26	0-45	0-63	0-60	1-39	1-57
107	0-09	0-24	0-40	1-43	2-18	2-34
108	0-03	0-13	0-24	2-37	3-07	3-18
Est vol		Thur 8,015 calls 13,218 puts				
Op Int Wed		43,559 calls 57,022 puts				

GERMAN GOVT BOND (LIFFE)
$250,000 marks; pts. of 100%

Strike	Calls–Settle			Puts–Settle		
Price	Jun	Jly	Aug	Jun	Jly	Aug
9300	1.11	.89	1.09	.05	.40	.60
9350	.70	.61	.81	.14	.62	.82
9400	.37	.39	.59	.31	.90	1.10
9450	.17	.24	.42	.61	1.25	1.43
9500	.06	.13	.29	1.00	1.64	1.80
9550	.02	.07	.21	1.46	2.08	2.22
Est vol		Thur 16,848 calls 15,270 puts				
Op Int Wed		177,252 calls 171,975 puts				

INDEX

S&P 500 STOCK INDEX (CME)
$500 times premium

Strike	Calls–Settle			Puts–Settle		
Price	May	Jun	Jly	May	Jun	Jly
515	12.40	14.75	20.45	0.75	3.15	4.75
520	7.95	10.90	16.65	1.30	4.30	5.90
525	4.25	7.60	13.20	2.60	5.95	7.35
530	1.75	4.95	10.05	5.10	8.30	9.15
535	0.60	3.00	7.45	8.95	11.30	11.50
540	0.20	1.70	5.20	....	....	....
Est vol 18,740			Wed 5,128 calls 14,-			
444 puts						
Op Int Wed		99,305 calls 186,105 puts				

OTHER OPTIONS

Final or settlement prices of selected contracts. Volume and open interest are totals in all contract months.

CORN (MCE)
1,000 bu.; cents per bu.

Strike	Calls–Settle			Puts–Settle		
Price	Jly	Sep	Dec	Jly	Sep	Dec
260	6⅜	15⅝	20	8½	13	14
Est vol 10			Wed 4 calls 0 puts			
Op int Wed			1,810 calls 59 puts			

EASTERN CATASTROPHE INS. (CBT)
$25,000 times ratio of losses/prem.

Strike	Calls–Settle			Puts–Settle		
Price	Dec	Mar	Jun	Dec	Mar	Jun
14.0	....	....	....	....	....	....
Est vol 0			Wed 0 calls 0 puts			
Op Int Wed			1,805 calls 0 puts			

GSCI (CME)
$250 times Prem.

Strike	Calls–Settle			Puts–Settle		
Price	Jun	Jly	Aug	Jun	Jly	Aug
179	....	....	....	....	....	....
Est vol 0			Wed 0 calls 0 puts			
Op Int Wed			1,308 calls 1,309 puts			

LIBOR – 1 Mo. (CME)
$3 million; pts. of 100%

Strike	Calls–Settle			Puts–Settle		
Price	Jun	Jly	Aug	Jun	Jly	Aug
9400	0.03	0.10	....	0.08	0.14	....
Est vol 50			Wed 130 calls 0 puts			
Op Int Wed			1,714 calls 817 puts			

LUMBER (CME)
160,000 bd .ft., $ per 1,000 bd.ft.

Strike	Calls–Settle			Puts–Settle		
Price	Jly	Sep	Nov	Jly	Sep	Nov
265	13.70	25.80	....	13.70	12.50	....
Est vol 19			Wed 40 calls 26 puts			
Op Int Wed			813 calls 449 puts			

NYSE COMPOSITE INDEX (NYFE)
$500 times premium

Strike	Calls–Settle			Puts–Settle		
Price	May	Jun	Jly	May	Jun	Jly
284	1.40	3.20	5.70	1.85	3.65	4.35
Est vol 44			Wed 19 calls 85 puts			
Op Int Wed			1,030 calls 1,701 puts			

OATS (CBT)
5,000 bu.; cents per bu.

Strike	Calls–Settle			Puts–Settle		
Price	Jly	Sep	Dec	Jly	Sep	Dec
150	6	11½	....	7½	....	....
Est vol 100			Wed 150 calls 55 puts			
Op Int Wed			1,365 calls 1,217 puts			

PLATINUM (NYM)
50 troy oz.; $ per troy oz.

Strike	Calls–Settle			Puts–Settle		
Price	Jun	Jly	Aug	Jun	Jly	Aug
430	....	8.80	....	4.50	....	
Est vol 291			Wed 305 calls 415 puts			
Op Int Wed			2,197 calls 2,924 puts			

SOYBEANS (MCE)
1,000 bu.; cents per bu.

Strike	Calls–Settle			Puts–Settle		
Price	Jly	Aug	Sep	Jly	Aug	Sep
575	10⅝	21½	28	16½	21¾	23½
Est vol 50			Wed 16 calls 2 puts			
Op Int Wed			2,704 calls 176 puts			

2 YR TREAS NOTE (CBT)
$200,000; pts. 32nds of 100%

Strike	Calls–Settle			Puts–Settle		
Price	Jun	Sep	Dec	Jun	Sep	Dec
10300	0-12	....	....	....	....	....
Est vol 0			Wed 0 calls 0 puts			
Op Int Wed			660 calls 2,614 puts			

WHEAT (KC)
5,000 bu.; cents per bu.

Strike	Calls–Settle			Puts–Settle		
Price	Jly	Sep	Dec	Jly	Sep	Dec
370	10	15½	24¼	12	18¼	17⅝
Est vol 19			Wed 63 calls 87 puts			
Op Int Wed			3,217 calls 3,844 puts			

Reasons for the Popularity of Futures Options

Futures options are more attractive to investors than options on the underlying asset when it is cheaper or more convenient to deliver futures contracts on the asset rather than the asset itself. This is true of many commodities. For example, it is much easier and more convenient to make or take delivery of a live hogs futures contract than it is to make or take delivery of the hogs themselves.

An important point about a futures option is that the exercise of the option does not usually lead to delivery of the underlying asset, since in most circumstances the underlying futures contract is closed out prior to delivery. Futures options are, therefore, normally settled in cash. This is appealing to many investors, particularly those with limited capital who may find it difficult to come up with the funds to buy the underlying asset when an option is exercised.

Another advantage sometimes cited for futures options is that the trading of futures and futures options are arranged in pits side by side in the same exchange. This facilitates hedging, arbitrage, and speculation. It also tends to make the markets more efficient.

A final point is that futures options tend to entail lower transactions costs than spot options in many situations.

Black's Model

In 1976, Black developed a model for pricing options on futures.[3] This model is based on the underlying assumption that the futures price, F, follows geometric Brownian motion:

$$dF = \mu F\, dt + \sigma\, dz$$

where μ is the expected growth rate in F, σ is its volatility, and dz is a Wiener process. As shown in Appendix 12B, this assumption leads to the futures price being treated in the same way as a security providing a continuous dividend yield equal to r. The European call price, c, and European put price, p, for a futures option are therefore given by equations (12.4) and (12.5) with S replaced by F and $q = r$:

$$c = e^{-r(T-t)}[FN(d_1) - XN(d_2)] \tag{12.10}$$

$$p = e^{-r(T-t)}[XN(-d_2) - FN(-d_1)] \tag{12.11}$$

where

$$d_1 = \frac{\ln(F/X) + (\sigma^2/2)(T - t)}{\sigma\sqrt{T - t}}$$

$$d_2 = \frac{\ln(F/X) - (\sigma^2/2)(T - t)}{\sigma\sqrt{T - t}} = d_1 - \sigma\sqrt{T - t}$$

Example 12.6

Consider a European put futures option on crude oil. Suppose that the time to maturity is four months, the current futures price is \$20, the strike price is \$20, the risk-free interest rate is 9% per annum, and the volatility of the futures price is 25% per annum. In this case, $F = 20$, $X = 20$, $r = 0.09$, $T - t = 0.3333$, and $\sigma = 0.25$. Since $\ln(F/X) = 0$,

$$d_1 = \frac{\sigma\sqrt{T - t}}{2} = 0.07216$$

$$d_2 = -\frac{\sigma\sqrt{T - t}}{2} = -0.07216$$

$$N(-d_1) = 0.4712 \qquad N(-d_2)$$

and the put price, p, is given by

$$p = e^{-0.09 \times 0.3333}(20 \times 0.5288 - 20 \times$$

or \$1.12.

[3] See F. Black, "The Pricing of Commodity Contracts," J.
(March 1976), 167–79.

The Expected Growth Rate of a Futures Price

The expected growth rate in the price of a stock that pays dividends at rate q is $r - q$ in a risk-neutral world. (This is because, with this growth rate, the total expected return in the form of dividends and capital gains is r.) Since a futures price behaves like a stock where the dividend yield, q, equals r, it follows that the expected growth rate in a futures price in a risk-neutral world is zero. This is as might be expected. It costs nothing to enter into a futures contract. The expected gain to the holder of a futures contract in a risk-neutral world should therefore be zero.

This result that the expected growth rate in a futures price in a risk-neutral world is zero is a very general one. It is true for all futures prices. It applies in the world where interest rates are stochastic as well as the world where they are constant.

Since the expected growth rate of the futures price is zero,

$$F = \hat{E}(F_T)$$

where F_T is the futures price at the maturity of the contract, F is the futures price today, and $\hat{E}$ denotes expected value in a risk-neutral world. Since $F_T = S_T$, where S_T is the spot price at time T, it follows that

$$F = \hat{E}(S_T) \tag{12.12}$$

We have therefore shown that for all assets the futures price equals the expected future spot price in a risk-neutral world.

Put–Call Parity

A put–call parity relationship for European futures options can be derived in a similar way as for ordinary options (see Section 7.6). If F_T is the futures price at maturity, a European call plus an amount of cash equal to $Xe^{-r(T-t)}$ has the terminal value

$$\max(F_T - X, 0) + X = \max(F_T, X)$$

An amount of cash equal to $Fe^{-r(T-t)}$ plus a futures contract plus a European put option has terminal value[4]

$$F + (F_T - F) + \max(X - F_T, 0) = \max(F_T, X)$$

Since the two portfolios are equivalent at maturity, it follows that they are worth the same today. The futures contract is worth zero today. Hence

$$c + Xe^{-r(T-t)} = p + Fe^{-r(T-t)} \tag{12.13}$$

the result we would expect from the argument in Section 12.1 since it nds to substituting $Fe^{-r(T-t)}$ for S in equation (7.3).

sumes no difference between forward and futures contracts.

Example 12.7

Suppose that the price of a European call option on silver futures for delivery in six months is 56 cents per ounce when the strike price is $8.50. Assume that the silver futures price for delivery in six months is currently $8.00 and the risk-free interest rate for an investment that matures in six months is 10% per annum. From a rearrangement of equation (12.13), the price of a European put option on silver futures with the same maturity and exercise date as the call option is

$$0.56 + 8.50e^{-0.5\times0.1} - 8.00e^{-0.5\times0.1} = 1.04$$

European Futures Options versus European Spot Options

The futures price of any asset equals its spot price at maturity of the futures contract. It follows that a European futures option is worth the same as the corresponding European option on the underlying asset if the futures contract has the same maturity as the option. This explains why the formulas in equations (12.8) and (12.9) for a European call option on spot foreign exchange in terms of the forward rate are identical to equations (12.10) and (12.11).

American Futures Options versus American Spot Options

Traded futures options are in practice usually American. Assuming that the risk-free rate of interest, r, is positive, there is always some chance that it will be optimal to exercise an American futures option early. American futures options are therefore worth more than their European counterparts. Unfortunately, no analytic formulas are available for valuing American futures options. Numerical procedures and analytic approximations are discussed in Chapter 15.

It is not generally true that an American futures option is worth the same as the corresponding American option on the underlying asset when the futures and options contract have the same maturity. Suppose, for example, that there is a normal market with futures prices consistently higher than spot prices prior to maturity. This is the case with most indices, gold, silver, low-interest currencies, and some commodities. An American call futures option must be worth more than the corresponding American call option on the underlying asset. This is because there are some situations when it will be exercised early, and in these situations, it will provide a greater profit to the holder. Similarly, an American put futures option must be worth less than the corresponding American put option on the underlying asset. If there is an inverted market with futures prices consistently lower than spot prices, as is the case with high-interest currencies and some commodities, the reverse must be true. American call futures options are worth less than the corresponding American call option on the underlying asset, while American put futures options are worth more than the corresponding American put option on the underlying asset.

The differences between American futures options and American asset options that have just been outlined are true when the futures contract expires later than the options contract as well as when the two expire at the same time. In fact,

the differences tend to be greater the later the futures contract expires. They are also true regardless of the assumptions that are made about the processes followed by the spot price and the futures price.

12.6 SUMMARY

The Black–Scholes formula for valuing European options on a non-dividend-paying stock can be extended to cover European options on a stock providing a continuous known dividend yield. In practice stocks do not provide continuous dividend yields. However, a number of other assets upon which options are written can be considered to be analogous to a stock providing a continuous dividend yield. In particular:

1. An index is analogous to a stock providing a continuous dividend yield. The dividend yield is the average dividend yield on the stocks comprising the index.
2. A foreign currency is analogous to a stock providing a continuous dividend yield where the dividend yield is the foreign risk-free interest rate.
3. A futures price is analogous to a stock providing a continuous dividend yield where the dividend yield is equal to the domestic risk-free interest rate.

The extension to Black–Scholes can therefore be used to value European options on indices, foreign currencies, and futures contracts. As we will see in Chapter 15, these analogies are also useful in valuing numerically American options on indices, currencies, and futures contracts.

Index options are settled in cash. Upon exercise of an index call option, the holder receives the amount by which the index exceeds the strike price at close of trading. Similarly, upon exercise of an index put option, the holder receives the amount by which the strike price exceeds the index at close of trading. Index options can be used for portfolio insurance. If the portfolio has a β of 1.0, it is appropriate to buy one put option for each $100S$ dollars in the portfolio, where S is the value of the index; otherwise, β put options should be purchased for each $100S$ dollars in the portfolio, where β is the beta of the portfolio calculated using the capital asset pricing model. The strike price of the put options purchased should reflect the level of insurance required.

Currency options are traded both on organized exchanges and over the counter. They can be used by corporate treasurers to hedge foreign exchange exposure. For example, a U.S. corporate treasurer who knows that sterling will be received by his or her company at a certain time in the future can hedge by buying put options that mature at that time. Similarly, a U.S. corporate treasurer who knows that sterling will be paid at a certain time in the future can hedge by buying call options which mature at that time.

Futures options require the delivery of the underlying futures contract upon exercise. When a call is exercised, the holder acquires a long futures position

plus a cash amount equal to the excess of the futures price over the strike price. Similarly, when a put is exercised, the holder acquires a short position plus a cash amount equal to the excess of the strike price over the futures price. The futures contract that is delivered typically expires slightly later than the option. If we assume that the two expiration dates are the same, a European futures option is worth exactly the same as the corresponding European option on the underlying asset. However, this is not true of American options. If the futures market is normal, an American call futures is worth more than the American call on the underlying asset, while an American put futures is worth less than the American put on the underlying asset. If the futures market is inverted, the reverse is true.

SUGGESTIONS FOR FURTHER READING

General

Merton, R. C., "Theory of Rational Option Pricing," *Bell Journal of Economics and Management Science*, 4 (Spring 1973), 141–83.

Stoll, H. R., and R. E. Whaley, "New Option Instruments; Arbitrageable Linkages and Valuation," *Advances in Futures and Options Research,* 1, pt. A (1986), 25–62.

On Options on Stock Indices

Chance, D. M., "Empirical Tests of the Pricing of Index Call Options," *Advances in Futures and Options Research*, 1, pt. A (1986), 141–66.

On Options on Currencies

Amin, K., and R. A. Jarrow, "Pricing Foreign Currency Options under Stochastic Interest Rates," *Journal of International Money and Finance,* 10 (1991), 310–329.

Biger, N., and J. Hull, "The Valuation of Currency Options," *Financial Management*, 12 (Spring 1983), 24–28.

Bodurtha, J. N., and G. R. Courtadon, "Tests of an American Option Pricing Model on the Foreign Currency Options Market," *Journal of Financial and Quantitative Analysis*, 22 (June 1987), 153–67.

Garman, M. B., and S. W. Kohlhagen, "Foreign Currency Option Values," *Journal of International Money and Finance*, 2 (December 1983), 231–37.

Grabbe, J. O., "The Pricing of Call and Put Options on Foreign Exchange," *Journal of International Money and Finance*, 2 (December 1983), 239–53.

On Options on Futures

Black, F., "The Pricing of Commodity Contracts," *Journal of Financial Economics*, 3 (March 1976), 167–79.

Brenner, M., G. Courtadon, and M. Subrahmanyam, "Options on the Spot and Options on Futures," *Journal of Finance*, 40 (December 1985), 1303–17.

Ramaswamy, K., and S. M. Sundaresan, "The Valuation of Options on Futures Contracts," *Journal of Finance*, 40 (December 1985), 1319–40.

Wolf, A., "Fundamentals of Commodity Options on Futures," *Journal of Futures Markets*, 2 (1982), 391–408.

QUESTIONS AND PROBLEMS

12.1. A portfolio is currently worth $10 million and has a beta of 1.0. The S&P 100 is currently standing at 250. Explain how a put option on the S&P 100 with a strike of 240 can be used to provide portfolio insurance.

12.2. "Once we know how to value options on a stock paying a continuous dividend yield, we know how to value options on stock indices, currencies, and futures." Explain this statement.

12.3. Explain the difference between a call option on yen and a call option on yen futures.

12.4. Explain how currency options can be used for hedging.

12.5. Calculate the value of a three-month at-the-money European call option on a stock index when the index is at 250, the risk-free interest rate is 10% per annum, the volatility of the index is 18% per annum, and the dividend yield on the index is 3% per annum.

12.6. Consider an American call futures option where the futures contract and the option contract expire at the same time. Under what circumstances is the futures option worth more than the corresponding American option on the underlying asset?

12.7. Calculate the value of a five-month European put futures option when the futures price is $19, the strike price is $20, the risk-free interest rate is 12% per annum, and the volatility of the futures price is 20% per annum.

12.8. Suppose that an exchange constructs a stock index which tracks the return, including dividends, on a certain portfolio. Explain how you would value (a) futures contracts; (b) European options on the index.

12.9. The S&P index currently stands at 348 and has a volatility of 30% per annum. The risk-free rate of interest is 7% per annum and the index provides a dividend yield of 4% per annum. Calculate the value of a three-month European put with strike price 350.

12.10. Suppose that the spot price of the Canadian dollar is U.S. $0.75 and that the Canadian dollar–U.S. dollar exchange rate has a volatility of 4% per annum. The risk-free rates of interest in Canada and the United States are 9% and 7% per annum, respectively. Calculate the value of a European call option with strike price 0.75 and exercise date in nine months.

12.11. Calculate the implied volatility of soybean futures prices from the following information concerning a European put on soybean futures:

Current futures price	525
Strike price	525
Risk-free rate	6% per annum
Time to maturity	5 months
Put price	20

12.12. Show that the put–call parity relationship for European index options is

$$c + Xe^{-r(T-t)} = p + Se^{-q(T-t)}$$

where q is the dividend yield on the index, c is the price of a European call option, p is the price of a European put option, and both options have strike price X and maturity T.

12.13. What is the put–call parity relationship for European currency options?

12.14. Show that if C is the price of an American call with strike price X and maturity T on a stock providing a dividend yield of q, and P is the price of an American put on the same stock with the same strike price and exercise date:

$$Se^{-q(T-t)} - X < C - P < S - Xe^{-r(T-t)}$$

where S is the stock price, r is the risk-free interest rate, and $r > 0$. (*Hint*: To obtain the first half of the inequality, consider possible values of:

Portfolio A: a European call option plus an amount X invested at the risk-free rate

Portfolio B: an American put option plus $e^{-q(T-t)}$ of stock with dividends being reinvested in the stock

To obtain the second half of the inequality consider possible values of:

Portfolio C: an American call option plus an amount $Xe^{-r(T-t)}$ invested at the risk-free rate

Portfolio D: a European put option plus one stock with dividends being reinvested in the stock)

12.15. Show that if C is the price of an American call option on a futures contract when the strike price is X and the maturity is T, and P is the price of an American put on the same futures contract with the same strike price and exercise date,

$$Fe^{-r(T-t)} - X < C - P < F - Xe^{-r(T-t)}$$

where F is the futures price and r is the risk-free rate. Assume that $r > 0$ and that there is no difference between forward and futures contracts. (*Hint*: Use an analogous approach to that indicated for Problem 12.14.)

*12.16. If the price of currency A expressed in terms of the price of currency B follows the process assumed in Section 12.4, what is the process followed by the price of currency B expressed in terms of currency A?

12.17. Would you expect the volatility of a stock index to be greater or less than the volatility of a typical stock? Explain your answer.

12.18. A mutual fund announces that the salaries of its fund managers will depend on the performance of the fund. If the fund loses money, the salaries will be zero. If the fund makes a profit, the salaries will be proportional to the profit. Describe the salary of a fund manager as a derivative. How is a fund manager motivated to behave with this type of remuneration package?

12.19. Does the cost of portfolio insurance increase or decrease as the beta of the portfolio increases? Explain your answer.

12.20. Suppose that a portfolio is worth $60 million and the S&P 500 is at 300. If the value of the portfolio mirrors the value of the index, what options should be purchased to provide protection against the value of the portfolio falling below $54 million in one year's time?

12.21. Consider again the situation in Problem 12.20. Suppose that the portfolio has a beta of 2.0, that the risk-free interest rate is 5% per annum, and that the dividend yield on both the portfolio and the index is 3% per annum. What options should be purchased to provide protection against the value of the portfolio falling below $54 million?

12.22. Consider
   (a) A call CAP on the S&P 500 (traded on the CBOT) with a strike price of 300 (see Section 12.3 for a discussion of this instrument).
   (b) A bull spread created from European calls on the S&P 500 with strike prices of 300 and 330 and the same maturity as the CAP.

   What is the difference between the two? Which is worth more?

*12.23. In Section 12.5 it is noted that a futures price is analogous to a security providing a continuous dividend yield at rate r. By considering a forward contract on the futures price and using results from Chapter 3, show that the forward price equals the futures price when interest rates are constant.

12.24. Can an option on the deutschemark–yen exchange rate be created from two options, one on the dollar–deutschemark exchange rate, the other on the dollar–yen exchange rate? Explain your answer.

APPENDIX 12A: DERIVATION OF DIFFERENTIAL EQUATION SATISFIED BY A DERIVATIVE DEPENDENT ON A STOCK PROVIDING A CONTINUOUS DIVIDEND YIELD

Define f as the price of a derivative dependent on a stock providing a continuous dividend yield at rate q. We suppose that the stock price, S, follows the process

$$dS = \mu S\, dt + \sigma S\, dz$$

where dz is a Wiener process. The variables μ and σ are the expected proportional growth rate in the stock price and the volatility of the stock price. Since the stock price provides a continuous dividend yield, μ is not equal to the expected return on the stock.

Since f is a function of S and t, it follows from Ito's lemma that

$$df = \left(\frac{\partial f}{\partial S}\mu S + \frac{\partial f}{\partial t} + \frac{1}{2}\frac{\partial^2 f}{\partial S^2}\sigma^2 S^2 \right) dt + \frac{\partial f}{\partial S}\sigma S\, dz$$

Similarly to Section 11.5, we can set up a portfolio consisting of

$$-1: \quad \text{derivative}$$

$$+\frac{\partial f}{\partial S}: \quad \text{stock}$$

If Π is the value of the portfolio,

$$\Pi = -f + \frac{\partial f}{\partial S} S \tag{12A.1}$$

and the change, $\Delta\Pi$, in the value of the portfolio in time Δt is as given by equation (11.14):

$$\Delta\Pi = \left(-\frac{\partial f}{\partial t} - \frac{1}{2}\frac{\partial^2 f}{\partial S^2}\sigma^2 S^2\right)\Delta t$$

In time Δt the holder of the portfolio earns capital gains equal to $\Delta\Pi$ and dividends equal to

$$qS\frac{\partial f}{\partial S}\Delta t$$

Define ΔW as the change in the wealth of the portfolio holder in time Δt. It follows that

$$\Delta W = \left(-\frac{\partial f}{\partial t} - \frac{1}{2}\frac{\partial^2 f}{\partial S^2}\sigma^2 S^2 + qS\frac{\partial f}{\partial S}\right)\Delta t \tag{12A.2}$$

Since this expression is independent of the Wiener process, the portfolio is instantaneously riskless. Hence

$$\Delta W = r\Pi\Delta t \tag{12A.3}$$

Substituting from equations (12A.1) and (12A.2) into equation (12A.3) gives

$$\left(-\frac{\partial f}{\partial t} - \frac{1}{2}\frac{\partial^2 f}{\partial S^2}\sigma^2 S^2 + qS\frac{\partial f}{\partial S}\right)\Delta t = r\left(-f + \frac{\partial f}{\partial S}S\right)\Delta t$$

so that

$$\frac{\partial f}{\partial t} + (r-q)S\frac{\partial f}{\partial S} + \frac{1}{2}\sigma^2 S^2\frac{\partial^2 f}{\partial S^2} = rf \tag{12A.4}$$

This is the differential equation that must be satisfied by f.

APPENDIX 12B: DERIVATION OF DIFFERENTIAL EQUATION SATISFIED BY A DERIVATIVE DEPENDENT ON A FUTURES PRICE

Suppose that the futures price F follows the process

$$dF = \mu F\, dt + \sigma F\, dz \tag{12B.1}$$

where dz is a Wiener process and σ is constant. Since f is a function of F and t, it follows from Ito's lemma that

$$df = \left(\frac{\partial f}{\partial F}\mu F + \frac{\partial f}{\partial t} + \frac{1}{2}\frac{\partial^2 f}{\partial F^2}\sigma^2 F^2\right)dt + \frac{\partial f}{\partial F}\sigma F\, dz \tag{12B.2}$$

Consider a portfolio consisting of

$$-1: \quad \text{derivative}$$

$$+\frac{\partial f}{\partial F}: \quad \text{futures contracts}$$

Define Π as the value of the portfolio and let $\Delta\Pi$, Δf, and ΔF be the change in Π, f, and F in time Δt, respectively. Since it costs nothing to enter into a futures contract,

$$\Pi = -f \tag{12B.3}$$

In time Δt, the holder of the portfolio earns capital gains equal to $-\Delta f$ from the derivative and income of

$$\frac{\partial f}{\partial F}\Delta F$$

from the futures contract. Define ΔW as the total change in wealth of the portfolio holder in time Δt. It follows that

$$\Delta W = \frac{\partial f}{\partial F}\Delta F - \Delta f$$

The discrete versions of equations (12B.1) and (12B.2) are

$$\Delta F = \mu F\, \Delta t + \sigma F \Delta z$$

and

$$\Delta f = \left(\frac{\partial f}{\partial F}\mu F + \frac{\partial f}{\partial t} + \frac{1}{2}\frac{\partial^2 f}{\partial F^2}\sigma^2 F^2\right)\Delta t + \frac{\partial f}{\partial F}\sigma F \Delta z$$

where $\Delta z = \epsilon\sqrt{\Delta t}$ and ϵ is a random sample from a standardized normal distribution. It follows that

$$\Delta W = \left(-\frac{\partial f}{\partial t} - \frac{1}{2}\frac{\partial^2 f}{\partial F^2}\sigma^2 F^2 \right)\Delta t \qquad (12B.4)$$

This is riskless. Hence it must also be true that

$$\Delta W = r\Pi\, \Delta t \qquad (12B.5)$$

Substituting for Π from equation (12B.3), equations (12B.4) and (12B.5) give

$$\left(-\frac{\partial f}{\partial t} - \frac{1}{2}\frac{\partial^2 f}{\partial F^2}\sigma^2 F^2 \right)\Delta t = -rf\, \Delta t$$

Hence

$$\frac{\partial f}{\partial t} + \frac{1}{2}\frac{\partial^2 f}{\partial F^2}\sigma^2 F^2 = rf$$

This has the same form as equation (12A.4) with q set equal to r. We deduce that a futures price can be treated in the same way as a stock providing a dividend yield at rate r for the purpose of valuing derivatives.

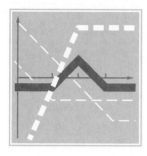

Chapter 1 3

General Approach to Pricing Derivatives

In this chapter we extend the ideas in Chapters 11 and 12 to present a general approach to pricing derivatives. It can be used when there are several underlying variables following continuous-time stochastic processes and does not require these variables to be the prices of traded securities.

The term *traded security* is here used to describe a traded asset that is held solely for investment by a significant number of people. Stocks, bonds, gold, and silver are all traded securities, but most commodities are not. The distinction between underlying variables that are the prices of traded securities and those that are not is an important one in the valuation of derivatives. We have already seen this in Chapter 3 in the context of forward and futures contracts. In general, when an underlying variable is the price of a traded security, the risk-neutral valuation result shows that investor attitudes to risk are irrelevant to the relationship between the price of the derivative and value of the underlying variable. When the underlying variable is not the price of a traded security, these risk attitudes may be important.

13.1 SINGLE UNDERLYING VARIABLE

In this section we consider the properties of derivatives dependent on the value of a single variable, θ, that follows a stochastic process

$$\frac{d\theta}{\theta} = m\,dt + s\,dz \qquad (13.1)$$

where dz is a Wiener process. The parameters m and s are the expected growth rate in θ and the volatility of θ, respectively. We assume that they depend only on θ and t. We do not assume that θ is the price of a traded security. It could be something as far removed from financial markets as the temperature in the center of New Orleans.

Suppose that f_1 and f_2 are the prices of two derivatives dependent only on θ and time. These could be options or other securities that are defined so that they provide a payoff equal to some function of θ at some future time. The processes followed by f_1 and f_2 can be determined from Ito's lemma. We suppose that they

288

are

$$\frac{df_1}{f_1} = \mu_1 \, dt + \sigma_1 \, dz$$

and

$$\frac{df_2}{f_2} = \mu_2 \, dt + \sigma_2 \, dz$$

where μ_1, μ_2, σ_1, and σ_2 are functions of θ and t, and dz is the same Wiener process as in equation (13.1). The discrete versions of these processes are

$$\Delta f_1 = \mu_1 f_1 \, \Delta t + \sigma_1 f_1 \, \Delta z \tag{13.2}$$

$$\Delta f_2 = \mu_2 f_2 \, \Delta t + \sigma_2 f_2 \, \Delta z \tag{13.3}$$

We can eliminate the Δz by forming an instantaneously riskless portfolio consisting of $\sigma_2 f_2$ of the first derivative and $-\sigma_1 f_1$ of the second derivative. If Π is the value of the portfolio,

$$\Pi = (\sigma_2 f_2) f_1 - (\sigma_1 f_1) f_2 \tag{13.4}$$

and

$$\Delta\Pi = \sigma_2 f_2 \, \Delta f_1 - \sigma_1 f_1 \, \Delta f_2$$

Substituting from equations (13.2) and (13.3), this becomes

$$\Delta\Pi = (\mu_1 \sigma_2 f_1 f_2 - \mu_2 \sigma_1 f_1 f_2) \, \Delta t \tag{13.5}$$

Since Π is instantaneously riskless, it must earn the risk-free rate. Hence

$$\Delta\Pi = r\Pi \, \Delta t$$

Substituting into this equation from equations (13.4) and (13.5) gives

$$\mu_1 \sigma_2 - \mu_2 \sigma_1 = r\sigma_2 - r\sigma_1$$

or

$$\frac{\mu_1 - r}{\sigma_1} = \frac{\mu_2 - r}{\sigma_2} \tag{13.6}$$

Market Price of Risk

Define λ as the value of each side in equation (13.6), so that

$$\frac{\mu_1 - r}{\sigma_1} = \frac{\mu_2 - r}{\sigma_2} = \lambda$$

Dropping subscripts, we have shown that if f is the price of a security dependent only on θ and t with

$$df = \mu f \, dt + \sigma f \, dz \tag{13.7}$$

then

$$\frac{\mu - r}{\sigma} = \lambda \tag{13.8}$$

The parameter λ is, in general, dependent on both θ and t, but it is not dependent on the nature of the derivative f. It is known as the *market price of risk* of θ. The variables μ and σ are the expected return and volatility of f.[1]

The market price of risk of θ measures the trade-offs between risk and return that are made for securities dependent on θ. Equation (13.8) can be written

$$\mu - r = \lambda \sigma \tag{13.9}$$

For an intuitive understanding of this equation, we note that the variable σ can be loosely interpreted as the quantity of θ-risk present in f. On the right-hand side of the equation we are therefore multiplying the quantity of θ-risk by the price of θ-risk. The left-hand side is the expected return in excess of the risk-free interest rate that is required to compensate for this risk. Many readers will notice an analogy between equation (13.9) and the capital asset pricing model, which relates the expected excess return on a stock to its risk.

Example 13.1

Consider a security whose price is positively related to the price of oil but depends on no other stochastic variables. Suppose that it provides an expected return of 12% per annum and has a volatility of 20% per annum. Assume that the risk-free interest rate is 8% per annum. It follows that the market price of risk of oil is $(0.12 - 0.08)/0.2 = 0.2$. Note that oil is not a traded security. Therefore, its market price of risk cannot be calculated from equation (13.8) by setting μ equal to the expected return from an investment in oil and σ equal to the volatility of oil prices.

Differential Equation

Using Ito's lemma, the parameters μ and σ in equation (13.7) are given by

$$\mu f = \frac{\partial f}{\partial t} + m\theta \frac{\partial f}{\partial \theta} + \frac{1}{2} s^2 \theta^2 \frac{\partial^2 f}{\partial \theta^2}$$

and

$$\sigma f = s\theta \frac{\partial f}{\partial \theta}$$

Substituting these into equation (13.9), we obtain the following differential equation that must be satisfied by f:

$$\frac{\partial f}{\partial t} + \theta \frac{\partial f}{\partial \theta}(m - \lambda s) + \frac{1}{2} s^2 \theta^2 \frac{\partial^2 f}{\partial \theta^2} = rf \tag{13.10}$$

---

[1]Strictly speaking, one of σ and $-\sigma$ is the volatility of f. If f is positively related to θ (so that $\partial f/\partial \theta$ is positive), σ is positive and equals the volatility of f. But if f is negatively related to θ, then σ is negative and the volatility of f equals $-\sigma$.

Equation (13.10) is structurally very similar to the Black–Scholes differential equation (11.15). With S replaced by θ and $q = r - m + \lambda s$, it is the same as the differential equation (12A.4) for valuing a derivative dependent on an asset providing a known dividend yield, q. This observation leads to a way of extending the risk-neutral valuation result in Section 11.6 so that it applies when the variables underlying a derivative are not the prices of traded securities.

Risk-Neutral Valuation with a Single Underlying Variable

Any solution to equation (12A.4) for S is a solution to (13.10) for θ, and vice versa, when the substitution

$$q = r - m + \lambda s$$

is made. As explained in Section 12.2, we know how to solve (12A.4) using risk-neutral valuation. This involves setting the drift of S equal to $r - q$ and discounting expected payoffs at the risk-free interest rate. It follows that we can solve equation (13.10) by setting the drift of θ equal to

$$r - (r - m + \lambda s) = m - \lambda s$$

and discounting expected payoffs at the risk-free interest rate.

The approach to valuing a derivative is therefore to reduce the drift of θ by λs, from m to $m - \lambda s$, and then behave as though the world is risk neutral. The risk-neutral valuation result in Chapter 11 is a particular case of this more general result. To see this, suppose that θ is the price of a non-dividend-paying stock. From equation (13.9),

$$m - r = \lambda s$$

or

$$m - \lambda s = r$$

which shows that changing the expected growth rate of θ to $m - \lambda s$ is the same as setting the return from the stock equal to the risk-free rate of interest.

Example 13.2

The current price of copper is 80 cents per pound and the risk-free interest rate is 5% per annum. The expected growth rate in the price of copper is 2% per annum and its volatility is 20% per annum. The market price of the risk associated with copper is 0.5. Assume that a contract is traded which allows the holder to receive 1,000 pounds of copper at no cost in six months' time. In this case, $m = 0.02$, $\lambda = 0.5$, and $s = 0.2$. The expected growth rate of the price of copper in a risk-neutral world is

$$m - \lambda s = 0.02 - 0.5 \times 0.2 = -0.08$$

or -8% per annum. The expected payoff from the contract in a risk-neutral world is therefore $1,000 \times 0.80e^{-0.08 \times 0.5} = 768.63$. Discounting for six months at 5% per annum, we estimate the current value of the contract to be 749.65.

It is worth noting that our extension of the risk-neutral valuation argument is more subtle than it first appears. When θ is not the price of a traded security, the risk-neutral valuation argument does not necessarily tell us anything about what would happen in a risk-neutral world. It simply states that changing the expected growth rate of θ from m to $m - \lambda s$ and then behaving as though the world is risk neutral gives the correct values for derivatives.[2] For convenience, however, we will refer to a world where expected growth rates are changed from m to $m - \lambda s$ as a risk-neutral world.

13.2 INTEREST RATE RISK

An interest rate is an example of a variable that is not the price of a traded security. In this section we discuss the nature of the market price of interest rate risk.

The returns on the stocks and bonds in a typical portfolio are negatively related to changes in interest rates. As interest rates decrease, bond and stock prices tend to increase; as interest rates increase, bond and stock prices tend to decrease. Consider adding to the portfolio a security whose price is positively related to one particular interest rate, say, the 1-year interest rate. This security will tend to have the effect of reducing rather than increasing the risk in the portfolio. This is because, as interest rates rise, the fall in the value of the stocks and bonds in the portfolio is offset by an increase in the value of the security; as interest rates fall, the rise in the value of the stocks and bonds in the portfolio is offset by a decrease in the value of the security. This means that the holder of the portfolio will be happy with an expected return from the security which is less than the risk-free interest rate.

Suppose that the interest rate is denoted by θ and follows the process in equation (13.1), while the security under consideration has a price f and follows the process in equation (13.7). Since θ and f are positively related, σ is positive. From the argument just given, $\mu < r$. It follows from equation (13.8) that the market price of risk of the interest rate is negative.

A negative market price of risk for an interest rate means that its expected growth rate in the risk-neutral world is greater than its expected growth rate in the real world. The expected value of an interest rate in a risk-neutral world is approximately equal to its forward interest rate.[3] A negative market price of risk therefore implies that forward rates are greater than expected future spot rates. This result is consistent with liquidity preference theory, which was introduced in Section 4.1.

---

[2]To illustrate this point, suppose that θ is the temperature in the center of New Orleans. The process followed by θ clearly does not depend on the risk preferences of human beings, but we might nevertheless have to adjust the drift of the process when valuing derivatives dependent on θ.

[3]The expected value of an interest rate in the risk-neutral world is exactly equal to the futures interest rate as discussed in Section 12.5.

Example 13.3

Consider two securities, both of which are positively dependent on the 90-day interest rate. Suppose that the first one has an expected return of 3% per annum and a volatility of 20% per annum, and the second one has a volatility of 30% per annum. Assume that the instantaneous risk-free rate of interest is 6% per annum. The market price of interest rate risk is, using the return and volatility for the first security, $(0.03 - 0.06)/0.2 = -0.15$. From a rearrangement of equation (13.9), the expected return from the second security is therefore $0.06 - 0.15 \times 0.3 = 0.015$ or 1.5% per annum.

13.3 SECURITIES DEPENDENT ON SEVERAL STATE VARIABLES

Appendices 13A and 13B extend the results in Section 13.1 to securities whose prices depend on several underlying variables. Appendix 13A provides a version of Ito's lemma that covers functions of several variables. Appendix 13B derives a differential equation that must be satisfied by all derivatives dependent on a set of state variables that follow Ito processes.

Suppose that n variables, $\theta_1, \theta_2, \ldots, \theta_n$, follow stochastic processes of the form

$$\frac{d\theta_i}{\theta_i} = m_i \, dt + s_i \, dz_i \tag{13.11}$$

for $i = 1, 2, \ldots, n$, where the dz_i are Wiener processes. The parameters m_i and s_i are expected growth rates and volatilities and may be functions of the θ_i and time. Appendix 13A shows that the process for the price, f, of a security that is dependent on the θ_i has the form

$$\frac{df}{f} = \mu \, dt + \sum_{i=1}^{n} \sigma_i \, dz_i \tag{13.12}$$

In this equation, μ is the expected return from the security and $\sigma_i \, dz_i$ is the component of the risk of this return attributable to θ_i.

Appendix 13B shows that

$$\mu - r = \sum_{i=1}^{n} \lambda_i \sigma_i \tag{13.13}$$

where λ_i is the market price of risk for θ_i. This equation relates the expected excess return that investors require on the security to the λ_i and σ_i. The term $\lambda_i \sigma_i$ measures the extent to which the return required by investors on a security is affected by the dependence of the security on θ_i. If $\lambda_i \sigma_i = 0$, there is no effect; if $\lambda_i \sigma_i > 0$, investors require a higher return to compensate them for the risk arising

from θ_i; if $\lambda_i \sigma_i < 0$, the dependence of the security on θ_i causes investors to require a lower return than would otherwise be the case. The $\lambda_i \sigma_i < 0$ situation occurs when the variable has the effect of reducing rather than increasing the risks in the portfolio of a typical investor.

Example 13.4

A stock price depends on three underlying variables: the price of oil, the price of gold, and the performance of the whole stock market. Suppose that the market prices of risk for these variables are 0.2, −0.1, and 0.4, respectively. Suppose also that the σ_i factors in equation (13.12) corresponding to the three variables have been estimated as 0.05, 0.1, and 0.15, respectively. The excess return on the stock over the risk-free rate is

$$0.2 \times 0.05 - 0.1 \times 0.1 + 0.4 \times 0.15 = 0.06$$

or 6.0% per annum. If variables other than those considered affect f, this result is still true provided that the market price of risk for each of these other variables is zero.

Equation (13.13) is closely related to arbitrage pricing theory, which was developed by Ross in 1976.[4] The continuous-time version of the capital asset pricing model (CAPM) can be regarded as a particular case of the equation. CAPM argues that an investor requires excess returns to compensate for any risk that is correlated to the risk in the return from the stock market but requires no excess return for other risks. Risks that are correlated with the return from the stock market are referred to as *systematic;* other risks are referred to as *nonsystematic.* If CAPM is true, λ_i is proportional to the instantaneous correlation between changes in θ_i and the return from the market. When θ_i is instantaneously uncorrelated with the return from the market, λ_i is zero.

Risk-Neutral Valuation with Several Underlying Variables

Our risk-neutral valuation arguments in Section 13.1 concerning differential equation (13.10) can be extended to cover the more general differential equation (13B.11) in Appendix 13B. A derivative can always be valued as if the world were risk neutral, provided that the expected growth rate of each underlying variable is assumed to be $m_i - \lambda_i s_i$ rather than m_i. The volatility of the variables and the coefficient of correlation between variables are not changed. This result was first developed by Cox, Ingersoll, and Ross and represents an important extension to the basic risk-neutral valuation argument.[5]

Suppose that a derivative which is dependent on θ_i $(1 \leq i \leq n)$ provides a payoff at time T. To value the derivative, it is necessary to set the expected

---

[4]See S. A. Ross, "The Arbitrage Theory of Capital Asset Pricing," *Journal of Economic Theory*, 13 (December 1976), 343–62.

[5]See lemma 4 in J. C. Cox, J. E. Ingersoll, and S. A. Ross, "An Intertemporal General Equilibrium Model of Asset Prices," *Econometrica*, 53 (1985), 363–84.

growth rate of each θ_i equal to $m_i - \lambda_i s_i$ while keeping the volatility of each θ_i equal to s_i and the instantaneous correlation between θ_i and θ_k equal to ρ_{ik} for all i and k. The value of the derivative is then the expected payoff discounted to the present at the risk-free rate of interest. Thus the value f of a security that pays off f_T at time T is given by

$$f = e^{-r(T-t)}\hat{E}(f_T) \tag{13.14}$$

where $\hat{E}$ denotes expected value in a risk-neutral world (i.e., a world where the growth rate in θ_i is $m_i - \lambda_i s_i$).

If r is a stochastic variable, it is treated in the same way as the other θ_i's. The growth rate (or proportional drift rate) in r is, for the purposes of all calculations, reduced by $\lambda_r s_r$, where λ_r is the market price of the risk associated with r and s_r is the volatility of r.[6] To value a derivative, it is necessary to calculate the expected payoff in a risk-neutral world conditional on the particular path followed by r. This expected payoff is then discounted at the average value of r on the path and the expected value is taken over all possible paths. Thus the value, f, of a derivative that pays off f_T at time T is given by

$$f = \hat{E}[e^{-\bar{r}(T-t)}f_T] \tag{13.15}$$

where $\bar{r}$ is the average risk-free interest rate between t and T.

Equations (13.14) and (13.15) are true when the payoff, f_T, is some function of the paths followed by the underlying variables as well as when the payoff depends only on the final values of the variables. In the former situation, f is termed a *path-dependent derivative*. A number of types of path-dependent securities are discussed in Chapter 18.

Example 13.5

Consider a security that pays off \$100 at time T if the price of stock A is above X_A and the price of stock B is above X_B. We assume that prices of the two stocks are uncorrelated and that no dividends are paid. Using risk-neutral valuation, the value of the security is $100 Q_A Q_B e^{-r(T-t)}$, where Q_A is the probability of stock A's price being above X_A at time T in a risk-neutral world and Q_B is the probability of stock B's price being above X_B at time T in a risk-neutral world. It can be shown that

$$Q_A = N\left[\frac{\ln(S_A/X_A) + (r - \sigma_A^2/2)(T-t)}{\sigma_A\sqrt{T-t}}\right]$$

$$Q_B = N\left[\frac{\ln(S_B/X_B) + (r - \sigma_B^2/2)(T-t)}{\sigma_B\sqrt{T-t}}\right]$$

where S_A and S_B are the current prices of stock A and stock B, and σ_A and σ_B are the volatilities of stock A and stock B.

---

[6] As discussed in Section 13.2, λ_r can be expected to be negative, so that the growth rate is higher in a risk-neutral world.

Equivalent Martingale Measures

The risk-neutral valuation approach is sometimes referred to as using an *equivalent martingale measure*. A *martingale* is a zero-drift stochastic process. Harrison and Kreps show that in a world where interest rates are zero and there are no arbitrage opportunities, there exists a unique equivalent martingale measure under which the price of any non-income-producing security equals its expected future price.[7]

A full discussion of this result is beyond the scope of this book. It is easy to see that the equivalent martingale measure result is consistent with the risk-neutral valuation results that we have presented in this book. When interest rates are zero, the risk-neutral valuation result tells us that we can set the drifts of all securities equal to zero and value the securities by using a zero discount rate. Setting the drifts equal to zero creates the equivalent martingale measure. Using a zero discount rate means that the price today equals the expected future price.

The equivalent martingale measure theory can be extended to a world where interest rates are nonzero (and possibly stochastic). Define h as the value of an instrument that is worth \$1 today and is invested at each moment in time at the instantaneous risk-free rate. We change our units of measurement so that the prices of all other securities are defined in "units of h" rather than in dollars. This means that if the dollar price of a security is f, the price in units of h is f/h. With this change of numeraire we move to a situation where interest rates are zero and the equivalent martingale measure arguments are valid.

13.4 IS IT NECESSARY TO ESTIMATE THE MARKET PRICE OF RISK?

The analysis so far is interesting from a theoretical point of view but leaves one big unanswered question: How do we get an estimate of λ, the market price of risk of a variable, and m, its expected growth rate? Luckily it turns out that we can avoid having to make a direct estimate of either of these variables in many situations. There are a number of approaches:

1. Futures prices can be used to provide direct information on the process followed by a variable in a risk-neutral world. For a consumption commodity that has an actively traded futures market, it is therefore not usually necessary to estimate m and λ directly. We explain this in more detail in Section 13.5.

2. When a derivative depends on variables whose risk-neutral processes are unknown, it is sometimes possible to overcome the problem by looking at

---

[7]See J. M. Harrison and D. M. Kreps, "Martingales and Arbitrage in Multiperiod Securities Markets," *Journal of Economic Theory*, 20 (1979), 381–408.

the derivative or its underlying variables in a different way. We give an example of this in Section 13.6.

3. When we are modeling interest rates, it turns out that the current term structure leads us directly to the processes followed by interest rates in the risk-neutral world. We never need to estimate the real-world processes. This is explained in Chapter 17.

13.5 DERIVATIVES DEPENDENT ON COMMODITY PRICES

Most commodities are held primarily for consumption and cannot be considered as traded securities. Their market prices of risk are therefore liable to enter into the pricing of derivatives. Luckily it turns out that we can finesse the problem of estimating the market price of risk by using futures prices.

Define:

   S: commodity price

   $F(\tau)$: futures price for a contract on the commodity that matures at time τ.

If the derivative depends on the commodity price at only one time, T, we can assume that the variable underlying the derivative is $F(T)$ because $S = F(T)$ at time T. As explained in Chapter 12, $F(T)$ follows a zero-drift stochastic process in a risk-neutral world.

For American options and other derivatives that depend on the commodity price at more than one time, we need the process followed by the commodity price in a risk-neutral world. From equation (12.12) we know that the expected price of the commodity at time t in a risk-neutral world is $F(t)$. If we assume that the growth rate in the commodity price is dependent only on time and that the volatility of the commodity price is constant, it follows that the risk-neutral process for the commodity price has the form

$$\frac{dS}{S} = \mu(t)\,dt + \sigma\,dz \tag{13.16}$$

where

$$\mu(t) = \frac{\partial}{\partial t}[\ln F(t)]$$

Example 13.6

Suppose that the futures prices of live cattle at the end of July 1997 are as follows:

August 1997	62.20
October 1997	60.60
December 1997	62.70
February 1998	63.37

| April 1998 | 64.42 |
| June 1998 | 64.40 |

These can be used to estimate the expected growth rate in live cattle prices in a risk-neutral world. For example, the expected growth rate in live cattle prices between October and December 1997 in a risk-neutral world is

$$\ln \frac{62.70}{60.60} = 0.034$$

or 3.4% with continuous compounding. On an annualized basis this is 20.4% per annum.

As a simple illustration of the valuation of a derivative, consider one that will pay off at the end of July 1998 an amount equal to the average price of live cattle during the preceding year. As an approximation, the average price of live cattle during the previous year in a risk-neutral world is the average of the six futures prices just given (i.e., it is 62.95 cents). Assuming that the risk-free rate of interest is 10% per annum, the value of the derivative is

$$62.95e^{-0.1} = 56.96 \text{ cents}$$

Convenience Yields

The convenience yield for a commodity was introduced in Chapter 3. It is a measure of the benefits realized from ownership of the physical commodity that are not realized by the holders of a futures contract. If y is the convenience yield and u is the storage cost, the commodity behaves like a traded security that provides a return equal to $y - u$. In a risk-neutral world its growth is therefore

$$r - (y - u) = r - y + u$$

The convenience yield of a commodity can be related to its market price of risk. From the analysis in the first part of this chapter, the expected growth of the commodity price in a risk-neutral world is $m - \lambda s$, where m is its expected growth in the real world, s its volatility, and λ is its market price of risk. It follows that

$$m - \lambda s = r - y + u$$

or

$$y = r + u - m + \lambda s$$

13.6 QUANTOS

An interesting application of the concepts in this chapter is to what are termed *quantos*. These are derivatives where there are two currencies involved. The payoff is defined in terms of the values of variables measured in the first currency and the payoff is made in the second currency.

Consider a forward contract maturing at time T on the Nikkei 225 stock average. Define:

$S(t)$: Nikkei index measured in yen at time t
$Q(t)$: value of U.S. \$1 in yen at time t
K: delivery price measured in yen
q: dividend yield on the Nikkei index
r: domestic (U.S. dollar) risk-free rate
r_f: risk-free rate in Japan
F: forward price for the contract

If the payoff from the forward contract is

$$S(T) - K \text{ yen}$$

the contract is a regular forward contract since both the underlying variable, $S(t)$ and the payoff are measured in yen. The forward price is $S(t)e^{(r_f - q)(T-t)}$ yen, as explained Section 3.7.

If the payoff is

$$S(T) - K \text{ dollars}$$

the contract is a quanto since $S(t)$ is measured in yen and the payoff is in dollars.[8] It is tempting to argue that the futures price is $S(t)e^{(r-q)(T-t)}$ dollars. This is not correct. The no-arbitrage arguments given in Chapter 3 for index futures do not apply because we cannot trade an asset that is worth $S(t)$ dollars at time t. To make this point clear, suppose that the Nikkei index is 23,000, 23,050, and 23,025 on three successive days. We can trade a portfolio that is worth 23,000 yen, 23,050 yen, and 23,025 yen on the three days. But we cannot trade a portfolio that is worth \$23,000, \$23,050, and \$23,025 on the three days.

The problem in valuing a quanto security that pays off $S(T) - K$ dollars is that we do not know the process followed in a risk-neutral world by the variable $S(t)$ dollars. We solve this problem by noting that $S(t)$ dollars is the same as $S(t)Q(t)$ yen. From the viewpoint of a Japanese investor the payoff from the quanto is

$$[S(T) - K]Q(T) \text{ yen}$$

Using risk-neutral valuation, the value of the quanto is

$$e^{-r_f(T-t)}\hat{E}[S(T)Q(T) - KQ(T)] \text{ yen}$$

or

$$e^{-r_f(T-t)}\{\hat{E}[S(T)Q(T)] - K\hat{E}[Q(T)]\} \text{ yen}$$

---

[8]The contract has the same structure as the CME futures contract on the Nikkei Stock Average discussed in Section 3.7.

where $\hat{E}$ denotes expectations in a world that is risk neutral from the viewpoint of a yen investor. The forward price is the value of K that makes this zero. Hence

$$F = \frac{\hat{E}[S(T)Q(T)]}{\hat{E}[Q(T)]} \tag{13.17}$$

We know that from the point of view of a Japanese investor, $Q(t)$ grows in a risk-neutral world at an expected rate of $r_f - r$, so that

$$\hat{E}[Q(T)] = Q(t)e^{(r_f - r)(T-t)} \tag{13.18}$$

To evaluate $\hat{E}[S(t)Q(t)]$, we note that

$$dS(t) = (r_f - q)S(t)\,dt + \sigma_S S(t)\,dz_S$$

$$dQ(t) = (r_f - r)Q(t)\,dt + \sigma_Q Q(t)\,dz_Q \tag{13.19}$$

where σ_S and σ_Q are the volatilities of S and Q, and dz_S and dz_Q are Wiener processes. From Ito's lemma in Appendix 12A, the process followed by $S(t)Q(t)$ is

$$d[S(t)Q(t)] = (r_f - q + r_f - r + \rho\sigma_S\sigma_Q)S(t)Q(t)\,dt$$
$$+ S(t)Q(t)(\sigma_S\,dz_S + \sigma_Q\,dz_Q)$$

where ρ is the instantaneous correlation between S and Q. This shows that the variable $S(t)Q(t)$ follows geometric Brownian motion with an expected drift in the risk-neutral world of $2r_f - q - r + \rho\sigma_S\sigma_Q$. Hence

$$\hat{E}[S(T)Q(T)] = S(t)Q(t)e^{(2r_f - q - r + \rho\sigma_S\sigma_Q)(T-t)} \tag{13.20}$$

From equations (13.17), (13.18), and (13.20)[9]

$$F = S(t)e^{(r_f - q + \rho\sigma_S\sigma_Q)(T-t)} \tag{13.21}$$

Using the result in equation (12.12), the process followed by $S(t)$ dollars in the risk-neutral world has drift $r_f - q + \rho\sigma_S\sigma_Q$. From the point of view of a U.S. investor it behaves like a dollar-denominated stock that pays a continuous dividend yield of q^*, where

$$r - q^* = r_f - q + \rho\sigma_S\sigma_Q$$

or

$$q^* = r - r_f + q - \rho\sigma_S\sigma_Q$$

This observation enables us to value other derivatives dependent on the Nikkei index that pay off in dollars. For example, equation (11.1), with q replaced by q^*,

---

[9]Note that if the exchange rate, $Q(t)$, had been defined as the number of dollars per yen, the sign of ρ would be reversed and equation (13.21) would be

$$F = S(t)e^{(r_f - q - \rho\sigma_S\sigma_Q)(T-t)}$$

can be used to value a European call option paying off $\max[S(T) - X, 0]$ dollars at time T.

A General Result

The Nikkei index, when used to calculate a yen payoff, has a risk-neutral rate of $r_f - q$. Equations (12.12) and (13.21) show that, when it is used to calculate a dollar payoff, it has a risk-neutral growth rate of $r_f - q + \rho \sigma_S \sigma_Q$.

This illustrates a general result in the pricing of derivatives. When using risk-neutral valuation to value a derivative that provides a payoff in a certain currency, the risk-neutral processes for all the underlying variables should be from the perspective of that currency. If it is known that a variable, θ, has a risk-neutral process

$$d\theta = \hat{m}\theta \, dt + s\theta \, dz$$

from the perspective of currency B, its risk-neutral process from the perspective of currency A is

$$d\theta = (\hat{m} + \rho s \sigma_Q)\theta \, dt + s\theta \, dz \qquad (13.22)$$

where σ_Q is the volatility of the exchange rate, Q, between A and B and ρ is the correlation between Q and θ. The variable Q is expressed as the number of units of currency B per unit of currency A.

To illustrate this result we consider the variables Q and $1/Q$. The variable Q is the number of units of currency B per unit of currency A. Its risk-neutral process is

$$dQ = [r_B - r_A]Q \, dt + \sigma_Q Q \, dz \qquad (13.23)$$

where r_A and r_B are the short-term interest rates in currencies A and B. By applying Ito's lemma we get the risk-neutral process for $1/Q$ as

$$d(1/Q) = [r_A - r_B + \sigma_Q^2](1/Q) \, dt - \sigma_Q(1/Q) \, dz \qquad (13.24)$$

This seems a strange result. Since $1/Q$ is the number of units of currency A per unit of currency B, we expect it to have a risk-neutral growth rate of $r_A - r_B$, not $r_A - r_B + \sigma_Q^2$. The result is known as *Siegel's paradox*.

Siegel's paradox can be explained as follows. Equation (13.23) is the risk-neutral process for Q from the perspective of currency B. Equation (13.24) therefore gives the process for $1/Q$ from the perspective of currency B. The variable $1/Q$ has a volatility of σ_Q and the correlation between Q and $1/Q$ is -1. It follows from equation (13.22) that the risk-neutral growth rate of $1/Q$ must be reduced by σ_Q^2 when we consider the world from the perspective of currency A rather than currency B. This reduces the risk-neutral growth rate to the value we expect of $r_A - r_B$.

13.7 SUMMARY

In Chapter 3 we showed that there is an important difference between valuing forward or futures contracts on an asset that is held primarily for investment by a significant number of investors, and valuing forward or futures contracts on an asset that is held primarily for consumption. In this chapter we have shown that the same distinction is important for other derivatives. The value of a derivative is independent of an underlying variable's growth rate and its market price of risk when the variable is a traded security. However, it is liable to depend on both of these parameters for other variables.

The key result in this chapter is the extension of risk-neutral valuation. We have shown that when valuing derivatives, we can always behave as though the world is risk neutral, provided that we also reduce the expected growth rate of each underlying variable by the product of its volatility and its market price of risk. This adjusted growth rate can be referred to as the *risk-neutral growth rate*.

Luckily, the risk-neutral growth rate can be estimated in many situations without first estimating the actual growth rate and the market price of risk. For example, when a variable is the price of a traded security, its risk-neutral growth rate is the risk-free interest rate less the dividend yield on the security; when a variable is the price of a commodity, estimates of its risk-neutral growth rate can be calculated from futures prices.

Quantos present a challenge for the analyst. These are derivatives where the payoff is made in a currency A while the underlying variables are defined in a different currency B. It is important to recognize that the risk-neutral growth rate of an underlying variable depends on one's perspective. The risk-neutral growth rate from the perspective of an investor in currency A is different from that from the perspective of an investor in currency B. When risk-neutral valuation is used for a quanto, care must be taken to ensure that all stochastic processes are risk-neutral from the perspective of the currency in which the payoff is made.

SUGGESTIONS FOR FURTHER READING

Cox J. C., J. E. Ingersoll, and S. A. Ross, "An Intertemporal General Equilibrium Model of Asset Prices," *Econometrica*, 53 (1985), 363–84.

Garman, M., "A General Theory of Asset Valuation Under Diffusion State Processes," Working Paper 50, University of California, Berkeley, 1976.

Harrison, J. M., and D. M. Kreps, "Martingales and Arbitrage in Multiperiod Securities Markets," *Journal of Economic Theory*, 20 (1979), 381–408.

Harrison, J. M., and S. R. Pliska, "Martingales and Stochastic Integrals in the Theory of Continuous Trading," *Stochastic Processes and Their Applications,* (1981), 215–60.

Hull, J. C., and A. White, "An Overview of the Pricing of Contingent Claims," *Canadian Journal of Administrative Sciences*, 5 (September 1988), 55–61.

Reiner, E., "Quanto Mechanics," *RISK,* March 1992.

Jamshidian, F., "Corralling Quantos," *RISK,* March 1994.

QUESTIONS AND PROBLEMS

13.1. How is the market price of risk defined for a variable that is not the price of a traded security?

13.2. Suppose that the market price of risk for gold is zero. If the storage costs are 1% per annum and the risk-free rate of interest is 6% per annum, what is the expected growth rate in the price of gold?

*13.3. A security's price is positively dependent on two variables: the price of copper and the yen–dollar exchange rate. Suppose that the market price of risk for these variables is 0.5 and 0.1, respectively. If the price of copper were held fixed, the volatility of the security would be 8% per annum; if the yen–dollar exchange rate were held fixed, the volatility of the security would be 12% per annum. The risk-free interest rate is 7% per annum. What is the expected rate of return from the security? If the two variables are uncorrelated with each other, what is the volatility of the security?

13.4. An oil company is set up solely for the purpose of exploring for oil in a certain small area of Texas. Its value depends primarily on two stochastic variables: the price of oil and the quantity of proven oil reserves. Discuss whether the market price of risk for the second of these two variables is likely to be positive, negative, or zero.

*13.5. Deduce the differential equation for a derivative dependent on the prices of two non-dividend-paying traded securities by forming a riskless portfolio consisting of the derivative and the two traded securities. Verify that the differential equation is the same as the one given in equation (13B.11).

*13.6. A forward contract provides a payoff at time T of $(S_T - K)$ yen, where S_T is the dollar price of gold at time T and K is the delivery price measured in dollars. Assuming that storage costs are zero and defining other variables as necessary, calculate the forward price.

13.7. The convenience yield for soybean oil is 5% per annum, the storage costs are 1% per annum, the risk-free interest rate is 6% per annum, and the expected growth in the price of soybean oil is zero. What is the relationship between the six-month futures price and the expected price in six months?

13.8. The market price of risk for copper is 0.5, the volatility of copper prices is 20% per annum, the spot price is 80 cents per pound, and the six-month futures price is 75 cents per pound. What is the expected proportional growth rate in copper prices over the next six months?

*13.9. Suppose that an interest rate, x, follows the process

$$dx = a(x_0 - x)\,dt + c\,\sqrt{x}\;dz$$

where a, x_0, and c are positive constants. Suppose further that the market price of risk for x is λ. How should the drift rate in x be adjusted when the extension of the risk-neutral valuation argument is used to value a derivative?

13.10. A security pays off $S_1 S_2$ at time T, where S_1 is the level of the S&P 500 index and S_2 is the price of oil. Assume that both S_1 and S_2 follow geometric Brownian motion and are uncorrelated. Defining other variables as necessary, calculate the value of the security at time t.

*13.11. Using risk-neutral valuation arguments, show that an option to exchange one IBM share for two Kodak shares in six months has a value that is independent of the level of interest rates.

13.12. Consider a commodity with constant volatility, σ. Assuming that the risk-free interest rate is constant, show that in a risk-neutral world,

$$\ln S_T \sim \phi \left[\ln F - \frac{\sigma^2}{2}(T - t),\ \sigma\sqrt{T - t} \right]$$

where S_T is the value of the commodity at time T and F is the futures price for a contract maturing at time T.

*13.13. What is the formula for the price of a European call option on a foreign index when the strike price is in dollars and the index is translated into dollars at a predetermined exchange rate? What difference does it make if the index is translated into dollars at the exchange rate prevailing at the time of exercise?

APPENDIX 13A: GENERALIZATION OF ITO'S LEMMA

Ito's lemma as presented in Appendix 10A provides the process followed by a function of a single stochastic variable. Here we present a generalized version of Ito's lemma for the process followed by a function of several stochastic variables.

Suppose that a function, f, depends on the n variables $x_1, x_2, \ldots, x_n$ and time, t. Suppose further that x_i follows an Ito process with instantaneous drift a_i and instantaneous variance b_i^2 ($1 \le i \le n$), that is,

$$dx_i = a_i\, dt + b_i\, dz_i \tag{13A.1}$$

where dz_i is a Wiener process ($1 \le i \le n$). Each a_i and b_i may be any function of all the x_i's and t. A Taylor series expansion of f gives

$$\Delta f = \sum_i \frac{\partial f}{\partial x_i}\Delta x_i + \frac{\partial f}{\partial t}\Delta t + \frac{1}{2}\sum_i \sum_j \frac{\partial^2 f}{\partial x_i\, \partial x_j}\Delta x_i\, \Delta x_j$$

$$+ \frac{1}{2}\sum_j \frac{\partial^2 f}{\partial x_i\, \partial t}\Delta x_i \Delta t + \cdots \tag{13A.2}$$

Equation (13A.1) can be discretized as

$$\Delta x_i = a_i\, \Delta t + b_i \epsilon_i \sqrt{\Delta t}$$

where ϵ_i is a random sample from a standardized normal distribution. The correlation, ρ_{ij}, between dz_i and dz_j is defined as the correlation between ϵ_i and ϵ_j. In Appendix 10A it was argued that

$$\lim_{\Delta t \to 0} \Delta x_i^2 = b_i^2\, dt$$

Similarly,

$$\lim_{\Delta t \to 0} \Delta x_i \, \Delta x_j = b_i b_j \rho_{ij} \, dt$$

As $\Delta t \to 0$, the first three terms in the expansion of Δf in equation (13A.2) are of order Δt. All other terms are of higher order. Hence

$$df = \sum_i \frac{\partial f}{\partial x_i} dx_i + \frac{\partial f}{\partial t} dt + \frac{1}{2} \sum_i \sum_j \frac{\partial^2 f}{\partial x_i \partial x_j} b_i b_j \rho_{ij} \, dt$$

This is the generalized version of Ito's lemma. Substituting for dx_i from equation (13A.1) gives

$$df = \left(\sum_i \frac{\partial f}{\partial x_i} a_i + \frac{\partial f}{\partial t} + \frac{1}{2} \sum_i \sum_j \frac{\partial^2 f}{\partial x_i \partial x_j} b_i b_j \rho_{ij} \right) dt + \sum_i \frac{\partial f}{\partial x_i} b_i \, dz_i$$

$$(13A.3)$$

APPENDIX 13B: DERIVATION OF THE GENERAL DIFFERENTIAL EQUATION SATISFIED BY DERIVATIVES

Consider a certain derivative security that depends on n state variables and time, t. We make the assumption that there are a total of at least $n + 1$ traded securities (including the one under consideration) whose prices depend on some or all of the n state variables. In practice, this is not unduly restrictive. The traded securities may be options with different strike prices and exercise dates, forward contracts, futures contracts, bonds, stocks, and so on. We assume that no dividends or other income is paid by the $n + 1$ traded securities.[10] Other assumptions are similar to those made in Section 11.4 to derive the Black–Scholes equation.

The n state variables are assumed to follow continuous-time Ito diffusion processes. We denote the ith state variable by θ_i ($1 \le i \le n$) and suppose that

$$d\theta_i = m_i \theta_i \, dt + s_i \theta_i \, dz_i \qquad (13B.1)$$

where dz_i is a Wiener process and the parameters, m_i and s_i, are the expected growth rate in θ_i and the volatility of θ_i. The m_i and s_i can be functions of any of the n state variables and time. Other notation used is as follows:

ρ_{ik}: correlation between dz_i and dz_k ($1 \le i, k \le n$)
f_j: price of the jth traded security ($1 \le j \le n + 1$)
r: instantaneous (i.e., very short-term) risk-free rate

---

[10]This is not restrictive. A non-dividend-paying security can always be obtained from a dividend-paying security by reinvesting the dividends in the security.

One of the f_j is the price of the security under consideration. The short-term risk-free rate, r, may be one of the n state variables.

Since the $n + 1$ traded securities are all dependent on the θ_i, it follows from Ito's lemma in Appendix 13A that the f_j follow diffusion processes:

$$df_j = \mu_j f_j \, dt + \sum_i \sigma_{ij} f_j \, dz_i \tag{13B.2}$$

where

$$\mu_j f_j = \frac{\partial f_j}{\partial t} + \sum_i \frac{\partial f_j}{\partial \theta_i} m_i \theta_i + \frac{1}{2} \sum_{i,k} \rho_{ik} s_i s_k \theta_i \theta_k \frac{\partial^2 f_j}{\partial \theta_i \, \partial \theta_k} \tag{13B.3}$$

$$\sigma_{ij} f_j = \frac{\partial f_j}{\partial \theta_i} s_i \theta_i \tag{13B.4}$$

In these equations, μ_j is the instantaneous mean rate of return provided by f_j and σ_{ij} is the component of the instantaneous standard deviation of the rate of return provided by f_j, which may be attributed to the θ_i.

Since there are $n + 1$ traded securities and n Wiener processes in equation (13B.2), it is possible to form an instantaneously riskless portfolio, Π, using the securities. Define k_j as the amount of the jth security in the portfolio, so that

$$\Pi = \sum_j k_j f_j \tag{13B.5}$$

The k_j must be chosen so that the stochastic components of the returns from the securities are eliminated. From equation (13B.2) this means that

$$\sum_j k_j \sigma_{ij} f_j = 0 \tag{13B.6}$$

for $1 \leq i \leq n$. The return from the portfolio is then given by

$$d\Pi = \sum_j k_j \mu_j f_j \, dt$$

The cost of setting up the portfolio is $\sum_j k_j f_j$. If there are no arbitrage opportunities, the portfolio must earn the risk-free interest rate, so that

$$\sum_j k_j \mu_j f_j = r \sum_j k_j f_j \tag{13B.7}$$

or

$$\sum_j k_j f_j (\mu_j - r) = 0 \tag{13B.8}$$

Equations (13B.6) and (13B.8) can be regarded as $n + 1$ homogeneous linear equations in the k_j's. The k_j's are not all zero. From a well-known theorem in linear algebra, equations (13B.6) and (13B.8) can be consistent only if

$$f_j(\mu_j - r) = \sum_i \lambda_i \sigma_{ij} f_j \tag{13B.9}$$

or

$$\mu_j - r = \sum_i \lambda_i \sigma_{ij} \tag{13B.10}$$

for some λ_i ($1 \le i \le n$), which are dependent only on the state variables and time. This proves the result in equation (13.13).

Substituting from equations (13B.3) and (13B.4) into equation (13B.9), we obtain

$$\frac{\partial f_j}{\partial t} + \sum_i \frac{\partial f_j}{\partial \theta_i} m_i \theta_i + \frac{1}{2} \sum_{i,k} \rho_{ik} s_i s_k \theta_i \theta_k \frac{\partial^2 f_j}{\partial \theta_i \partial \theta_k} - r f_j = \sum_i \lambda_i \frac{\partial f_j}{\partial \theta_i} s_i \theta_i$$

which reduces to

$$\frac{\partial f_j}{\partial t} + \sum_i \theta_i \frac{\partial f_j}{\partial \theta_i} (m_i - \lambda_i s_i) + \frac{1}{2} \sum_{i,k} \rho_{ik} s_i s_k \theta_i \theta_k \frac{\partial^2 f_j}{\partial \theta_i \partial \theta_k} = r f_j$$

Dropping the subscripts to f, we deduce that any security whose price, f, is contingent on the state variables $\theta_i (1 \le i \le n)$ and time, t, satisfies the second-order differential equation

$$\frac{\partial f}{\partial t} + \sum_i \theta_i \frac{\partial f}{\partial \theta_i} (m_i - \lambda_i s_i) + \frac{1}{2} \sum_{i,k} \rho_{ik} s_i s_k \theta_i \theta_k \frac{\partial^2 f}{\partial \theta_i \partial \theta_k} = r f \tag{13B.11}$$

The particular derivative security that is obtained is determined by the boundary conditions that are imposed on equation (13B.11).

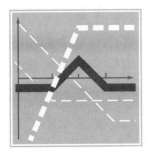

Chapter 14

The Management of Market Risk

A financial institution that sells an option or other derivative to a client in the over-the-counter markets is faced with the problem of managing its risk. If the option happens to be the same as one that is traded on an exchange, the financial institution can neutralize its exposure by buying on the exchange the same option as it has sold. But when the option has been tailored to the needs of a client and does not correspond to the standardized products traded by exchanges, hedging the exposure is far more difficult. In this chapter we discuss some of the alternative approaches to this problem. The analysis presented is applicable to market makers in options on an exchange as well as to financial institutions.

There are several dimensions to the risks faced by an options trader. For instance, the price of a foreign exchange option depends on the underlying exchange rate, the volatility of the exchange rate, and two interest rates. In each case the relationship is nonlinear. For example, a 0.02 increase in the exchange rate does not have twice the effect on the option price of a 0.01 increase. There are two main approaches (not mutually exclusive) to managing market risk. One involves quantifying and controlling each of the risks separately. The other involves carrying out a scenario analysis where the impact on the option position of alternative future scenarios is evaluated. In this chapter we describe both approaches.

A problem closely related to hedging option positions is that of creating options synthetically. Portfolio managers are sometimes interested in creating a put option on a portfolio synthetically to ensure that the value of the portfolio does not fall below a certain level. In the last part of this chapter we discuss how this can be done and the reasons why it does not always work well.

14.1 EXAMPLE

In this section and the next two sections we use as an example the position of a financial institution that has sold for $300,000 a European call option on 100,000 shares of a non-dividend-paying stock. We assume that the stock price is $49, the strike price is $50, the risk-free interest rate is 5 percent per annum, the stock price volatility is 20 percent per annum, the time to maturity is 20 weeks, and the

expected return from the stock is 13 percent per annum.[1] With our usual notation this means that

$$S = 49 \qquad X = 50 \qquad r = 0.05 \qquad \sigma = 0.20 \qquad T - t = 0.3846 \qquad \mu = 0.13$$

Financial institutions do not normally write call options on individual stocks, but this is a convenient example with which to develop our ideas. The points that will be made apply to other types of options and to other derivatives.

The Black–Scholes price of the option is about $240,000. The financial institution has therefore sold the option for $60,000 more than its theoretical value. It is faced with the problem of hedging its exposure.

14.2 NAKED AND COVERED POSITIONS

One strategy open to the financial institution is to do nothing. This is sometimes referred to as a *naked position*. If the call is exercised, the financial institution will have to buy 100,000 shares at the market price prevailing in 20 weeks to cover the call. The cost to the financial institution will then be 100,000 times the amount by which the stock price exceeds the strike price. For example, if after 20 weeks the stock price is $60, the option costs the financial institution $1,000,000. This is considerably greater than the $300,000 premium received. A naked position works well if the stock price is below $50 at the end of the 20 weeks. The option then costs the financial institution nothing and it makes a profit of $300,000 on the whole deal.

As an alternative to a naked position, the financial institution can adopt a *covered position*. This involves buying 100,000 shares as soon as the option has been sold. If the option is exercised, this strategy works well, but in other circumstances it could prove to be expensive. For example, if the stock price drops to $40, the financial institution loses $900,000 on its stock position. Again, this is considerably greater than the $300,000 charged for the option. Put–call parity shows that the exposure from writing a covered call is the same as the exposure from writing a naked put.

Neither a naked position nor a covered position provides a satisfactory hedge. If the assumptions underlying the Black–Scholes formula hold, the cost to the financial institution should always be $240,000 on average for both approaches.[2] But on any one occasion the cost is liable to range from zero to over $1,000,000. A perfect hedge would ensure that the cost is always $240,000, that is, that the standard deviation of the cost of writing the option and hedging it is zero.

---

[1]It was shown in Chapter 11 that the expected return is irrelevant to the pricing of the option. However, it can have some bearing on the effectiveness of a particular hedging scheme.

[2]More precisely, the present value of the expected cost is $240,000 for both approaches assuming that appropriate risk-adjusted discount rates are used.

14.3 A STOP-LOSS STRATEGY

One hedging idea that is sometimes proposed involves what is known as a *stop-loss strategy*.[3] To illustrate the basic idea, consider an institution that has written a European call option with strike price X to buy one unit of a stock. The hedging scheme involves buying the stock as soon as its price rises above X, and selling as soon as it falls below X. The objective is to hold a naked position whenever the stock price is less than X and a covered position whenever the stock price is greater than X. The scheme is designed to ensure that the institution owns the stock at time T if the option closes in the money and does not own it if the option closes out of the money. It appears to produce payoffs that are the same as the payoffs on the option. In the situation illustrated in Figure 14.1, the stop-loss strategy involves buying the stock at time t_1, selling it at time t_2, buying it at time t_3, selling it at time t_4, buying it at time t_5, and delivering it at time T.

We denote the stock price at time t by $S(t)$. The cost of setting up the hedge initially is $S(0)$ if $S(0) > X$ and zero otherwise. At first blush, the total cost, Q, of writing and hedging the option would appear to be given by

$$Q = \max[S(0) - X, 0] \tag{14.1}$$

since all purchases and sales subsequent to time zero are made at price X. If this were correct, the hedging scheme would work perfectly in the absence of

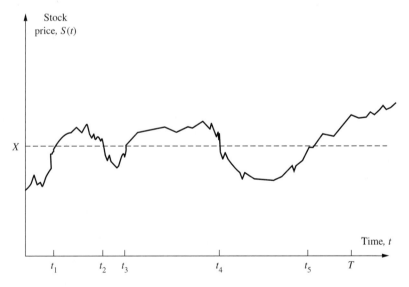

Figure 14.1   Stop-loss strategy.

[3] For a fuller analysis of the scheme, see J. Hull and A. White, "Hedging through the Cap: Implications for Market Efficiency, Hedging, and Option Pricing," *International Options Journal,* 4 (1987), 17–22.

transactions costs. Furthermore, the cost of hedging the option would always be less than its Black–Scholes price. Thus one could earn riskless profits by writing options and hedging them.

There are two basic reasons why equation (14.1) is incorrect. The first is that the cash flows to the hedger occur at different times and must be discounted. The second is that purchases and sales cannot be made at exactly the same price X. This second point is critical. If we assume a risk-neutral world with zero interest rates, we can justify ignoring the time value of money. But we cannot legitimately assume that both purchases and sales are made at the same price. If markets are efficient, the hedger cannot know whether when the stock price equals X, it will continue above or below X.

As a practical matter, purchases must be made at $X + \delta$ and sales must be made at $X - \delta$, for some positive δ. Thus every purchase and subsequent sale includes a cost (apart from transactions costs) of 2δ. A natural response to this on the part of the hedger is to reduce δ. Assuming that stock prices change continuously, δ can be made arbitrarily small by monitoring the prices closely. However, as δ is made smaller, the expected number of trades increases. The cost per trade is reduced, but this is offset by an increase in the expected frequency of trading. As $\delta \longrightarrow 0$, the expected number of trades tends to infinity.

The stop-loss strategy, although superficially attractive, does not work particularly well as a hedging scheme. Consider, for example, its use for an out-of-the-money option. If the stock price never crosses the line $S(t) = X$, the hedging scheme costs nothing. But if the path of the stock price crosses the line $S(t) = X$ many times, the scheme is liable to be quite expensive. Monte Carlo simulation can be used to assess the overall performance of the scheme. Table 14.1 shows the results for the option considered in Section 14.2. It assumes that the stock price is observed at the end of time intervals of length Δt and calculates hedge performance measure as the ratio of the standard deviation of the cost of writing the option and hedging it to the Black–Scholes price of the option.[4] (Each result is based on 1,000 sample paths for the stock price and has a standard error of about 2%.) It appears to be impossible to produce a performance measure for the scheme which is below 0.70 regardless of how small Δt is made.

TABLE 14.1   Performance of Stop-Loss Strategy

Hedge performance measure = ratio of standard deviation of cost of option to theoretical price of option

Δt (weeks)	5	4	2	1	0.5	0.25
Performance Measure	1.02	0.93	0.82	0.77	0.76	0.76

[4]The precise hedging rule used was as follows. If the stock price moves from below X to above X in a time interval of length Δt, it is bought at the end of the interval. If it moves from above X to below X in the time interval, it is sold at the end of the interval. Otherwise, no action is taken.

14.4 MORE SOPHISTICATED HEDGING SCHEMES

Most option traders use more sophisticated hedging schemes than those that have been described so far. As a first step, they attempt to make their portfolio immune to small changes in the price of the underlying asset in the next small interval of time. This is known as *delta hedging*. They then look at what are known as *gamma* and *vega*. Gamma is the rate of change of delta with respect to the asset's price; vega is the rate of change of the portfolio with respect to the asset's volatility. By keeping gamma close to zero, a portfolio can be made relatively insensitive to fairly large changes in the price of the asset; by keeping vega close to zero, it can be made insensitive to changes in the asset's volatility. Option traders may also look at *theta* and *rho*. Theta is the rate of change of the option portolio with the passage of time; rho is its rate of change with respect to the risk-free interest rate. They may also carry out a *scenario analysis* investigating how the value of their position will be impacted by alternative future scenarios. In the next few sections we discuss these approaches in more detail.

14.5 DELTA HEDGING

The *delta* of a derivative, Δ, was introduced in Chapter 9. It is defined as the rate of change of its price with respect to the price of the underlying asset.[5] It is the slope of the curve that relates the derivative's price to the underlying asset price.

Consider a call option on a stock. Figure 14.2 shows the relationship between the call price and the underlying stock price. When the stock price corresponds to point A, the option price corresponds to point B and the Δ of the call is the slope of the line indicated. As an approximation,

$$\Delta = \frac{\Delta c}{\Delta S}$$

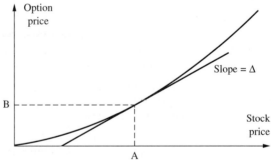

Figure 14.2   Calculation of delta.

[5]More formally, $\Delta = \partial f / \partial S$, where f is the price of the derivative and S is the price of the underlying asset.

where ΔS is a small change in the stock price and Δc is the corresponding change in the call price.

Assume that the delta of the call option is 0.6. This means that when the stock price changes by a small amount, the option price changes by about 60% of that amount. Suppose that the option price is $10 and the stock price is $100. Imagine an investor who has sold 20 option contracts, that is, options to buy 2,000 shares. The investor's position could be hedged by buying $0.6 \times 2,000 = 1,200$ shares. The gain (loss) on the option position would tend to be offset by the loss (gain) on the stock position. For example, if the stock price goes up by $1 (producing a gain of $1,200 on the shares purchased), the option price will tend to go up by $0.6 \times \$1 = \$0.60$ (producing a loss of $1,200 on the options written); if the stock price goes down by $1 (producing a loss of $1,200 on the shares purchased), the option price will tend to go down by $0.60 (producing a gain of $1,200 on the options written).

In this example, the delta of the investor's option position is $0.6 \times (-2,000) = -1,200$. In other words, the investor loses $1,200 \Delta S$ on the options when the stock price increases by ΔS. The delta of the stock is by definition 1.0 and the long position in 1,200 shares has a delta of $+1,200$. The delta of the investor's total position (short 2,000 call options; long 1,200 shares) is therefore zero. The delta of the position in the underlying asset offsets the delta of the option position. A position with a delta of zero is referred to as being *delta neutral.*

It is important to realize that the investor's position remains delta hedged (or delta neutral) for only a relatively short period of time. This is because delta changes with both changes in the stock price and the passage of time. In practice, when delta hedging is implemented, the hedge has to be adjusted periodically. This is known as *rebalancing.* In our example, the stock price might increase to $110 by the end of three days. As indicated by Figure 14.2, an increase in the stock price leads to an increase in delta. Suppose that delta rises from 0.60 to 0.65. This would mean that an extra $0.05 \times 2,000 = 100$ shares would have to be purchased to maintain the hedge. Hedging schemes such as this that involve frequent adjustments are known as *dynamic hedging schemes.*

Delta is closely related to the Black–Scholes analysis. Black and Scholes showed that it is possible to set up a riskless portfolio consisting of a position in a derivative on a stock and a position in the stock. Expressed in terms of Δ, their portfolio is

$$- 1: \text{ derivative}$$
$$+ \Delta: \text{ shares of the stock}$$

Using our new terminology, we can say that Black and Scholes valued options by setting up a delta-neutral position and arguing that the return on the position in a short period of time equals the risk-free interest rate.

Delta of Forward Contracts

Equation (3.6) shows that when the price of a non-dividend-paying stock changes by ΔS, with all else remaining the same, the value of a forward contract

on the stock also changes by ΔS. The delta of a forward contract on one share of a non-dividend-paying stock is therefore 1.0. This means that a short forward contract on one share can be hedged by purchasing one share, while a long forward contract on one share can be hedged by shorting one share. These two hedging schemes are "hedge and forget" schemes in the sense that no changes need to be made to the position in the stock during the life of the contract. As already mentioned, when an option or other more complicated derivative is being hedged, delta hedging is not a hedge-and-forget scheme. If the hedge is to be effective, the position in the stock must be rebalanced frequently.

Deltas of European Calls and Puts

For a European call option on a non-dividend-paying stock, it can be shown that

$$\Delta = N(d_1)$$

where d_1 is defined in equation (11.22). Using delta hedging for a short position in a European call option therefore involves keeping a long position of $N(d_1)$ shares at any given time. Similarly, using delta hedging for a long position in a European call option involves maintaining a short position of $N(d_1)$ shares at any given time.

For a European put option on a non-dividend-paying stock, delta is given by

$$\Delta = N(d_1) - 1$$

This is negative, which means that a long position in a put option should be hedged with a long position in the underlying stock, and a short position in a put option should be hedged with a short position in the underlying stock. The variation of the delta of a call option and a put option with the stock price is shown in Figure 14.3. Figure 14.4 shows typical patterns for the variation of delta with time to maturity for at-the-money, in-the-money, and out-of-the-money options.

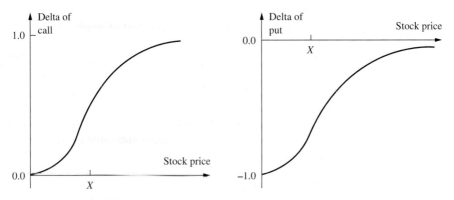

Figure 14.3   Variation of delta with the stock price for a call option and a put option on a non-dividend-paying stock.

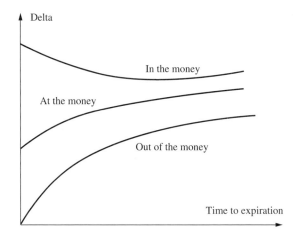

Figure 14.4   Typical pattern for variation of delta with the time to maturity for a call option.

Simulations

Tables 14.2 and 14.3 provide two simulations of the operation of delta hedging for the example in Section 14.1. The hedge is assumed to be adjusted or rebalanced weekly. In both tables delta is calculated initially as 0.522. This means that as soon as the option is written, $2,557,800 must be borrowed to buy 52,200 shares at a price of $49. An interest cost of $2,500 is incurred in the first week.

In Table 14.2 the stock price falls to $48\frac{1}{8}$ by the end of the first week. This reduces the delta to 0.458, and 6,400 shares are sold to maintain the hedge. This realizes $308,000 in cash and the cumulative borrowings at the end of week 1 are reduced to $2,252,300. During the second week the stock price reduces to $47\frac{3}{8}$ and delta declines again; and so on. Toward the end of the life of the option it becomes apparent that the option will be exercised and delta approaches 1.0. By week 20, therefore, the hedger has a fully covered position. The hedger receives $5,000,000 for the stock held, so that the total cost of writing the option and hedging it is $263,400.

Table 14.3 illustrates an alternative sequence of events which are such that the option closes out of the money. As it becomes progressively clearer that the option will not be exercised, delta approaches zero. By week 20 the hedger has a naked position and has incurred costs totaling $256,600.

In Tables 14.2 and 14.3 the costs of hedging the option, when discounted to the beginning of the period, are close to but not exactly the same as the Black–Scholes price of $240,000. If the hedging scheme worked perfectly, the cost of hedging would, after discounting, be exactly equal to the theoretical price of the option on every simulation. The reason that there is a variation in the cost of delta hedging is that the hedge is rebalanced only once a week. As rebalancing takes place more frequently, the uncertainty in the cost of hedging is reduced.

TABLE 14.2 Simulation of Delta Hedging; Option Closes in the Money; Cost of Option to Writer = $263,400

Week	Stock Price	Delta	Shares Purchased	Cost of Shares Purchased (thousands of dollars)	Cumulative Cost (incl. interest, in thousands of dollars)	Interest Cost (thousands of dollars)
0	49	0.522	52,200	2,557.8	2,557.8	2.5
1	$48\frac{1}{8}$	0.458	(6,400)	(308.0)	2,252.3	2.2
2	$47\frac{3}{8}$	0.400	(5,800)	(274.8)	1,979.7	1.9
3	$50\frac{1}{4}$	0.596	19,600	984.9	2,966.5	2.9
4	$51\frac{3}{4}$	0.693	9,700	502.0	3,471.3	3.3
5	$53\frac{1}{8}$	0.774	8,100	430.3	3,904.9	3.8
6	53	0.771	(300)	(15.9)	3,892.8	3.7
7	$51\frac{7}{8}$	0.706	(6,500)	(337.2)	3,559.3	3.4
8	$51\frac{3}{8}$	0.674	(3,200)	(164.4)	3,398.4	3.3
9	53	0.787	11,300	598.9	4,000.5	3.8
10	$49\frac{7}{8}$	0.550	(23,700)	(1,182.0)	2,822.3	2.7
11	$48\frac{1}{2}$	0.413	(13,700)	(664.4)	2,160.6	2.1
12	$49\frac{7}{8}$	0.542	12,900	643.4	2,806.1	2.7
13	$50\frac{3}{8}$	0.591	4,900	246.8	3,055.6	2.9
14	$52\frac{1}{8}$	0.768	17,700	922.6	3,981.2	3.8
15	$51\frac{7}{8}$	0.759	(900)	(46.7)	3,938.3	3.8
16	$52\frac{7}{8}$	0.865	10,600	560.5	4,502.6	4.3
17	$54\frac{7}{8}$	0.978	11,300	620.1	5,127.0	4.9
18	$54\frac{5}{8}$	0.990	1,200	65.6	5,197.5	5.0
19	$55\frac{7}{8}$	1.000	1,000	55.9	5,258.3	5.1
20	$57\frac{1}{4}$	1.000	0	0.0	5,263.4	

Table 14.4 shows statistics on the performance of delta hedging from 1,000 simulations of stock price movements for our example. As in Table 14.1, the performance measure is the ratio of the standard deviation of the cost of writing the option and hedging it to the Black–Scholes price of the option. It is clear that delta hedging is a great improvement over the stop-loss strategy. Unlike the stop-loss strategy, the performance of delta hedging gets steadily better as the hedge is monitored more frequently.

Delta hedging aims to keep the total wealth of the financial institution as close to unchanged as possible. Initially, the value of the written option is

TABLE 14.3   Simulation of Delta Hedging; Option Closes out of the
Money; Cost of Option to Writer = $256,600

Week	Stock Price	Delta	Shares Purchased	Cost of Shares Purchased (thousands of dollars)	Cumulative Cost (incl. interest, in thousands of dollars)	Interest Cost (thousands of dollars)
0	49	0.522	52,200	2,557.8	2,557.8	2.5
1	$49\frac{3}{4}$	0.568	4,600	228.9	2,789.1	2.7
2	52	0.705	13,700	712.4	3,504.2	3.4
3	50	0.579	(12,600)	(630.0)	2,877.6	2.8
4	$48\frac{3}{8}$	0.459	(12,000)	(580.5)	2,299.8	2.2
5	$48\frac{1}{4}$	0.443	(1,600)	(77.2)	2,224.8	2.1
6	$48\frac{3}{4}$	0.475	3,200	156.0	2,383.0	2.3
7	$49\frac{5}{8}$	0.540	6,500	322.6	2,707.8	2.6
8	$48\frac{1}{4}$	0.420	(12,000)	(579.0)	2,131.4	2.0
9	$48\frac{1}{4}$	0.410	(1,000)	(48.2)	2,085.2	2.0
10	$51\frac{1}{8}$	0.658	24,800	1,267.9	3,355.1	3.2
11	$51\frac{1}{2}$	0.692	3,400	175.1	3,533.5	3.4
12	$49\frac{7}{8}$	0.542	(15,000)	(748.1)	2,788.7	2.7
13	$49\frac{7}{8}$	0.538	(400)	(20.0)	2,771.5	2.7
14	$48\frac{3}{4}$	0.400	(13,800)	(672.7)	2,101.4	2.0
15	$47\frac{1}{2}$	0.236	(16,400)	(779.0)	1,324.4	1.3
16	48	0.261	2,500	120.0	1,445.7	1.4
17	$46\frac{1}{4}$	0.062	(19,900)	(920.4)	526.7	0.5
18	$48\frac{1}{8}$	0.183	12,100	582.3	1,109.5	1.1
19	$46\frac{5}{8}$	0.007	(17,600)	(820.6)	290.0	0.3
20	$48\frac{1}{8}$	0.000	(700)	(33.7)	256.6	

TABLE 14.4   Performance of Delta Hedging

Hedge performance measure = ratio of standard deviation of cost of option
to theoretical price of option

Time between Hedge Rebalancing (weeks)	5	4	2	1	0.5	0.25
Performance Measure	0.43	0.39	0.26	0.19	0.14	0.09

$240,000. In the situation depicted in Table 14.2, the value of the option can be calculated as $414,500 in week 9. Thus the financial institution has lost $174,500 on its option position between week 0 and week 9. Its cash position, as measured by the cumulative cost, is $1,442,700 worse in week 9 than in week 0. The value of the shares held has increased from $2,557,800 to $4,171,100 between week 0 and week 9. The net effect of all this is that the overall wealth of the financial institution has changed by only $3,900 during the nine-week period.

Where the Cost Comes From

The delta-hedging scheme in Tables 14.2 and 14.3 in effect creates a long position in the option synthetically. This neutralizes the short position arising from the option that has been written. The scheme generally involves selling stock just after the price has gone down and buying stock just after the price has gone up. It might be termed a buy high–sell low scheme! The cost of $240,000 comes from the average difference between the price paid for the stock and the price realized for it. Of course, the simulations in Tables 14.2 and 14.3 are idealized in that they assume that the volatility is constant and that there are no transactions costs.

Delta of Other European Options

For European call options on a stock index paying a dividend yield q,

$$\Delta = e^{-q(T-t)}N(d_1)$$

where d_1 is defined as in equation (12.4). For European put options on the stock index,

$$\Delta = e^{-q(T-t)}[N(d_1) - 1]$$

For European call options on a currency,

$$\Delta = e^{-r_f(T-t)}N(d_1)$$

where r_f is the foreign risk-free interest rate and d_1 is defined as in equation (12.6). For European put options on a currency,

$$\Delta = e^{-r_f(T-t)}[N(d_1) - 1]$$

For European futures call options,

$$\Delta = e^{-r(T-t)}N(d_1)$$

where d_1 is defined as in equation (12.10), and for European futures put options,

$$\Delta = e^{-r(T-t)}[N(d_1) - 1]$$

Example 14.1

A bank has written a six-month European option to sell £1,000,000 at an exchange rate of 1.6000. Suppose that the current exchange rate is 1.6200, the risk-free interest rate in the

United Kingdom is 13% per annum, the risk-free interest rate in the United States is 10% per annum, and the volatility of sterling is 15%. In this case $S = 1.6200$, $X = 1.6000$, $r = 0.10$, $r_f = 0.13$, $\sigma = 0.15$, and $T - t = 0.5$. The delta of a put option on a currency is

$$[N(d_1) - 1]e^{-r_f(T-t)}$$

where d_1 is given by equation (12.6):

$$d_1 = 0.0287$$

$$N(d_1) = 0.5115$$

The delta of the put option is therefore $(0.5115 - 1)e^{-0.13 \times 0.5} = -0.458$. This is the delta of a long position in one put option. The delta of the bank's total short position is $-1,000,000$ times this or $+458,000$. Delta hedging therefore requires that a short sterling position of £458,000 be set up initially. This short sterling position has a delta of $-458,000$ and neutralizes the delta of the option position. As time passes, the short position must be changed.

Using Futures

In practice, delta hedging is often carried out using a position in futures rather than one in the underlying asset. The contract that is used does not have to mature at the same time as the derivative. For ease of exposition we assume that a futures contract is on one unit of the underlying asset.
Define:

T^*: maturity of futures contract

H_A: required position in asset at time t for delta hedging

H_F: alternative required position in futures contracts at time t for delta hedging

If the underlying asset is a non-dividend-paying stock, the futures price, F, is from equation (3.5) given by

$$F = Se^{r(T^*-t)}$$

When the stock price increases by ΔS, the futures price increases by $\Delta S e^{r(T^*-t)}$. The delta of the futures contract is therefore $e^{r(T^*-t)}$. Thus $e^{-r(T^*-t)}$ futures contracts have the same sensitivity to stock price movements as one stock. Hence

$$H_F = e^{-r(T^*-t)}H_A$$

When the underlying asset is a stock or stock index paying a dividend yield q, a similar argument shows that

$$H_F = e^{-(r-q)(T^*-t)}H_A \tag{14.2}$$

When it is a currency

$$H_F = e^{-(r-r_f)(T^*-t)}H_A$$

Example 14.2

Consider again the option in Example 14.1. Suppose that the bank decides to hedge using nine-month currency futures contracts. In this case $T^* - t = 0.75$ and

$$e^{-(r-r_f)(T^*-t)} = 1.0228$$

so that the short position in currency futures required for delta hedging is $1.0228 \times 458,000 = £468,442$. Since each futures contract is for the purchase or sale of £62,500, this means that (to the nearest whole number) seven contracts should be shorted.

It is interesting to note that the delta of a futures contract is different from the delta of the corresponding forward. This is true even when interest rates are constant and the forward price equals the futures price. Consider the situation where the underlying asset is a non-dividend-paying stock. The delta of a futures contract on one unit of the asset is $e^{r(T^*-t)}$, whereas the delta of a forward contract on one unit of the asset is, as discussed earlier, 1.0.

Delta of a Portfolio

In a portfolio of options and other derivatives where there is a single underlying asset, the delta of the portfolio is a weighted sum of the deltas of the individual derivatives in the portfolio. If a portfolio, Π, consists of an amount, w_i, of derivative i ($1 \le i \le n$), the delta of the portfolio is given by

$$\Delta = \sum_{i=1}^{n} w_i \, \Delta_i$$

where Δ_i is the delta of ith derivative. This can be used to calculate the position in the underlying asset, or in a futures contract on the underlying asset, necessary to carry out delta hedging. When this position has been taken, the delta of the portfolio is zero and the portfolio is referred to as being delta neutral.

Example 14.3

Consider a financial institution that has the following three positions in options to buy or sell German marks:

1. A long position in 100,000 call options with strike price 0.55 and exercise date in three months. The delta of each option is 0.533.
2. A short position in 200,000 call options with strike price 0.56 and exercise date in five months. The delta of each option is 0.468.
3. A short position in 50,000 put options with strike price 0.56 and exercise date in two months. The delta of each option is -0.508.

The delta of the whole portfolio is

$$0.533 \times 100,000 - 200,000 \times 0.468 - 50,000 \times (-0.508) = -14,900$$

This means that the portfolio can be made delta neutral with a long position of 14,900 marks.

A six-month futures contract could also be used to achieve delta neutrality in this example. Suppose that the risk-free rate of interest is 8% per annum in the United States and 4% per annum in Germany. The number of marks that must be bought in the futures market for delta neutrality is

$$14{,}900e^{-(0.08-0.04)\times0.5} = 14{,}605$$

14.6 THETA

The *theta* of a portfolio of derivatives, Θ, is the rate of change of the value of the portfolio with respect to time with all else remaining the same.[6] It is sometimes referred to as the *time decay* of the portfolio. For a European call option on a non-dividend-paying stock,

$$\Theta = -\frac{SN'(d_1)\sigma}{2\sqrt{T-t}} - rXe^{-r(T-t)}N(d_2)$$

where d_1 and d_2 are defined as in equation (11.22) and

$$N'(x) = \frac{1}{\sqrt{2\pi}}e^{-x^2/2}$$

For a European put option on the stock,

$$\Theta = -\frac{SN'(d_1)\sigma}{2\sqrt{T-t}} + rXe^{-r(T-t)}N(-d_2)$$

For a European call option on a stock index paying a dividend at rate q,

$$\Theta = -\frac{SN'(d_1)\sigma e^{-q(T-t)}}{2\sqrt{T-t}} + qSN(d_1)e^{-q(T-t)} - rXe^{-r(T-t)}N(d_2)$$

where d_1 and d_2 are defined as in equation (12.4). The formula for $N'(x)$ is given in Section 11.8. For a European put option on the stock index

$$\Theta = -\frac{SN'(d_1)\sigma e^{-q(T-t)}}{2\sqrt{T-t}} - qSN(-d_1)e^{-q(T-t)} + rXe^{-r(T-t)}N(-d_2)$$

With q equal to r_f, these last two equations give thetas for European call and put options on currencies. With q equal to r and S equal to F, they give thetas for European futures options.

Example 14.4

Consider a four-month put option on a stock index. The current value of the index is 305, the strike price is 300, the dividend yield is 3% per annum, the risk-free interest rate is

---

[6]More formally, $\Theta = \partial\Pi/\partial t$, where Π is the value of the portfolio.

8% per annum, and the volatility of the index is 25% per annum. In this case, $S = 305$, $X = 300$, $q = 0.03$, $r = 0.08$, $\sigma = 0.25$, and $T - t = 0.3333$. The option's theta is

$$-\frac{SN'(d_1)\sigma e^{-q(T-t)}}{2\sqrt{T-t}} - qSN(-d_1)e^{-q(T-t)} + rXe^{-r(T-t)}N(-d_2) = -18.15$$

This means that if 0.01 year (or 2.5 trading days) passes with no changes to the value of the index or its volatility, the value of the option declines by 0.1815.

   Theta is usually negative for an option.[7] This is because as the time to maturity decreases, the option tends to become less valuable. The variation of Θ with stock price for a call option on a stock is shown in Figure 14.5. When the stock price is very low, theta is close to zero. For an at-the-money call option, theta is large and negative. As the stock price becomes larger, theta tends to $-rXe^{-rT}$. Figure 14.6 shows typical patterns for the variation of Θ with the time to maturity for in-the-money, at-the-money, and out-of-the-money call options.
   Theta is not the same type of hedge parameter as delta and gamma. This is because there is some uncertainty about the future stock price, but there is no uncertainty about the passage of time. It does not make sense to hedge against the effect of the passage of time on an option portfolio. As we will see in Section 14.7, if theta is large in absolute terms, either delta or gamma must be large. If both the delta and gamma of an option position are zero, theta indicates that the value of the position will grow at the risk-free rate.

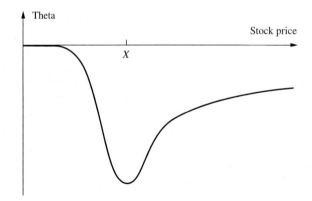

Figure 14.5   Variation of theta of a European call option with stock price.

---

[7] An exception to this could be an in-the-money European put option on a non-dividend-paying stock or an in-the-money European call option on a currency with a very high interest rate.

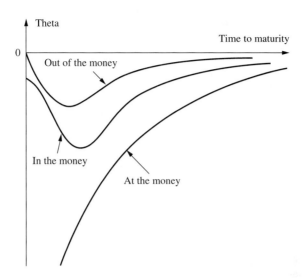

Figure 14.6 Typical patterns for variation of theta of a European call option with time to maturity.

14.7 GAMMA

The *gamma*, Γ, of a portfolio of derivatives on an underlying asset is the rate of change of the portfolio's delta with respect to the price of the underlying asset.[8] If gamma is small, delta changes only slowly and adjustments to keep a portfolio delta neutral need only be made relatively infrequently. However, if gamma is large in absolute terms, delta is highly sensitive to the price of the underlying asset. It is then quite risky to leave a delta-neutral portfolio unchanged for any length of time. Figure 14.7 illustrates this point. When the stock price moves from S to S', delta hedging assumes that the option price moves from C to C' when in actual fact it moves from C to C''. The difference between C' and C'' leads to a hedging error. The error depends on the curvature of the relationship between the option price and the stock price. Gamma measures this curvature.[9]

Suppose that ΔS is the change in the price of an underlying asset in a small interval of time, Δt, and $\Delta \Pi$ is the corresponding change in the price of the portfolio. If terms such as Δt^2, which are of higher order than Δt, are ignored, Appendix 14A shows that for a delta-neutral portfolio,

$$\Delta \Pi = \Theta \Delta t + \frac{1}{2} \Gamma \Delta S^2 \tag{14.3}$$

---

[8]More formally, $\Gamma = \partial^2 \Pi / \partial S^2$, where Π is the value of the portfolio.

[9]Indeed, the gamma of an option is sometimes referred to by practitioners as its curvature.

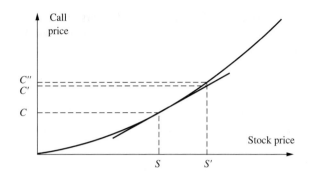

Figure 14.7   Error in delta hedging.

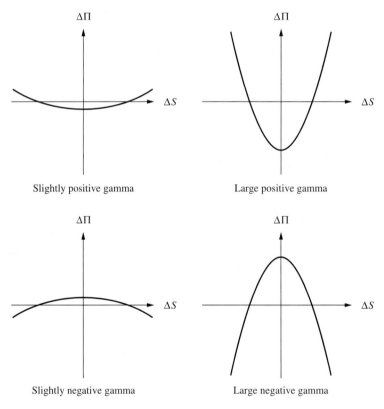

Figure 14.8   Alternative relationships between $\Delta\Pi$ and ΔS for a delta-neutral port-folio.

where Θ is the theta of the portfolio. Figure 14.8 shows the nature of this relationship between $\Delta\Pi$ and ΔS. When gamma is positive, theta tends to be negative.[10] The portfolio declines in value if there is no change in the S, but increases in value if there is a large positive or negative change in S. When gamma is negative, theta tends to be positive and the reverse is true; the portfolio increases in value if there is no change in S but decreases in value if there is a large positive or negative change in S. As the absolute value of gamma increases, the sensitivity of the value of the portfolio to S increases.

Example 14.5

Suppose that the gamma of a delta-neutral portfolio of options on an asset is $-10,000$. Equation (14.3) shows that if a change of $+2$ or -2 in the price of the asset occurs over a short period of time, there is an unexpected decrease in the value of the portfolio of approximately $0.5 \times 10,000 \times 2^2 = \$20,000$.

Making a Portfolio Gamma Neutral

A position in the underlying asset or in a futures contract on the underlying asset has zero gamma. The only way a financial institution can change the gamma of its portfolio is by taking a position in a traded option. Suppose that a delta-neutral portfolio has gamma equal to Γ and a traded option has a gamma equal to Γ_T. If the number of traded options added to the portfolio is w_T, the gamma of the portfolio is

$$w_T\Gamma_T + \Gamma$$

Hence the position in the traded option necessary to make the portfolio gamma neutral is $-\Gamma/\Gamma_T$. Of course, including the traded option is liable to change the delta of the portfolio, so the position in the underlying asset (or futures contract on the underlying asset) then has to be changed to maintain delta neutrality. Note that the portfolio is only gamma neutral instantaneously. As time passes, gamma neutrality can be maintained only if the position in the traded option is adjusted so that it is always equal to $-\Gamma/\Gamma_T$.

Example 14.6

Suppose that a portfolio is delta neutral and has a gamma of $-3,000$. The delta and gamma of a particular traded call option are 0.62 and 1.50, respectively. The portfolio can be made gamma neutral by including a long position of

$$\frac{3,000}{1.5} = 2,000$$

traded call options in the portfolio. However, the delta of the portfolio will then change from zero to $2,000 \times 0.62 = 1,240$. A quantity, 1,240, of the underlying asset must therefore be sold from the portfolio to keep it delta neutral.

---

[10]It will be shown in Section 14.8 that

$$\Theta + \frac{1}{2}\sigma^2 S^2\Gamma = r\Pi$$

for a delta-neutral portfolio.

Making a portfolio gamma neutral can be regarded as a first correction for the fact that the position in the underlying asset (or futures contracts on the underlying asset) cannot be changed continuously when delta hedging is used.

Calculation of Gamma

For a European call or put option on a non-dividend-paying stock, the gamma is given by

$$\Gamma = \frac{N'(d_1)}{S\sigma\sqrt{T-t}}$$

where d_1 is defined as in equation (11.22) and $N'(x)$ is given in Section 11.8. This is always positive and varies with S in the way indicated in Figure 14.9.

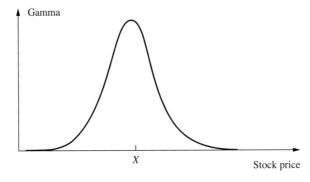

Figure 14.9   Typical patterns for variation of gamma with stock price for an option.

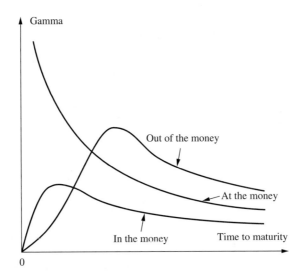

Figure 14.10   Variation of gamma with time to maturity for a stock option.

Typical patterns for the variation of gamma with time to maturity for out-of-the-money, at-the-money, and in-the-money options is shown in Figure 14.10. For an at-the-money option, gamma increases as the time to maturity decreases. Short-life at-the-money options have very high gammas, which means that the value of the option holder's position is highly sensitive to jumps in the stock price.

For a European call or put option on a stock index paying a continuous dividend at rate q,

$$\Gamma = \frac{N'(d_1)e^{-q(T-t)}}{S\sigma\sqrt{T-t}}$$

where d_1 is defined as in equation (12.4). This formula gives the gamma for a European option on a currency when q is put equal to the foreign risk-free rate and gives the gamma for a European futures option with $q = r$ and $S = F$.

Example 14.7

Consider a four-month put option on a stock index. Suppose that the current value of the index is 305, the strike price is 300, the dividend yield is 3% per annum, the risk-free interest rate is 8% per annum, and volatility of the index is 25% per annum. In this case, $S = 305$, $X = 300$, $q = 0.03$, $r = 0.08$, $\sigma = 0.25$, and $T - t = 0.3333$. The gamma of the index option is given by

$$\frac{N'(d_1)e^{-q(T-t)}}{S\sigma\sqrt{T-t}} = 0.00857$$

Thus an increase of 1 in the index increases the delta of the option by approximately 0.00857.

14.8 RELATIONSHIP AMONG DELTA, THETA, AND GAMMA

The Black–Scholes differential equation (11.15) that must be satisfied by the price, f, of any derivative on a non-dividend-paying stock is

$$\frac{\partial f}{\partial t} + rS\frac{\partial f}{\partial S} + \frac{1}{2}\sigma^2 S^2\frac{\partial^2 f}{\partial S^2} = rf$$

Since

$$\Theta = \frac{\partial f}{\partial t} \qquad \Delta = \frac{\partial f}{\partial S} \qquad \Gamma = \frac{\partial^2 f}{\partial S^2}$$

it follows that

$$\Theta + rS\Delta + \frac{1}{2}\sigma^2 S^2\Gamma = rf \tag{14.4}$$

This is true for portfolios of derivatives on a non-dividend-paying security as well as for individual derivatives.

For a delta-neutral portfolio, $\Delta = 0$ and

$$\Theta + \frac{1}{2}\sigma^2 S^2 \Gamma = rf$$

This shows that when Θ is large and positive, gamma tends to be large and negative, and vice versa. In a delta-neutral portfolio, theta can be regarded as a proxy for gamma.

14.9 VEGA

Up to now we have implicitly assumed that the volatility of the asset underlying a derivative is constant. In practice, volatilities change over time. This means that the value of a derivative is liable to change because of movements in volatility as well as because of changes in the asset price and the passage of time.

The *vega* of a portfolio of derivatives, $\mathcal{V}$, is the rate of change of the value of the portfolio with respect to the volatility of the underlying asset.[11] If vega is high in absolute terms, the portfolio's value is very sensitive to small changes in volatility. If vega is low in absolute terms, volatility changes have relatively little impact on the value of the portfolio.

A position in the underlying asset or in a futures contract has zero vega. However, the vega of a portfolio can be changed by adding a position in a traded option. If $\mathcal{V}$ is the vega of the portfolio and $\mathcal{V}_T$ is the vega of a traded option, a position of $-\mathcal{V}/\mathcal{V}_T$ in the traded option makes the portfolio instantaneously vega neutral. Unfortunately, a portfolio that is gamma neutral will not in general be vega neutral, and vice versa. If a hedger requires a portfolio to be both gamma and vega neutral, at least two traded derivatives dependent on the underlying asset must usually be used.

Example 14.8

Consider a portfolio that is delta neutral, with a gamma of $-5,000$ and a vega of $-8,000$. Suppose that a traded option has a gamma of 0.5, a vega of 2.0, and a delta of 0.6. The portfolio can be made vega neutral by including a long position in 4,000 traded options. This would increase delta to 2,400 and require that 2,400 units of the asset be sold to maintain delta neutrality. The gamma of the portfolio would change from $-5,000$ to $-3,000$.

To make the portfolio gamma and vega neutral, we suppose that there is a second traded option with a gamma of 0.8, a vega of 1.2, and a delta of 0.5. If w_1 and w_2 are the amounts of the two traded options included in the portfolio, we require that

$$-5,000 + 0.5w_1 + 0.8w_2 = 0$$

$$-8,000 + 2.0w_1 + 1.2w_2 = 0$$

The solution to these equations is $w_1 = 400$, $w_2 = 6,000$. The portfolio can therefore be made gamma and vega neutral by including 400 of the first traded option and 6,000 of the

---

[11]More formally, $\mathcal{V} = \partial\Pi/\partial\sigma$, where Π is the value of the portfolio. Vega is also sometimes referred to as lambda, kappa, or sigma.

second traded option. The delta of the portfolio after the addition of the positions in the two traded options is $400 \times 0.6 + 6,000 \times 0.5 = 3,240$. Hence 3,240 units of the asset would have to be sold to maintain delta neutrality.

For a European call or put option on a non-dividend-paying stock, vega is given by

$$\mathcal{V} = S\sqrt{T-t}\,N'(d_1)$$

where d_1 is defined as in equation (11.22). The formula for $N'(x)$ is given in Section 11.8. For a European call or put option on a stock or stock index paying a continuous dividend yield at rate q,

$$\mathcal{V} = S\sqrt{T-t}\,N'(d_1)e^{-q(T-t)}$$

where d_1 is defined as in equation (12.4). This equation gives the vega for a European currency option with q replaced by r_f. It also gives the vega for a European futures option with q replaced by r, and S replaced by F. The vega of an option is always positive. The general way in which it varies with S is shown in Figure 14.11.

Calculating vega from the Black–Scholes pricing formula is an approximation. This is because one of the assumptions underlying Black–Scholes is that volatility is constant. Ideally, we would like to calculate vega from a model in which volatility is assumed to be stochastic. This is considerably more complicated. Luckily, it can be shown that the vega calculated from a stochastic volatility model is very similar to the Black–Scholes vega.[12] Stochastic volatility models are discussed in Chapter 19.

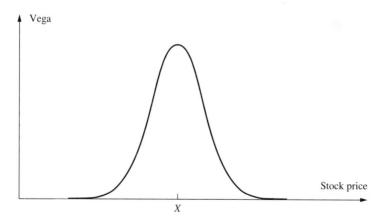

Figure 14.11   Variation of vega with stock price for an option.

[12] See J. Hull and A. White, "The Pricing of Options on Assets with Stochastic Volatilities," *Journal of Finance,* 42 (June 1987), 281–300; J. Hull and A. White, "An Analysis of the Bias in Option Pricing Caused by a Stochastic Volatility," *Advances in Futures and Options Research,* 3 (1988), 27–61.

Gamma neutrality corrects for the fact that time elapses between hedge rebalancing. Vega neutrality corrects for a variable σ. As might be expected, whether it is best to use an available traded option for vega or gamma hedging depends on the time between hedge rebalancing and the volatility of the volatility.[13]

Example 14.9

Consider again the put option in Example 14.7. Its vega is given by

$$S\sqrt{T-t}\,N'(d_1)e^{-q(T-t)} = 66.44$$

Thus a 1% or 0.01 increase in volatility (from 25% to 26%) increases the value of the option by approximately 0.6644.

14.10 RHO

The *rho* of a portfolio of derivatives is the rate of change of the value of the portfolio with respect to the interest rate.[14] It measures the sensitivity of the value of a portfolio to interest rates. For a European call option on a non-dividend-paying stock,

$$\text{rho} = X(T-t)e^{-r(T-t)}N(d_2)$$

and for a European put option on the stock,

$$\text{rho} = -X(T-t)e^{-r(T-t)}N(-d_2)$$

where d_2 is defined as in equation (11.22). These same formulas apply to European call and put options on stocks and stock indices paying a dividend yield at rate q, and to European call and put options on futures contracts, when appropriate changes are made to the definition of d_2.

Example 14.10

Consider again the four-month put option on a stock index. The current value of the index is 305, the strike price is 300, the dividend yield is 3% per annum, the risk-free interest rate is 8% per annum, and the volatility of the index is 25% per annum. In this case, $S = 305, X = 300, q = 0.03, r = 0.08, \sigma = 0.25, T - t = 0.333$. The option's rho is

$$-X(T-t)e^{-r(T-t)}N(-d_2) = -42.57$$

This means that for a one-percentage-point or 0.01 increase in the risk-free interest rate (from 8% to 9%), the value of the option decreases by 0.4257.

---

[13] For a discussion of this issue, see J. Hull and A. White, "Hedging the Risks from Writing Foreign Currency Options," *Journal of International Money and Finance,* 6 (June 1987), 131–52.

[14] More formally, rho equals $\partial\Pi/\partial r$, where Π is the value of the portfolio.

In the case of currency options, there are two rhos corresponding to the two interest rates. The rho corresponding to the domestic interest rate is given by previous formulas. The rho corresponding to the foreign interest rate for a European call on a currency is given by

$$\text{rho} = -(T - t)e^{-r_f(T-t)}SN(d_1)$$

while for a European put it is

$$\text{rho} = (T - t)e^{-r_f(T-t)}SN(-d_1)$$

14.11 SCENARIO ANALYSIS

It would be wrong to give the impression that option traders are continually re-balancing their portfolios to maintain delta neutrality, gamma neutrality, vega neutrality, and so on. In practice, transactions costs make frequent rebalancing very expensive. Rather than trying to eliminate all risks, option traders therefore usually concentrate on assessing risks and deciding whether they are acceptable. They tend to use delta, gamma, and vega measures to quantify the different aspects of the risk inherent in their option portfolios. If the downside risk is acceptable, no adjustment is made to the portfolio; if it is unacceptable, they take an appropriate position in either the underlying asset or another derivative.

In addition to monitoring risks such as delta, gamma, and vega, option traders often also carry out a scenario analysis. This involves calculating the gain/loss on their portfolio over a specified period under a variety of different scenarios. The time period chosen is likely to depend on the liquidity of the instruments. Typically, it is one day, one week, or one month. The scenarios can be either chosen by management or generated by a model.

Consider a bank with a portfolio of options on a foreign currency. There are two main variables upon which the value of the portfolio depends. These are the exchange rate and the exchange rate volatility. Suppose that the exchange rate is currently 1.0000 and its volatility is 10% per annum. The bank could calculate a table such as Table 14.5 showing the profit/loss experienced during a two-week period under different scenarios. This table considers seven different exchange rates and three different volatilities. Since a one-standard-deviation move in the exchange rate during a two-week period is about 0.02, the exchange rate moves considered are approximately one, two, and three standard deviations.

In Table 14.5 the greatest loss is in the lower right corner of the table. This corresponds to the volatility increasing to 12% and the exchange rate moving up to 1.06. It should be noted that the nature of an options portfolio is such that the greatest losses do not always correspond to one of the four corners of the table. Suppose, for example, that a bank's portfolio consists of a reverse butterfly spread (see Section 8.2). The greatest loss will be experienced if the exchange rate stays where it is.

TABLE 14.5   Profit/Loss Realized in Two Weeks Under Different
Scenarios in Millions of Dollars

	Exchange Rate						
Volatility	0.94	0.96	0.98	1.00	1.02	1.04	1.06
8%	+102	+55	+25	+6	−10	−34	−80
10%	+80	+40	+17	+2	−14	−38	−85
12%	+60	+25	+9	−2	−18	−42	−90

Stress Testing

One form of scenario analysis involves what is known as *stress testing*. This involves testing the effect on a portfolio of extreme movements in the underlying variables. The scenarios considered are often the worst cases taken from 10 or 20 years of historical data. For example, in the case of an equity options portfolio, stress testing might involve evaluating how well the portfolio would stand up to the stock market crash experienced in October 1987.

Monte Carlo Simulation

Monte Carlo simulation is a tool that can be used to evaluate the probabilities of different gains/losses being realized over a future period. Movements in market prices and volatilities are simulated and a complete probability distribution for the gain/loss on a bank's portfolio over the specified period is obtained. Monte Carlo simulation can be used to evaluate the risks on a portfolio where there are a number of different underlying assets, providing the relevant correlations are known. In this way a bank can judge the benefits achieved from diversification. More details on the mechanics of carrying out Monte Carlo simulations are provided in Chapter 15.

Value at Risk

A key question in the management of market risk is "How bad can things get?" What is known as the *value at risk* approach attempts to answer this. When implementing this approach the first step is to decide on a confidence level. This could be 95%, 98%, or 99%. We then calculate the loss that has the property that it will not be exceeded at the chosen confidence level. This is the value at risk. For example, if a 99% confidence limit is chosen, the value at risk corresponds to the one percentile point on the probability distribution of gains and losses.

For a portfolio of instruments that are linearly dependent on the underlyings, the value at risk increases as the square root of how far ahead we are looking. Thus the 25-day value at risk is approximately five times the one-day value at risk. The same is not true of portfolios that involve options and other nonlinear derivatives. This is because of the effect of gamma and vega risks.

14.12 PORTFOLIO INSURANCE

Portfolio managers holding a well-diversified stock portfolio are sometimes interested in insuring themselves against the value of the portfolio dropping below a certain level. One way of doing this is by holding, in conjunction with the stock portfolio, put options on a stock index. This strategy was discussed in Chapter 12.

Consider, for example, a fund manager with a $30 million portfolio whose value mirrors the value of the S&P 500. Suppose that the S&P 500 is standing at 300 and the manager wishes to insure against the value of the portfolio dropping below $29 million in the next six months. One approach is to buy 1,000 six-month put option contracts on the S&P 500 with a strike price of 290 and a maturity in six months. If the index drops below 290, the put options will become in the money and provide the manager with compensation for the decline in the value of the portfolio. Suppose, for example, that the index drops to 270 at the end of 6 months. The value of the manager's stock portfolio is likely to be about $27 million. Since each option contract is on 100 times the index, the total value of the put options is $2 million. This brings the value of the entire holding back up to $29 million. Of course, insurance is not free. In this example the put options could cost the portfolio manager as much as $1 million.

Creating Options Synthetically

An alternative approach open to the portfolio manager involves creating the put options synthetically. This involves taking a position in the underlying asset (or futures on the underlying asset) so that the delta of the position is maintained equal to the delta of the required option. If more accuracy is required, the next step is to use traded options to match the gamma and vega of the required option. The position necessary to create an option synthetically is the reverse of that necessary to hedge it. This is a reflection of the fact that a procedure for hedging an option involves the creation of an equal and opposite option synthetically.

There are two reasons why it may be more attractive for the portfolio manager to create the required put option synthetically than to buy it in the market. The first is that options markets do not always have the liquidity to absorb the trades that managers of large funds would like to carry out. The second is that fund managers often require strike prices and exercise dates that are different from those available in traded options markets.

The synthetic option can be created from trades in stocks themselves or from trades in index futures contracts. We first examine the creation of a put option by trades in the stocks themselves. Consider again the fund manager with a well-diversified portfolio worth $30 million who wishes to buy a European put on the portfolio with a strike price of $29 million and an exercise date in six months. Recall that the delta of a European put on an index is given by

$$\Delta = e^{-q(T-t)}[N(d_1) - 1] \qquad (14.5)$$

where, with the usual notation,

$$d_1 = \frac{\ln(S/X) + (r - q + \sigma^2/2)(T - t)}{\sigma \sqrt{T - t}}$$

Since, in this case, the fund manager's portfolio mirrors the index, this is also the delta of a put on the portfolio when it is regarded as a single security. The delta is negative. Accordingly, to create the put option synthetically, the fund manager should ensure that at any given time a proportion

$$e^{-q(T-t)}[1 - N(d_1)]$$

of the stocks in the original \$30 million portfolio have been sold and the proceeds invested in riskless assets. As the value of the original portfolio declines, the delta of the put becomes more negative and the proportion of the portfolio sold must be increased. As the value of the original portfolio increases, the delta of the put becomes less negative and the proportion of the portfolio sold must be decreased (i.e., some of the original portfolio must be repurchased).

Using this strategy to create portfolio insurance means that at any given time funds are divided between the stock portfolio on which insurance is required and riskless assets. As the value of the stock portfolio increases, riskless assets are sold and the position in the stock portfolio is increased. As the value of the stock portfolio declines, the position in the stock portfolio is decreased and riskless assets are purchased. The cost of the insurance arises from the fact that the portfolio manager is always selling after a decline in the market and buying after a rise in the market.

Use of Index Futures

Using index futures to create portfolio insurance can be preferable to using the underlying stocks, provided that the index futures market is sufficiently liquid to handle the required trades. This is because the transactions costs associated with trades in index futures are generally less than those associated with the corresponding trades in the underlying stocks. The portfolio manager considered earlier would keep the \$30 million stock portfolio intact and short index futures contracts. From equations (14.2) and (14.5), the dollar amount of futures contracts shorted as a proportion of the value of the portfolio should be

$$e^{-q(T-t)}e^{-(r-q)(T^*-t)}[1 - N(d_1)] = e^{q(T^*-T)}e^{-r(T^*-t)}[1 - N(d_1)]$$

where T^* is the maturity date of the futures contract. If the portfolio is worth K_1 times the index and each index futures contract is on K_2 times the index, this means that the number of futures contracts shorted at any given time should be

$$e^{q(T^*-T)}e^{-r(T^*-t)}[1 - N(d_1)]\frac{K_1}{K_2}$$

Example 14.11

In the example given at the beginning of this section, suppose that the volatility of the market is 25% per annum, the risk-free interest rate is 9% per annum, and the dividend yield on the market is 3% per annum. In this case, $S = 300$, $X = 290$, $r = 0.09$, $q = 0.03$, $\sigma = 0.25$, and $T - t = 0.5$. The delta of the option that is required is

$$e^{-q(T-t)}[N(d_1) - 1] = -0.322$$

Hence, if trades in the portfolio are used to create the option, 32.2% of the portfolio should be sold initially. If nine-month futures contracts on the S&P 500 are used, $T^* - T = 0.25$, $T^* - t = 0.75$, $K_1 = 100,000$, $K_2 = 500$, so that the number of futures contracts shorted should be

$$e^{q(T^*-T)}e^{-r(T^*-t)}[1 - N(d_1)]\frac{K_1}{K_2} = 61.6$$

An important issue when put options are created synthetically for portfolio insurance is the frequency with which the portfolio manager's position should be adjusted or rebalanced. With no transaction costs, continuous rebalancing is optimal. However, as transactions costs increase, the optimal frequency of rebalancing declines. This issue is discussed by Leland.[15]

Up to now we have assumed that the portfolio mirrors the index. As discussed in Chapter 12, the hedging scheme can be adjusted to deal with other situations. The strike price for the options used should be the expected level of the market index when the portfolio's value reaches its insured value. The number of index options used should be β times the number of options that would be required if the portfolio had a beta of 1.0.

Example 14.12

Suppose that the risk-free rate of interest is 5% per annum, the S&P 500 stands at 500, and the value of a portfolio with a beta of 2.0 is $10 million. Suppose that the dividend yield on the S&P 500 is 3%, the dividend yield on the portfolio is 2%, and that the portfolio manager wishes to insure against a decline in the value of the portfolio to below $9.3 million in the next year. If the value of the portfolio declines to $9.3 million at the end of the year, the total return (after taking account of the 2% dividend yield) is approximately -5% per annum. This is 10% per annum less than the risk-free rate. We expect the market to perform 5% worse than the risk-free rate (i.e., to provide zero return) in these circumstances. Hence, we expect a 3% decline in the S&P 500 since this index does not take any account of dividends. The correct strike price for the put options that are created is therefore 485. The number of put options required is beta times the value of the portfolio divided by the value of the index, or 40,000 (i.e., 400 contracts).

To illustrate that this answer is at least approximately correct, suppose that the portfolio's value drops to $8.3 million. With dividends it provides a return of approximately -15% per annum. This is approximately 20% per annum less than the risk-free rate.

---

[15] See H. E. Leland, "Option Pricing and Replication with Transactions Costs," *Journal of Finance*, 40 (December 1985), 1283–1301.

The S&P 500 plus dividends on the S&P 500 can be expected to provide a return that is 10% per annum less than the risk-free rate. This means that the index will reduce by 8%, to 460. The 40,000 put options with a strike price of 485 will pay off $1 million, as required.

When β is not equal to 1.0 and the fund manager wishes to use trades in the portfolio to create the option, the portfolio can be regarded as a single security. As an approximation, the volatility of the portfolio can be assumed to be equal to β times the volatility of the market index.[16]

October 19, 1987 and Stock Market Volatility

Creating put options on the index synthetically does not work well if the volatility of the index changes rapidly or if the index exhibits large jumps. On Monday, October 19, 1987, the Dow Jones Industrial Average dropped by over 500 points. Portfolio managers who had insured themselves by buying traded put options survived this crash well. Those who had chosen to create put options synthetically found that they were unable to sell either stocks or index futures fast enough to protect their position.

We have already (in Section 11.11) raised the issue of whether volatility is caused solely by the arrival of new information or whether trading itself generates volatility. Portfolio insurance schemes such as those just described have the potential to increase volatility. When the market declines, they cause portfolio managers either to sell stock or to sell index futures contracts. This may accentuate the decline. The sale of stock is liable to drive down the market index further in a direct way. The sale of index futures contracts is liable to drive down futures prices. This creates selling pressure on stocks via the mechanism of index arbitrage (see Chapter 3) so that the market index is liable to be driven down in this case as well. Similarly, when the market rises, the portfolio insurance schemes cause portfolio managers either to buy stock or to buy futures contracts. This may accentuate the rise.

In addition to formal portfolio insurance schemes, we can speculate that many investors consciously or subconsciously follow portfolio insurance schemes of their own. For example, an investor may be inclined to enter the market when it is rising, but will sell when it is falling, to limit his or her downside risk.

Whether portfolio insurance schemes (formal or informal) affect volatility depends on how easily the market can absorb the trades that are generated by portfolio insurance. If portfolio insurance trades are a very small fraction of all trades, there is likely to be no effect. But as portfolio insurance becomes more widespread, it is liable to have a destabilizing effect on the market.

---

[16]This is exactly true only if beta is calculated on the basis of the returns in very small time intervals. By contrast, the argument in Example 14.12 is exactly true only if beta is calculated on the basis of returns in time intervals of length equal to the life of the option being created.

Brady Commission Report

The report of the Brady commission on the October 19, 1987, crash provides some interesting insights into the effect of portfolio insurance on the market at that time.[17] The Brady commission estimates that $60 billion to $90 billion of equity assets were under portfolio insurance administration in October 1987. During the period Wednesday, October 14, 1987, to Friday, October 16, 1987, the market declined by about 10 percent, with much of this decline taking place on the Friday afternoon. This should have generated at least $12 billion of equity or index futures sales as a result of portfolio insurance schemes.[18] In fact, less than $4 billion were sold, which means that portfolio insurers approached the following week with huge amounts of selling already dictated by their models. The Brady commission estimated that on Monday, October 19, sell programs by three portfolio insurers accounted for almost 10 percent of the sales on the New York Stock Exchange, and that portfolio insurance sales amount to 21.3 percent of all sales in index futures markets. It seems likely that portfolio insurance caused some downward pressure on the market. It is significant that in aggregate, portfolio insurers executed only a relatively small proportion of the total trades generated by their models. Needless to say, the popularity of portfolio insurance schemes that are based solely on dynamic trading in stocks and futures has declined considerably since October 1987.

14.13 SUMMARY

Financial institutions offer a variety of option products to their clients. Often, the options do not correspond to the standardized products traded by exchanges. This presents the financial institutions with the problem of hedging their exposure. Naked and covered positions leave them subject to an unacceptable level of risk. One strategy that is sometimes proposed is a stop-loss strategy that involves holding a naked position when an option is out of the money and converting it to a covered position as soon as the option moves in the money. Surprisingly, the strategy does not work well.

The delta, Δ, of an option is the rate of change of its price with respect to the price of the underlying asset. Delta hedging involves creating a position with zero delta (sometimes referred to as a delta-neutral position). Since the delta of the underlying asset is 1.0, one way of doing this is to take a position of $-\Delta$ in the underlying asset for each long option being hedged. The delta of an option changes over time. This means that the position in the underlying asset has to be frequently adjusted.

---

[17]See "Report of the Presidential Task Force on Market Mechanisms," January 1988.

[18]To put this in perspective, on Monday, October 19, all previous records were broken when 604 million shares worth $21 billion were traded on the New York Stock Exchange. Approximately $20 billion of S&P 500 futures contracts were traded on that day.

Once an option position has been made delta neutral, the next stage is often to look at its gamma. The gamma of an option is the rate of change of its delta with respect to the price of the underlying asset. It is a measure of the curvature of the relationship between the option price and the asset price. The impact of this curvature on the performance of delta hedging can be reduced by making an option position gamma neutral. If Γ is the gamma of the position being hedged, this is usually achieved by taking a position in a traded option that has a gamma of $-\Gamma$.

Delta and gamma hedging are both based on the assumption that the volatility of the underlying asset is constant. In practice, volatilities do change over time. The vega of an option, or an option portfolio, measures the rate of change of its value with respect to volatility. If a trader wishes to hedge an option position against volatility changes, he or she can make the position vega neutral. Like the procedure for creating gamma neutrality, this usually involves taking an offsetting position in a traded option. If the trader wishes to achieve both gamma and vega neutrality, two traded options are usually required.

Two other measures of the risk of an option position are theta and rho. Theta measures the rate of change of the value of the position with respect to the passage of time with all else remaining constant; rho measures the rate of change of the value of the position with respect to the short-term interest rate with all else remaining constant.

Another approach to risk management is scenario analysis. This involves calculating the gain/loss on a portfolio over a specified period of time under a number of scenarios. The scenarios can be chosen by management or generated using Monte Carlo simulation. A popular measure related to scenario analysis is what is known as the value at risk. This is the loss over a specified period of time that will not be exceeded with a 95%, 99%, or other specified confidence level.

Portfolio managers are sometimes interested in creating put options synthetically for the purposes of insuring an equity portfolio. They can do this either by trading the portfolio or by trading index futures on the portfolio. Trading the portfolio involves splitting the portfolio between equities and risk-free securities. As the market declines, more is invested in risk-free securities. As the market increases, more is invested in equities. Trading index futures involves keeping the equity portfolio intact and selling index futures. As the market declines, more index futures are sold; as it rises fewer are sold. This works reasonably well in normal market conditions. However, on Monday, October 19, 1987, when the Dow Jones Industrial Average dropped by over 500 points, it worked badly. Portfolio insurers were unable to sell either stocks or index futures fast enough to protect their positions.

SUGGESTIONS FOR FURTHER READING

On Hedging Option Positions

Boyle, P. P., and D. Emanuel, "Discretely Adjusted Option Hedges," *Journal of Financial Economics,* 8 (1980), 259–82.

Dillman, S., and J. Harding, "Life after Delta: the Gamma Factor," *Euromoney,* Supplement (February 1985), 14–17.

Figlewski, S. "Options Arbitrage in Imperfect Markets," *Journal of Finance,* 44 (December 1989), 1289–1311.

Galai, D., "The Components of the Return from Hedging Options Against Stocks," *Journal of Business,* 56 (January 1983), 45–54.

Hull, J., and A. White, "Hedging the Risks from Writing Foreign Currency Options," *Journal of International Money and Finance,* 6 (June 1987), 131–52.

On Portfolio Insurance

Asay, M., and C. Edelberg, "Can a Dynamic Strategy Replicate the Returns on an Option?" *Journal of Futures Markets,* 6 (Spring 1986), 63–70.

Bookstaber, R., and J. A. Langsam, "Portfolio Insurance Trading Rules," *Journal of Futures Markets,* 8 (February 1988), 15–31.

Etzioni, E. S., "Rebalance Disciplines for Portfolio Insurance," *Journal of Portfolio Insurance,* 13 (Fall 1986), 59–62.

Leland, H. E., "Option Pricing and Replication with Transactions Costs," *Journal of Finance,* 40 (December 1985), 1283–1301.

Leland, H. E., "Who Should Buy Portfolio Insurance," *Journal of Finance,* 35 (May 1980), 581–94.

Rubinstein, M., "Alternative Paths for Portfolio Insurance," *Financial Analysts Journal,* 41 (July–August 1985), 42–52.

Rubinstein, M., and H. E. Leland, "Replicating Options with Positions in Stock and Cash," *Financial Analysts Journal,* 37 (July–August 1981), 63–72.

Schwartz, E. S., "Options and Portfolio Insurance," *Finanzmarkt und Portfolio Management,* 1 (1986), 9–17.

Tilley, J. A., and G. O. Latainer, "A Synthetic Option Framework for Asset Allocation," *Financial Analysts Journal,* 41 (May–June 1985), 32–41.

QUESTIONS AND PROBLEMS

14.1. What does it mean to assert that the delta of a call option is 0.7? How can a short position in 1,000 call options be made delta neutral when the delta of each option is 0.7?

14.2. Calculate the delta of an at-the-money six-month European call option on a non-dividend-paying stock when the risk-free interest rate is 10% per annum and the stock price volatility is 25% per annum.

14.3. What does it mean to assert that the theta of an option position is −0.1 when time is measured in years? If a trader feels that neither a stock price nor its implied volatility will change, what type of option position is appropriate?

14.4. What is meant by the gamma of an option position? Consider the situation of an option writer when the gamma of his or her position is large and negative and the delta is zero. What are the risks?

14.5. "The procedure for creating an option position synthetically is the reverse of the procedure for hedging the option position." Explain this statement.

14.6. Why did portfolio insurance not work well on October 19, 1987?

*14.7. A deposit instrument offered by a bank guarantees that investors will receive a return during a six-month period that is the greater of (a) zero; and (b) 40% of the return provided by a market index. A person is planning to invest \$100,000 in the instrument. Describe the payoff as an option on the index. Assuming that the risk-free rate of interest is 8% per annum, the dividend yield on the index is 3% per annum, and the volatility of the index is 25% per annum, is the product a good deal?

14.8. The Black–Scholes price of an out-of-the-money call option with a strike price of \$40 is \$4.00. A trader who has written the option plans to use the stop-loss strategy in Section 14.3. The trader's plan is to buy at $40\frac{1}{8}$ and to sell at $39\frac{7}{8}$. Estimate the expected number of times the stock will be bought or sold.

*14.9. Use the put–call parity relationship to derive for a non-dividend-paying stock the relationship between:
(a) The delta of a European call and the delta of a European put.
(b) The gamma of a European call and the gamma of a European put.
(c) The vega of a European call and the vega of a European put.
(d) The theta of a European call and the theta of a European put.

14.10. Suppose that a stock price is currently \$20 and that a call option with strike price \$25 is created synthetically using a position in the stock that is changed frequently. Consider the following two scenarios:
(a) Stock price increases steadily from \$20 to \$35 during the life of the option.
(b) Stock price oscillates wildly, ending up at \$35.
Which scenario would make the synthetically created option more expensive? Explain your answer.

14.11. What is the delta of a short position in 1,000 European call options on silver futures? The options mature in eight months and the futures contract underlying the option matures in nine months. The current nine-month futures price is \$8.00 per ounce, the strike price of the options is \$8.00, the risk-free interest rate is 12% per annum, and the volatility of silver is 18% per annum.

14.12. In Problem 14.11, what initial position in nine-month silver futures is necessary for delta hedging? If silver itself is used, what is the initial position? If one-year silver futures are used, what is the initial position? Assume no storage costs for silver.

14.13. A company uses delta hedging to hedge a portfolio of long positions in put and call options on a currency. Which of the following would give the most favorable result?
(a) A virtually constant spot rate.
(b) Wild movements in the spot rate.
Explain your answer.

14.14. Repeat Problem 14.13 for a financial institution with a portfolio of short positions in put and call options on a currency.

14.15. A financial institution has just sold some seven-month European call options on the Japanese yen. Suppose that the spot exchange rate is 0.80 cent per yen, the strike price is 0.81 cent per yen, the risk-free interest rate in the United States is 8%

per annum, the risk-free interest rate in Japan is 5% per annum, and the volatility of the yen is 15% per annum. Calculate the delta, gamma, vega, theta, and rho of the option. Interpret each number.

14.16. A financial institution has the following portfolio of over-the-counter options on sterling:

Type	Position	Delta of Option	Gamma of Option	Vega of Option
Call	−1,000	0.50	2.2	1.8
Call	−500	0.80	0.6	0.2
Put	−2,000	−0.40	1.3	0.7
Call	−500	0.70	1.8	1.4

A traded option is available which has a delta of 0.6, a gamma of 1.5, and a vega of 0.8.

(a) What position in the traded option and in sterling would make the portfolio both gamma neutral and delta neutral?

(b) What position in the traded option and in sterling make the portfolio both vega neutral and delta neutral?

14.17. Consider again the situation in Problem 14.16. Suppose that a second traded option with a delta of 0.1, a gamma of 0.5, and a vega of 0.6 is available. How could the portfolio be made delta, gamma, and vega neutral?

*14.18. Under what circumstances is it possible to make a position in an over-the-counter European option on a stock index both gamma neutral and vega neutral by introducing a single traded European option into the portfolio?

14.19. A fund manager has a well-diversified portfolio that mirrors the performance of the S&P 500 and is worth $90 million. The value of the S&P 500 is 300 and the portfolio manager would like to buy insurance against a reduction of more than 5% in the value of the portfolio over the next six months. The risk-free interest rate is 6% per annum. The dividend yield on both the portfolio and the S&P 500 is 3%, and the volatility of the index is 30% per annum.

(a) If the fund manager buys traded European put options, how much would the insurance cost?

(b) Explain carefully alternative strategies open to the fund manager involving traded European call options, and show that they lead to the same result.

(c) If the fund manager decides to provide insurance by keeping part of the portfolio in risk-free securities, what should the initial position be?

(d) If the fund manager decides to provide insurance by using nine-month index futures, what should the initial position be?

14.20. Repeat Problem 14.19 on the assumption that the portfolio has a beta of 1.5. Assume that the dividend yield on the portfolio is 4% per annum.

14.21. Show by substituting for Θ, Δ, Γ, and f that the relationship in equation (14.4) is true for:

(a) A single European call option on a non-dividend-paying stock.

(b) A single European put option on a non-dividend-paying stock.

(c) Any portfolio of European put and call options on a non-dividend-paying stock.

14.22. What is the equation corresponding to equation (14.4) for a portfolio of derivatives on a currency?

14.23. Suppose that $70 billion of equity assets are the subject of portfolio insurance schemes. Assume that the schemes are designed to provide insurance against the value of the assets declining by more than 5% within one year. Making whatever estimates you find necessary, calculate the value of the stock or futures contracts that the administrators of the portfolio insurance schemes will attempt to sell if the market falls by 23% in a single day.

APPENDIX 14A: TAYLOR SERIES EXPANSIONS AND HEDGE PARAMETERS

The various hedging alternatives open to the manager of a portfolio of derivatives can be illustrated using a Taylor series expansion of the change in the value of the portfolio in a short period of time. If the volatility of the underlying asset is assumed to be constant, the value of the portfolio, Π, is a function of the asset price, S, and time t. The Taylor series expansion gives

$$\Delta\Pi = \frac{\partial \Pi}{\partial S}\Delta S + \frac{\partial \Pi}{\partial t}\Delta t + \frac{1}{2}\frac{\partial^2 \Pi}{\partial S^2}\Delta S^2 + \frac{1}{2}\frac{\partial^2 \Pi}{\partial t^2}\Delta t^2 + \frac{\partial^2 \Pi}{\partial S \partial t}\Delta S \Delta t + \cdots$$

$$(14A.1)$$

where $\Delta\Pi$ and ΔS are the change in Π and S in a small time interval Δt. Delta hedging eliminates the first term on the right-hand side. The second term is non-stochastic. The third term (which is of order Δt) can be made zero by ensuring that the portfolio is gamma neutral as well as delta neutral. Other terms are of higher order than Δt.

For a delta-neutral portfolio, the first term on the right-hand side of equation (14A.1) is zero, so that

$$\Delta\Pi = \Theta \Delta t + \frac{1}{2}\Gamma \Delta S^2$$

when terms of higher order than Δt are ignored. This is equation (14.3).

When the volatility of the underlying asset is assumed to be variable, Π is a function of σ, S, and t. Equation (14A.1) then becomes

$$\Delta\Pi = \frac{\partial \Pi}{\partial S}\Delta S + \frac{\partial \Pi}{\partial \sigma}\Delta\sigma + \frac{\partial \Pi}{\partial t}\Delta t + \frac{1}{2}\frac{\partial^2 \Pi}{\partial S^2}\Delta S^2 + \frac{1}{2}\frac{\partial^2 \Pi}{\partial \sigma^2}\Delta\sigma^2 + \cdots$$

where $\Delta\sigma$ is the change in σ in time Δt. In this case, delta hedging eliminates the first term on the right-hand side. The second term is eliminated by making the portfolio vega neutral. The third term is nonstochastic. The fourth term is eliminated by making the portfolio gamma neutral.

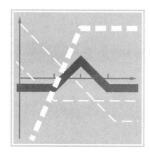

Chapter 15

Numerical Procedures

In this chapter we discuss three numerical procedures that can be used to value derivatives when exact formulas are not available. One of these procedures, Monte Carlo simulation, is useful for derivatives where the payoff is dependent on the history of the underlying variable or where there are several underlying variables. The other two procedures involve the use of trees and finite difference methods. Unlike Monte Carlo simulation, they can be used for derivatives where the holder has early exercise decisions to make prior to maturity. In this chapter we show how all the procedures can be used to calculate hedge parameters such as delta, gamma, and vega. We also present an analytic approximation for American options. For ease of exposition we assume that the current time (usually denoted by t) is zero throughout this chapter except in the appendix.

15.1 BINOMIAL TREES

In Chapter 9 we introduced one- and two-step binomial trees for non-dividend-paying stocks and showed how they lead to valuations for European and American options. These trees are very imprecise models of reality and were used only for illustrative purposes. A more realistic model is one that assumes stock price movements are composed of a large number of small binomial movements. This is the assumption that underlies a widely used numerical procedure that was first proposed by Cox, Ross, and Rubinstein.[1]

Consider the evaluation of an option on a non-dividend-paying stock. We start by dividing the life of the option into a large number of small time intervals of length Δt. We assume that in each time interval the stock price moves from its initial value of S to one of two new values, Su and Sd. This model is illustrated in Figure 15.1. In general, $u > 1$ and $d < 1$. The movement from S to Su is therefore an "up" movement and the movement from S to Sd is a "down" movement. The probability of an up movement will be denoted by p. The probability of a down movement is $1 - p$.

[1]See J. C. Cox, S. A. Ross, and M. Rubinstein, "Option Pricing: A Simplified Approach," *Journal of Financial Economics*, 7 (October 1979), 229–63.

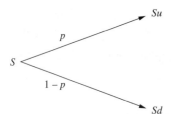

Figure 15.1   Stock price movements in time Δt under the binomial model.

Risk-Neutral Valuation

In Chapters 9 and 11 we introduced what is known as the risk-neutral valuation principle. This states that any security dependent on a stock price can be valued on the assumption that the world is risk neutral. It means that for the purposes of valuing an option (or any other derivative), we can assume that:

1. The expected return from all traded securities is the risk-free interest rate.
2. Future cash flows can be valued by discounting their expected values at the risk-free interest rate.

When using a binomial tree we make use of this result. The tree is designed to represent the behavior of a stock price in a risk-neutral world.

Determination of p, u, and d

The parameters p, u, and d must give correct values for the mean and variance of stock price changes during a time interval of length Δt. Since we are working in a risk-neutral world, the expected return from a stock is the risk-free interest rate, r.[2] Hence the expected value of the stock price at the end of a time interval of length Δt is $Se^{r\Delta t}$, where S is the stock price at the beginning of the time interval. It follows that

$$Se^{r\Delta t} = pSu + (1 - p)Sd \tag{15.1}$$

or

$$e^{r\Delta t} = pu + (1 - p)d \tag{15.2}$$

From equation (11.4) the variance of the change in the stock price in a small time interval Δt is $S^2 e^{2r\Delta t}(e^{\sigma^2 \Delta t} - 1)$. Since the variance of a variable Q is defined as $E\left(Q^2\right) - [E(Q)]^2$, where E denotes expected value, it follows that

$$S^2 e^{2r\Delta t}(e^{\sigma^2 \Delta t} - 1) = pS^2 u^2 + (1 - p)S^2 d^2 - S^2[pu + (1 - p)d]^2$$

---

[2]In practice, r is usually set equal to the zero-coupon yield on a bond maturing at the same time as the option. Section 15.4 shows how r can be made a function of time.

or

$$e^{2r\Delta t + \sigma^2 \Delta t} = pu^2 + (1 - p)d^2 \tag{15.3}$$

Equations (15.2) and (15.3) impose two conditions on p, u, and d. A third condition used by Cox, Ross, and Rubinstein is

$$u = \frac{1}{d}$$

It can be shown that the three conditions imply

$$p = \frac{a - d}{u - d} \tag{15.4}$$

$$u = e^{\sigma \sqrt{\Delta t}} \tag{15.5}$$

$$d = e^{-\sigma \sqrt{\Delta t}} \tag{15.6}$$

where

$$a = e^{r\Delta t} \tag{15.7}$$

and terms of higher order than Δt are ignored.[3]

Tree of Stock Prices

The complete tree of stock prices that is considered when the binomial model is used is illustrated in Figure 15.2. At time zero, the stock price, S, is known. At time Δt, there are two possible stock prices, Su and Sd; at time $2\Delta t$, there are three possible stock prices, Su^2, S, and Sd^2; and so on. In general, at time $i\Delta t$, $i + 1$ stock prices are considered. These are

$$Su^j d^{i-j} \qquad j = 0, 1, \ldots, i$$

Note that the relationship $u = 1/d$ is used in computing the stock price at each node of the tree in Figure 15.2. For example, $Su^2 d = Su$. Note also that the tree recombines in the sense that an up movement followed by a down movement leads to the same stock price as a down movement followed by an up movement. This considerably reduces the number of nodes on the tree.

---

[3] As an alternative we can exactly solve equations (15.2) and (15.3) subject to $u = 1/d$, to obtain

$$u = \frac{(a^2 + b^2 + 1) + \sqrt{(a^2 + b^2 + 1)^2 - 4a^2}}{2a}$$

$$p = \frac{a - d}{u - d}$$

where

$$a = e^{r\Delta t}$$

$$b^2 = a^2(e^{\sigma^2 \Delta t} - 1)$$

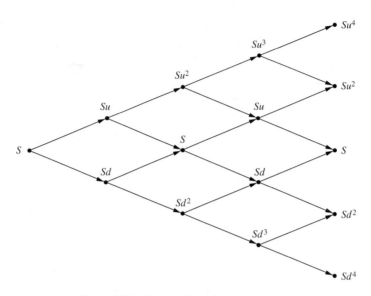

Figure 15.2   Tree used to value a stock option.

Working Backward through the Tree

Options are evaluated by starting at the end of the tree (time T) and working backward. The value of the option is known at time T. For example, a put option is worth $\max(X - S_T, 0)$ and a call option is worth $\max(S_T - X, 0)$, where S_T is the stock price at time T and X is the strike price. Since a risk-neutral world is being assumed, the value at each node at time $T - \Delta t$ can be calculated as the expected value at time T discounted at rate r for a time period Δt. Similarly, the value at each node at time $T - 2\Delta t$ can be calculated as the expected value at time $T - \Delta t$ discounted for a time period Δt at rate r, and so on. If the option is American, it is necessary to check at each node to see whether early exercise is preferable to holding the option for a further time period Δt. Eventually, by working back through all the nodes, the value of the option at time zero is obtained.

Example 15.1

Consider a five-month American put option on a non-dividend-paying stock when the stock price is \$50, the strike price is \$50, the risk-free interest rate is 10% per annum, and the volatility is 40% per annum. With our usual notation, this means that $S = 50$, $X = 50$, $r = 0.10$, $\sigma = 0.40$, and $T = 0.4167$. Suppose that we divide the life of the option into five intervals of length one month ($= 0.0833$ year) for the purposes of constructing a binomial tree. Then $\Delta t = 0.0833$ and using equations (15.4) to (15.7),

$$u = e^{\sigma \sqrt{\Delta t}} = 1.1224 \qquad d = e^{-\sigma \sqrt{\Delta t}} = 0.8909$$

$$a = e^{r \Delta t} = 1.0084 \qquad p = \frac{a - d}{u - d} = 0.5076$$

$$1 - p = 0.4924$$

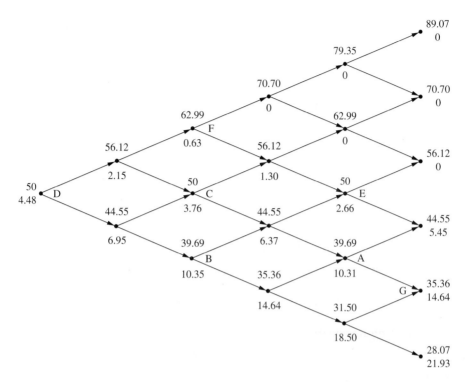

Figure 15.3   Binomial tree for American put on non-dividend-paying stock (Example 15.1).

Figure 15.3 shows the binomial tree. At each node there are two numbers. The top one shows the stock price at the node; the lower one shows the value of the option at the node. The probability of an up movement is always 0.5076; the probability of a down movement is always 0.4924.

The stock price at the jth node ($j = 0, 1, \ldots, i$) at time $i\Delta t$ is calculated as $Su^j d^{i-j}$. For example, the stock price at the node labeled A ($i = 4$, $j = 1$) is $50 \times 1.1224 \times 0.8909^3 = \$39.69$. The option prices at the final nodes are calculated as $\max(X - S_T, 0)$. For example, the option price at node G is $50 - 35.36 = 14.64$.

The option prices at the penultimate nodes are calculated from the option prices at the final nodes. First, we assume no exercise of the option at the nodes. This means that the option price is calculated as the present value of expected option price in time Δt. For example, at node E the option price is calculated as

$$(0.5076 \times 0 + 0.4924 \times 5.45)e^{-0.10 \times 0.0833} = 2.66$$

while at node A it is calculated as

$$(0.5076 \times 5.45 + 0.4924 \times 14.64)e^{-0.10 \times 0.0833} = 9.90$$

We then check to see if early exercise is preferable to waiting. At node E, early exercise would give a value for the option of zero since both the stock price and strike price are $50. Clearly it is best to wait. The correct value for the option at node E is therefore $2.66.

At node A it is a different story. If the option is exercised it is worth $50.00 − $39.69 or $10.31. This is more than $9.90. If node A is reached, the option should therefore be exercised and the correct value for the option at node A is $10.31. Option prices at earlier nodes are calculated in a similar way. Note that it is not always best to exercise an option early when it is in the money. Consider node B. If the option is exercised, it is worth $50.00 − $39.69 or $10.31. However, if it is held, it is worth

$$(0.5076 \times 6.37 + 0.4924 \times 14.64)e^{-0.10 \times 0.0833} = 10.35$$

The option should therefore not be exercised at this node, and the correct option value at the node is $10.35.

Working back through the tree, we find the value of the option at the initial node to be $4.48. This is our numerical estimate for the option's current value. In practice, a smaller value of Δt, and many more nodes, would be used. The true value of the option, obtained using a very small value of Δt, is $4.29.

Expressing the Approach Algebraically

Suppose that the life of an American put option on a non-dividend-paying stock is divided into N subintervals of length Δt. Define $f_{i,j}$ as the value of an American option at the jth node at time $i\Delta t$ for $0 \leq i \leq N, 0 \leq j \leq i$. We will refer to this as the value of the option at the (i, j) node. The stock price at the (i, j) node is $Su^j d^{i-j}$. Since the value of an American put at its expiration date is $\max(X - S_T, 0)$, we know that

$$f_{N,j} = \max(X - Su^j d^{N-j}, 0) \qquad j = 0, 1 \ldots, N$$

There is a probability, p, of moving from the (i, j) node at time $i\Delta t$ to the $(i + 1, j + 1)$ node at time $(i + 1)\Delta t$, and a probability $1 - p$ of moving from the (i, j) node at time $i\Delta t$ to the $(i + 1, j)$ node at time $(i + 1)\Delta t$. Assuming no early exercise, risk-neutral valuation gives

$$f_{i,j} = e^{-r\Delta t}[p f_{i+1,j+1} + (1 - p)f_{i+1,j}]$$

for $0 \leq i \leq N - 1$ and $0 \leq j \leq i$. When early exercise is taken into account, this value for $f_{i,j}$ must be compared with the option's intrinsic value, and we obtain

$$f_{i,j} = \max\{X - Su^j d^{i-j}, e^{-r\Delta t}[p f_{i+1,j+1} + (1 - p)f_{i+1,j}]\}$$

Note that because the calculations start at time T and work backward, the value at time $i\Delta t$ captures not only the effect of early exercise possibilities at time $i\Delta t$, but also the effect of early exercise at subsequent times. In the limit as Δt tends to zero, an exact value for the American put is obtained. In practice, $N = 30$ usually gives reasonable results.

Estimating Delta and Other Hedge Parameters

It will be recalled that the delta, Δ, of an option is the rate of change of its price with respect to the underlying stock price. In other words,

$$\Delta = \frac{\Delta f}{\Delta S}$$

where ΔS is a small change in the stock price and Δf is the corresponding small change in the option price. At time Δt we have an estimate, f_{11}, for the option price when the stock price is Su; and an estimate, f_{10}, for the option price when the stock price is Sd. In other words, when $\Delta S = Su - Sd$, the value of Δf is $f_{11} - f_{10}$. An estimate of Δ at time Δt is therefore:

$$\Delta = \frac{f_{11} - f_{10}}{Su - Sd} \qquad (15.8)$$

To determine gamma, Γ, we note that we have two estimates of Δ at time $2\Delta t$. When $S = (Su^2 + S)/2$ (halfway between the second and third node), delta is $(f_{22} - f_{21})/(Su^2 - S)$; when $S = (S + Sd^2)/2$ (halfway between the first and second node) delta is $(f_{21} - f_{20})/(S - Sd^2)$. The difference between the two values of S is h, where

$$h = 0.5(Su^2 - Sd^2)$$

Gamma is the change in delta divided by h:

$$\Gamma = \frac{[(f_{22} - f_{21})/(Su^2 - S)] - [(f_{21} - f_{20})/(S - Sd^2)]}{h} \qquad (15.9)$$

These procedures provide estimates of delta at time Δt and of gamma at time $2\Delta t$. In practice, these are often used as estimates of delta and gamma at time zero as well. If slightly more accuracy is required for delta and gamma, it makes sense to start the binomial tree at time $-2\Delta t$ and assume that the stock price is S at this time. The required estimate of the price of the option is then f_{21} (rather than f_{00}). More nodes have to be evaluated, but three different values of S are considered at time zero: Sd^2, S, and Su^2. An estimate of delta is

$$\Delta = \frac{f_{22} - f_{20}}{Su^2 - Sd^2}$$

and equation (15.9) provides the estimate of gamma.

A further hedge parameter that can be obtained directly from the tree is theta, Θ. This is the rate of change of the option price with time when all else is kept constant. If the tree starts at time zero, an estimate of theta is

$$\Theta = \frac{f_{21} - f_{00}}{2\Delta t} \qquad (15.10)$$

If the tree starts at time $-2\Delta t$, a symmetrical estimate of theta can be obtained:

$$\Theta = \frac{f_{42} - f_{00}}{4\Delta t}$$

Vega can be calculated by making a small change, $\Delta\sigma$, in the volatility and constructing a new tree to obtain a new value of the option (Δt should be kept the

same). The estimate of vega is

$$\mathcal{V} = \frac{f^* - f}{\Delta\sigma}$$

where f and f^* are the estimates of the option price from the original and the new tree, respectively. Rho can be calculated similarly.

Example 15.2

Consider again Example 15.1. From Figure 15.3 $f_{1,0} = 6.95$ and $f_{1,1} = 2.15$. Equation (15.8) gives an estimate of delta of

$$\frac{2.15 - 6.95}{56.12 - 44.55} = -0.41$$

From equation (15.9), an estimate of the gamma of the option can be obtained from the values at nodes B, C, and F as

$$\frac{[(0.63 - 3.76)/(62.99 - 50.00)] - [(3.76 - 10.35)/(50.00 - 39.69)]}{11.65} = 0.034$$

From equation (15.10), an estimate of the theta of the option can be obtained from the values at nodes D and C as

$$\frac{3.76 - 4.48}{0.1667} = -4.3$$

These are of course only rough estimates. They become progressively better as the number of time steps on the tree is increased.

15.2 USING THE BINOMIAL TREE FOR OPTIONS ON INDICES, CURRENCIES, AND FUTURES CONTRACTS

The binomial tree approach to valuing options on non-dividend-paying stocks can easily be adapted to valuing American calls and puts on a stock providing a continuous dividend yield at rate q. Since the dividends provide a return of q, the stock price itself must on average in a risk-neutral world provide a return of $r - q$. Hence equation (15.1) becomes

$$Se^{(r-q)\Delta t} = pSu + (1 - p)Sd$$

so that (15.2) becomes

$$e^{(r-q)\Delta t} = pu + (1 - p)d$$

It turns out that equations (15.4), (15.5), and (15.6) are still correct but with

$$a = e^{(r-q)\Delta t} \tag{15.11}$$

The binomial tree numerical procedure can therefore be used exactly as before with this new value of a.

It will be recalled from Chapter 12 that stock indices, currencies, and futures contracts can, for the purposes of option evaluation, be considered as stocks paying continuous dividend yields. In the case of a stock index, the relevant dividend yield is the dividend yield on the stock portfolio underlying the index; in the case of a currency, it is the foreign risk-free interest rate; in the case of a futures contract, it is the domestic risk-free interest rate. The binomial tree approach can therefore be used to value options on stock indices, currencies, and futures contracts.

Example 15.3

Consider a four-month American call option on index futures where the current futures price is 300, the exercise price is 300, the risk-free interest rate is 8% per annum, and the volatility of the index is 40% per annum. We divide the life of the option into four 1-month periods for the purposes of constructing the tree. In this case, $F = 300, X = 300$, $r = 0.08, \sigma = 0.4, T = 0.3333$, and $\Delta t = 0.0833$. Since a futures contract is analogous to a stock paying dividends at a continuous rate r, q should be set equal to r in equation (15.11). This gives $a = 1$. The other parameters necessary to construct the tree are

$$u = e^{\sigma \sqrt{\Delta t}} = 1.1224 \qquad d = \frac{1}{u} = 0.8909$$

$$p = \frac{a - d}{u - d} = 0.4713 \qquad 1 - p = 0.5287$$

The tree is shown in Figure 15.4. (The upper number is the futures price; the lower number is the option price.) The estimated value of the option is 25.54.

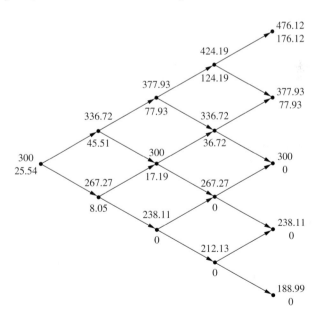

Figure 15.4   Binomial tree for American call option on an index futures contract (Example 15.3).

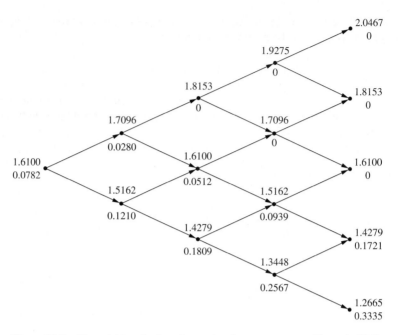

Figure 15.5   Binomial tree for American put option on a currency (Example 15.4).

Example 15.4

Consider a one-year American put option on the British pound. The current exchange rate is 1.6100, the strike price is 1.6000, the U.S. risk-free interest rate is 8% per annum, the sterling risk-free interest rate is 10% per annum, and the volatility of the sterling exchange rate is 12% per annum. In this case, $S = 1.61, X = 1.60, r = 0.08, r_f = 0.10, \sigma = 0.12$, and $T = 1.0$. We divide the life of the option into four 3-month periods for the purposes of constructing the tree so that $\Delta t = 0.25$. In this case $q = r_f$ and equation (15.11) gives

$$a = e^{(0.08-0.10)\times 0.25} = 0.9950$$

The other parameters necessary to construct the tree are

$$u = e^{\sigma\sqrt{\Delta t}} = 1.0618 \qquad d = \frac{1}{u} = 0.9418$$

$$p = \frac{a-d}{u-d} = 0.4433 \qquad 1-p = 0.5567$$

The tree is shown in Figure 15.5. (The upper number is the exchange rate; the lower number is the option price.) The estimated value of the option is $0.0782.

15.3 BINOMIAL MODEL FOR A DIVIDEND-PAYING STOCK

We now move on to the more tricky issue of how the binomial model can be used for a dividend-paying stock. As in Chapter 11, the word *dividend* will, for the

purposes of our discussion, be used to refer to the reduction in the stock price on the ex-dividend date as a result of the dividend.

Known Dividend Yield

If it is assumed that there is a single dividend and the dividend yield, (i.e., the dividend as a proportion of the stock price) is known, then the tree takes the form shown in Figure 15.6 and can be analyzed in a similar manner to that just described. If the time $i\Delta t$ is prior to the stock going ex-dividend, the nodes on the tree correspond to stock prices

$$Su^j d^{i-j} \qquad j = 0, 1, \ldots, i$$

where u and d are defined as in equations (15.5) and (15.6). If the time $i\Delta t$ is after the stock goes ex-dividend, the nodes correspond to stock prices

$$S(1 - \delta)u^j d^{i-j} \qquad j = 0, 1, \ldots, i$$

where δ is the dividend yield. Several known dividend yields during the life of an option can be dealt with similarly. If δ_i is the total dividend yield associated with all ex-dividend dates between time zero and time $i\Delta t$, the nodes at time $i\Delta t$ correspond to stock prices

$$S(1 - \delta_i)u^j d^{i-j}$$

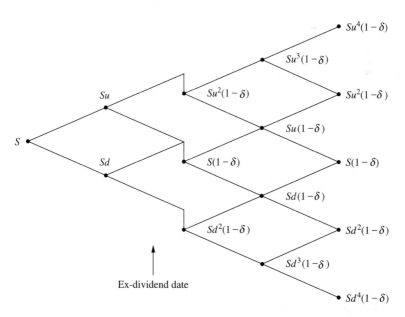

Figure 15.6   Tree when stock pays a known dividend yield at one particular time.

Known Dollar Dividend

In some situations, the most realistic assumption is that the dollar amount of the dividend rather than the dividend yield is known in advance. If the volatility of the stock, σ, is assumed constant, the tree then takes the form shown in Figure 15.7. It does not recombine, which means that the number of nodes that have to be evaluated, particularly if there are several dividends, is liable to become very large. Suppose that there is only one dividend, that the ex-dividend date, τ, is between $k\Delta t$ and $(k + 1)\Delta t$, and that the dollar amount of the dividend is D. When $i \leq k$, the nodes on the tree at time $i\Delta t$ correspond to stock prices

$$Su^j d^{i-j} \qquad j = 0, 1, 2, \ldots, i$$

as before. When $i = k + 1$, the nodes on the tree correspond to stock prices

$$Su^j d^{i-j} - D \qquad j = 0, 1, 2, \ldots, i$$

When $i = k + 2$, the nodes on the tree correspond to stock prices

$$(Su^j d^{i-1-j} - D)u \qquad \text{and} \qquad (Su^j d^{i-1-j} - D)d$$

for $j = 0, 1, 2, \ldots, i - 1$, so that there are $2i$ rather than $i + 1$ nodes. At time $(k + m)\Delta t$, there are $m(k + 1)$ rather than $k + m + 1$ nodes.

The problem can be simplified by assuming, as in the analysis of European options in Section 11.12, that the stock price has two components: a part that is

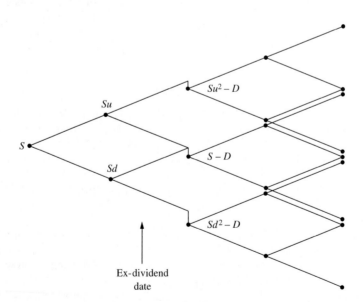

Figure 15.7   Tree when dollar amount of dividend is assumed known and volatility is assumed constant.

uncertain and a part that is the present value of all future dividends during the life of the option. Suppose, as before, that there is only one ex-dividend date, τ, during the life of the option and that $k\Delta t \leq \tau \leq (k + 1)\Delta t$. The value of the uncertain component, S^*, at time $i\Delta t$ is given by

$$S^* = S \qquad \text{when } i\Delta t > \tau$$

and

$$S^* = S - De^{-r(\tau - i\Delta t)} \qquad \text{when } i\Delta t \leq \tau$$

where D is the dividend. Define σ^* as the volatility of S^* and assume that σ^* rather than σ is constant. (In general $\sigma^* > \sigma$.) The parameters p, u, and d can be calculated from equations (15.4), (15.5), (15.6), and (15.7) with σ replaced by σ^* and a tree can be constructed in the usual way to model S^*. By adding to the stock price at each node the present value of future dividends (if any), the tree can be converted into another tree that models S. At time $i\Delta t$, the nodes on this tree correspond to the stock prices

$$S^* u^j d^{i-j} + De^{-r(\tau - i\Delta t)} \qquad j = 0, 1, \ldots, i$$

when $i\Delta t < \tau$ and

$$S^* u^j d^{i-j} \qquad j = 0, 1, \ldots, i$$

when $i\Delta t > \tau$. This approach, which has the advantage of being consistent with the approach for European options in Section 11.12, succeeds in achieving a situation where the tree recombines so that there are $i + 1$ nodes at time $i\Delta t$. It can be generalized in a straightforward way to deal with the situation where there are several dividends.

Example 15.5

Consider a five-month put option on a stock that is expected to pay a single dividend of $2.06 during the life of the option. The initial stock price is $52, the strike price is $50, the risk-free interest rate is 10% per annum, the volatility is 40% per annum, and the ex-dividend date is in $3\frac{1}{2}$ months.

We first construct a tree to model S^*, the stock price less the present value of future dividends during the life of the option. Initially, the present value of the dividend is

$$2.06e^{-0.2917 \times 0.1} = 2.00$$

The initial value of S^* is therefore 50.0. Assuming that the 40% per annum volatility refers to S^*, Figure 15.3 provides a binomial tree for S^*. (S^* has the same initial value and volatility as the stock price upon which Figure 15.3 was based.) Adding the present value of the dividend at each node leads to Figure 15.8, which is a binomial model for S. The probabilities at each node are, as in Figure 15.3, 0.5076 for an up movement and 0.4924 for a down movement. Working back through the tree in the usual way gives the option price as $4.43.

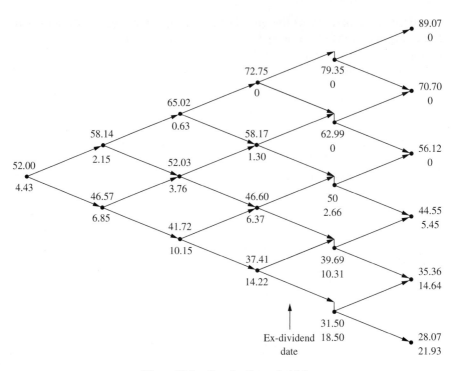

Figure 15.8   Tree for Example 15.5.

15.4 EXTENSIONS OF THE BASIC TREE APPROACH

In Chapter 18 we describe how tree approaches can be extended to handle options dependent on two underlying variables and some types of path-dependent derivatives. We also discuss how they can be used to value barrier options. Here we point out some relatively minor extensions of the basic methodology.

Time-Dependent Interest Rates

The usual assumption when American options are being valued is that interest rates are constant. When the term structure is steeply upward or downward sloping, this may not be a satisfactory assumption. It is more appropriate to assume that the interest rate for a period of length Δt in the future equals the current forward interest rate for that period. The process for a non-dividend-paying stock is then

$$\frac{dS}{S} = r(t)\,dt + \sigma\,dz$$

We can construct a binomial tree as before with a being a function of time:

$$a(t) = e^{r(t)\Delta t} \tag{15.12}$$

This does not change the geometry of the tree since u and d do not depend on a. The probabilities at the nodes are[4]

$$p = \frac{a(t) - d}{u - d}$$

$$1 - p = \frac{u - a(t)}{u - d}$$

A similar modification of the basic tree can be used to value index options, foreign exchange options, and futures options.

Commodity Prices

As explained in Section 13.5, the average growth rate in a commodity price in a risk-neutral world can be deduced from futures prices. If it is assumed that the commodity price has a constant volatility and a drift rate that is independent of its price, the process for the commodity price has the form

$$\frac{dS}{S} = \mu(t)\, dt + \sigma\, dz$$

This can be represented in the form of a tree using the same approach as that just described for a stock with a time-dependent interest rate. In practice, commodity prices seem to exhibit some mean reversion. To reflect mean reversion in the tree we can use a trinomial tree approach similar to that described in Chapter 17 for interest rates.

Control Variate Technique

A technique known as the *control variate technique* can be used for the evaluation of an American option.[5] This involves using the same tree to calculate both the value of the American option, f_A, and the value of the corresponding European option, f_E. We also calculate the Black–Scholes price of the European option, f_{BS}. The error given by the tree in the pricing of the European option is assumed equal to that given by the tree in the pricing of the American option. This gives the estimate of the price of the American option to be

$$f_A + f_{BS} - f_E$$

To illustrate this approach, Figure 15.9 values the option in Figure 15.3 on the assumption that it is European. The price obtained is \$4.31. From the Black–Scholes formula, the true European price of the option is \$4.08. The estimate of the American price in Figure 15.3 is \$4.48. The control variate estimate of the

---

[4]For a sufficiently large number of time steps, these probabilities are always positive.

[5]See J. Hull and A. White, "The Use of the Control Variate Technique in Option Pricing," *Journal of Financial and Quantitative Analysis*, 23 (September 1988), 237–51.

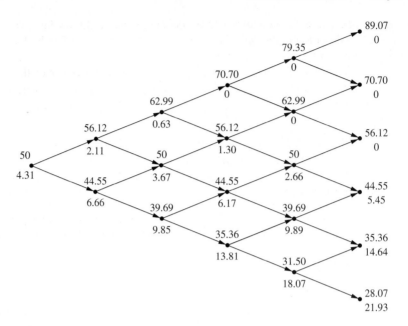

Figure 15.9   Tree for European version of option in Figure 15.3. At each node, the upper number is the stock price, and the lower number is the option price.

American price is therefore

$$4.48 + 4.08 - 4.31 = 4.25$$

The true American price, as mentioned earlier, is 4.29. The control variate approach does therefore produce a considerable improvement over the basic tree estimate of 4.48 in this case. The control variate technique in effect involves using the tree to calculate the difference between the European and the American price rather than the American price itself. We will give a further application of the technique when we discuss Monte Carlo simulation later in this chapter.

15.5 ALTERNATIVE PROCEDURES FOR CONSTRUCTING TREES

The original Cox, Ross, and Rubinstein approach is not the only way of building a binomial tree. Instead of imposing the assumption $u = 1/d$ on equations (15.2) and (15.3), we can set $p = 0.5$. A solution to the equations when terms of higher order than Δt are ignored is then

$$u = e^{(r-\sigma^2/2)\Delta t + \sigma\sqrt{\Delta t}}$$

$$d = e^{(r-\sigma^2/2)\Delta t - \sigma\sqrt{\Delta t}}$$

When the stock provides a continuous dividend yield equal to q, the variable r becomes $r - q$ in these formulas. This allows trees with $p = 0.5$ to be built for indices, foreign exchange, and futures.

This alternative tree-building procedure has the advantage over the Cox, Ross, and Rubinstein that the probabilities are always 0.5 regardless of the value of σ or the number of time steps.[6] Its disadvantage is that it is not as easy to calculate delta, gamma, and rho from the tree.

Example 15.6

Consider a nine-month American call option on the Canadian dollar. The current exchange rate is 0.7900, the strike price is 0.8000, the U.S. risk-free interest rate is 6% per annum, the Canadian risk-free interest rate is 10% per annum, and the volatility of the exchange rate is 4% per annum. In this case, $S = 0.79$, $X = 0.80$, $r = 0.06$, $r_f = 0.10$, $\sigma = 0.04$, and $T = 0.75$. We divide the life of the option into three-month periods for the purposes of constructing the tree so that $\Delta t = 0.25$. We set the probabilities on each branch to 0.5 and

$$u = e^{(0.06-0.10-0.0016/2)0.25+0.04\sqrt{0.25}} = 1.0098$$

$$d = e^{(0.06-0.10-0.0016/2)0.25-0.04\sqrt{0.25}} = 0.9703$$

The tree for the exchange rate is shown in Figure 15.10. The tree gives the value of the option as $0.0016.

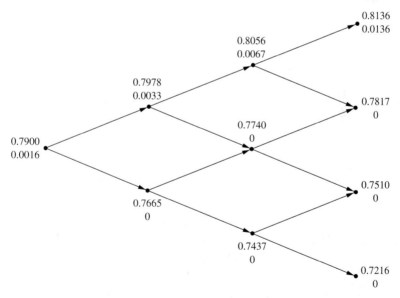

Figure 15.10   Binomial tree for American call option on the Canadian dollar. At each node, the uppermost number is the spot exchange rate and the lower number is the option price. All probabilities are 0.5.

---

[6]The Cox, Ross, and Rubinstein tree has the disadvantage that it leads to negative probabilities when $\sigma < |(r - q)\sqrt{\Delta t}|$. The alternative procedure described here does not have this drawback.

Trinomial Trees

Trinomial trees can be used as an alternative to binomial trees. The general form of the tree is as shown in Figure 15.11. Suppose that p_u, p_m, and p_d are the probabilities of up, middle, and down movements at each node and Δt is the length of the time step. For a non-dividend-paying stock, parameter values that match the mean and standard deviation of price changes when terms of higher order than Δt are ignored are

$$u = e^{\sigma \sqrt{3\Delta t}}$$

$$d = \frac{1}{u}$$

$$p_d = -\sqrt{\frac{\Delta t}{12\sigma^2}}\left(r - \frac{\sigma^2}{2}\right) + \frac{1}{6}$$

$$p_m = \frac{2}{3}$$

$$p_u = \sqrt{\frac{\Delta t}{12\sigma^2}}\left(r - \frac{\sigma^2}{2}\right) + \frac{1}{6}$$

For a stock paying a continuous dividend at rate q, we replace r by $r - q$ in these equations. Calculations for a trinomial tree are analogous to those for a binomial tree. The trinomial tree approach proves to be equivalent to the explicit finite difference method, described in Section 15.8.

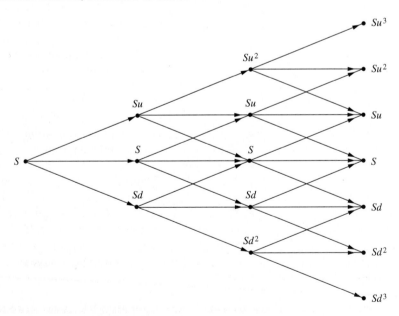

Figure 15.11   Trinomial stock price tree.

15.6 MONTE CARLO SIMULATION

We will use the term *European-style derivative* to describe a derivative where
the holder has no decisions to make during its life, and the term *American-style
derivative* to refer to a derivative where there are early exercise or other decisions
that may have to be made. Consider a European-style derivative that pays off f_T
at time T. From equation (13.15), its value at time zero is given by

$$f = \hat{E}(f_T e^{-\bar{r}T}) \tag{15.13}$$

where $\hat{E}$ denotes expectations in a risk-neutral world and $\bar{r}$ is the average instantaneous risk-free interest rate between time zero and time T. If the risk-free interest
rate is assumed to be known with certainty, equation (15.13) simplifies to

$$f = e^{-\bar{r}T}\hat{E}(f_T) \tag{15.14}$$

and $\bar{r}$ equals the yield on a zero-coupon bond maturing at time T. Monte Carlo
simulation is a procedure for estimating the value of a European-style derivative
from either equation (15.13) or (15.14).

One Underlying Variable

Consider first the situation where a derivative depends on only one underlying stochastic variable. Suppose first that this is not an interest rate, so that
equation (15.14) can be used. One possible path for the variable is simulated
in a risk-neutral world using a method similar to that described in Section 10.4
for simulating a stock price. This enables a payoff for the derivative to be calculated. This payoff can be regarded as a random sample from the set of all possible
payoffs. A second path for the variable is sampled and a second sample payoff obtained. Further sample paths give further sample payoffs. After a large number,
say 10,000, payoffs have been calculated, $\hat{E}(f_T)$ can be estimated as the arithmetic average of them. The current value of the derivative can then be calculated
using equation (15.14). Alternatively, we can discount each sample payoff as it
is calculated and then take the arithmetic average of the results. The calculation
of a single payoff or discounted payoff will be referred to as a *simulation trial*.
Thus the simulation just described consists of 10,000 simulation trials.

If the variable is the short-term risk-free interest rate, r, or some variable
related to r, the Monte Carlo simulation procedure is similar to that just described
except that the discount rate is different for each trial. Paths for r in a risk-neutral
world are simulated. On each simulation trial, both the average value of r during
the life of the derivative and the payoff from the derivative must be calculated.
Before proceeding to the next simulation trial, the payoff from the derivative must
be discounted at this average value of r and the result stored. After a large number
of simulation trials, the arithmetic average of the discounted payoffs is calculated.
From equation (15.13), this provides an estimate of f.

To describe Monte Carlo simulation more formally when there is one un-
derlying variable, we suppose that the variable is θ. Define s as the volatility of θ

and $\hat{m}$ as its growth rate in a risk-neutral world. For the purposes of carrying out the simulation, the life of the derivative is divided into N subintervals of length Δt. The discrete version of the process for θ in a risk-neutral world is

$$\Delta\theta = \hat{m}\theta\Delta t + s\theta\epsilon\sqrt{\Delta t} \qquad (15.15)$$

where $\Delta\theta$ is the change in θ in time Δt and ϵ is a random sample from a standardized normal distribution.[7] To carry out one simulation trial, N independent random samples must be drawn from a standardized normal distribution. When these are substituted into equation (15.15), the values of $\Delta\theta$ at times $0, \Delta t, 2\Delta t, \ldots, T$ are calculated. This provides a simulated path for θ and enables a sample payoff for the derivative to be calculated.

Several Underlying Variables

When there are several variables, the paths of each one must be sampled on each simulation trial. The payoff from the derivative is calculated on each simulation trial from the sample paths. If the instantaneous risk-free interest rate, r, is a function of the state variables, the average value of r, $\bar{r}$, must also be calculated on each simulation trial. The payoff is discounted at $\bar{r}$ before the next simulation trial is begun. It should be emphasized that the stochastic processes for all variables, including r, must, for the purposes of the simulation, be the processes that the variables would follow in a risk-neutral world.

Suppose that there are n variables, $\theta_i (1 \leq i \leq n)$. Define s_i as the volatility of θ_i, $\hat{m}_i$ as the expected growth rate of θ_i in a risk-neutral world, and ρ_{ik} as the instantaneous correlation between θ_i and θ_k. As in the single-variable case, the life of the derivative must be divided into N subintervals of length Δt. The discrete version of the process for θ_i is then

$$\Delta\theta_i = \hat{m}_i\theta_i\Delta t + s_i\theta_i\epsilon_i\sqrt{\Delta t} \qquad (15.16)$$

where $\Delta\theta_i$ is the change in θ_i in time Δt and ϵ_i is a random sample from a standardized normal distribution. The coefficient of correlation between ϵ_i and ϵ_k is ρ_{ik} for $1 \leq i, k \leq n$. One simulation trial involves obtaining N samples of the $\epsilon_i (1 \leq i \leq n)$ from a multivariate standardized normal distribution. These are substituted into equation (15.16) to produce simulated paths for each θ_i and enable a sample value for the derivative to be calculated.

Monte Carlo simulation can without difficulty be extended to cover situations where payoffs occur at different times during the life of a derivative, but it cannot easily be used for American-style derivatives.

---

[7]When θ follows geometric Brownian motion (i.e., $\hat{m}$ and s are constant), it is slightly more accurate to assume that $(\theta + \Delta\theta)/\theta$ is lognormally distributed. Using the results in Section 11.1, it can be shown that equation (15.15) becomes

$$\theta + \Delta\theta = \theta\exp\left[\left(\hat{m} - \frac{s^2}{2}\right)\Delta t + s\epsilon\sqrt{\Delta t}\right]$$

Generating the Random Samples

Most programming languages incorporate routines for sampling a random number between 0 and 1. An approximate sample from a univariate standardized normal distribution can be obtained from the formula

$$\epsilon = \sum_{i=1}^{12} R_i - 6 \tag{15.17}$$

where the R_i are independent random numbers between 0 and 1 $(1 \leq i \leq 12)$ and ϵ is the required sample from $\phi(0, 1)$. This approximation is satisfactory for most purposes.

If samples from a standardized bivariate normal distribution are required, an appropriate procedure is as follows. Independent samples x_1 and x_2 from a univariate standardized normal distribution are obtained as just described. The required samples ϵ_1 and ϵ_2 are then calculated as follows:

$$\epsilon_1 = x_1$$

$$\epsilon_2 = \rho x_1 + x_2 \sqrt{1 - \rho^2}$$

where ρ is the correlation between the variables in the bivariate distribution.

For an n-variate normal distribution where the coefficient of correlation between variable i and variable j is $\rho_{i,j}$, we first sample n independent variables x_i $(1 \leq i \leq n)$ from univariate standardized normal distributions. The required samples are ϵ_i $(1 \leq i \leq n)$, where

$$\epsilon_i = \sum_{k=1}^{k=i} \alpha_{ik} x_k$$

For ϵ_i to have the correct variance and the correct correlation with the ϵ_j $(1 \leq j < i)$, we must have

$$\sum_k \alpha_{ik}^2 = 1$$

and

$$\sum_k \alpha_{ik} \alpha_{jk} = \rho_{i,j}$$

The first sample, ϵ_1, is set equal to x_1. These equations for the α's can be solved so the ϵ_2 is calculated from x_1 and x_2, ϵ_3 is calculated from x_1, x_2, and x_3, and so on.[8]

---

[8] If the equations for the α's do not have real solutions, the assumed correlation structure is impossible. An example of an impossible correlation structure when $n = 3$ is $\rho_{12} = 0.9$, $\rho_{13} = 0.9$, and $\rho_{23} = 0$.

Number of Trials

The number of simulation trials carried out depends on the accuracy required. If M independent trials are carried out as described above, it is usual to calculate the standard deviation as well as the mean of the discounted payoffs given by the simulation trials for the derivative. Denote the mean by μ and the standard deviation by ω. The variable μ is the simulation's estimate of the value of the derivative. The standard error of the estimate is

$$\frac{\omega}{\sqrt{M}}$$

A 95% confidence interval for the price, f, of the derivative is therefore given by

$$\mu - \frac{1.96\omega}{\sqrt{M}} < f < \mu + \frac{1.96\omega}{\sqrt{M}}$$

This shows that our uncertainty about the value of the derivative is inversely proportional to the square root of the number of trials. To double the accuracy of a simulation, we must quadruple the number of trials; to increase the accuracy by a factor of 10, the number of trials must increase by a factor of 100; and so on.

Applications

Monte Carlo simulation tends to be numerically more efficient than other procedures when there are three or more stochastic variables. This is because the time taken to carry out a Monte Carlo simulation increases approximately linearly with the number of variables, whereas the time taken for most other procedures increases exponentially with the number of variables. Monte Carlo simulation has the advantage that it provides a standard error for the estimates that are made. It is an approach that can accommodate complex payoffs and complex stochastic processes. It can be used when the payoff depends on some function of the whole path followed by a variable, not just its terminal value. A limitation of the Monte Carlo simulation approach is that it can be used only for European-style derivatives.

Hedge parameters can be calculated using Monte Carlo simulation. Suppose that we are interested in the rate of change of f with q, where f is the value of the derivative and q is the value of an underlying variable or a parameter. First, Monte Carlo simulation is used in the usual way to calculate an estimate, f, for the value of the derivative. A small increase, Δq, is then made in the value of q, and a new value for the derivative, f^*, is calculated *using the same random number streams* as for f. An estimate for the hedge parameter is given by

$$\frac{f^* - f}{\Delta q}$$

The number of time intervals, N, should be kept the same for estimating both f and f^*.

15.7 VARIANCE REDUCTION PROCEDURES

If the simulation is carried out as described so far, a very large value of M is usually necessary to estimate f with reasonable accuracy. This is expensive in terms of computation time. In this section we examine a number of variance reduction procedures that can lead to dramatic savings.

Antithetic Variable Technique

In the antithetic variable technique, a simulation trial involves calculating two values of the derivative. The first value, f_1, is calculated in the usual way; the second value, f_2, is calculated by changing the sign of all the samples from standard normal distributions. (If ϵ is the sample used to calculate the first value, $-\epsilon$ is used to calculate the second value.) The sample value of the derivative calculated from the simulation trial is the average of the two calculated values. This works well because when one value is above the true value, the other tends to be below, and vice versa.

Denote $\overline{f}$ as the average of f_1 and f_2:

$$\overline{f} = \frac{f_1 + f_2}{2}$$

The final estimate of the value of the derivative is the average of the $\overline{f}$'s. If ω is the standard deviation of the $\overline{f}$'s, and M is the number of simulation trials (i.e., the number of pairs of values calculated), the standard error of the estimate is $\omega / \sqrt{M}$.

Control Variate Technique

We have already given one example of the control variate technique in connection with the use of trees to value American options (see Section 15.4). The control variate technique is applicable when there are two similar derivatives, A and B. Security A is the security under consideration; security B is a security that is similar to security A and for which an analytic solution is available. Two simulations using the same random number streams and the same Δt are carried out in parallel. The first is used to obtain an estimate, f_A^*, of the value of A; the second is used to obtain an estimate, f_B^*, of the value of B. A better estimate of the value of A, f_A, is then obtained using the formula

$$f_A = f_A^* - f_B^* + f_B \tag{15.18}$$

where f_B is the known true value of B. Hull and White provide an example of the use of the control variate technique when evaluating the effect of stochastic volatility on the price of a European call option.[9] In this case, f_A is the value

[9]See J. Hull and A. White, "The Pricing of Options on Assets with Stochastic Volatilities," *Journal of Finance*, 42 (June 1987), 281–300.

of the option assuming stochastic volatility and f_B is its value assuming constant volatility. The latter is known analytically.

Importance Sampling

Importance sampling is best explained with an example. Suppose that we wish to calculate the price of a deep-out-of-the-money call option with strike price X. If we sample paths in the usual way, most of the paths will lead to zero payoff. This is a waste of computation time since the zero-payoff paths contribute very little to the determination of the value of the option. We therefore try to choose only important paths, that is, paths where the stock price is above X at maturity.

If F is the unconditional probability distribution function for the stock price and k is the probability (known analytically) of the stock price being greater than X at maturity, then $G = F/k$ is the probability distribution of the stock price conditional on the stock price being greater than X. To implement importance sampling, we sample from G rather than F. The estimate of the value of the option is the average discounted payoff multiplied by k.

Stratified Sampling

Stratified sampling involves dividing the underlying probability distribution into ranges or intervals and sampling from each interval according to its probability. If a large number of intervals are used, the mean or median conditional on being in an interval can be used as a representative value for the interval. (When sampling from the interval, we then always pick its representative value.) Curran shows results from using this procedure to value both European call options and path-dependent options.[10] In the case of a standard normal distribution when there are n intervals, we can calculate the representative value for the ith interval as

$$N^{-1}\left(\frac{i - 0.5}{n}\right)$$

where N^{-1} is the inverse cumulative normal distribution. For example, when $n = 4$ the representative values corresponding to the four intervals are $N^{-1}(0.125)$, $N^{-1}(0.375)$, $N^{-1}(0.625)$, $N^{-1}(0.875)$. The function N^{-1} can be calculated iteratively using the approximation to the N given in Section 11.8. An alternative approach is suggested by Moro.[11]

Moment Matching

Moment matching involves adjusting the samples taken from a standardized normal distribution so that the first, second, and possibly higher, moments

---

[10] See M. Curran, "Strata Gems," *RISK,* March 1994, pp. 70–71.

[11] See B. Moro, "The Full Monte," *RISK,* February 1985, pp. 57–58.

are matched. Suppose that the normal distribution samples used to calculate the change in the value of a particular variable over a particular time period are ϵ_i $(1 \leq i \leq n)$. To match the first two moments, we calculate the mean of the samples, m, and the standard deviation of the samples, s. We then define adjusted samples y_i $(1 \leq i \leq n)$ as

$$y_i = \frac{\epsilon_i - m}{s}$$

These adjusted samples have the correct mean of zero and the correct standard deviation of 1.0. We use the adjusted samples for all calculations.

Moment matching saves computation time but can lead to memory problems since every number sampled must be stored until the end of the simulation. Moment matching is sometimes also termed *quadratic resampling*. It is often used in conjunction with the antithetic variable technique. Since the latter automatically matches all odd moments, the goal of moment matching then becomes that of matching the second moment and possibly the fourth moment.

Using Quasi-Random Sequences

A quasi-random sequence (also called a *low-discrepancy* sequence) is a sequence of representative samples from a probability distribution.[12] Descriptions of the use of quasi-random sequences appear in Joy et al., Brotherton-Ratcliffe, and Press et al.[13] Quasi-random sequences have the advantage that the standard error is proportional to $1/M$ rather than $1/\sqrt{M}$, where M is the sample size.

Quasi-random sampling is similar to stratified sampling. The objective is to sample representative values for the underlying variables. In stratified sampling it is assumed that we know in advance how many samples will be taken. A quasi-random sampling scheme is more flexible. The samples are taken in such a way that we are always "filling in" gaps between existing samples. At each stage of the simulation the points sampled are roughly evenly spaced throughout the probability space.

Figure 15.12 shows points generated in two dimensions using a procedure suggested by Sobol'.[14] It can be seen that successive points do tend to fill in the gaps left by previous points.

---

[12] The term *quasi-random* is a misnomer. A quasi-random sequence is totally deterministic.

[13] See C. Joy, P. P. Boyle, and K. S. Tan, "Quasi Monte Carlo Methods in Numerical Finance," Working Paper, University of Waterloo, Waterloo, Ontario N2L 3G1; R. Brotherton-Ratcliffe, "Monte Carlo Motoring," *RISK*, December 1994, pp. 53–58; W. H. Press, S. A. Teukolsky, W. T. Vetterling, and B. P. Flannery, *Numerical Recipes in C: The Art of Scientific Computing*, 2nd ed. (Cambridge: Cambridge University Press, 1992).

[14] See I. M. Sobol', *USSR Computational Mathematics and Mathematical Physics*, 7, 4 (1967), 86–112. A description of Sobol's procedure is in Press et al. (1992).

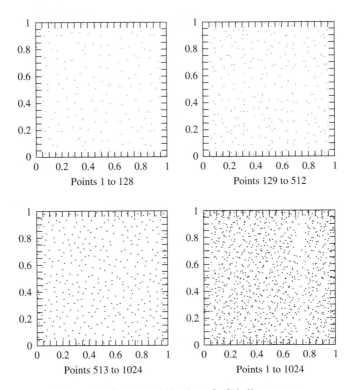

Figure 15.12 First 1024 points of a Sobol' sequence.

15.8 FINITE DIFFERENCE METHODS

Finite difference methods value a derivative by solving the differential equation that the derivative satisfies. The differential equation is converted into a set of difference equations and the difference equations are solved iteratively.

To illustrate the approach, we consider how it might be used to value an American put option on a non-dividend-paying stock. The differential equation that the option must satisfy is

$$\frac{\partial f}{\partial t} + rS\frac{\partial f}{\partial S} + \frac{1}{2}\sigma^2 S^2 \frac{\partial^2 f}{\partial S^2} = rf \qquad (15.19)$$

A number of equally spaced times between the current time, zero, and the maturity of the option, T, are chosen. We suppose that $\Delta t = T/N$ and consider the following $N + 1$ times:

$$0, \Delta t, 2\Delta t, \ldots, T$$

A number of equally spaced stock prices are also chosen. We suppose that $S_{\max}$ is a stock price which is sufficiently high that, when it is reached, the put has

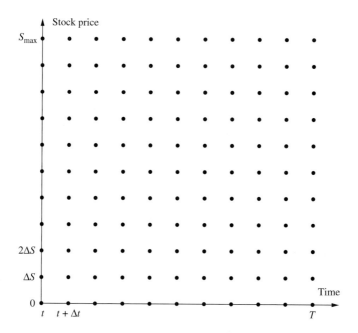

Figure 15.13   Grid for finite difference approach.

virtually no value. We define $\Delta S = S_{\max}/M$ and consider a total of $M + 1$ stock prices:

$$0, \Delta S, 2\,\Delta S, \ldots, S_{\max}$$

One of these is assumed to be the current stock price.

This general approach is represented diagrammatically in Figure 15.13. A grid consisting of a total of $(M + 1)(N + 1)$ points is constructed. The (i, j) point on the grid is the point that corresponds to time $i\Delta t$ and stock price $j\Delta S$. We will use the variable $f_{i,j}$ to denote the value of the option at the (i, j) point.

Implicit Finite Difference Method

For an interior point (i, j) on the grid, $\partial f/\partial S$ can be approximated as

$$\frac{\partial f}{\partial S} = \frac{f_{i,j+1} - f_{i,j}}{\Delta S} \tag{15.20}$$

or as

$$\frac{\partial f}{\partial S} = \frac{f_{i,j} - f_{i,j-1}}{\Delta S} \tag{15.21}$$

Equation (15.20) is known as the *forward difference approximation*; equation (15.21) is known as the *backward difference approximation*. We use a more

symmetrical approximation by averaging the two:

$$\frac{\partial f}{\partial S} = \frac{f_{i,j+1} - f_{i,j-1}}{2\,\Delta S} \tag{15.22}$$

For $\partial f/\partial t$ we will use a forward difference approximation so that the value at time $i\Delta t$ is related to the value at time $(i + 1)\Delta t$:

$$\frac{\partial f}{\partial t} = \frac{f_{i+1,j} - f_{i,j}}{\Delta t} \tag{15.23}$$

The backward difference approximation for $\partial f/\partial S$ at the (i, j) point is given by equation (15.21). The backward difference at the $(i, j + 1)$ point is

$$\frac{f_{i,j+1} - f_{i,j}}{\Delta S}$$

Hence a finite difference approximation for $\partial^2 f/\partial S^2$ at the (i, j) point is

$$\frac{\partial^2 f}{\partial S^2} = \left(\frac{f_{i,j+1} - f_{i,j}}{\Delta S} - \frac{f_{i,j} - f_{i,j-1}}{\Delta S} \right) \bigg/ \Delta S$$

or

$$\frac{\partial^2 f}{\partial S^2} = \frac{f_{i,j+1} + f_{i,j-1} - 2f_{i,j}}{\Delta S^2} \tag{15.24}$$

Substituting equations (15.22), (15.23), and (15.24) into the differential equation (15.19) and noting that $S = j\Delta S$ gives

$$\frac{f_{i+1,j} - f_{i,j}}{\Delta t} + rj\,\Delta S\frac{f_{i,j+1} - f_{i,j-1}}{2\,\Delta S} + \tfrac{1}{2}\sigma^2 j^2 \Delta S^2 \frac{f_{i,j+1} + f_{i,j-1} - 2f_{i,j}}{\Delta S^2} = rf_{i,j}$$

for $j = 1, 2, \ldots, M - 1$ and $i = 0, 1, \ldots, N - 1$. Rearranging terms, we obtain

$$a_j f_{i,j-1} + b_j f_{i,j} + c_j f_{i,j+1} = f_{i+1,j} \tag{15.25}$$

where

$$a_j = \tfrac{1}{2}rj\Delta t - \tfrac{1}{2}\sigma^2 j^2 \Delta t$$

$$b_j = 1 + \sigma^2 j^2 \Delta t + r\Delta t$$

$$c_j = -\tfrac{1}{2}rj\Delta t - \tfrac{1}{2}\sigma^2 j^2 \Delta t$$

The value of the put at time T is $\max[X - S_T, 0]$ where S_T is the stock price at time T. Hence

$$f_{N,j} = \max[X - j\Delta S, 0] \qquad j = 0, 1, \ldots, M \tag{15.26}$$

The value of the put option when the stock price is zero is X. Hence

$$f_{i,0} = X \qquad i = 0, 1, \ldots, N \tag{15.27}$$

The value of the option tends to zero as the stock price tends to infinity. We may therefore use the approximation

$$f_{i,M} = 0 \qquad i = 0, 1, \ldots, N \tag{15.28}$$

Equations (15.26), (15.27), and (15.28) define the value of the put option along the three edges of the grid in Figure 15.13, where $S = 0$, $S = S_{\max}$, and $t = T$. It remains to use Equation (15.25) to arrive at the value of f at all other points. First the points corresponding to time $T - \Delta t$ are tackled. Equation (15.25) with $i = N - 1$ gives $M - 1$ simultaneous equations:

$$a_j f_{N-1,j-1} + b_j f_{N-1,j} + c_j f_{N-1,j+1} = f_{N,j} \tag{15.29}$$

for $j = 1, 2, \ldots, M - 1$. The right-hand sides of these equations are known from equation (15.26). Furthermore, from equations (15.27) and (15.28),

$$f_{N-1,0} = X \tag{15.30}$$

$$f_{N-1,M} = 0 \tag{15.31}$$

Thus equations (15.29) are $M - 1$ equations which can be solved for the $M - 1$ unknowns: $f_{N-1,1}, f_{N-1,2}, \ldots, f_{N-1,M-1}$.[15] After this has been done, each value of $f_{N-1,j}$ is compared with $X - j\Delta S$. If $f_{N-1,j} < X - j\Delta S$, early exercise at time $T - \Delta t$ is optimal and $f_{N-1,j}$ is set equal to $X - j\Delta S$. The nodes corresponding to time $T - 2\Delta t$ are handled in a similar way, and so on. Eventually, $f_{0,1}, f_{0,2}, f_{0,3}, \ldots, f_{0,M-1}$ are obtained. One of these is the option price of interest.

The control variate technique can be used in conjunction with finite difference methods. The same grid is used to value an option that is similar to the one under consideration but for which an analytic valuation is available. Equation (15.18) is then used.

Example 15.7

Table 15.1 shows the result of using the implicit finite difference method as just described for pricing the option in Example 15.1. Values of 20, 10, and 5 were chosen for M, N, and ΔS, respectively. Thus the option price is evaluated at \$5 stock price intervals between \$0 and \$100 and at half-month time intervals throughout the life of the option. The option price given by the grid is \$4.07. The same grid gives the price of the corresponding European option as \$3.91. The true European price given by the Black–Scholes formula is \$4.08. The control variate estimate of the American price is therefore

$$4.07 + 4.08 - 3.91 = \$4.24$$

This is reasonably close to the true value of \$4.29.

---

[15]This does not involve inverting a matrix. The first equation in (15.29) can be used to express $f_{N-1,2}$ in terms of $f_{N-1,1}$; the second equation can be used to express $f_{N-1,3}$ in terms of $f_{N-1,1}$; and so on. The final equation provides a value for $f_{N-1,1}$, which can then be used to determine the other $f_{N-1,j}$.

TABLE 15.1 Grid to Value Option in Example 15.1 Using Implicit Finite Difference Methods

Stock Price (dollars)	Time to Maturity (Months)										
	5	$4\frac{1}{2}$	4	$3\frac{1}{2}$	3	$2\frac{1}{2}$	2	$1\frac{1}{2}$	1	$\frac{1}{2}$	0
100	0.00	0.00	0.00	0.00	0.00	0.00	0.00	0.00	0.00	0.00	0.00
95	0.02	0.02	0.01	0.01	0.00	0.00	0.00	0.00	0.00	0.00	0.00
90	0.05	0.04	0.03	0.02	0.01	0.01	0.00	0.00	0.00	0.00	0.00
85	0.09	0.07	0.05	0.03	0.02	0.01	0.01	0.00	0.00	0.00	0.00
80	0.16	0.12	0.09	0.07	0.04	0.03	0.02	0.01	0.00	0.00	0.00
75	0.27	0.22	0.17	0.13	0.09	0.06	0.03	0.02	0.01	0.00	0.00
70	0.47	0.39	0.32	0.25	0.18	0.13	0.08	0.04	0.02	0.00	0.00
65	0.82	0.71	0.60	0.49	0.38	0.28	0.19	0.11	0.05	0.02	0.00
60	1.42	1.27	1.11	0.95	0.78	0.62	0.45	0.30	0.16	0.05	0.00
55	2.43	2.24	2.05	1.83	1.61	1.36	1.09	0.81	0.51	0.22	0.00
50	4.07	3.88	3.67	3.45	3.19	2.91	2.57	2.17	1.66	0.99	0.00
45	6.58	6.44	6.29	6.13	5.96	5.77	5.57	5.36	5.17	5.02	5.00
40	10.15	10.10	10.05	10.01	10.00	10.00	10.00	10.00	10.00	10.00	10.00
35	15.00	15.00	15.00	15.00	15.00	15.00	15.00	15.00	15.00	15.00	15.00
30	20.00	20.00	20.00	20.00	20.00	20.00	20.00	20.00	20.00	20.00	20.00
25	25.00	25.00	25.00	25.00	25.00	25.00	25.00	25.00	25.00	25.00	25.00
20	30.00	30.00	30.00	30.00	30.00	30.00	30.00	30.00	30.00	30.00	30.00
15	35.00	35.00	35.00	35.00	35.00	35.00	35.00	35.00	35.00	35.00	35.00
10	40.00	40.00	40.00	40.00	40.00	40.00	40.00	40.00	40.00	40.00	40.00
5	45.00	45.00	45.00	45.00	45.00	45.00	45.00	45.00	45.00	45.00	45.00
0	50.00	50.00	50.00	50.00	50.00	50.00	50.00	50.00	50.00	50.00	50.00

Explicit Finite Difference Method

The implicit finite difference method has the advantage that it is very robust. It always converges to the solution of the differential equation as ΔS and Δt approach zero.[16] One of the disadvantages of the implicit finite difference method is that $M - 1$ simultaneous equations have to be solved in order to calculate the $f_{i,j}$'s from the $f_{i+1,j}$'s. The method can be simplified if the values of $\partial f/\partial S$ and $\partial^2 f/\partial S^2$ at point (i, j) on the grid are assumed to be the same as at point $(i + 1, j)$. Equations (15.22) and (15.24) then become

$$\frac{\partial f}{\partial S} = \frac{f_{i+1,j+1} - f_{i+1,j-1}}{2\,\Delta S}$$

$$\frac{\partial^2 f}{\partial S^2} = \frac{f_{i+1,j+1} + f_{i+1,j-1} - 2f_{i+1,j}}{\Delta S^2}$$

The difference equation is

$$\frac{f_{i+1,j} - f_{i,j}}{\Delta t} + rj\Delta S \frac{f_{i+1,j+1} - f_{i+1,j-1}}{2\Delta S}$$

$$+ \frac{1}{2}\sigma^2 j^2 \Delta S^2 \frac{f_{i+1,j+1} + f_{i+1,j-1} - 2f_{i+1,j}}{\Delta S^2} = rf_{i,j}$$

or

$$f_{i,j} = a_j^* f_{i+1,j-1} + b_j^* f_{i+1,j} + c_j^* f_{i+1,j+1} \tag{15.32}$$

where

$$a_j^* = \frac{1}{1 + r\Delta t}\left(-\tfrac{1}{2}rj\Delta t + \tfrac{1}{2}\sigma^2 j^2 \Delta t\right)$$

$$b_j^* = \frac{1}{1 + r\Delta t}(1 - \sigma^2 j^2 \Delta t)$$

$$c_j^* = \frac{1}{1 + r\Delta t}\left(\tfrac{1}{2}rj\Delta t + \tfrac{1}{2}\sigma^2 j^2 \Delta t\right)$$

This creates what is known as the *explicit finite difference method*. Figure 15.14 shows the difference between the implicit and explicit methods. The implicit method leads to equation (15.25), which gives a relationship between three different values of the option at time $i\Delta t$ (i.e., $f_{i,j-1}$, $f_{i,j}$, and $f_{i,j+1}$) and one value of the option at time $(i + 1)\Delta t$ (i.e., $f_{i+1,j}$). The explicit method leads to equation (15.32), which gives a relationship between one value of the option at time $i\Delta t$ (i.e., $f_{i,j}$) and three difference values of the option at time $(i + 1)\Delta t$ (i.e., $f_{i+1,j-1}$, $f_{i+1,j}$, $f_{i+1,j+1}$).

---

[16] A useful rule of thumb for finite difference methods is that ΔS should be kept proportional to $\sqrt{\Delta t}$ as they approach zero.

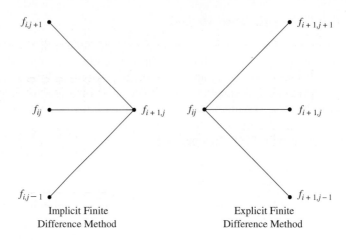

Implicit Finite
Difference Method

Explicit Finite
Difference Method

Figure 15.14   Difference between implicit and explicit finite difference methods.

Example 15.8

Table 15.2 shows the result of using the explicit version of the finite difference method for pricing the option in Example 15.1. As in Example 15.7, values of 20, 10, and 5 were chosen for M, N, and ΔS, respectively. The option price given by the grid is $4.26.[17]

Change of Variable

It is computationally more efficient to use finite difference methods with $\ln S$ rather than S as the underlying variable. Define $Z = \ln S$. Equation (15.19) becomes

$$\frac{\partial f}{\partial t} + \left(r - \frac{\sigma^2}{2} \right)\frac{\partial f}{\partial Z} + \tfrac{1}{2}\sigma^2\frac{\partial^2 f}{\partial Z^2} = rf$$

The grid then evaluates the derivative for equally spaced values of Z rather than for equally spaced values of S. The difference equation for the implicit method becomes

$$\frac{f_{i+1,j} - f_{i,j}}{\Delta t} + (r - \sigma^2/2)\frac{f_{i,j+1} - f_{i,j-1}}{2\Delta Z} + \tfrac{1}{2}\sigma^2\frac{f_{i,j+1} + f_{i,j-1} - 2f_{i,j}}{\Delta Z^2} = rf_{i,j}$$

or

$$\alpha_j f_{i,j-1} + \beta_j f_{i,j} + \gamma_j f_{i,j+1} = f_{i+1,j} \qquad (15.33)$$

---

[17]The negative numbers and other inconsistencies in the top left-hand part of the grid will be explained later.

TABLE 15.2 Grid to Value Option in Example 15.1 Using Explicit Finite Difference Method

Stock Price (dollars)	Time to Maturity (Months)										
	5	$4\frac{1}{2}$	4	$3\frac{1}{2}$	3	$2\frac{1}{2}$	2	$1\frac{1}{2}$	1	$\frac{1}{2}$	0
100	0.00	0.00	0.00	0.00	0.00	0.00	0.00	0.00	0.00	0.00	0.00
95	0.06	0.00	0.00	0.00	0.00	0.00	0.00	0.00	0.00	0.00	0.00
90	−0.11	0.05	0.00	0.00	0.00	0.00	0.00	0.00	0.00	0.00	0.00
85	0.28	−0.05	0.05	0.00	0.00	0.00	0.00	0.00	0.00	0.00	0.00
80	−0.13	0.20	0.00	0.05	0.00	0.00	0.00	0.00	0.00	0.00	0.00
75	0.46	0.06	0.20	0.04	0.06	0.00	0.00	0.00	0.00	0.00	0.00
70	0.32	0.46	0.23	0.25	0.10	0.09	0.00	0.00	0.00	0.00	0.00
65	0.91	0.68	0.63	0.44	0.37	0.21	0.14	0.00	0.00	0.00	0.00
60	1.48	1.37	1.17	1.02	0.81	0.65	0.42	0.27	0.00	0.00	0.00
55	2.59	2.39	2.21	1.99	1.77	1.50	1.24	0.90	0.59	0.00	0.00
50	4.26	4.08	3.89	3.68	3.44	3.18	2.87	2.53	2.07	1.56	0.00
45	6.76	6.61	6.47	6.31	6.15	5.96	5.75	5.50	5.24	5.00	5.00
40	10.28	10.20	10.13	10.06	10.01	10.00	10.00	10.00	10.00	10.00	10.00
35	15.00	15.00	15.00	15.00	15.00	15.00	15.00	15.00	15.00	15.00	15.00
30	20.00	20.00	20.00	20.00	20.00	20.00	20.00	20.00	20.00	20.00	20.00
25	25.00	25.00	25.00	25.00	25.00	25.00	25.00	25.00	25.00	25.00	25.00
20	30.00	30.00	30.00	30.00	30.00	30.00	30.00	30.00	30.00	30.00	30.00
15	35.00	35.00	35.00	35.00	35.00	35.00	35.00	35.00	35.00	35.00	35.00
10	40.00	40.00	40.00	40.00	40.00	40.00	40.00	40.00	40.00	40.00	40.00
5	45.00	45.00	45.00	45.00	45.00	45.00	45.00	45.00	45.00	45.00	45.00
0	50.00	50.00	50.00	50.00	50.00	50.00	50.00	50.00	50.00	50.00	50.00

where

$$\alpha_j = \frac{\Delta t}{2\Delta Z}(r - \sigma^2/2) - \frac{\Delta t}{2\Delta Z^2}\sigma^2$$

$$\beta_j = 1 + \frac{\Delta t}{\Delta Z^2}\sigma^2 + r\Delta t$$

$$\gamma_j = -\frac{\Delta t}{2\Delta Z}(r - \sigma^2/2) - \frac{\Delta t}{2\Delta Z^2}\sigma^2$$

The difference equation for the explicit method becomes

$$\frac{f_{i+1,j} - f_{i,j}}{\Delta t} + (r - \sigma^2/2)\frac{f_{i+1,j+1} - f_{i+1,j-1}}{2\Delta Z}$$
$$+ \frac{1}{2}\sigma^2\frac{f_{i+1,j+1} + f_{i+1,j-1} - 2f_{i+1,j}}{\Delta Z^2} = rf_{i,j}$$

or

$$\alpha_j^* f_{i+1,j-1} + \beta_j^* f_{i+1,j} + \gamma_j^* f_{i+1,j+1} = f_{i,j} \tag{15.34}$$

where

$$\alpha_j^* = \frac{1}{1 + r\Delta t}\left(-\frac{\Delta t}{2\Delta Z}(r - \sigma^2/2) + \frac{\Delta t}{2\Delta Z^2}\sigma^2\right) \tag{15.35}$$

$$\beta_j^* = \frac{1}{1 + r\Delta t}\left(1 - \frac{\Delta t}{\Delta Z^2}\sigma^2\right) \tag{15.36}$$

$$\gamma_j^* = \frac{1}{1 + r\Delta t}\left(\frac{\Delta t}{2\Delta Z}(r - \sigma^2/2) + \frac{\Delta t}{2\Delta Z^2}\sigma^2\right) \tag{15.37}$$

The change of variable approach has the property that α_j, β_j, and γ_j as well as α_j^*, β_j^*, and γ_j^* are independent of j. It can be shown that it is numerically most efficient to set $\Delta Z = \sigma\sqrt{3\Delta t}$.

Relation to Trinomial Tree Approaches

The explicit finite difference method is very similar to the trinomial tree approach. In the expressions for a_j^*, b_j^*, and c_j^* in equation (15.32), we can interpret terms as follows:

$-\frac{1}{2}rj\Delta t + \frac{1}{2}\sigma^2 j^2\Delta t$: probability of stock price decreasing from $j\Delta S$ to $(j - 1)\Delta S$ in time Δt

$1 - \sigma^2 j^2\Delta t$: probability of stock price remaining unchanged at $j\Delta S$ in time Δt

$\frac{1}{2}rj\Delta t + \frac{1}{2}\sigma^2 j^2\Delta t$: probability of stock price increasing from $j\Delta S$ to $(j + 1)\Delta S$ in time Δt

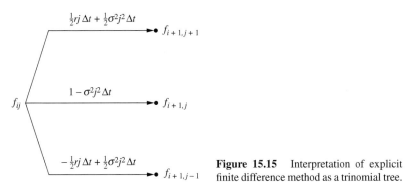

$$\tfrac{1}{2}rj\,\Delta t + \tfrac{1}{2}\sigma^2 j^2\,\Delta t$$

$f_{i+1,j+1}$

$$1 - \sigma^2 j^2\,\Delta t$$

f_{ij} $f_{i+1,j}$

$$-\tfrac{1}{2}rj\,\Delta t + \tfrac{1}{2}\sigma^2 j^2\,\Delta t$$

$f_{i+1,j-1}$

Figure 15.15   Interpretation of explicit finite difference method as a trinomial tree.

This interpretation is illustrated in Figure 15.15. The three probabilities sum to unity. They give the expected increase in the stock price in time Δt as $rj\Delta S\Delta t = rS\Delta t$. This is the expected increase in a risk-neutral world. For small values of Δt, they also give the variance of the change in the stock price in time Δt as $\sigma^2 j^2 \Delta S^2 \Delta t = \sigma^2 S^2 \Delta t$. This corresponds to the stochastic process followed by S. The value of f at time $i\Delta t$ is calculated as the expected value of f at time $(i+1)\Delta t$ in a risk-neutral world discounted at the risk-free rate.

For the explicit version of the finite difference method to work well, the three "probabilities"

$$-\tfrac{1}{2}rj\Delta t + \tfrac{1}{2}\sigma^2 j^2\Delta t$$

$$1 - \sigma^2 j^2\Delta t$$

$$\tfrac{1}{2}rj\Delta t + \tfrac{1}{2}\sigma^2 j^2\Delta t$$

should all be positive. In Example 15.8, $1 - \sigma^2 j^2\Delta t$ is negative when $j \geq 13$ (i.e., when $S \geq 65$). This explains the negative option prices and other inconsistencies in the top left-hand part of Table 15.2. This example illustrates the main problem associated with the explicit finite difference method. Because the probabilities in the associated tree may be negative, it does not necessarily produce results which converge to the solution of the differential equation.[18]

When the change-of-variable approach is used [see equations (15.34) to (15.37)], the probability that $Z = \ln S$ will decrease by ΔZ is

$$-\frac{\Delta t}{2\Delta Z}(r - \sigma^2/2) + \frac{\Delta t}{2\Delta Z^2}\sigma^2$$

---

[18]J. Hull and A. White, "Valuing Derivative Securities Using the Explicit Finite Difference Method," *Journal of Financial and Quantitative Analysis*, 25 (March 1990), 87–100, show how this problem can be overcome. In the situation considered here it is sufficient to construct the grid in $\ln S$ rather than S to ensure convergence.

The probability that it will stay the same is

$$-\frac{\Delta t}{2\Delta Z}(r - \sigma^2/2) + \frac{\Delta t}{2\Delta Z^2}\sigma^2$$

The probability that it will increase by ΔZ is

$$\frac{\Delta t}{2\Delta Z}(r - \sigma^2/2) + \frac{\Delta t}{2\Delta Z^2}\sigma^2$$

These three movements in Z correspond to the stock price changing from S to $Se^{-\Delta z}$, S, and $Se^{\Delta z}$ respectively. If we set $\Delta Z = \sigma\sqrt{3\Delta t}$, the tree and the probabilities are identical to those for the trinomial tree approach discussed in Section 15.5.

Other Finite Difference Methods

Many of the other finite difference methods that have been proposed have some of the features of the explicit finite difference method and some features of the implicit finite difference method.

In what is known as the *hopscotch method* we alternate between the explicit and implicit calculations as we move from node to node. This is illustrated in Figure 15.16. At each time we first do all the calculations at the "explicit nodes" in the usual way. We can then deal with the "implicit nodes" without solving a set of simultaneous equations. This is because the values at the adjacent nodes have already been calculated.

The *Crank–Nicholson* scheme is an average of the explicit and implicit methods. For the implicit method equation (15.25) gives

$$f_{i,j} = a_j f_{i-1,j-1} + b_j f_{i-1,j} + c_j f_{i-1,j+1}$$

For the explicit method equation (15.32) gives

$$f_{i-1,j} = a_j^* f_{i,j-1} + b_j^* f_{i,j} + c_j^* f_{i,j+1}$$

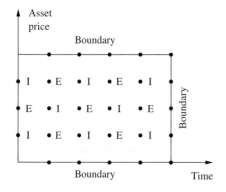

Figure 15.16 Hopscotch method. I indicates node at which implicit calculations are done; E indicates node at which explicit calculations are done.

The Crank–Nicholson method averages these two equations to obtain

$$f_{i,j} + f_{i-1,j} = a_j f_{i-1,j-1} + b_j f_{i-1,j} + c_j f_{i-1,j+1} + a_j^* f_{i,j-1} + b_j^* f_{i,j} + c_j^* f_{i,j+1}$$

Putting

$$g_{i,j} = f_{i,j} - a_j^* f_{i,j-1} - b_j^* f_{i,j} - c_j^* f_{i,j+1}$$

we obtain

$$g_{i,j} = a_j f_{i-1,j-1} + b_j f_{i-1,j} + c_j f_{i-1,j+1} - f_{i-1,j}$$

This shows that implementing the Crank–Nicholson method is similar to implementing the implicit finite difference method. The advantage of the Crank–Nicholson method is that it has faster convergence than either the explicit or implicit method.

Applications of Finite Difference Methods

Finite difference methods can be used for the same types of derivative pricing problems as tree approaches. They can handle American-style as well as European-style derivatives but cannot easily be used in situations where the payoff from a derivative depends on the past history of the underlying variable. Finite difference methods can, at the expense of a considerable increase in computer time, be used when there are several state variables. The grid in Figure 15.13 then becomes multidimensional.

The method for calculating hedge statistics is similar to that used for trees. Delta, gamma, and theta can be calculated directly from the $f_{i,j}$ values on the grid. For vega, it is necessary to make a small change to volatility and recalculate the value of the derivative using the same grid.

15.9 ANALYTIC APPROXIMATIONS IN OPTION PRICING

As an alternative to the numerical procedures described so far in this chapter, a number of analytic approximations to the valuation of American options have been suggested. The best known of these is a quadratic approximation approach originally suggested by MacMillan and extended by Barone-Adesi and Whaley.[19] It can be used to value American calls and puts on stocks, stock indices, currencies, and futures contracts. It involves estimating the difference, v, between the European option price and the American option price. Since both the European and American option satisfy the same differential equation, v must also

[19]See L. W. MacMillan, "Analytic Approximation for the American Put Option," *Advances in Futures and Options Research*, 1 (1986), 119–39; G. Barone-Adesi and R. E. Whaley, "Efficient Analytic Approximation of American Option Values," *Journal of Finance*, 42 (June 1987), 301–20.

satisfy the differential equation. MacMillan, and Barone-Adesi and Whaley show that when an approximation is made, the differential equation can be solved using standard methods. More details on the approach are presented in Appendix 15A.

15.10 SUMMARY

In this chapter we have presented three different numerical procedures for valuing derivatives when no analytic solution is available. These involve the use of trees, Monte Carlo simulation, and finite difference methods.

Binomial trees assume that in each short interval of time, Δt, a stock price either moves up by a proportional amount, u, or down by a proportional amount, d. The sizes of u and d and their associated probabilities are chosen so that the change in the stock price has the correct mean and standard deviation in a risk-neutral world. Derivative prices are calculated by starting at the end of the tree and working backward. For an American option, the value at a node is the greater of the value if it is exercised immediately and the discounted expected value if it is held for a further period of time Δt.

Monte Carlo simulation involves using random numbers to sample many different paths that the variables underlying the derivative could follow in a risk-neutral world. For each path the payoff is calculated and discounted at the risk-free interest rate. The arithmetic average of the discounted payoffs is the estimate of the value of the derivative.

Finite difference methods solve the underlying differential equation by converting it to a difference equation. They are similar to tree approaches in that the computations work back from the end of the life of the derivative to the beginning. The explicit finite difference method is functionally the same as using a trinomial tree. The implicit finite difference method is more complicated but has the advantage that the user does not have to take any special precautions to ensure convergence.

The method that is chosen in practice is likely to depend on the characteristics of the derivative being evaluated and the accuracy required. Monte Carlo simulation, which works forward from the beginning to the end of the life of a security, can only be used for European-style derivatives but can cope with a great deal of complexity as far as the payoffs are concerned. It becomes relatively more efficient as the number of underlying variables increases. Tree approaches and finite difference methods, which work from the end of the life of a security to the beginning, can accommodate American-style as well as European-style derivatives. However, they are very difficult to apply when the payoffs depend on the past history of the state variables as well as on their current values. Also, they are liable to become computationally quite time consuming when three or more variables are involved. As an alternative to numerical procedures a number of analytic approximations have been suggested. The best known of these was

suggested by MacMillan and extended by Barone-Adesi and Whaley. It is described in Appendix 15A.

SUGGESTIONS FOR FURTHER READING

On Tree Approaches

Boyle, P. P., "A Lattice Framework for Option Pricing with Two State Variables," *Journal of Financial and Quantitative Analysis*, 23 (March 1988), 1–12.

Cox, J., S. Ross, and M. Rubinstein, "Option Pricing: A Simplified Approach," *Journal of Financial Economics*, 7 (October 1979), 229–64.

Rendleman, R., and B. Bartter, "Two State Option Pricing," *Journal of Finance*, 34 (1979), 1092–1110.

On Monte Carlo Simulation

Boyle, P. P., "Options: A Monte Carlo Approach," *Journal of Financial Economics*, 4 (1977), 323–38.

Brotherton-Ratcliffe, R., "Monte Carlo Motoring," *RISK*, December 1994, pp. 53–58.

Curran, M., "Strata Gems," *RISK*, March 1994, pp. 70–71.

Joy, C., P. P. Boyle, and K. S. Tan, "Quasi Monte Carlo Methods in Numerical Finance," Working Paper, University of Waterloo, Waterloo, Ontario N2L 3G1.

Moro, B. "The Full Monte," *RISK*, February 1985, pp. 57–58.

Press, W. H., S. A. Teukolsky, W. T. Vetterling, and B. P. Flannery, *Numerical Recipes in C: The Art of Scientific Computing*, 2nd ed. Cambridge: Cambridge University Press, 1992.

Sobol', I. M., *USSR Computational Mathematics and Mathematical Physics*, 7, 4 (1967), 86–112.

On Finite Difference Methods

Brennan, M. J., and E. S. Schwartz, "Finite Difference Methods and Jump Processes Arising in the Pricing of Contingent Claims: A Synthesis," *Journal of Financial and Quantitative Analysis*, 13 (September 1978), 462–74.

Brennan, M. J., and E. S. Schwartz, "The Valuation of American Put Options," *Journal of Finance*, 32 (May 1977), 449–62.

Courtadon, G., "A More Accurate Finite Difference Approximation for the Valuation of Options," *Journal of Financial and Quantitative Analysis*, 17 (December 1982), 697–705.

Hull, J., and A. White, "Valuing Derivative Securities Using the Explicit Finite Difference Method," *Journal of Financial and Quantitative Analysis*, 25 (March 1990), 87–100.

Schwartz, E. S., "The Valuation of Warrants: Implementing a New Approach," *Journal of Financial Economics*, 4 (1977), 79–94.

Wilmott, P., J. Dewynne, and S. Howison, *Option Pricing: Mathematical Models and Computation.* Oxford: Oxford Financial Press, 1993.

On Analytic Approximations

Barone-Adesi, G., and R. E. Whaley, "Efficient Analytic Approximation of American Option Values," *Journal of Finance*, 42 (June 1987), 301–20.

Carr, P., R. Jarrow, and R. Myneni, "Alternative Characterizations of American Put Options," *Mathematical Finance,* 2 (1992), 87–106.

Geske, R., and H. E. Johnson, "The American Put Valued Analytically," *Journal of Finance*, 39 (December 1984), 1511–24.

Johnson, H. E., "An Analytic Approximation to the American Put Price," *Journal of Financial and Quantitative Analysis*, 18 (March 1983), 141–48.

MacMillan, L. W. "Analytic Approximation for the American Put Option," *Advances in Futures and Options Research*, 1 (1986), 119–39.

QUESTIONS AND PROBLEMS

15.1. Which of the following can be estimated for an American option by constructing a single binomial tree: delta, gamma, vega, theta, rho?

15.2. Calculate the price of a three-month American put option on a non-dividend-paying stock when the stock price is $60, the strike price is $60, the risk-free interest rate is 10% per annum, and the volatility is 45% per annum. Use a binomial tree with a time interval of one month.

15.3. Explain how the control variate technique is implemented when a tree is used to value American options.

15.4. Calculate the price of a nine-month American call option on corn futures when the current futures price is 198 cents, the strike price is 200 cents, the risk-free interest rate is 8% per annum, and the volatility is 30% per annum. Use a binomial tree with a time interval of three months.

15.5. Consider an option that pays off the amount by which the final stock price exceeds the minimum stock price achieved during the life of the option. Can this be valued using the binomial tree approach? Explain your answer.

15.6. "For a dividend-paying stock, the tree for the stock price does not recombine; but the tree for the stock price less the present value of future dividends does recombine." Explain this statement.

15.7. Show that the probabilities in a Cox, Ross, and Rubinstein binomial tree are negative when the condition in footnote 6 holds.

15.8. How would you use the binomial tree approach to value an American option on a stock index when the dividend yield on the index is a function of time?

15.9. Explain why the Monte Carlo simulation approach cannot be used for American-style derivatives.

15.10. A one-year American put option on a non-dividend-paying stock has an exercise price of $18. The current stock price is $20, the risk-free interest rate is 15% per annum, and the volatility of the stock price is 40% per annum. Divide the year into four 3-month time intervals and use the tree approach to estimate the value of the option. Use the control variate technique to improve this estimate.

15.11. A one-year American call option on silver futures has an exercise price of $9. The current futures price is $8.50, the risk-free rate of interest is 12% per annum, and the volatility of the futures price is 25% per annum. Divide the year into four 3-month time intervals and use the tree approach to estimate the value of the option. Use the control variate technique to improve this estimate. Estimate the option's delta.

15.12. A two-month American put option on the Major Market Index has an exercise price of 480. The current level of the index is 484, the risk-free interest rate is 10% per annum, the dividend yield on the index is 3% per annum, and the volatility of the index is 25% per annum. Divide the life of the option into four half-month periods and use the tree approach to estimate the value of the option.

15.13. A six-month American call option on a stock is expected to pay dividends of $1 per share at the end of the second month and the fifth month. The current stock price is $30, the exercise price is $34, the risk-free interest rate is 10% per annum, and the volatility of the part of the stock price that will not be used to pay the dividends is 30% per annum. Divide the life of the option into six one-month periods and use the tree approach to estimate the value of the option. Compare your answer to that given by Black's approximation (see Section 11.12). Estimate the delta and theta of the option from your tree.

15.14. How can the control variate approach improve the estimate of the delta of an American option when the tree approach is used?

*15.15. Suppose that Monte Carlo simulation is being used to evaluate a European call option on a non-dividend-paying stock when the volatility is stochastic. Explain why it is necessary to calculate six values of the option in each simulation trial when both the control variable and the antithetic variable technique are used.

*15.16. Explain how equations (15.25) to (15.28) change when the finite difference method is being used to evaluate an American call option on a currency.

*15.17. An American put option on a non-dividend-paying stock has four months to maturity. The exercise price is $21, the stock price is $20, the risk-free rate of interest is 10% per annum, and the volatility is 30% per annum. Use the explicit version of the finite difference approach to value the option. Use stock price intervals of $4 and time intervals of one month.

*15.18. The current value of the British pound is $1.60 and the volatility of the pound–dollar exchange rate is 15% per annum. An American call option has an exercise price of $1.62 and a time to maturity of one year. The risk-free rates of interest in the United States and the United Kingdom are 6% per annum and 9% per annum, respectively. Use the explicit finite difference method to value the option. Consider exchange rate intervals of 0.20 and time intervals of 3 months. (*Hint*: Only exchange rates between 0.80 and 2.40 need to be considered).

*15.19. Suppose that, as an approximation, it is assumed that the term structure of interest rates is flat for one year and that

$$dr = (a - r)b \, dt + rc \, dz$$

where a, b, and c are known constants; r is the interest rates for maturities up to one year; and dz is a Wiener process. Discuss the problems in using a binomial tree to represent movements in r.

15.20. The spot price of copper is $0.60 per pound. Suppose that the futures prices (dollars per pound) are as follows:

> 3 months   0.59
> 6 months   0.57
> 9 months   0.54
> 12 months   0.50

The volatility of the price of copper is 40% per annum and the risk-free rate is 6% per annum. Use a binomial tree to value an American call option on copper with an exercise price of $0.60 and a time to maturity of one year. Divide the life of the option into four 3-month periods for the purposes of constructing the tree.

15.21. Use the binomial tree in Problem 15.20 to value a security that pays off x^2 in one year where x is the price of copper.

*15.22. When do the boundary conditions for $S = 0$ and $S \longrightarrow \infty$ affect the estimates of derivative prices in the explicit finite difference method?

*15.23. How can finite difference methods be used when there are known dividends?

*15.24. A company has issued a three-year convertible bond that has a face value of $25 and can be exchanged for two of the company's shares at any time. The company can call the issue forcing conversion when the share price is greater than or equal to $18. Assuming that the company will force conversion at the earliest opportunity, what are the boundary conditions for the price of the convertible? Describe how you would use finite difference methods to value the convertible assuming constant interest rates. Assume there is no risk of the company defaulting.

15.25. Provide formulas that can be used for obtaining three random samples from standard normal distributions when the correlation between sample i and sample j is $\rho_{i,j}$.

APPENDIX 15A: ANALYTIC APPROXIMATION TO AMERICAN OPTION PRICES OF MACMILLAN, AND BARONE-ADESI AND WHALEY

Consider an option on a stock providing a continuous dividend yield equal to q. We will denote the difference between the American and European option price by v. Since both the American and the European option prices satisfy the Black–Scholes differential equation, v also does so. Hence

$$\frac{\partial v}{\partial t} + (r - q)S\frac{\partial v}{\partial S} + \tfrac{1}{2}\sigma^2 S^2 \frac{\partial^2 v}{\partial S^2} = rv$$

For convenience we define

$$\tau = T - t$$
$$h(\tau) = 1 - e^{-r\tau}$$

$$\alpha = \frac{2r}{\sigma^2}$$

$$\beta = \frac{2(r-q)}{\sigma^2}$$

We also write, without loss of generality,

$$v = h(\tau)g(S, h)$$

With appropriate substitutions and variable changes, this gives

$$S^2 \frac{\partial^2 g}{\partial S^2} + \beta S \frac{\partial g}{\partial S} - \frac{\alpha}{h} g - (1-h)\alpha \frac{\partial g}{\partial h} = 0$$

The approximation which is used involves assuming that the final term on the left-hand side is zero, so that

$$S^2 \frac{\partial^2 g}{\partial S^2} + \beta S \frac{\partial g}{\partial S} - \frac{\alpha}{h} g = 0 \qquad (15A.1)$$

The term that is ignored is generally fairly small. When τ is large, $1 - h$ is close to zero; when τ is small, $\partial g / \partial h$ is close to zero.

The American call and put prices will, as usual, be denoted by $C(S)$ and $P(S)$, where S is the stock price, and the corresponding European call and put prices will be denoted by $c(S)$ and $p(S)$. Equation (15A.1) can be solved using standard techniques. After boundary conditions have been applied, it is found that

$$C(S) = \begin{cases} c(S) + A_2 \left(\dfrac{S}{S^*} \right)^{\gamma_2} & \text{when } S < S^* \\ S - X & \text{when } S \geq S^* \end{cases}$$

The variable S^* is the critical price of the stock above which the option should be exercised. It is estimated by solving the equation

$$S^* - X = c(S^*) + \left\{ 1 - e^{-q(T-t)}N[d_1(S^*)] \right\} \frac{S^*}{\gamma_2}$$

iteratively. For a put option, the valuation formula is

$$P(S) = \begin{cases} p(S) + A_1 \left(\dfrac{S}{S^{**}} \right)^{\gamma_1} & \text{when } S > S^{**} \\ X - S & \text{when } S \leq S^{**} \end{cases}$$

The variable S^{**} is the critical price of the stock below which the option should be exercised. It is estimated by solving the equation

$$X - S^{**} = p(S^{**}) - \left\{ 1 - e^{-q(T-t)}N[-d_1(S^{**})] \right\} \frac{S^{**}}{\gamma_1}$$

iteratively. The other variables that have been used here are

$$\gamma_1 = \left[-(\beta - 1) - \sqrt{(\beta - 1)^2 + \frac{4\alpha}{h}} \right] \Big/ 2$$

$$\gamma_2 = \left[-(\beta - 1) + \sqrt{(\beta - 1)^2 + \frac{4\alpha}{h}} \right] \Big/ 2$$

$$A_1 = -\left(\frac{S^{**}}{\gamma_1} \right) \left\{ 1 - e^{-q(T-t)} N[-d_1(S^{**})] \right\}$$

$$A_2 = \left(\frac{S^*}{\gamma_2} \right) \left\{ 1 - e^{-q(T-t)} N[d_1(S^*)] \right\}$$

$$d_1(S) = \frac{\ln(S/X) + (r - q + \sigma^2/2)(T - t)}{\sigma \sqrt{T - t}}$$

As pointed out in Chapter 12, options on stock indices, currencies, and futures contracts are analogous to options on a stock providing a continuous dividend with the dividend yield constant. Hence the quadratic approximation approach can easily be applied to all of these types of options.

Chapter 16

Interest Rate Derivatives and the Use of Black's Model

Interest rate derivatives are instruments whose payoffs are dependent in some way on the level of interest rates. In the 1980s and early 1990s the volume of trading in interest rate derivatives in both the over-the-counter and exchange-traded markets increased very fast. Many new products were developed to meet particular needs of end users. A key challenge for derivatives practitioners has been to find robust procedures for pricing and hedging these products.

Interest rate derivatives are more difficult to value than equity and foreign exchange derivatives. There are a number of reasons for this:

1. The probabilistic behavior of an individual interest rate is much more complicated than that of a stock price or exchange rate.
2. For the valuation of many products it is necessary to develop a model describing the probabilistic behavior of the entire yield curve.
3. The volatilities of different points on the yield curve are different.
4. Interest rates are used for discounting as well as for defining the payoff from the derivative.

In this chapter, which is the first of two chapters on interest rate derivatives, we review some of the products that trade and how they are used. We also discuss some relatively simple valuation models that are widely used. These models are in the spirit of the original Black–Scholes model for European stock options. They are appropriate for derivatives whose payoffs depend only on the value of a single variable (e.g., an interest rate or a bond price) observed at one particular point in time. The models assume that the probability distribution of the variable at that point in time is lognormal. For ease of exposition we assume that the current time is zero throughout this chapter.

16.1 EXCHANGE–TRADED INTEREST RATE OPTIONS

The most popular exchange-traded interest rate options are those on Treasury bond futures, Treasury note futures, and Eurodollar futures. Table 12.4 shows the closing prices for these securities on May 11, 1995. A Treasury bond futures option is an option to enter a Treasury bond futures contract. As mentioned in Chapter 4, one Treasury bond futures contract is for the delivery of $100,000

of Treasury bonds. The price of a Treasury bond future option is quoted as a percentage of the face value of the underlying Treasury bonds to the nearest $\frac{1}{64}$ of 1%. Table 12.4 gives the price of the September call futures option on Treasury bonds as 2-40 or $2\frac{40}{64}$% of the debt principal when the strike price is 108 (implying that one contract would cost $2,625). The quotes for options on Treasury notes are similar.

An option on Eurodollar futures is an option to enter into a Eurodollar futures contract. As explained in Chapter 4, the asset underlying a Eurodollar futures contract is a $1 million three-month deposit. When the Eurodollar quote changes by one basis point or 0.01, there is a gain or loss on the contract of $25. Similarly, in the pricing of options on Eurodollar futures, one basis point represents $25. Table 12.4 gives the price of the CME September call futures option on Eurodollars as 0.56% when the strike price is 93.50. This implies that one contract would cost $56 \times \$25 = \$1,400$.

Interest rate futures contracts work in the same way as other futures contracts discussed in Chapter 12. For example, the payoff from a call is $\max(F - X, 0)$, where F is the futures price at the time of exercise and X is the strike price. In addition to the cash payoff the option holder obtains a long position in the futures contract when he or she exercises and the option writer obtains a corresponding short position.

Interest rate futures prices increase when bond prices increase (i.e., when interest rates fall). They decrease when bond prices decrease (i.e., when interest rates rise). An investor who thinks that short-term interest rates will rise can speculate by buying put options on Eurodollar futures, while an investor who thinks that they will fall can speculate by buying call options on Eurodollar futures. An investor who thinks that long-term interest rates will rise can speculate by buying put options on Treasury note futures or Treasury bond futures, while an investor who thinks they will fall can speculate by buying call options on these instruments.

Example 16.1

Suppose that it is February and the futures price for the June Eurodollar contract is 93.82. (This corresponds to a three-month Eurodollar interest rate of 6.18% per annum.) The price of a call option on this contract with a strike price of 94.00 is quoted as 0.20. This option could be attractive to an investor who feels that interest rates are likely to come down. Suppose that short-term interest rates do reduce by about 100 basis points over the next three months and the investor exercises the call when the Eurodollar futures price is 94.78. (This corresponds to a three-month Eurodollar interest rate of 5.22% per annum.) The payoff is $25 \times 78 = \$1,950$. The cost of the contract is $20 \times 25 = \$500$. The investor's profit is therefore $1,450.

Example 16.2

Suppose that it is August and the futures price for the December Treasury bond contract traded on the CBOT is 96-09 (or $96\frac{9}{32} = 96.28125$). The yield on long-term government bonds is about 8.4 percent per annum. An investor who feels that this yield will fall by December might choose to buy December calls with a strike price of 98. Assume that the

price of these calls is 1-04 (or $1\frac{4}{64}$ = 1.0625% of the principal). If long-term rates fall to 8% per annum and the Treasury bond futures price rises to 100-00, the investor will make a net profit per $100 of bond futures of

$$100.00 - 98.00 - 1.0625 = 0.9375$$

Since one option contract is for the purchase or sale of instruments with a face value of $100,000, the investor would make a profit of $937.50 per option contract bought.

16.2 EMBEDDED BOND OPTIONS

Some bonds contain embedded call and put options. For example, a *callable bond* contains provisions that allow the issuing firm to buy back the bond at a predetermined price at certain times in the future. The holder of such a bond has sold a call option to the issuer. The strike price or call price in the option is the predetermined price that must be paid by the issuer to the holder. Callable bonds usually cannot be called for the first few years of their life. After that the call price is usually a decreasing function of time. For example, in a 10-year callable bond, there might be no call privileges for the first two years. After that the issuer might have the right to buy the bond back at a price of 110 in years 3 and 4 of its life, at a price of 107.5 in years 5 and 6, at a price of 106 in years 7 and 8, and at a price of 103 in years 9 and 10. The value of the call option is reflected in the quoted yields on bonds. Bonds with call features generally offer higher yields than bonds with no call features.

A *puttable bond* contains provisions that allow the holder to demand early redemption at a predetermined price at certain times in the future. The holder of such a bond has purchased a put option on the bond as well as the bond itself. Since the put option increases the value of the bond to the holder, bonds with put features provide lower yields than bonds with no put features. A simple example of a puttable bond is a 10-year retractible bond where the holder has the right to be repaid at the end of five years.

A number of interest rate instruments have embedded bond options. For example, early redemption privileges on fixed-rate deposits are analogous to the put features of a bond. Prepayment privileges on fixed-rate loans are analogous to the call features of a bond. Also, loan commitments made by a bank or other financial institution are put options. Consider, for example, the situation where a bank quotes a five-year interest rate of 12% per annum to a potential borrower and states that the rate is good for the next two months. The client has in effect obtained the right to sell a five-year bond with a 12% coupon to the financial institution for its face value any time within the next two months.

16.3 MORTGAGE-BACKED SECURITIES

A type of interest rate option is embedded in what is known as a *mortgage-backed security* (MBS). This security has become very popular in recent years. It is

created when a financial institution decides to sell part of its residential mortgage portfolio to investors. The mortgages sold are put into a pool and investors acquire a stake in the pool by buying units. The units are known as mortgage-backed securities. A secondary market is usually created for the units so that investors can sell them to other investors as desired. An investor who owns units representing X percent of a certain pool is entitled to X percent of the principal and interest cash flows received from the mortgages in the pool.

The mortgages in a pool are generally guaranteed by a government-related agency such as the Government National Mortgage Association (GNMA) or the Federal National Mortgage Association (FNMA) so that investors are protected against defaults. This makes an MBS sound like a regular fixed-income security issued by the government. In fact, there is a critical difference between an MBS and a regular fixed-income investment. This is that the mortgages in an MBS pool have prepayment privileges. These prepayment privileges can be quite valuable to the householder. For example, in the United States mortgages typically last for 25 years and can be prepaid at any time. In other words, the householder has a 25-year American-style option to put the mortgage back to the lender at its face value.

In practice prepayments on mortgages occur for a variety of reasons. Sometimes interest rates have fallen and the owner of the house decides to refinance at a lower rate of interest. On other occasions a mortgage is prepaid simply because the house is being sold. A critical element in valuing an MBS is the determination of what is known as the *prepayment function*. This is a function describing expected prepayments on the underlying pool of mortgages at a time t in terms of the yield curve at time t and other relevant variables.

A prepayment function would be very unreliable as a predictor of actual prepayment experience for an individual mortgage. When many similar mortgage loans are combined in the same pool, there is a "law of large numbers" effect at work and prepayments can be predicted from an analysis of historical data more accurately. As already mentioned, prepayments are not always motivated by pure interest rate considerations. Nevertheless, there is a tendency for prepayments to be more likely when interest rates are low than when they are high. This means that investors require a higher rate of interest on an MBS than on other fixed-income securities to compensate for the prepayment options they have written.

Collateralized Mortgage Obligations

The MBSs we have described so far are sometimes referred to as *pass-throughs*. All investors receive the same return and bear the same prepayment risk. Not all mortgage-backed securities work in this way. In a *collateralized mortgage obligation* (CMO) the investors are divided into a number of classes and rules are developed for determining how principal repayments are channeled to different classes.

As an example of a CMO consider an MBS where investors are divided into three classes: class A, class B, and class C. All the principal repayments (both

those that are scheduled and those that are prepayments) are channeled to class A investors until investors in this class have been completely paid off. Principal repayments are then channeled to class B investors until these investors have been completely paid off. Finally, principal repayments are channeled to class C investors. In this situation class A investors bear the most prepayment risk. The class A securities can be expected to last less long than the class B securities, which in turn can be expected to last less long than the class C securities.

The objective of this type of structure is to create classes of securities that are more attractive to institutional investors than those created by the simpler pass-through MBS. The prepayment risks assumed by the different classes depend on the par value in each class. For example, class C bears very little prepayment risk if the par values in classes A, B, and C are 400, 300, and 100, respectively. It bears rather more prepayment risk in the situation where the par values in the classes are 100, 200, and 500.

IOs and POs

In what is known as a *stripped MBS*, principal payments are separated from interest payments. All principal payments are channeled to one class of security, known as a *principal only* (PO). All interest payments are channeled to another class of security known as an *interest only* (IO). Both IOs and POs are risky investments. As prepayment rates increase, a PO becomes more valuable and an IO becomes less valuable. As prepayment rates decrease, the reverse happens. In a PO, a fixed amount of principal is returned to the investor, but the timing is uncertain. A high rate of prepayments on the underlying pool leads to the principal being received early (which is, of course, good news for the holder of the PO). A low rate of prepayments on the underlying pool delays the return of the principal and reduces the yield provided by the PO. In the case of an IO the total of the cash flows received by the investor is not certain. The higher the rate of prepayments, the lower the total cash flows received by the investor, and vice versa.

16.4 OPTION-ADJUSTED SPREAD

The types of models that can be used to price mortgage-backed securities and bonds with embedded options are discussed in Chapter 17. A critical input to any model that is chosen is the zero-coupon yield curve. This is a curve, generated in the way described in Chapter 4, that describes the relationship between yield and maturity for zero-coupon bonds that have no embedded options.

In addition to calculating theoretical prices for embedded options and mortgage-backed securities, traders also like to compute what is known as the *option-adjusted spread* (OAS). This is a measure of the spread over the yields on government Treasury bonds provided by the instrument when all options have been taken into account.

To calculate an OAS for an instrument, it is first priced using the zero-coupon government Treasury curve as the input to the pricing model. The price of the instrument given by the model is compared to the price in the market. A series of iterations is then used to determine the parallel shift to the input Treasury curve that causes the model price equal to the market price. This parallel shift is the OAS.

To illustrate the nature of the calculations, suppose that the market price is $102.00 and that the price calculated using the Treasury curve is $103.27. As a first trial we might choose to try a 60-basis-point parallel shift to the Treasury zero curve. Suppose that this gives a price of $101.20 for the instrument. This is less than the market price of $102.00 and means that a parallel shift somewhere between 0 and 60 basis points will lead to the model price being equal to the market price. It is natural to use linear interpolation to calculate

$$60 \times \frac{103.27 - 102.00}{103.27 - 101.20} = 36.81$$

or 36.81 basis points as the next trial shift. Suppose that this gives a price of $101.95. This indicates that the OAS is slightly less than 36.81 basis points. Linear interpolation suggests that the next trial shift be

$$36.81 \times \frac{103.27 - 102.00}{103.27 - 101.95} = 35.41$$

or 35.41 basis points; and so on.

16.5 BLACK'S MODEL

Since the Black–Scholes model was first published in 1973, it has become a very popular tool. As explained in Chapter 12, the model has been extended so that it can be used to value options on foreign exchange, options on indices, and options on futures contracts. Traders have become very comfortable with both the lognormal assumption that underlies the model and the volatility measure that describes uncertainty. It is not surprising that there have been attempts to extend the model so that it covers interest rate derivatives.

The extension of the Black–Scholes model that is most widely used in the interest rate area is Black's model, which was published in 1976.[1] This was originally developed for valuing options on commodity futures and has been described in Section 12.5. In this section we review the model and show that it can be extended so that it provides a flexible framework for valuing a wide range of European options. In later sections we provide a number of examples of the application of Black's model to interest rate options.

---

[1] See F. Black, "The Pricing of Commodity Contracts," *Journal of Financial Economics,* 3 (March 1976), 167–79.

Using Black's Model to Price European Options

Consider a European call option on a variable V. Assume that interest rates are nonstochastic and define:

- T: maturity date of the option
- F: futures price of V for a contract with maturity T
- X: strike price of the option
- r: zero-coupon yield for maturity T
- σ: volatility of F
- V_T: value of V at time T
- F_T: value of F at time T

The option pays off $\max(V_T - X, 0)$ at time T. Since $F_T = V_T$, we can also regard the option as paying off $\max(F_T - X, 0)$ at time T. As shown in Section 12.5, Black's model gives the value, c, of the option at time zero as

$$c = e^{-rT}[FN(d_1) - XN(d_2)] \tag{16.1}$$

where

$$d_1 = \frac{\ln(F/X) + \sigma^2 T/2}{\sigma \sqrt{T}}$$

$$d_2 = \frac{\ln(F/X) - \sigma^2 T/2}{\sigma \sqrt{T}} = d_1 - \sigma \sqrt{T}$$

The value, p, of the corresponding put option is given by

$$p = e^{-rT}[XN(-d_2) - FN(-d_1)] \tag{16.2}$$

Extensions of Black's Model

Black's model assumes that the volatility of F is constant. We can relax this assumption somewhat. Since we are valuing a European option, we do not care about the values of V or F prior to time T. We just require V to have a lognormal probability distribution at time T. From equation (12.12), F is the expected value of V_T in a risk-neutral world and it can be shown that sufficient conditions for us to be able to use risk-neutral valuation to deduce equations (16.1) and (16.2) are the following:

1. The probability distribution of V_T is is lognormal.
2. The standard deviation of $\ln V_T$ is $\sigma \sqrt{T}$.
3. Interest rates are nonstochastic.

As pointed out in Section 3.6, futures prices and forward prices are the same when interest rates are nonstochastic. The variable F can therefore be defined as the forward price of V for a contract maturing at time T.

To summarize, we can use equations (16.1) and (16.2) to value European options in any situation where interest rates are assumed to be nonstochastic and the underlying variable is assumed to be lognormal at the maturity of the option. The variable F in the equations can be defined as the forward price of the underlying variable for a contract with maturity T.

Since we are not necessarily assuming geometric Brownian motion for the evolution of either V or F, it is not strictly correct to refer to the variable σ as a volatility. It is, in reality, nothing more than a variable with the property that $\sigma\sqrt{T}$ is the standard deviation of $\ln V_T$. To emphasize this point we will refer to σ as the *volatility measure* for V at time T.

As a further extension of Black's model we can allow the time when the payoff is made to be different from T. Assume that the payoff on the option is calculated from the value of the variable V at time T, but that the payoff is delayed until time T^* where $T^* \geq T$. In this case it is necessary to discount the payoff from time T^* instead of from time T. We define r^* as the zero-coupon yield for maturity T^* and equations (16.1) and (16.2) become

$$c = e^{-r^*T}[FN(d_1) - XN(d_2)] \qquad (16.3)$$

$$p = e^{-r^*T}[XN(-d_2) - FN(-d_1)] \qquad (16.4)$$

where

$$d_1 = \frac{\ln(F/X) + \sigma^2 T/2}{\sigma\sqrt{T}}$$

$$d_2 = \frac{\ln(F/X) - \sigma^2 T/2}{\sigma\sqrt{T}} = d_1 - \sigma\sqrt{T}$$

Applications to Interest Rates

Equations (16.1) to (16.4) are frequently used to value interest rate options. The variable V is typically an interest rate, a bond price, or a spread between two interest rates. The variable F is set equal to the forward price of V.[2] The variables r and r^* that are used for discounting purposes are the zero-coupon yields calculated from the initial term structure.

When Black's model is used in this way, there appear to be two approximations:

1. The forward price of V is assumed to be equal to its futures price and therefore equal to the expected value of V_T in a risk-neutral world. But forward and futures prices are not equal when interest rates are stochastic.
2. Interest rates are assumed to be constant for discounting purposes even though they are assumed to be stochastic when the payoff from the option is calculated.

---

[2]When V is an interest rate, a "convexity adjustment" to F is sometimes necessary. This is discussed later in the chapter.

As it happens these two approximations have offsetting effects.[3] Black's model when used to value European interest rate options therefore has a stronger theoretical basis than might be supposed.

16.6 EUROPEAN BOND OPTIONS

A European bond option is an option to buy or sell a bond for a certain price on a certain date. If the bond price at the maturity of the option is assumed to be lognormal, equations (16.1) and (16.2) can be use to price the option with F equal to the forward bond price. The variable σ is defined so that $\sigma\sqrt{T}$ is the standard deviation of the logarithm of the bond price at the maturity of the option.

As explained in Chapter 4, F can be calculated from the spot bond price, B, using the formula

$$F = (B - I)e^{rT} \tag{16.5}$$

where I is the present value of the coupons that will be paid during the life of the option. In this formula both the spot bond price and the forward bond price are cash prices rather than quoted prices. The relationship between cash and quoted bond prices is explained in Section 4.3.

The strike price, X, in equations (16.1) and (16.2) should be the cash strike price. In choosing the correct value for X, the precise terms of the option are therefore important. If the strike price is defined as the cash amount that is exchanged for the bond when the option is exercised, X should be put equal to this strike price. If the strike price is the quoted price applicable when the option is exercised (as it is in most exchange-traded bond options), X should be set equal to the strike price plus accrued interest at the expiration date of the option. (As mentioned in Chapter 4, traders refer to the quoted price of a bond as the "clean price" and the cash price as the "dirty price.")

Example 16.3

Consider a 10-month European call option on a 9.75-year bond with a face value of $1,000. (When the option matures the bond will have eight years and 11 months remaining.) Suppose that the current cash bond price is $960, the strike price is $1,000, the ten-month risk-free interest rate is 10% per annum, and the volatility measure for the bond price in 10 months is 9% per annum. The bond pays a semiannual coupon of 10% and coupon payments of $50 are expected in three months and nine months. (This means that the accrued interest is $25 and the quoted bond price is $935.) We suppose that the three-month and nine-month risk-free interest rates are 9.0% and 9.5% per annum, respectively. The present value of the coupon payments is therefore

$$50e^{-0.25\times0.09} + 50e^{-0.75\times0.095} = 95.45$$

---

[3]See, for example, F. Jamshidian, "Options and Futures Evaluation with Deterministic Volatilities," *Mathematical Finance*, 3, 2 (1993) 149–59.

or $95.45. The bond forward price is from equation (16.5) given by

$$F = (960 - 95.45)e^{0.1 \times 0.8333} = 939.68$$

(a) If the strike price is the cash price that would be paid for the bond on exercise, the parameters for equation (16.1) are $F = 939.68$, $X = 1000$, $r = 0.1$, $\sigma = 0.09$, and $T = 0.8333$. The price of the call option is $9.49.
(b) If the strike price is the quoted price that would be paid for the bond on exercise, one month's accrued interest must be added to X since the maturity of the option is one month after a coupon date. This produces a value for X of

$$1{,}000 + 50 \times 0.16667 = 1{,}008.33$$

The values for the other parameters in equation (16.1) are unchanged (i.e., $F = 939.68$, $r = 0.1$, $\sigma = 0.09$, and $T = 0.8333$). The price of the option is $7.97.

Figure 16.1 shows how the standard deviation of the logarithm of a bond's price changes with time. The standard deviation is zero today since there is no uncertainty about the bond's price today. It is also zero at the bond's maturity since we know that the bond's price will equal its face value at maturity. Between today and the maturity of the bond, the standard deviation first increases and then decreases. From Section 16.5, the volatility measure, σ, that should be used when a European option on the bond is valued is

$$\frac{\text{standard deviation of logarithm of bond price at maturity of option}}{\sqrt{\text{time to maturity of option}}}$$

Figure 16.2 shows a typical pattern for σ as a function of the life of the option. In general, σ declines as the life of the option increases. It also tends to be an increasing function of the life of the bond when the life of the option is held fixed.

Yield Volatilities

The volatilities that are quoted for bond options are often yield volatility measures rather than price volatility measures. The duration concept, introduced

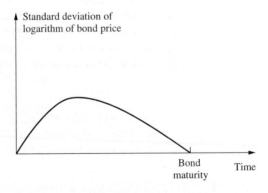

Figure 16.1   Standard deviation of logarithm of bond price as a function of time.

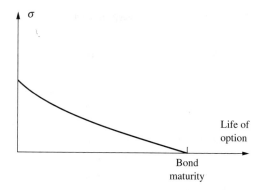

Figure 16.2   Variation of volatility measure, σ, for bond with life of option.

in Chapter 4, is used by the market to convert a quoted yield volatility into a price volatility. Suppose that D is the modified duration of the forward bond underlying the option as defined in Chapter 4. The relationship between the change in the bond's price, B, and its yield, y, at the maturity of the option is

$$\frac{\Delta B}{B} \approx -D\,\Delta y$$

or

$$\frac{\Delta B}{B} \approx -Dy\frac{\Delta y}{y}$$

This suggests that the volatility measure, σ, used in Black's model can be approximately related to the corresponding yield volatility measure, σ_y, using

$$\sigma = Dy\sigma_y \tag{16.6}$$

When a yield volatility is quoted for a bond option, the implicit assumption is usually that it will be converted to a price volatility using equation (16.6) and that this will then be used in conjunction with equation (16.1) or (16.2) to obtain a price.

16.7 INTEREST RATE CAPS

A popular interest rate option offered by financial institutions in the over-the-counter market is an *interest rate cap*. Interest rate caps are designed to provide insurance against the rate of interest on a floating-rate loan rising above a certain level. This level is known as the *cap rate*. When a cap on a loan and the loan itself are both provided by the same financial institution, the cost of the options underlying the cap is often incorporated into the interest rate charged. When they are provided by different financial institutions, an up-front payment for the cap is likely to be required.

A Cap as a Portfolio of Interest Rate Options

The operation of a cap is illustrated in Figure 16.3. A cap guarantees that the rate charged on a loan at any given time will be the lesser of the prevailing rate and the cap rate. Suppose that the rate on a loan, where the principal amount is $10 million, is reset every three months equal to three-month LIBOR, and that a financial institution has capped the rate at 10% per annum. (Since the payments are made quarterly, this cap rate is also expressed with quarterly compounding.)

To fulfill its obligations under the cap agreement, the financial institution must pay to the borrower at the end of each quarter (in millions of dollars)

$$0.25 \times 10 \times \max(R - 0.1, 0)$$

where R is the three-month LIBOR rate (expressed with quarterly compounding) at the beginning of the quarter. For example, when the three-month LIBOR rate at the beginning of the quarter is 11% per annum, the financial institution must pay $0.25 \times 10,000,000 \times 0.01 = \$25,000$ at the end of the quarter. When it is 9% per annum, the financial institution is not required to pay anything. The expression $\max(R - 0.1, 0)$ is the payoff from a call option on R. The cap can therefore be viewed as a portfolio of call options on R with the payoffs from the options occurring three months in arrears. The individual options comprising a cap are sometimes referred to as *caplets*.

In general, if the cap rate is R_X, the principal is L, and interest payments are made at times $\tau, 2\tau, \ldots, n\tau$ from the beginning of the life of the cap, the writer of the cap is required to make a payment at time $(k + 1)\tau$ given by

$$\tau L \max(R_k - R_X, 0) \tag{16.7}$$

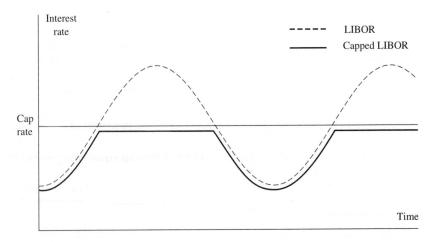

Figure 16.3   Borrower's effective interest rate with a floating-rate loan and an interest rate cap.

where R_k is the value at time $k\tau$ of the rate being capped. This is a call option on the rate observed at time $k\tau$ with the payoff occurring at time $(k + 1)\tau$. Caps are normally structured so that there is no payoff at time τ based on the rate at time 0. There are therefore potential payoffs from a cap at times $2\tau, 3\tau, \ldots, n\tau$.

A Cap as a Portfolio of Bond Options

It is interesting to note that a cap can be also be characterized as a portfolio of put options on discount bonds with payoffs on the puts occurring at the time they are calculated. The payoff in equation (16.7) at time $(k + 1)\tau$ is equivalent to

$$\frac{\tau L}{1 + \tau R_k} \max(R_k - R_X, 0)$$

at time $k\tau$. A few lines of algebra show that this reduces to

$$\max\left[L - \frac{L(1 + R_X\tau)}{1 + \tau R_k}, 0\right] \tag{16.8}$$

The expression

$$\frac{L(1 + R_X\tau)}{1 + \tau R_k}$$

is the value at time $k\tau$ of a discount bond that pays off $L(1 + R_X\tau)$ at time $(k+1)\tau$. The expression in equation (16.8) is therefore the payoff from a put option with maturity $k\tau$ on a discount bond with maturity $(k + 1)\tau$ when the face value of the bond is $L(1 + R_X\tau)$ and the strike price is L. This proves the assertion that an interest rate cap is a portfolio of European put options on discount bonds.

Floors and Collars

Interest rate floors and interest rate collars (which are sometimes called floor–ceiling agreements) are defined analogously to caps. A *floor* places a lower limit on the interest rate that will be charged. *Collars* specify both the upper and lower limits for the rate that will be charged. Analogously to an interest rate cap, an interest rate floor is a portfolio of put options on interest rates or a portfolio of call options on discount bonds. It is often written by the borrower of floating-rate funds. A collar is a combination of a long position in a cap and a short position in a floor. It is usually constructed so that the price of the cap equals the price of the floor. The net cost of the collar is then zero.

There is a put–call parity relationship between the prices of caps and floors. This is

$$\text{cap price} \ = \ \text{floor price} \ + \ \text{swap price}$$

In this relationship the cap and floor have the same strike price, R_X. The swap is an agreement to receive floating and pay the fixed rate of R_X with no exchange of

payments on the first reset date.[4] All three instruments have the same life and the same frequency of payments. This result can easily be seen to be true by noting that a long position in the cap combined with a short position in the floor provides the same cash flows as the swap.

Valuation of Caps and Floors

As shown in equation (16.7), the caplet corresponding to the rate observed at time $k\tau$ provides a payoff at time $(k + 1)\tau$ of

$$\tau L \max(R_k - R_X, 0)$$

If the rate R_k is assumed to be lognormal with a volatility measure σ_k, equation (16.3) gives the value of this caplet as

$$\tau L e^{-r^*(k+1)\tau}[F_k N(d_1) - R_X N(d_2)] \tag{16.9}$$

where

$$d_1 = \frac{\ln(F_k / R_X) + \sigma_k^2 k\tau/2}{\sigma_k \sqrt{k\tau}}$$

$$d_2 = \frac{\ln(F_k / R_X) - \sigma_k^2 k\tau/2}{\sigma_k \sqrt{k\tau}} = d_1 - \sigma \sqrt{k\tau}$$

and F_k is the forward rate for the period between time $k\tau$ and $(k + 1)\tau$. The value of the corresponding floorlet is, from equation (16.4),

$$\tau L e^{-r^*(k+1)\tau}[R_X N(-d_2) - F_k N(-d_1)] \tag{16.10}$$

In these equation r^* is a continuously compounded zero rate for a maturity of $(k + 1)\tau$. Both R_X and F_k are expressed with a compounding frequency of τ.

Example 16.4

Consider a contract that caps the interest rate on a $10,000 loan at 8% per annum (with quarterly compounding) for three months starting in one year. This is a caplet and could be one element of a cap. Suppose that the forward interest rate for a three-month period starting in one year is 7% per annum (with quarterly compounding); the current 15-month interest rate is 6.5% per annum (with continuous compounding); and the volatility measure for the three-month rate underlying the caplet is 20% per annum. In equation (16.9), $F_k = 0.07$, $\tau = 0.25$, $L = 10,000$, $R_X = 0.08$, $r^* = 0.065$, $\sigma_k = 0.20$, and $k\tau = 1.0$. Since

$$d_1 = \frac{\ln 0.875 + 0.02}{0.20} = -0.5677$$

$$d_2 = d_1 - 0.20 = -0.7677$$

---

[4]Note that swaps are usually structured so that the τ-period rate at time zero determines an exchange of payments at time τ. As mentioned earlier, caps and floors are usually structured so that there is no payoff at time τ. This difference explains why we have to exclude the first exchange of payments on the swap.

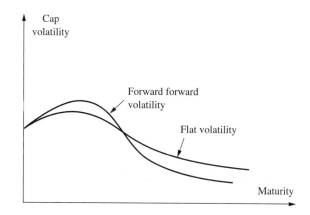

Figure 16.4   Volatility hump.

the caplet price is

$$0.25 \times 10,000e^{-0.065 \times 1.25}[0.07N(-0.5677) - 0.08N(-0.7677)] = 5.19$$

or $5.19.

Each caplet must be valued separately using equation (16.9). One approach is to use a different volatility measure, σ, for each caplet. The volatility measures are then referred to as *forward forward volatilities*. An alternative approach is to use the same volatility measure for all the caplets comprising any particular cap but to vary this volatility according to the life of the cap. The volatilities used are then referred to as *flat volatilities*. The volatilities quoted by brokers are usually flat volatilities. However, many traders like to work with forward forward volatilities since it allows them to identify underpriced and overpriced caplets. Options on Eurodollar futures are very similar to caplets and the implied forward forward volatilities for caplets on three-month LIBOR are frequently compared with those calculated from the prices of Eurodollar futures options.

Figure 16.4 shows a typical pattern for a forward forward volatility and flat volatility as a function of maturity. (In the case of forward forward volatility, the maturity is the maturity of a caplet; in the case of flat volatility, it is the maturity of a cap.) The flat volatilities are akin to cumulative averages of the forward forward volatilities and therefore exhibit less variability. As indicated by Figure 16.4, we usually observe a "hump" in the volatilities at about the one- to two-year point. This hump is observed both when the volatilities are implied from option prices and when they are calculated from historical data. No really convincing explanation for its existence has been put forward.

16.8 EUROPEAN SWAP OPTIONS

Swap options or *swaptions* are options on interest rate swaps and are another increasingly popular type of interest rate option. They give the holder the right to

enter into a certain interest rate swap at a certain time in the future. (The holder does not, of course, have to exercise this right.) Many large financial institutions that offer interest rate swap contracts to their corporate clients are also prepared to sell them swaptions or buy swaptions from them.

To give an example of how a swaption might be used, consider a company that knows that in six months it will enter into a five-year floating-rate loan agreement with resets every six months and knows that it will wish to swap the floating interest payments for fixed interest payments to convert the loan into a fixed-rate loan. (See Chapter 5 for a discussion of how swaps can be used in this way.) At a cost the company could enter into a swaption giving it the right to receive six-month LIBOR and pay a certain fixed rate of interest, say 12% per annum, for a five-year period starting in six months. If the fixed rate on a regular five-year swap in six months turns out to be less than 12% per annum, the company will choose not to exercise the swaption and will enter into a swap agreement in the usual way. However, if it turns out to be greater than 12% per annum, the company will choose to exercise the swaption and will obtain a swap at more favorable terms than those available in the market.

Swaptions, when used in the way that has just been described, provide companies with a guarantee that the fixed rate of interest they will pay on a loan at some future time will not exceed some level. They are an alternative to forward swaps (sometimes called *deferred swaps*). Forward swaps involve no up-front cost but have the disadvantage that they obligate the company to enter into a swap agreement. With a swaption, the company is able to benefit from favorable interest rate movements while acquiring protection from unfavorable interest rate movements. The difference between a swaption and a forward swap is analogous to the difference between an option on foreign exchange and a forward contract on foreign exchange.

Relation to Bond Options

It will be recalled from Chapter 5 that an interest rate swap can be regarded as an agreement to exchange a fixed-rate bond for a floating-rate bond. At the start of a swap, the value of the floating-rate bond always equals the principal amount of the swap. A swaption can therefore be regarded as an option to exchange a fixed-rate bond for the principal amount of the swap. If a swaption gives the holder the right to pay fixed and receive floating, it is a put option on the fixed-rate bond with strike price equal to the principal. If a swaption gives the holder the right to pay floating and receive fixed, it is a call option on the fixed-rate bond with a strike price equal to the principal.

Valuation of European Swaptions

European swaptions are frequently valued by assuming that the swap rate at the maturity of the option is lognormal. Consider a swaption where we have the right to pay a rate R_X and receive floating on a swap that will last n years starting

in T years. We suppose that there are m payments per year under the swap and that the principal is L.

Suppose that the swap rate at the maturity of the swap option is R. (Both R and R_X are expressed with a compounding frequency of m times per year.) By comparing the cash flows on a swap where the fixed rate is R with the cash flows on a swap where the fixed rate is R_X, we see that the payoff from the swaption consists of a series of cash flows equal to

$$\frac{L}{m}\max(R - R_X, 0)$$

The cash flows are received m times per year for the n years of the life of the swap; that is, they are received at times $T + 1/m, T + 2/m, \ldots, T + mn/m$, measured in years from today. Each cash flow is the payoff from a call option on R with strike price R_X.

Suppose that $t_i = T + i/m$. Using equation (16.3), the value of the cash flow received at time t_i is

$$\frac{L}{m}e^{-r_i t_i}[FN(d_1) - R_X N(d_2)]$$

where

$$d_1 = \frac{\ln(F/R_X) + \sigma^2 T/2}{\sigma\sqrt{T}}$$

$$d_2 = \frac{\ln(F/R_X) - \sigma^2 T/2}{\sigma\sqrt{T}} = d_1 - \sigma\sqrt{T}$$

F is the forward swap rate, and r_i is the continuously compounded zero-coupon interest rate for a maturity of t_i.

The total value of the swaption is

$$\sum_{i=1}^{mn} \frac{L}{m}e^{-r_i t_i}[FN(d_1) - R_X N(d_2)]$$

Defining A as the value of a contract that pays \$1 at times t_i $(1 \le i \le mn)$, the value of the swaption becomes

$$\frac{LA}{m}[FN(d_1) - R_X N(d_2)] \tag{16.11}$$

where

$$A = \sum_{i=1}^{mn} e^{-r_i t_i}$$

If the swaption gives the holder the right to receive a fixed rate of R_X instead of paying it, the payoff from the swaption is

$$\frac{L}{m} \max(R_X - R, 0)$$

This is a put option on R. As before, the payoffs are received at times t_i ($1 \leq i \leq mn$). Equation (16.4) gives the value of the swaption as

$$\frac{LA}{m}[R_X N(-d_2) - FN(-d_1)] \qquad (16.12)$$

Example 16.5

Suppose that the LIBOR yield curve is flat at 6% per annum with continuous compounding. Consider a swaption that gives the holder the right to pay 6.2% in a three-year swap starting in five years. The volatility measure for the swap rate is 20%. Payments are made semiannually and the principal is $100. In this case

$$A = e^{-0.06 \times 5.5} + e^{-0.06 \times 6} + e^{-0.06 \times 6.5} + e^{-0.06 \times 7} + e^{-0.06 \times 7.5} + e^{-0.06 \times 8} = 4.0071$$

A rate of 6% per annum with continuous compounding translates into 6.09% with semiannual compounding. It follows that in this example $F = 0.0609$, $X = 0.062$, $T = 5$, $\sigma = 0.2$, so that

$$d_1 = \frac{\ln(0.0609/0.062) + 0.2^2 \times 5/2}{0.2\sqrt{5}} = 0.1836$$

$$d_2 = d_1 - 0.2\sqrt{5} = -0.2636$$

From equation (16.11) the value of the swaption is

$$\frac{100 \times 4.0071}{2}[0.0609 \times N(0.1836) - 0.062 \times N(-0.2636)] = 2.07$$

or $2.07.

16.9 ACCRUAL SWAPS

An extension of Black's model can be used to value what are known as *accrual swaps*. These are swaps where the interest on one side accrues only when the floating reference rate is in a certain range. Sometimes the range remains fixed during the entire life of the swap; sometimes it is reset periodically.

As a simple example of an accrual swap, consider a deal where a fixed rate, Q, is exchanged for three-month LIBOR every quarter. We suppose that the fixed rate accrues only on days when three-month LIBOR is below 8% per annum. Suppose that the principal is L. In a normal swap the fixed-rate payer would pay $0.25QL$ on each payment date. In an accrual swap this is changed to QLn_1/n_2, where n_1 is the number of business days in the preceding period for which three-month LIBOR was below 8% and n_2 is the total number of business days in the

year. The fixed-rate payer saves QL/n_2 on days when the fixed rate is above 8%. The fixed-rate payer's position can be considered to be equivalent to a regular swap plus a series of binary options, one for each day of the life of the swap.[5] The binary options pay off QL/n_2 when three-month LIBOR is above 8%.

To generalize, we suppose that the LIBOR cutoff rate (8% in the case above) is R_X and that payments are exchanged every τ years. Consider day i during the life of the swap. Suppose that the forward LIBOR rate on day i is F_i and its volatility measure is σ_i. The risk-neutral probability that LIBOR is less than the R_X is $N(d_2)$, where

$$ d_2 = \frac{\ln(F_i/R_X) - \sigma_i^2 t_i/2}{\sigma_i \sqrt{t_i}} $$

and t_i is the time in years until the ith day. The payoff from the binary option is realized at the swap payment date following day i. We suppose that this is at time s_i. If r_i is the zero-coupon interest rate for a maturity of s_i, the value of the binary option corresponding to day i is

$$ \frac{QL}{n_2} e^{-r_i s_i} N(d_2) $$

The total value of the binary options is obtained by summing this expression for every day in the life of the swap.[6]

16.10 SPREAD OPTIONS

Spread options are instruments that provide a payoff dependent on the spread between two interest rates. In some cases the rates are both calculated from the same yield curve. (An example would be the situation where the spread is calculated as three-month LIBOR less the five-year swap rate.) In other cases two different yield curves are involved. (An example here would be the situation where the spread is calculated as the excess of the three-month LIBOR rate over the three-month Treasury bill rate.)

When the spread is always positive, it is sometimes reasonable to assume that it is lognormal at the maturity of the option.[7] Black's model can be used.

---

[5]A binary option is an option that pays off a fixed amount if the value of the underlying is in a certain range. It is discussed in Chapter 18.

[6]In practice, good results can be obtained by basing calculations on a relatively small number of equally spaced days during the life of the swap. As discussed in Section 16.11, a small convexity adjustment to the forward rates is in theory necessary because the time lag between the interest rate being observed and the corresponding payoff on the binary option is less than τ. In practice this is usually ignored.

[7]An example of a spread that is always positive is the excess of the three-month LIBOR rate over the three-month Treasury bill rate.

Equations (16.1) and (16.2) with F equal to the forward value of the spread and $\sigma\sqrt{T}$ equal to the standard deviation of the logarithm of the spread.[8]

When the spread is liable to be positive or negative, one approach is to assume that it is normally distributed centered on its forward value. Another is to assume that each of the two rates from which the spread is calculated is lognormal and that there is a correlation between the rates. In this case the expected value of each rate is its forward rate (adjusted as appropriate for convexity) and a different volatility measure can be assumed for each rate. The value of the option is the discounted expected payoff. This can be calculated using a three-dimensional tree or Monte Carlo simulation or some other tool. (For a discussion of procedures for constructing three-dimensional trees, see Chapter 18.)

16.11 CONVEXITY ADJUSTMENTS

As discussed in Section 4.2, a forward interest rate equals the yield on the corresponding forward bond. For example, the forward rate for the period between year 3 and year 4 is the yield calculated from the forward price of a zero-coupon bond lasting between these times. As indicated in Section 16.5, when valuing interest rate derivatives using Black's model, it is appropriate to set the expected price of a bond in a risk-neutral world equal to its forward price and then assume that interest rates are constant when discounting. It is not always correct to set an interest rate equal to the forward interest rate in a risk-neutral world since the relationship between bond prices and bond yields is nonlinear. If the forward price of a zero-coupon bond lasting between three and four years is 90, this can be assumed to be the expected bond price for the purposes of using Black's model. The forward interest rate for the period between three and four years is 11.11% with annual compounding. This is not the expected bond yield (i.e., it is not the expected one-year interest rate in three years' time). The amount by which the expected interest rate exceeds the forward rate is known as a *convexity adjustment*.

The way in which the convexity adjustment arises is illustrated in Figure 16.5, which shows the relationship between bond prices and bond yields. For simplicity we suppose that there are only three possible bond prices, B_1, B_2, and B_3, and that they are equally likely. They are equally spaced so that $B_2 - B_1 = B_3 - B_2$. The bond prices translate into three equally likely yields: Y_1, Y_2, and Y_3. The latter are not equally spaced. The variable, Y_2, is the forward bond yield since it is the yield given by the forward bond price. The expected bond yield is the average of Y_1, Y_2, and Y_3 and is clearly greater than Y_2. The difference between Y_2 and the expected bond yield is the convexity adjustment.

---

[8]The convexity adjustments described in the next section should be made to forward rates used to calculate the forward spread.

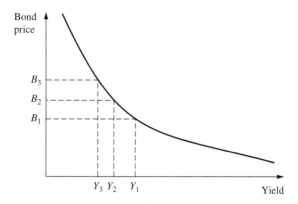

Figure 16.5   Convexity adjustment.

When Is a Convexity Adjustment Necessary?

Interest rate derivatives are often structured so that there is a lag between the time when the interest rate is observed and the time when the corresponding payoff occurs. Consider, for example, a "plain vanilla" interest rate swap where six-month LIBOR is exchanged for a fixed rate of interest. As explained in Chapter 5, the swap is designed so that there is a lag of six months between LIBOR being observed and the corresponding payment occurring. As another example consider an instrument that provides a cap on the three-month interest rate. As explained in Section 16.7, this is usually structured so that the rate is observed at one point in time and the corresponding payoff occurs three months later. In general, when the payoff on a derivative depends on the τ-period rate, it is common to incorporate a time lag of τ between the rate being observed and the corresponding payoff taking place. We refer to this as the *natural time lag*.

When an interest rate derivative is structured so that it incorporates a natural time lag, it is not usually necessary to make a convexity adjustment. This general rule applies to most of the interest rate derivatives that are commonly encountered. To understand the reason for the rule, suppose that R is the τ-period interest rate observed at time T. Consider a cash flow of $100R\tau$ that is received at time $T + \tau$ under certain states of the world. This is equivalent to a cash flow of

$$\frac{100R\tau}{1 + R\tau} = 100\left(1 - \frac{1}{1 + R\tau}\right)$$

at time T. Since $1/(1 + R\tau)$ is the price of a discount bond, its expected value in a risk-neutral world can be assumed to be the forward bond price when Black's model is used. Suppose that F is the forward interest rate for the period between times T and $T + \tau$. Since this is defined as the yield calculated from the forward bond price

$$\hat{E}\left[\frac{1}{1 + R\tau}\right] = \frac{1}{1 + F\tau}$$

where $\hat{E}$ denotes expected value in the risk-neutral world being considered. It follows that

$$\hat{E}\left[\frac{100R\tau}{1 + R\tau}\right] = 100\left(1 - \frac{1}{1 + F\tau}\right)$$

$$= \frac{100F\tau}{1 + F\tau}$$

This indicates that we can set the mean of the probability distribution for R equal to F provided that we discount from time $T + \tau$ to time T at rate F.

This analysis shows why instruments such as caps, "plain vanilla" interest rate swaps, and FRAs, which incorporate natural time lags, can be valued by assuming that the expected future interest rate is the forward rate. For other instruments, which do not incorporate natural time lags into the way the payoff is defined, the expected future interest rate should be assumed to be the forward rate plus a convexity adjustment.

Example 16.6

Consider a derivative that provides a payoff equal to the one-year zero-coupon rate in three years multiplied by $100. If the payoff is made at the end of four years the derivative incorporates a natural time lag and the value of the derivative is

$$100Fe^{-4r^*}$$

where r^* is the four-year risk-free interest rate and F is the forward interest rate for the period between the end of year 3 and the end of year 4. If the payoff is made at the end of three years, the derivative does not incorporate a natural time lag and the value of the derivative is

$$100(F + c)e^{-3r}$$

where r is the three-year risk-free interest rate and c is a convexity adjustment.

Calculating the Convexity Adjustment

We now provide a way of calculating the convexity adjustment when the payoff from an interest rate derivative does not incorporate the natural interest-rate time lag.

Suppose that it is now time zero and the payoff from a derivative takes place at time T. Assume that the payoff depends on a bond yield observed at time T. Assume further that this bond yield is lognormal with volatility measure σ. Define F as the forward bond yield for a forward contract with maturity T and $P(y)$ as the price of the bond as a function of its yield y.

Brotherton-Ratcliffe and Iben show that an analytic approximation for the convexity adjustment that must be made to F is[9]

---

[9]See R. Brotherton-Ratcliffe and B. Iben, "Yield Curve Applications of Swap Products," Chapter 15 of *Advanced Strategies in Financial Risk Management,* R. Schwartz and C. Smith (eds.), (New York: New York Institute of Finance, 1993).

$$-0.5F^2\sigma^2T\frac{P''(F)}{P'(F)} \tag{16.13}$$

where $P'(y)$ and $P''(y)$ denote the first and second partial derivatives of P with respect to y. This means we should assume that the expected interest rate in a risk-neutral world is

$$F - 0.5F^2\sigma^2T\frac{P''(F)}{P'(F)}$$

rather than F. This result is proved in Appendix 16A.

Example 16.7

Consider an instrument that provides a payoff in three years equal to the one-year zero-coupon interest rate (annually compounded) at that time multiplied by $100. Suppose that the zero rate for all maturities is 10% per annum with annual compounding and the volatility measure for the one-year rate in three years is 20%. In this case the payoff depends on the yield on a zero-coupon bond:

$$P(y) = \frac{1}{1+y}$$

$$P'(y) = -\frac{1}{(1+y)^2}$$

$$P''(y) = \frac{2}{(1+y)^3}$$

The forward rate F is 0.1, so that $P'(F) = -0.8264$ and $P''(F) = 1.5026$. From equation (16.13) the convexity adjustment

$$0.5 \times 0.1^2 \times 0.2^2 \times 3 \times \frac{1.5026}{0.8264} = 0.00109$$

or 10.9 basis points. We should assume a forward rate of 0.10109 ($= 10.109\%$) rather than 0.1 when valuing the instrument. Using risk-neutral valuation, the instrument is worth

$$100 \times \frac{0.10109}{1.1^3} = 7.60$$

or $7.60.

Derivatives with Payoffs Dependent on Swap Rates

Up to now we have assumed that the derivative depends on a zero-coupon interest rate. In some instances the underlying rate is a swap rate. A swap rate is an interest rate designed to provide multiple payments, one on each payment date of the underlying swap. If the derivative is structured so that its payoffs mirror this payment pattern, it is appropriate to set the expected swap rate equal to the forward swap rate in a risk-neutral world when Black's model is used. This is what we did in the case of the European swaption in Section 16.8. It was the

correct approach because the swaption can be viewed as providing multiple pay-offs, one for each swap payment date.

If a derivative depends on a swap rate but its payoffs do not correspond to the payment pattern on a swap, a convexity adjustment to the forward swap rate is necessary. Appendix 16A shows that if the payoff from a derivative takes place at time T and depends on a swap rate observed at time T, the convexity adjustment is given by equation (16.13) with the following adjustments to the definitions of the variables:

F: forward swap rate

$P(y)$: price at time T of a bond that provides coupons equal to the forward swap rate over the life of the swap as function of its yield y

σ: volatility measure for the swap rate at time T

Example 16.8

Consider an instrument that provides a payoff in three years equal to the three-year swap rate at that time multiplied by \$100. Suppose that payments are made annually on the swap, that the zero rate for all maturities is 12% per annum with annual compounding, and that the volatility measure for the three-year swap rate in three years is 22%. In this case

$$P(y) = \frac{F}{1 + y} + \frac{F}{(1 + y)^2} + \frac{1 + F}{(1 + y)^3}$$

$$P'(y) = -\frac{F}{(1 + y)^2} - \frac{2F}{(1 + y)^3} - 3\frac{(1 + F)}{(1 + y)^4}$$

$$P''(y) = \frac{2F}{(1 + y)^3} + \frac{6F}{(1 + y)^4} + \frac{12(1 + F)}{(1 + y)^5}$$

The forward swap rate F is 0.12, so that $P'(F) = -2.4018$ and $P''(F) = 8.2546$. From equation (16.13) the convexity adjustment

$$0.5 \times 0.12^2 \times 0.22^2 \times 3 \times \frac{8.2546}{2.4018} = 0.0036$$

or 36 basis points. We should assume a forward swap rate of 0.1236 ($= 12.36\%$) rather than 0.12 when valuing the instrument. Using risk-neutral valuation, the instrument is worth

$$100 \times \frac{0.1236}{1.12^3} = 8.80$$

or \$8.80.

Constant-Maturity Swaps

An example of an actively traded instrument where it is necessary to make convexity adjustments is a *constant-maturity swap*. This is a swap where on each payment date a swap rate is exchanged for a fixed rate of interest. An example

is a swap that lasts for 10 years, has a principal of $100, and has semiannual payment dates. On each payment date one side pays a fixed rate of 8% applied to the principal of $100. The other side pays the current five-year swap rate applied to a principal of $100.

We made the point in Section 5.3 that "plain vanilla" interest rate swaps can be valued by assuming that forward rates are realized. It should be clear from the analysis we have just presented that a similar result does not apply to constant-maturity swaps. The correct way to value a constant-maturity swap is to assume that convexity-adjusted forward swap rates are realized. This means that we first calculate a forward swap rate for each payment date. We apply the convexity adjustment discussed above to each of the forward swap rates and assume that these adjusted forward swap rates are realized.

16.12 SUMMARY

Interest rate options arise in practice in many different ways. For example, options on Treasury bond futures, Treasury note futures, and Eurodollar futures are actively traded by exchanges. Many traded bonds include features that are options. The loans and deposit instruments offered by financial institutions often contain hidden options. Mortgage-backed securities contain embedded interest rate options that represent the prepayment options granted by the lenders of mortgage funds to borrowers. In the over-the-counter market, instruments such as caps and swap options trade actively.

Black's model provides a popular approach for valuing European-style interest rate options. The essence of Black's model is that the value of the variable underlying the option is assumed to be lognormal at the maturity of the option. In the case of a European bond option, Black's model assumes that the underlying bond price is lognormal at the option's maturity. For a cap, Black's model assumes that the interest rate underlying each of the constituent caplets is lognormally distributed. In the case of a swap option, Black's model assumes that the underlying swap rate is lognormally distributed.

Extensions of Black's model can be used to value accrual swaps and spread options. An accrual swap is a swap where interest on one side accrues only when the floating reference lies within a certain range. A spread option is an option that provides a payoff dependent on the spread between two interest rates.

When Black's model is used, the expected value of the underlying lognormal variable in the risk-neutral world can usually be assumed to be equal to its forward value. An exception is when the derivative is structured so that its payoff does not reflect the way in which interest is normally paid on a loan or a deposit instrument. It is then necessary to make what is termed a convexity adjustment to the forward rate. The convexity adjustment arises from the curvature present in the relationship between bond prices and bond yield. It can be estimated analytically.

SUGGESTIONS FOR FURTHER READING

Black, F., "The Pricing of Commodity Contracts," *Journal of Financial Economics,* 3 (March 1976), 167–79.

Brotherton-Ratcliffe, R., and B. Iben, "Yield Curve Applications of Swap Products," Chapter 15 of *Advanced Strategies in Financial Risk Management,* R. Schwartz and C. Smith (eds.), New York Institute of Finance, New York, 1993.

QUESTIONS AND PROBLEMS

16.1. A corporation knows that it will have $5 million to invest for 90 days in three months and wishes to guarantee that a certain interest rate will be obtained. What position in exchange-traded interest rate options provides a hedge against interest rate moves?

16.2. A company caps three-month LIBOR at 10% per annum. The principal amount is $20 million. On a reset date, three-month LIBOR is 12% per annum. What payment would this lead to under the cap? When would the payment be made?

16.3. How is a mortgage-backed security created? Explain why mortgage-backed securities are more risky than regular fixed-income instruments such as government bonds.

16.4. Explain why a swaption can be regarded as a type of bond option.

16.5. An analyst asserts that the option-adjusted spread for a particular mortgage-backed security offering is 155 basis points. Explain carefully what this means.

16.6. Use Black's model to value a one-year European put option on a 10-year bond. Assume that the current value of the bond is $125, the strike price is $110, the one-year interest rate is 10% per annum, the bond's price volatility measure is 8% per annum, and the present value of the coupons that will be paid during the life of the option is $10.

16.7. Suppose that the LIBOR yield curve is flat at 8% with annual compounding. A swaption gives the holder the right to receive 7.6% in a five-year swap starting in four years. Payments are made annually. The volatility measure for the swap rate is 25% per annum and the principal is $1 million. Use Black's model to price the swaption.

16.8. In the accrual swap discussed in the text, the fixed side accrues only when the floating reference rate lies below a certain level. Discuss how the analysis can be extended to cope with the situation where the fixed side accrues only when the floating reference rate is above one level and below another.

16.9. Explain whether any convexity adjustments are necessary when
  (a) We wish to value a spread option that pays off every quarter the excess (if any) of the five-year swap rate over the three-month LIBOR rate applied to a principal of $100. The payoff occurs 90 days after the rates are observed.
  (b) We wish to value a spread option that pays off every quarter the greater of three-month LIBOR rate minus the three-month Treasury bill rate minus 50 basis points and zero. The payoff occurs 90 days after the rates are observed.

16.10. Explain carefully how you would use (a) forward forward volatilities and (b) flat volatilities to value a five-year cap.

16.11. Calculate the price of an option that caps the three-month rate starting in 18 months time at 13% (quoted with quarterly compounding) on a principal amount of $1,000. The volatility measure for the interest rate for the period in question is 12% per annum (quoted with quarterly compounding), the 18-month risk-free interest rate (continuously compounded) is 11.5% per annum, and the volatility of the forward rate is 12% per annum.

16.12. Suppose that an implied Black volatility for a five-year option on a 10-year bond is used to price a nine-year option on the bond. Would you expect the resultant price to be too high or too low? Explain.

16.13. Consider an eight-month European put option on a Treasury bond that currently has 14.25 years to maturity. The current bond price is $910, the exercise price is $900, and the volatility measure for the bond price is 10% per annum. A coupon of $35 will be paid by the bond in three months. The risk-free interest rate is 8% for all maturities up to one year. Use Black's model to determine the price of the option. Consider both the case where the strike price corresponds to the cash price of the bond and the case where it corresponds to the quoted price.

16.14. Calculate delta, gamma, and vega in Problem 16.13 when the strike price corresponds to the quoted price. Explain how they can be interpreted.

16.15. Calculate the price of a cap on the three-month LIBOR rate in nine months' time when the principal amount is $1,000. Use Black's model and the following information:

Quoted nine-month Eurodollar futures price = 92
Interest-rate volatility implied by a nine-month Eurodollar option
   = 15% per annum
Current 12-month interest rate with continuous compounding
   = 7.5% per annum
Cap rate = 8% per annum with quarterly compounding

16.16. Calculate delta, gamma, and vega in Problem 16.15. Explain how they can be interpreted.

16.17. Calculate the value of a four-year European call option on a five-year bond using Black's model. The five-year bond price is $105, the price of a four-year bond with the same coupon is $102, the strike price is $100, the four-year risk-free interest rate is 10% per annum with continuous compounding, and the volatility of measure for the bond price in four years is 2% per annum.

16.18. Consider a European bond option on a Treasury bill where the Treasury bill matures 90 days after the end of the life of the option. Is the value of the option always an increasing function of the option maturity? Explain your answer.

16.19. What other instrument is the same as a five-year zero-cost collar where the strike price of the cap equals the strike price of the floor? What does the common strike price equal?

16.20. Derive a put–call parity relationship for European bond options.

16.21. Derive a put–call parity relationship for European swap options.

16.22. Explain why there is an arbitrage opportunity if the implied Black (flat) volatility for a cap is different from that for a floor.

16.23. Does the lognormal bond price model permit bond yields to become negative? Explain your answer.

16.24. Suppose that in Example 16.4 of Section 16.7 the payoff occurs in one year (i.e., when the interest rate is observed) rather than in 15 months. What difference does this make to the inputs to Black's model?

16.25. The yield curve is flat at 10% per annum with annual compounding. Calculate the value of an instrument where in five years' time the two-year swap rate (with annual compounding) is received and a fixed rate of 10% is paid. Both are applied to a notional principal of $100. Assume that payments are exchanged annually and that the volatility measure for the swap rate is 20% per annum. Explain why the value of the instrument is different from zero.

*16.26. Suppose that the yield, R, on a discount bond follows the process

$$dR + \mu\, dt + \sigma\, dz$$

where μ and σ are functions of R and t, and dz is a Wiener process. Show that the volatility of the discount bond price declines to zero as it approaches maturity.

16.27. In a vanilla swap the floating payment made on a payment date is calculated using the floating rate at the preceding payment date. In an "in arrears swap" the floating rate on a payment date is calculated from the floating rate observed on that payment date. Describe how you would value an in arrears swap.

16.28. Suppose that the LIBOR yield curve is flat at 8% (with continuous compounding). The payoff from a derivative occurs in four years. It is equal to the five-year rate minus the two-year rate at this time applied to a principal of $100 with both rates being continuously compounded. (The payoff can be positive or negative.) Calculate the value of the derivative. Assume that the volatility measure for all rates is 25%.

APPENDIX 16A: PROOF OF THE CONVEXITY ADJUSTMENT FORMULA

In this appendix we prove the result in equation (16.13) and show how it can be extended to cover forward swap rates. Suppose that the payoff from a derivative at time T depends on a bond yield observed at that time. Define:

        F: forward bond yield for a forward contract with maturity T

    $P(y)$:   price of the bond at time T as a function of its yield y

        σ: volatility measure of the bond yield

Expanding $P(y)$ in a Taylor series about $y = F$ yields

$$P(y) \approx P(F) + (y - F)P'(F) + 0.5(y - F)^2 P''(F)$$

where $P'(y)$ and $P''(y)$ are the first and second partial derivatives of the bond price with respect to its yield. Taking expectations in a risk-neutral world gives

$$\hat{E}[P(y)] \approx P(F) + [\hat{E}(y) - F]P'(F) + 0.5F^2\sigma^2 P''(F)T$$

Since $\hat{E}[P(y)]$ is the forward bond price in the risk-neutral world being considered (see Section 16.5), it follows from the way F is defined that

$$\hat{E}[P(y)] = P(F)$$

Hence

$$[\hat{E}(y) - F] \approx -0.5F^2\sigma^2\frac{P''(F)T}{P'(F)}$$

An estimate of the expected bond yield is therefore

$$F - 0.5F^2\sigma^2 T\frac{P''(F)}{P'(F)}$$

This is the result in equation (16.13).

Consider next the problem of calculating the convexity adjustment for a forward swap rate. Define:

F: forward swap rate

$P(y)$: price at time T of a bond that provides coupons equal to the forward swap rate over the life of the swap as a function of its yield y

σ: volatility measure for the swap rate at time T

The analysis above shows that an estimate of the expected yield on a bond whose coupon equals the forward swap rate is

$$F - 0.5F^2\sigma^2 T\frac{P''(F)}{P'(F)}$$

This is not exactly the same as the expected swap rate, but we can expect the two to be very close. The formula for estimating the convexity adjustment for a forward swap rate is therefore essentially the same as that for a regular forward interest rate.

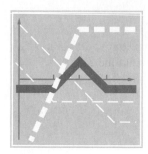

Chapter 17

Interest Rate Derivatives and Models of the Yield Curve

The models for pricing interest rate options that were presented in Chapter 16 make the assumption that the probability distribution of an interest rate, a bond price, or some other variable at a future point in time is lognormal. They are widely used for valuing instruments such as caps, European bond options, and European swap options. However, they do have limitations. They do not provide a description of the way in which interest rates evolve over time. Consequently, they cannot be used for valuing many of the interest rate derivatives that currently trade such as American-style interest rate options, callable bonds, index amortizing swaps, and structured notes.

In this chapter we discuss an approach aimed at overcoming the limitations of the models in Chapter 16. It involves constructing what is known as a *yield curve model* or *term structure model*. This is a model that describes the probabilistic behavior of all rates. Yield curve models are more complicated than the models used to describe a stock price or an exchange rate. This is because they are concerned with movements in an entire yield curve—not with changes to a single variable. As time passes, the individual interest rates in the term structure change. In addition, the shape of the curve itself is liable to change.

In this chapter we consider both *equilibrium models* and *no-arbitrage models.* In an equilibrium model the initial term structure is an output from the model; in a no-arbitrage model it is an input to the model.

17.1 INTRODUCTION TO EQUILIBRIUM MODELS

Equilibrium models usually start with assumptions about economic variables and derive a process for the short-term risk-free rate, r. They then explore what the process implies for bond prices and option prices. The short rate, r, at time t is the rate that applies to an infinitesimally short period of time at time t. It is sometimes referred to as the *instantaneous short rate.* It is important to emphasize that it is not the process for r in the real world that matters. As discussed in Chapter 13, bond prices, option prices, and other derivative prices depend only on the process followed by r in a risk-neutral world.

From the analysis in Chapter 13 [in particular, equation (13.15)], the value of an interest-rate derivative that provides a payoff of f_T at time T is

$$\hat{E}\left[e^{-\bar{r}(T-t)}f_T\right] \tag{17.1}$$

where $\bar{r}$ is the average value of r in the time interval between t and T, and $\hat{E}$ denotes expected value in a risk-neutral world.

Define $P(t, T)$ as the price at time t of discount bond that pays off \$1 at time T. From equation (17.1),

$$P(t, T) = \hat{E}\left[e^{-\bar{r}(T-t)}\right] \tag{17.2}$$

If $R(t, T)$ is the continuously compounded interest rate at time t for a term of $T - t$,

$$P(t, T) = e^{-R(t,T)(T-t)} \tag{17.3}$$

so that

$$R(t, T) = -\frac{1}{T-t}\ln P(t, T) \tag{17.4}$$

and from equation (17.2),

$$R(t, T) = -\frac{1}{T-t}\ln\hat{E}\left[e^{-\bar{r}(T-t)}\right] \tag{17.5}$$

This equation enables the term structure of interest rates at any given time to be obtained from the value of r at that time and the risk-neutral process for r. It shows that once we have fully defined the process for r, we have fully defined everything about the initial term structure and how it can evolve at all future times.

17.2 ONE-FACTOR MODELS

In a one-factor model, the process for r involves only one source of uncertainty. Usually the short rate is described in a risk-neutral world by an Ito process of the form

$$dr = m(r)\,dt + s(r)\,dz$$

The instantaneous drift, m, and instantaneous standard deviation, s, are assumed to be functions of r, but independent of time. The assumption of a single factor is not as restrictive as it might appear. A one-factor model implies that all rates move in the same direction over any short time interval, but not that they all move by the same amount. It does not, as is sometimes supposed, imply that the term structure always has the same shape. A fairly rich pattern of term structures can occur under a one-factor model.

In the next few sections we consider several one-factor equilibrium models:

$m(r) = \mu r$; $s(r) = \sigma r$ (Rendleman and Bartter model)

$m(r) = a(b - r)$; $s(r) = \sigma$ (Vasicek model)

$m(r) = a(b - r)$; $s(r) = \sigma \sqrt{r}$ (Cox, Ingersoll, and Ross model)

17.3 THE RENDLEMAN AND BARTTER MODEL

In Rendleman and Bartter's model the risk-neutral process for r is[1]

$$dr = \mu r\, dr + \sigma r\, dz$$

This means that r follows geometric Brownian motion. The process for r is of the same type as that assumed for a stock price in Chapter 10. The process has a constant expected growth rate of μ and a constant volatility of σ. It can be represented using a binomial tree similar to the one used for stocks in Chapter 15. The parameters u, d, and p are as follows:

$$u = e^{\sigma \sqrt{\Delta t}}$$

$$d = e^{-\sigma \sqrt{\Delta t}}$$

$$p = \frac{a - d}{u - d}$$

where

$$a = e^{\mu \Delta t}$$

The way in which an interest rate tree is used is explained later in this chapter.

Mean Reversion

Rendleman and Bartter's assumption that the short-term interest rate behaves like a stock price is less than ideal. One important difference between interest rates and stock prices is that interest rates appear to be pulled back to some long-run average level over time. This phenomenon, known as *mean reversion,* is not captured by the Rendleman and Bartter model. When r is high, mean reversion tends to cause it to have a negative drift; when r is low, mean reversion tends to cause it to have a positive drift. Mean reversion is illustrated in Figure 17.1.

---

[1] See R. Rendleman and B. Bartter, "The Pricing of Options on Debt Securities," *Journal of Financial and Quantitative Analysis,* 15 (March 1980), 11–24.

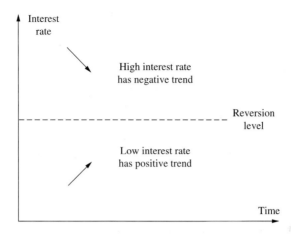

Figure 17.1   Mean reversion.

There are compelling economic arguments in favor of mean reversion. When rates are high, the economy tends to slow down and there is less requirement for funds on the part of borrowers. As a result, rates decline. When rates are low, there tends to be a high demand for funds on the part of borrowers. As a result, rates tend to rise.

17.4 THE VASICEK MODEL

In Vasicek's model the risk-neutral process for r is

$$dr = a(b - r)\,dt + \sigma\,dz$$

where a, b, and σ are constants.[2] This model incorporates mean reversion. The short rate is pulled to a level b at rate a. Superimposed upon this "pull" is a normally distributed stochastic term $\sigma\,dz$.

Vasicek shows that equation (17.2) can be used to obtain the following expression for the price at time t of a zero-coupon bond that pays \$1 at time T:

$$P(t, T) = A(t, T)e^{-B(t,T)r(t)} \tag{17.6}$$

In this equation $r(t)$ is the value of r at time t,

$$B(t, T) = \frac{1 - e^{-a(T-t)}}{a} \tag{17.7}$$

---

[2]See O. A. Vasicek, "An Equilibrium Characterization of the Term Structure," *Journal of Financial Economics*, 5 (1977), 177–88.

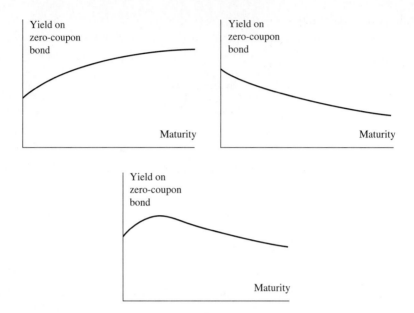

Figure 17.2   Possible shapes of term structure when Vasicek's model is used.

and

$$A(t, T) = \exp\left[\frac{(B(t, T) - T + t)(a^2 b - \sigma^2/2)}{a^2} - \frac{\sigma^2 B(t, T)^2}{4a} \right] \quad (17.8)$$

When $a = 0$, $B(t, T) = T - t$ and $A(t, T) = \exp[\sigma^2(T - t)^3/6]$.

Using equation (17.4) yields

$$R(t, T) = -\frac{1}{T - t} \ln A(t, T) + \frac{1}{T - t} B(t, T) r(t) \quad (17.9)$$

showing that the entire term structure can be determined as a function of $r(t)$ once a, b, and σ have been chosen. The shape can be upward sloping, downward sloping, or slightly "humped" (see Figure 17.2). Equation (17.9) shows that $R(t, T)$ is linearly dependent on $r(t)$. This means that the value of $r(t)$ determines the level of the term structure at time t. The general shape of the term structure at time t is independent of $r(t)$ but does depend on t.

Valuing European Options on Zero-Coupon Bonds

Jamshidian has shown that options on zero-coupon bonds can be valued using Vasicek's model.[3] The price at time t of a European call option maturing

[3] See F. Jamshidian, "An Exact Bond Option Pricing Formula," *Journal of Finance,* 44 (March 1989), 205–9.

at time T on a zero-coupon bond is

$$LP(t, s)N(h) - XP(t, T)N(h - \sigma_P) \tag{17.10}$$

where L is the bond principal, s is the bond maturity,

$$h = \frac{1}{\sigma_P} \ln \frac{LP(t, s)}{P(t, T)X} + \frac{\sigma_P}{2}$$

$$\sigma_P = \frac{\sigma}{a}[1 - e^{-a(s-T)}]\sqrt{\frac{1 - e^{-2a(T-t)}}{2a}}$$

and X is the strike price. The price of a European put option on the bond is

$$XP(t, T)N(-h + \sigma_P) - LP(t, s)N(-h) \tag{17.11}$$

When $a = 0$, $\sigma_P = \sigma(s - T)\sqrt{T - t}$.

Valuing European Options on Coupon-Bearing Bonds

Jamshidian also shows that the prices of options on coupon-bearing bonds can be obtained from the prices of options on zero-coupon bonds in a one-stochastic-variable model such as Vasicek's where all rates are positively related to r. Consider a European call option with exercise price X and maturity T on a coupon-bearing bond. Suppose that the bond provides a total of n cash flows after the option matures. Let the ith cash flow be c_i and occur at time s_i ($1 \le i \le n; s_i > T$). Define:

r^*: value of the short rate r at time T that causes the coupon-bearing bond price to equal the strike price

X_i: value at time T of zero-coupon bond paying off \$1 at time s_i when $r = r^*$

When bond prices are known analytically as a function of r (as they are in Vasicek's model), r^* can be obtained very quickly using an iterative procedure such as the Newton–Raphson method, which is explained in footnote 1 of Chapter 4.

The variable $P(T, s_i)$ is the price at time T of a zero-coupon bond maturing at time s_i. The payoff from the option is therefore

$$\max\left[0, \sum_{i=1}^{n} c_i P(T, s_i) - X\right]$$

Since all rates are increasing functions of r, all bond prices are decreasing functions of r. This means that the coupon-bearing bond is worth more than X at time T and should be exercised if and only if $r < r^*$. Furthermore, the zero-coupon bond maturing at time s_i that underlies the coupon-bearing bond is worth more than $c_i X_i$ at time T if and only if $r < r^*$. The payoff from the option is therefore

$$\sum_{i=1}^{n} c_i \max[0, P(T, s_i) - X_i]$$

This shows that the option on the coupon-bearing bond is the sum of n options on the underlying zero-coupon bonds. A similar argument applies to European put options on coupon-bearing bonds.

Example 17.1

Suppose that $a = 0.1$, $b = 0.1$, and $\sigma = 0.02$ in Vasicek's model with the initial value of the short rate being 10% per annum. Consider a three-year European put option with a strike price of $98 on a bond that will mature in five years. Suppose that the bond has a face value of $100 and pays a coupon of $5 every six months. At the end of three years the bond can be regarded as the sum of four zero-coupon bonds. If the short-term interest rate is r at the end of the three years, the value of the bond is, from equation (17.6),

$$5A(3, 3.5)e^{-B(3,3.5)r} + 5A(3, 4)e^{-B(3,4)r} + 5A(3, 4.5)e^{-B(3,4.5)r} + 105A(3, 5)e^{-B(3,5)r}$$

Using the expressions for $A(t, T)$ and $B(t, T)$ in equations (17.7) and (17.8), this becomes

$$5 \times 0.9988e^{-0.4877r} + 5 \times 0.9952e^{-0.9516r} + 5 \times 0.9895e^{-1.3929r} + 105 \times 0.9819e^{-1.8127r}$$

To apply Jamshidian's procedure, we must find, r^*, the value of r for which this bond price equals the strike price of 98. An iterative procedure shows that $r^* = 0.10952$. When r has this value, the values of the four zero-coupon bonds underlying the coupon-bearing bond are 4.734, 4.484, 4.248, and 84.535. The option on the coupon-bearing bond is therefore the sum of four options on zero-coupon bonds:

1. A three-year option with strike price 4.734 on a 3.5-year zero-coupon bond with a face value of 5
2. A three-year option with strike price 4.484 on a four-year zero-coupon bond with a face value of 5
3. A three-year option with strike price 4.248 on a 4.5-year zero-coupon bond with a face value of 5
4. A three-year option with strike price 84.535 on a five-year zero-coupon bond with a face value of 105

To illustrate the pricing of these options, consider the fourth. From equation (17.6), $P(0, 3) = 0.7419$ and $P(0, 5) = 0.6101$. Also, $\sigma_P = 0.05445$, $h = 0.4161$, $L = 105$, and $X = 84.535$. Equation (17.11) gives the value of the option as 0.8085. Similarly, the value of the first, second, and third options are, respectively, 0.0125, 0.0228, and 0.0314. The value of the option under consideration is therefore $0.0125 + 0.0228 + 0.0314 + 0.8085 = 0.8752$.

17.5 THE COX, INGERSOLL, AND ROSS MODEL

In Vasicek's model the short-term interest rate, r, at a future time is normally distributed and can be negative. Cox, Ingersoll, and Ross have proposed an alternative model where rates are always nonnegative.[4] The risk-neutral process for r in

---

[4]See J. C. Cox, J. E. Ingersoll, and S. A. Ross, "A Theory of the Term Structure of Interest Rates," *Econometrica*, 53 (1985), 385–407.

their model is

$$dr = a(b - r) dt + \sigma \sqrt{r} dz$$

This has the same mean-reverting drift as Vasicek, but the stochastic term has a standard deviation proportional to $\sqrt{r}$. This means that as the short-term interest rate increases, its standard deviation increases.

Cox, Ingersoll, and Ross show that in their model, bond prices have the same general form as in Vasicek's model:

$$P(t, T) = A(t, T)e^{-B(t,T)r}$$

but the functions $B(t, T)$ and $A(t, T)$ are different:

$$B(t, T) = \frac{2(e^{\gamma(T-t)} - 1)}{(\gamma + a)(e^{\gamma(T-t)} - 1) + 2\gamma}$$

and

$$A(t, T) = \left[\frac{2\gamma e^{(a+\gamma)(T-t)/2}}{(\gamma + a)(e^{\gamma(T-t)} - 1) + 2\gamma} \right]^{2ab/\sigma^2}$$

with $\gamma = \sqrt{a^2 + 2\sigma^2}$. As in the case of Vasicek's model, upward-sloping, downward-sloping, and slightly humped yield curves are possible. The long rate, $R(t, T)$, is linearly dependent on $r(t)$. This means that the value of $r(t)$ determines the level of the term structure at time t. The general shape of the term structure at time t is independent of $r(t)$, but does depend on t.

Cox, Ingersoll, and Ross provide formulas for European call and put options on zero-coupon bonds. These involve integrals of the noncentral chi-square distribution. European options on coupon-bearing bonds can be valued using Jamshidian's approach in a similar way to that described for Vasicek's model.

17.6 TWO-FACTOR MODELS

A number of researchers have investigated the properties of two-factor equilibrium models. For example, Brennan and Schwartz have developed a model where the process for the short rate reverts to a long rate, which in turn follows a stochastic process.[5] The long rate is chosen as the yield on a perpetual bond that pays $1 per year. Since the yield on this bond is the reciprocal of its price, Ito's lemma can be used to calculate the process followed by the yield from the process followed by the price of the bond. The fact that the bond is a traded security simplifies the analysis since we know that the growth rate of its price in a risk-neutral world must be the risk-free interest rate less its yield.

[5] See M. J. Brennan and E. S. Schwartz, "A Continuous Time Approach to Pricing Bonds," *Journal of Banking and Finance,* 3 (July 1979), 133–55; M. J. Brennan and E. S. Schwartz, "An Equilibrium Model of Bond Pricing and a Test of Market Efficiency," *Journal of Financial and Quantitative Analysis,* 17, 3 (September 1982), 301–29.

Another two-factor model has been proposed by Longstaff and Schwartz.[6] These authors start with a general equilibrium model of the economy and derive a term structure model in which there is a stochastic volatility. The model proves to be analytically quite tractable.

17.7 INTRODUCTION TO NO-ARBITRAGE MODELS

The disadvantage of the equilibrium models presented in the the preceding few sections is that they do not automatically fit today's term structure. By choosing the parameters judiciously, they can be made to provide an approximate fit to many of the term structures that are encountered in practice. But the fit is not usually an exact one and in some cases there are significant errors. Most traders find this unsatisfactory. Not unreasonably, they argue that they can have very little confidence in the price of a bond option when the model does not price the underlying bond correctly. A 1% error in the price of the underlying bond can lead to a 25% error in an option price.

In this section we present some general theoretical background material on what are known as *no-arbitrage models.* These are models designed to be exactly consistent with today's term structure. We assume that the term structure depends on only one factor and indicate how the results can be extended to several factors.

Notation

We will adopt the following notation:

$P(t, T)$: price at time t of a discount (i.e., zero-coupon) bond with principal \$1 maturing at time T

Ω_t: vector of past and present values of interest rates and bond prices at time t that are relevant for determining bond price volatilities at that time

$v(t, T, \Omega_t)$: volatility of $P(t, T)$

$f(t, T_1, T_2)$: forward rate as seen at time t for the period between time T_1 and time T_2

$F(t, T)$: instantaneous forward rate as seen at time t for a contract maturing at time T

$r(t)$: short-term risk-free interest rate at time t

$dz(t)$: Wiener process driving term structure movements

The variable $F(t, T)$ is the limit of $f(t, T, T + \Delta t)$ as Δt tends to zero.

---

[6]See F. A. Longstaff and E. S. Schwartz, "Interest Rate Volatility and the Term Structure: A Two Factor General Equilibrium Model," *Journal of Finance,* 47, 4 (September 1992), 1259–82.

Time Zero

One notational issue is liable to cause confusion as we move from equilibrium models to no-arbitrage models. This concerns the use of the variable t. Throughout most of this book, it has been convenient to regard the variable t as representing today. For example, in the Black–Scholes equation in Chapter 11, $T - t$ is the time from today until the end of the life of the option. For the rest of this chapter it will be inappropriate to think of time t in this way. Time t ($t \geq 0$) is some general time (either today or in the future) at which we are considering the model. Today will be denoted by time zero. This means that $r(0)$, $P(0, T)$, and $F(0, T)$ are known for all T.

Processes for Discount Bond Prices and Forward Rates

Assuming just one factor, the risk-neutral process for $P(t, T)$ has the form

$$dP(t, T) = r(t)P(t, T)\, dt + v(t, T, \Omega_t)P(t, T)\, dz(t) \qquad (17.12)$$

This equation reflects the fact that since a discount bond is a traded security providing no income, its expected return at time t in a risk-neutral world must be $r(t)$. As its argument Ω_t indicates, the volatility, v, can in the most general form of the model be any well-behaved function of past and present interest rates and bond prices. But since a bond's price volatility declines to zero at maturity, we must have [7]

$$v(t, t, \Omega_t) = 0$$

From equations (4.1) and (17.4), the forward rate, $f(t, T_1, T_2)$, can be related to discount bond prices as follows:

$$f(t, T_1, T_2) = \frac{\ln[P(t, T_1)] - \ln[P(t, T_2)]}{T_2 - T_1} \qquad (17.13)$$

From (17.12) and Ito's lemma,

$$d\ln[P(t, T_1)] = \left[r(t) - \frac{v(t, T_1, \Omega_t)^2}{2} \right] dt + v(t, T_1, \Omega_t)\, dz(t)$$

and

$$d\ln[P(t, T_2)] = \left[r(t) - \frac{v(t, T_2, \Omega_t)^2}{2} \right] dt + v(t, T_2, \Omega_t)\, dz(t)$$

so that

$$df(t, T_1, T_2) = \frac{v(t, T_2, \Omega_t)^2 - v(t, T_1, \Omega_t)^2}{2(T_2 - T_1)}\, dt + \frac{v(t, T_1, \Omega_t) - v(t, T_2, \Omega_t)}{T_2 - T_1}\, dz(t)$$

$$(17.14)$$

---

[7] The $v(t, t, \Omega_t) = 0$ condition is equivalent to the assumption that all discount bonds have finite drifts at all times. If the volatility of the bond does not decline to zero at maturity, an infinite drift may be necessary to ensure that the bond's price equals its face value at maturity.

Equation (17.14) shows that the risk-neutral process for f depends only on the v's. It depends on r and the P's only to the extent that the v's themselves depend on these variables.

When we put $T_1 = T$ and $T_2 = T + \Delta T$ in equation (17.14) and then take limits as ΔT tends to zero, $f(t, T_1, T_2)$ becomes $F(t, T)$, the coefficient of $dz(t)$ becomes $v_T(t, T, \Omega_t)$, and the coefficient of dt becomes

$$\frac{1}{2} \frac{\partial [v(t, T, \Omega_t)^2]}{\partial T} = v(t, T, \Omega_t) v_T(t, T, \Omega_t)$$

where the subscript denotes a partial derivative. It follows that

$$dF(t, T) = v(t, T, \Omega_t) v_T(t, T, \Omega_t) \, dt - v_T(t, T, \Omega_t) \, dz(t) \qquad (17.15)$$

Once the function $v(t, T, \Omega_t)$ has been specified, the risk-neutral processes for the $F(t, T)$'s are known. The $v(t, T, \Omega_t)$'s are therefore sufficient to define fully a one-factor interest rate model.

Equation (17.15) shows that there is a link between the drift and standard deviation of an instantaneous forward rate. Heath, Jarrow, and Morton were the first to point this out.[8] Integrating $v_T(t, \tau, \Omega_t)$ between $\tau = t$ and $\tau = T$, we obtain

$$v(t, T, \Omega_t) - v(t, t, \Omega_t) = \int_t^T v_T(t, \tau, \Omega_t) \, d\tau$$

Since $v(t, t, \Omega_t) = 0$, this becomes

$$v(t, T, \Omega_t) = \int_t^T v_T(t, \tau, \Omega_t) \, d\tau$$

If $m(t, T, \Omega_t)$ and $s(t, T, \Omega_t)$ are the instantaneous drift and standard deviation of $F(t, T)$ so that

$$dF(t, T) = m(t, T, \Omega_t) \, dt + s(t, T, \Omega_t) \, dz$$

it follows from equation (17.15) that

$$m(t, T, \Omega_t) = s(t, T, \Omega_t) \int_t^T s(t, \tau, \Omega_t) \, d\tau \qquad (17.16)$$

Extension to Several Factors

The Heath, Jarrow, and Morton result can be extended to the situation where there are several independent factors. Suppose that

$$dF(t, T) = m(t, T, \Omega_t) \, dt + \sum_i s_k(t, T, \Omega_t) \, dz_k \qquad (17.17)$$

---

[8] See D. Heath, R. Jarrow, and A. Morton, "Bond Pricing and the Term Structure of Interest Rates; A New Methodology," *Econometrica*, 60, 1 (1992), 77–105.

Then a similar analysis to that just given shows that

$$m(t, T, \Omega_t) = \sum_k s_k(t, T, \Omega_t) \int_t^T s_k(t, \tau, \Omega_t) \, d\tau \tag{17.18}$$

Extension to Discrete Case

We now consider the process followed by Δt-period forward rates rather than instantaneous forward rates. Define $m_{i,j}$ and $s_{i,j}$ as the drift and standard deviation of the forward rate for the period between times $j\Delta t$ and $(j + 1)\Delta t$ as seen at time $i\Delta t$. This means that

$$df(t, j\Delta t, j\Delta t + \Delta t) = m_{i,j} \, dt + s_{i,j} \, dz$$

when $t = i\Delta t$. From equation (17.14) it follows that

$$m_{i,j} = \frac{v_{i,j+1}^2 - v_{i,j}^2}{2 \, \Delta t}$$

$$s_{i,j} = \frac{v_{i,j+1} - v_{i,j+1}}{\Delta t}$$

where $v_{i,j}$ is the value of $v(t, T, \Omega_t)$ when $t = i\Delta t$ and $T = j\Delta t$. Since $v_{i,i} = 0$, these equations lead to the result

$$\sum_{j=i}^k m_{i,j} = \frac{1}{2}\Delta t \left(\sum_{j=i}^k s_{i,j} \right)^2 \tag{17.19}$$

Setting $k = i$ allows $m_{i,i}$ to be calculated from $s_{i,i}$; setting $k = i + 1$ then allows $m_{i,i+1}$ to be calculated from $m_{i,i}$, $s_{i,i}$, and $s_{i,i+1}$; and so on.

The Process for the Short Rate

We go back to the one-factor continuous time model for forward rates in equation (17.15) and derive the risk-neutral process for the short rate, $r(t)$. Since

$$F(t, t) = F(0, t) + \int_0^t dF(\tau, t)$$

and $r(t) = F(t, t)$, it follows from (17.15) that

$$r(t) = F(0, t) + \int_0^t v(\tau, t, \Omega_\tau)v_t(\tau, t, \Omega_\tau) \, d\tau + \int_0^t v_t(\tau, t, \Omega_\tau) \, dz(\tau)$$

Differentiating with respect to t and using $v(t, t, \Omega_t) = 0$ [9]

$$dr(t) = F_t(0, t)\, dt + \left\{ \int_0^t [v(\tau, t, \Omega_\tau) v_{tt}(\tau, t, \Omega_\tau) + v_t(\tau, t, \Omega_\tau)^2]\, d\tau \right\} dt$$

$$+ \left\{ \int_0^t v_{tt}(\tau, t, \Omega_\tau)\, dz(\tau) \right\} dt + [v_t(\tau, t, \Omega_\tau)|_{\tau = t}]\, dz(t)$$

It is interesting to examine the terms on the right-hand side of this equation. The first and fourth terms are straightforward. The first term shows that one component of the drift in r is the slope of the initial forward rate curve. The fourth term shows that the instantaneous standard deviation of r is $v_t(\tau, t, \Omega_\tau)|_{\tau=t}$. The second and third terms are more complicated, particularly when v is stochastic. The second term depends on the history of v because it involves $v(\tau, t, \Omega_\tau)$ when $\tau < t$. The third term depends on the history of both v and dz. The two terms are therefore liable to cause the process for r to be non-Markov.

17.8 MODELING FORWARD RATES

One approach to modeling the term structure is to use equation (17.17) and estimate the $s_k(t, T, \Omega_t)$'s. Equation (17.18) can then be used to calculate the drifts, $m(t, T, \Omega_t)$. This has become known as the Heath, Jarrow, and Morton (HJM) approach. The set of all forward rate volatilities is sometimes referred to as the *volatility structure*.

Heath, Jarrow, and Morton have proposed a two-factor lognormal model for forward rates:

$$dF(t, T) = m(t, T, \Omega_t)\, dt + \sigma_1(t, T) F(t, T)\, dz_1 + \sigma_2(t, T) F(t, T)\, dz_2$$

$$(17.20)$$

where dz_1 and dz_2 are uncorrelated, and σ_1 and σ_2 are functions only of $T - t$. The σ_1 and σ_2 functions can be estimated from historical data using statistical techniques such as factor analysis and principal components analysis. Figure 17.3 shows typical results. The variable $\sigma_1(t, T)$ is approximately constant. This means that the $\sigma_1(t, T) F(t, T) dz_1$ term in equation (17.20) gives a roughly parallel shift in the forward curve. The variable $\sigma_2(t, T)$ changes sign as $T - t$ increases. This means that the $\sigma_2(t, T) F(t, T) dz_2$ term in equation (17.20) gives a twist in the forward curve where long rates move in the opposite direction to short rates. In any short period of time the change in the yield curve given by equation (17.20) is a combination of a parallel shift and a twist.

---

[9]The stochastic calculus in this equation may be unfamiliar to some readers. To interpret what is going on, we can replace integral signs with summation signs and d's with Δ's. For example, $\int_0^t v(\tau, t, \Omega_\tau) v_t(\tau, t, \Omega_\tau)\, d\tau$ becomes $\sum_{i=1}^n v(i\Delta t, t, \Omega_i) v_t(i\, \Delta t, t, \Omega_i)\, \Delta t$, where $\Delta t = t/n$.

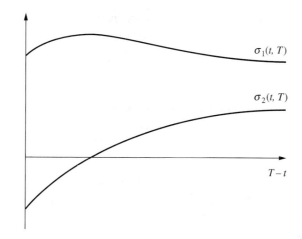

Figure 17.3 First two factors describing term structure moves.

Unfortunately, most models of the forward rate [including the one in equation (17.20)] are non-Markov. This means that it is not possible to represent the behavior of the term structure using a recombining tree. Figure 17.4 shows what happens when a binomial tree is used for a general one-factor model of forward rates. An up movement followed by a down movement does not lead to the same term structure as a down movement followed by an up movement. In general, after n time steps there are 2^n nodes in such a model. This severely limits the number of time steps that can be used and makes computations extremely slow.

Since a complete knowledge of the behavior of the short rate is sufficient to determine the initial term structure and how it can evolve, we can regard the tree in Figure 17.4 as a tree in the short rate. Our discussion of the process for the short rate, r, in the preceding section explains why the HJM tree does not usually recombine. In the general HJM model, the process for r is non-Markov. To know the stochastic behavior of r over a short period of time in the future, we need to know not only the value of r at the beginning of the period but also the path it followed in reaching that value.[10]

Monte Carlo Simulation

Monte Carlo simulation, introduced in Chapter 15, can be used to implement a general non-Markov model of the term structure. It is a useful (if somewhat slow) tool for testing the effect of different volatility structures on European option prices. One of its limitations is that it cannot be used for American-style options.

The time over which the simulation is to be carried out is divided into n intervals of length Δt. The simulation can then be carried out by discretizing the

---

[10]Note that this does not lead to a market inefficiency since r is not the price of a traded security.

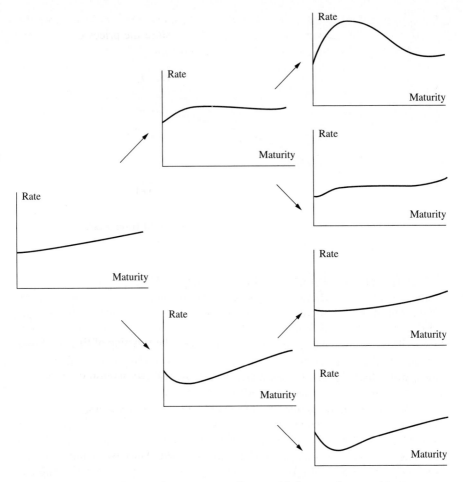

Figure 17.4   Tree for term structure in a non-Markov one-factor model.

process for forward rates. In the one-factor case the continuous-time stochastic process

$$dF(t, T) = m(t, T, \Omega_t) \, dt + s(t, T, \Omega_t) \, dz$$

for the forward rate becomes

$$F_{i+1,j} - F_{i,j} = m_{i,j} \, \Delta t + s_{i,j} \epsilon \sqrt{\Delta t}$$

where $F_{i,j}$ is $f(i\Delta t, j\Delta t, j\Delta t + \Delta t)$; that is $F_{i,j}$ the forward rate as seen at time $i\Delta t$ for the period between $j\Delta t$ and $(j+1)\Delta t$. The variable ϵ is a random sample from a unit normal distribution, $m_{i,j}$ and $s_{i,j}$ are the values of $m(t, T, \Omega_t)$ and $s(t, T, \Omega_t)$ when $t = i\Delta t$ and $T = j\Delta t$. The values of the $m_{i,j}$'s can be calculated from the $s_{i,j}$'s using equation (17.16), but better results are achieved if the discrete-time result in equation (17.19) is used.

The problems of calculating the $m_{i,j}$'s can be avoided if bond prices rather than forward rates are simulated. At time $i\Delta t$ we store the prices of bonds that have maturities $j\Delta t$ for $i + 1 \leq j \leq n$. The equation

$$\frac{dP(t, T)}{P(t, T)} = r(t)\, dt + v(t, T, \Omega_t)\, dz$$

becomes

$$\frac{P_{i+1,j} - P_{i,j}}{P_{i,j}} = \frac{1}{P_{i,i+1}} - 1 + v_{i,j}\epsilon \sqrt{\Delta t}$$

or

$$P_{i+1,j} = P_{i,j}\left(\frac{1}{P_{i,i+1}} + v_{i,j}\epsilon \sqrt{\Delta t}\right)$$

where $P_{i,j}$ is the price at time $i\, \Delta t$ of a bond maturing at time $j\, \Delta t$.

Extensions of these approaches can accommodate several factors.

17.9 DEVELOPING MARKOV MODELS

To avoid the problems associated with nonrecombining trees, an alternative to the HJM approach has become popular. This involves specifying a Markov model for the short rate where the drift is a function of time. The function of time is chosen to make the model consistent with the initial term structure. As we will see in the next few sections, many models developed in this way are natural extensions of the equilibrium models discussed earlier in the chapter.

There is a key difference between modeling r and modeling either bond prices or instantaneous forwards. When we model bond prices or instantaneous forwards, the initial values of the variables ensure that we are consistent with the initial term structure, but the model is usually non-Markov. When we model r directly, it is easy to ensure that the model is Markov, but the initial value of the variable ensures only that we are consistent with the short end of the term structure. We examine next several no-arbitrage Markov models of the short rate.

17.10 HO AND LEE MODEL

Ho and Lee proposed the first no-arbitrage model of the term structure in a paper in 1986.[11] They presented the model in the form of a binomial tree of bond prices. There were two parameters: the short-rate standard deviation and the market price risk of the short rate. It has since been shown that the continuous-time limit of the model is

$$dr = \theta(t)\, dt + \sigma\, dz$$

---

[11] See T. S. Y. Ho and S.-B. Lee, "Term Structure Movements and Pricing Interest Rate Contingent Claims," *Journal of Finance*, 41 (December 1986), 1011–29.

where σ, the instantaneous standard deviation of the short rate, is constant and $\theta(t)$ is a function of time chosen to ensure that the model fits the initial term structure. The variable $\theta(t)$ defines the average direction in which r moves at time t. This is independent of the level of r. It can be calculated from the initial term structure using

$$\theta(t) = F_t(0, t) + \sigma^2 t$$

where the subscript denotes differentiation with respect to t. It is interesting to note that Ho and Lee's parameter concerned with the market price of risk is a redundant variable. This is analogous to risk preferences being irrelevant in the pricing of stock options. As an approximation $\theta(t)$ equals $F_t(0, t)$. This means that the average direction in which the short rate will be moving in the future is approximately equal to the slope of the instantaneous forward curve.

In the Ho and Lee model, discount bonds and European options on discount bonds can be valued analytically. The expression for the price of a discount bond at time t in terms of the short rate is

$$P(t, T) = A(t, T)e^{-r(t)(T-t)}$$

where

$$\ln A(t, T) = \ln \frac{P(0, T)}{P(0, t)} - (T - t)\frac{\partial \ln P(0, t)}{\partial t} - \frac{1}{2}\sigma^2 t(T - t)^2$$

As discussed in Section 17.7, today is time zero. Times t and T are general times in the future with $T \geq t$. These equations therefore define the price of a discount bond at a future time t in terms of the short rate at time t and the prices of bonds today. The latter can be calculated from today's term structure. The partial derivative $\partial \ln P(0, t)/\partial t$ can be approximated by

$$\frac{\ln P(0, t + \epsilon) - \ln P(0, t - \epsilon)}{2\epsilon}$$

where ϵ is small length of time such as 0.01 years. The volatility at time t of a discount bond maturing at time T in the Ho and Lee model is

$$v(t, T, \Omega_t) = \sigma(T - t)$$

The standard deviation of all forward rates is σ.

The price at time zero of a call option that matures at time T on a discount bond maturing at time s is

$$LP(0, s)N(h) - XP(0, T)N(h - \sigma_P)$$

where L is the face value of the bond, X is its strike price,

$$h = \frac{1}{\sigma_P} \ln \frac{LP(0, s)}{P(0, T)X} + \frac{\sigma_P}{2}$$

and

$$\sigma_P = \sigma(s - T)\sqrt{T}$$

The price of a put option on the bond is

$$XP(0, T)N(-h + \sigma_P) - LP(0, s)N(-h)$$

European options on coupon-bearing bonds can be valued by decomposing them into a portfolio of European options on discount bonds using the approach suggested by Jamshidian described in Section 17.4 (see Example 17.1). American options and other derivatives can be valued by constructing a tree using either the approach described by Ho and Lee or the approach described later in this chapter.

The Ho and Lee model has the advantage that it is a Markov analytically tractable model. It is easy to apply and provides an exact fit to the current term structure of interest rates. One disadvantage of the model is that it gives the user very little flexibility in choosing the volatility structure. All spot and forward rates have the same instantaneous standard deviation, σ. A related disadvantage of the model is that it has no mean reversion. Regardless of how high or low interest rates are at a particular point in time, the average direction in which interest rates move over the next short period of time is always the same.

17.11 HULL AND WHITE MODEL

In a paper published in 1990, Hull and White explored extensions of the Vasicek model that provide an exact fit to the initial term structure.[12] The version of the extended Vasicek's model that they suggest is

$$dr = (\theta(t) - ar) dt + \sigma dz \qquad (17.21)$$

or

$$dr = a\left[\frac{\theta(t)}{a} - r\right] dt + \sigma dz$$

where a and σ are constants. The Hull–White model can be characterized as the Ho and Lee model with mean reversion at rate a. Alternatively, it can be characterized as the Vasicek model with a time-dependent reversion level. At time t the short rate reverts to $\theta(t)/a$ at rate a. The Ho and Lee model is a particular case of this Hull–White model with $a = 0$.

The model has the same amount of analytic tractability as Ho and Lee. The $\theta(t)$ function can be calculated from the initial term structure:

$$\theta(t) = F_t(0, t) + aF(0, t) + \frac{\sigma^2}{2a}(1 - e^{-2at}) \qquad (17.22)$$

The last term in this equation is usually fairly small. If we ignore it, the equation implies that the drift of the process for r at time t is $F_t(0, t) + a[F(0, t) - r]$. This

---

[12] See J. Hull and A. White, "Pricing Interest Rate Derivative Securities," *Review of Financial Studies,* 3, 4 (1990), 573–92.

shows that on average r approximately follows the slope of the initial instantaneous forward rate curve. When it gets away from that curve, it reverts back to it at rate a.

Bond prices are given by

$$P(t, T) = A(t, T)e^{-B(t,T)r(t)} \tag{17.23}$$

where

$$B(t, T) = \frac{1 - e^{-a(T-t)}}{a} \tag{17.24}$$

and

$$\ln A(t, T) = \ln \frac{P(0, T)}{P(0, t)} - B(t, T)\frac{\partial \ln P(0, t)}{\partial t} - \frac{1}{4a^3}\sigma^2(e^{-aT} - e^{-at})^2(e^{2at} - 1) \tag{17.25}$$

Equations (17.23), (17.24), and (17.25) define the price of a discount bond at a future time t in terms of the short rate at time t and the prices of bonds today. The latter can be calculated from today's term structure. As in the case of the Ho and Lee model, the partial derivative $\partial \ln P(0, t)/\partial t$ in equation (17.25) can be approximated by

$$\frac{\ln P(0, t + \epsilon) - \ln P(0, t - \epsilon)}{2\epsilon}$$

where ϵ is a small length of time such as 0.01 years.

The price at time zero of a call option that matures at time T on a discount bond maturing at time s is

$$LP(0, s)N(h) - XP(0, T)N(h - \sigma_P)$$

where L is the face value of the bond, X is its strike price,

$$h = \frac{1}{\sigma_P} \ln \frac{LP(0, s)}{P(0, T)X} + \frac{\sigma_P}{2}$$

and

$$\sigma_P = \frac{\sigma}{a}[1 - e^{-a(s-T)}]\sqrt{\frac{1 - e^{-2aT}}{2a}}$$

The price of a put option on the bond is

$$XP(0, T)N(-h + \sigma_P) - LP(0, s)N(-h)$$

These option pricing formulas are the same as those given for the Vasicek model in equations (17.10) and (17.11) with $t = 0$. They are also equivalent to using Black's model as described in Section 16.6. The variable σ_P is the standard deviation of the logarithm of the bond price at time T and the volatility measure for the bond used in Black's model is $\sigma_P/\sqrt{T}$. European options on coupon-bearing bonds can be valued using the Jamshidian decomposition into options on discount bonds described in Section 17.4.

The volatility structure in the Hull–White model is determined by both σ and a. The model can represent a wider range of volatility structures than Ho and Lee.[13] The volatility at time t of a bond maturing at time T is

$$v(t, T, \Omega_t) = \frac{\sigma}{a}[1 - e^{-a(T-t)}]$$

The instantaneous standard deviation at time t of the zero-coupon interest rate maturing at time T is

$$\frac{\sigma}{a(T-t)}[1 - e^{-a(T-t)}]$$

and the instantaneous standard deviation of the T-maturity instantaneous forward rate is $\sigma e^{-a(T-t)}$. These functions are shown in Figure 17.5. The parameter

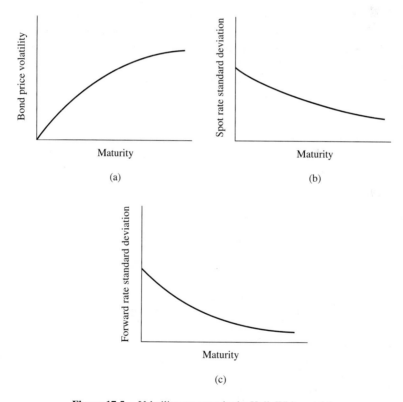

Figure 17.5   Volatility structure in the Hull–White model.

[13]For a still wider range of volatility structures, Hull and White developed a two-factor model in which the short rate reverts to a level which is itself stochastic. See J. Hull and A. White, "Numerical Procedures for Implementing Term Structure Models II: Two-Factor Models," *Journal of Derivatives,* 2, 2 (Winter 1994), 37–48.

σ determines the short rate's instantaneous standard deviation. The reversion rate parameter, a, determines the curvature in Figure 17.5a and the rate at which standard deviations decline with maturity in Figure 17.5b and c. The higher a, the greater the curvature and the greater the decline. When $a = 0$, the model reduces to Ho and Lee. Discount bond price volatilities are a linear function of maturity and the instantaneous standard deviations of both spot and forward rates are constant.

17.12 INTEREST RATE TREES

An interest rate tree is a discrete-time representation of the stochastic process for the short rate in much the same way as a stock price tree is a discrete-time representation of the process followed by a stock price. If the time step on the tree is Δt, the rates on the tree are the continuously compounded Δt-period rates. The usual assumption when a tree is built is that the Δt-period rate follows the same stochastic process as the instantaneous rate in the corresponding continuous-time model. The main difference between interest rate trees and stock price trees is in the way in which discounting is done. In a stock price tree the discount rate is usually assumed to be the same at each node. In an interest rate tree the discount rate varies from node to node.

It often proves to be convenient to use a trinomial rather than a binomial tree for interest rates. The main advantage of a trinomial tree is that it provides an extra degree of freedom, making it easier for the tree to represent features of the interest rate process such as mean reversion. As pointed out in Section 15.7, using a trinomial tree is equivalent to using the explicit finite difference method.

Illustration of Use of Trinomial Trees

To illustrate how trinomial interest rate trees are used to value derivatives, we consider the simple example shown in Figure 17.6. This is a two-step tree with each time step being one year in length. We assume that the up, middle, and down probabilities are 0.25, 0.50, and 0.25 respectively, at each node. The assumed short rate (which is, in this case, the continuously compounded one-year rate) is shown as the upper number at each node.[14]

The tree is used to value a derivative that provides a payoff at the end of the second time step of

$$\max[100(r - 0.11), 0]$$

where r is the Δt-period rate (in this case, the one-year rate). The calculated value of this derivative is the lower number at each node. At the final nodes, the value

---

[14]We explain later how the probabilities and rates on an interest rate tree are determined.

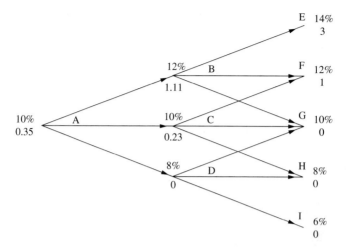

Figure 17.6   Example of the use of trinomial trees.

of the derivative equals the payoff. At node E, for example, the value is $100 \times (0.14 - 0.11) = 3$. At earlier nodes the value of the derivative is calculated using the rollback procedure explained in Chapter 15. At node B the one-year interest rate is 12%. This is used for discounting to obtain the value of the derivative at node B from its values at nodes E, F, and G as

$$[0.25 \times 3 + 0.5 \times 1 + 0.25 \times 0]e^{-0.12 \times 1} = 1.11$$

At node C the one-year interest rate is 10%. This is used for discounting to obtain the value of the derivative at node C as

$$(0.25 \times 1 + 0.5 \times 0 + 0.25 \times 0)e^{-0.1 \times 1} = 0.23$$

At the initial node A the interest rate is also 10% and the value of the derivative is

$$(0.25 \times 1.11 + 0.5 \times 0.23 + 0.25 \times 0)e^{-0.1 \times 1} = 0.35$$

Nonstandard Branching

Hull and White propose variations to the standard branching pattern on a trinomial tree.[15] The standard branching pattern, which is used at all nodes in Figure 17.6, is shown in Figure 17.7a. It is "up one/straight along/down one." One alternative to this is "up two/up one/straight along," which is shown in

[15] See J. Hull and A. White, "One-Factor Interest Rate Models and the Valuation of Interest Rate Derivative Securities," *Journal of Financial and Quantitative Analysis,* 28 (1993), 235–54.

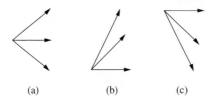

(a)   (b)   (c)

Figure 17.7   Alternative branching methods in a trinomial tree.

Figure 17.7b. This proves useful for incorporating mean reversion when interest rates are very low. A third branching method shown in Figure 17.7c is "straight along/one down/two down." This is useful for incorporating mean reversion when interest rates are very high. We illustrate the use of different branching methods in the next section.

17.13 A GENERAL TREE-BUILDING PROCEDURE

In an article published in 1994, Hull and White explain a robust two-stage procedure for constructing trinomial trees to represent a wide range of one-factor models.[16] In this section we first explain how the procedure can be used for the Hull–White model and then show how it can be extended to represent other models.

First Stage

The Hull–White model is

$$dr = [\theta(t) - ar]\,dt + \sigma\,dz$$

The first stage in building a tree for this model is to build a tree for a variable r^* that is initially zero and follows the process

$$dr^* = -ar^*\,dt + \sigma\,dz$$

This process is symmetrical about $r^* = 0$. The variable $r^*(t + \Delta t) - r^*(t)$ is normally distributed. If terms of higher order than Δt are ignored, the expected value of $r^*(t + \Delta t) - r^*(t)$ is $-ar^*(t)\,\Delta t$ and the variance of $r^*(t + \Delta t) - r^*(t)$ is $\sigma^2\,\Delta t$.

The spacing between interest rates on the tree, Δr, is set to equal

$$\Delta r = \sigma\sqrt{3\,\Delta t}$$

where Δt is the length of each time step. Theoretical work in numerical procedures suggests that this is a good choice of Δr from the viewpoint of error minimization.

---

[16] See J. Hull and A. White, "Numerical Procedures for Implementing Term Structure Models I: Single Factor Models," *Journal of Derivatives,* 2, 1 (1994), 7–16.

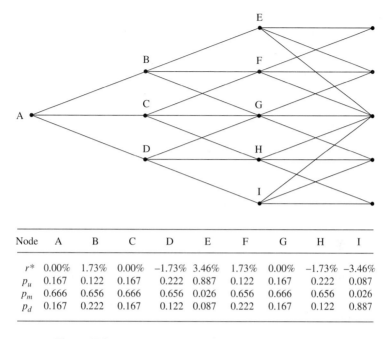

Node	A	B	C	D	E	F	G	H	I
r^*	0.00%	1.73%	0.00%	−1.73%	3.46%	1.73%	0.00%	−1.73%	−3.46%
p_u	0.167	0.122	0.167	0.222	0.887	0.122	0.167	0.222	0.087
p_m	0.666	0.656	0.666	0.656	0.026	0.656	0.666	0.656	0.026
p_d	0.167	0.222	0.167	0.122	0.087	0.222	0.167	0.122	0.887

Figure 17.8   Tree for r^* in Hull–White model (the first stage).

Our objective during the first stage is to build a tree similar to that shown in Figure 17.8, where the nodes are evenly spaced in r^* and t. To do this we must resolve which of the three branching methods shown in Figure 17.7 will apply at each node. This will determine the overall shape of the tree. Once this is done, the branching probabilities must also be calculated.

Define (i, j) as the node for which $t = i \, \Delta t$ and $r^* = j \, \Delta r$. The branching method that is used at a node must lead to all three probabilities being positive. Most of the time the branching in Figure 17.7a is appropriate. When $a > 0$, it is necessary to switch from the branching in Figure 17.7a to the branching in Figure 17.7c for a sufficiently large j. Similarly, it is necessary to switch from the branching in Figure 17.7a to the branching in Figure 17.7b when j is sufficiently negative. Define j_{max} as the value of j where we switch from the Figure 17.7a branching to the Figure 17.7c branching and j_{min} as the value of j where we switch from the Figure 17.7a branching to the Figure 17.7b branching. Hull and White show that probabilities are always positive if we set j_{max} equal to the smallest integer greater than $0.184/(a\Delta t)$ and j_{min} equal to $-j_{max}$.

Define p_u, p_m, and p_d as the probabilities of the highest, middle, and lowest branches emanating from the node. The probabilities are chosen to match the expected change and variance of the change in r^* over the next time interval Δt. The probabilities must also sum to unity. This leads to three equations in the three probabilities.

If the branching pattern from node (i, j) is as in Figure 17.7a the three equations for p_u, p_m, and p_d are

$$p_u \, \Delta r - p_d \, \Delta r = -aj \, \Delta r \, \Delta t$$

$$p_u \, \Delta r^2 + p_d \, \Delta r^2 = \sigma^2 \Delta t + a^2 j^2 \Delta r^2 \Delta t^2$$

$$p_u + p_m + p_d = 1$$

Using $\Delta r^2 = 3\sigma^2 \Delta t$, the solution to these equations is

$$p_u = \frac{1}{6} + \frac{a^2 j^2 \Delta t^2 - aj \, \Delta t}{2}$$

$$p_m = \frac{2}{3} - a^2 j^2 \Delta t^2$$

$$p_d = \frac{1}{6} + \frac{a^2 j^2 \Delta t^2 + aj \, \Delta t}{2}$$

Similarly, if the branching has the form shown in Figure 17.7b, the probabilities are

$$p_u = \frac{1}{6} + \frac{a^2 j^2 \Delta t^2 + aj \, \Delta t}{2}$$

$$p_m = -\frac{1}{3} - a^2 j^2 \Delta t^2 - 2aj \, \Delta t$$

$$p_d = \frac{7}{6} + \frac{a^2 j^2 \Delta t^2 + 3aj \, \Delta t}{2}$$

Finally, if the branching has the form shown in Figure 17.7c, the probabilities are

$$p_u = \frac{7}{6} + \frac{a^2 j^2 \Delta t^2 - 3aj \, \Delta t}{2}$$

$$p_m = -\frac{1}{3} - a^2 j^2 \Delta t^2 + 2aj \, \Delta t$$

$$p_d = \frac{1}{6} + \frac{a^2 j^2 \Delta t^2 - aj \, \Delta t}{2}$$

To illustrate the first stage of the tree construction, suppose that $\sigma = 0.01$, $a = 0.1$, and $\Delta t = 1$ year. In this case $\Delta r = 0.01\sqrt{3} = 0.0173$, j_{max} is set equal to the smallest integer greater than $0.184/0.1$, and $j_{min} = -j_{max}$. This means that $j_{max} = 2$ and $j_{min} = -2$ and the tree is as shown in Figure 17.8. The probabilities on the branches emanating from each node are shown below the tree and are calculated using the equations above for p_u, p_m, and p_d.

Note that the probabilities at each node in Figure 17.8 depend only on j. For example, the probabilities at node B are the same as the probabilities at node F. Furthermore, the tree is symmetrical. The probabilities at node D are the mirror image of the probabilities at node B.

Second Stage

The second stage in the tree construction is to convert the tree for r^* into a tree for r. This is accomplished by displacing the nodes on the r^*-tree so that the initial term structure is exactly matched. Define

$$\alpha(t) = r(t) - r^*(t)$$

Since

$$dr = [\theta(t) - ar] \, dt + \sigma \, dz$$

and

$$dr^* = -ar^* \, dt + \sigma \, dz$$

it follows that

$$d\alpha = [\theta(t) - a\alpha(t)] \, dt$$

Solving this yields

$$\alpha(t) = e^{-at} \left[r(0) + \int_0^t e^{aq} \theta(q) \, dq \right]$$

Substituting the analytic expression for $\theta(t)$ given in equation (17.22), this reduces to

$$\alpha(t) = F(0, t) + \frac{\sigma^2}{2a^2} (1 - e^{-at})^2 \tag{17.26}$$

Equation (17.26) provides an exact continuous-time relationship between r and r^*. It is possible to use this to create a tree for r from the corresponding tree for r^*. The approach is to set the interest rates on the r-tree at time $i\Delta t$ to be equal to the corresponding interest rates on the r^*-tree plus $\alpha(i\Delta t)$ while keeping the probabilities the same. Although satisfactory for most purposes, the tree for r that is produced in this way is not exactly consistent with the initial term structure. This is because continuous-time α's are used in a discrete-time model. An alternative procedure is to calculate the α's iteratively so that the initial term structure is matched exactly. We now explain this approach. It provides a tree-building procedure that can be extended to models where there are no analytic results.

Define α_i as the value of r at time $i\Delta t$ on the r-tree minus the corresponding value of r^* at time $i\Delta t$ on the r^*-tree. Define $Q_{i, j}$ as the present value of a security

that pays off \$1 if node (i, j) is reached and zero otherwise. The α_i and $Q_{i,j}$ can be calculated using forward induction in such a way that the initial term structure is matched exactly.

Illustration of Second Stage

Suppose that the t-year continuously compounded zero rate in the example in Figure 17.8 is $0.08 - 0.05e^{-0.18t}$. (This corresponds approximately to the term structure in the United States at the beginning of 1994.) The value of $Q_{0,0}$ is 1. The value of α_0 is chosen to give the right price for a zero-coupon bond maturing at time Δt. That is, α_0 is set equal to the initial Δt-period interest rate. Since $\Delta t = 1$ in this example, $\alpha_0 = 0.0382$. This defines the position of the initial node on the r-tree in Figure 17.9. The next step is to calculate the values of $Q_{1,1}$, $Q_{1,0}$, and $Q_{1,-1}$. There is a probability of 0.1667 that the (1, 1) node is reached and the discount rate for the first time step is 3.82%. The value of $Q_{1,1}$ is therefore $0.1667e^{-0.0382} = 0.1604$. Similarly, $Q_{1,0} = 0.6417$ and $Q_{1,-1} = 0.1604$.

Once $Q_{1,1}$, $Q_{1,0}$, and $Q_{1,-1}$ have been calculated, we are in a position to determine α_1. This is chosen to give the right price for a zero-coupon bond maturing at time 2 Δt. Since $\Delta r = 0.0173$ and $\Delta t = 1$, the price of this bond as seen at node B is $e^{-(\alpha_1 + 0.0173)}$. Similarly, the price as seen at node C is $e^{-\alpha_1}$ and the

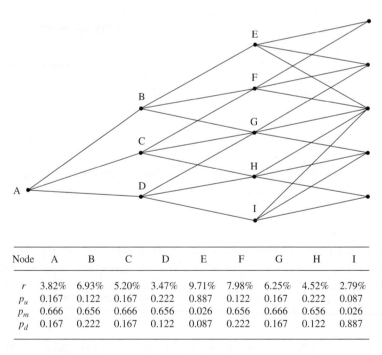

Node	A	B	C	D	E	F	G	H	I
r	3.82%	6.93%	5.20%	3.47%	9.71%	7.98%	6.25%	4.52%	2.79%
p_u	0.167	0.122	0.167	0.222	0.887	0.122	0.167	0.222	0.087
p_m	0.666	0.656	0.666	0.656	0.026	0.656	0.666	0.656	0.026
p_d	0.167	0.222	0.167	0.122	0.087	0.222	0.167	0.122	0.887

Figure 17.9   Tree for r in Hull–White model (the second stage).

price as seen at node D is $e^{-(\alpha_1 - 0.0173)}$. The price as seen at the initial node A is therefore

$$Q_{1,1}e^{-(\alpha_1 + 0.0173)} + Q_{1,0}e^{-\alpha_1} + Q_{1,-1}e^{-(\alpha_1 - 0.0173)} \qquad (17.27)$$

From the initial term structure this bond price should be $e^{-0.04512 \times 2} = 0.9137$. Substituting for the Q's in equation (17.27), we obtain

$$0.1604e^{-(\alpha_1 + 0.0173)} + 0.6417e^{-\alpha_1} + 0.1604e^{-(\alpha_1 - 0.0173)} = 0.9137$$

or

$$e^{-\alpha_1}(0.1604e^{-0.0173} + 0.6417 + 0.1604e^{0.0173}) = 0.9137$$

or

$$\alpha_1 = \ln\left[\frac{0.1604e^{-0.0173} + 0.6417 + 0.1604e^{0.0173}}{0.9137}\right] = 0.0520$$

This means that the central node at time Δt in the tree for r corresponds to an interest rate of 5.20%. (See Figure 17.9.)

The next step is to calculate $Q_{2,2}$, $Q_{2,1}$, $Q_{2,0}$, $Q_{2,-1}$, and $Q_{2,-2}$. The calculations can be shortened by using previously determined Q values. Consider $Q_{2,1}$ as an example. This is the value of a security that pays off \$1 if node F is reached and zero otherwise. Node F can be reached only from nodes B and C. The interest rates at these nodes are 6.93% and 5.20%, respectively. The probabilities associated with the B–F and C–F branches are 0.656 and 0.167. The value at node B of a security that pays \$1 at node F is therefore $0.656e^{-0.0693}$. The value at node C is $0.167e^{-0.0520}$. The variable, $Q_{2,1}$, is $0.656e^{-0.0693}$ times the present value of \$1 received at node B plus $0.167e^{-0.0520}$ times the present value of \$1 received at node C; that is,

$$Q_{2,1} = 0.656e^{-0.0693} \times 0.1604 + 0.167e^{-0.0520} \times 0.6417 = 0.1997$$

Similarly, $Q_{2,2} = 0.0183$, $Q_{2,0} = 0.4737$, $Q_{2,-1} = 0.2032$, and $Q_{2,-2} = 0.0189$.

The next step in producing the r-tree in Figure 17.9 is to calculate α_2. After that, the $Q_{3,j}$'s can then be computed. We can then calculate α_3; and so on.

Formulas for α's and Q's

To express the approach more formally, we suppose that the $Q_{i,j}$'s have been determined for $i \le m$ $(m \ge 0)$. The next step is to determine α_m so that the tree correctly prices a discount bond maturing at $(m + 1) \Delta t$. The interest rate at node (m, j) is $\alpha_m + j \Delta r$, so that the price of a discount bond maturing at time $(m + 1) \Delta t$ is given by

$$P_{m+1} = \sum_{j=-n_m}^{n_m} Q_{m,j} \exp[-(\alpha_m + j \Delta r)\Delta t] \qquad (17.28)$$

where n_m is the number of nodes on each side of the central node at time $m \, \Delta t$. The solution of this equation is

$$\alpha_m = \frac{\ln \sum_{j=-n_m}^{n_m} Q_{m,j} e^{-j\Delta r \Delta t} - \ln P_{m+1}}{\Delta t}$$

Once α_m has been determined, the $Q_{i,j}$ for $i = m + 1$ can be calculated using

$$Q_{m+1,j} = \sum_k Q_{m,k} q(k, j) \exp[-(\alpha_m + k \, \Delta r) \, \Delta t]$$

where $q(k, j)$ is the probability of moving from node (m, k) to node $(m + 1, j)$ and the summation is taken over all values of k for which this is nonzero.

Extension to Other Models

The procedure that has just been outlined can be extended to more general models of the form

$$df(r) = [\theta(t) - af(r)] \, dt + \sigma \, dz$$

This family of models has the property that they can fit any term structure.[17]
We start by setting $x = f(r)$ so that

$$dx = [\theta(t) - ax] \, dt + \sigma \, dz$$

The first stage is to build a tree for x on the assumption that $\theta(t) = 0$ and the initial value of x is zero. The procedure here is identical to the procedure already outlined for building the tree such as that in Figure 17.8.

As in Figure 17.9 we then displace the nodes at time $i \, \Delta t$ by an amount α_i to provide an exact fit to the initial term structure. The equations for determining α_i and $Q_{i,j}$ inductively are slightly different from those for the $f(r) = r$ case. $Q_{0,0} = 1$. Suppose that the $Q_{i,j}$'s have been determined for $i \leq m$ ($m \geq 0$). The next step is to determine α_m so that the tree correctly prices an $(m + 1)\Delta t$ discount bond. Define g as the inverse function of f so that the Δt-period interest rate at the jth node at time $m \, \Delta t$ is

$$g(\alpha_m + j\Delta x)$$

The price of a discount bond maturing at time $(m + 1)\Delta t$ is given by

$$P_{m+1} = \sum_{j=-n_m}^{n_m} Q_{m,j} \exp[-g(\alpha_m + j\Delta x)\Delta t] \tag{17.29}$$

---

[17]Not all no-arbitrage models have this property. For example, the extended-CIR model, considered by Cox, Ingersoll, and Ross (1985) and Hull and White (1990), which has the form

$$dr = [\theta(t) - ar] \, dt + \sigma \sqrt{r} \, dz$$

cannot fit yield curves where the forward rate declines sharply. This is because the process is not well defined when $\theta(t)$ is negative.

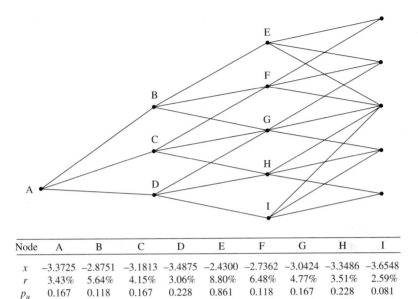

Node	A	B	C	D	E	F	G	H	I
x	−3.3725	−2.8751	−3.1813	−3.4875	−2.4300	−2.7362	−3.0424	−3.3486	−3.6548
r	3.43%	5.64%	4.15%	3.06%	8.80%	6.48%	4.77%	3.51%	2.59%
p_u	0.167	0.118	0.167	0.228	0.861	0.118	0.167	0.228	0.081
p_m	0.666	0.654	0.666	0.654	0.058	0.654	0.666	0.654	0.058
p_d	0.167	0.228	0.167	0.118	0.081	0.228	0.167	0.118	0.861

Figure 17.10   Tree for lognormal model.

This equation can be solved using a numerical procedure such as Newton–Raphson. When $m = 0$, $\alpha_0 = f(r_0)$.

Once α_m has been determined, the $Q_{i,j}$ for $i = m + 1$ can be calculated using

$$Q_{m+1,j} = \sum_k Q_{m,k} q(k, j) \exp[-g(\alpha_m + k\Delta x)\Delta t]$$

where $q(k, j)$ is the probability of moving from node (m, k) to node $(m + 1, j)$ and the summation is taken over all values of k for which this is nonzero.

Figure 17.10 shows the results of applying the procedure to the model

$$d \ln(r) = [\theta(t) - a \ln(r)] \, dt + \sigma \, dz$$

when $a = 0.22$, $\sigma = 0.25$, $\Delta t = 0.5$, and the t-year zero-coupon yield is $0.08 - 0.05e^{-0.18t}$.

Using Analytic Results in Conjunction with Trees

When a tree is constructed for the Hull–White model, the analytic results in Sections 17.10 and 17.11 can be used to provide the complete term structure and European option prices at each node. It is important to recognize that the variable r in the analytic results is the instantaneous short rate, while the r's on the Hull–White tree are Δt-period rates. The two should not be assumed to be

interchangeable. Denoting the instantaneous short rate by r and the Δt period rate by R, equation (17.23) shows that the instantaneous r can be calculated from the Δt-period r as

$$r = \frac{R\Delta t + \ln A(t, t + \Delta t)}{B(t, t + \Delta t)} \tag{17.30}$$

To calculate the term structure at a node of the Hull–White tree, we first use equation (17.30) to get the instantaneous short rate at the node. We then use equation (17.23) to determine other rates.

Example

As an example of the implementation of the model, we use the data in Table 17.1. Data points for maturities between those indicated were generated using linear interpolation.

The zero curve was used to price a 3-year ($= 3 \times 365$ day) option on a zero-coupon bond that will expire in 9 years ($= 9 \times 365$ days). Interest rates were assumed to follow the Hull–White ($f(r) = r$) model. The strike price was 63, $a = 0.1$, and $\sigma = 0.01$. The tree was constructed out to the end of the life of the option. The zero-coupon bond prices at the final nodes were calculated analytically as described in the preceding section. As shown in Table 17.2, the results from the tree are consistent with the analytic price of the option.

TABLE 17.1   DM Zero Curve, July 8, 1994.
All rates continuously compounded.

Maturity	Days	Rate
3 days	3	5.01772
1 month	31	4.98284
2 months	62	4.97234
3 months	94	4.96157
6 months	185	4.99058
1 year	367	5.09389
2 years	731	5.79733
3 years	1,096	6.30595
4 years	1,461	6.73464
5 years	1,826	6.94816
6 years	2,194	7.08807
7 years	2,558	7.27527
8 years	2,922	7.30852
9 years	3,287	7.39790
10 years	3,653	7.49015

Data courtesy of A. A. J. Pelsser, ABN Amro.

TABLE 17.2   Value of Three-Year Put Option on a Nine-Year Zero-Coupon Bond with a Strike of 63

$a = 0.1$ and $\sigma = 0.01$; zero curve as in Table 17.1

Steps	Tree	Analytic
10	1.8658	1.8093
30	1.8234	1.8093
50	1.8093	1.8093
100	1.8144	1.8093
200	1.8097	1.8093
500	1.8093	1.8093

This example provides a good test of one's implementation of the model because the gradient of the zero curve changes sharply immediately after the expiration of the option. Small errors in the construction and use of the tree are liable to have a big effect on the option values obtained. For example, when 100 time steps are used, the value of the option is reduced by about $0.25 if we make the mistake of assuming that the Δt-period rate is the instantaneous rate.

Changing the Length of the Time Step

It is possible to change the length of the time step in the tree. Suppose that the nodes are at times $t_0, t_1, t_2, \ldots, t_n$. When the x^* tree is constructed, the vertical spacing between nodes at time t_{i+1} is set equal to $\sigma \sqrt{3(t_{i+1} - t_i)}$. The branching method is as indicated in Figure 17.11. From any given node at time t_i, we branch to one of three adjacent nodes at time t_{i+1}. Suppose that x_i^* is the value of x^* at time t_i. The central node we branch to at time t_{i+1} is chosen to be the node closest to the expected value of x^*; that is, it is the node closest to $x_i^* - a(t_{i+1} - t_i)x_i^*$. The probabilities are determined so that the mean and standard deviation of the change in x^* are matched. The tree for x is constructed from the tree for x^* as in the constant-time-step case.

Cash Flows between Nodes

Another issue in the construction of the tree concerns cash flows that occur between nodal dates. Suppose that a cash flow occurs at time τ when the immediately preceding nodal date is t_i and the immediately following nodal date is t_{i+1}.

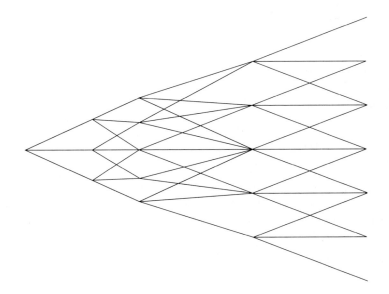

Figure 17.11   Changing the length of the time step.

One approach is to discount the cash flow from time τ to the nodes at time t_i using estimates of the $\tau - t_i$ rates prevailing at the nodes at time t_i.[18] Another approach is to assume that a proportion $(\tau - t_i)/(t_{i+1} - t_i)$ of the cash flow occurs at time t_{i+1} while the remainder occurs at time t_i.[19] A final approach is to avoid the problem altogether by changing the length of the time step so that every payment date is also a nodal date.

Calibration

The Black–Scholes stock option model has the simplifying feature that it involves only one volatility parameter. The usual procedure for calibrating the model to the market is to infer this parameter from the market prices of actively traded stock options. The models presented here are more complicated than Black–Scholes in that they involve two volatility parameters, a and σ. The parameter σ determines the overall volatility of the short rate. The parameter a determines the relative volatilities of long and short rates.

The parameters can be implied simultaneously from broker quotes or other market data on the prices of interest rate options. The procedure is to choose the values of a and σ that minimize

$$\sum_i (P_i - V_i)^2$$

where P_i is the market price of the ith interest rate option and V_i is the price given by the model for the ith interest rate option. The minimization is accomplished using an iterative search "hill-climbing" technique. This procedure is particularly easy in the case of the Hull–White model, where the prices of caps and swap options can be calculated analytically.

Hedge Statistics

One of the attractive features of the Hull–White tree is that it can easily be used to produce accurate hedge statistics. The calculation of a hedge statistic for an interest rate derivative generally involves computing the impact on its price of a small change in either the term structure or one of the volatility parameters. When the term structure is changed, the position of the central nodes on the tree change, but the branching probabilities and the position of the rest of the nodes relative to the central nodes remain the same. When σ is changed, the vertical spacing between the nodes changes, but the probabilities remain the same. When a changes the probabilities change while the geometry of the tree stays the same.

Several different delta measures are typically calculated for the Hull–White model. Each one corresponds to a different shift in the zero curve. Note that the

---

[18] In the case of the Hull–White model, these rates can be calculated analytically.

[19] This approach has the effect of apportioning the cash flow to nodal dates while ensuring that the expected time when the cash flow occurs is correct.

objective is usually to hedge against all the shifts in the term structure that can occur, not just those that are consistent with the model being assumed.[20] A number of different approaches can be used to generate the shifts that are considered:

1. Divide the zero curve into a number of sections (or "buckets"). Shift the rates in each bucket by a small amount, keeping the rest of the zero curve the same.

2. Divide the forward curve into a number of sections (or "buckets"). Shift the rates in each bucket by a small amount, keeping the rest of the forward curve the same.

3. Consider the instruments from which the zero curve was originally computed. Shift the yields or rates on one of these instruments by a small amount, keeping the rest unchanged.

4. Consider two shifts corresponding to the two factors in Figure 17.3 (i.e., an approximately parallel shift and a twist).

Two vegas are usually calculated for the Hull–White model. These correspond to the two volatility parameters a and σ. The first vega is the partial derivative with respect to a; the second is the partial derivative with respect to σ. One possible gamma measure is the second partial derivative with respect to r. This can be calculated directly from the tree. An alternative is the second partial derivative with respect to a parallel shift in the zero curve.

17.14 NONSTATIONARY MODELS

The models discussed in the preceding sections have involved only one function of time, $\theta(t)$. Some authors have suggested extending the models by making a or σ (or both) functions of time. In their 1990 paper, for example, Hull and White produced results for the model in equation (17.21) when a and σ are functions of time. In 1990, Black, Derman, and Toy suggested a procedure for building a binomial tree that is equivalent to using the model

$$d \ln r = \left[\theta(t) + \frac{\sigma'(t)}{\sigma(t)} \ln(r) \right] dt + \sigma(t) dz$$

The volatilities of all rates at time zero are matched.[21] In 1991, Black and Karasinski suggested a procedure involving time steps of varying lengths for building

---

[20]This may seem strange but is consistent with the way all option-pricing models are used. We hedge against the assumptions of the model as well as against the variables the model assumes to be stochastic. As an analogy consider the Black–Scholes model. Even though this assumes that volatility is constant, we hedge against changes in volatility.

[21]See F. Black, E. Derman, and W. Toy, "A One-Factor Model of Interest Rates and Its Application to Treasury Bond Options," *Financial Analysts Journal,* January–February 1990, pp. 33–39.

a binomial tree for the more general model[22]

$$d \ln r = \left[\theta(t) - a(t) \ln(r) \right] dt + \sigma(t) dz$$

The trinomial tree-building procedure in Section 17.13 can be extended to accommodate a and σ being functions of time. As in the constant a and σ case, we first build a tree for x^* where

$$dx^* = -a(t)x^* dt + \sigma(t) dz$$

The spacing between the nodes at time t_{i+1} is chosen to be

$$\sigma(i\,\Delta t)\,\sqrt{3(t_{i+1} - t_i)}$$

From any given node at time t_i we branch to one of three adjacent nodes at time t_{i+1}. Suppose that x_i^* is the value of x_i^* at time t_i. The central node we branch to at time t_{i+1} is chosen to be the node closest to the expected value of x^*; that is, it is the node closest to $x_i^* - a(t_i)(t_{i+1} - t_i)x_i^*$. The probabilities are determined similarly to the constant-time-step case, so that the mean and standard deviation of the change in x^* is matched. The tree for x is calculated from the tree for x^* as in the constant a and σ case.

The $a(t)$ and $\sigma(t)$ can be set in advance of the numerical procedure. Alternatively, it is not difficult to devise an iterative procedure that chooses $a(t)$ and $\sigma(t)$ so that the initial prices of caps or European swap options (or both) are matched. When used for $x = \ln(r)$, this type of tree-building procedure has the advantage over the one suggested by Black and Karasinski that the length of the time step is under the control of the user.

It is deceptively appealing to introduce extra degrees of freedom into a one-factor Markov model to match exactly the prices of caps and swap options in the market. The disadvantage of the approach is that it leads to a nonstationary volatility structure. The volatility term structure being implied by the model in the future is liable to be quite different from that existing in the market today. This can result in unacceptable biases when derivatives are priced. By fitting a one-factor Markov interest model to today's option prices, we are unwittingly making a statement about how the volatility term structure will evolve in the future. Using all the degrees of freedom in the model to fit the volatility exactly constitutes an overparameterization of the model.[23]

17.15 FORWARD RATES AND FUTURES RATES

Eurodollar futures contracts are often used to construct a LIBOR zero-coupon yield curve. As mentioned in Section 4.5, it is inappropriate to assume that the Eurodollar futures rate is a forward interest rate.

---

[22]See F. Black and P. Karasinski, "Bond and Option Pricing when Short Rates Are Lognormal," *Financial Analysts Journal,* July–August 1991, pp. 52–59.

[23]This point is discussed further in J. Hull and A. White, "Using Hull–White Interest Rate Trees," *Journal of Derivatives,* Spring 1996.

Since $\hat{E}[r(t)] = \alpha(t)$ in the Hull–White model, it follows from equation (17.26) that

$$\hat{E}[r(t)] = F(0, t) + \frac{\sigma^2}{2a^2}(1 - e^{-at})^2$$

or

$$\hat{E}[r(t)] = F(0, t) + \frac{\sigma^2 B(0, t)^2}{2}$$

From equations (17.4) and (17.23),

$$R(t_1, t_2) = -\frac{1}{t_2 - t_1} \ln[A(t_1, t_2)] + \frac{1}{t_2 - t_1} B(t_1, t_2) r(t)$$

so that

$$\hat{E}[R(t_1, t_2)] = -\frac{1}{t_2 - t_1} \ln[A(t_1, t_2)] + \frac{1}{t_2 - t_1} B(t_1, t_2) \left[F(0, t_1) + \frac{\sigma^2 B(0, t_1)^2}{2} \right]$$

From equation (17.25),

$$\ln A(t, T) = -(T - t) f(0, t, T) + B(t, T) F(0, t) - \frac{1}{4a} \sigma^2 B(t, T)^2 (1 - e^{-2at})$$

Using this equation in conjunction with the preceding one yields

$$\hat{E}[R(t_1, t_2)] = f(0, t_1, t_2) + \frac{B(t_1, t_2)}{t_2 - t_1}[B(t_1, t_2)(1 - e^{-2at_1}) + 2aB(0, t_1)^2]\frac{\sigma^2}{4a}$$

$$(17.31)$$

Since the futures price of a variable equals its expected future price in a risk-neutral world, $\hat{E}[R(t_1, t_2)]$ is the futures value of the rate between times t_1 and t_2. The variable $f(0, t_1, t_2)$ is the forward rate between times t_1 and t_2. Equation (17.31) therefore shows that the futures rate should be reduced by

$$\frac{B(t_1, t_2)}{t_2 - t_1}[B(t_1, t_2)(1 - e^{-2at_1}) + 2aB(0, t_1)^2]\frac{\sigma^2}{4a}$$

to obtain the forward rate. This adjustment is sometimes referred to as a *convexity adjustment*.[24] When $a = 0$ the adjustment becomes $\sigma^2 t_1 t_2 / 2$. As the following example will show, the adjustment can be significant for long-maturity futures contracts.

Example 17.2

Consider the situation where $a = 0.05$ and $\sigma = 0.015$ and we wish to calculate a forward rate when the eight-year Eurodollar futures price is 94. In this case $t_1 = 8$, $t_2 = 8.25$,

---

[24]It is quite different from the convexity adjustment to forward rates discussed in Section 16.11.

$B(t_1, t_2) = 0.2484$, $B(0, t_1) = 6.5936$, and the convexity adjustment is

$$\frac{0.2484}{0.25}[0.2484(1 - e^{-2\times0.05\times8}) + 2 \times 0.05 \times 6.5936^2]\frac{0.015^2}{4 \times 0.05} = 0.0050$$

or 0.50%. The futures rate is 6% per annum with quarterly compounding or 5.96% with continuous compounding. The forward rate is therefore $5.96 - 0.50 = 5.46\%$ per annum with continuous compounding.

17.16 SUMMARY

The traditional models of the term structure used in finance are known as equilibrium models. These are useful for understanding potential relationships between variables in the economy but have the disadvantage that the initial term structure is an output from the model rather than an input to it. When valuing derivatives it is important that the model used be consistent with the initial term structure observed in the market. No-arbitrage models are designed to have this property. They take the initial term structure as given and define how it can evolve. Choosing between the various no-arbitrage models that have been suggested involves some difficult trade-offs.

No-arbitrage models can be developed as models of bond prices or as models of forward rates or as models of the short rate. In this chapter we have shown that these three approaches are equivalent. If we choose to model discount bond prices, we set the expected return from each bond equal to the risk-free rate. Any bond price volatility function can be used provided that each bond's volatility declines to zero at its maturity. If we choose to model forward rates, there is a relationship between drifts and standard deviations that must be satisfied. If we choose to model the short rate, the drift is usually chosen to be a function of time that makes the model exactly consistent with the initial yield curve.

When modeling bond prices or forward rates, we are free to choose the volatilities in any way we wish. Unfortunately, the result is usually a non-Markov model that must be implemented using Monte Carlo simulation or a non-recombining tree. When the short rate is modeled, the resulting model is generally Markov. However, we do not have complete freedom to specify the volatilities of all rates at all times. It is possible to make a Markov model exactly consistent with any set of initial volatilities, but the rate volatilities implied by the model at future times are liable to be quite different from the initial rate volatilities.

In this chapter we have provided a detailed description of methods for building trees for some of the one-factor Markov models that are commonly used in practice. The simplest one-factor model is the Ho–Lee model. This has the advantage that it is analytically tractable. Its chief disadvantage is that it implies that all rates are equally variable at all times. The Hull–White model is a version of the Ho–Lee model that includes mean reversion. It allows a richer description of the volatility environment while preserving its analytic tractability. Lognormal

one-factor models have the advantage that they avoid the possibility of negative interest rates, but, unfortunately, they have no analytic tractability.

SUGGESTIONS FOR FURTHER READING

Equilibrium Approaches to Modeling the Term Structure

Brennan, M. J., and E. S. Schwartz, "An Equilibrium Model of Bond Pricing and a Test of Market Efficiency," *Journal of Financial and Quantitative Analysis,* 17, 3 (September 1982), 301–29.

Courtadon, G., "The Pricing of Options on Default-Free Bonds," *Journal of Financial and Quantitative Analysis,* 17 (March 1982), 75–100.

Cox, J. C., J. E. Ingersoll, and S. A. Ross, "A Theory of the Term Structure of Interest Rates," *Econometrica,* 53 (1985), 385–407.

Jamshidian, F., "An Exact Bond Option Pricing Formula," *Journal of Finance,* 44 (March 1989), 205–9.

Longstaff, F. A., and E. S. Schwartz, "Interest Rate Volatility and the Term Structure: A Two Factor General Equilibrium Model," *Journal of Finance,* 47, 4 (September 1992), 1259–82.

Rendleman, R., and B. Bartter, "The Pricing of Options on Debt Securities," *Journal of Financial and Quantitative Analysis,* 15 (March 1980), 11–24.

Schaefer, S. M., and E. S. Schwartz, "Time-Dependent Variance and the Pricing of Options," *Journal of Finance,* 42 (December 1987), 1113–28.

Vasicek, O. A., "An Equilibrium Characterization of the Term Structure," *Journal of Financial Economics,* 5 (1977), 177–88.

No-Arbitrage Models

Amin, K., and A. Morton, "Implied Volatility Functions in Arbitrage-Free Term Structure Models," *Journal of Financial Economics,* 35 (1994), 141–180.

Black, F., "Interest Rates as Options," *Journal of Finance,* 50, 5 (1995), pp. 1371–76.

Black, F., E. Derman, and W. Toy, "A One-Factor Model of Interest Rates and Its Application to Treasury Bond Options," *Financial Analysts Journal,* January–February 1990, 33–39.

Black, F., and P. Karasinski, "Bond and Option Pricing When Short Rates Are Lognormal," *Financial Analysts Journal,* July–August, 1991, pp. 52–59.

Burghardt, G., and B. Hoskins, "A Question of Bias," *RISK,* March 1995.

Cheyette, O., "Term Structure Dynamics and Mortgage Valuation," *Journal of Fixed Income,* March 1992, pp. 28–41.

Heath, D., R. Jarrow, and A. Morton, "Bond Pricing and the Term Structure of Interest Rates: A Discrete Time Approximation," *Journal of Financial and Quantitative Analysis,* 25, 4 (December 1990), 419–40.

Heath, D., R. Jarrow, and A. Morton, "Bond Pricing and the Term Structure of the Interest Rates: A New Methodology," *Econometrica,* 60, 1 (1992), 77–105.

Heath, D., R. Jarrow, A. Morton, and M. Spindel, "Easier Done Than Said," *RISK,* May 1993, pp. 77–80.

Ho, T. S. Y., and S.-B. Lee, "Term Structure Movements and Pricing Interest Rate Contingent Claims," *Journal of Finance,* 41 (December 1986), 1011–29.

Hull, J., and A. White, "Bond Option Pricing Based on a Model for the Evolution of Bond Prices," *Advances in Futures and Options Research,* 6 (1993), 1–13.

Hull, J., and A. White, "Branching Out," *RISK,* January 1994, pp. 34–37.

Hull, J., and A. White, "In the Common Interest," *RISK,* March 1992, pp. 64–68.

Hull, J., and A. White, "Numerical Procedures for Implementing Term Structure Models I: Single-Factor Models," *Journal of Derivatives,* 2, 1 (Fall 1994), 7–16.

Hull, J., and A. White, "Numerical Procedures for Implementing Term Structure Models II: Two-Factor Models," *Journal of Derivatives,* 2, 2 (Winter 1994), 37–48.

Hull, J., and A. White, "One-Factor Interest Rate Models and the Valuation of Interest Rate Derivative Securities," *Journal of Financial and Quantitative Analysis,* 28 (June 1993), 235–54.

Hull, J., and A. White, "Pricing Interest Rate Derivative Securities," *Review of Financial Studies,* 3, 4 (1990), 573–92.

Hull, J., and A. White, " The Pricing of Options on Interest Rate Caps and Floors Using the Hull–White Model," *Journal of Financial Engineering,* 2, 3, (1993), 287–96.

Hull, J., and A. White, "Using Hull–White Interest Rate Trees," *Journal of Derivatives,* Spring 1996, 26–36.

Hull, J., and A. White, "Valuing Derivative Securities Using the Explicit Finite Difference Method," *Journal of Financial and Quantitative Analysis,* 25 (March 1990), 87–100.

Jarrow, R. A., *Modeling Fixed Income Securities and Interest Rate Options,* McGraw-Hill: New York, 1995.

Jarrow, R. A., and S. M. Turnbull, "Delta, Gamma, and Bucket Hedging of Interest Rate Derivatives," *Applied Mathematical Finance,* 1 (1994), 21–48.

Jeffrey, A., "Single Factor Heath-Jarrow-Morton Term Structure Models Based on Markov Spot Interest Rate Dynamics," *Journal of Financial and Quantitative Analysis,* 30 (1995), 619–42.

Li, A., P. Ritchken, and L. Sankarasubramanian, "Lattice Models for Pricing American Interest Rate Claims," *Journal of Finance,* 50, 2 (June 1995), 719–37.

Pelsser, A. A. J., "Efficient Methods for Valuing and Managing Interest Rate and Other Derivative Securities," PhD Thesis, Erasmus University, Rotterdam, 1996.

Riccardo, R., *Interest Rate Option Models,* John Wiley & Sons, 1996.

Ritchken, P., and L. Sankarasubramanian, "Volatility Structures of Forward Rates and the Dynamics of the Term Structure," *Mathematical Finance,* 5 (1995), 55–72.

QUESTIONS AND PROBLEMS

17.1. What is the difference between an equilibrium model and a no-arbitrage model?

17.2. If a stock price were mean reverting or followed a path-dependent process there would be a market inefficiency. Why is there not a market inefficiency when the short-term interest rate does so?

17.3. Suppose that the short rate is currently 4% and its standard deviation is 1% per annum. What happens to the standard deviation when the short rate increases to 8% in (a) Vasicek's model; (b) Rendleman and Bartter's model; and (c) the Cox, Ingersoll, and Ross model?

17.4. Explain the difference between a one-factor and a two-factor interest rate model.

17.5. Explain the difference between a Markov and a non-Markov interest rate model.

17.6. Can the approach described in Section 17.4 for decomposing an option on a coupon-bearing bond into a portfolio of options on discount bonds be used in conjunction with a two-factor model? Explain your answer.

17.7. Suppose that $a = 0.1$ and $b = 0.1$ in both the Vasicek and the Cox, Ingersoll, Ross model. In both models, the initial short rate is 10% and the initial standard deviation of the short rate is 2%. Compare the prices given by the models for a discount bond that matures in year 10.

17.8. Suppose that $a = 0.1$, $b = 0.08$, and $\sigma = 0.015$ in Vasicek's model with the initial value of the short rate being 5%. Calculate the price of a one-year European call option on a discount bond with a principal of $100 that matures in three years when the strike price is $87.

17.9. Repeat Problem 17.8 valuing a European put option with a strike of $87. What is the put–call parity relationship between the prices of European call and put options? Show that the put and call option prices satisfy put–call parity in this case.

17.10. Suppose that $a = 0.50$, $b = 0.08$, and $\sigma = 0.015$ in Vasicek's model with the initial short-term interest rate being 6%. Calculate the price of a 2.1-year European call option on a bond that will mature in three years. Suppose that the bond pays a coupon of 5% semiannually. The face value of the bond is 100 and the strike price of the option is 99. The strike price is the cash price (not the quoted price) that will be paid for the bond.

17.11. Use the answer to Problem 17.10 and put–call parity arguments to calculate the price of a put option that has the same terms as the call option in Problem 17.10.

17.12. In the Hull–White model, $a = 0.08$ and $\sigma = 0.01$. Calculate the price of a one-year European call option on a discount bond that will mature in five years when the term structure is flat at 10%, the face value of the bond is $100, and the strike price is $68.

17.13. Repeat the calculations in Problems 17.10 for the Hull–White model. Assume that the initial term structure is flat at 6% with semiannual compounding.

17.14. In the Hull–White model, $a = 0.1$ and $\sigma = 0.015$. Calculate the price of a three-month European put option on a 15-month bond with a 12% (semiannual) coupon. Assume that the bond principal is $100, the cash strike price is $100, and the initial zero-coupon interest rate for a maturity of t years is

$$0.09 + 0.02t$$

17.15. What is the process followed by the forward rate, $F(t, T)$, in the Ho–Lee model?

17.16. What is the process followed by the forward rate, $F(t, T)$, in the Hull–White model?

17.17. Using the formulas given in the text, show that the drift rate of the short rate at time t in the Ho and Lee model is $G_t(0, t)$, where $G(t, T)$ is the instantaneous futures rate as seen at time t for a contract maturing at time T.

17.18. Using the formulas given in the text, show that the drift rate of the short rate at time t in the Hull and White model is $G_t(0, t) + a[G(0, t) - r]$, where $G(t, T)$ is the instantaneous futures rate as seen at time t for a contract maturing at time T.

17.19. Suppose that $a = 0.05, \sigma = 0.015$, and the term structure is flat at 10%. Construct a trinomial tree for the Hull–White model where there are three time steps, each one year in length.

17.20. Construct a trinomial tree for the Ho and Lee model where $\sigma = 0.02$ and the initial zero-coupon interest rate for a maturity of t years is $0.07 + 0.01t$. Use two time steps, each six months long. Calculate the value of a zero-coupon bond with a remaining life of one year at the ends of the final nodes of the tree. Use the tree to value a one-year European call option on the bond with a strike price of 90.Compare the price given by the tree with the analytic price.

Calculate the price of a two-year zero-coupon bond from the tree in Figure 17.6.

Calculate the price of a two-year bond zero-coupon from the tree in Figure 17.9 and verify that it agrees with the initial term structure.

Calculate the price of an 18-month zero-coupon bond from the tree in Figure 17.10 and verify that it agrees with the initial term structure.

17.24. Construct a trinomial tree for the Hull–White model when $\sigma = 0.014, a = 0.2$ and the initial zero-coupon interest rate for a maturity of t is $0.08 + 0.01\sqrt{t}$. Use three time steps, each six months long. Calculate the value of a zero-coupon bond with a remaining life of three years (i.e., a bond maturing 4.5 years from today) at the ends of the final nodes of the tree. Use the tree to value an 18-month European call option on the bond with a strike price of 75. Compare the price given by the tree with the analytic price.

17.25. Suppose that $a = 0.1, \sigma = 0.02$ in the Hull–White model, and a 10-year Eurodollar futures quote is 92. What is the forward rate for the period between 10.0 and 10.25 years?

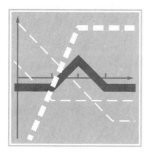

Chapter 18

Exotic Options

Derivatives with more complicated payoffs than the standard European or American calls and puts are sometimes referred to as *exotic options*. Most exotic options trade in the over-the-counter market and are designed by financial institutions to meet the requirements of their clients.

In this chapter we describe different types of exotic options and present some new valuation techniques. For ease of exposition, we assume that the current time is zero. Also, unless otherwise stated we consider the underlying asset to be a stock paying a continuous dividend yield at rate q. As discussed in Chapter 12, for an option on a stock index we set q equal to the dividend yield on the index; for an option on a currency we set q equal to the foreign risk-free rate; for an option on a futures contract we set q equal to the domestic risk-free rate. The arguments in Chapter 13 show that for an option on a commodity we can set q equal to the convenience yield net of storage costs; equivalently, we can set $r - q$ equal to the rate at which futures prices grow with the maturity of the contract.

18.1 TYPES OF EXOTIC OPTIONS

In this section we describe a number of different types of exotic options and present analytic results where they are available. We use a categorization of exotic options similar to that in an excellent series of articles written by Eric Reiner and Mark Rubinstein for *RISK* magazine in 1991 and 1992.

Packages

A package is a portfolio consisting of standard European calls, standard European puts, forward contracts, cash, and the underlying asset itself.[1] We discussed a number of different types of packages in Chapter 8: bull spreads, bear spreads, butterfly spreads, straddles, strangles, and so on.

---

[1] We could omit standard European puts from the list of securities in a package since put–call parity shows that a standard European put can always be created from a standard European call, cash, and the underlying asset. Similarly, we could omit forward contracts since they can be created from a position in the underlying asset.

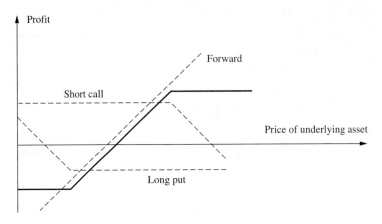

Figure 18.1   Construction of a range forward contract.

Often financial institutions like to design a package so that it has zero initial cost. One example of a zero-cost package is a *range forward contract*.[2] This was mentioned in Chapter 1. It consists of a long forward contract combined with a long position in a put and a short position in a call (see Figure 18.1). The strike prices are chosen so that the initial value of the call equals the initial value of the put. Since the value of the forward contract is zero initially, the value of the whole package is also zero. A range forward contract has a similar type of payoff pattern to a bull spread, which was discussed in Chapter 8.

A regular option can be converted into a zero-cost product by deferring payment for the option until maturity. If c is the cost of the option when payment is made at time zero, then $A = ce^{rT}$ is the cost when payment is made at time T, the maturity of the option. The payoff is then $\max(S - X, 0) - A$ or $\max(S - X - A, -A)$. When the strike price, X, equals the forward price, other names for a deferred payment option are break forward, Boston option, forward with optional exit, and cancelable forward.

Nonstandard American Options

In a standard American option, exercise can take place at any time during the life of the option and the exercise price is always the same. In practice, the American options that trade do not always have these standard features.

One type of nonstandard American option is known as a *Bermudan option*. In this, early exercise is restricted to certain dates during the life of the option. An example of a Bermudan option would be an American swap option that can be exercised only on dates when swap payments are exchanged.

---

[2] Other names used for a range forward contract are zero-cost collar, flexible forward, cylinder option, option fence, min-max, and forward band.

Other types of nonstandard American options sometimes occur in the warrants issued by a company on its own stock. It is often the case that early exercise is possible during part of the life of the option, but not during all of its life. Sometimes the strike price increases with the passage of time. For example, in a five-year warrant the strike price might be $30 during the first two years, $32 during the next two years, and $33 during the final year.

Forward Start Options

Forward start options are options that are paid for now but will start at some time in the future. They are sometimes used in employee incentive schemes. The terms of the option are usually chosen so that the options will be at the money at the time they start.

Consider a forward start call option that will start at time t_1 and mature at time t_2 when the underlying asset is a non-dividend-paying stock . Suppose that the stock price at time zero is S and the stock price at time t_1 is S_1. To value the option, we note from the Black–Scholes formula that the value of an at-the-money call option is proportional to the stock price. The value of the forward start option at time t_1 is therefore cS_1/S, where c is the value at time zero of an at-the-money option that lasts for $t_2 - t_1$. Using risk-neutral valuation, the value of the forward start option at time zero is

$$e^{-rt_1}\hat{E}\left[c\frac{S_1}{S}\right]$$

where $\hat{E}$ denotes expectations in a risk-neutral world. Since c and S are known and $\hat{E}[S_1] = Se^{rt_1}$, it follows that the value of the forward start option is c. In other words, the value of the forward start option is exactly the same as the value of a regular at-the-money option with the same life as the forward start option.

If the stock pays dividends at rate q, then $\hat{E}[S_1] = Se^{(r-q)t_1}$ and the previous analysis shows that the value of the forward start option is ce^{-qt_1}.

Compound Options

Compound options are options on options. There are four main types of compound options: a call on a call, a put on a call, a call on a put, and a put on a put. Compound options have two strike prices and two exercise dates. Consider, for example, a call on a call. On the first exercise date, T_1, the holder of the compound option is entitled to pay the first strike price, X_1, and receive a call option. The call option gives the holder the right to buy the underlying asset for the second strike price, X_2, on the second exercise date, T_2. The compound option will be exercised on the first exercise date only if the value of the option on that date is greater than the first strike price.

When the usual geometric Brownian motion assumption is made, European-style compound options can be valued analytically in terms of integrals of the

bivariate normal distribution.[3] With our usual notation the value at time zero of a European call option on a call option is

$$Se^{-qT_2}M(a_1, b_1; \sqrt{T_1/T_2}) - X_2e^{-rT_2}M(a_2, b_2; \sqrt{T_1/T_2}) - e^{-rT_1}X_1N(a_2)$$

where

$$a_1 = \frac{\ln(S/S^*) + (r - q + \sigma^2/2)T_1}{\sigma\sqrt{T_1}} \qquad a_2 = a_1 - \sigma\sqrt{T_1}$$

$$b_1 = \frac{\ln(S/X_2) + (r - q + \sigma^2/2)T_2}{\sigma\sqrt{T_2}} \qquad b_2 = b_1 - \sigma\sqrt{T_2}$$

The function M is the cumulative bivariate normal distribution function as defined in Appendix 11B. The variable S^* is the stock price at time T_1 for which the option price at time T_1 equals X_1. If the actual stock price is above S^* at time T_1, the first option will be exercised; if it is not above S^*, the option expires worthless.

With similar notation the value of a European put on a call is

$$X_2e^{-rT_2}M(-a_2, b_2; -\sqrt{T_1/T_2}) - Se^{-qT_2}M(-a_1, b_1; -\sqrt{T_1/T_2}) + e^{-rT_1}X_1N(-a_2)$$

The value of a European call on a put is

$$X_2e^{-rT_2}M(-a_2, -b_2; \sqrt{T_1/T_2}) - Se^{-qT_2}M(-a_1, -b_1; \sqrt{T_1/T_2}) - e^{-rT_1}X_1N(-a_2)$$

The value of a European put on a put is

$$Se^{-qT_2}M(a_1, -b_1; -\sqrt{T_1/T_2}) - X_2e^{-rT_2}M(a_2, -b_2; -\sqrt{T_1/T_2}) + e^{-rT_1}X_1N(a_2)$$

A procedure for computing M is provided in Appendix 11B.

"As You Like It" Options

An "as you like it" option (sometimes referred to as a *chooser option*) has the feature that after a specified period of time, the holder can choose whether the option is a call or a put. Suppose that the time at which the choice is made is t_1. The value of the "as you like it" option at this time is

$$\max(c, p)$$

where c is the value of the call underlying the option and p is the value of the put underlying the option.

If the options underlying the "as you like it" option are both European and have the same strike price, put–call parity can be used to provide a valuation formula. Suppose that S_1 is the stock price at time t_1, X is the strike price, t_2 is the maturity of the options, and r is the risk-free interest rate. Put–call parity implies that

$$\max(c, p) = \max(c, c + Xe^{-r(t_2-t_1)} - S_1e^{-q(t_2-t_1)})$$

$$= c + e^{-q(t_2-t_1)}\max(0, Xe^{-(r-q)(t_2-t_1)} - S_1)$$

[3] See R. Geske, "The Valuation of Compound Options," *Journal of Financial Economics*, 7 (1979), 63–81; M. Rubinstein, "Double Trouble," *RISK*, December 1991–January 1992.

This shows that the "as you like it" option is a package consisting of:

1. A call option with strike price X and maturity t_2.
2. $e^{-q(t_2-t_1)}$ put options with strike price $Xe^{-(r-q)(t_2-t_1)}$ and maturity t_1.

As such, it can readily be valued.

More complex "as you like it" options can be defined where the call and the put do not have the same strike price and time to maturity. They are then not packages but have the same types of features as compound options.

Barrier Options

Barrier options are options where the payoff depends on whether the underlying asset's price reaches a certain level during a certain period of time. In Chapter 12 we met one particular type of barrier option: the CAPs that trade on the CBOT. These are options designed so that the payoff cannot exceed $30. This means that a call CAP is exercised automatically on a day when the index reaches a barrier equal to the strike price plus $30; a put CAP is exercised automatically on a day when the index reaches a barrier equal to the strike price less $30.

A number of different types of barrier options regularly trade in the over-the-counter market. They are attractive to some market participants because they are less expensive than the corresponding regular options. These barrier options can be classified as either *knock-out options* or *knock-in options*. A knock-out option is an option that ceases to exist when the underlying asset price reaches a certain barrier. A knock-in option is an option that comes into existence only when the underlying asset price reaches a barrier.

Equations (12.4) and (12.5) show that the values at time zero of a regular call and put option are

$$c = Se^{-qT}N(d_1) - Xe^{-rT}N(d_2)$$
$$p = Xe^{-rT}N(-d_2) - Se^{-qT}N(-d_1)$$

where

$$d_1 = \frac{\ln(S/X) + (r - q + \sigma^2/2)T}{\sigma\sqrt{T}}$$

and

$$d_2 = \frac{\ln(S/X) + (r - q - \sigma^2/2)T}{\sigma\sqrt{T}} = d_1 - \sigma\sqrt{T}$$

A *down-and-out call* is one type of knock-out option. It is a regular call option that ceases to exist if the asset price reaches a certain barrier level, H. The barrier level is below the initial stock price. The corresponding knock-in option is a *down-and-in call*. This is a regular call that comes into existence only if the asset price reaches the barrier level.

If H is less than or equal to the strike price, X, the value of a down-and-in call at time zero is given by

$$c_{di} = Se^{-qT}(H/S)^{2\lambda}N(y) - Xe^{-rT}(H/S)^{2\lambda-2}N(y - \sigma\sqrt{T})$$

where

$$\lambda = \frac{r - q + \sigma^2/2}{\sigma^2}$$

$$y = \frac{\ln[H^2/(SX)]}{\sigma\sqrt{T}} + \lambda\sigma\sqrt{T}$$

Since the value of a regular call equals the value of a down-and-in call plus the value of a down-and-out call, the value of a down-and-out call is given by

$$c_{do} = c - c_{di}$$

If $H \geq X$, then

$$c_{do} = SN(x_1)e^{-qT} - Xe^{-rT}N(x_1 - \sigma\sqrt{T})$$
$$- Se^{-qT}(H/S)^{2\lambda}N(y_1) + Xe^{-rT}(H/S)^{2\lambda-2}N(y_1 - \sigma\sqrt{T})$$

and

$$c_{di} = c - c_{do}$$

where

$$x_1 = \frac{\ln(S/H)}{\sigma\sqrt{T}} + \lambda\sigma\sqrt{T}$$

$$y_1 = \frac{\ln(H/S)}{\sigma\sqrt{T}} + \lambda\sigma\sqrt{T}$$

An *up-and-out call* is a regular call option that ceases to exist if the asset price reaches a barrier level H that is higher than the current asset price. An *up-and-in call* is a regular call option that comes into existence only if the barrier is reached. When H is less than or equal to X, the value of the up-and-out call, c_{uo}, is zero and the value of the up-and-in call, c_{ui}, is c. When H is greater than X,

$$c_{ui} = SN(x_1)e^{-qT} - Xe^{-rT}N(x_1 - \sigma\sqrt{T}) - Se^{-qT}(H/S)^{2\lambda}[N(-y) - N(-y_1)]$$
$$+ Xe^{-rT}(H/S)^{2\lambda-2}[N(-y + \sigma\sqrt{T}) - N(-y_1 + \sigma\sqrt{T})]$$

and

$$c_{uo} = c - c_{ui}$$

Put barrier options are defined similarly to call barrier options. An *up-and-out put* is a put option that ceases to exist when a barrier H that is greater than the current stock price is reached. An *up-and-in put* is a put that comes into existence only if the barrier is reached. When the barrier, H, is greater than or equal to the

strike price, X, their prices are

$$p_{ui} = -Se^{-qT}(H/S)^{2\lambda}N(-y) + Xe^{-rT}(H/S)^{2\lambda-2}N(-y + \sigma\sqrt{T})$$

and

$$p_{uo} = p - p_{ui}$$

When H is less than or equal to X,

$$p_{uo} = -SN(-x_1)e^{-qT} + Xe^{-rT}N(-x_1 + \sigma\sqrt{T})$$
$$+ Se^{-qT}(H/S)^{2\lambda}N(-y_1) - Xe^{-rT}(H/S)^{2\lambda-2}N(-y_1 + \sigma\sqrt{T})$$

and

$$p_{ui} = p - p_{uo}$$

A *down-and-out put* is a put option that ceases to exist when a barrier less than the current asset price is reached. A *down-and-in put* is a put option that comes into existence only when the barrier is reached. When the barrier is greater than the strike price, $p_{do} = 0$ and $p_{di} = p$. When the barrier is less than the strike price,

$$p_{di} = -SN(-x_1)e^{-qT} + Xe^{-rT}N(-x_1 + \sigma\sqrt{T}) + Se^{-qT}(H/S)^{2\lambda}[N(y) - N(y_1)]$$
$$- Xe^{-rT}(H/S)^{2\lambda-2}[N(y - \sigma\sqrt{T}) - N(y_1 - \sigma\sqrt{T})]$$

and

$$p_{do} = p - p_{di}$$

All of these valuations make the usual assumption that the probability distribution for the stock price at a future time is lognormal. It should be noted that the price of a barrier option can be quite sensitive to this lognormal assumption.

An important issue for barrier options is the frequency with which the stock price, S, is observed for purposes of determining whether the barrier has been reached. The analytic formulas given in this section assume that S is observed continuously. Often, the terms of a contract state that S is observed once a day. For example, in S&P CAPs, S is observed at the close of trading each day.

Binary Options

Binary options are options with discontinuous payoffs. A simple example of a binary option is a *cash-or-nothing call*. This pays off nothing if the stock price ends up below the strike price and pays a fixed amount, Q, if it ends up above the strike price. In a risk-neutral world, the probability of the stock price being above the strike price at the maturity of an option is, with our usual notation, $N(d_2)$. The value of a cash or nothing call is therefore $Qe^{-rT}N(d_2)$.

Another type of binary option is an *asset-or-nothing call*. This pays off nothing if the underlying stock price ends up below the strike price and pays an amount equal to the stock price itself if it ends up above the strike price. With our usual notation, the value of an asset-or-nothing call is $Se^{-qT}N(d_1)$. A regular

option is equivalent to a long position in an asset-or-nothing call, and a short position in a cash-or-nothing call where the cash payoff equals the strike price.

An accrual swap (see Section 16.9) can be regarded as a regular swap combined with a portfolio of binary options.

Lookback Options

The payoffs from lookback options depend on the maximum or minimum stock price reached during the life of the option. The payoff from a European-style lookback call is the amount by which the final stock price exceeds the minimum stock price achieved during the life of the option. The payoff from a European-style lookback put is the amount by which the maximum stock price achieved during the life of the option exceeds the final stock price.

Valuation formulas have been produced for European lookbacks.[4] The value of a European lookback call at time zero is

$$
Se^{-qT}N(a_1) - Se^{-qT}\frac{\sigma^2}{2(r-q)}N(-a_1) - S_{\min}e^{-rT}\left[N(a_2) - \frac{\sigma^2}{2(r-q)}e^{Y_1}N(-a_3)\right]
$$

where

$$
a_1 = \frac{\ln(S/S_{\min}) + (r - q + \sigma^2/2)T}{\sigma\sqrt{T}}
$$

$$
a_2 = a_1 - \sigma\sqrt{T}
$$

$$
a_3 = \frac{\ln(S/S_{\min}) + (-r + q + \sigma^2/2)T}{\sigma\sqrt{T}}
$$

$$
Y_1 = -\frac{2(r - q - \sigma^2/2)\ln(S/S_{\min})}{\sigma^2}
$$

and $S_{\min}$ is the minimum stock price achieved to date. (If the lookback has just been originated, $S_{\min} = S$.)

The value of a European lookback put is

$$
S_{\max}e^{-rT}\left[N(b_1) - \frac{\sigma^2}{2(r-q)}e^{Y_2}N(-b_3)\right] + Se^{-qT}\frac{\sigma^2}{2(r-q)}N(-b_2) - Se^{-qT}N(b_2)
$$

where

$$
b_1 = \frac{\ln(S_{\max}/S) + (-r + q + \sigma^2/2)T}{\sigma\sqrt{T}}
$$

$$
b_2 = b_1 - \sigma\sqrt{T}
$$

---

[4]See B. Goldman, H. Sosin, and M. A. Gatto, "Path-Dependent Options: Buy at the Low, Sell at the High," *Journal of Finance,* 34 (December 1979), 1111–27; M. Garman, "Recollection in Tranquility," *RISK,* March 1989.

$$b_3 = \frac{\ln(S_{max}/S) + (r - q - \sigma^2/2)T}{\sigma\sqrt{T}}$$

$$Y_2 = \frac{2(r - q - \sigma^2/2)\ln(S_{max}/S)}{\sigma^2}$$

and S_{max} is the maximum stock price achieved to date. (If the lookback has just been originated, $S_{max} = S$.)

Example 18.1

Consider a newly issued lookback put on a non-dividend-paying stock where the stock price is 50, the stock price volatility is 40% per annum, the risk-free rate is 10% per annum, and the time to maturity is three months. In this case $S_{max} = 50$, $S = 50$, $r = 0.1$, $q = 0$, $\sigma = 0.4$, and $T = 0.25$. From the formulas just given, $b_1 = -0.025$, $b_2 = -0.225$, $b_3 = 0.025$, and $Y_2 = 0$, so that the value of the lookback put is 7.79. A newly issued lookback call on the same stock is worth 8.04.

A lookback call is a way in which the holder can buy the underlying asset at the lowest price achieved during the life of the option. Similarly, a lookback put is a way in which the holder can sell the underlying asset at the highest price achieved during the life of the option. The underlying asset in a lookback option is often a commodity. As with barrier options, the value of a lookback option is liable to be sensitive to the frequency with which the asset price is observed for the purposes of computing the maximum or minimum. The formulas above assume that the asset price is observed continuously.

Asian Options

Asian options are options where the payoff depends on the average price of the underlying asset during at least some part of the life of the option. The payoff from an *average price call* is $\max(0, S_{ave} - X)$ and that from an *average price put* is $\max(0, X - S_{ave})$, where S_{ave} is the average value of the underlying asset calculated over a predetermined averaging period. Average price options are less expensive than regular options and are arguably more appropriate than regular options for meeting some of the needs of corporate treasurers. Suppose that a U.S. corporate treasurer expects to receive from the company's German subsidiary a cash flow of 100 million deutschemarks spread evenly over the next year. The treasurer is likely to be interested in an option that guarantees that the average exchange rate realized during the year is above some level. An average price put option can achieve this more effectively than regular put options.

Another type of Asian option is an average strike option. An *average strike call* pays off $\max(0, S - S_{ave})$, while an *average strike put* pays off $\max(0, S_{ave} - S)$. Average strike options can guarantee that the average price paid for an asset in frequent trading over a period of time is not greater than the final price. Alternatively, it can guarantee that the average price received for an asset in frequent trading over a period of time is not less than the final price.

If the underlying asset price, S, is assumed to be lognormally distributed and S_{ave} is a geometric average of the S's, analytic formulas are available for valuing European average price options.[5] This is because the geometric average of a set of lognormally distributed variables is also lognormal. In a risk-neutral world it can be shown that the probability distribution of the geometric average of a stock price over a certain period is the same as that of the stock price if the stock's expected growth rate is set equal to $(r - q - \sigma^2/6)/2$ (rather than $r - q$) and its volatility is set equal to $\sigma/\sqrt{3}$ (rather than σ). A geometric average price option can therefore be treated like a regular option with the volatility set equal to $\sigma/\sqrt{3}$ and the dividend yield equal to

$$r - \frac{1}{2}\left(r - q - \frac{\sigma^2}{6}\right) = \frac{1}{2}\left(r + q + \frac{\sigma^2}{6}\right)$$

When, as is more common, Asian options are defined in terms of arithmetic averages, analytic pricing formulas are not available. This is because the distribution of the arithmetic average of a set of lognormal distributions does not have analytically tractable properties. However, there is an analytic approximation for valuing average price options on the arithmetic average. This involves calculating the first two moments of the probability distribution of the arithmetic average exactly and then assuming that distribution of the arithmetic average is the lognormal distribution with the same first two moments.[6]

Define

$$M_1 = \frac{e^{(r-q)T} - 1}{(r - q)T}$$

and

$$M_2 = \frac{2e^{[2(r-q)+\sigma^2]T}}{(r - q + \sigma^2)(2r - 2q + \sigma^2)T^2} + \frac{2}{(r - q)T^2}\left[\frac{1}{2(r - q) + \sigma^2} - \frac{e^{(r-q)T}}{r - q + \sigma^2}\right]$$

The first and second moments of the arithmetic average as seen at time zero for a period of time T are SM_1 and S^2M_2. It follows from equations (11.3) and (11.4) that if we make the lognormal approximation, we should treat an average price option like a regular option with dividend yield q_A and volatility σ_A, where

$$e^{(r-q_A)T} = M_1 \qquad e^{[2(r-q_A)+\sigma_A^2]T} = M_2$$

These two equations can be solved to yield

$$q_A = r - \frac{\ln M_1}{T} \qquad \sigma_A^2 = \frac{\ln M_2}{T} - 2(r - q_A)$$

---

[5] See A. Kemna and A. Vorst, "A Pricing Method for Options Based on Average Asset Values," *Journal of Banking and Finance*, 14 (March 1990), 113–29.

[6] See S. M. Turnbull and L. M. Wakeman, "A Quick Algorithm for Pricing European Average Options," *Journal of Financial and Quantitative Analysis*, 26 (September 1991), 377–89.

Example 18.2

Consider a newly issued average price call option on a non-dividend-paying stock where the stock price is 50, the strike price is 50, the stock price volatility is 40% per annum, the risk-free rate is 10% per annum, and the time to maturity is one year. In this case $S = 50$, $X = 50$, $r = 0.1$, $q = 0$, $\sigma = 0.4$, and $T = 1$. If the average is a geometric average, we can value the option as a regular option with the volatility equal to $0.4/\sqrt{3}$, or 23.09%, and dividend yield equal to $(0.1 + 0.4^2/6)/2$, or 6.33%. The value of the option is 5.13. If the average is an arithmetic average, we first calculate $M_1 = 1.05$ and $M_2 = 1.17$. The formulas in the text show that we can approximately value the option as a regular option with volatility equal to 23.54% and dividend yield equal to 4.96%. The value of the option is 5.62.

This analysis assumes that the remaining life of the option is at least as great as the averaging period. It can be generalized to cover the situation where some prices used to determine the average have already been observed. Suppose that the averaging period is composed of a period of length t_1 over which prices have already been observed and a period of length t_2 in the future. Suppose that the average stock price during the first time period is $\overline{S}$. The payoff from an average price call is

$$\max\left(\frac{\overline{S}t_1 + S_{ave}t_2}{t_1 + t_2} - X, 0\right)$$

where S_{ave} is the average stock price during the remaining part of the averaging period. This is the same as

$$\frac{t_2}{t_1 + t_2} \max(S_{ave} - X^*, 0)$$

where

$$X^* = \frac{t_1 + t_2}{t_2}X - \frac{t_1}{t_2}\overline{S}$$

The option can therefore be valued in the same way as an option whose remaining life is greater than the averaging period provided that we change the strike price from X to X^* and multiply the result by $t_2/(t_1 + t_2)$.

Options to Exchange One Asset for Another

Options to exchange one asset for another (sometimes referred to as *exchange options*) arise in various contexts. An option to buy deutschemarks with Swiss francs is, from the point of view of a U.S. investor, an option to exchange one foreign currency asset for another foreign currency asset. A stock tender offer is an option to exchange shares in one stock for shares in another stock.

A formula for valuing a European option to give up an asset worth S_1 and receive in return an asset worth S_2 was first produced by Margrabe.[7] Suppose that S_1 and S_2 both follow geometric Brownian motion with volatilities σ_1 and σ_2. Suppose further that the instantaneous correlation between S_1 and S_2 is ρ, and the yields provided by S_1 and S_2 are q_1 and q_2. The value of the option at time zero is

$$S_2 e^{-q_2 T} N(d_1) - S_1 e^{-q_1 T} N(d_2)$$

where

$$d_1 = \frac{\ln(S_2/S_1) + (q_1 - q_2 + \sigma^2/2)T}{\sigma\sqrt{T}}$$

$$d_2 = d_1 - \sigma\sqrt{T}$$

and

$$\sigma = \sqrt{\sigma_1^2 + \sigma_2^2 - 2\rho\sigma_1\sigma_2}$$

It is interesting to note that these formulas are independent of the risk-free rate r. This is because, as r increases, the growth rate of both asset prices in a risk-neutral world increases, but this is offset by an increase in the discount rate. The variable σ is the volatility of S_2/S_1. Comparisons with the formulas in Chapter 12 show that this option price is the same as the price of S_1 European call options on an asset worth S_2/S_1 when the strike price is 1, the risk-free interest rate is q_1, and the dividend yield on the asset is q_2. Mark Rubinstein shows that the American version of this option can be characterized similarly for valuation purposes.[8] It can be regarded as S_1 American options to buy an asset worth S_2/S_1 for 1 when the risk-free interest rate is q_1 and the dividend yield on the asset is q_2. The option can therefore be valued as described in Chapter 15 using a binomial tree.

It is worth noting that an option to obtain the better or worse of two assets can be regarded as a position in one of the assets combined with an option to exchange it for the other asset:

$$\min(S_1, S_2) = S_2 - \max(S_2 - S_1, 0)$$

$$\max(S_1, S_2) = S_1 + \max(S_2 - S_1, 0)$$

Options Involving Several Assets

Options involving two or more risky assets are sometimes referred to as *rainbow options*. One example is the bond futures contract traded on the CBOT that was described in Chapter 4. The party with the short position is allowed to choose between a large number of different bonds when making delivery. Another

---

[7] See W. Margrabe, "The Value of an Option to Exchange One Asset for Another," *Journal of Finance*, 33 (March 1978), 177–86.

[8] See M. Rubinstein, "One for Another," *RISK*, July–August 1991.

example is what is known as a *basket option*. This is an option whose payoff depends on the value of a portfolio of assets. A third example is a LIBOR-Contingent FX option. This is an option whose payoff occurs only if a prespecified interest rate is within a certain range at maturity.

Options involving several underlying assets can sometimes be valued analytically when appropriate assumptions are made. For example, basket options are often valued by assuming that the value of the portfolio of assets comprising the basket is lognormal rather than that each of the assets taken individually is lognormal.

18.2 BASIC NUMERICAL PROCEDURES

The numerical procedures described in Chapter 15 can often be adapted to cope with exotic options. Monte Carlo simulation is the natural tool to use for European-style path-dependent options when analytic results are not available. When sampling a path for the underlying asset, we keep track of the relevant functions of the path (e.g., the average asset price, the maximum asset price, or the minimum asset price). This allows the sample values of the derivative to be obtained.

A binomial or trinomial tree can be used to value all non-path-dependent options. The nature of the option governs the rules that are used when we roll back through the tree. For example, in a down-and-out option the rules are as for a regular option except that the value of the option is set equal to zero when the underlying asset's price is below the knockout barrier; in a Bermudan option we test for early exercise at time t only when the time interval between t and $t + \Delta t$ includes a date where early exercise is allowed; and so on. An "as you like it" option where the underlying options are American has the complication that when rolling back through the tree, we must value both a call and a put. For the nodes that correspond to the date where the choice is made, the value of the security is set equal to the greater of the value of the call and the value of the put. We roll back from these nodes to the present in the usual way.

18.3 PATH-DEPENDENT DERIVATIVES

The main problem in using Monte Carlo simulation to value path-dependent derivatives is that the computation time necessary to achieve the required level of accuracy can be unacceptably high. Also, American-style path-dependent derivatives cannot be handled. In this section we show how the binomial and trinomial tree methods presented in Chapters 15 and 17 can be extended to cope with path-dependent derivatives.[9] The procedure we propose can handle American-style

---

[9]This approach was suggested in J. Hull and A. White, "Efficient Procedures for Valuing European and American Path-Dependent Options," *Journal of Derivatives,* Fall 1993, 21–31.

path-dependent derivatives and is computationally more efficient than Monte Carlo simulation for European-style path-dependent derivatives.

For the procedure to work, two conditions must be satisfied:

1. The payoff from the derivative depends on a single function, F, of the path followed by the underlying stochastic variable.

2. The value of F at time $\tau + \Delta t$ can be calculated from the value of F at time τ and the value of the underlying asset at time $\tau + \Delta t$.

Illustration Using Lookback Options

As a first illustration of the procedure we consider an American lookback put option on a non-dividend-paying stock.[10] If exercised at time τ, this pays off the amount by which the maximum stock price between time 0 and time τ exceeds the current stock price. We suppose that the initial stock price is $50, the stock price volatility is 40 percent per annum, the risk-free interest rate is 10 percent per annum, the total life of the option is 3 months, and that stock price movements are represented by a three-step binomial tree. Using the notation in Chapter 15, this means that $S = 50$, $\sigma = 0.4$, $r = 0.10$, $\Delta t = 0.08333$, $u = 1.1224$, $d = 0.8909$, $a = 1.0084$, and $p = 0.5073$.

The tree is shown in Figure 18.2. The top number at each node is the stock price. The next level of numbers at each node shows the possible maximum stock prices achievable on paths leading to the node. The final level of numbers shows the values of the derivative corresponding to each of the possible maximum stock prices.

The values of the derivative at the final nodes of the tree are calculated as the maximum stock price less the actual stock price. To illustrate the rollback procedure, suppose that we are at node A, where the stock price is $50. The maximum stock price achieved so far is either 56.12 or 50. Consider first the situation where it is 50. If there is an up movement, the maximum stock price becomes 56.12 and the value of the derivative becomes zero. If there is a down movement, the maximum stock price stays at 50 and the value of the derivative becomes 5.45. Assuming no early exercise, the value of the derivative at A when the maximum achieved so far is 50 is therefore

$$(0 \times 0.5073 + 5.45 \times 0.4927)e^{-0.1 \times 0.08333} = 2.66$$

Clearly, it is not worth exercising at node A in these circumstance since the payoff from doing so is zero. A similar calculation for the situation where the maximum value at node A is 56.12 gives the value of the derivative at node A, without early exercise, to be

$$(0 \times 0.5073 + 11.57 \times 0.4927)e^{-0.1 \times 0.08333} = 5.65$$

---

[10]This example is used as a first illustration of the general procedure for handling path dependence. We give a more efficient approach to valuing lookback options in the next section.

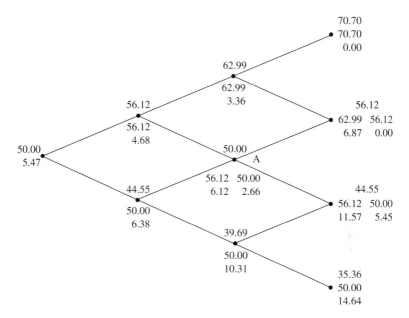

Figure 18.2 Tree for valuing an American lookback option.

In this case, early exercise is optimal since it gives a value of 6.12 and is the optimal strategy. Rolling back through the tree in this way gives the value of the derivative as $5.47.

Generalization

The approach just described is computationally feasible when the number of alternative values of the path function, F, at each node does not grow too fast as n, the number of time steps, is increased. The example we used, a lookback option, presents no problems since the number of alternative values for the maximum asset price at a node in a binomial tree with n time steps is never greater than n.

Luckily, the approach can be extended to cope with situations where there are a very large number of different possible values of the path function at each node. The basic idea is as follows. At a node we carry out calculations for a small number of representative values of F. When the value of the derivative is required for other values of the path function, we calculate it from the known values using interpolation.

The first stage is to work forward through the tree establishing the maximum and minimum values of the path function at each node. Assuming the value of the path function at time $\tau + \Delta t$ depends only on the value of the path function at time τ and the value of the underlying variable at time $\tau + \Delta t$, the maximum and minimum values of the path function for the nodes at time $\tau + \Delta t$ can be calculated in a straightforward way from those for the nodes at time τ. The

second stage is to choose representative values of the path function at each node. There are a number of approaches. A simple rule is to choose the representative values as the maximum value, the minimum value, and a number of other values that are equally spaced between the maximum and the minimum. As we roll back through the tree, we value the derivative for each of representative values of the path function.

We illustrate the nature of the calculation by considering the problem of valuing the average price call option that was considered in Example 18.2. We suppose that the payoff depends on the arithmetic average stock price. The initial stock price is 50, the strike price is 50, the risk-free interest rate is 10%, the stock price volatility is 40%, the time to maturity is one year, and the number of time steps on the tree is 20. In this case the binomial tree parameters are $\Delta t = 0.05$, $u = 1.0936$, $d = 0.9144$, $p = 0.5056$, and $1 - p = 0.4944$. The path function is the arithmetic average of the stock price.

Figure 18.3 shows the calculations that would be carried out in one small part of the tree. Node X is the central node at time 0.2 year (at the end of the fourth time step). Nodes Y and Z are the two nodes at time 0.25 year that can be reached from node X. The stock price at node X is 50. Forward induction shows that the maximum average stock price that is achievable in reaching node X is 53.83. The minimum is 46.65. (We include both the initial and final stock prices when calculating the average.) From node X we branch to one of the two nodes, Y and Z. At node Y the stock price is 54.68 and the bounds for the average are 47.99 and 57.39. At node Z the stock price is 45.72 and the bounds for the average stock price are 43.88 and 52.48.

We suppose that we have chosen the representative values of the average to be four equally spaced values at each node. This means that at node X we

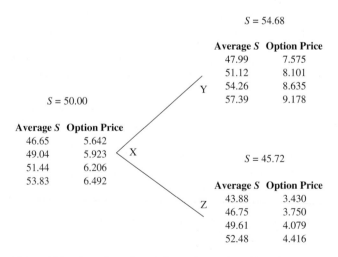

Figure 18.3   Part of tree for valuing option on the arithmetic average.

consider the averages 46.65, 49.04, 51.44, and 53.83. At node Y we consider the averages 47.99, 51.12, 54.26, and 57.39. At node Z we consider the averages 43.88, 46.75, 49.61, and 52.48. We assume that backward induction has already been used to calculate the value of the option for each of the alternative values of the average at nodes Y and Z. The values are shown in Figure 18.3. For example, at node Y when the average is 51.12, the value of the option is 8.101.

Consider the calculations at node X for the case when the average is 51.44. If the stock price moves up to node Y, the new average will be

$$\frac{5 \times 51.44 + 54.68}{6} = 51.98$$

The value of the derivative at node Y for this average can be found by interpolating between the values when the average is 51.12 and when it is 54.26. It is

$$\frac{(51.98 - 51.12) \times 8.635 + (54.26 - 51.98) \times 8.101}{54.26 - 51.12} = 8.247$$

Similarly, if the stock price moves down to node Z, the new average will be

$$\frac{5 \times 51.44 + 45.72}{6} = 50.49$$

and by interpolation the value of the derivative is 4.182.

The value of the derivative at node X when the average is 51.44 is therefore

$$(0.5056 \times 8.247 + 0.4944 \times 4.182)e^{-0.1 \times 0.05} = 6.206$$

The other values at node X are calculated similarly. Once the values at all nodes at time 0.2 year have been calculated in this way, we can move on to the nodes at time 0.15 year.

The value given by the full tree for the option at time zero is 7.17. As the number of time steps and the number of averages considered at each node is increased, the value of the option converges to the correct answer. With 60 time steps and 100 averages at each node, the value of the option is 5.58. The analytic approximation for the value of the option calculated in Example 18.2 is 5.62.

A key advantage of the method described here is that it can handle American options. The calculations are as we have described them except that we test for early exercise at each node for each of the alternative values of the path function at the node. (In practice, the early exercise decision is liable to depend on both the value of the path function and the value of the underlying asset.) Consider the American version of the average price call we have considered here. The value calculated using the 20-step tree and four averages at each node is 7.77. With 60 time steps and 100 averages the value is 6.17.

Applications and Extensions of the Approach

The approach that has been described can be used in a wide range of different situations. The two conditions that must be satisfied were listed at the

beginning of this section. Efficiency is improved somewhat if quadratic rather than linear interpolation is used at each node.

An interesting application of the approach is to index amortizing swaps and mortgage-backed securities. For these derivatives we can construct a trinomial tree for interest rates as described in Chapter 17 and define the path function at each node as the remaining principal.[11]

18.4 LOOKBACK OPTIONS

A number of researchers have suggested a simple approach to valuing lookback options.[12] To illustrate it, we again consider the American-style lookback put in Figure 18.2. When exercised this provides a payoff equal to the excess of the maximum stock price over the current stock price. We define $F(t)$ as the maximum stock price achieved up to time t and set

$$Y(t) = \frac{F(t)}{S(t)}$$

We next use the Cox, Ross, and Rubinstein tree for the stock price to produce a tree for Y. Initially, Y is 1 since $F = S$ at time zero. If there is an up movement in S during the first time step, both F and S increase by a proportional amount u and Y continues to be 1. If there is a down movement in S during the first time step, F stays the same, so that $Y = 1/d = u$. Continuing with these types of arguments we produce the tree shown in Figure 18.4 for Y. (Note that in this example $u = 1.1224$, $d = 0.8909$, $a = 1.0084$, and $p = 0.5073$). The rules defining the geometry of the tree are

1. When $Y = 1$ at time t, it is either u or 1 at time $t + \Delta t$.
2. When $Y = u^m$ at time t for $m \geq 1$, it is either u^{m+1} or u^{m-1} at time $t + \Delta t$.

An up movement in Y corresponds to a down movement in the stock price, and vice versa. The probability of an up movement in Y is therefore always $1 - p$ and the probability of a down movement in Y is always p.

We use the tree to value the American lookback option in units of the stock price rather than in dollars. In dollars the payoff from the option is

$$SY - S$$

[11]For a discussion of the use of the approach for index amortizing swaps, see J. Hull and A. White, "Finding the Keys," *RISK*, September 1993.

[12]The approach was proposed by E. Reiner in a lecture at Berkeley. It is also suggested in S. Babbs, "Binomial Valuation of Lookback Options," Working Paper, Midland Global Markets, 1992; and T. H. F. Cheuk and T. C. F. Vorst, "Lookback Options and the Observation Frequency: A Binomial Approach," Working Paper, Erasmus University, Rotterdam.

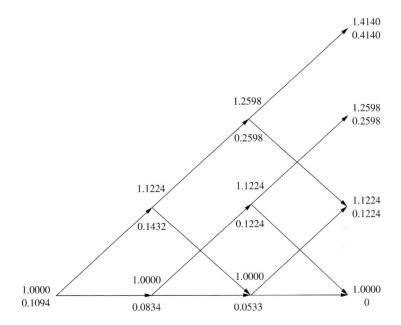

Figure 18.4   Efficient procedure for valuing an American-style lookback option.

In stock price units the payoff from the option therefore is

$$Y - 1$$

We roll back through the tree in the usual way, valuing a derivative that provides this payoff except that we adjust for the fact that the stock price (i.e., the unit of measurement) is different at different nodes. If $f_{i,j}$ is the value of the lookback at the jth node time $i\Delta t$, the rollback procedure gives

$$f_{i,j} = \max\{Y - 1, e^{-r\Delta t}[(1 - p)f_{i+1,j+1}d + pf_{i+1,j-1}u]\}$$

when $j \geq 1$. Note the fact that $f_{i+1,j+1}$ is multiplied by d and $f_{i,j}$ is multiplied by u in this equation. This is to take into account the fact that the stock price at node (i, j) is the unit of measurement. The stock price at node $(i + 1, j + 1)$, which is the unit of measurement for $f_{i+1,j+1}$, is d times the stock price at node (i, j) and the stock price at node $(i + 1, j - 1)$, which is the unit of measurement for $f_{i+1,j-1}$, is u times the stock price at node (i, j). Similarly when $j = 0$ the rollback procedure gives

$$f_{i,j} = \max\{Y - 1, e^{-r\Delta t}[(1 - p)f_{i+1,j+1}d + pf_{i+1,j}u]\}$$

The calculations for our example are shown in Figure 18.4. The tree estimates the value of the option at time zero (in stock price units) as 0.1094. This means that the dollar value of the option is $0.1094 \times 50 = 5.47$. This is the same as the value calculated from the tree in Figure 18.2. For a given number of time

steps, the two procedures are equivalent. The advantage of the procedure described here is that it avoids explicitly considering two state variables at each node.

The value of the option given by the tree in Figure 18.4 when it is European is 5.26. The exact value of the European option as shown in Example 18.1 is 7.79. The value given by the tree converges slowly to this as the number of time steps is increased. For example, with 100, 500, 1,000, and 5,000 time steps the values given by the tree for the European option in our example are 7.24, 7.54, 7.61, and 7.71.

The tree approach has the advantage over the analytic results that it can cope with American-style options. Also, in circumstances where the stock price is observed once a day for the purposes of calculating the maximum or minimum, a tree with Δt set equal to one day may well give a better answer for European options than the analytic results. This is because the analytic results assume that the stock price is observed continuously.

18.5 BARRIER OPTIONS

When a binomial or trinomial tree is used in the usual way to value a barrier option, convergence is slow. A large number of time steps are required to obtain a reasonably accurate result. The reason for this that the barrier being assumed by the tree is different from the true barrier.[13] We define the *inner barrier* as the barrier formed by nodes just on the inside of the true barrier (i.e., closer to the center of the tree) and the *outer barrier* as the barrier formed by nodes just outside the true barrier (i.e., farther away from the center of the tree). Figure 18.5 shows the inner and outer barrier for a trinomial tree on the assumption that the true barrier is horizontal. Figure 18.6 does the same for a binomial tree. The usual tree calculations implicitly assume that the outer barrier is the true barrier because the barrier conditions are first used at nodes on this barrier. There are two alternative approaches for overcoming this problem. For both, it turns out to be more efficient to use a trinomial tree rather than a binomial tree.

Positioning Nodes on the Barriers

Suppose that there are two horizontal barriers, B_1 and B_2, with $B_1 > B_2$ and that the underlying stock price follows geometric Brownian motion. In a trinomial tree there are three possible movements in the asset's price at each node: up by a proportional amount u; stay the same; and down by a proportional amount d where $d = 1/u$. We can always choose u so that nodes lie on both barriers. The condition that must be satisfied by u is

$$B_2 = B_1 u^N$$

---

[13] See P. P. Boyle and S. H. Lau, "Bumping Up Against the Barrier with the Binomial Method," *Journal of Derivatives* 1, 4 (Summer 1994), 6–14, for a discussion of this.

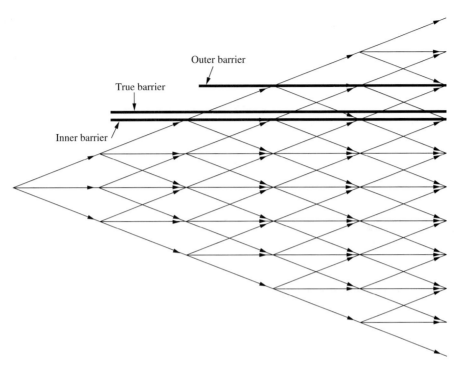

Outer barrier

True barrier

Inner barrier

Figure 18.5   Barriers assumed by trinomial trees.

or

$$\ln B_2 = \ln B_1 + N \ln u$$

for some integer N.

When discussing trinomial trees in Section 15.7, the value suggested for u was $e^{\sigma \sqrt{3\Delta t}}$ so that $\ln u = \sigma \sqrt{3\Delta t}$. In the situation considered here a good rule is to choose $\ln u$ as close as possible to this value consistent with the condition given above. This means that we set

$$\ln u = \frac{\ln B_2 - \ln B_1}{N}$$

where

$$N = \text{int}\left[\frac{\ln B_2 - \ln B_1}{\sigma \sqrt{3\Delta t}} + 0.5\right]$$

Normally, the trinomial stock price tree is constructed so that the central node is the initial stock price. In this case the stock price at the first node is the initial stock price. After that we choose the central node of the tree to be $B_1 u^M$, where M is the integer that makes this quantity as close as possible to the initial

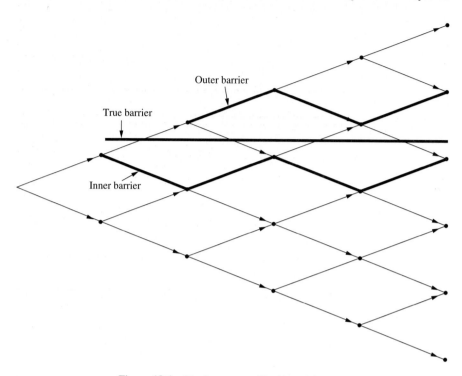

Figure 18.6   Barriers assumed by binomial trees.

stock price; that is,

$$M = \text{int}\left[\frac{\ln S - \ln B_1}{\ln u} + 0.5\right]$$

This leads to a tree of the form shown in Figure 18.7. The probabilities on all branches of the tree are chosen as usual to match the first two moments of the stochastic process followed by the asset price.

Adjusting for Nodes Not Lying on Barriers

An alternative procedure for coping with barriers is to make no changes to the tree and adjust for the fact that the barrier is specified incorrectly by the tree.[14] The first step is to calculate an inner barrier and an outer barrier, as described earlier. We then roll back through the tree, calculating two values of the derivative on the nodes that form the inner barrier. The first of these values is obtained by assuming that the inner barrier is correct; the second is obtained by assuming that the outer barrier is correct. A final estimate for the value of the derivative on the

---

[14]The procedure we describe here is similar to that in E. Derman, I. Kani, D. Ergener, and I. Bardhan, "Enhanced Numerical Methods for Options with Barriers," Working Paper, Goldman Sachs, May 1995.

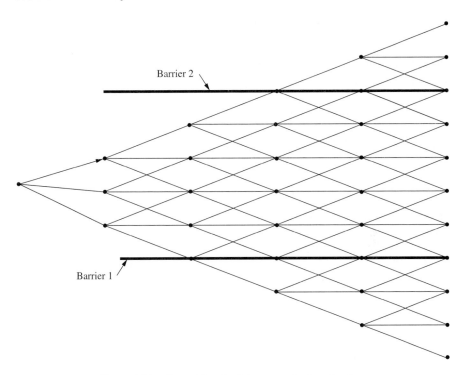

Figure 18.7   Tree with nodes lying on each of two barriers.

inner barrier is then obtained by interpolating between these two values. Suppose that at time $i\Delta t$ the true barrier is 0.2 from the inner barrier and 0.6 from the outer barrier. Suppose further that the value of the derivative on the inner barrier is 0 if the inner barrier is assumed to be correct and 1.6 if the outer barrier is assumed to be correct. The interpolated value on the inner barrier is 0.4. Once we have obtained a value for the derivative at all nodes on all inner barriers, we can roll back through the tree to obtain the initial value of the derivative in the usual way.

For a single horizontal barrier, this approach is equivalent to the following:

1. Calculate the price of the derivative on the assumption that the inner barrier is the true barrier.
2. Calculate the value of the derivative on the assumption that the outer barrier is the true barrier.
3. Interpolate between the two prices.

Its big advantage is that it can be generalized to situations where there is more than one barrier, to situations where the barriers are nonhorizontal, and to situations where the nodes on the tree do not lie along horizontal lines. For example, it can be used in conjunction with the trinomial interest rate trees described in Chapter 17 to value a variety of interest rate barrier options.

18.6 OPTIONS ON TWO CORRELATED ASSETS

Another tricky numerical problem is that of valuing rainbow options, i.e., options dependent on two assets whose prices are correlated. A number of alternative approaches have been suggested.

Transforming Variables

It is relatively easy to construct a tree in three dimensions to represent the movements of two *uncorrelated* variables. The procedure is as follows. First we construct a two-dimensional tree for each variable separately. We then combine these two two-dimensional trees into a single three-dimensional tree. The probabilities on the branches of the three-dimensional tree are the product of the corresponding probabilities on the two-dimensional trees. Suppose, for example, that the variables are stock prices, S_1 and S_2. Each can be represented in two dimensions by a Cox, Ross, and Rubinstein binomial tree. Suppose that S_1 has a probability p_1 of moving up by a proportional amount u_1 and a probability $1 - p_1$ of moving down by a proportional amount d_1. Suppose further that S_2 has a probability p_2 of moving up by a proportional amount u_2 and a probability $1 - p_2$ of moving down by a proportional amount d_2. In the three-dimensional tree there are four branches emanating from each node. The probabilities are

$$p_1 p_2: \ S_1 \text{ increases}; \ S_2 \text{ increases}$$
$$p_1(1 - p_2): \ S_1 \text{ increases}; \ S_2 \text{ decreases}$$
$$(1 - p_1)p_2: \ S_1 \text{ decreases}; \ S_2 \text{ increases}$$
$$(1 - p_1)(1 - p_2): \ S_1 \text{ decreases}; \ S_2 \text{ decreases}$$

Consider next the situation where S_1 and S_2 are correlated. We suppose that the risk-neutral processes are:

$$dS_1 = (r - q_1)S_1 \, dt + \sigma_1 S_1 \, dz_1$$
$$dS_2 = (r - q_2)S_2 \, dt + \sigma_2 S_2 \, dz_2$$

and the instantaneous correlation between the Wiener processes, dz_1 and dz_2, is ρ. This means that

$$d \ln S_1 = (r - q_1 - \sigma_1^2/2) \, dt + \sigma_1 \, dz_1$$
$$d \ln S_2 = (r - q_2 - \sigma_2^2/2) \, dt + \sigma_2 \, dz_2$$

We define two new uncorrelated variables,[15]

$$x_1 = \sigma_2 \ln S_1 + \sigma_1 \ln S_2$$
$$x_2 = \sigma_2 \ln S_1 - \sigma_1 \ln S_2$$

---

[15]This idea was suggested in J. Hull and A. White "Valuing Derivative Securities Using the Explicit Finite Difference Method," *Journal of Financial and Quantitative Analysis*, 25 (1990), 87–100.

These variables follow the processes

$$dx_1 = [\sigma_2(r - q_1 - \sigma_1^2/2) + \sigma_1(r - q_2 - \sigma_2^2/2)] \, dt + \sigma_1\sigma_2 \sqrt{2(1 + \rho)} \, dz_A$$

$$dx_2 = [\sigma_2(r - q_1 - \sigma_1^2/2) - \sigma_1(r - q_2 - \sigma_2^2/2)] \, dt + \sigma_1\sigma_2 \sqrt{2(1 - \rho)} \, dz_B$$

where dz_A and dz_B are uncorrelated Wiener processes.

The variables x_1 and x_2 can be modeled using two separate binomial trees. In time Δt, x_i has a probability p_i of increasing by h_i and a probability $1 - p_i$ of decreasing by h_i. The variables h_i and p_i are chosen so that the tree gives correct values for the first two moments of the distribution of x_1 and x_2. Since they are uncorrelated the two trees can be combined into a single three-dimensional tree, as already described.

At each node of the tree, S_1 and S_2 can be calculated from x_1 and x_2 using the inverse relationships

$$S_1 = \exp\left[\frac{x_1 + x_2}{2\sigma_2}\right] \qquad S_2 = \exp\left[\frac{x_1 - x_2}{2\sigma_1}\right]$$

To value a derivative we roll back through the tree in three dimensions.

Changing the Geometry of Tree

Rubinstein has suggested a way of building a three-dimensional tree for two correlated stock prices by using a nonrectangular arrangement of the nodes.[16] From a node (S_1, S_2) where the first stock price is S_1 and the second stock price is S_2, we have a 0.25 chance of moving to each of the following:

$$(S_1 u_1, S_2 A)$$

$$(S_1 u_1, S_2 B)$$

$$(S_1 d_1, S_2 C)$$

$$(S_2 d_1, S_2 D)$$

where

$$u_1 = \exp[(r - q_1 - \sigma_1^2/2)\Delta t + \sigma_1 \sqrt{\Delta t}]$$

$$d_1 = \exp[(r - q_1 - \sigma_1^2/2)\Delta t - \sigma_1 \sqrt{\Delta t}]$$

$$A = \exp[r - q_2 - \sigma_2^2/2 + \sigma_2 \sqrt{\Delta t}(\rho + \sqrt{1 - \rho^2})]$$

$$B = \exp[r - q_2 - \sigma_2^2/2 + \sigma_2 \sqrt{\Delta t}(\rho - \sqrt{1 - \rho^2})]$$

$$C = \exp[r - q_2 - \sigma_2^2/2 - \sigma_2 \sqrt{\Delta t}(\rho - \sqrt{1 - \rho^2})]$$

$$D = \exp[r - q_2 - \sigma_2^2/2 - \sigma_2 \sqrt{\Delta t}(\rho + \sqrt{1 - \rho^2})]$$

---

[16] See M. Rubinstein, "Return to Oz," *RISK*, November 1994, pp. 67–70.

When the correlation is zero this method is equivalent to constructing separate trees for S_1 and S_2 using the alternative binomial tree construction method in Section 15.7.

Adjusting the Probabilities

A third approach to building a three-dimensional tree for S_1 and S_2 involves first assuming no correlation and then adjusting the probabilities at each node to reflect the correlation. We use the alternative binomial tree construction method for each of S_1 and S_2 in Section 15.7. This method has the property that all probabilities are 0.5. When the two binomial trees are combined on the assumption that there is no correlation, the probabilities are as follows:

	S_1-move	
S_2-move	Down	Up
Up	0.25	0.25
Down	0.25	0.25

When we adjust these probabilities to reflect the correlation, they become

	S_1-move	
S_2-move	Down	Up
Up	$0.25(1-\rho)$	$0.25(1+\rho)$
Down	$0.25(1+\rho)$	$0.25(1-\rho)$

Hull and White have shown how this type of approach can be used for interest rate trees.[17] A trinomial tree for interest rates in one currency can be combined with a trinomial tree for interest rates in another currency to provide a three-dimensional tree, with nine branches emanating from each node, to model both interest rates simultaneously.

18.7 HEDGING ISSUES

Before trading an exotic option it is important for a financial institution to assess not only how it should be priced, but also the difficulties that are likely to be experienced in hedging it. The general approach described in Chapter 14 involving the monitoring of delta, gamma, vega, and so on, can be used.

---

[17]See J. Hull and A. White, "Numerical Procedures for Implementing Term Structure Models II: Two-Factor Models," *Journal of Derivatives,* Winter 1994, pp. 37–48.

Some exotic options are easier to hedge using the underlying asset than the corresponding plain vanilla option. An example is an average price option where the averaging period is the whole life of the option and the underlying asset is a stock price. As time passes, we observe more of the stock prices that will constitute the final average upon which the payoff is based. This means that our uncertainty about the payoff decreases with the passage of time. As a result, the option becomes progressively easier to hedge. In the final few days, the delta of the option always approaches zero since price movements in the final few days have very little impact on the payoff.

Barrier options can in certain circumstances be significantly more difficult to hedge than regular options. Consider a down-and-out call option on a currency when the exchange rate is 0.0005 above the barrier. If the barrier is hit, the option is worth nothing. If the barrier is not hit, the option may prove to be quite valuable. In this situation the delta of the option is discontinuous at the barrier and hedging using conventional techniques is difficult. The approach in Section 18.8 is often more appropriate.

18.8 STATIC OPTIONS REPLICATION

Hedging an option position involves replicating the opposite position. The procedures described in Chapter 14 involve what is sometimes referred to as *dynamic options replication*. They require the position in the hedging assets to be rebalanced frequently and can be quite expensive because of the transaction costs involved.

An alternative approach that can sometimes be used for exotic options is *static options replication*.[18] This involves searching for a portfolio of actively traded options that approximately replicate the exotic option under consideration. The basic principle is as follows. If two portfolios are worth the same on a certain boundary, they are also worth the same at all interior points of the boundary.

Consider as an example a nine-month up-and-out call option on a non-dividend-paying stock where the stock price is 50, and the strike price is 50, the barrier is 60, the risk-free interest rate is 10% per annum, and the volatility is 30% per annum. Suppose that $c(S, t)$ is the value of the option at time t for a stock price of S. We can use any boundary in (S, t) space for the purposes of producing the replicating portfolio. The natural boundary is

$$c(S, 0.75) = \max(S - 50, 0) \qquad \text{when } S < 60$$

$$c(60, t) = 0 \qquad\qquad\qquad \text{when } 0 \le t \le 0.75$$

There are many ways that we can approximately match this boundary using regular options. The natural instrument to match the first boundary is a regular

[18] See E. Derman, D. Ergener, and I. Kani, "Static Options Replication," *Journal of Derivatives* 2, 4 (Summer 1995), 78–95.

nine-month European call option with a strike price of 50. The first instrument introduced into the replicating portfolio is therefore likely to be one unit of this option. (We refer to this option as option 1.) One way of then proceeding is as follows. We divide the life of the option into a number of time steps and choose options that satisfy the second boundary condition at the beginning of each time step.

Suppose that we choose time steps of three months. The first instrument we choose should lead to the second boundary being matched at $t = 0.5$. In other words, it should lead to the value of the complete replicating portfolio being zero when $t = 0.5$ and $S = 60$. The option should have the property that it has zero value on the first boundary since this has already been matched. One possibility is a regular nine-month European call option with a strike price of 60. (We will refer to this as option 2.) Black–Scholes formulas show that this is worth 4.33 at the six-month point when $S = 60$. They also show that the position in option 1 is worth 11.54 at the point. The position we require in option 2 is therefore $-11.54/4.33 = -2.66$.

We next move on to matching the second boundary condition at $t = 0.25$. The option used should have the property that it has zero value on all boundaries that have been matched so far. One possibility is a regular six-month European call option with a strike price of 60. (We refer to this as option 3.) This is worth 4.33 at the three-month point when $S = 60$. Our position in options 1 and 2 is worth -4.21 at this point. The position we require in option 3 is therefore $4.21/4.33 = 0.97$.

Finally, we match the second boundary condition at $t = 0$. For this we use a regular three-month European option with a strike price of 60. (We refer to this as option 4.) Similarly to the above, our position in option 4 is calculated to be 0.28.

The portfolio chosen ($+1$ unit of option 1, -2.66 units of option 2, $+0.97$ unit of option 3, and $+0.23$ unit of option 4) is worth 0.73 at time zero when the stock price is 50. This compares with 0.31 given by the analytic formula for the up-and-out call earlier in this chapter. The replicating portfolio is more expensive than the up-and-out option because it matches the latter at only three points on the second boundary. If we use the same scheme but match at 18 points on the second boundary (using options that mature every half month), the value of the replicating portfolio reduces to 0.38. If 100 points are matched, the value reduces further to 0.32.

To hedge a derivative, we short the portfolio that replicates its boundary conditions. The hedge portfolio is always likely to be somewhat more expensive than the theoretical price of the derivative but has the advantage over delta hedging that it does not require frequent rebalancing. The static replication approach can be used for a wide range of derivatives. The user has a great deal of flexibility in choosing the boundary that is to be matched and the options that are to be used. However, the user must unwind the portfolio when any part of the boundary is reached.

18.9 SUMMARY

Exotic options are options with rules governing the payoff that are more complicated than standard options. We have discussed 11 different categories of exotic options: packages, nonstandard American options, forward start options, compound options, "as you like it" options, barrier options, binary options, lookback options, Asian options, options to exchange one asset for another, and options involving several assets. Some can be valued using straightforward extensions of the procedures that we have developed for European and American calls and puts; some can be valued analytically, but using much more complicated formulas than those for regular European calls and puts; and some require special numerical procedures.

The natural technique to use for valuing path-dependent options is Monte Carlo simulation. This has the disadvantage of being fairly slow and unable to handle American-style derivatives. Luckily, trees can be used to value many types of path-dependent derivatives. The approach is to choose representative values for the underlying path function at each node of the tree and calculate the value of the derivative for each alternative value of the path function as we roll back through the tree.

Lookback options can be handled more easily than other path-dependent options. Instead of constructing a tree to represent movements in the stock price, we construct a tree to represent movements in a variable that is the maximum (or minimum) stock price divided by the actual stock price. The option is then valued in stock price units rather than in dollars.

Trees can be used to value many types of barrier options, but the convergence of the option value to the correct value as the number of time steps is increased tends to be slow. One approach to improving convergence is to arrange the geometry of the tree so that nodes always lie on the barriers. Another is to use an interpolation scheme to adjust for the fact that the barrier being assumed by the tree is different from the true barrier.

One way of valuing options dependent on the prices of two correlated assets is to apply a transformation to the asset price to create two new uncorrelated variables. These two variables are each modeled with trees and the trees are then combined to form a single three-dimensional tree. At each node of the tree, the inverse of the transformation gives the asset prices. A second approach is to arrange the positions of nodes on the three-dimensional tree to reflect the correlation. A third approach is start with a tree that assumes no correlation between the variables and then adjust the probabilities on the tree to reflect the correlation.

Some exotic options are easier to hedge than the corresponding regular options, others are more difficult. In general, Asian options are easier to hedge because the payoff becomes progressively more certain as we approach maturity. Barrier options can be more difficult to hedge because delta is liable to be discontinuous at the barrier. One approach to hedging an exotic option, known as static

options replication, is to find a portfolio of regular options whose value matches the value of the exotic option on some boundary. The exotic option is hedged by shorting this portfolio.

SUGGESTIONS FOR FURTHER READING

Boyle, P. P., J. Evnine, and S. Gibbs, "Numerical Evaluation of Multivariate Contingent Claims," *Review of Financial Studies,* 2 2 (1989), 241–50.

Boyle, P. P., and S. H. Lau, "Bumping Up Against the Barrier with the Binomial Method," *Journal of Derivatives* 1, 4 (Summer 1994), 6–14.

Conze, A., and Viswanathan, "Path Dependent Options: The Case of Lookback Options," *Journal of Finance,* 46 (1991), 1893–1907.

Curran, M., "Beyond Average Intelligence," *RISK,* October 1992, pp. 60–62.

Derman, E., D. Ergener, and I. Kani, "Static Options Replication," *Journal of Derivatives,* 2, 4 (Summer 1995), 78–95.

Garman M. "Recollection in Tranquility," *RISK,* March 1989.

Geske R., "The Valuation of Compound Options," *Journal of Financial Economics,* 7 (1979), 63–81.

Goldman B., H. Sosin, and M. A. Gatto, "Path Dependent Options: Buy at the Low, Sell at the High," *Journal of Finance,* 34 (December 1979), 1111–27.

Hudson M., "The Value of Going Out," *RISK,* March 1991.

Hull, J., and A. White, "Efficient Procedures for Valuing European and American Path-Dependent Options," *Journal of Derivatives,* Fall 1993, pp. 21–31.

Hull, J., and A. White, "Finding the Keys," *RISK,* September 1993.

Johnson, H. "Options on the Maximum and Minimum of Several Assets," *Journal of Financial and Quantitative Analysis,* 22, 3 (September 1987), 277–83.

Kemna, A., and A. Vorst, "A Pricing Method for Options Based on Average Asset Values," *Journal of Banking and Finance,* 14 (March 1990), 113–29.

Levy, E., "Pricing European Average Rate Currency Options," *Journal of International Money and Finance,* 11 (1992), 474–91.

Levy, E., and S. M. Turnbull, "Average Intelligence," *RISK,* February 1992, pp. 53–59.

Margrabe, W., "The Value of an Option to Exchange One Asset for Another," *Journal of Finance,* 33 (March 1978), 177–86.

Ritchken, P., L. Sankarasubramanian, and A. M. Vijh, "The Valuation of Path Dependent Contracts on the Average," *Management Science,* 39 (1993), 1202–13.

Rubinstein, M., "Double Trouble," *RISK,* December 1991–January 1992.

Rubinstein, M., "One for Another," *RISK,* July–August 1991.

Rubinstein, M., "Options for the Undecided," *RISK,* April 1991.

Rubinstein, M., "Pay Now, Choose Later," *RISK,* February 1991.

Rubinstein, M., "Somewhere Over the Rainbow," *RISK,* November 1991.

Rubinstein, M., "Two in One," *RISK,* May 1991.

Rubinstein, M., and E. Reiner, "Breaking Down the Barriers," *RISK,* September 1991.

Rubinstein, M., and E. Reiner, "Unscrambling the Binary Code," *RISK,* October 1991.

Stulz, R., "Options on the Minimum or Maximum of Two Assets," *Journal of Financial Economics,* 10 (1982), 161–85.

Turnbull, S. M., and L. M. Wakeman, "A Quick Algorithm for Pricing European Average Options," *Journal of Financial and Quantitative Analysis,* 26 (September 1991), 377–89.

QUESTIONS AND PROBLEMS

18.1. Explain the difference between a forward start option and an "as you like it" option.

18.2. Describe the payoff from a portfolio consisting of a lookback call and a lookback put with the same maturity.

18.3. Consider an "as you like it" option where the holder has the right to choose between a European call and a European put at any time during a two-year period. The maturity dates and strike prices for the calls and puts are the same regardless of when the choice is made. Is it ever optimal to make the choice before the end of the two-year period? Explain your answer.

18.4. Suppose that c_1 and p_1 are the prices of a European average price call and a European average price put with strike X and maturity T, c_2 and p_2 are the prices of a European average strike call and European average strike put with maturity T, and c_3 and p_3 are the prices of a regular European call and a regular European put with strike price X and maturity T. Show that

$$c_1 + c_2 - c_3 = p_1 + p_2 - p_3$$

18.5. The text derives a decomposition of a particular type of "as you like it" option into a call maturing at time t_2 and a put maturing at time t_1. Derive an alternative decomposition into a call maturing at time t_1 and a put maturing at time t_2.

18.6. Section 18.1 gives two formulas for a down-and-out call. The first applies to the situation where the barrier, H, is less than or equal to the strike price, X. The second applies to the situation where $H \geq X$. Show that the two formulas are the same when $H = X$.

18.7. Explain why a down-and-out put is worth zero when the barrier is greater than the strike price.

18.8. Use a three-time-step tree to value an American lookback call option on a currency when the initial exchange rate is 1.6, the domestic risk-free rate is 5% per annum, the foreign risk-free interest rate is 8% per annum, the exchange rate volatility is 15%, and the time to maturity is 18 months. Use the approach in Section 18.3.

18.9. Repeat Problem 18.8 using the approach in Section 18.4

18.10. Use a three-time-step tree to value an American put option on the geometric average of the price of a non-dividend-paying stock when the stock price is $40, the strike price is $40, the risk-free interest rate is 10% per annum, the volatility is

35% per annum, and the time to maturity is three months. The geometric average is measured from today until the option matures.

18.11. Suppose that the strike price of an American call option on a non-dividend-paying stock grows at rate g. Show that if g is less than the risk-free rate, r, it is never optimal to exercise the call early.

18.12. How can the value of a forward start put option on a non-dividend-paying stock be calculated if it is agreed that the strike price will be 10% greater than the stock price at the time the option starts?

*18.13. If a stock price follows geometric Brownian motion, what process does $A(t)$ follow where $A(t)$ is the arithmetic average stock price between time zero and time t?

18.14. Explain why Asian options are much easier than barrier options to hedge using the underlying.

18.15. Calculate the price of a 1-year European option to give up 100 ounces of silver in exchange for 1 ounce of gold. The current prices of gold and silver are $380 and $4, respectively; the risk-free interest rate is 10% per annum; the volatility of each commodity price is 20%; and the correlation between the two prices is 0.7. Ignore storage costs.

18.16. Is a European down-and-out option on an asset worth the same as a European down-and-out option on the asset's futures price for a futures contract maturing at the same time as the option?

*18.17. **(a)** What put–call parity relationship exists between the price of a European call on a call and a European put on a call? Show that the formulas given in the text satisfy the relationship.

(b) What put–call parity relationship exists between the price of a European call on a put and a European put on a put? Show that the formulas given in the text satisfy the relationship.

18.18. Does a lookback call become more valuable or less valuable as we increase the frequency with which we observe the asset price in calculating the minimum?

18.19. Does a down-and-out call become more valuable or less valuable as we increase the frequency with which we observe the asset price in determining whether the barrier has been crossed? What is the answer to the same question for a down-and-in call?

18.20. Explain why a regular European call option is the sum of a down-and-out European call and a down-and-in European call. Is the same true for American call options?

18.21. Consider an average price call option that pays $\max(S_{ave} - X, 0)$ at time T where S_{ave} is the average stock price calculated from time t_0 to time T and X is the strike price. The stock pays no dividends.

(a) Explain why there is a formula for valuing the option exactly when the average is a geometric average, but not when it is an arithmetic average.

(b) There is one particular case when the option is on the arithmetic average and can be valued analytically. This is when it is being valued at some time t between t_0 and T and the average A calculated so far satisfies

$$A(t - t_0) > X(T - t_0)$$

Show that in this case the option is certain to be exercised and derive its value in terms of X, t_0, t, T, A, the stock price at time t, and the risk-free interest rate.

18.22. What is the value of a derivative that pays off $100 in six months if the S&P 500 index is greater than 500 and zero otherwise. Assume that the current level of the index is 480, the risk-free rate is 8% per annum, the dividend yield on the index is 3% per annum, and the volatility of the index is 20%.

18.23. What is the value in dollars of a derivative that pays off £10,000 in one year provided that the dollar-sterling exchange rate is greater than 1.5000 at that time. The current exchange rate is 1.4800. The dollar and sterling interest rates are 4% and 8% per annum respectively. The volatility of the exchange rate is 12% per annum.

18.24. In a three-month down-and-out call option on silver futures the strike price is $20 per ounce and the barrier is $18. The current futures price is $19, the risk-free interest rate is 5%, and the volatility of silver futures is 40% per annum. Explain how the option works and calculate its value. What is the value of a regular call option on silver futures with the same terms? What is the value of a down-and-in call option on silver futures with the same terms?

18.25. A new European-style lookback call option on a stock index has a maturity of nine months. The current level of the index is 400, the risk-free rate is 6% per annum, the dividend yield on the index is 4% per annum, and the volatility of the index is 20%. Use the approach in Section 18.4 to value the option and compare your answer to the result from using the analytic valuation formula.

18.26. Estimate the value of a new six-month European-style average price call option on a non-dividend-paying stock. The initial stock price is $30, the strike price is $30, the risk-free interest rate is 5%, and the stock price volatility is 30%.

18.27. Explain how you would use static options replication to hedge a derivative that pays off $100 in six months provided that a stock price stays within the range of $40 to $60 during that period.

Chapter 19

Alternatives to Black–Scholes for Option Pricing

In this chapter we consider a number of alternatives to the usual assumption of geometric Brownian motion for stock prices. We start by considering the adjustments that must be made to the Black–Scholes model when the volatility and the interest rate are known functions of time. We then move on to consider a variety of other models. These include models where the underlying asset price follows a jump process rather than a continuous process and models where the volatility is stochastic. We discuss the pricing biases that will be observed if the Black–Scholes formula is used when, in reality, stock price movements correspond to one of these other models. We also discuss the volatility smile, the volatility term structure, and the implied tree approach to valuing exotic options. We explain the GARCH approach to modeling volatility changes and provide a brief review of some of the empirical research on option pricing.

For ease of exposition, most of the results in this chapter are presented in the context of valuing options on non-dividend-paying stocks, but much of the discussion of pricing biases is equally applicable to options on stock indices, currencies, and futures contracts.

19.1 KNOWN CHANGES IN THE INTEREST RATE AND VOLATILITY

When the risk-free interest rate is a known function of time, the Black–Scholes formulas for valuing European call and put options on a stock are correct, with r replaced by the average instantaneous risk-free rate during the remaining life of the option. Similarly, when the volatility is a known function of time, the Black–Scholes formulas are true with the variance rate, σ^2, replaced by its average value during the remaining life of the option.

These results can be derived using risk-neutral valuation. They are useful in some situations. If the volatility of a stock is expected to rise steadily from 20% to 30% during the life of an option, it would be appropriate to use a volatility of

about 25% when valuing the option.[1] Also, if the term structure of interest rates indicates that the short rate is likely to change during the life of an option, this can be taken into account when choosing r. Usually, r is, as a matter of course, set equal to the rate of interest on an instrument that matures at the same time as the option rather than as the current instantaneous interest rate.[2]

19.2 MERTON'S STOCHASTIC INTEREST RATE MODEL

Results for the valuation of options when the interest rate is stochastic have been produced by Merton.[3] Consider a European option maturing at time T. Define $P(t, T)$ as the value at time t of a discount bond paying \$1 at time T. Merton assumes that $P(t, T)$ follows the process

$$\frac{dP(t, T)}{P(t, T)} = \mu_P \, dt + \sigma_P \, dz_P$$

The variable μ_P is the growth rate in the bond price and is stochastic; σ_P is the volatility of $P(t, T)$, and is assumed to be a known function of only t and T; dz_P is a Wiener process. Merton shows that the European call and put prices are given by

$$c = SN(d_1) - P(t, T)XN(d_2)$$
$$p = P(t, T)XN(-d_2) - SN(-d_1)$$

where

$$d_1 = \frac{\ln(S/X) - \ln P(t, T) + \hat{\sigma}^2(T - t)/2}{\hat{\sigma}\sqrt{T - t}}$$

$$d_2 = d_1 - \hat{\sigma}\sqrt{T - t}$$

$$\hat{\sigma}^2(T - t) = \int_t^T (\sigma^2 + \sigma_P^2 - 2\rho\sigma\sigma_P) \, dt \qquad (19.1)$$

The parameter, σ, is the volatility of the stock and ρ is the instantaneous correlation between the stock and bond prices.

---

[1] Setting σ^2 equal to the average variance rate during the life of an option is not quite the same as setting σ equal to the average volatility, but in practice there is very little difference between the two. If, in this example, the volatility increases linearly from 20% per annum to 30% per annum, the correct value to use for σ can be shown to be 25.17% per annum.

[2] The issue as to whether the interest rate should be the risk-free rate or some other rate reflecting the creditworthiness of the option writer will be discussed in Chapter 20.

[3] See R. C. Merton, "Theory of Rational Option Pricing," *Bell Journal of Economics and Management Science,* 4 (Spring 1973), 141–83.

The variable $P(t, T)$ is given by

$$P(t, T) = e^{-R(t,T)(T-t)}$$

where $R(t, T)$ is the rate of interest on a riskless bond that matures at time T. Merton's model is therefore the same as the Black–Scholes model with:

1. The instantaneous interest rate, r, replaced by the rate of interest, $R(t, T)$, on a riskless bond maturing at the same time as the option.
2. The stock price volatility, σ, replaced by $\hat{\sigma}$ [see equation (19.1)].

Merton's model provides support for using $R(t, T)$ rather than r in the Black–Scholes model. For most traded options it can be shown that $\hat{\sigma}$ is close to σ.[4] The volatility adjustment therefore has little effect on the option price.[5]

    Merton's model requires the volatility of a discount bond to be a known function of time. It is consistent with the Vasicek, Ho–Lee, and Hull–White interest rate models discussed in Chapter 17. It is not consistent with other term structure models where the volatility of a bond price is a function of both the bond price itself and time.

19.3 PRICING BIASES

The critical determinant of the price of a European stock option is the terminal stock price distribution. Up to now we have assumed that this is lognormal. In this section we consider the effects of departures from lognormality. The general approach is similar to that taken by Jarrow and Rudd.[6]

    Figure 19.1 shows four ways in which the true terminal distribution can be different from a lognormal distribution while still giving the same mean and standard deviation for the stock price return. In Figure 19.1a, both tails are thinner than the lognormal distribution; in Figure 19.1d, both tails are fatter; in Figure 19.1b and c, one tail is thinner and the other is fatter.

    It is instructive to consider the biases that would be observed if the Black–Scholes model were used to price options in the four situations. Consider first a call option that is significantly out of the money. It has a positive value only if there is a large increase in the stock price. Its value therefore depends only on

---

[4]This is because σ_P is usually very much smaller than σ. For a one-year option on a stock, a high initial value for σ_P would be 2% per annum, and this would decline to zero during the life of the option. Typically, σ is about 30%.

[5]Stock and bond prices are generally positively correlated so that $\rho > 0$. If $\sigma_P < 2\rho\sigma$, it follows from equation (19.1) that $\hat{\sigma} < \sigma$. The effect of the volatility adjustment is then to reduce the price of the option.

[6]R. Jarrow and A. Rudd, "Approximate Option Valuation for Arbitrary Stochastic Processes," *Journal of Financial Economics,* 10 (November 1982), 347–69.

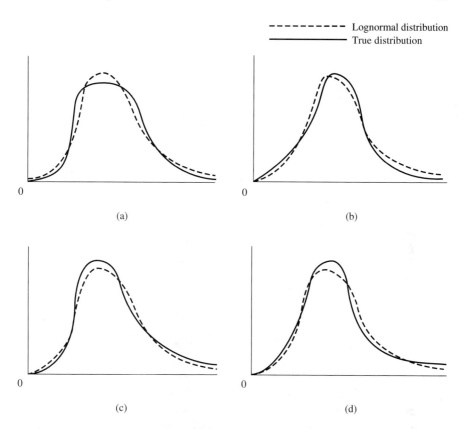

Figure 19.1   Alternative terminal stock price distributions: dashed line, lognormal distribution; solid line, true distribution.

the right tail of the terminal stock price distribution. The fatter this tail, the more valuable the option is. Consequently, Black–Scholes will tend to underprice out-of-the-money calls in Figure 19.1c and d, and overprice out-of-the-money calls in Figure 19.1a and b. Consider next a put option that is significantly out of the money. It has a positive value only if there is a large decrease in the stock price. Its value therefore depends only on the left tail of the terminal stock price distribution. The fatter this tail, the more valuable the option is. Black–Scholes will therefore tend to underprice out-of-the-money puts in Figure 19.1b and d, and overprice out-of-the-money puts in Figure 19.1a and c.

To obtain the biases for in-the-money options, we can use put–call parity. With the usual notation, put–call parity (see Section 7.6) gives

$$p + S = c + Xe^{-r(T-t)}$$

This relationship is independent of the shape of the terminal stock price distribution. If the European call with price c is out of the money, the corresponding

TABLE 19.1　Biases Corresponding to Alternative Stock Prices Distributions in Figure 19.1

Distribution	Characteristics	Biases
Figure 19.1a	Both tails thinner	Black–Scholes overprices out-of-the-money and in-the-money calls and puts.
Figure 19.1b	Left tail fatter; right tail thinner	Black–Scholes overprices out-of-the-money calls and in-the-money puts. It underprices out-of-the-money puts and in-the-money calls.
Figure 19.1c	Left tail thinner; right tail fatter	Black–Scholes overprices out-of-the-money puts and in-the-money calls. It underprices in-the-money puts and out-of-the-money calls.
Figure 19.1d	Both tails fatter	Black–Scholes underprices out-of-the-money and in-the-money calls and puts.

European put with price p is in the money, and vice versa. Consequently, an in-the-money European put must exhibit the same pricing biases as an out-of-the-money European call. Similarly, an in-the-money European call must exhibit the same pricing biases as an out-of-the-money European put. The biases are therefore as indicated in Table 19.1.

19.4 ALTERNATIVE MODELS

In this section we discuss a number of alternatives to the Black–Scholes model and explain how they can give rise to some of the biases mentioned in the preceding section.

Stochastic Volatility

The pricing bias caused by a stochastic volatility depends on the correlation between the volatility and the asset price. When the correlation is significantly positive, the situation is as in Figure 19.1c. The Black–Scholes model tends to underestimate the price for out-of-the-money call options and overestimate the price for out-of-the-money put options. The reason is as follows. When the stock price increases, volatility tends to increase. This means that very high stock prices

are more likely than under geometric Brownian motion. When the stock price decreases, volatility tends to decrease. This means that very low stock prices are less likely than under geometric Brownian motion.

When the correlation is significantly negative, the situation is as in Figure 19.1b. Black–Scholes tends to overestimate the price of out-of-the-money call options and underestimate the price of out-of-the-money put options. This is because when the stock price increases, volatility tends to decrease, making it less likely that really high stock prices will be achieved. When the stock price decreases, volatility tends to increase, making it more likely that really low stock prices will be achieved.

Finally, when the correlation is close to zero, the situation is as in Figure 19.1d. Black–Scholes tends to underprice deep-out-of-the-money and deep-in-the-money options. Stochastic volatility models are considered further in Section 19.6.

Compound Option Model

The equity in a levered firm can be viewed as a call option on the value of the firm. To see this, suppose that the value of the firm is V and the face value of outstanding debt is A. Suppose further that all the debt matures at a single time, T^*. If $V < A$ at time T^*, the value of the equity at this time is zero since all the company's assets go to the bondholders. If $V > A$ at time T^*, the value of the equity at this time is $V - A$. Thus the equity is a European call option on V with maturity T^* and exercise price A.

An option on stock of the firm that expires earlier than T^* can be regarded as an option on an option on V or a compound option (see Chapter 18). This has been analyzed by Geske.[7] The state variable underlying the value of the stock option is the firm value, V, rather than the stock price, S. Geske assumes that σ_V, the volatility of V, is constant and that the amount of debt, A, is also constant. The volatility of S is then negatively correlated with V. When V decreases, leverage increases and the volatility of S increases. When V increases, leverage decreases and the volatility of S decreases. From the arguments concerning stochastic volatility, this means that the pricing biases correspond to Figure 19.1b. Relative to Black–Scholes, the compound option model overprices out-of-the-money calls and in-the-money puts. It also underprices in-the-money calls and out-of-the-money puts.

Under Geske's model, the Black–Scholes formula gives S as a function of V:

$$S = VN(d_1) - Ae^{-r(T^*-t)}N(d_2) \qquad (19.2)$$

[7]See R. Geske, "The Valuation of Compound Options," *Journal of Financial Economics*, 7 (1979), 63–81.

where

$$d_1 = \frac{\ln(V/A) + (r + \sigma_V^2/2)(T^* - t)}{\sigma_V \sqrt{T^* - t}}$$

$$d_2 = d_1 - \sigma_V \sqrt{T^* - t}$$

The formula for pricing a European call option using the compound option model is given in Appendix 19A. It is more complicated than the Black–Scholes formula in that it requires a knowledge of the face value of the debt and the maturity of the debt.

Displaced Diffusion Model

Rubinstein has proposed what is known as a *displaced diffusion model* for stock option pricing.[8] In this model, the firm is assumed to hold two categories of assets: risky assets, which have a constant volatility, and riskless assets, which provide a return, r. There is also assumed to be a certain fixed amount of default-free debt. If α is the initial proportion of the total assets of the firm which are risky and β is the initial debt-to-equity ratio, a key parameter, a, in the model is defined by

$$a = \alpha(1 + \beta)$$

If $a > 1$, the amount of debt in the displaced diffusion model exceeds the riskless assets. Netting the riskless assets off against the debt, the model becomes very similar to the compound option model and leads to biases that correspond to Figure 19.1b. Unlike the compound option model, the displaced diffusion model does not take into account the possibility of default on the debt. In a situation where the value of the assets is less than the face value of the debt, the model assumes that the value of the equity is negative.

If $a < 1$, the amount of debt is less than the amount of riskless assets. The model then has properties that are markedly different from the properties of the compound option model. Netting off the debt against the riskless assets, we can write

$$S = S_A + S_B$$

where S is the stock price, S_A is the value of the risky assets, and S_B is the value of net riskless assets. When S_A increases quickly, S increases and the volatility of S also increases. This is because risky assets have become a proportionately larger part of S. Similarly, when S_A decreases quickly, both S and the volatility of S decrease. It follows that the volatility and stock price are positively correlated. From the arguments concerning stochastic volatility, this means that the biases correspond to Figure 19.1c.

[8] See M. Rubinstein, "Displaced Diffusion Option Pricing," *Journal of Finance*, 38 (March 1983), 213–17.

The formula for pricing a European call under the displaced diffusion model is given in Appendix 19A. It will be recalled that in valuing options on stocks paying known dividends, we assumed that the stock price can be divided into a riskless component which is used to pay the dividends and a risky component with a constant volatility. This is a version of the displaced diffusion model with zero debt.

Constant Elasticity of Variance Model

The constant elasticity of variance model was proposed by Cox and Ross.[9] In this model the stock price has a volatility of $\sigma S^{-\alpha}$ for some α where $0 \leq \alpha \leq 1$.[10] Thus the volatility decreases as the stock price increases.

The rationale for the constant elasticity of variance model is that all firms have fixed costs that have to be met regardless of the firm's operating performance. When the stock price declines, we can presume that the firm's operating performance has declined and the fixed costs have the effect of increasing volatility. When the stock price increases, the reverse happens and the fixed costs have the effect of decreasing volatility. One type of fixed cost is that arising from financial leverage. In general concept, the constant elasticity of variance model is therefore similar to the compound option model. The formulas for pricing options under the general constant elasticity of variance model are relatively complicated and are not reproduced in this book. Since the volatility is negatively related to the stock price, the arguments in Section 19.3 show that the biases correspond to Figure 19.1b.

When $\alpha = 1$, the stock price volatility is inversely proportional to the stock price. This gives rise to a simple version of the constant elasticity of variance model known as the *absolute diffusion model*. The formula for pricing a European call under the absolute diffusion model is given in Appendix 19A. The model is easy to apply. Unfortunately, it has a weakness in that it allows stock prices to become negative.

The Pure Jump Model

The models considered so far have involved the stock price changing continuously. We now consider a model where the stock price follows a jump process. This was first suggested by Cox and Ross and elaborated on in a later paper by Cox, Ross, and Rubinstein.[11] The model is illustrated in Figure 19.2. In each

---

[9]See J. C. Cox and S. A. Ross, "The Valuation of Options for Alternative Stochastic Processes," *Journal of Financial Economics,* 3 (March 1976), 145–66.

[10]More formally, the model for the stock price is

$$dS = \mu S\, dt + \sigma S^{1-\alpha}\, dz$$

[11] See J. C. Cox and S. A. Ross, "The Pricing of Options for Jump Processes," Working Paper 2-75, Rodney L. White Center for Financial Research, University of Pennsylvania, April 1975; J. C. Cox, S. A. Ross, and M. Rubinstein, "Option Pricing: A Simplified Approach," *Journal of Financial Economics,* 7 (September 1979), 229–63.

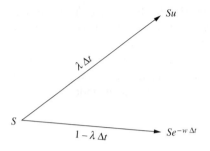

Figure 19.2   Stock price changes under the pure jump model.

small interval of time, Δt, the stock price has a probability $\lambda \Delta t$ of moving from S to Su and a probability of $1 - \lambda \Delta t$ of moving from S to $Se^{-w\Delta t}$. Most of the time, the stock price declines at rate w. However, occasionally it exhibits jumps equal to $u - 1$ times the current stock price.

In the limit as $\Delta t \longrightarrow 0$, jumps occur according to a Poisson process at rate λ. The terminal stock price distribution is log-Poisson and the price of a call is as given in Appendix 19A. It is easy to see that the pure jump model leads to the situation in Figure 19.1c. Arguably, the model is unrealistic in that jumps can only be positive.

The Jump Diffusion Model

Merton has suggested a model in which the stock price has jumps superimposed upon a geometric Brownian motion.[12] Define

μ: expected return from stock

λ: rate at which jumps happen

k: average jump size measured as a proportional increase in the stock price

The proportional jump size is assumed to be drawn from a probability distribution in the model. The average growth rate from the jumps is λk. This means that the expected growth rate provided by the geometric Brownian motion is $\mu - \lambda k$.[13]

The key assumption made by Merton is that the jump component of the stock's return represents nonsystematic risk (i.e., risk not priced in the econ-

---

[12]See R. C. Merton, "Option Pricing When Underlying Stock Returns Are Discontinuous," *Journal of Financial Economics,* 3 (March 1976), 125–44.

[13]More formally, the model is

$$\frac{dS}{S} = (\mu - \lambda k)\,dt + \sigma\,dz + dq$$

where dz is a Wiener process, dq is the Poisson process generating the jumps, and σ is the volatility of the geometric Brownian motion. The processes dz and dq are assumed to be independent.

omy).[14] This means that a Black–Scholes type of portfolio, which eliminates the uncertainty arising from the geometric Brownian motion, must earn the riskless rate. This leads to the pricing formula in Appendix 19A.

As one might expect, jump processes give rise to fatter tails than do continuous processes. A model where jumps can be either positive or negative therefore leads to the situation in Figure 19.1d. Black–Scholes formulas underprice calls and puts when they are either significantly in the money or significantly out of the money.

19.5 OVERVIEW OF PRICING BIASES

Table 19.2 summarizes the results from Section 19.4. In addition to being categorized according to the terminal stock price distribution, the various models can be categorized according to whether the bias increases or decreases as the time to maturity increases. The biases caused by a stochastic volatility become a larger percentage of the option price as the time to maturity increases. The reason for this is easy to understand. Just as the effect of volatility on the standard deviation of the stock price distribution increases as we look farther ahead, so the distortions to that distribution caused by uncertainties in the volatility become greater as we look farther ahead. For a similar reason, the biases in the compound option model become more pronounced as the time to maturity increases.

Jumps are different in that they produce proportionately greater effects when the time to maturity of the option is small. When we look sufficiently far into the future, jumps tend to get "averaged out" so that the stock price distribution arising from jumps is almost indistinguishable from that arising from continuous changes.

19.6 STOCHASTIC VOLATILITY

One assumption in Black–Scholes that is clearly not true is the assumption that volatility is constant. Practitioners find it necessary to change the volatility parameter frequently when using Black–Scholes to value options.

Hull and White consider the following stochastic volatility model for the risk-neutral behavior of a stock price:

$$\frac{dS}{S} = r\,dt + \sqrt{V}\,dz_S$$

$$dV = a(b - V)\,dt + \xi V^{\alpha} S\,dz_V$$

---

[14]This assumption is important because it turns out that we cannot apply risk-neutral valuation to situations where the size of the jump is systematic. For a discussion of this point, see E. Naik and M. Lee, "General Equilibrium Pricing of Options on the Market Portfolios with Discontinuous Returns," *Review of Financial Studies,* 3 (1990), 493–521.

TABLE 19.2   Categorization of Models According to Shape of Terminal Stock Price Distribution

Figure 19.1b	Figure 19.1c	Figure 19.1d
Compound option model	Displaced diffusion model when $a < 1$	Jump diffusion model Stochastic volatility model when stock price and volatility have zero correlation
Displaced diffusion model when $a > 1$	Pure jump model	
Constant elasticity of variance model	Stochastic volatility model when stock price and volatility are positively correlated	
Stochastic volatility model when stock price and volatility are negatively correlated		

where a, b, ξ, and α are constant, and dz_S and dz_V are Wiener processes. The variable, V, in this model is the stock's variance rate. It is the square of its volatility. The variance rate is assumed to revert to a level b at rate a.

Hull and White show that when volatility is stochastic but uncorrelated with the stock price, the price of a European option is the Black–Scholes price integrated over the probability distribution of the average variance rate during the life of the option.[15] Thus a European call price is

$$\int c(\overline{V})g(\overline{V}) d\overline{V}$$

where $\overline{V}$ is the average value of the variance rate, σ^2, c is the Black–Scholes price expressed as a function of $\overline{V}$, and g is the probability density function of $\overline{V}$ in a risk-neutral world. Hull and White compared the price given by their stochastic volatility model with the price given by Black–Scholes when the variance rate in Black–Scholes is put equal to the average value of $\overline{V}$. They found that Black–Scholes overprices options that are at the money or close to the money, and underprices options that are deep in or deep out of the money. This is consistent with the bias given in Section 19.4 for the zero-correlation case.

In the situation where the stock price and volatility are correlated, there is no simple result. Option prices can be obtained using Monte Carlo simulation.

---

[15] See J. C. Hull and A. White, "The Pricing of Options on Assets with Stochastic Volatilities," *Journal of Finance,* 42 (June 1987), 281–300. This result is independent of the process followed by the variance rate.

In the particular case where $\alpha = 0.5$, a series expansion for the option price can be derived.[16]

For options that last less than a year, the pricing impact of a stochastic volatility is fairly small in absolute terms. It becomes progressively larger as the life of the option increases. The pricing impact in percentage terms can be quite large for deep-out-of-the-money options. The impact of a stochastic volatility on the performance of delta hedging is always significant. It is important that practitioners monitor vega, even in situations where the impact of stochastic volatility on pricing is negligible.

GARCH

One technique for modeling volatility that has become popular is generalized autoregressive conditional heteroskedasticity (GARCH). In this section we explain the ideas behind the most commonly used GARCH model, GARCH(1,1).[17] Define:

σ_i: volatility of asset price at time $i\Delta t$

μ: average return on the asset

r_i: actual return on the asset at time $i\Delta t$

ϵ_i: $r_i - \mu$

The variable ϵ_i^2 can be characterized as the most recent information about the variance of asset returns at time $i\Delta t$. GARCH(1,1) relates the variance of asset returns at time $i\Delta t$ to the variance of asset returns at time $(i - 1)\Delta t$ and ϵ_i^2. The equation is

$$\sigma_i^2 = \omega + \alpha \epsilon_{i-1}^2 + \beta \sigma_{i-1}^2 \tag{19.3}$$

where ω, α, and β are constants. These three constants are estimated using maximum likelihood methods. If we write $\omega = (1 - \alpha - \beta)V$, equation (19.3) becomes

$$\sigma_i^2 = V(1 - \alpha - \beta) + \alpha \epsilon_{i-1}^2 + \beta \sigma_{i-1}^2 \tag{19.4}$$

This shows that the variance rate at time $i\Delta t$ is a weighted average of:

1. A constant long-run average variance rate, V
2. The previous variance rate, σ_{i-1}^2
3. The most recent news about the variance rate, ϵ_{i-1}^2

---

[16]For details of this series expansion, see J. C. Hull and A. White, "An Analysis of the Bias in Option Pricing Caused by a Stochastic Volatility," *Advances in Futures and Options Research,* 3 (1988), 27–61. An alternative approach to obtaining analytic results when $\alpha = 0.5$ is provided by S. L. Heston, "A Closed Form Solution for Options with Stochastic Volatility with Applications to Bond and Currency Options," *Review of Financial Studies,* 6, 2 (1993), 327–43.

[17]For a discussion of GARCH(1,1) see T. Bollerslev, "Generalized Autoregressive Conditional Heteroskedasticity," *Journal of Econometrics,* 31 (1986), 307–27.

By repeatedly substituting for σ on the right-hand side of equation (19.3), we obtain

$$\sigma_i^2 = \frac{\omega}{1 - \beta} + \alpha \sum_{j=1}^{\infty} \beta^{j-1} \epsilon_{i-j}^2$$

This shows that the variance rate at any given time is a constant plus the weighted average of all past ϵ's. The parameter β can be interpreted as a "decay rate." It defines the relative importance of the different ϵ's in determining the current variance rate. For example, if $\beta = 0.5$, ϵ_{i-1}^2 is twice as important as ϵ_{i-2}^2; ϵ_{i-2}^2 is twice as important as ϵ_{i-3}^2; and so on.

From equation (19.4), the variance rate at time $i\Delta t$ is

$$\sigma_i^2 = V + \alpha(\epsilon_{i-1}^2 - V) + \beta(\sigma_{i-1}^2 - V)$$

For a time $k\Delta t$ in the future, this becomes

$$\sigma_{i+k}^2 = V + \alpha(\epsilon_{i+k-1}^2 - V) + \beta(\sigma_{i+k-1}^2 - V)$$

The expected value of ϵ_{i+k-1}^2 is σ_{i+k-1}^2. Hence

$$E[\sigma_{i+k}^2 - V] = (\alpha + \beta)E[\sigma_{i+k-1}^2 - V]$$

Using this equation repeatedly yields

$$E[\sigma_{i+k}^2 - V] = (\alpha + \beta)^k (\sigma_i^2 - V)$$

or

$$E[\sigma_{i+k}^2] = V + (\alpha + \beta)^k (\sigma_i^2 - V)$$

Since $\alpha + \beta < 1$, the final term in this equation becomes progressively smaller as k increases. Our forecasts of the future variance rate tend to V as we look further and further ahead. The GARCH(1,1) therefore has some of the same properties as mean reverting stochastic volatility models discussed earlier in this section.

19.7 HOW BLACK–SCHOLES IS USED IN PRACTICE

It will be clear from the discussion so far in this chapter that Black–Scholes provides a less-than-perfect description of the real world. Stock prices and other asset prices exhibit more complicated behavior than geometric Brownian motion. Why, then, do practitioners continue to use Black–Scholes?

One reason is the model is easy to use. There is only one parameter that is not directly observable in the market. This is the volatility. Practitioners can infer volatilities from option prices and option prices from volatilities in an unambiguous way. The more complicated models that have been discussed in this chapter involve several unobservable parameters and are much less easy to use.

Another reason for the popularity of Black–Scholes is that practitioners have developed what might be termed "tricks of the trade" to finesse its imperfections. The rest of this section and the next provides a brief review of these "tricks of the trade."

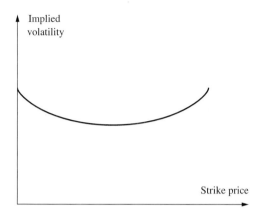

Figure 19.3   Volatility smile for foreign exchange options.

Volatility Smile

Practitioners frequently calculate what is known as the *volatility smile*. This is a plot of implied volatility of an option as a function of its strike price. A typical volatility smile for options on a foreign exchange is shown in Figure 19.3. Out-of-the-money and in-the-money options both tend to have higher implied volatilities than at-the-money options.[18] This is consistent with Figure 19.1d and could be explained by a jump diffusion model or by a stochastic volatility model where the underlying asset price and its volatility are uncorrelated.

Figure 19.4 shows the implied volatilities for options on the S&P 500 on May 5, 1993 as a function of strike price.[19] This is more a "grimace" than a smile and is typical of the pattern observed for equities. Figure 19.4 is consistent with Figure 19.1b. Implied volatilities are greater for low-strike-price options than for high-strike-price options. The effect could be produced by the compound option model, the displaced diffusion model with $a > 1$, the constant elasticity of variance model, or a stochastic volatility model where the stock price and volatility are negatively correlated.

Volatility Term Structure

Practitioners also like to calculate what is known as the *volatility term structure*. This is a plot of the variation of the implied volatility with the time to maturity of the option. Figure 19.5 shows the volatility term structure for options on the S&P 500 on May 5, 1993.[20] It can be seen that the implied volatility was an increasing function of option maturity at this time.

[18]For this purpose it is appropriate to define an at-the-money option as an option where the strike price equals the forward price of the asset.

[19]This figure is taken from E. Derman and I. Kani, "The Volatility Smile and Its Implied Tree," Quantitative Strategies Publications, Goldman Sachs, January 1994.

[20]This diagram also comes from E. Derman and I. Kani, "The Volatility Smile and Its Implied Tree," Quantitative Strategies Publications, Goldman Sachs, January 1994.

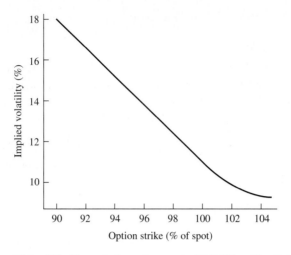

Figure 19.4 Volatility smile for options on the S&P 500 on May 5, 1993.

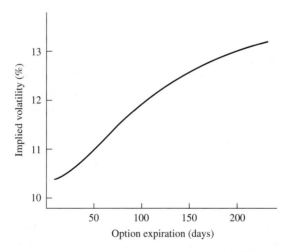

Figure 19.5 Volatility term structure for options on the S&P 500 on May 5, 1993.

TABLE 19.3 Volatility Matrix (ATM = At the Money)

	ATM less 2 SDs	ATM less 1 SD	ATM	ATM plus 1 SD	ATM plus 2 SDs
1 MM	14.2	13.0	12.0	12.8	13.6
3 MM	14.2	13.0	12.0	12.8	13.6
6 MM	14.7	13.5	12.5	13.3	14.1
1 YR	15.9	14.8	13.5	14.5	15.5
2 YR	16.6	15.3	14.0	15.0	16.0
5 YR	16.6	15.5	14.4	15.2	16.0

Volatility Matrices

A common approach to coping with the imperfections in Black–Scholes is to construct a matrix of implied volatilities. An example is shown in Table 19.3.[21] One dimension of the matrix is strike price; the other is time to maturity. The main body of the matrix shows implied volatilities calculated from the Black–Scholes model. At any given time, some of the entries in the matrix are likely to correspond to options for which reliable market data are available. The volatilities for these options can be calculated directly from their market prices and entered into the table. The rest of the matrix is determined using linear interpolation.

When a new option has to be valued, practitioners look up the appropriate volatility in the table. For example, when valuing a nine-month option with a strike price one standard deviation below the at-the-money (ATM) strike price, practitioners would interpolate between 13.5 and 14.8 to obtain a volatility of 14.15%. This is the volatility that would be used in the Black–Scholes formula or in the construction of a binomial tree.

The Role of the Model

How important is the pricing model if practitioners are prepared to use a different volatility for every deal? In practice, an option pricing model is often no more than a tool for understanding the volatility environment and for pricing illiquid securities consistently with the market prices of actively traded securities. If practitioners stopped using Black–Scholes and switched to, say, the constant elasticity of variance model, the matrix of volatilities would change and the shape of the smile would change. But arguably the prices quoted in the market would not change appreciably.

19.8 IMPLIED TREES

The implied tree methodology is a way in which practitioners have tried to reflect volatility smiles and time to maturity effects in the pricing of exotic options.[22] The usual geometric Brownian motion model for the behavior of stock prices in a risk-neutral world is

$$dS = rS\,dt + \sigma S\,dz$$

with r and σ constant. The implied tree method assumes that

$$dS = r(t)S\,dt + \sigma(S, t)\,dz$$

---

[21] At-the-money could be defined as the forward price of the underlying asset for the purposes of Table 19.3.

[22] For a discussion of the implied tree methodology, see E. Derman and I. Kani, "The Volatility Smile and Its Implied Tree," Quantitative Strategies Publications, Goldman Sachs, January 1994; E. Derman and I. Kani, "Riding on a Smile," *RISK*, February 1994, pp. 32–39; B. Dupire, "Pricing with a Smile," *RISK*, 7 (February 1994), 18–20; M. Rubinstein, "Implied Binomial Trees," *Journal of Finance*, 49, 3 (July 1994), 771–818.

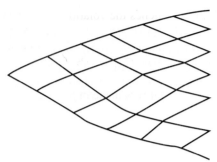

Figure 19.6   Implied tree.

where the functions r and σ are chosen to match a matrix of option prices such as those shown in Table 19.3. An implied tree is a binomial tree of asset price movements of the general form shown in Figure 19.6.

An implied tree is constructed using forward induction. To understand the approach, note that there are $n + 1$ nodes at time $n\,\Delta t$.[23] Assume that the tree has already been constructed up to time $(n - 1)\Delta t$. The next step involves:

1. Choosing the positions of the $n + 1$ nodes at time $n\,\Delta t$.
2. Choosing the n "up" probabilities on the branches between times $(n - 1)\Delta t$ and $n\,\Delta t$. (The "down" probabilities are 1 minus the "up" probabilities.)

These choices provide $2n + 1$ degrees of freedom.

The short rate for the period between $(n - 1)\Delta t$ and $n\,\Delta t$ is set equal to the forward rate. The expected return from the stock at each of the nodes at time $(n - 1)\Delta t$ must equal this short rate. This uses up n degrees of freedom. The tree is also constructed to ensure that n European style options maturing at time $n\,\Delta t$ are priced correctly. These options have strike prices equal to the stock prices at the nodes at time $(n - 1)\Delta t$.[24] This uses up an additional n degrees of freedom. The final degree of freedom is used up in ensuring that the center of the tree equals today's stock price.

The requirements just mentioned lead to $2n + 1$ equations in $2n + 1$ unknowns. By solving the equations we are able to advance the construction of the tree by one time step. One aspect of the algorithm is that negative probabilities must be avoided. If a particular probability does turn out to be negative, it is necessary to introduce a rule to override the option price responsible for the negative probability.

The implied tree methodology has the advantage that all options are priced consistently with actively traded options. The main disadvantage is that we may

[23] The brief description of the implied tree methodology here is based on the work of E. Derman and I. Kani.

[24] In practice it is necessary to interpolate between the implied volatilities of actively traded options to determine implied volatilities for the options used in the tree construction. These implied volatilities are then converted into option prices using Black–Scholes.

be pushing a one-factor model too far. The tree matches the volatility smile and volatility term structure observed in the market today. However, the tree itself implies a volatility smile and volatility term structure in the future. These may be quite different from those observed in the market today. Caution should therefore be exercised in using an implied tree to price deals that are dependent on the volatility observed at a future time.[25] A similar point was made in Section 17.14 in connection with yield curve models.

19.9 EMPIRICAL RESEARCH

There are a number of problems in carrying out empirical research to test the Black–Scholes and other option pricing models. The first problem is that any statistical hypothesis about how options are priced has to be a joint hypothesis to the effect that (1) the option pricing formula is correct, and (2) markets are efficient. If the hypothesis is rejected, it may be the case that (1) is untrue, (2) is untrue, or both (1) and (2) are untrue. A second problem is that the stock price volatility is an unobservable variable. One approach is to estimate the volatility from historical stock price data. Alternatively, implied volatilities can be used in some way. A third problem for the researcher is to make sure that data on the stock price and option price are synchronous. For example, if the option is thinly traded, it is not likely to be acceptable to compare closing option prices with closing stock prices. This is because the closing option price might correspond to a trade at 1:00 p.m., while the closing stock price corresponds to a trade at 4:00 p.m. Here we present some examples of the type of empirical research that has been carried out.

Black and Scholes and Galai have tested whether it is possible to make excess returns above the risk-free rate of interest by buying options that are undervalued by the market (relative to the theoretical price) and selling options that are overvalued by the market (relative to the theoretical price).[26] A riskless delta-neutral portfolio is assumed to be maintained at all times by trading the underlying stocks on a regular basis as described in Section 14.5. Black and Scholes used data from the over-the-counter options market where options are dividend protected. Galai used data from the Chicago Board Options Exchange (CBOE) where options are not protected against the effects of cash dividends. Galai used Black's approximation as described in Section 11.12 to incorporate the effect of anticipated dividends into the option price. Both of the studies showed that in the absence of transactions costs, significant excess returns over the risk-free rate could be obtained by buying undervalued options and selling overvalued options.

---

[25] An example of such a deal is a compound option.

[26] See F. Black and M. Scholes, "The Valuation of Option Contracts and a Test of Market Efficiency," *Journal of Finance,* 27 (May 1972), 399–418; D. Galai, "Tests of Market Efficiency and the Chicago Board Options Exchange," *Journal of Business,* 50 (April 1977), 167–97.

It is possible that these excess returns were available only to market makers, and that when transactions costs are considered, they vanish.

A number of researchers have chosen to make no assumptions about the process followed by stock prices and have tested whether arbitrage strategies can be used to make a riskless profit in options markets. Garman provides a computational procedure for finding any arbitrage possibilities that exist in a given situation.[27] One study by Klemkosky and Resnick which is frequently cited tests whether the relationship in equation (7.9) is ever violated.[28] It concludes that some small arbitrage profits were possible from using the relationship. These were due mainly to the overpricing of American calls.

Chiras and Manaster have carried out a volatility study using CBOE data which compares the weighted implied volatility from options on a stock at a point in time with the volatility calculated from historical data.[29] They found that the former provides a much better forecast of the volatility of the stock price during the life of the option. However, there is no general agreement on this. Some subsequent research has reached the opposite conclusion. Chiras and Manaster also tested to see whether it was possible to make above-average returns by buying options with low implied standard deviations and selling options with high implied standard deviations. This strategy showed a profit of 10 percent per month. The Chiras and Manaster study can be interpreted as providing good support for the Black–Scholes model while showing that the CBOE was inefficient in some respects.

MacBeth and Merville have tested the Black–Scholes model using a different approach.[30] They looked at different call options on the same stock at the same time and compared the volatilities implied by the option prices. The stocks chosen were AT&T, Avon, Kodak, Exxon, IBM, and Xerox, and the time period considered was the year 1976. They found that implied volatilities tended to be relatively high for in-the-money options and relatively low for out-of-the-money options. A relatively high implied volatility is indicative of a relatively high option price, and a relatively low implied volatility is indicative of a relatively low option price. Therefore, if it is assumed that Black–Scholes prices at-the-money options correctly, it can be concluded that out-of-the-money call options are overpriced by Black–Scholes and in-the-money call options are underpriced by Black–Scholes. These effects become more pronounced as the time to maturity increases and the degree to which the option is in or out of the money increases. MacBeth and Merville's results are consistent with the displaced

[27]M. B. Garman, "An Algebra for Evaluating Hedge Portfolios," *Journal of Financial Economics,* 3 (October 1976), 403–27.

[28]R. C. Klemkosky, and B. G. Resnick, "Put–Call Parity and Market Efficiency," *Journal of Finance,* 34 (December 1979), 1141–55.

[29]D. Chiras and S. Manaster, "The Information Content of Stock Prices and Test of Market Efficiency," *Journal of Financial Economics,* 6 (September 1978), 213–34.

[30]See J. D. MacBeth and L. J. Merville, "An Empirical Examination of the Black–Scholes Call Option Pricing Model," *Journal of Finance,* 34 (December 1979), 1173–86.

diffusion model when $a > 1$, the compound option model, the absolute diffusion model, and the stochastic volatility model when the stock price and volatility are negatively correlated.

Rubinstein has carried out a study similar to the MacBeth and Merville study, but using a far larger data set and a different time period.[31] He looked at all reported trades on the 30 most active Chicago Board Option Exchange options classes between August 23, 1976 and August 31, 1978. Special care was taken to incorporate the effects of dividends and early exercise. Rubinstein compared implied volatilities of matched pairs of call options that differed either only as far as exercise price was concerned or only as far as maturity was concerned. He found that his time period could be conveniently divided into two subperiods: August 23, 1976 to October 21, 1977 and October 22, 1977 to August 31, 1978. For the first period, his results were consistent with those of MacBeth and Merville. However, for the second period, the opposite result from MacBeth and Merville was obtained; that is, implied volatilities were relatively high for out-of-the-money options and relatively low for in-the-money options. Throughout the entire period Rubinstein found that for out-of-the-money options, short-maturity options had significantly higher implied volatilities than long-maturity options. The results for at-the-money and in-the-money options were less clear cut.

No single alternative to the Black–Scholes model seems superior for both of Rubinstein's time periods. Indeed, it is difficult to imagine a model that leads to the changes in the biases that were observed between the first time period and the second time period. Possibly macroeconomic variables affect stock option prices in a way that is as yet not fully understood. At present, there do not seem to be any really compelling arguments for using any of the models introduced earlier in this chapter in preference to Black–Scholes for stock options.

A number of authors have researched the pricing of options on assets other than stocks. For example, Shastri and Tandon, and Bodurtha and Courtadon have examined the market prices of currency options;[32] Shastri and Tandon in another paper have examined the market prices of futures options;[33] Chance has examined the market prices of index options.[34] The authors find that the Black–Scholes model and its extensions misprice some options. There appears to be

---

[31] See M. Rubinstein, "Nonparametric Tests of Alternative Options Pricing Models Using All Reported Trades and Quotes on the 30 Most Active CBOE Options Classes from August 23, 1976 through August 31, 1978," *Journal of Finance,* 40 (June 1985), 455–80.

[32] See K. Shastri and K. Tandon, "Valuation of Foreign Currency Options: Some Empirical Tests," *Journal of Financial and Quantitative Analysis,* 21, (June 1986), 145–60; J. N. Bodurtha and G. R. Courtadon, "Tests of an American Option Pricing Model on the Foreign Currency Options Market," *Journal of Financial and Quantitative Analysis,* 22 (June 1987), pp. 153–68.

[33] See K. Shastri and K. Tandon, "An Empirical Test of a Valuation Model for American Options on Futures Contracts," *Journal of Financial and Quantitative Analysis,* 21 (December 1986), 377–92.

[34] See D. M. Chance, "Empirical Tests of the Pricing of Index Call Options," *Advances in Futures and Options Research,* 1, pt. A (1986), 141–66.

some evidence, for example, that currencies follow jump processes and that currency option prices are consistent with Figure 19.1d. However, the mispricing was not sufficient in most cases to present profitable opportunities to investors when transactions costs and bid–ask spreads were taken into account. In their two papers, Shastri and Tandon point out that even for a market maker, some time must elapse between a profitable opportunity being identified and action being taken. This delay, even if it is only to the next trade, can be sufficient to eliminate the profitable opportunity.

In an interesting study, Lauterbach and Schultz investigated the pricing of warrants.[35] They conclude that the biases are consistent with Figure 19.1b. The constant elasticity of variance model with $\alpha = 0.5$ gave a better fit to the data than did the Black–Scholes model. From Table 19.2 we see that Lauterbach and Schultz's results are also consistent with the compound option pricing model, the displaced diffusion model where $a > 1$, and the stochastic volatility model where the stock price and interest rate are negatively correlated. Their results were found to persist throughout a 10-year time period.

19.10 SUMMARY

The Black–Scholes model and its extensions assume that the probability distribution of the stock price at any given future time is lognormal. If this assumption is incorrect, there are liable to be biases in the prices produced by the model. If the right tail of the true distribution is fatter than the right tail of the lognormal distribution, there will be a tendency for the Black–Scholes model to underprice out-of-the-money calls and in-the-money puts. If the left tail of the true distribution is fatter than the left tail of the lognormal distribution, there will be a tendency for the Black–Scholes model to underprice out-of-the-money puts and in-the-money calls. When either tail is too thin relative to the lognormal distribution, the opposite biases are observed.

A number of alternatives to the Black–Scholes model have been suggested. These include models where the future volatility of a stock price is uncertain, models where the company's equity is assumed to be an option on its assets, and models where the stock price experiences occasional jumps rather than continuous changes. The models can be categorized according to the biases they give rise to. It is interesting to note that biases arising from jumps become less pronounced as an option's life increases, while biases arising in other ways become more pronounced as the option life increases.

The imperfections in Black–Scholes are evidenced by the fact that practitioners need to change the volatility parameter on a regular basis to reflect the latest market information. They are also evidenced by the fact that both practitioners

---

[35] See B. Lauterbach and P. Schultz, "Pricing Warrants: An Empirical Study of the Black–Scholes Model and Its Alternatives," *Journal of Finance*, 4, 4 (September 1990), 1181–1210.

and researchers find that implied volatilities depend on strike price (the volatility smile effect) and on time to maturity (the volatility term structure effect). Despite these imperfections the Black–Scholes model and its extensions are still widely used for valuing options. The model imperfections are handled by using volatility matrices. These matrices are constructed from the latest implied volatility data and incorporate both the volatility smile and the volatility term structure. Implied trees are a way of going one step further than this and incorporating the volatility smiles and the volatility term structure into the pricing of exotic options.

SUGGESTIONS FOR FURTHER READING

On Alternative Models

Black, F., "How to Use the Holes in Black–Scholes," *RISK,* March 1988.

Cox, J. C., and S. A. Ross, "The Valuation of Options for Alternative Stochastic Processes," *Journal of Financial Economics*, 3 (March 1976), 145–66.

Cox, J. C., S. A. Ross, and M. Rubinstein, "Option Pricing: A Simplified Approach," *Journal of Financial Economics*, 7 (September 1979), 229–63.

Derman, E., and I. Kani, "Riding on a Smile," *RISK,* February 1994, pp. 32–39.

Dupire, B., "Pricing with a Smile," *RISK,* February 1994, pp. 18–20.

Geske, R., "The Valuation of Compound Options," *Journal of Financial Economics,* 7 (1979), 63–81.

Heston, S. L., "A Closed Form Solution for Options with Stochastic Volatility with Applications to Bond and Currency Options," *Review of Financial Studies,* 6, 2 (1993), 327–43.

Hull, J. C., and A. White, "An Analysis of the Bias in Option Pricing caused by a Stochastic Volatility," *Advances in Futures and Options Research,* 3 (1988), 27–61.

Hull, J. C., and A. White, "The Pricing of Options on Assets with Stochastic Volatilities," *Journal of Finance,* 42 (June 1987), 281–300.

Merton, R. C., "Option Pricing When Underlying Stock Returns Are Discontinuous," *Journal of Financial Economics,* 3 (March 1976), 125–44.

Merton, R. C., "Theory of Rational Option Pricing," *Bell Journal of Economics and Management Science,* 4 (Spring 1973), 141–83.

Rubinstein, M., "Displaced Diffusion Option Pricing," *Journal of Finance,* 38 (March 1983), 213–17.

Rubinstein, M., "Implied Binomial Trees," *Journal of Finance,* 49, 3 (July 1994), 771–818.

On Empirical Research

Black, F., and M. Scholes, "The Valuation of Option Contracts and a Test of Market Efficiency," *Journal of Finance,* 27 (May 1972), 399–418.

Bodurtha, J. N., and G. R. Courtadon, "Tests of an American Option Pricing Model on the Foreign Currency Options Market," *Journal of Financial and Quantitative Analysis,* 22 (June 1987), 153–68.

Bollerslev, T., "Generalized Autoregressive Conditional Heteroskedasticity," *Journal of Econometrics,* 31 (1986), 307–27.

Chance, D. M., "Empirical Tests of the Pricing of Index Call Options," *Advances in Futures and Options Research,* 1, pt. A (1986), 141–66.

Chiras, D., and S. Manaster, "The Information Content of Option Prices and a Test of Market Efficiency," *Journal of Financial Economics,* 6 (September 1978), 213–34.

Cumby, R., S. Figlewski, and J. Hasbrouck, "Forecasting Volatilities and Correlations with EGARCH Models," *Journal of Derivatives,* 1, 2 (Winter 1993), 51–63.

Engle, R. F., "Autoregressive Conditional Heteroscedasticity with Estimates of the Variance of United Kingdom Inflation," *Econometrica,* 50 (1982), 987–1007.

Galai, D., "Tests of Market Efficiency and the Chicago Board Options Exchange," *Journal of Business,* 50 (April 1977), 167–97.

Harvey, C. R., and R. E. Whaley, "Dividends and S&P 100 Index Option Valuations," *Journal of Futures Markets,* 12 (1992), 123–37.

Harvey, C. R., and R. E. Whaley, "Market Volatility Prediction and the Efficiency of the S&P 100 Index Option Market," *Journal of Financial Economics,* 31 (1992), 43–73.

Harvey, C. R., and R. E. Whaley, "S&P 100 Index Option Volatility," *Journal of Finance,* 46 (1991), 1551–61.

Klemkosky, R. C., and B. G. Resnick, "Put–Call Parity and Market Efficiency," *Journal of Finance,* 34 (December 1979), 1141–55.

Lauterbach, B., and P. Schultz, "Pricing Warrants: An Empirical Study of the Black–Scholes Model and Its Alternatives," *Journal of Finance,* 4, 4 (September 1990), 1181–1210.

MacBeth, J. D., and L. J. Merville, "An Empirical Examination of the Black–Scholes Call Option Pricing Model," *Journal of Finance,* 34 (December 1979), 1173–86.

Noh, J., R. F. Engle, and A. Kane, "A Test of Efficiency for the S&P 500 Index Options Market Using Variance Forecasts," *Journal of Derivatives,* 2 (1994), 17–30.

Rubinstein, M., "Nonparametric Tests of Alternative Option Pricing Models Using All Reported Trades and Quotes on the 30 Most Active CBOE Option Classes from August 23, 1976 through August 31, 1978," *Journal of Finance,* 40 (June 1985), 455–80.

Shastri, K., and K. Tandon, "An Empirical Test of a Valuation Model for American Options on Futures Contracts," *Journal of Financial and Quantitative Analysis,* 21 (December 1986), 377–92.

Shastri, K., and K. Tandon, "Valuation of Foreign Currency Options: Some Empirical Tests," *Journal of Financial and Quantitative Analysis,* 21 (June 1986), 145–60.

Xu, X., and S. J. Taylor, "The Term Structure of Volatility Implied by Foreign Exchange Options," *Journal of Financial and Quantitative Analysis,* 29 (1994), 57–74.

QUESTIONS AND PROBLEMS

19.1.   What option pricing biases are likely to be observed when:
  (a) Both tails of the stock price distribution are thinner than those of the lognormal distribution?

(b) The right tail is thinner, and the left tail is fatter, than that of a lognormal distribution?

19.2. What biases are caused by an uncertain volatility when the stock price is positively correlated with volatility?

19.3. What biases are caused by jumps in the movements of a stock price? Are these biases likely to be more pronounced for a six-month option than for a three-month option?

19.4. Assume that a stock price follows the compound option model. The Black–Scholes model is used to calculate implied volatilities for call and put options with different exercise prices and different times to maturity. What patterns would you expect to observe in the implied volatilities?

19.5. Why are the biases (relative to Black–Scholes) for the market prices of in-the-money call options usually the same as the biases for the market prices of out-of-the-money put options?

19.6. A stock price is currently $20. Tomorrow, news is expected to be announced that will either increase the price by $5 or decrease the price by $5. What are the problems in using Black–Scholes to value options on the stock?

19.7. What are the major problems in testing a stock option pricing model empirically?

*19.8. At time t a stock price is S. Suppose that the time interval between t and T is divided into two subintervals of length t_1 and t_2. During the first subinterval, the risk-free interest rate and volatility are r_1 and σ_1, respectively. During the second subinterval, they are r_2 and σ_2, respectively. Assume that the world is risk neutral.

   (a) Use the results in Chapter 11 to determine the stock price distribution at time T in terms of r_1, r_2, σ_1, σ_2, t_1, t_2, and S.

   (b) Suppose that $\bar{r}$ is the average interest rate between time t and T and that $\bar{V}$ is the average variance rate between times t and T. What is the stock price distribution at time T in terms of $\bar{r}$, $\bar{V}$, $T - t$, and S?

   (c) What are the results corresponding to (a) and (b) when there are three subintervals with different interest rates and volatilities?

   (d) Show that if the risk-free rate, r, and the volatility, σ, are known functions of time, the stock price distribution at time T in a risk-neutral world can be calculated using equation (11.2) on the assumption that (1) the risk-free rate is constant and equal to the average value of r, and (2) the variance rate is constant and equal to the average value of σ^2.

   (e) Prove the result in Section 19.1.

19.9. A company has two classes of stock, one voting and one nonvoting. Both pay the same dividends and the voting stock always sells for a 10% premium over the nonvoting stock. If the volatility of the total equity is constant, is the Black–Scholes formula correct for valuing European options on the voting stock? Explain your answer.

19.10. Assume that a stock price follows the jump diffusion model. The Black–Scholes model is used to calculate implied volatilities for call and put options with different exercise prices and different times to maturity. What patterns would you expect to observe in the implied volatilities?

19.11. Repeat Problem 19.10 assuming that the stock price follows a stochastic volatility model with the stock price and its volatility positively correlated.

19.12. Suppose that a foreign currency exchange rate follows a jump process and has a stochastic volatility that is uncorrelated with the exchange rate. What sort of biases would you expect in the option prices observed in the market relative to those given by the Black–Scholes formulas? Assume that implied volatilities are calculated on the basis of at-the-money options.

19.13. Consider a firm with no riskless assets and a certain amount of debt. Does the displaced diffusion model or the compound option model give a higher value for a call option? Which model gives a higher value for a put option? Explain your answer.

19.14. Option traders sometimes refer to deep out-of-the-money options as being options on volatility. Why do you think they do this?

APPENDIX 19A: PRICING FORMULAS FOR ALTERNATIVE MODELS

In this appendix we present for reference European call option pricing formulas for some of the models considered in the chapter. European put option prices can be obtained from the call prices using put–call parity.

Compound Option Model

The value of a European call on a non-dividend-paying stock is given by

$$c = VM\left(a_1, b_1; \sqrt{\frac{\tau_1}{\tau_2}}\right) - Ae^{-r\tau_2}M\left(a_2, b_2; \sqrt{\frac{\tau_1}{\tau_2}}\right) - Xe^{-r\tau_1}N(a_2)$$

where

$$a_1 = \frac{\ln(V/V^*) + (r + \frac{1}{2}\sigma_V^2)\tau_1}{\sigma_V\sqrt{\tau_1}}$$

$$b_1 = \frac{\ln(V/A) + (r + \frac{1}{2}\sigma_V^2)\tau_2}{\sigma_V\sqrt{\tau_2}}$$

$$a_2 = a_1 - \sigma_V\sqrt{\tau_1}$$

$$b_2 = b_1 - \sigma_V\sqrt{\tau_2}$$

$$\tau_1 = T - t$$

$$\tau_2 = T^* - t$$

The function $M(a, b; \rho)$ is the cumulative probability in the standardized bivariate normal distribution that the first variable is less than a and the second variable is less than b when the coefficient of correlation between the variables is ρ. A procedure for evaluating it numerically is given in Appendix 11B. The variable V^* is the value of V at time T, which gives $S = X$. This can be determined numerically from equation (19.2). Other notation is defined in Section 19.4.

Displaced Diffusion Model

The price of a European call option on a stock using the displaced diffusion model is

$$c = aSN(d_1) - (X - bS)e^{-r(T-t)}N(d_2)$$

where

$$d_1 = \frac{\ln[aS/(X - bS)] + \left(r - \sigma_R^2/2\right)(T - t)}{\sigma_R \sqrt{T - t}}$$

$$d_2 = d_1 - \sigma_R \sqrt{T - t}$$

$$a = \alpha(1 + \beta)$$

$$b = (1 - a)e^{r(T-t)}$$

In this formula, α is the initial proportion of the total assets that are risky, β is the initial debt-to-equity ratio, and σ_R is the volatility of the risky assets. If there are known dividends, their value compounded to time T at the risk-free rate should be subtracted from b.

Absolute Diffusion Model

The price of a European call option on a stock using the absolute diffusion model is

$$c = (S - Xe^{-r(T-t)})N(y_1) + (S + Xe^{-r(T-t)})N(y_2) + v[n(y_1) - n(y_2)]$$

where

$$v = \sigma \sqrt{\frac{1 - e^{-2r(T-t)}}{2r}}$$

$$y_1 = \frac{S - Xe^{-r(T-t)}}{v}$$

$$y_2 = \frac{-S - Xe^{-r(T-t)}}{v}$$

$$n(y) = \frac{1}{\sqrt{2\pi}} e^{-y^2/2}$$

This formula assumes that zero is an absorbing barrier for the stock price.

Pure Jump Model

Using the pure jump model the European call option price is given by

$$c = S\Psi(x; y) - Xe^{-r(T-t)}\Psi\left(x, \frac{y}{u}\right)$$

where

$$\Psi(\alpha; \beta) = \sum_{i=\alpha}^{\infty} \frac{e^{-\beta}\beta^i}{i!}$$

$$y = \frac{(r + w)(T - t)u}{u - 1}$$

and x is the smallest nonnegative integer that is greater than

$$\frac{\ln(X/S) + w(T - t)}{\ln u}$$

Jump Diffusion Model

The simplest form of Merton's jump diffusion model is when the logarithm of the size of the proportional jump has a normal distribution. Assume that the standard deviation of the normal distribution is δ. The European call option price can then be written

$$c = \sum_{n=0}^{\infty} \frac{e^{-\lambda'\tau}(\lambda'\tau)^n}{n!} f_n$$

where $\tau = T - t$ and $\lambda' = \lambda(1 + k)$. The variable f_n is the Black–Scholes option price when the instantaneous variance rate is

$$\sigma^2 + \frac{n\delta^2}{\tau}$$

and the risk-free rate is

$$r - \lambda k + \frac{n\gamma}{\tau}$$

where $\gamma = \ln(1 + k)$.

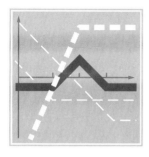

Chapter 20

Credit Risk and Regulatory Capital

When valuing a derivative, it is customary to assume that there is no risk of default. For an exchange-traded option, this assumption is usually a reasonable one since most exchanges have been very successful in organizing trading to ensure that their contracts are always honored. Unfortunately, the no-default assumption is far less defensible in the over-the-counter market. In recent years, this market has become increasingly important. Dealing with credit risk issues has become a major activity for both banks and bank regulators.

The main overall concern of bank regulators is to ensure that a bank's capital reflects the risks it is bearing. The traditional approach they have adopted has been to specify minimum levels for balance sheet ratios: for example, the ratio of equity to total assets. This became inappropriate in the late 1980s because derivatives such as swaps and options, which do not appear on the balance sheet, had begun to account for a significant proportion of the total risk. A scheme proposed by the Bank for International Settlements (BIS) in 1988 has achieved widespread acceptance by central banks throughout the world.[1] In this scheme, each on- and off-balance sheet item is assigned a weight reflecting its relative credit risk and minimum levels are set for the ratio of bank capital to total risk-weighted exposure. Regulators are now extending the scheme to require capital for market risk as well as credit risk.

In addition to ensuring that they satisfy the capital requirements imposed by regulators, financial institutions are faced with the problem of adjusting the prices of off-balance sheet items to reflect credit risk. They must ensure that their bid–offer spreads are large enough to provide compensation for possible defaults. In many financial institutions there has been a tendency to categorize credit risks as either acceptable or unacceptable and then to price all acceptable credit risks in much the same way. It seems likely that this will change as methods for quantifying credit risk become more widely accepted.

In this chapter we discuss the impact of credit risk on the pricing of derivatives and provide some details concerning the BIS regulatory requirements. We also cover the pricing of convertibles. For ease of exposition we assume that the current time is zero rather than t.

---

[1]Bank for International Settlements, "Proposals for International Convergence of Capital Adequacy Standards," July 1988.

20.1 BACKGROUND

For a financial institution to make a credit loss on a derivative, two conditions must be satisfied:

1. The counterparty must default.
2. The no-default value of the contract to the financial institution must be positive. (In other words, the contract must be an asset rather than a liability to the financial institution.)

There is no need for the second condition when we are considering the possibility of a credit loss on an option, since this is always an asset to one party (the purchaser) and a liability to the other party (the writer). The second condition is relevant for a contract such as a swap or a forward contract that can become either an asset or a liability to the financial institution. If the counterparty gets into financial difficulties when a contract has a positive value to the counterparty and a negative value to the financial institution, it is reasonable to assume that the contract will be sold to another party or be taken over by the liquidator in such a way that there is no real change in the financial institution's position. On the other hand, if the counterparty gets into financial difficulties when the contract has a negative value to the counterparty and a positive value to the financial institution, the counterparty may default on the contract and the financial institution is liable to make a loss equal to the positive value it has in the contract. This situation is illustrated in Figure 20.1. The financial institution's possible loss (i.e., exposure) at any given time is an optionlike function of the value of the contract. Expressed algebraically, the exposure is

$$\max(V, 0)$$

where V is the no-default value of the contract to the financial institution.

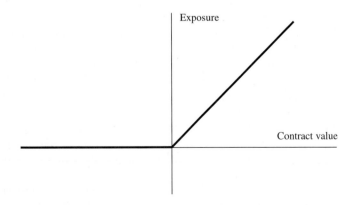

Figure 20.1   Exposure as a function of contract value.

The Independence Assumption

When defaults are possible, there are two groups of variables affecting the value of a derivative to a financial institution:

1. The variables affecting its value in a no-default world.
2. The variables affecting the occurrence of defaults by the counterparty and the proportional recovery made in the event of a default.

Hull and White examine a general model for pricing the option in terms of these two sets of variables.[2] The results in this chapter are based largely on their analysis.

The most general case of the model is quite cumbersome and requires a full specification of the relationships between the two sets of variables. An assumption that considerably simplifies the analysis is that the variables in group 1 are independent of the variables in group 2. Unless otherwise mentioned, we make this assumption throughout the rest of the chapter. We refer to the assumption as the *independence assumption.*

One requirement for the independence assumption is that the value of the contract under consideration have a negligible bearing on the ability of the counterparty of meet its liabilities as they become due. This means that the contract must be a very small part of the counterparty's portfolio of assets and liabilities or that the contract's risk must be hedged entirely by the counterparty. When the counterparty is a large financial institution, this requirement is likely to be met. Most large financial institutions have large portfolios of derivatives and sophisticated systems for ensuring that they are not unduly exposed to movements in the values of any one underlying market variable.

The independence assumption can be criticized on the grounds that market variables (e.g., interest rates) affect the performance of particular sectors of the world economy and therefore the chance of defaults. However, this may not be as serious a problem for the independence assumption as it sounds. A great deal of time often elapses between a movement in market variables and the resultant defaults by companies. Defaults can therefore be expected to be only very weakly related to the values of market variables at the time when the default occurs. (An example may help to illustrate the point being made here. High interest rates in the early 1980s caused problems in many sectors, but most of the resulting defaults, bankruptcies, and loan losses occurred a few years later, when rates were much lower.)

The independence assumption provides a good robust starting point for an evaluation of the impact of credit risk and provides a basis for incorporating credit risk into the systems used by financial institutions. In particular cases where

---

[2]See J. Hull and A. White, "The Impact of Default Risk on the Prices of Options and Other Derivative Securities," *Journal of Banking and Finance,* 19, 2 (May 1995), 299–322, and "The Price of Default," *RISK,* September 1992, pp. 101–3.

the assumption is clearly inappropriate, a trader can use judgment to adjust the assessment of the credit risk upward or downward.

The Credit Risk of Bonds

Bond traders have developed procedures for taking credit risk into account when pricing corporate bonds. They use the information provided by agencies such as Standard & Poor's and Moody's to assign a credit rating (e.g., AAA, AA, A, and BBB) to all issuers of corporate bonds. They then collect market data on actively traded bonds to calculate a generic zero-coupon yield curve for each credit rating category. (See Section 4.1 for how zero-coupon yields can be calculated from bond yields using the bootstrap method.) These zero-coupon yield curves are then used to value other bonds.

We now show how a zero-coupon yield curve for corporate bonds can be used to provide estimates of expected default losses on bonds. We take as our example an A-rated corporate bond. Define

$y(T)$:   yield on a zero-coupon A-rated corporate bond maturing at time T

$y^*(T)$:   yield on a zero-coupon Treasury bond maturing at time T

$B(T)$:   price of a zero-coupon A-rated corporate bond with a principal of $1 maturing at time T

$B^*(T)$:   price of a zero-coupon Treasury bond with a principal of $1 maturing at time T

$h(T)$:   expected loss from defaults on the T-year A-rated bond as a proportion of the bond's no-default value

In general, $y(T) > y^*(T)$, and $B(T) < B^*(T)$. Treasury bonds are default-free. We can conjecture that, if markets are operating efficiently, the lower price of the A-rated bond should exactly compensate the bond holder for his or her expected default losses. This means that the present value of the expected loss from defaults on the T-year A-rated zero-coupon bond equals $B^*(T) - B(T)$, so that

$$h(T) = \frac{B^*(T) - B(T)}{B^*(T)}$$

Since

$$B(T) = e^{-y(T)T}$$

and

$$B^*(T) = e^{-y^*(T)T}$$

it follows that

$$h(T) = \frac{e^{-y^*(T)T} - e^{-y(T)T}}{e^{-y^*(T)T}} = 1 - e^{-[y(T)-y^*(T)]T} \tag{20.1}$$

TABLE 20.1   Calculation of $h(T)$, the Expected Default Loss from a T-year A-Rated Corporate Bond, as a Proportion of its No-Default Value

T	$y^*(T)$	$y(T)$	$h(T)$
1	0.0500	0.0525	0.002497
2	0.0500	0.0550	0.009950
3	0.0500	0.0570	0.020781
4	0.0500	0.0585	0.033428
5	0.0500	0.0595	0.046390

Example 20.1

Consider the data in Table 20.1. The Treasury zero-curve is flat at 5% per annum. The spreads over Treasuries for corporate bonds with maturities of one, two, three, four, and five years are 25, 50, 70, 85, and 95 basis points respectively. The expected loss from defaults as a proportion of no-default value, as calculated from equation (20.1), is shown in the final column of the table. Consider for example a two-year bond. The expected loss from defaults as a proportion of the no-default value is

$$1 - e^{-(0.0550-0.0500)\times2} = 0.009950$$

or 0.9950%.

The adjustments for credit risk that are made in the bond market can be used as a basis for calculating the expected cost of default losses on derivatives.[3] In addition to the independence assumption already discussed, we assume that in the event of a default by the counterparty, the expected proportion of no-default value lost is the same both for the derivative and for bonds issued by the counterparty.[4]

20.2 ADJUSTING THE PRICES OF OPTIONS FOR CREDIT RISK

Consider a European option maturing at time T written by an A-rated corporation. Define

f: value of the option taking account of the possibility of a default
f^*: value of a similar default-free option

The relationship between these two variables is

$$f = f^* \frac{B(T)}{B^*(T)}$$

---

[3] The analysis we will present is based on J. Hull and A. White, "The Impact of Default Risk on the Prices of Options and Other Derivative Securities," *Journal of Banking and Finance*, 19, 2 (May 1995), 299–322. See also J. Hull and A. White, "The Price of Default," *RISK*, September 1992, 101–3.

[4] The corporate zero-coupon yield curve used in the analysis should be for bonds that will rank equally with the option in the event of default. Usually these are unsecured bonds.

or

$$f = f^* e^{-[y(T)-y^*(T)]T} \tag{20.2}$$

The reason for this is as follows. Since we are assuming that the bond ranks equally with the derivative in the event of a default, the proportion of the no-default value of the bond that is lost when a default occurs equals the proportion of the no-default value of the option that is lost. Losses from defaults are assumed to be independent of the behavior of the market variables that determine the value of the option and the value of the bond in a no-default world. The expected proportional loss from default is therefore the same for all realizations of these market variables and must be the same for both the option and the bond.

Example 20.2

Consider a 2-year over-the-counter option with a default-free value of $3. Suppose that a 2-year bond issued by the option writer that would rank equally with the option in the event of a default yields 150 basis points over similar Treasury issues. Default risk has the effect of reducing the option price to

$$3e^{-0.015 \times 2} = 2.911$$

or by about 3 percent.

This simple adjustment for credit risk is appropriate for all European-style derivatives that provide a nonnegative payoff at one particular point in time. Thus, in Example 20.2, default risk has the effect of reducing the price of any derivative that promises a nonnegative payoff in 2 years by about 3 percent.

Interpretation of the Rule

One interpretation of the adjustment rule is that we should use the "risky" discount rate, y, instead of the risk-free discount rate, y^*, when discounting payoffs from a derivative. Some care must be taken here. The risk-free interest rate enters into the valuation of a derivative in two ways: It is used to define the expected return from the underlying asset in a risk-neutral world, and it is used to discount the expected payoff. We should change the risk-free rate to the risky rate for discounting purposes, but not when determining expected returns in a risk-neutral world.

American Options

The impact of default risk on American options is more complicated than on European options. This is because the option holder's decision on early exercise may be influenced by new information, received during the life of the option, on the fortunes of the option writer. An example may help to illustrate the point here. Suppose that bank X sells a one-year call option on a non-dividend-paying stock to bank Y and that, during the following six months, bank X experiences a series of large well-publicized loan losses. Normally, the option would not be

exercised early. However, if the option is somewhat in the money at the end of the six months, bank Y might choose to exercise the option at this time rather than wait and risk bank X being liquidated before the option matures.

The proportional impact of default risk on the price of an American option is less than that for a similar European option. This is because early exercise shortens the life of an American option, making a loss from defaults less likely. Another general result is that American options subject to default risk are always exercised earlier than similar no-default options. It is interesting to note that options such as calls on non-dividend-paying stocks, which are never exercised early in a no-default world, should sometimes be exercised early when there is default risk. When the independence assumption is made, a lower bound to the value of an American option can be obtained by using the binomial tree in the usual way, but with the discount rate used between times t and $t + \Delta t$ being the forward rate calculated from the $y(T)$ yield curve.

20.3 CONTRACTS THAT CAN BE ASSETS OR LIABILITIES

We now move on to consider the impact of default risk on contracts, such as swaps and forward contracts, that can become either assets or liabilities. As before, we define f as the value of the derivative, taking account of possible defaults, and f^* as the no-default value of the derivative. For simplicity, suppose that defaults can occur only at times $t_1, t_2, \ldots, t_n$. Using the notation introduced in Section 20.1, equation (20.1) shows that the expected proportion of the no-default value lost between time zero and time t_i is

$$h(t_i) = 1 - e^{-[y(t_i)-y^*(t_i)]t_i}$$

Define u_i as the expected loss at time t_i as a proportion of the no-default value. Since defaults can occur only at times $t_1, t_2, \ldots, t_n$, it follows that

$$u_1 = h(t_1) \tag{20.3}$$

$$u_2 = h(t_2) - h(t_1)$$

$$u_3 = h(t_3) - h(t_2)$$

and so on. In general,

$$u_i = h(t_i) - h(t_{i-1}) \tag{20.4}$$

for $1 < i \leq n$.

Define v_i as the value at time zero of a derivative that pays off the exposure at time t_i; that is, a derivative that pays off $\max[f^*, 0]$ at time t_i. The independence assumption implies that the present value of the expected loss from defaults at time t_i is the present value of the expected exposure at time t_i multiplied by the expected proportional loss at this time. This is $u_i v_i$. The total expected loss is

therefore given by

$$f^* - f = \sum_{i=1}^{n} u_i v_i \qquad (20.5)$$

To illustrate the use of equation (20.5), suppose that a financial institution enters into a fixed-for-fixed foreign currency swap with an A-rated counterparty in which it receives interest in dollars and pays interest in sterling. Principals are exchanged at the end of the life of the swap. Suppose that the swap details are as follows:

Life of swap: five years
Frequency of payments: annual
Sterling interest exchanged: 10% per annum (compounded annually)
Dollar interest exchanged: 5% per annum (compounded annually)
Sterling principal: £50 million
Dollar principal: $100 million
Initial exchange rate: 2.0000
Volatility of exchange rate: 15%

We suppose that the sterling yield curve is flat at 10% per annum (annually compounded) and the dollar yield curve is flat at 5% per annum (annually compounded) with both interest rates being constant. We also suppose that one-, two-, three-, four-, and five-year zero coupon bonds issued by the counterparty would have yields that are spreads of 25, 50, 70, 85, and 95 basis points above the corresponding riskless rate.[5]

We assume that defaults can occur only on payment dates (that is, just before payments are due to be exchanged). This means that $n = 5$, $t_1 = 1$, $t_2 = 2$, $t_3 = 3$, $t_4 = 4$, and $t_5 = 5$. Since interest rates are assumed constant, we know that the value of the sterling bond underlying the swap at each possible default time is 55 million pounds. Similarly the value of the dollar bond underlying the swap at each possible default time is 105 million dollars. The value of the swap at time t_i in millions of dollars is therefore

$$105 - 55S(t_i)$$

where $S(t)$ is the dollar–sterling exchange rate at time t.

The variable v_i is the value of a derivative that pays off

$$\max[105 - 55S(t_i), 0] = 55 \max\left[\frac{105}{55} - S(t_i), 0\right]$$

millions of dollars at time t_i. This is a foreign currency put option. The variable v_i can therefore be obtained from equation (12.7). The spreads over Treasuries

---

[5] These spreads are expressed with continuous compounding and are the same as those in Table 20.1.

TABLE 20.2   Cost of Defaults in Millions of Dollars
on a Currency Swap with an A-rated Corporation
When Dollars Are Received and Sterling Is Paid

Maturity	u_i	v_i	$u_i v_i$
1	0.002497	5.9785	0.0149
2	0.007453	10.2140	0.0761
3	0.010831	13.5522	0.1468
4	0.012647	16.2692	0.2058
5	0.012962	18.4967	0.2398
Total			0.6834

in this example are the same as those in Table 20.1. The u_i can therefore be calculated by substituting the values of $h(T)$ from Table 20.1 into equations (20.3) and (20.4).

Table 20.2 shows the calculation of the cost of default from the u_i and v_i. The total cost of defaults is 0.6834 million dollars or 0.6834% of the principal. Table 20.3 shows a similar set of calculations for the situation in which the financial institution is paying dollars and receiving sterling. In this case v_i is the price of a foreign exchange call option maturing at time t_i. Table 20.3 shows that the expected cost of defaults is 0.2404 million dollars or 0.2404% of the principal.

This example illustrates the general rule that a financial institution has more default risk when it is receiving a low-interest-rate currency and paying a high-interest-rate currency than the other way round. The reason is that the high-interest-rate currency is expected to depreciate relative to the low-interest-rate currency, causing the low-interest-rate bond underlying the swap to appreciate in value relative to the high-interest-rate bond.

The total cost of defaults on a matched pair of swaps with two different A-rated counterparties is $0.6834 + 0.2403 = 0.9236$ million dollars or about 0.924% of the principal. Using a discount rate of 5% per annum this is equivalent to

TABLE 20.3   Cost of Defaults in Millions of Dollars
on a Currency Swap with an A-rated Corporation
When Dollars Are Paid and Sterling Is Received

Maturity	u_i	v_i	$u_i v_i$
1	0.002497	5.9785	0.0149
2	0.007453	5.8850	0.0439
3	0.010831	5.4939	0.0595
4	0.012647	5.0169	0.0634
5	0.012962	4.5278	0.0587
Total			0.2404

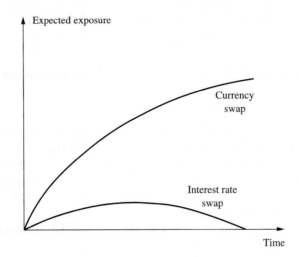

Figure 20.2   Expected exposure on a matched pair of interest rate swaps and a matched pair of currency swaps.

payments of about 0.21 million dollars per year for five years. Since the principal is 100 million dollars, 0.21 million dollars is 21 basis points. We have therefore shown that the financial institution should seek a bid–offer spread of about 21 basis points on a matched pair of currency swaps to compensate for credit risk when the exchange rate volatility is 15%.[6]

The impact of default risk on interest rate swaps is considerably less than that on currency swaps. Using similar data to that for the currency swap, the required total spread for a matched pair of interest rate swaps is about 2%. Figure 20.2 compares the expected exposure on a matched pair of offsetting interest rate swaps with the expected exposure on a matched pair of offsetting currency swaps. The expected exposure on a matched pair of interest rate swaps starts at zero, increases, and then decreases to zero. By contrast, the expected exposure on a matched pair of currency swaps increases steadily with the passage of time.[7]

The Continuous Time Analysis

The analysis just presented assumes that defaults can occur only at times t_1, $t_2, \ldots, t_n$. When we allow defaults to occur at any time, equation (20.5) becomes

$$f^* - f = \int_0^T u(t)v(t)\,dt \qquad (20.6)$$

---

[6] The total cost of defaults, and therefore the required bid–offer spread, on a matched pair of currency swaps is relatively insensitive to the interest rates in the two currencies, but the way in which the cost is split between the swaps does depend on the interest rates.

[7] This is largely because of the impact of the final exchange of principal in the currency swap. Sometimes currency swaps are negotiated without the final exchange of principal in order to reduce credit risk.

where

$$u(t) = \frac{\partial h(t)}{\partial t}$$

and $v(t)$ is the value of a derivative that pays off the exposure at time t. It can be shown that

$$u(t) = e^{-[y(t)-y^*(t)]t}\alpha(t)$$

where $\alpha(t)$ is the excess of the t-year instantaneous forward rate calculated from the $y(t)$ zero curve over that calculated from the $y^*(t)$ curve.

Equation (20.6) can be evaluated using numerical integration. For the example considered earlier, equation (20.6) gives the cost of defaults as 0.653% of principal when the financial institution is receiving dollars and as 0.211% of principal when it is paying dollars. The total cost of defaults on a matched pair of swaps is therefore given by equation (20.6) to be 0.864%. This compares with 0.924% given by equation (20.5).

Why is the cost of defaults given by equation (20.6) for a matched pair of currency swaps less than that given by equation (20.5)? The reason is that different assumptions are made about when the contract is valued for the purposes of determining the loss. Equation (20.6) assumes that the financial institution may recognize the counterparty as being in a default situation at any time, not just when it is due to receive payments from the counterparty. The financial institution's loss is based on the value of the contract at the time when the counterparty is observed to be in a default situation. The discrete analysis of equation (20.5) assumes that it is the value of the contract at the next payment date that determines the loss. In both cases the expected present value of the loss is equal to the value of a European option with a maturity equal to the time when the loss is calculated. Since European option prices usually increase with maturity, the loss is on average greater with the discrete analysis.

20.4 HISTORICAL DEFAULT EXPERIENCE

The historical default experience on bonds has been much less than that implied by bond prices.[8] Consider, for example, the performance of corporate bonds that have an A rating at the time of issue. A Moody's study using data for the period 1970 to 1994 shows that these bonds have a probability of 0.6% of defaulting during the first 5 years. A similar Standard & Poor's study using data for the period 1981 to 1993 shows that they have a probability of 0.84% of defaulting during this period. These numbers are both much lower than the 4.64% estimate of the cost of defaults in Table 20.1.

The Table 20.1 estimate is based on a 95-basis-point spread between the five-year corporate zero-coupon rate and the five-year Treasury zero-coupon rate.

---

[8]For an analysis of historical default experience, see E. I. Altman, "Measuring Corporate Bond Mortality and Performance," *Journal of Finance,* 44 (1989), 902–22.

This is not an unreasonable estimate of this spread for an A-rated bond. Even when the spread is reduced to 25 basis points, default losses are 1.24%, which is still significantly higher than the historical default experience.[9]

There are a number of possible reasons for differences between estimates of default losses calculated from bond prices and those calculated from actual default experience. It may be that bond traders are factoring into bond prices the possibility of "depression scenarios" much worse than anything seen during the period covered by the Moody's and Standard & Poor's data. It is also arguable that corporate bonds have more systematic (that is, nondiversifiable) risk than Treasury bonds and should provide bond holders with a return that reflects this risk as well as expected default losses. A final point is that part of the higher return on corporate bonds may be compensation for their lower liquidity than Treasury bonds.

Should the estimates of $h(t)$ that are used to adjust derivative prices for credit risk be based on bond prices or on historical default experience? This is a tricky question. It may not be appropriate to include the part of the excess corporate bond return that is compensation for liquidity in the pricing of some derivatives. However, to the extent that the excess return is compensation for systematic risk and depression scenarios, it should be taken into account in the pricing of derivatives.

20.5 VALUATION OF CONVERTIBLE BONDS

It is appropriate at this point to discuss the valuation of convertible bonds. These are bonds issued by a company where the holder has the option to exchange the bonds for the company's stock at certain times in the future. The exchange ratio (i.e., the amount of stock obtained in exchange for one bond) may be a function of time. The bonds are usually callable. This means that the issuer has the right to buy back the bonds. The call price (i.e., the price at which the bonds can be bought back) is often a function of time. The holder has the right to convert the bonds once they have been called. The call feature is therefore often a way of forcing conversion at a time earlier than the holder would otherwise choose.

One approach to valuing a convertible is to use a one-factor model where the company's stock price is assumed to be stochastic and interest rates are assumed to be deterministic. We build a stock price tree where the growth rate in the stock price at time t is the risk-free forward interest rate $w^*(t)$.[10] The life of the tree should equal the life of the convertible. The value of the convertible at the

---

[9]Furthermore, the Moody's and Standard & Poor's numbers may overstate the historical cost of defaults somewhat since they do not take account of any recoveries of principal made by the bond holder when the bonds default.

[10]This refinement of the Cox, Ross, and Rubinstein tree was discussed in Section 15.4. Strictly speaking $w^*(t)$ should be the Δt forward rate rather than the instantaneous forward rate. In the limit there is no difference.

final nodes of the tree can be calculated based on any conversion options that the holder has at that time. We then roll back through the tree in the usual way. At nodes where the terms of the instrument allow conversion we test whether conversion is optimal. We also test whether the position of the issuer can be improved by calling the bonds. If so, we assume that the bonds are called and retest whether conversion is optimal. This is equivalent to setting the value at a node equal to

$$\max[\min(Q_1, Q_2), Q_3]$$

where Q_1 is the value given by the rollback (assuming that the bond is neither converted nor called at the node), Q_2 is call price, and Q_3 is the value if conversion takes place. As we roll back through the tree, we must add in interest payments (if there has been no conversion) and dividend payments (if conversion has taken place).

One complication is the choice of a discount rate. Suppose first that the convertible is certain to remain a bond. It is then appropriate to use a discount rate corresponding to the creditworthiness of the issuer. This means that at time t we use the forward "risky" rate $w(t)$. The effect of this is that all the cash flows on the bond get discounted at the appropriate risky rate and the value of the bond today corresponds to its value in the market.

Suppose next that the bond is certain to be converted. It is then appropriate to use the risk-free rate, $w^*(t)$, as the discount rate at each node. This is because the standard risk-neutral valuation arguments for equity derivatives are independent of the creditworthiness of the company that issued the equity.

In practice we are usually uncertain as to whether the bond will be exercised. Consider a particular node at time t where the stock price is S. There is a (risk-neutral) probability $\pi(t, S)$ that the bond will be converted and a probability $1 - \pi(t, S)$ that it will not be converted. We set the discount rate at the node equal to $\pi w^*(t) + (1 - \pi)w(t)$. This discount rate can be calculated inductively as we roll back through the tree.[11] Suppose that at a particular node we branch up with probability p to a node where the discount rate is w_u and down to a node where it is w_d. The correct discount rate to use when we roll back is

$$pw_u + (1 - p)w_d$$

Once we have rolled back we test whether the bond should be converted or called. If neither is optimal, this is the discount rate associated with the node for future calculations. If it turns out to be optimal to call or convert the bond, the discount rate is changed to $w^*(t)$ at the node.

Example 20.3

As a simple example of the procedure for valuing convertibles, consider a nine-month discount bond issued by company XYZ with a face value of $100. Suppose that it can

---

[11] This idea is described in "Valuing Convertible Bonds as Derivatives," Quantitative Strategies Research Notes, Goldman Sachs, November 1994.

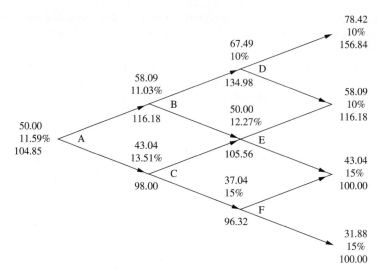

Figure 20.3   Tree for valuing convertible in Example 20.3.

be exchanged for 2 shares of company XYZ's stock at any time during the nine months. Assume also that it is callable for $115 at any time. We assume that the initial stock price is $50, its volatility is 30% per annum, and there are no dividends. The risk-free yield curve will be assumed to be flat at 10% per annum. The yield curve corresponding to bonds issued by company XYZ will be assumed to be flat at 15%. Figure 20.3 shows the stock price tree that can be used to value this convertible. The top number at each node is the stock price; the middle number is the discount rate used when cash flows are discounted back to the node from subsequent nodes; the final number at each node is the value of the convertible. The tree parameters are $u = 1.1618$, $d = 0.8607$, $a = 1.0253$, and $p = 0.5467$. At the final nodes the convertible is worth $\max(100, 2S_T)$, where S_T is the stock price. As we roll back through the tree, we test whether conversion is optimal and whether the bond should be called. We also calculate the appropriate discount rate. At node D, rollback gives the value of the bond as

$$(0.5467 \times 156.84 + 0.4533 \times 116.18)e^{-0.1\times0.25} = 134.98$$

The holder of the bond is indifferent as to whether he or she converts since the conversion value is also 134.98. The issuer is also indifferent as to whether the bond is called. This is because if it is called, the holder will immediately convert and the value will remain at 134.98. The correct discount rate at node D is 10% since the conversion is bound to take place at some stage if node D is reached. At node F the correct discount rate is 15% since the convertible is certain not to be converted if this node is reached. At node E the correct discount rate is

$$0.5467 \times 10 + 0.4533 \times 15 = 12.27\%$$

The value of the convertible at this node is

$$(0.5467 \times 116.18 + 0.4533 \times 100)e^{-0.1227\times0.25} = 105.56$$

Clearly, the bond should be neither converted nor called. At node B the discount rate used for the roll back calculations is a weighted average of the 10% at node D and the 12.27% at node E. This is

$$0.5467 \times 10 + 0.4533 \times 12.27 = 11.03\%$$

and the value of the convertible at node B given by the rollback calculations is

$$(0.5467 \times 134.99 + 0.4533 \times 105.56)e^{-0.1103 \times 0.25} = 118.34$$

It is optimal for the issuer to call the bond at node B since this will cause immediate conversion and leads to a value of 116.18 at the node. For the purposes of calculating the discount rate at node A we assume a discount rate of 10% at node B, reflecting the fact that conversion takes place at this node. The correct discount rate at node A is therefore

$$0.5467 \times 10 + 0.4533 \times 13.51 = 11.59$$

The value of the derivative at node A is

$$(0.5467 \times 116.18 + 0.4533 \times 98.00)e^{-0.1159 \times 0.25} = 104.85$$

If the bond had no conversion option, its value would be

$$100e^{-0.75 \times 0.15} = 89.36.$$

The value of the conversion option is therefore $104.85 - 89.36 = 15.49$.

20.6 THE BIS CAPITAL REQUIREMENTS

Regulatory authorities require that the following BIS requirements be satisfied:

$$\frac{\text{tier 1 capital}}{\text{risk-adjusted exposure}} > 4\%$$

$$\frac{\text{tier 1 plus tier 2 capital}}{\text{risk-adjusted exposure}} > 8\%$$

Tier 1 capital is shareholder's equity not including goodwill. Tier 2 capital consists of subordinated debt, loan reserves, and other sorts of long-term capital that is not equity.

Risk-adjusted exposure equals the total of risk-adjusted on-balance exposure and risk-adjusted off-balance sheet exposure. Risk-adjusted on-balance sheet exposure equals to the sum of

$$\text{principal} \times \text{risk weight}$$

for each asset. The risk weight for a commercial loan is 1.0; the risk weight for some other types of assets is less than 1.0. For example, residential mortgages have a risk weight of 0.5; Treasury bills have a risk weight of 0.0; loans to banks have a risk weight of 0.2; and so on. Consider a bank with the following

on-balance sheet assets

Commercial loans $10 million
Residential mortgages $30 million

The risk-adjusted exposure is $10 + 0.5 \times 30 = \$25$ million. The tier 1 (equity) capital required to support the assets would be $0.04 \times 25 = \$1$ million. In addition, tier 1 plus tier 2 capital would have to be greater than $0.08 \times 25 = \$2$ million.

For off-balance sheet contracts there are a variety of rules. Consider interest rate swaps. The first step is to calculate

current exposure + add-on factor

The current exposure is the greater of the current value of the swap and zero (see Figure 20.1). The add-on factor, as a percentage of the notional principal, is calculated as indicated in Table 20.4. The current exposure + add-on factor is multiplied by the risk weight of the counterparty to give the risk-adjusted exposure. For this purpose corporate counterparties are given a risk weight of 0.5.

As an example, consider a three-year interest rate swap with a corporate counterparty that has a current value of $10,000 and a notional principal of $1 million. The add-on factor is $5,000 and the risk-adjusted exposure would be calculated as $15,000 \times 0.5 = \$7,500$. If the swap were with a bank (risk-weight = 0.2), the risk-weighted exposure would be $15,000 \times 0.2 = \$3,000$.

When a swap or other derivative is being negotiated, it is important to realize that it is not only the capital requirement at the time the contract is negotiated that is important. Prudent financial planning requires that we calculate possible future capital requirements during the life of the derivative. Many financial institutions carry out Monte Carlo simulations to determine confidence limits for their regulatory capital at future times.

Internal Capital Allocation

The BIS capital requirements do not distinguish between different corporate counterparties. A counterparty with a AAA rating is treated the same as one with a BBB rating. For internal use, some financial institutions have developed more

TABLE 20.4   Percent of Notional Principal Added to Current Exposure to Obtain Capital Requirements for Swaps

Residual Maturity (years)	Interest-Rate Contracts (%)	Single Currency Floating/Floating Swaps	Exchange-Rate Contracts (%)
<1	Nil	Nil	1.0
>1	0.5	Nil	5.0

sophisticated capital allocation procedures. An amount of capital is allocated to each deal entered into by a financial institution and traders are evaluated on the basis of their return on capital employed. This has the advantage that it motivates traders to take credit risk into account when quoting prices. One way of allocating capital internally is to charge a trader an amount of capital proportional to $f^* - f$. The framework described earlier in this chapter can be used to calculate $f^* - f$.

Netting

A contentious issue in the evaluation of credit risk concerns what is known as *netting*. Most derivatives contracts state that if a counterparty defaults on one contract, it must default on all contracts. This has led banks to argue that when exposures and capital requirements are calculated, a swap with a negative value should be allowed to offset a swap with a positive value when the counterparty is the same in the two cases. Consider all the swaps that a bank has with a particular counterparty. Without netting, the bank's exposure at a future time is the payoff from a portfolio of options. With netting, it is the payoff from an option on a portfolio. The latter is never greater than, and is often considerably less than, the former. Regulatory authorities have become progressively more sympathetic to the use of netting in the calculation of capital requirements.

Capital for Market Risk

At the time of writing, regulators are planning to require banks to keep capital for market risks in addition to credit risks.[12] A number of alternatives for how the capital charge can be calculated for options have been proposed. Three of these are:

1. Calculate the capital charge from the delta, gamma, and vega measures. The theoretical foundations underlying this approach are the Taylor series expansion for the change in the value of a portfolio over a short period of time shown in Appendix 14A.
2. Carry out a scenario analysis to produce an output similar to Table 14.5. Base the required capital on the worst-case outcome shown by the table.
3. Use an internal model. In this case the capital charge is to be based on the value at risk for a period of 10 business days with a confidence limit of 99%. (See Section 14.12 for a discussion of the value at risk approach.)

Systemic Risk

In addition to ensuring that individual banks have enough capital to support the risks they are taking, regulators are concerned about what is known as

---

[12]See "Proposal to Issue a Supplement to the Basle Capital Accord to Cover Market Risks," Consultative Proposal by Basle Committee on Bank Supervision, Basle, April 1995.

systemic risk. This is the risk of several large financial institutions defaulting on their contracts at the same time, causing a severe strain on the financial system. The argument is that when one large financial institution runs into financial difficulties and defaults on its derivative transactions, there could be a "chain reaction." Other large financial institutions would experience losses because of the defaults on their contracts with the first financial institution. They, too, might get into financial difficulties and default their transactions; and so on. What is the chance of derivatives causing a problem of this magnitude? This is a hotly debated issue. Regulators argue that even if the chance is very small, say 1 in 10,000, it is something that should be protected against.

20.7 REDUCING EXPOSURE TO CREDIT RISK

There are a number of ways in which a financial institution can reduce the default risk in a derivatives contract. For example:

1. It can set credit limits for every counterparty. Most financial institutions do this. The credit limit is usually a limit on the total exposure of the financial institution to the counterparty. Traders are denied the authority to enter into a new trade with the counterparty if it would lead to the credit limit being exceeded.

2. It can ask the counterparty to post collateral and agree that the amount of collateral posted will be adjusted periodically to reflect the value of the derivatives contract to the counterparty. Ideally the collateral should be at least equal to the financial institution's exposure at any given time. This type of collateralization is similar to the margin requirements of futures exchanges and, if implemented carefully, can eliminate virtually all credit risk. It requires the two parties to agree on a valuation model for the contract and to agree to a rate of interest paid on the collateral. Sometimes collateral is posted by both sides and is held by a third party.

3. The payoffs on contracts can sometimes be designed to reduce credit risk. Consider, for example, a financial institution wishing to buy an option from a counterparty with a lower credit risk. It might insist on a zero-cost package that involves the option premium being paid in arrears (see Section 18.1 for a discussion of this type of instrument). This reduces the company's exposure arising from the option position.

4. Another way of reducing default risk is to include what are termed *downgrade triggers* in the contract. These state that if the credit rating of the counterparty falls below a certain level, say A, the contract is closed out using a predetermined formula with one side paying a cash amount to the other side. Downgrade triggers lead to a significant reduction in credit risk, but they do not completely eliminate all credit risk. If there is a big jump

in the credit rating of the counterparty, say from AA to Default, in a short period of time, the financial institution may still suffer a credit loss.

Credit Derivatives

A further way of reducing credit risk is through the use of *credit derivatives*. There are a number of different types of credit derivatives. Examples are

1. A forward contract on a corporate bond
2. A forward contract on the spread between a corporate bond yield and the Treasury yield
3. A swap where the cash flows from a corporate bond are paid and the cash flows from a Treasury instrument are received
4. A *Credit Risk Option* (CRO), where the writer agrees to compensate the seller for a prespecified fall in the credit rating of a corporation

To reduce its credit exposure to a corporation, a financial institution could short the first contract or take a long position in one of the other three contracts.

AAA-Rated Subsidiaries

AAA-rated companies are in a strong negotiating position in derivatives markets. This has led some financial institutions, which do not themselves have AAA ratings, to set up subsidiaries with AAA ratings for the purposes of trading derivatives. The subsidiary is well capitalized initially by the parent company, and the parent company agrees to inject more capital as needed according to a prearranged formula. If the parent company fails to inject the required capital, all derivative transactions entered into by the subsidiary are closed out. The parent company guarantees the subsidiary, but the subsidiary does not guarantee the parent company.

20.8 SUMMARY

As the volume of trading in the over-the-counter markets has increased, it has become important to assess the effect of default risk on derivative prices. In this chapter we have presented some of the ways in which this can be done. If we are prepared to assume that the variables concerned with defaults are independent of the variables determining the value of the security in a no-default world, the impact of defaults on derivatives can be derived from the impact of defaults on bonds analytically. In the case of contracts that are unambiguously assets, default risk is taken into account by increasing the interest rate that is used for discounting.

Capital requirements for banks throughout the world are determined using the Bank for International Settlements proposals. In these, each on- and off-balance sheet item is assigned a weight reflecting its relative credit risk. This

weight depends on both the nature of the contract and the counterparty. Minimum levels are set for the ratio of capital to risk-weighted exposure. Regulatory authorities are moving toward requiring capital for market risk as well as credit risk.

SUGGESTIONS FOR FURTHER READING

Altman, E. I., "Measuring Corporate Bond Mortality and Performance," *Journal of Finance,* 44, (1989), 902–22.

Bank for International Settlements, "Proposals for International Convergence of Capital Adequacy Standards," July 1988.

Belton, T. M., "Credit Risk in Interest Rate Swaps," Working Paper, Board of Governors of Federal Reserve System, 1987.

Cooper, I., and A. Mello, "The Default Risk of Swaps," *Journal of Finance,* 46 (1991), 597–620.

Goldman Sachs, "Valuing Convertible Bonds as Derivatives," Quantitative Strategies Research Notes, Goldman Sachs, November 1994.

Group of Thirty, "Derivatives: Practices and Principles," Washington, D.C., 1993.

Hull, J., "Assessing Credit Risk in a Financial Institution's Off-Balance Sheet Commitments," *Journal of Financial and Quantitative Analysis,* 24 (1989), 489–501.

Hull, J., and A. White, "The Impact of Default Risk on the Prices of Options and Other Derivative Securities," *Journal of Banking and Finance,* 19, 2 (May 1995), 299–322.

Hull, J., and A. White, "The Price of Default," *RISK,* September 1992, 101–3.

Jarrow, R. A., and S. M. Turnbull, "Pricing Options on Derivative Securities Subject to Credit Risk," *Journal of Finance,* 50 (1995), 53–85.

Johnson, H., and R. Stulz, "The Pricing of Options Under Default Risk," *Journal of Finance,* 42 (1987), 267–80.

Jonkhart, M. J. L., "On the Term Structure of Interest Rates and the Risk of Default: An Analytical Approach," *Journal of Banking and Finance,* 3 (1979), 253–62.

Merton, R. C., "On the Pricing of Corporate Debt: The Risk Structure of Interest Rates," *Journal of Finance,* 2 (1974), 449–470.

Rodriguez, R. J., "Default Risk, Yield Spreads, and Time to Maturity," *Journal of Financial and Quantitative Analysis,* 23 (1988), 111–17.

Wall, L. D., and K.-W. Fung, "Evaluating the Credit Exposure of Interest Rate Swap Portfolios," Working Paper 87-8, Federal Reserve Board of Atlanta, 1987.

Yawitz, J. B., K. J. Maloney, and L. H. Ederington, "Taxes, Default Risk, and Yield Spreads," *Journal of Finance,* 4 (1985), 1127–40.

QUESTIONS AND PROBLEMS

20.1. Suppose that the spread between the yield on a three-year zero-coupon riskless bond and a three-year zero-coupon bond issued by a corporation is 1%. By how

much does Black–Scholes overstate the value of a three-year option sold by a corporation?

20.2. "A long forward contract subject to default risk is a combination of a short position in a no-default put and a long position in a call subject to default risk." Explain this statement.

20.3. Explain why the credit exposure on a matched pair of forward contracts resembles a straddle.

20.4. Explain why the impact of credit risk on a matched pair of interest rate swaps tends to be less than that on a matched pair of currency swaps.

20.5. A bank has the following assets: $200 million of Treasury bills, $100 million of loans to corporations, $50 million of residential mortgages, and $150 million of loans to other banks. What are the capital requirements?

20.6. "When a bank is negotiating currency swaps, it should try to ensure that it is receiving the lower interest rate currency from a company with a low credit risk." Explain.

*20.7. Show that equation (20.2) is a particular case of equation (20.6).

20.8. Does put–call parity hold when there is default risk? Explain your answer.

20.9. A company enters into a one-year forward contract to sell $100 for DM150. The contract is initially at the money. In other words, the forward exchange rate is 1.50. The one-year dollar risk-free rate of interest is 5% per annum. The one-year dollar rate of interest at which the counterparty can borrow is 6% per annum. The exchange rate volatility is 12% per annum. What is the present value of the cost of defaults on the contract? Assume that defaults are recognized only at the end of the life of the contract.

20.10. Suppose that in Problem 20.9, the six-month forward rate is also 1.50 and the six-month dollar risk-free interest rate is 5% per annum. Suppose further that the six-month dollar rate of interest at which the counterparty can borrow is 5.5% per annum. What is the present value of the cost of defaults assuming that defaults are recognized either at the six-month point or at the one-year point?

20.11. Consider an 18-month discount bond with a face value of $100 that can be converted into five shares of the company's stock at any time during its life. Suppose that the current share price is $20, no dividends are paid on the stock, the risk-free rate for all maturities is 6% per annum with continuous compounding, and the share price volatility is 25% per annum. Assume that the yield on nonconvertible bonds issued by the company is 10% per annum for all maturities. The bond callable at $110. Use three-time-step tree to calculate the value of the bond. What is the value of the conversion option?

20.12. A three-year convertible bond with a face value of $100 has been issued by company ABC. It pays a coupon of $5 at the end of each year. It can be converted into ABC's equity as follows. At the end of the first year it can be exchanged for 3.6 shares immediately after the coupon has been paid. At the end of the second year it can be exchanged for 3.5 shares immediately after the coupon has been paid. The current share price is $25, no dividends are paid on the stock, and the stock price volatility is 25%. The risk-free interest rate is 5% with continuous compounding. The yield on bonds issued by company ABC is 7% with continuous compounding. Use a three-step tree to calculate the value of the bond. How much is the conversion option worth?

20.13. What difference does it make to the value of the bond in Problem 20.12 if it is callable at any time during the first two years for 115? How much is the call option worth?

20.14. Discuss how you would value the credit derivatives listed in Section 20.7.

20.15. Suppose that a financial institution has entered into a swap dependent on the sterling interest rate with counterparty X and into an exactly offsetting swap with counterparty Y. Which of the following statements are true, and which are false?

    (a) The total present value of the cost of defaults is the present value of the cost of defaults on the contract with X plus the present value of the cost of defaults on the contract with Y.

    (b) The expected exposure in one year on both contracts is the sum of the expected exposure on the contract with X and the expected exposure on the contract with Y.

    (c) The 95% upper confidence limit for the exposure in one year on both contracts is the sum of the 95% upper confidence limit for the exposure in one year on the contract with X and the 95% upper confidence limit for the exposure in one year on the contract with Y.

20.16. Explain how you would extend the analysis in Sections 20.2 and 20.3 to evaluate total expected default costs on all outstanding derivative transactions with a particular counterparty. Consider both the case where there is no netting and the case where netting is permissible.

20.17. "When netting is allowed, the incremental effect of a new derivative transaction on total expected default costs with a particular counterparty can be negative." Explain this statement.

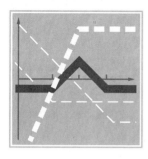

C h a p t e r 2 1

Review of Key Concepts

Although much of this book has focused on options, the reader should by now have realized that there are certain key concepts that are important in the analysis of all derivatives. In this final chapter we review some of these concepts.

21.1 RISKLESS HEDGES

The pricing of derivatives involves the construction of riskless hedges from traded securities. For a hedge to be riskless, it must be totally independent of any stochastic variables. If the prices of two traded securities depend on one underlying stochastic variable, it is possible to set up a hedge, consisting of a position in the two securities, which is riskless. More generally, if the prices of $N + 1$ traded securities depend on N underlying stochastic variables, it is possible to set up a hedge, consisting of a position in the $N + 1$ traded securities, which is independent of all N stochastic variables and is therefore riskless.

A riskless hedge must earn the risk-free rate of interest. This fact can be used to obtain a differential equation that derivatives must satisfy. In the situation where all the stochastic variables underlying a derivative are the prices of traded securities, a riskless hedge can be set up using these securities together with the derivative. In the situation where some or all of the underlying state variables are not the prices of traded securities, the riskless hedge must consist of a position in several different derivatives.

It is important to realize that a differential equation which is derived by setting up a riskless hedge does not have a unique solution. Indeed, any security that is contingent on the stochastic variables under consideration must satisfy the same differential equation. The particular security that is obtained is determined by the specification of the boundary conditions.

Derivatives can be classified according to whether the riskless hedges that are set up are permanently riskless or only instantaneously riskless. For forward contracts on a traded security, a permanently riskless hedge can be set up consisting of the forward contract and the underlying security. In the case of options and other more complicated derivatives, the hedge that is set up is only instantaneously riskless. To remain riskless it must be rebalanced continuously. It is

interesting to note that a futures contract can in this context be viewed as being intermediate between forward contracts and options. A hedge that is set up between a futures contract and the underlying security is not permanently riskless, but it needs to be rebalanced only once per day to remain riskless.

21.2 TRADED SECURITIES VERSUS OTHER UNDERLYING VARIABLES

In the context of pricing derivatives, a traded security can be defined as any asset that is held solely for investment purposes by a significant number of investors. Silver is a traded security according to this definition, whereas copper is not. There is an important difference between the situation where a derivative depends only on the prices of traded securities and the situation where it depends on the values of other variables. When an underlying variable is a traded security, the price of an option is independent of the expected drift rate of the underlying variable and the market price of its risk. When the underlying variable is not a traded security, these parameters are relevant. This difference arises from the fact that only traded securities can be included in the construction of a riskless hedge.

21.3 RISK-NEUTRAL VALUATION

The risk-neutral valuation argument is a very simple argument that is at the heart of much of the analysis of derivatives. If a derivative depends only on the prices of traded securities, the differential equation for its price does not involve parameters that are affected by risk preferences. It follows that the price of the derivative in a world where all investors are risk neutral must be the same as its price in the real world. For the purposes of valuing the derivative, it is therefore permissible to assume that all investors are risk neutral.

This assumption simplifies the analysis considerably. In a risk-neutral world, the expected return from any traded security is the risk-free rate. Furthermore, the expected payoffs from any derivative are discounted at the risk-free rate to get its present value. It should be emphasized that the risk-neutrality assumption does not mean that the derivative is being valued only for the case of a risk-neutral world. Its value in a risk-neutral world happens to be the same as its value in other worlds where investors are risk averse.

It turns out that when some or all of the variables underlying a derivative are not the prices of traded securities, an extension of the risk-neutral valuation argument can be used. It is still permissible to assume that the world is risk neutral provided that the expected growth rate in each variable is chosen in an appropriate way. The correct expected growth rate is in theory equal to the actual growth rate reduced by the product of the variable's market price of risk and

its volatility. If the variable is a commodity price, futures prices can be used to provide information about the correct growth rate. If the variable is the short-term interest rate, the current yield curve can be used to provide this information.

21.4 THOSE BIG LOSSES

No book on derivatives would be complete without some reference to the huge losses of some derivatives market participants (e.g., Gibson Greetings, Procter and Gamble, Kidder Peabody, Orange County, and Barings) in the early 1990s. These losses received a great deal of publicity and made many people very wary of derivatives. Some nonfinancial corporations have announced plans to reduce their use of derivatives. The level of interest in some of the more exotic products offered by dealers has declined.

The stories behind the losses emphasize that derivatives can be used for hedging or speculation; that is, they can be used either to reduce risks or to take risks. The losses were experienced because derivatives were used inappropriately. People who had an implicit or explicit mandate to manage risks prudently decided to take big bets on the future direction of market variables.

The lesson to be learned from the losses is the importance of *internal controls*. Senior management within a company should issue a clear and unambiguous policy statement about how derivatives are to be used and the extent to which it is permissible for employees to take positions on movements in market variables. They should then institute controls to ensure that the policy is carried out. It is a recipe for disaster to give one or two people complete authority to trade derivatives without a close monitoring of the risks being taken.

21.5 A FINAL WORD

I hope that this book has stimulated the reader's interest in derivatives. I have certainly found the task of organizing my own knowledge of the subject to write this book a rewarding one.

What does the future hold for the analysis of derivatives? It is always tempting to answer a question such as this by saying that all the important discoveries have already been made. I do not think this is true for the analysis of derivatives. A great deal of research—both theoretical and empirical—is carried out each year by financial institutions and by academics. New derivatives are being developed at an exciting pace. There can be little doubt that important new ideas and new results will continue to emerge.

Major Exchanges

Major Exchanges Throughout the World
Trading Futures and Options, with Their Official Abbreviations

Agrarische Termijnmarkt Amsterdam	ATA
American Stock Exchange	AMEX
Australian Options Market	AOM
Belgian Futures & Options Exchange	BELFOX
Bolsa de Mercadorias y Futuros, Brazil	BM&F
Chicago Board of Trade	CBOT
Chicago Board Options Exchange	CBOE
Chicago Mercantile Exchange	CME
Coffee, Sugar & Cocoa Exchange, New York	CSCE
Commodity Exchange, New York	COMEX
Copenhagen Stock Exchange	FUTOP
Deutsche Termin Börse, Germany	DTB
European Options Exchange	EOE
Financiële Termijnmarkt Amsterdam	FTA
Finnish Options Market	FOM
Hong Kong Futures Exchange	HKFE
International Petroleum Exchange, London	IPE
Irish Futures & Options Exchange	IFOX
Kansas City Board of Trade	KCBT
Kobe Rubber Exchange	KRE
Kuala Lumpur Commodity Exchange	KLCE
London Commodity Exchange	LCE
London International Financial Futures & Options Exchange	LIFFE
London Metal Exchange	LME
London Securities and Derivatives Exchange	OMLX
Manila International Futures Exchange	MIFE
Marché à Terme International de France	MATIF
Marché de Options Négociables de Paris	MONEP
MEFF Renta Fija and Variable, Spain	MEFF
Mercado de Futuros y Opciones S.A., Argentina	MERFOX
MidAmerica Commodity Exchange	MidAm
Minneapolis Grain Exchange	MGE

Major Exchanges Throughout the World
Trading Futures and Options, with Their
Official Abbreviations (*continued*)

Montreal Exchange	ME
New York Cotton Exchange	NYCE
New York Futures Exchange	NYFE
New York Mercantile Exchange	NYMEX
New York Stock Exchange	NYSE
New Zealand Futures & Options Exchange	NZFOE
Osaka Grain Exchange	OGE
Osaka Securities Exchange	OSA
ÖTOB Aktiengesellschaft	ÖTOB
Pacific Stock Exchange	PSE
Philadelphia Stock Exchange	PHLX
Singapore International Financial Futures Exchange	SIMEX
Stockholm Options Market	OM
Swiss Options and Financial Futures Exchange	SOFFEX
Sydney Futures Exchange	SFE
Tokyo Grain Exchange	TGE
Tokyo International Financial Futures Exchange	TIFFE
Toronto Stock Exchange	TSE
Vancouver Stock Exchange	VSE
Winnipeg Commodity Exchange	WCE

Glossary of Notation

A guide to the main ways in which symbols are used in this book is given below. Symbols that appear in only one small part of the book may not be listed here but are always defined at the place where they are first used.

a: Growth rate of underlying variable in a risk-neutral world in a binomial model during time Δt. For example, when the underlying variable is a non-dividend-paying stock, $a = e^{r\Delta t}$; when it is a currency, $a = e^{(r-r_f)\Delta t}$; and so on. The variable a is also used in Chapter 10 as the drift rate in a generalized Wiener process. In Chapter 17 it is the reversion rate in an interest rate process.

b: In Chapter 10, b^2 is the variance rate in a generalized Wiener process. In Chapter 17, b is the reversion level in an interest rate process.

c: Price of a European call option.

C: Price of an American call option.

d_1, d_2: Parameters in option pricing formulas. See, for example, equations (11.22) and (12.6).

d: Proportional down movement in a binomial model. If $d = 0.9$, value of variable moves to 90% of its previous value when there is a down movement.

D: In Chapter 7, D is the present value of dividends on a stock. In Chapter 4, D is used to denote duration.

D_i: The ith cash dividend payment.

$E(\cdot)$: Expected value of a variable.

$\hat{E}(\cdot)$: Expected value of a variable in a risk-neutral world.

f: Value of a derivative. The symbol, f_i, is the value of the ith derivative. The symbol f_T is the value of the derivative at time T.

F: Forward or futures price. The symbol F_T is the forward or futures price at time T. In Appendix 3A, F_i is the futures price at the end of day i.

$F(t, T)$: Instantaneous forward interest rate as seen at time t for a contract with maturity T.

$\mathcal{F}$: Value of one futures contract.

I: Present value of income on a security.

K: Delivery price in a forward contract.

$M(x, y, \rho)$: Cumulative probability in a bivariate normal distribution that the first variable is less than x and the second variable is less than y when the coefficient of correlation between the variables is ρ.

$N(x)$: Cumulative probability that a variable with a standardized normal distribution is less than x. A standardized normal distribution is a normal distribution with a mean of zero and standard deviation of 1.0. Thus $N(0) = 0.5$.

p: This is used in two major ways: The first is as the value of a European put option (e.g., Chapter 11). The second is as the probability of an up movement in binomial models (e.g., Chapter 15).

P: Value of an American put option. Also $P(t, T)$ is used as the price at time t of a discount bond maturing at time T.

q: Dividend yield rate.

r: Risk-free interest rate. Note that in Chapters 3, 4, 7, and 8, r is the risk-free rate between times t and T. Elsewhere in the book, it should usually be interpreted as the instantaneous (i.e., very short term) risk-free interest rate.

r_f: Instantaneous risk-free interest rate in a foreign country.

$\bar{r}$: Average instantaneous risk-free rate of interest during the life of a derivative.

$R(t, T)$: Risk-free interest rate at time t for an investment maturing at time T.

S: Price of asset underlying a derivative. In different parts of the book, S is used to refer to the price of a currency, the price of a stock, the price of a stock index, and the price of a commodity.

S_T: Value of S at time T.

t: Usually t denotes the current time measured from some reference point in the past. Note that in Sections 17.7 to 17.11 we define time zero as today and use t to denote some general future time.

T: Time at maturity of a derivative.

u: Proportional up movement in a binomial model. For example, $u = 1.2$ indicates that the variable increases by 20% when an up movement occurs. The symbol u is also used to denote the storage costs per unit time as a proportion of the price of an asset.

$\mathcal{V}$: Vega of a derivative or portfolio of derivatives.

X: Strike price of an option.

Γ: Gamma of a derivative or portfolio of derivatives.

Δ: Delta of a derivative or portfolio of derivatives.

Δx: Small change in x for any variable x.

ϵ: Random sample from a standardized normal distribution.

η: Continuously compounded return on a stock.

Θ: Theta of a derivative or portfolio of derivatives.

Π: Value of a portfolio of derivatives.

ρ: Coefficient of correlation.

σ: Usually this is the volatility of an asset (i.e., it corresponds to the standard deviation of proportional changes in the asset's price). Note that in Chapter 2 σ_F and σ_S are the standard deviation of F and S at the hedge maturity. Also in the Ho–Lee and Hull–White models (Chapter 17), σ is the instantaneous standard deviation of the short rate.

$\phi(m, s)$: Normal distribution with mean m and standard deviation s.

Table for $N(x)$ When $x \leq 0$

This table shows values of $N(x)$ for $x \leq 0$. The table should be used with interpolation. For example,

$$N(-0.1234) = N(-0.12) - 0.34[N(-0.12) - N(-0.13)]$$
$$= 0.4522 - 0.34 \times (0.4522 - 0.4483)$$
$$= 0.4509$$

x	0.00	0.01	0.02	0.03	0.04	0.05	0.06	0.07	0.08	0.09
-0.0	0.5000	0.4960	0.4920	0.4880	0.4840	0.4801	0.4761	0.4721	0.4681	0.4641
-0.1	0.4602	0.4562	0.4522	0.4483	0.4443	0.4404	0.4364	0.4325	0.4286	0.4247
-0.2	0.4207	0.4168	0.4129	0.4090	0.4052	0.4013	0.3974	0.3936	0.3897	0.3859
-0.3	0.3821	0.3783	0.3745	0.3707	0.3669	0.3632	0.3594	0.3557	0.3520	0.3483
-0.4	0.3446	0.3409	0.3372	0.3336	0.3300	0.3264	0.3228	0.3192	0.3156	0.3121
-0.5	0.3085	0.3050	0.3015	0.2981	0.2946	0.2912	0.2877	0.2843	0.2810	0.2776
-0.6	0.2743	0.2709	0.2676	0.2643	0.2611	0.2578	0.2546	0.2514	0.2483	0.2451
-0.7	0.2420	0.2389	0.2358	0.2327	0.2296	0.2266	0.2236	0.2206	0.2177	0.2148
-0.8	0.2119	0.2090	0.2061	0.2033	0.2005	0.1977	0.1949	0.1922	0.1894	0.1867
-0.9	0.1841	0.1814	0.1788	0.1762	0.1736	0.1711	0.1685	0.1660	0.1635	0.1611
-1.0	0.1587	0.1562	0.1539	0.1515	0.1492	0.1469	0.1446	0.1423	0.1401	0.1379
-1.1	0.1357	0.1335	0.1314	0.1292	0.1271	0.1251	0.1230	0.1210	0.1190	0.1170
-1.2	0.1151	0.1131	0.1112	0.1093	0.1075	0.1056	0.1038	0.1020	0.1003	0.0985
-1.3	0.0968	0.0951	0.0934	0.0918	0.0901	0.0885	0.0869	0.0853	0.0838	0.0823
-1.4	0.0808	0.0793	0.0778	0.0764	0.0749	0.0735	0.0721	0.0708	0.0694	0.0681
-1.5	0.0668	0.0655	0.0643	0.0630	0.0618	0.0606	0.0594	0.0582	0.0571	0.0559
-1.6	0.0548	0.0537	0.0526	0.0516	0.0505	0.0495	0.0485	0.0475	0.0465	0.0455
-1.7	0.0446	0.0436	0.0427	0.0418	0.0409	0.0401	0.0392	0.0384	0.0375	0.0367
-1.8	0.0359	0.0351	0.0344	0.0336	0.0329	0.0322	0.0314	0.0307	0.0301	0.0294
-1.9	0.0287	0.0281	0.0274	0.0268	0.0262	0.0256	0.0250	0.0244	0.0239	0.0233
-2.0	0.0228	0.0222	0.0217	0.0212	0.0207	0.0202	0.0197	0.0192	0.0188	0.0183
-2.1	0.0179	0.0174	0.0170	0.0166	0.0162	0.0158	0.0154	0.0150	0.0146	0.0143
-2.2	0.0139	0.0136	0.0132	0.0129	0.0125	0.0122	0.0119	0.0116	0.0113	0.0110
-2.3	0.0107	0.0104	0.0102	0.0099	0.0096	0.0094	0.0091	0.0089	0.0087	0.0084
-2.4	0.0082	0.0080	0.0078	0.0075	0.0073	0.0071	0.0069	0.0068	0.0066	0.0064
-2.5	0.0062	0.0060	0.0059	0.0057	0.0055	0.0054	0.0052	0.0051	0.0049	0.0048
-2.6	0.0047	0.0045	0.0044	0.0043	0.0041	0.0040	0.0039	0.0038	0.0037	0.0036
-2.7	0.0035	0.0034	0.0033	0.0032	0.0031	0.0030	0.0029	0.0028	0.0027	0.0026
-2.8	0.0026	0.0025	0.0024	0.0023	0.0023	0.0022	0.0021	0.0021	0.0020	0.0019
-2.9	0.0019	0.0018	0.0018	0.0017	0.0016	0.0016	0.0015	0.0015	0.0014	0.0014
-3.0	0.0014	0.0013	0.0013	0.0012	0.0012	0.0011	0.0011	0.0011	0.0010	0.0010
-3.1	0.0010	0.0009	0.0009	0.0009	0.0008	0.0008	0.0008	0.0008	0.0007	0.0007
-3.2	0.0007	0.0007	0.0006	0.0006	0.0006	0.0006	0.0006	0.0005	0.0005	0.0005
-3.3	0.0005	0.0005	0.0005	0.0004	0.0004	0.0004	0.0004	0.0004	0.0004	0.0003
-3.4	0.0003	0.0003	0.0003	0.0003	0.0003	0.0003	0.0003	0.0003	0.0003	0.0002
-3.5	0.0002	0.0002	0.0002	0.0002	0.0002	0.0002	0.0002	0.0002	0.0002	0.0002
-3.6	0.0002	0.0002	0.0001	0.0001	0.0001	0.0001	0.0001	0.0001	0.0001	0.0001
-3.7	0.0001	0.0001	0.0001	0.0001	0.0001	0.0001	0.0001	0.0001	0.0001	0.0001
-3.8	0.0001	0.0001	0.0001	0.0001	0.0001	0.0001	0.0001	0.0001	0.0001	0.0001
-3.9	0.0000	0.0000	0.0000	0.0000	0.0000	0.0000	0.0000	0.0000	0.0000	0.0000
-4.0	0.0000	0.0000	0.0000	0.0000	0.0000	0.0000	0.0000	0.0000	0.0000	0.0000

Table for $N(x)$ When $x \geq 0$

This table shows values of $N(x)$ for $x \geq 0$. The table should be used with interpolation. For example,

$$N(0.6278) = N(0.62) + 0.78[N(0.63) - N(0.62)]$$
$$= 0.7324 + 0.78 \times (0.7357 - 0.7324)$$
$$= 0.7350$$

x	0.00	0.01	0.02	0.03	0.04	0.05	0.06	0.07	0.08	0.09
0.0	0.5000	0.5040	0.5080	0.5120	0.5160	0.5199	0.5239	0.5279	0.5319	0.5359
0.1	0.5398	0.5438	0.5478	0.5517	0.5557	0.5596	0.5636	0.5675	0.5714	0.5753
0.2	0.5793	0.5832	0.5871	0.5910	0.5948	0.5987	0.6026	0.6064	0.6103	0.6141
0.3	0.6179	0.6217	0.6255	0.6293	0.6331	0.6368	0.6406	0.6443	0.6480	0.6517
0.4	0.6554	0.6591	0.6628	0.6664	0.6700	0.6736	0.6772	0.6808	0.6844	0.6879
0.5	0.6915	0.6950	0.6985	0.7019	0.7054	0.7088	0.7123	0.7157	0.7190	0.7224
0.6	0.7257	0.7291	0.7324	0.7357	0.7389	0.7422	0.7454	0.7486	0.7517	0.7549
0.7	0.7580	0.7611	0.7642	0.7673	0.7704	0.7734	0.7764	0.7794	0.7823	0.7852
0.8	0.7881	0.7910	0.7939	0.7967	0.7995	0.8023	0.8051	0.8078	0.8106	0.8133
0.9	0.8159	0.8186	0.8212	0.8238	0.8264	0.8289	0.8315	0.8340	0.8365	0.8389
1.0	0.8413	0.8438	0.8461	0.8485	0.8508	0.8531	0.8554	0.8577	0.8599	0.8621
1.1	0.8643	0.8665	0.8686	0.8708	0.8729	0.8749	0.8770	0.8790	0.8810	0.8830
1.2	0.8849	0.8869	0.8888	0.8907	0.8925	0.8944	0.8962	0.8980	0.8997	0.9015
1.3	0.9032	0.9049	0.9066	0.9082	0.9099	0.9115	0.9131	0.9147	0.9162	0.9177
1.4	0.9192	0.9207	0.9222	0.9236	0.9251	0.9265	0.9279	0.9292	0.9306	0.9319
1.5	0.9332	0.9345	0.9357	0.9370	0.9382	0.9394	0.9406	0.9418	0.9429	0.9441
1.6	0.9452	0.9463	0.9474	0.9484	0.9495	0.9505	0.9515	0.9525	0.9535	0.9545
1.7	0.9554	0.9564	0.9573	0.9582	0.9591	0.9599	0.9608	0.9616	0.9625	0.9633
1.8	0.9641	0.9649	0.9656	0.9664	0.9671	0.9678	0.9686	0.9693	0.9699	0.9706
1.9	0.9713	0.9719	0.9726	0.9732	0.9738	0.9744	0.9750	0.9756	0.9761	0.9767
2.0	0.9772	0.9778	0.9783	0.9788	0.9793	0.9798	0.9803	0.9808	0.9812	0.9817
2.1	0.9821	0.9826	0.9830	0.9834	0.9838	0.9842	0.9846	0.9850	0.9854	0.9857
2.2	0.9861	0.9864	0.9868	0.9871	0.9875	0.9878	0.9881	0.9884	0.9887	0.9890
2.3	0.9893	0.9896	0.9898	0.9901	0.9904	0.9906	0.9909	0.9911	0.9913	0.9916
2.4	0.9918	0.9920	0.9922	0.9925	0.9927	0.9929	0.9931	0.9932	0.9934	0.9936
2.5	0.9938	0.9940	0.9941	0.9943	0.9945	0.9946	0.9948	0.9949	0.9951	0.9952
2.6	0.9953	0.9955	0.9956	0.9957	0.9959	0.9960	0.9961	0.9962	0.9963	0.9964
2.7	0.9965	0.9966	0.9967	0.9968	0.9969	0.9970	0.9971	0.9972	0.9973	0.9974
2.8	0.9974	0.9975	0.9976	0.9977	0.9977	0.9978	0.9979	0.9979	0.9980	0.9981
2.9	0.9981	0.9982	0.9982	0.9983	0.9984	0.9984	0.9985	0.9985	0.9986	0.9986
3.0	0.9986	0.9987	0.9987	0.9988	0.9988	0.9989	0.9989	0.9989	0.9990	0.9990
3.1	0.9990	0.9991	0.9991	0.9991	0.9992	0.9992	0.9992	0.9992	0.9993	0.9993
3.2	0.9993	0.9993	0.9994	0.9994	0.9994	0.9994	0.9994	0.9995	0.9995	0.9995
3.3	0.9995	0.9995	0.9995	0.9996	0.9996	0.9996	0.9996	0.9996	0.9996	0.9997
3.4	0.9997	0.9997	0.9997	0.9997	0.9997	0.9997	0.9997	0.9997	0.9997	0.9998
3.5	0.9998	0.9998	0.9998	0.9998	0.9998	0.9998	0.9998	0.9998	0.9998	0.9998
3.6	0.9998	0.9998	0.9999	0.9999	0.9999	0.9999	0.9999	0.9999	0.9999	0.9999
3.7	0.9999	0.9999	0.9999	0.9999	0.9999	0.9999	0.9999	0.9999	0.9999	0.9999
3.8	0.9999	0.9999	0.9999	0.9999	0.9999	0.9999	0.9999	0.9999	0.9999	0.9999
3.9	1.0000	1.0000	1.0000	1.0000	1.0000	1.0000	1.0000	1.0000	1.0000	1.0000
4.0	1.0000	1.0000	1.0000	1.0000	1.0000	1.0000	1.0000	1.0000	1.0000	1.0000

Author Index

A

Abramowitz, M., 243
Aitchison, J., 229
Allen, S. L., 107
Altman, E. I., 527, 536
Amin, K., 281, 453
Asay, M., 339

B

Babbs, S., 474
Bank for International Settlements (BIS), 517, 533, 536
Bardhan, I., 478
Barone-Adesi, G., 379, 381, 382
Bartter, B., 207, 381, 418, 453
Basle Committee on Bank Supervision, 533
Becker, H. P., 191
Beckers, S., 247
Belton, T. M., 536
Bhattacharya, M., 172, 174
Bicksler, J., 134
Biger, N., 281
Black, F., 228, 240, 244, 252, 254, 255(3), 277, 281, 313, 392, 412, 449, 450, 453(3), 507, 511(2)
Blattberg, R., 255
Bodurtha, J. N., 281, 509, 511
Bollerslev, T., 501, 512
Bookstaber, R. M., 191, 339
Boyle, P. P., 338, 367, 381(3), 476, 486(2)
Brady commission, 337
Brealey, R. A., 223
Brennan, M. J., 281, 381(2), 423(2), 453
Brenner, M., 281
Brotherton-Ratcliffe, R., 367, 381, 408, 412
Brown, J. A. C., 229
Brown, R. L., 143
Burghardt, G., 453

C

Carabini, C. E., 57, 72
Carr, P., 382

Chance, D. M., 41, 154, 191, 281, 509, 512
Chang, E. C., 71, 72
Chen, A. H., 56, 72, 134
Cheuk, T. H. F., 474
Cheyette, O., 453
Chiang, R., 107(2)
Chicago Board of Trade (CBOT), 41, 42
Chicago Board Options Exchange (CBOE), 154(2)
Chiras, D. P., 247, 508, 512
Clasing, H. K., 154
Conze, A., 486
Cooper, I., 536
Cootner, P. H., ed. 223
Cornell, B., 56, 72
Courtadon, G. R., 281(2), 381, 453, 509, 511
Cox, D. R., 223
Cox, J. C., 72, 76, 154, 194, 207, 255, 295, 302, 343, 345, 358, 359, 381, 422, 423, 444, 453, 497(3), 511(2)
Culp, C., 38, 42
Cumby, R., 512
Curran, M., 366, 381, 486

D

Degler, W. H., 191
Derman, E., 449, 453, 478, 483, 486, 503(2), 505(2), 506, 511
Dewynne, J., 381
Dillman, S., 339
Drezner, Z., 260
Duffie, D., 42
Dupire, B., 505, 511
Dusak, K., 70, 72

E

Easterwood, J. C., 107
Edelberg, C., 339
Ederington, L. H., 42, 536
Emanuel, D., 338
Engle, R. F., 512(2)

Ergener, D., 478, 483, 486
Etzioni, E. S., 339
Evnine, J., 486

F

Fabozzi, F. J., 107
Fama, E. F., 247, 255
Feller, W., 223
Figlewski, S., 107, 339, 512
Flannery, B. P., 367, 381
Franckle, C. T., 42
French, D. W., 248
French, K. R., 56, 72, 247, 248
Fung, K.-W., 536

G

Galai, D., 172(2), 174(2), 244, 339, 507,
    512
Garman, M. B., 281, 302, 464, 486, 508
Gastineau, G., 154, 191
Gatto, M. A., 464, 486
Gay, G. D., 107
Geske, R., 252(2), 255(2), 259, 382, 460,
    486, 495, 511
Gibbs, S., 486
Goldman, B., 464, 486
Goldman Sachs, 529, 536
Gonedes, N., 255
Gould, J. P., 172, 174
Grabbe, J. O., 281
Gray, R. W., 70, 72
Group of Thirty, 536

H

Hamson, J. M., 302
Harding, J., 339
Harrison, J. M., 296, 302
Harvey, C. R., 512(3)
Hasbrouck, J., 512
Heath, D., 426, 428, 453(2), 454
Hennigar, E., 107
Hicks, J. R., 68, 72
Hill, J. M., 42
Ho, T. S. Y., 431, 433, 454
Horn, F. F., 42
Hoskins, B., 453
Houthakker, H. S., 70, 72
Howison, S., 381
Hudson, M., 486
Hull, J. C., 134(2), 281, 302, 310, 329(2), 330,
    339, 357, 365, 377, 381, 433, 435, 437,
    438, 439, 444, 449, 450, 454(10), 469,
    474, 480, 482, 486(2), 500, 501, 511(2),
    519, 521(2), 536(3)

I

Ibbotson, R. G., 219
Iben, B., 408, 412
Ingersoll, J. E., 72, 76, 295, 302, 422, 423, 444,
    453
International Swaps and Derivatives Association
    (ISDA), 134
Ito, K., 220, 225

J

Jamshidian, F., 302, 395, 420, 421, 433,
    453
Jarrow, R. A., 72, 281, 382, 426, 428,
    453(2), 454(3), 492, 536
Jeffrey, A., 454
Johnson, H. E., 253, 382(2), 486, 536
Johnson, L. L., 42
Jones, F. J., 42
Jonkhart, M. J. L., 536
Joy, C., 367, 381

K

Kane, A., 512
Kane, E. J., 72
Kani, I., 478, 483, 486, 503(2), 505(2), 506,
    511
Kapner, K. R., 134
Karasinski, P., 450, 453
Kemna, A., 466, 486
Keynes, J. M., 68, 72
Kleinstein, A. D., 107
Klemkosky, R. C., 107, 172(2), 174(2), 508,
    512
Kohlhagen, S. W., 281
Kolb, R. W., 42, 107(3)
Kon, S. J., 255
Kopprasch, R. W., 191
Kreps, D. M., 296, 302

L

Langsam, J. A., 339
Lasser, D. J., 107
Latainer, G. O., 339
Latane, H., 247
Lau, S. H., 476, 486
Lauterbach, B., 244, 510, 512
Layard-Liesching, R., 134
Lee, M., 499
Lee, S.-B., 431, 433, 454
Leland, H. E., 335, 339(3)
Levy, E., 486(2)
Li, A., 454
Longstaff, F. A., 424, 453

M

MacBeth, J. D., 508, 512
MacMillan, L. W., 379, 381, 382
Maloney, K. J., 536
Manaster, S., 247, 508, 512
Margrabe, W., 72, 468, 486
Marshall, J. F., 134
McMillan, L. G., 154, 191
Mello, A., 536
Merton, R. C., 174(2), 255(2), 263, 281, 491,
    498, 511(2), 536
Merville, L. J., 508, 512
Miller, H. D., 223
Miller, M., 38, 42
Moro, B., 366, 381
Morton, A., 426, 428, 453(3), 454
Myneni, R., 382

N

Naik, E., 499
Nikkhah, S., 33, 42
Noh, J., 512

O

Oldfield, G. S., 72

P

Park, H. Y., 56, 72
Pelsser, A. A. J., 446, 454
Pliska, S. R., 302
Press, W. H., 367, 381
Pringle, J. J., 134

R

Ramaswamy, K., 282
Reiff, W. W., 107
Reiner, E., 302, 457, 474, 487(2)
Reinganum, M., 56, 72
Rendleman, R., 57, 72, 207, 247, 381, 418, 453
Resnick, B. G., 107(2), 172(2), 174(2), 508, 512
Riccardo, R., 454
Richard, S., 72
Richardson, M., 255
Ritchken, P., 454(2), 486
Rodriguez, R. J., 536
Roll, R., 248, 252, 256, 259
Ross, S. A., 72, 76, 194, 207, 255, 294, 295,
    302, 343, 345, 358, 359, 381, 422, 423,
    444, 453, 497(3), 511(2)
Rubinstein, M., 154, 194, 207, 339(2), 343, 345,
    358, 359, 381, 457, 460, 468, 481, 486(6),
    487(2), 496, 497, 505, 509, 511(3), 512
Rudd, A., 492

S

Sankarasubramanian, L., 454(2), 486
Schaefer, S. M., 453
Schneeweis, T., 42
Schneller, M., 244
Scholes, M., 228, 240, 244, 255(2), 313, 507,
    511
Schultz, P., 244, 510, 512
Schwartz, E. S., 339, 381(3), 380, 423(2), 424,
    453(2)
Schwartz, E. W., 42
Schwartz, R., ed. 408, 412
Senchak, A. J., 107
Shastri, K., 509(2), 512(2)
Sinquefield, R. A., 219
Slivka, R., 191
Smith, C., ed. 408, 412
Smith, C. W., 134, 255
Smith, T., 255
Smithson, C. W., 134
Sobol', I. M., 367, 381
Sosin, H., 464, 486
Spindel, M., 454
Stegun, I., 243
Stoll, H. R., 172, 174, 281
Stulz, R. M., 42, 487, 536
Subrahmanyam, M., 281
Sundaresan, M., 72, 282

T

Tan, K. S., 367, 381
Tandon, K., 509(2), 512(2)
Taylor, S. J., 512
Telser, L. G., 70, 72
Teukolsky, S. A., 367, 381
Teweles, R. J., 42
Tilley, J. A., 339
Toy, W., 449, 453
Turnbull, S. M., 134, 454, 466, 486, 487,
    536

V

Vasicek, O. A., 419, 453
Veit, W. T., 107
Vetterling, W. T., 367, 381
Vijh, A. M., 486
Viswanath, P. V., 72
Viswanathan, 486
Vorst, A. C. F., 466, 474, 486

W

Wakeman, L. M., 134, 466, 487
Wall, L. D., 134, 536
Welch, W. W., 191

Whaley, R. E., 247, 252, 253, 256, 259, 281,
    379, 381, 382, 512(3)
White, A., 134, 302, 310, 329(2), 330, 339, 357,
    365, 377, 381, 433, 435, 437, 438, 439,
    444, 449, 450, 454(10), 469, 474, 480,
    482, 486(2), 500, 501, 511(2), 519, 521(2),
    536(2)
Wilmott, P., 381
Wolf, A., 282

X

Xu, X., 512

Y

Yates, J. W., 191
Yawitz, J. B., 536

Subject Index

A

AAA-rated subsidiaries, 535
absolute diffusion model, 497, 515 appendix 19A
accounting and tax, 38–40, 151–3
accrual swaps, 404–5, 464
accrued interest, 90, 395
All Ordinaries Share Price Index, 58
alternative (option pricing) models, 494–9
 formulas for, 514–16 appendix 19A
American options, 5
 analytic approximation, prices, 379–80, 384–6
  appendix 15A
 binomial tree, 203–4
 call and put prices, relationship between,
  169–70
 calls, early exercise of, 162–5, 250–1
 calls (dividends), exact valuation of, 259
  appendix 11A
 delta (Δ) of, 349
 dividends and, 250–1
 early exercise of (dividends), 171
 early exercise of (no dividends), 162–7
 futures options vs. spot options, 279–80
 path-dependent, 469–74
 puts, early exercise of, 165–7
 puts, no exact analytic formula, 242
 standard, 458
 valuation of, 343–81
American Stock Exchange. *See* AMEX
American-style
 Asian options, 472–3 figure 18.3
 average price calls, 472–3 figure 18.3
 average strike calls, 473
 derivatives, 361, 522
 interest rate options, 416
 lookback options, 474–6 figure 18.4
 options to exchange one asset for another, 468
 path-dependent derivatives, 469–74
American swap options, 458
AMEX, 138, 147
amortizing swaps, 131
analytic approximation to American option
 prices, 379–80, 384–6 appendix 15A

antithetic variable technique (simulation), 365
APT, 294
arbitrage, 12–13, 48
 arguments, 51, 52, 62, 65, 163, 168
 cross-border (tax), 152
 definition of, 12
 index, 59–60
 no, assumption, 13, 145, 158, 195, 235, 236
 opportunities, 12, 28, 30, 49, 96–7, 172–3
 triple witching hour, 30
arbitrage pricing theory (APT), 294
arbitrageurs, 12–13. *See also under* arbitrage
arithmetic
 average, Asian option, 466, 472–3 figure 18.3
 mean vs. geometric mean, 232n
Asian options, 140, 465–7
 arithmetic average, 466, 472–3 figure 18.3
 geometric average, 466
 See also average price; average strike
ask price, 146
asset or nothing call, 463
assets
 consumption vs. investment, 45, 65–7 (*see
  also* traded securities)
 swaps to transform, using, 114
 underlying contracts, 17, 138–9
assigned investor (OCC), 151
"as you like it" options, 460–1, 469
at-the-money options, 141, 314, 322, 327,
 505n
average
 price calls, 465, 472–3 figure 18.3, 483
 price puts, 465, 483
 strike calls, 465, 473
 strike puts, 465

B

backwardation (futures), normal, 69
backward induction, 473, 529
Bank for International Settlements. *See under*
 BIS
Bankers Trust, 9

Barings, 541
barrier options, 461–3, 476–9, 483
  nodes not lying on the barriers, 478–9
    figure 18.7
  positioning nodes on the barriers, 476–8
    figures 18.5–6
basis, 32
  alternative definition, 32n
  gross (clearing), 24
  net (clearing), 24
  rollover (futures), 37
  strengthening of, 32
  weakening of, 32
basis risk, 32–4
  alternative definition, 34n
  and choice of delivery month, 34
  and choice of underlying, 34
basket options, 469
Basle Committee on Bank Supervision. *See
    under* BIS
bearish calendar spreads, 186
bear spreads, 181–3, 182 figure 8.4, 457
Bermudan options, 140, 458, 469
beta (β), 61, 335–6, 336n
  futures to change, using, 62
  index options to change, using, 267–8
bid–ask spreads, 117n, 146, 148, 517, 526n
bid price, 146
binary options, 405, 405n, 463–4
binomial trees, 194–206, 343–60
  algebraically expressed, 348
  American options using, valuing, 203–4
  commodity prices, 357
  control variate techniques using, 357–8
  Cox, Ross, and Rubinstein model, 194, 343,
    345, 358–9, 359n, 474, 480
  delta (Δ) using, estimating, 204–5
  exotic options, 469, 476, 480–2
  extension of, 356–8
  generalizations, 196–7, 201–2
  hedge parameters using, estimating, 348–50
  for indices, futures, and currencies, 350–2
  one-step, 194–6, 199
  in practice, using, 205–6
  Rendleman and Bartter model, 418–19
  stock's expected return, relevance of, 197–8,
    309n
  for stocks with dividends, 352–5
  time-dependent interest rates, 356–7
  time steps, 201, 202, 205n, 206, 348
  two-step, 199–202
  See also under trinomial trees
BIS, 517, 532
  Basle Committee on Bank Supervision,
    533n
  capital requirements, the, 531–2
  See also under credit risk

bivariate normal distribution function,
    cumulative, 260 appendix 11B, 460
Black and Karasinski model, 449–50
Black, Derman, and Toy model, 449
"Black Monday," 60, 332, 336, 337
Black–Scholes differential equation
  assumptions for, 236
  boundary conditions of, 238
  derivation of, 235–7
  underlying concepts, 235–7
Black–Scholes pricing formulas, 240–2
  alternative models, 494–9, 514–16 appendix
    19A
  how used in practice, 502–5
  properties of, 242
  role of the model, 505
  for stocks options (continuous dividend yield),
    263–4
  for warrants, 244–6
Black's approximation, 252–3
Black's model, 392–5
  for caps and floors, 400–1
  for futures options, 277
  for interest rate derivatives, 387–411, 434
board broker, 147
bond. *See under* bonds
bond options
  and duration, 396–7
  embedded, 389
  European, 395–7
  exchange-traded, 387–9, 395
  and swaptions, 402
  Treasury, 387–9
  valuing caps and floors using, 400–1
  yield volatilities, 396–7
bond options, valuation of
  Black's model, 393
  Cox, Ingersoll, and Ross model, 418, 422–3
  Heath, Jarrow, and Morton model, 428–31
  Ho and Lee model, 431–3, 434, 435, 436,
    492
  Hull and White model, 433–6, 445, 448, 449,
    451, 492
  Rendleman and Bartter model, 418–19
  two-factor equilibrium models, 423–4
  Vasicek model, 418, 419–22, 423, 433, 434,
    492
bonds
  callable, 153, 389, 416, 528–31
  cheapest-to-deliver, 92–3
  convertible, 153, 528–31
  corporate, day count conventions, 85
  coupon-bearing, 80
  credit risk of, 520–1
  discount (*see* zero–coupon)
  equivalent yield, 98
  municipal, day count conventions, 85

par yield, 122
perpetual, 423
price process, bond, 425–6
price volatility, bond, 425
puttable, 389
Standard Oil's bond issue, 9
valuing currency swaps, using, 128
valuing interest rate swaps, using, 121–3
zero-coupon, 78
See also under Treasury bonds
bootstrap method, 82, 122
Boston options, 458
bottom
    straddles, 188, 187 figure 8.10
    vertical combinations, 188–90
boundary conditions, differential equation, 238,
    307, 539
bounds (option prices), 159–62
    lower, empirical research on, 172
    lower, on stocks (dividends), 170–1, 262
    lower, on stocks (no dividends), 160–2
    upper, 159–60
Brady commission report, 337
break forward, 458
Brotherton-Ratcliffe and Iben convexity
    adjustment formula proof, 414–15 appendix
    16A
Brownian motion, 210
    geometric, 217, 228, 268n, 362n, 418, 459,
    468, 490, 495, 498, 499, 502, 505
buckets (yield curve sections), 449
bullish calendar spreads, 186
bull spreads, 179–81, 179 figure 8.2, 457, 458
butterfly spreads, 183–5, 183 figure 8.6, 457

C

CAC-40 Index, 57
calendar
    spreads, 185–6, 185 figure 8.8
    days vs. trading days (volatility), 233, 248–9
callable bonds, 153, 389, 416
call options, 5
    asset or nothing, 463
    average price, 465, 472–3 figure 18.3, 483
    average strike, 465, 473
    cash or nothing, 463
    covered, 150, 177
    definition of, 5
    open interest, 145
    volume, 145
cancelable forward, 458
capital
    allocation, internal, 532–3
    asset pricing model (CAPM), 61, 290, 294
    for market risk, 533
    regulatory (*see under* credit risk)

requirements, BIS, 531–2
requirements, simulation of, 532
tier 1 and tier 2, 531
caplets, 398
CAPM, 61, 290, 294
cap rate, 397
caps (interest rate), 397–401, 398 figure 16.3,
    408
    caplets, 398
    cap rate, 397
    flat volatilities, 401
    forward forward volatilities, 401
    reset date, first, 400, 400n
    valuing, as a portfolio of bond options, 399
    valuing, as a portfolio of interest rate options,
    398–9
    See also floors
CAPS, S&P, 266, 461, 463
cash
    or nothing call, 463
    settlement, 29–30, 139, 265, 276
CBOE, 138, 146, 154, 266, 507, 508, 509
CBOT, 4, 16, 18, 19, 24, 31, 41, 42, 89, 91,
    139, 461, 468
CBT. *See* CBOT
CFTC, 30, 151
cheapest-to-deliver bond (CBOT T-bond
    futures), 92–3
Chicago
    Board of Trade (*see* CBOT)
    Board Options Exchange (*see* CBOE)
    Mercantile Exchange (*see under* CME)
chi-square distribution, noncentral, 423
choice of contract (basis risk)
    delivery month, 34
    underlying, 34
chooser option, 460–1
"clean price" (T-bond), 90, 395
clearinghouse, exchange, 23
clearing margin, 23
closing out positions, 17, 31
CME, 4, 17, 18, 19, 20, 31, 35, 57, 62,
    63, 99
    IMM, division of, 63, 273
CMOs, 390–1
CMS swaps, 131
CMT swaps, 131
CMX. *See* COMEX
collars, 399–400
    zero-cost, 458n
collateral, 534
collateralized mortgage obligations. *See* CMOs
combinations (options), 187–90
    bottom vertical, 188–90
    straddles, 187–8, 187 figure 8.10, 457
    strangles, 188–90, 189 figure 8.12, 457
    straps, 188, 189 figure 8.11

combinations (options) (*Cont.*)
  strips, 188, 189 figure 8.11
  top vertical, 190
COMEX, 20, 28
commercial paper rate, 130
commission brokers, 16
commissions (options), 147–8
Commodity
  Exchange, Inc (*see* COMEX)
  Futures Trading Commission (*see* CFTC)
commodity
  convenience yields, 67, 298
  futures, 65–8
  prices, derivatives dependent on, 297–8
  prices, mean reversion of, 357
  swaps, 131
companies
  Bankers Trust, 9
  Barings, 541
  Gibson Greetings, 541
  Goldman Sachs, 529n, 536
  Kidder Peabody, 541
  Metallgesellschaft, 38, 38n
  Moody's, 520, 527, 528, 528n
  Orange County, 541
  Procter and Gamble, 541
  S&P, 273, 520, 527, 528, 528n
  Standard Oil, 9
comparative advantage (swaps)
  argument, 118–21
  credit rating, 120
  criticism of, argument, 120–1
  tax, 126
compound
  option model, 495–6, 514 appendix 19A
  options, 459–60, 461
compounding frequency, 98n, 103n, 230n
  continuous compounding, 46–8
  conversion formulas, 47–8
  day count conventions, 85–6
constant elasticity of variance model, 497
constant-maturity
  convexity adjustment for, swap, 410–1
  swap rate (CMS) swaps, 131
  Treasury rate (CMT) swaps, 131
consumption vs. investment assets, 45, 65–7. *See also* traded securities
contango (futures), 69
contingent claims, 1, 219
continuous
  compounding, 46–8
  dividend yield, 54–5, 261–3, 284–5 appendix 12A
  time, 209
  variable, 209
control variate techniques
  finite difference methods used with, 371

Monte Carlo simulation, 365–6
  trees, 357–8
convenience yields, 67, 298
conversion factors, 90–2
convertible bonds, 153
  valuation of, 528–31
convexity, 104
convexity adjustments
  forward rate to expected interest rate, 394n, 405n, 406–11, 414–15 appendix 16A, 451n
  futures rate to forward rate, 450–2, 451n
"corner the market," 31
corporate zero curve, 520
correlated assets, options on two, 480–2
  geometry of the tree, changing, 481–2
  probabilities, adjusting, 482
  variables, transforming, 480–1
correlation
  and choice of futures contracts, 34
  instantaneous, 468, 480, 491
cost of carry, 67–8
coupon-bearing
  bonds, 80
  bond yield curve, 80
counterparty, 50, 122, 132
covered
  calls, 150, 177
  and naked positions, 309
Cox, Ingersoll, and Ross (CIR) model, 418, 422–3
  extended-CIR model, 444n
Cox, Ross, and Rubinstein model, 194, 343, 345, 358–9, 359n, 474, 480
Crank–Nicholson (finite difference) method, 378–9
credit
  derivatives, 535
  limits, 534
  rating, 120, 520, 532, 535
  risk option (CRO), 535
credit risk, 491n, 517–36
  background, 518
  of bonds, 520–1
  capital requirements, the BIS, 531–3
  currency vs. interest rate swaps, 526 figure 20.2
  "depression scenarios," 528
  forwards for, adjusting price of, 523–7
  historical default experience, 527–8
  independence assumption, 519–20
  market risk vs., 132–3
  netting, 533
  option prices for, adjusting, 521–3
  reducing exposure to, 534–5
  repo rate and, 50
  of swaps, 120–1, 132–3, 523–7
cross-currency futures and options. *See* quantos

CTN. *See* NYCE
cumulative
   bivariate normal distribution function, 260
      appendix 11B, 460
   normal distribution function, 241, 243–4
currency exchange. *See under* foreign
      exchange (FX)
currency options, 269–73, 330n
   quotes, 270
   valuation of, 270–3
currency risk, 127
currency swaps, 125–8
   credit risk of, 132, 523–7
   definition of, 125
   valuing, using bonds, 128
   valuing, using forward contracts, 129–30
   without final exchange of principal, 526n
curvature (options), 323n. *See also under*
      gamma (Γ)
cycles (stock options), expiration, 140
cylinder options, 458n

D

daily price movement limits, 19
day
   count conventions, 85–6
   trade, 23
days (volatility), calendar days vs. trading,
      233
decay
   rate, 502
   time, 321 (*see also under* theta)
deep-out-of-the-money options, 246, 365
default risk. *See under* credit risk
deferred
   payment options, 458
   swaps, 131, 402
delivery
   arrangements, 18–19
   cash settlement, 29–30, 139, 265, 276
   choice, 68
   choice of, month, 34
   location, 18–19
   months, 19, 34
   price, 2
delta (Δ), 204, 312–21, 312n, 448, 482–3, 501,
      533
   of American options, 348–9
   discontinuous, 483
   of European calls and puts, 314
   of European options, 318–19
   of forward contracts, 313–14
   of forwards vs. futures, 320
   of portfolios, 320–1
   theta (Θ), and gamma (Γ), relationship among,
      327–8

delta hedging, 204, 312–21, 312n, 484
   cost of, 318
   forwards vs. futures, 320
   futures, using, 319–20
delta-neutral portfolios, 313, 325n, 507
"depression scenarios," 528
derivative pricing
   for commodities, 297–8
   cross-currency (*see* quantos)
   quantos, 299–301
   underlying variable, with a single,
      288–92
   underlying variables, with several,
      294–6
derivatives, 1, 220
   American-style, 361, 522
   credit, 535
   European-style, 361, 368, 522
   history-dependent, 295
diagonal spreads, 187
differential equation
   Black–Scholes, derivation of, 237–9
   boundary conditions, 238, 307, 539
   futures price, 286–7 appendix 12B
   general, derivation of, 305–7 appendix 13B
   for stocks (continuous dividend yields),
      284–5 appendix 12A
   underlying variable, for single, 290–1
diff (differential) swap, 131
dilution and warrants, 244–6
"dirty price" (T-bond), 90, 395
discontinuous delta, 483
discount
   bonds, valuing European options on, 420–1
   bonds (*see* zero-coupon bonds)
   instruments (T-bill), 95
   rate, 97
   rate for swaps, 12n
discrete
   time, 209
   variable, 209
displaced diffusion model, 496–7, 514–15
      appendix 19A
dividend, 141, 158, 170–1, 172, 249–53, 263,
      352–5
   seasonal nature of, 268
   yield, 54–5, 261, 352
DJIA, 58, 336
domestic rho, 330
Dow Jones Industrial Average. *See* DJIA
down-and-in options, 461, 463
down-and-out options, 461, 463, 469, 483
downgrade triggers, 534
drift rate, expected, 214, 215
   constant, 215
   instantaneous, 216, 426
   See also under rate of return

duration, 100–2
  bond options and, 396–7
  hedging using, 102–4
  limitations of, 104–6
  modified, 102, 397
duration-based hedge ratio, 103, 103n
dynamic
  hedging schemes, 313
  options replication, 483

E

early exercise, 162–7
  credit information, effect of, 522
  dividends on, effect of, 170–1
  of stock calls (no dividends), 162–5
  of stock puts (no dividends), 165–7
early redemption privileges, 389
efficient markets, weak form of, 201, 310n
embedded bond options, 153, 389
empirical research/evidence
  on Black–Scholes and other option pricing
    models, 507–10
  on futures price and expected future spot
    price, 70–1
  on futures prices vs. forward prices, 56
  on options, 172–3
end of month options. *See* "EOM" options
"EOM" options, 270
equilibrium models, 416–17
  one-factor, 417–18
  two-factor, 423–4
equity swaps, 131
equivalent martingale measures, 296
Eurocurrency markets, 111
Eurodollar
  futures contracts, 99–100
  futures options, 387–8
  interest rate, 99
European options, 5
  Black's model to price, using, 393
  on bonds, 395–7
  delta (Δ) of, 314, 318–19
  dividends and, 249–50
  futures options vs. spot options, 279
  on interest rate swaps (*see under*
    swaptions)
European-style
  derivatives, 361, 368, 522
  lookback options, 464–5
exchange risk, 127
exchange options, 467–8
exchanges
  AMEX, 138, 147
  CBOE, 138, 149, 266, 507, 508, 509
  CBOT, 4, 16, 18, 19, 24, 31, 89, 91, 139,
    461, 468

CME, 4, 17, 18, 19, 20, 31, 35, 57, 62, 63, 99
COMEX, 20, 28
IMM, 63, 273
NYCE, 17
NYMEX, 19, 28, 33n, 35
NYSE, 57, 59, 60, 138, 337n
PHLX, 138, 147, 269, 270
PSE, 138
Tokyo Stock Exchange, 57
exchange-traded
  bond options, 387–9, 395
  options, 138–9, 517
  stock options, 138, 172
ex-dividend date, 59, 142, 235, 249–50
exercise
  date, 5
  limits, 143
  price, 5
exotic options, 9, 457–86, 505
  American options, nonstandard, 458–9
  Asian options, 140, 465–7, 472–3
    figure 18.3
  "as you like it" options, 460–1, 469
  barrier options, 461–3, 476–9, 483
  basket options, 469
  Bermudan options, 140, 458, 469
  binary options, 405, 405n, 463–4
  chooser options, 460–1
  compound options, 459–60, 461
  cylinder options, 458n
  exchange options, 467–8
  exchange one asset for another, options to,
    467–8
  flexible forwards, 10, 458n
  flex options, 142, 266
  forward band, 458n
  forward start options, 459
  hedging issues, 482–3
  implied trees, 505–7
  knock-in options, 461
  knock-out options, 461
  LIBOR-contingent FX options, 469
  lookback options, 464–5, 474–6
    figure 18.4
  min-max, 458n
  numerical procedures, basic, 469
  option fence, 458n
  OTC options, 139–40, 457
  packages, 457–8, 461, 534
  rainbow options, 468–9, 480
  several assets, options involving, 468–9
  static options replication, 483–4
  warrants, 153, 244–6, 459, 510
  zero-cost collar, 458n
  See also under American-style
exotics. *See under* exotic options
expectations theory, 86

expected
rate of return, 215, 216, 219, 231–2, 309n
return (ambiguous nature of term), 232
drift rate, 214, 215, 216
expiration
cycles (stock options), 140
date of options, 5, 140–1
explicit finite difference methods, 373–4
three-dimensional trees, relation to, 480n
trinomial trees, relation to, 360, 376–8, 436
exposure
derivatives credit risk, optionlike nature of,
518 figure 20.1
risk-adjusted, 531–2
See also under risk
extendible swaps, 131

F

factor analysis (statistics), 428
FASB
Statement No. 52, Foreign Currency
Translation, 39
Statement No. 80, Accounting for Futures
Contracts, 39
Federal
National Mortgage Association (*see* FNMA)
Reserve Board, 30
Financial Accounting Standards Board. *See*
FASB
finite difference methods, 368–79
application of, 379
change of variable (ln S rather than S), 374–6,
377n
control variate techniques used in conjunction
with, 371
Crank–Nicholson method, 378–9
explicit finite difference method, 360, 373–4,
376–8, 436, 480n
hedge parameters using, estimating, 379
hopscotch method, 378
See also under implicit finite difference
methods
fixed for floating, exchange of, 112–4
flat volatilities, 401
flexible forwards, 10, 458n
flex options, 142, 266
floating
for fixed, exchange of, 112–4
interest rates (*see under* LIBOR)
reference rates, 130
floor broker, 146
floor–ceiling agreements, 399
floorlets (floors), 400
floors (interest rate), 399–400, 400–1. *See also*
under caps
FNMA, 390

foreign
currency (*see under* currency)
exchange (FX) quotes, 65
exchange (FX) risk, 127
rho, 331
forward
band, 458n
curve (*see under* forward rate curve)
flexible, 10, 458n
induction, 442, 472, 506
interest rates (*see under* forward rate)
with optional exit, 458
start options, 459
swaps, 131, 402
forward contracts, 1
for credit risk, adjusting price of, 523–7
definition of, 1
delivery price of, 1
delta (Δ) of, 313–14
futures, comparison with, 4, 40 table 2.3
Ito's lemma, application to, 221
long positions in, 1
options, comparison with, 5
payoffs from, 2
on securities with known cash incomes, 52–4
on securities with known dividend yields,
54–5
on securities with no income, 51–2
short positions in, 1
value of (general result), 55
forward forward volatilities, 401
forward prices, 45–72
of currencies, 63–4
definition of, 2
forward contract values vs., 50
futures prices vs., 55–7, 56n, 76–7
appendix 3A
summary of results (investment assets), 71
table 3.4
forward rate, 424
agreements (*see* FRAs)
discrete, 427
instantaneous, 81, 424, 426, 435, 527
modeling the, 428–31
process, 426
volatilities (*see* volatility structure)
forward rate curves, 81
buckets (sections), 449
instantaneous, 432
forwards. *See under* forward contracts
FRAs, 87–8, 96, 408
FT-SE 100 Index, 57
futures contracts, 3
accounting and tax, 38–40
asset (underlying), 17, 21n
cash settlement of, 29–30
closing out positions, 17

futures contracts (*Cont.*)
  on commodities, 65–7
  converging to spot prices, prices of, 28–9
  on currencies, 63–4
  daily price movement limits, 19
  definition of, 3
  delivery arrangements, 18–19
  delivery month of, 19
  and delta hedging, 319–20
  on Eurodollars, 99–100
  forwards, comparison with, 4, 40 table 2.3
  on gold and silver, 65
  hedging using, 31–5
  initial margin for, 20
  interest rate, 78–106
  lifetime highs and lows, 27
  limits in, position, 20
  maintenance margin for, 21, 22
  margin account, 20
  margin call, 21
  margins, operation of, 20–4
  markets for, 16–28
  marking to market, 20–1, 22
  optimal number of, 61
  options, comparison with, 5
  options on, 139, 273–80
  position limits in, 20
  positions, closing out, 17
  prices of, 45–72
  quotes, 19, 24–8
  size of, 18
  specifications for, 17–20
  spot price, price converging to, 28–9
  on stock indices, 57–62
  tax, accounting and, 38–40
  Treasury bill, 95–9
  Treasury bonds and Treasury notes, 88–95
  variation margin for, 21
futures options, 139, 273–80
  American, vs. American spot options, 279–80
  Black's model, 277, 392–5
  cash settlement, 276
  definition of, 139, 273
  differential equation for, 286–7 appendix 12B
  on Eurodollar, 387–8
  European, vs. European spot options, 279
  put–call parity, 278–9
  on Treasury bonds, 387–9
  on Treasury notes, 387–8
  valuation of, 277, 393
futures prices, 45–72
  of commodities, 65–7
  of currencies, 63–4
  and expected future spot prices, 68–71, 278
  forward prices vs., 55–7, 56n, 76–7
    appendix 3A
  market price of risk, used to determine, 297

of stock indices, 59
summary of results for investment assets, 71
  table 3.4

G

gamma (Γ), 312, 323–7, 323n, 449, 482, 501,
  533
  of American options, 349
  of European options, 326–7
  theta (Θ), and delta (Δ), relationship among,
    327–8
  and value at risk, 332
gamma-neutral portfolios, 325–6
gap management, 106
GARCH, 501–2
general differential equation, derivation of,
  305–7 appendix 13B
generalized
  autoregressive conditional heteroskedasticity
    (*see* GARCH)
  Wiener process, 212–15, 214 figure 10.2
geometric
  average, 232n
  average, Asian options, 466
  Brownian motion, 217, 228, 268n, 362n, 418,
    459, 468, 490, 495, 498, 499, 502, 505
Gibson Greetings, 541
GNMA, 390
Goldman Sachs, 529n, 536
  Commodity Index. *See* GSCI
Government National Mortgage Association. *See*
  GNMA
Greeks, the, 312
  with binomial trees, estimating, 348–50
  delta (Δ), 204–5, 312–21, 312n, 448, 482–3,
    501, 533
  gamma (Γ), 312, 323–7, 323n, 449, 482, 501,
    533
  with Monte Carlo simulation, estimating, 368
  rho, 312, 330–1
  theta (Θ), 312, 321–2
  theta (Θ), delta (Δ), and gamma (Γ),
    relationship among, 327–8
  vega, 312, 328–30, 350, 449, 482, 501, 533
  See also under specific heading
gross basis (clearing), 24
Group of Thirty, 536
GSCI, 58

H

Heath, Jarrow, and Morton model, 428–31
hedge
  duration-based, ratio, 103, 103n
  long, 31
  optimal, ratio, 35–7

price-sensitivity, ratio, 103, 103n
rolling the, forward, 34, 37–8
short, 31
"hedge and forget" schemes, 314
hedge parameters
 finite difference methods, 379
 interest rate derivatives, 448–9
 Monte Carlo simulation, 364
 Taylor series expansion and, 342 appendix
  14A, 533
hedgers, 11
hedging strategies, 449n
 duration-based, 102–4
 dynamic hedging schemes, 313
 exotics, hedging issues for, 482–3
 expected return and effectiveness of, 309n
 futures, using, 31–5
 index futures, using, 61–2, 334–6
 index options, using, 266–8
 rolling forward, 37–8
 simulation of, 315–18
 stop-loss, 310–11, 310n
 synthetic options, using, 318, 333–4
historical default experience, 527–8
history-dependent derivatives, 295
Ho and Lee model, 431–3, 433, 434, 435, 436,
  492
hopscotch (finite difference) method, 378
Hull and White model, 433–6, 445, 448, 449,
  451, 492
 first stage (trinomial tree), 439 figure 17.8
 second stage (trinomial tree), 442 figure 17.9
Hunt brothers, 31n

I

ICONs, 9–10
IMM, 63, 273
implicit finite difference methods, 369–71
 backward difference approximation, 369
 forward difference approximation, 369
 See also under finite difference methods
implied
 forward forward volatilities, 401
 repo rate, 96
 trees, 505–7
implied volatilities, 246–7
 deep-out-of-the-money options, 246
 parameter calibration (trinomial trees), 448
 weighted-average, 247
importance sampling (simulation), 366
independence assumption (credit risk), 519–20
index
 amortizing (rate) swaps, 131, 416, 474,
  474n
 arbitrage, 59–60
 currency option notes (*see* ICONs)

futures, stock, 57–62
 options, 139, 264–9
indexed principal swaps, 131, 416, 474, 474n
indication pricing schedule (swaps), 116
indices
 All Ordinaries Share Price Index, 58
 CAC-40 Index, 57
 DJIA, 58, 336
 FT-SE 100 Index, 57
 GSCI, 58
 MMI, 58, 265, 266
 Nikkei 225 Stock Average, 57, 62, 153, 299,
  299n, 301
 NYSE Composite, 58, 273
 S&P 100, 139, 265, 266
 S&P 400 (MidCap), 57
 S&P 500, 29, 57, 59, 60, 139, 265, 266, 333,
  337n
induction
 backward, 473, 529
 forward, 442, 472, 506
initial
 margin, 20, 148–50
 term structure, 431, 432, 433, 442, 443, 444
inner barrier, 476, 478, 479
instantaneous
 correlation, 468, 480, 491
 expected drift rate, 216, 417, 426
 forward rate, 81, 424, 426, 435, 527
 short rate (*see under* short rate)
 standard deviation, 417, 426, 432, 433, 435,
  436
 variance rate, 216
interest only (MBSs). *See* IO
interest rate derivatives, valuation of. *See under*
  bond options, valuation of
interest rates
 bid–ask spreads, 526n
 caps on (*see under* caps)
 collars on, 399–400
 derivative securities on, 387–411
 floating for fixed, exchange of, 112–14
 floors on, 399–400
 futures on, 78–106
 known changes in the, 490–1
 nonparallel shifts in, 105–6, 449
 nonstochastic, 393
 options on, 387–411
 parallel shifts in, 392, 449
 rho, sensitivity to change in, 330
 spot and forward, 78–80
 stochastic, 491–2
 time-dependent (trees), 356–7
 See also under short rate; term structure
interest rate models. *See under* term structure
  models
interest rate risk, 292–3

interest rate swaps
  CMS swaps, 131
  CMT swaps, 131
  diff (differential) swaps, 131
  European options on (*see under* swaptions)
  financial intermediary, role of, 115–16
  floating reference rates, 130
  forward swaps, 402
  indexed principal swaps, 131
  mechanics of, 111–18
  "plain vanilla," 111, 114, 116, 123n, 407, 408,
    411
  pricing schedules for, 116–17
  spread differentials of, 120
  spread over LIBOR, guaranteed, 120n
  valuing, using bonds, 121–3
  valuing, using FRAs, 123–5, 123n
  warehousing of, 117–18
interest rate trees, 436–8
  nonstandard branching, 437–8
internal capital allocation, 532–3
International
  Monetary Market (division of CME). *See*
    IMM
  Swaps and Derivatives Association. *See* ISDA
interpolation, 473, 479
  linear, 84, 392, 474, 505
  quadratic, 474
in-the-money options, 141, 314, 322, 327
intrinsic value (options), 142
inverse cumulative normal distribution, 366
inverted market (futures price), 28
investment vs. consumption assets, 45, 65–7. *See
  also* traded securities
IO (MBSs), 391
irregularities, trading, 31
ISDA, 134
Ito process, 215, 417
Ito's lemma, 220–2, 237, 423, 425
  derivation of, 225–7 appendix 10A
  forward contracts, application to, 221
  generalization of, 304–5 appendix 13A
  stock price, application to the logarithm of,
    221–2

J

Jamshidian approach, valuation of European
  options on
  coupon-bearing bonds, 421–2, 433, 434
  discount bonds, 420–1
Japanese Nikkei. *See* Nikkei 225 Stock Average
jump diffusion model, 498–9, 516 appendix
  19A
jump model, pure, 497–8, 515–16 appendix
  19A
jumps, 336, 497–8

K

kappa, 328n. *See also under* vega
Kidder Peabody, 541
knock-in options, 461
knock-out options, 461
known dividend yield, 54–5, 261, 284–5
  appendix 12A

L

lambda, 328n. *See also under* vega
last trading day, 19, 30
lattice approach. *See* binomial trees; trinomial
  trees
LEAPS, 141, 266
lemma. *See under* Ito's lemma
liabilities, using swaps to transform, 114–15
LIBOR, 99, 111–12
  -contingent FX options, 469
  floating reference rates, 130
  zero-coupon, curve, 100
licensing futures exchanges, 30
limit
  down, 19
  move, 19
  order, 16, 146, 147
  up, 19
limits
  daily price movement, 19
  exercise, 143
  position, 20, 31, 143
linear interpolation, 84, 392, 474, 505
liquidity, 528
  choice of futures contract, 34
  futures vs. forwards, 56n
  preference theory, 86, 293
locals, 16
lognormal
  assumption, 387, 392, 393, 395, 402, 463,
    466, 492
  distribution, 228, 229, 230 figure 11.1, 387,
    493 figure 19.1
London Interbank Offer Rate. *See under* LIBOR
long
  hedge, 31
  positions, 1, 7
Long Term Credit Bank of Japan, 10
long-term equity anticipation securities. *See*
  LEAPS
lookback options, 464–5, 470–1, 474–6 figure 18.4
low-discrepancy sequences, 366–7. *See*
  quasi-random sequences

M

maintenance margin, 21, 22
Major Market Index. *See* MMI

margin
  account, 20, 148–50
  call, 21
  clearing, 23
  initial, 20
  maintenance, 21, 22
  requirements, 31
  variation, 21
margins, 20–4, 56n, 148–50
  operation of, 20–4
  for stock options, 148
market
  "corner the…," 31
  efficiency, weak-form, 210, 310n
  inverted (futures price), 28
  maker, 146, 148, 308, 510
  marking to, 20–1, 22
  mixed (futures price), 28
  normal (futures price), 28
  order, 16
  OTC, 1, 139, 142, 308, 397, 457, 517
  price of risk, 289–90, 296–7, 540
  segmentation theory, 86
market risk
  credit risk vs., 132–3
  management of, 308–38
  regulatory capital for, 517, 533
marking to market, 20–1, 22
Markov
  non-, 428, 429, 431
  process, 209
  property, 209–10, 431, 433, 450
matched pair of swaps. *See* offsetting swaps
martingale, 296
MBSs, 389–91, 474
  collateralized mortgage obligations (CMO), 390–1
  interest only (IO), 391
  passthroughs, 390
  prepayment risk, 390, 391
  principal only (PO), 391
  stripped, 391
mean. *See under* normal distribution
mean reversion, 357, 418–19 figure 17.1, 438
  stochastic reversion level, 435n
  time-dependent reversion level, 433
Merton's stochastic interest rate model, 491–2
Metallgesellschaft, 38, 38n
min-max, 458n
mixed market (futures price), 28
MMI, 58, 265, 266
model
  absolute diffusion, 497, 515 appendix 19A
  binomial, 194–6, 199–202, 343–60, 469
  Black and Karasinski, 449–50
  Black, Derman, and Toy, 449
  Black's (*see under* Black's model)

Black's approximation, 252–3
Black–Scholes, 240–2
capital asset pricing, 61, 294
compound option, 495–6, 514 appendix 19A
constant elasticity of variance, 497
Cox, Ingersoll, and Ross, 418, 422–3
Cox, Ross, and Rubinstein, 194, 343, 345, 358–9, 359n, 474, 480
displaced diffusion, 496–7, 514–15 appendix 19A
empirical research, option pricing models, 507–10
equilibrium (term structure) models, 416–24
Heath, Jarrow, and Morton, 428–31
Ho and Lee, 431–3, 433, 434, 435, 436, 492
Hull and White, 433–6, 445, 448, 449, 451, 492
jump diffusion, 498–9, 516 appendix 19A
Merton's stochastic interest rate, 491–2
no-arbitrage (term structure) models, 424–49
nonstationary (term structure) models, 449–50
pure jump, 497–8, 515–16 appendix 19A
Rendleman and Bartter, 418–19
Roll, Geske, and Whaley formula, 252–3, 259 appendix 11A
stock price, 215–17
term structure models, 416–52
Vasicek, 418, 419–22, 423, 433, 434, 492
yield curve models, 416–52
See also under specific heading
modified duration, 102, 397
moment matching (simulation), 366–7
moneyness (options), 141, 314, 322, 327
Monte Carlo simulation, 343, 361–4, 500
  application of, 364
  of capital requirements, 532
  European-style path-dependent options, 469, 470
  hedge parameters with, estimating, 364
  non-Markov term structure, 429–31
  in scenario analysis, 332
  simulation trials, 361, 364
  standard error of the estimate, 364, 365
  of stock price, 217–19
  trials, number of, 364
  underlying variable, with one, 361–2
  underlying variables, with several, 362
  See also under variance reduction procedures
Moody's, 520, 527, 528, 528n
mortgage-backed securities. *See* MBSs
municipal bond tax-exempt rate, 131

N

naked
  and covered positions, 309
  options, 149

National Futures Association. *See* NFA
natural time lag, 407
negative probabilities in trees, 357n, 359n
net basis (clearing), 24
netting, 533
neutral calendar spreads, 186
newspaper quotes. *See under* quotes
Newton–Raphson procedure, 84, 84n, 246n, 421, 445
New York
  Cotton Exchange (*see* NYCE)
  Mercantile Exchange (*see* NYMEX)
  Stock Exchange Composite Index (*see* NYSE Composite)
  Stock Exchange (*see* NYSE)
NFA, 30
Nikkei 225 Stock Average
  arbitrage arguments not applicable, 62
  CME futures, 57, 62, 299n
  quantos (cross-currency derivatives), 299, 299n, 301
  warrants on, 153
no-arbitrage (term structure) models, 424–49
  discount bond prices, process for, 425–6, 425n
  discrete case, extension to, 427
  factors, extension to several factors, 426–7
  forward rates, process for, 425–6
  short rate, process for, 427–8
  time zero, 425
nominal rate of interest, 159
nonparallel shifts in interest rates, 105–6, 449
nonstationary (term structure) models, 449–50
nonstochastic interest rates, 393
nonsystematic risk, 69, 219n, 294, 498. *See also under* credit risk
non-traded securities, 291, 292, 297
normal
  backwardation (futures), 69
  distribution, 210, 211, 211n, 217, 228, 229, 231
  distribution, inverse cumulative, 366
  distribution, standardized, 210, 214, 217, 218, 226, 366
  distribution function, cumulative, 241, 243–4
  distribution function, cumulative bivariate, 260
    appendix 11B, 460
  market (futures price), 28
notice of intention to deliver, 29, 68
notional principal, 113
numerical integration, 527
numerical procedures, 343–81
  binomial trees, 343–50
  for exotic options, basic, 469
  finite difference methods, 368–79
  Monte Carlo simulation, 361–4
NYCE, 17
n-year zero-coupon yield, 78

NYM. *See* NYMEX
NYMEX, 19, 28, 33n, 35
NYSE, 57, 59, 60, 138, 337n
NYSE Composite, 58, 273

O

OAS, 391–2
OCC, 150–1, 153
October 19, 1987, 60, 332, 336, 337
offsetting
  contracts (swaps), 132
  order (options), 147
open
  interest, 27–8, 145
  positions, 31
optimal hedge ratio, 35–7
option-adjusted spread. *See* OAS
Option Clearing Corporation. *See* OCC
options, 4–9, 138
  American vs. European, 5
  assets (underlying), 138–9
  on bond futures, 387–9
  call, 5
  class, option, 141
  commissions, 147–8
  correlated assets, on two, 480–2
  credit risk (CROs), 535
  for credit risk, adjusting the prices of, 531–3
  cross-currency (*see* quantos)
  currency, 138–9, 269–73
  definition of, 5
  dividends and stock splits, 142–3
  dynamic options replication, 483
  embedded bond, 153, 389
  "EOM," 270
  exchange-traded, 138–9, 517
  exercise date, 5
  exercise price, 5
  exercising, 151
  expiration date, 5, 140–1
  flex, 142, 266
  foreign currency, 138–9
  on futures, 139, 273–80
  futures and forwards, comparison with, 5
  index, 139
  interest rate, 387–9
  intrinsic value, 142
  margin account,148–50
  margin not allowed, 148
  maturity, 5
  moneyness, 141, 314, 322, 327
  OTC, 139–140, 457
  payoffs from, 8–9
  positions, 7
  pricing models, alternative, 494–9, 514–16
    appendix 19A

put, 5
quantos, 299–301
quotes, 145
series, option, 141
specification of stock, 140–4
spread, 405–6, 406n
on stock indices, 138, 264–9
on stocks (known dividend yields), 261–3
stock splits and dividends, 142–3
on swaps, 131, 401–4
synthetic, 308, 318, 333–4
tax planning using, 152–3
time measures, two, 248
trading, 146–7
trading strategies, 177–90
wash sale rule, 152
See also under exotic options
options, valuation of
binomial model, using, 194–6, 199–202,
    350–60
Black–Scholes, 240–2
cross-currency (*see* quantos)
currency, 270–3
dividends and, 249–53
futures options, 277
for interest rate, 387–411, 393
numerical procedures, using, 343–81
quantos, 299–301
for stock indices, 268–9
for stocks (known dividend yields), 263–4
for two underlying assets, 480–2
Orange County, 541
order
book official, 146–7
limit, 16, 147
market, 16
offsetting, 147
OTC
markets, 1, 139, 142, 308, 397, 457, 517
options, 139–40, 457
outer barrier, 476, 478, 479
out-of-the-money options, 141, 314, 322, 327
overnight repo, 50
over-the-counter. *See under* OTC

P

Pacific Stock Exchange. *See* PSE
packages, 457–8, 461, 534
parallel shifts in the term structure, 392, 449
parity, put–call, 167–170, 171, 172, 178, 242,
    262–3, 278–9, 460, 493
par yield bonds, 122
passthroughs (MBSs), 390
path-dependent derivatives
American-style, generalization, 471–3
European-style, 469, 470

payoffs, 8–9
from bear spreads, 182 table 8.2
from bull spreads, 180 table 8.1
from butterfly spreads, 184 table 8.3
from European options, 8 figure 1.6
from forward contracts, 3 figure 1.1
from other combinations, 190 figure 8.13
from range forward contract, 458 figure 18.1
from straddles, 188 table 8.4
from strangles, 189 table 8.5
permanently riskless hedges. *See* "hedge and
    forget" schemes
perpetual bonds, 423
Philadelphia Stock Exchange. *See* PHLX
PHLX, 138, 147, 269, 270
pi (Π), 61, 237, 321n, 323n, 328n, 330n
"plain vanilla" (interest rate) swaps, 111, 114,
    116, 123n, 407, 408, 411
PO (MBSs), 391
Poisson process, 498
portfolio, value of. *See* pi (Π)
portfolio insurance, 266–7, 333–6
Brady commission report, 337
index futures, using, 334–6
index options, using, 266–7
synthetically, creating options, 333–4
position limits, 20, 31, 143
positions
closing out, 17, 31
open, 31
prepayment (MBSs)
function, 390
privileges, 389, 390
risk, 390, 391
price-sensitivity hedge ratio, 103, 103n
pricing
biases, 492–4 table 19.1, 499
derivatives, general approach to, 288–302
alternative option, models, 494–9, 514–16
    appendix 19A
schedules (swaps), 116–17
principal components analysis (statistics), 428
principal only (MBSs). *See* PO
probabilities
negative, in trees, 357n, 359n
risk-neutral, 197 (9.3), 198, 201, 202, 205n,
    206, 343, 344–5, 345n, 360
Procter and Gamble, 541
program trading, 60
protective puts, 177
PSE, 138
pure jump model, 497–8, 515–16 appendix 19A
put–call parity, 167–70, 171, 172, 178, 242,
    262–3, 278–9, 460, 493
put options, 5
American, no exact analytic formula, 242
average price, 465, 483

put options (*Cont.*)
average strike, 465
definition of, 5
open interest, 145
protective, 177
volume, 145
puttable
bonds, 389
swaps, 131

Q

quadratic
approximation (option pricing), 379–80,
384–6
interpolation, 474
resampling, 366
quantos (cross-currency derivatives),
299–301
quasi-random sequences (simulation), 367–8
quotes
currency options, 270
foreign exchange (FX) futures, 64
futures contract, 19, 24–8
lifetime highs and lows (futures), 27
options, newspaper, 145
stock options, newspaper, 145
Treasury bill price, 97
Treasury bond futures, 90

R

rainbow options, 468–9, 480
random samples, generating, 363
range forward contracts, 10, 458
rates of return
distribution of, 230–2
expected, 215, 216, 219, 231–2, 309n
See also under drift rate
rating, credit, 120, 520, 532, 535
rebalancing
hedges, 313, 539
portfolios, 236
and transactions costs, 335, 335n
regulatory
authorities, 30–1, 151, 517, 531–2
capital (*see under* credit risk)
Rendleman and Bartter model, 418–19
repo
implied, rate, 96
overnight, 50
rate, 50
term, 50
repurchase agreement. *See under* repo
reverse
butterfly spreads, 184, 331
calendar spreads, 186

reversion, mean, 357, 418–19 figure 17.1, 438
stochastic reversion level, 435n
time-dependent reversion level, 433
rho, 312, 330–331
domestic, 330
foreign, 331
risk
credit vs. market, 132–3
default (*see under* credit risk)
foreign exchange (FX), 127
interest rate, 292–3
market, management of, 308–38
market price of, 289–90, 296–7, 540
nondiversifiable, 219n
nonsystematic, 69, 219n, 294, 498
prepayment risk (MBSs), 390, 391
systematic (nondiversifiable), 69, 70, 294,
528
systemic, 533
value at, 332, 533
See also under basis risk; credit risk; market
risk
risk-adjusted exposure, 531–2
risk-free interest rate, 158
riskless
hedges, 539
portfolio, 235
profit (*see under* arbitrage)
risk-neutral
probabilities, 197 (9.3), 198, 201, 202, 205n,
206, 343, 344–5, 345n, 360
world, 198, 239
risk-neutral valuation, 194, 198–9, 239–40,
263–4, 344, 540–1
equivalent martingale measures, 296
forward contracts on stocks, applied to, 240
non-traded securities, extension to, 291
underlying variable, with a single, 291–2
underlying variables, with several, 294–6
Roll, Geske, and Whaley formula, 252–3, 259
appendix 11A
rolling
back through the tree, 346–8
the hedge forward, 34, 37–8
rollover basis (futures), 37

S

S&P, 273, 520, 527, 528, 528n. *See also under*
Standard and Poor's
100, 139, 265, 266
400 (MidCap), 57
500, 29, 57, 59, 60, 139, 265, 266, 333, 337n
CAPS, 266, 461, 463
scenario
analysis, 308, 312, 331–2, 449, 533
"depression," 528

SEC, 30, 151
Securities and Exchange Commission. *See* SEC
securities dependent on several state variables,
    293–6, 379
settlement
    cash, 29–30, 139, 265, 276
    for futures, 29–30
    price, 24, 29–30
short
    hedge, 31
    positions, 1, 7
    selling, 48
    squeeze, 48
short rate, 416, 417, 421, 424, 429, 433
    instantaneous, 445, 446
    known changes in the, 490–1
    Markov model, 431
    process, 427–8
    stochastic process for, 416, 423, 436
short-term risk-free rate. *See under* short rate
Siegel's paradox, 301
sigma (σ), 159, 328n. *See also under* variance;
    volatility
simulation
    of delta hedging, 315–18
    trials, 361, 364
    See also under Monte Carlo simulation
specialist system, 147
speculators, 11–12, 12n
spot interest rates, 78–80
spread
    differentials (swaps), 120
    options, 405–6, 406n
    over LIBOR (swaps), 120n
    transactions (futures), 23
spreads (options), 177–90
    bear, 181–3, 182 figure 8.4, 457
    bearish calendar, 186
    bull, 179–81, 179 figure 8.2, 457, 458
    bullish calendar, 186
    butterfly, 183–5, 183 figure 8.6, 457
    calendar, 185–6, 185 figure 8.8
    diagonal, 187
    neutral calendar, 186
    reverse butterfly, 184, 331
    reverse calendar, 186
    See also under payoffs
spreads, bid–ask, 117n, 146, 148, 517, 526n
standard
    deviation (*see under* instantaneous; normal
        distribution; variance; volatility)
    error of the estimate (simulations), 364, 365,
        368
Standard and Poor's, 273, 520, 527, 528, 528n.
    See also under S&P
    100 Index (*see* S&P 100)
    500 Index (*see* S&P 500)

CAPS (*see* S&P CAPS)
MidCap 400 Index (*see* S&P 400)
standardized normal distribution, 210, 214, 217,
    218, 226
Standard Oil, 9
state variables
    general differential equation, derivation of,
        305–7 appendix 13B
    securities dependent on several, 293–6, 379
static options replication, 483–4
step-up swaps, 131
stochastic
    calculus, 209, 428n
    interest rates, 491–2
    process, 209, 212, 226
    variables, 304, 539
    volatility, 329n, 494–5, 499–501
stock
    dividends, 142–3, 158, 249–53
    historical risk premium, 219
    splits, 142–3
stock indices, 57–8
    arbitrage on, 59–60
    futures on, 57–62
    futures prices of, 59
    options on, 138, 264–9
    valuation of options on, 268–9
stock option prices, 156–73
    assumptions and notation, 158–9
    bounds for, 159–62, 170–1, 262
    dividends on, effect of, 170–1
    factors affecting, 156–8, 157 table 7.1
stock options
    American calls (dividends), valuation of, 259
        appendix 11A
    exchange-traded, 138, 172
    margins for, 148
    quotes, newspaper, 145
    specification of, 140–4
    trading, 146–7
stock price, 156
    behavior, continuous-time version, 216 (10.6)
    behavior, discrete-time version, 217 (10.7)
    Ito's lemma, application to the logarithm of,
        221–2
    lognormal property of, 228–30
    model, 215–17
    parameters, 219
    simulation of, 217–19
    volatility, 159, 206, 216, 219
stop-loss strategy, 310–11
storage cost, 65, 67
straddle, 187–8
    bottom, 188, 187 figure 8.10
    purchase, 188, 187 figure 8.10
    top, 188
    write, 188

strangles, 188–90, 189 figure 8.12, 457
straps, 188, 189 figure 8.11
stratified sampling (simulation), 365
strengthening of the basis, 32
stress testing, 332
strike prices, 138, 156
stripped MBSs, 391
strips, 188, 189 figure 8.11
structured notes, 416
swaps, 111–33
  accrual, 404–5, 464
  assets using, transforming, 114
  caps and floors (*see under* caps)
  commodity, 131
  constant-maturity, 410–1
  credit risk of, 120–1, 132–3, 523–7
  currency, 125–8
  default, 132
  deferred, 131, 402
  definition of, 111, 130
  discount rate, 12n
  equity, 131
  extendible, 131
  financial intermediary, role of, 115–16
  forward, 131
  index amortizing (rate), 131, 416, 474, 474n
  interest rate, 111
  liability transformation, using, 114–15
  matched pair of (*see* offsetting contracts)
  notional principal, 113
  offsetting contracts, 132
  options on, 131, 401–4
  pricing schedule, indication, 116
  puttable, 131
  step-up, 131
  term structure, 125 figure 5.7
  warehousing of, 117–18, 128
  See also under comparative advantage
swaptions, 131, 401–4
  convexity adjustment, 409–10
  relation to bond options, 402
  valuation of, 402–4
synchronous data, 507
synthetic options, 308, 318, 333–4
systematic (nondiversifiable) risk, 69, 70,
    294. *See also under* market risk
systemic risk, 533

T

tax
  advantage (swaps), comparative, 126
  futures, 38–40, 56n
tax (options), 151–3
  factors and measuring volatility, 235
  planning, 152–3
  wash sale rule, 152

Taylor series, 225, 342 appendix 14A
terminal stock price distribution, 230, 492–3
    figure 19.3, 500 table 19.2
term repo, 50
term structure
  current, 297
  initial, 431, 432, 433, 442, 443, 444
  nonparallel shifts in the, 105–6, 449
  parallel shift in the, 392, 449
  and swap value, 125 figure 5.7
  volatility, 503–5, figure 19.5
term structure models, 416–52
  equilibrium models, 416–24
  no-arbitrage models, 424–49
  nonstationary models, 449–50
term structure theories, 86–7
  expectations theory, 86
  liquidity preference theory, 86, 293
  market segmentation theory, 86
theory
  arbitrage pricing (APT), 294
  expectations, 86
  liquidity preference, 86, 293
  market segmentation, 86
  of term structures, 86–7
theta (Θ), 312, 321–2
  of American options, 349
  delta (Δ), and gamma (Γ), relationship among,
      327–8
  time decay, 321
three-dimensional trees, 406, 480–2
tier 1 capital, 531
tier 2 capital, 531
time
  continuous, 209
  decay, 321 (*see also under* theta)
  discrete, 209
  to expiration, 157
  measures (options), two, 248
  steps (trees), 201, 202, 205n, 206, 348, 447
  theta (Θ), sensitivity to decay of, 321
  value (options), 142
time-dependent interest rates (trees), 356–7
Tokyo Stock Exchange, 57
top
  straddles, 188
  vertical combinations, 190
traded securities, 288, 305, 539, 540. *See
    also* consumption vs. investment assets;
      exchange-traded
traders, types of, 10–13
  arbitrageurs, 12–13
  hedgers, 11
  speculators, 11–12
trading
  days vs. calendar days (volatility), 233, 248–9
  irregularities, 31

last, day, 19, 30
program, 60
strategies involving options, 177–90
volatility, as the cause of, 248
volume (futures), 27–8
transactions costs, 12, 56n, 158, 172–3, 335, 335n
Treasury bills
day count conventions, 85
discount instrument, 95
floating reference rates, 130
futures on, 95–9, 98n
price quotes, 97–9, 98n
Treasury bonds, 90
clean price, 90
day count conventions, 85
dirty price, 90
Treasury bond futures, 18, 88–95
cheapest-to-deliver bond, 92–3
conversion factors for, 90–2
options on, 387–9
quoted futures price, determining the, 93–5
quotes, 19, 90
wild card play, 93
Treasury curve. *See under* zero curve
Treasury note futures, 18, 19, 88–95
options on, 387–8
trees
implied, 505–7
nonrecombining, 429
three-dimensional, 406, 480–2
See also under binomial trees; trinomial trees
trinomial trees, 360 figure 15.11, 436–8
analytic results in conjunction with, using, 445–7
branching probabilities of, 439–41, 448
calibration of volatility parameters for, 448
cash flows between nodes in, 447–8
commodity prices and, 357
exotic options, 469, 474, 476, 479, 482
explicit finite difference method, relation to, 360, 376–8, 436
interest rates and, 436–8
other models, extension to, 444–5
three-dimensional, 482
time step, changing the length of the, 447
tree-building procedure, general, 438–49
See also under binomial trees
triple witching hour, 30
true barrier, 476

U

underlying
choice of (basis risk), 34
delta (Δ), sensitivity to price of, 204, 312–21, 312n, 448, 482–3, 501

up-and-in options, 462
up-and-out options, 462, 483
uptick, 49
U.S. Treasury
bill (*see under* Treasury bills)
bond (*see under* Treasury bonds)
Department, 30
note futures contracts, 88–95

V

value at risk, 332, 533
variables
continuous, 209
discrete, 209
securities dependent on several state, 293–6
stochastic, 304, 539
variance
of actual vs. proportional change, 216
average, vs. average volatility, 491n
per unit time (*see* variance rate)
rate, 214, 215, 216
rate, constant, 215
rate, instantaneous, 216
of terminal stock price, 230
See also under volatility
variance reduction procedures (simulation), 364–8
antithetic variable technique, 364–5
control variate technique, 365
importance sampling, 365
low-discrepancy sequences (*see* quasi-random sequences)
moment matching, 366
quadratic resampling (*see* moment matching)
quasi-random sequences, 366–7
stratified sampling, 365–6
variation margin, 21
Vasicek model, 418, 419–22, 423, 433, 434, 492
Jamshidian approach, 420–2
vector for bond price volatilities, 424
vega, 312, 328–30, 350, 449, 482, 501, 533
stochastic volatility, 329n
and value at risk, 332
vega-neutral portfolios, 328
volatility, 157, 159, 216, 219
adjustment, 492, 492n
average, vs. average variance, 491n
causes of, 247–9, 336
estimation of, historical, 232–5
flat, 401
forward forward, 401
"hump," 401 figure 16.4
implied, 246–7
known changes in the, 490–1
low, and alternative tree construction, 358–9
matrix, 504–5 table 19.3

volatility (*Cont.*)
measure, 394, 396, 397, 401
measurement period, 233
smile, 503 figure 19.3, 504 figure 19.4, 505
stochastic, 329n, 494–5, 499–501
stock market, 336
stock price, 159, 206, 216, 219
structure, 428, 435 figure 17.5, 435n, 450
term structure, 503–5, figure 19.5
vector for bond price, 424
vega, sensitivity to changes in, 312, 328–30, 350, 449, 482, 501, 533
weighted-average implied, 247
yield, 396–7
See also under variance
volume of trading, 27–8, 145

W

Wall Street Journal, 24, 25–7, 28, 41, 57, 58, 64, 88, 89, 145, 264, 265, 271, 274–6
warehousing of swaps, 117–18, 128
warrants, 153, 244–6, 459, 510
wash sale rule (options), 152
weakening of the basis, 32
weak-form market efficiency, 210, 310n, 429n
Wiener process, 210–15, 213 figure 10.1, 237, 424, 480–1, 491, 500
generalized, 212–15, 214 figure 10.2, 215
wild card play (CBOT T-bond futures), 93
working backward. *See* rolling back through the tree

writing, 7
covered calls, 150, 177
naked options, 149

Y

yield curve. *See under* term structure; zero curve
yield curve models. *See under* term structure models
yield volatilities, 387, 396–7

Z

zero-cost
collar, 458n
package, 458, 534
zero-coupon
bonds, 78 (*see also* discount bonds)
LIBOR curve, 100
n-year, yield, 78
yield, 344n
zero-coupon yield curve. *See under* zero curve
zero curve, 446 table 17.1, 520
bootstrapping the, 82, 122
buckets (sections), 449
corporate, 520
definition of, 80
determination of, 82–4
option-adjusted spread (OAS), 391
shifts, 449
zero-drift stochastic process. *See* martingale